To Simon e
with my love.
May 2004.

Martin

A History of Theatre in Africa

This book aims to offer a broad history of theatre in Africa, covering the entire continent. The roots of African theatre are ancient and complex and lie in areas of community festival, seasonal rhythm and religious ritual, as well as in the work of popular entertainers and storytellers. Since the 1950s, in a movement that has paralleled the political emancipation of so much of the continent, there has also grown a theatre that comments back from the colonized world to the world of the colonists and explores its own cultural, political and linguistic identity. *A History of Theatre in Africa* offers a comprehensive yet accessible account of this long and varied chronicle and is written by a team of scholars in the field. Chapters include an examination of the concepts of 'history' and 'theatre' in Africa; North Africa; Francophone theatre; Anglophone West Africa; East Africa; Southern Africa; Lusophone African theatre; Mauritius and Réunion; and the African Diaspora.

MARTIN BANHAM is Emeritus Professor of Drama and Theatre Studies at the School of English, University of Leeds. His publications include *African Theatre Today* (1976), *The Cambridge Guide to African and Caribbean Theatre* (edited with Errol Hill and George Woodyard, 1994) and *The Cambridge Guide to World Theatre* (1988, and with subsequent editions as *The Cambridge Guide to Theatre*). He has written extensively on African Theatre in international journals and is co-editor with James Gibbs and Femi Osofisan of the annual journal, *African Theatre*.

A HISTORY OF
Theatre in Africa

Edited by Martin Banham

CAMBRIDGE
UNIVERSITY PRESS

PUBLISHED BY THE PRESS SYNDICATE OF THE UNIVERSITY OF CAMBRIDGE
The Pitt Building, Trumpington Street, Cambridge, United Kingdom

CAMBRIDGE UNIVERSITY PRESS
The Edinburgh Building, Cambridge, CB2 2RU, UK
40 West 20th Street, New York, NY 10011–4211, USA
477 Williamstown Road, Port Melbourne, VIC 3207, Australia
Ruiz de Alarcón 13, 28014 Madrid, Spain
Dock House, The Waterfront, Cape Town 8001, South Africa

http://www.cambridge.org

First published 2004

Printed in the United Kingdom at the University Press, Cambridge

Typeface Columbus 10.75/13.75 pt.   *System* LᴬTEX 2$_\varepsilon$ [TB]

A catalogue record for this book is available from the British Library

Library of Congress Cataloguing in Publication data
A history of theatre in Africa / edited by Martin Banham.
    p.   cm.
Includes bibliographical references and index.
ISBN 0 521 80813 8
1. Theatre – Africa – History.   2. Performing arts – Africa – History.
1. Banham, Martin.
PN 2969.H57   2003
792′.096 – dc21   2003055280

ISBN 0 521 80813 8 hardback

To the memory of Geoffrey Axworthy, Dele Charley,
Peter Lwanga, John Masanja, Rose Mbowa, Wale Ogunyemi,
Sonny Oti, Ola Rotimi: fine friends, great artists, with
the ancestors.

Contents

Contributors

DAPO ADELUGBA is Professor of Theatre Studies at the University of Ibadan. He has written widely on Nigerian theatre and is also extremely active as a director, having staged work by such leading Nigerian playwrights as Wale Ogunyemi and J. P. Clark in Nigeria and the UK.

SOLA ADEYEMI studied theatre arts at the University of Ibadan and then worked as a postgraduate on a comparative study of Yoruba and Zulu cultural performances at the University of Natal, South Africa. He is currently living in London and is completing his doctorate on a postcolonial study of the performances of Femi Osofisan.

ECKHARD BREITINGER is Professor of African Studies at Bayreuth University. He has held visiting professorships in several African universities, in Nigeria, Cameroon, Kenya and, substantially, Uganda. He is the editor and publisher of Bayreuth African Studies, a distinguished series concerned with African arts and culture that has published over fifty titles. Breitinger's contribution to the series includes editing *Theatre and Performance in Africa* (1994) and, with Yvette Hutchison, *History and Theatre in Africa* (2000).

CIARUNJI CHESAINA is a professor in the Department of Literature, University of Nairobi. She spent a considerable period as the High Commissioner for Kenya in the Republic of South Africa.

JOHN CONTEH-MORGAN, formerly of Fourah Bay College, University of Sierra Leone, is currently Associate Professor of French and Francophone Studies at Ohio State University and editor of *Research in African Literatures*. His publications include *Drama and Theatre in Francophone Africa* (Cambridge, 1994) and he was a major contributor to *The Cambridge Guide to Theatre* (Cambridge, 1995) and *The Routledge Encyclopedia of African Writers* (London, 2002). His translation of Paulin Hountondji's *The*

Struggle for Meaning: Reflections on Philosophy, Culture and Democracy in Africa was published by Ohio University Press in 2002.

JAMES GIBBS has taught at the Universities of Ghana, Malawi, Ibadan and Liège and is currently a senior lecturer at the University of the West of England, Bristol. He has published widely on African literature (including *Wole Soyinka*, London, 1986) and is co-editor, with Martin Banham and Femi Osofisan, of the annual journal, *African Theatre*.

YVETTE HUTCHISON is a South African teaching at King Alfred's College, Winchester. She is assistant editor of the *South African Theatre Journal*. Her doctorate was on the relationship between theatre, myth and history in post-1960s Kenya, Nigeria and South Africa.

DAVID KERR has taught at the Universities of Botswana and Malawi and at King Alfred's College, Winchester. He is currently Professor of Theatre Studies at the University of Malawi. His extensive writings on African theatre include *African Popular Theatre* (London, 1995) and *Dance, Media Entertainment and Popular Theatre in South-East Africa* (Bayreuth, 1998). He was guest editor of the fourth issue of the annual journal *African Theatre* (*African Theatre: Southern Africa*, Oxford, 2004).

ASHERI KILO is Senior Lecturer in Theatre Arts at the University of Buea, Cameroon, and is the co-ordinator of the drama and theatre arts programmes. She is a director of the university's theatre troupe.

AMANDINA LIHAMBA is Professor in the Department of Fine and Performing Arts at the University of Dar Es Salaam. She is also a performer, director and playwright and has worked in theatre for development within and outside Africa.

LUÍS R. MITRAS is a South African at present based in Lisbon. He has published on Lusophone literatures and has translated novels, short stories and poetry from Portuguese and Spanish. He is adjunct associate professor at the European Division of the University of Maryland.

ROSHNI MOONEERAM lectures in English linguistics at the University of Central England, Birmingham. Her doctoral thesis from the University of Leeds discussed the sociolinguistics and stylistics of the Creole language of Mauritius. She has contributed to Stanley Wells and Sarah Stanton's *Cambridge Companion to Shakespeare on Stage* (Cambridge, 2002), to the annual journal *African Theatre* (*African Theatre in Development*, Oxford, 1999) and to *Kunapipi*.

KHALID ALMUBARAK MUSTAFA graduated from the University of Khartoum, where he was chairperson of the Students Union. His doctorate was from the University of Bristol. He taught drama at the Universities of Khartoum and Kuwait, and was Dean of the Higher Institute of Music and Drama (Sudan) and Director of Khartoum University Press. His publications include *Arabic Drama: A Critical Introduction* (Khartoum, 1986), *Turabi's Islamist Venture* (Cairo, 2001), *Tilk AnNazra* (1978) – a collection of plays in classical Arabic – and a translation into Arabic of two volumes of British documents about Sudan (Omdurman, 2002). He is a published and performed playwright in both Arabic and English, and is a columnist and critic for *AlRayAlAm* (Sudan) and *AlHayat* (London).

EVAN MWANGI teaches literature at the University of Nairobi and at Ohio University, Athens, Ohio. He has co-edited (with Opiyo Mumma and Christopher Odhiambo) *Orientations of Drama, Theatre and Culture: Cultural Identity and Community Development* (Nairobi, 1998) and *Emerging Patterns for a Third Millennium: Drama / Theatre at the Equator Crossroads* (with Tobias Otieno and Opiyo Mumma; Nairobi, 1999).

OLU OBAFEMI is Professor of English at the University of Ilorin, Nigeria, and a playwright, theatre director and critic. His critical works include a major study entitled *Contemporary Nigerian Theatre* (Bayreuth, 1996). He is one of Nigeria's leading radical dramatists, with plays such as *Nights of a Mystical Beast* (1986), *Suicide Syndrome* (1988) and *Naira has no Gender* (1993). He is also a novelist and a poet, and has written on social and political issues facing Nigeria today. He has been a regular columnist in leading Nigerian newspapers since 1981.

OSITA OKAGBUE is Lecturer in Drama and Theatre Arts at Goldsmiths College, University of London. His essays on aspects of African and Caribbean theatre have appeared in *Contemporary Dramatists, Contemporary American Dramatists, New Literatures Review, African Writers, Who's Who in Contemporary World Theatre, Meditations on African Literature, South African Theatre Journal, Theatre Research International, Culture and Identity, The Continuum Companion to Twentieth-century Theatre, Contemporary Theatre Review* and *Okike*.

KOLE OMOTOSO is a Nigerian scholar who moved to South Africa in 1992. He is a professor in the Drama Department at the University of Stellenbosch and a research professor at the Centre for Theatre and Performance Studies, also at Stellenbosch. His publications include work on contemporary Arabic theatre and the theatre of the English-speaking Caribbean. A present research interest is a comparative study of Yoruba travelling theatre and Afrikaans travelling theatre.

JANE PLASTOW is Deputy Director of the Workshop Theatre and Director of the Centre for African Studies, both at the University of Leeds. She has published widely on African theatre and theatre for development, including *African Theatre and Politics* (Amsterdam, 1996), *Contemporary African Plays* (edited with Martin Banham; London, 1999) and – as guest editor – the third volume of the annual journal *African Theatre, African Theatre: Women* (Oxford, 2002).

KAMAL SALHI is Senior Lecturer in French and Francophone Studies at the School of Modern Languages and Cultures, University of Leeds, and Deputy Director of the Leeds University Centre for African Studies. His publications include *The Politics and Aesthetics of Kateb Yacine* (Lampeter, 1999) and, as editor, *African Theatre for Development: Art for Self-Determination* (Exeter, 1998). He is the founder and editor of the *International Journal of Francophone Studies*.

MOHAMED SHERIFF is a leading Sierra Leonian novelist, playwright and director. Co-founder (with Oumarr Farouk Sesay) of Pampana Communications Drama Company, he writes, directs and produces plays for radio, television and community theatre. His play *Just Me and Mama* won a prize in the BBC African Performance Radio Playwriting Competition in 1999 and was broadcast several times, on the BBC African and World Services. His theatre for development plays have been commissioned by, amongst others, UNICEF, UNDP, the National Commission for Democracy and Human Rights, and the Anti-Corruption Commission.

AHMED ZAKI is President of ITI Egypt and Professor of Drama at the Academy of Dramatic Arts, Cairo. He is a former Under-Secretary of Culture and Head of the Drama Sector. A director of over sixty plays, he was honoured at the Cairo International Festival for Experimental Theatre in 1992 for his contribution to theatre. He has written extensively on theatre and was the regional co-ordinator of volume IV of *The World Encyclopedia of Contemporary Theatre* (1999).

Acknowledgements

This volume was the initiative of Dr Victoria Cooper at Cambridge University Press and throughout its preparation she has offered great and generous support and shrewd (and helpfully pragmatic!) guidance. Jackie Warren, the production editor at the Press, and the copyeditor, Hilary Hammond, have both, with great professionalism and friendliness, smoothed a multitude of rough edges and saved me from many errors. There is a Sudanese proverb that says that he who shoots an arrow upwards into the sky should have his head protected – a protective role they have both performed!

I owe a considerable and special debt of gratitude to Judith Greenwood, who, in addition to undertaking the major task of creating the index, throughout the process of commissioning and editing read authors' manuscripts and discussed them with me, raising important queries, making constructive suggestions and generally offering invaluable intellectual support and personal encouragement. The final product owes much to her.

Lastly, to the individual contributors – scholars, practitioners, old and new friends and colleagues – my great thanks for their work and dedication to the project. They are the true dancers in the rich forest of African theatre.

Preface

To attempt a history of theatre in Africa is a daunting task. At the outset we have to decide what we mean by Africa, by theatre, and by history in this context. Resolving the first of these was relatively simple – a choice between a sub-Saharan Africa or the total continent including the Maghreb and Egypt. Don Rubin, in the volumes of *The World Encyclopedia of Contemporary Theatre* on Africa and the Arab World (1997 and 1999 respectively), decided to separate north Africa from Africa south of the Sahara, on the entirely persuasive grounds that the Arab world is a cultural unity. I made the same judgement in *The Cambridge Guide to African and Caribbean Theatre* (1994) and in the earlier *African Theatre Today* (London, 1976). On the other hand, as many of the contributors to this volume acknowledge and illustrate, historically there has been immense cultural interchange between all parts of the continent, and particularly from the Arab world into East and West Africa, and this is often most vividly identified and retained in aspects of performance. Hence my decision to seek to cover the whole continent, though accepting that on such a vast scale there are as many disconnections as there are connections. The second term, *theatre*, is more elusive and presents a greater problem. The variety of performance forms in African societies is immense, ranging from dance to storytelling, masquerade to communal festival, with a vibrant and generally more recent 'literary' and developmental theatre. All have to be celebrated and acknowledged in a 'history' (which I will come back to). Kole Omotoso, in his introductory chapter to this volume, helps us determine the interaction of various kinds of performance in creating theatre in African societies, and many other contributors return to this question. But, as the Nigerian scholar Yemi Ogunbiyi implies at the beginning of his *Drama and Theatre in Nigeria: A Critical Source Book* (Lagos, 1981), it is legitimate, whilst acknowledging the roots of religious ritual, festival and so forth, to refer to 'a robust theatrical tradition'. In this volume the word *theatre* is used in a way that embraces a wide range of aspects of performance – in truth we use it in its largest and most inclusive sense.

Finally, *history*. For a continent that can in some parts offer 5,000 years of record and documentation (as Ahmed Zaki observes of Egypt) and in others articulate its past significantly through oral narration, myth and legend, history cannot be one thing. A continent that has been invaded and colonised, and subject to the imposition of alien languages and governments, cannot have a convenient linear history. We are often asking 'Whose history?'; in South Africa, for instance, there are legitimate separate performance histories of both indigenous and settler cultures. But the apparent difficulty of finding a coherent pattern of history of African performance is also an opportunity to assert its defining and uniting quality – a sense of function. The roots of African theatre in ritual, seasonal rhythms, religion and communal communication are roots common to world theatre, but whereas it may be argued that European theatre, for instance, is at so great a distance from its functional roots as to be almost unaware of them, African theatre – even at the beginning of the twenty-first century – remains directly and immediately related to them. The contemporary literary playwright is likely to be drawing upon exactly the same performance imperative as the storyteller or the masquerade; the performer is still the necessary chronicler of time and experience. The late Joel Adedeji, in a posthumous essay entitled 'African Theatre: The Issue of an Historical Approach' (in D. Layiwola, ed., *Rethinking African Arts and Culture*, Cape Town, 2000), points to the difficulties of 'writing a history of an African art phenomenon which originates and proceeds from Oral Tradition, Oral History and what is now generally referred to as Oral Literature'. He points the historian again to '[T]he root elements of African theatre . . . the mimetic masks, the chant/song and the dance', and suggests that in order for him/her to be properly critical the methodology he/she uses may have to move beyond the recording of facts: 'it may be necessary to recreate the circumstances in which the work first manifested itself and was then developed'. Practical research has indeed informed many of the contributors to this volume.

The contributors to this volume are mainly scholars and theatre practitioners who are indigenous to the areas of Africa they are discussing or who have significant experience within the region. My invitation to each of them was to write not to a determined framework of theatre history but from their own insights and priorities. There are inevitably moments of overlap; old colonial borders may, for instance, give a Lusophone or a Francophone focus to specific chapters, but cultural communities and traditions subvert artificial boundaries. The volume is organised broadly on regional and linguistic terms. This is often more a matter of convenience (and access for the reader) than of absolute logic: indeed, this very act of organisation may confront us again with the question 'Whose history?' Conscious that the theatre and performance of Africa has spread well beyond the continent, I have included one chapter, from Osita Okagbue, on aspects of the diaspora. African-American theatre is, however, not included, as this would properly demand a study in its own terms.

My hope is that the reader will be reminded of the extraordinary complexity of African performance culture, of its richness, agelessness and beauty; that he or she will see much that offers coherence and continuity, even within diversity, on the vast stage of Africa.

Martin Banham

1 Concepts of history and theatre in Africa

KOLE OMOTOSO

The streets of my home-town, Akure, at present the state capital of Ondo State in the south-western part of Nigeria, constituted the ever-moving theatre in which my eyes first saw the performances of my Yoruba culture, history and rituals. Looking back, it is easy to see why a society recently reintroduced to another cryptographic culture, that of the Europeans, clung to its oral tradition while not throwing away the new form of memory preservation through writing. The missionaries had reduced the language to Romanized alphabets, stopping further development through Arabic script, the so-called *ajami* script. The Bible had been translated into Yoruba and biblical stories that were to provide themes for future dramatists were available to all and sundry in Yorubaland. Thus from about 1834 onwards the Church Missionary Society had begun to spread the alternative creation story narrated in Genesis.

Every town and village had churches commensurate with their size. To these churches were attached educational institutions, beginning with primary, secondary and vocational schools and colleges. Western education was accepted as the way forward for transforming the society. Parents and guardians put themselves out to educate their children and wards. The missionary schools and colleges converted pupils and students into their various denominations. Pupils were altar boys in the Catholic schools. Students joined choirs and went through the religious rituals of baptism, confirmation and the festival of harvest. Harvest festivals gave individual students and their parents the opportunity to show off their wealth by competing with other students in donating money and goods to the church, as chairman of the festival for their class. The fourteen Stations of the Cross ritual of the Catholics was a ceremony that those who were not Catholics by conversion found engaging and so interesting to attend and watch. The year of the Marian Congress, a once in a hundred year (or twenty-five years?) Catholic street parade, took place in 1956, and I ran and joined in the parade since I was then attending a Catholic primary school.

Islamic institutions did not bow out of the cultural scene with the arrival of the Christian proselytizers. Fulani jihadists had invaded the northern part of Yorubaland at the end of the eighteenth century and forced the Yoruba to move their capital, Oyo, further south into the forest area of their country. The Muslims had their mosques to which *madrasahs* (places of religious study) were attached. While mosques were not as numerous as the churches, their five times a day prayers preceded by the call of the *muezzin* ensured that they were not ignored. The annual month of fasting was also a time of sharing with the people of the town their culinary delicacies, even with those of us who were not fasting.

The same streets on which both Christian and Muslim rituals and festivals took place also constituted the playing spaces of the collective rituals and festivals of the Yoruba of Akure.

There were festivals devoted to the various Yoruba gods. The Ogun festivals divided into the women's Ogun festival and the men's Ogun festival. There were Ogun festivals for the various professions, such as motor mechanics and long-distance drivers, in which the use of iron and iron implements was prominent. Ogun is the god of war, of hunters and blacksmiths.

The *Egungun* (ancestor worship) festivals seemed to continue all year round since there were always different types of Egungun to enliven the people of the town. A particular egungun caught my fancy. It was usually dressed in a headgear that was bedecked with beautiful feathers, arranged prettily on its woven mask. It had a beard of woven cloth also decorated with smaller feathers but of the same colourfulness. It spoke in a deep guttural voice supposed to be that of the ancestors. It danced. It sang with a chorus of singers and drummers following. It played verbal games with the audience – the one that followed it faithfully and the audience it attracted as it stopped at every house of a notable of the town:

> You of larger than life lips, pull up your lips!
> You seem to stare at me with your drooping lips!

There was also the marathon race through designated routes in the town. Young men coming of age, men dedicated to the service of the Oba, the king, whose title is Deji of Akure, ran this annual race. I do not know what prize they collected at the end of it. It was not competitive beyond the ability to finish the race. The song that accompanied this race spoke of the king sitting waiting and warning all the cowards to stay back because there was no place in the race for the idle.

We would leave the streets and go into the school hall and there would be a magician who had obtained the permission of the headmaster to entertain the pupils with his magical performances. He would have spent seven days and seven nights at the burial ground and the whirlwind would have carried him away to the land of the spirits to teach him these magical performances.

On another occasion it would be the travelling theatre performing at the town hall that evening and we would be encouraged to go. The play would be *Nebuchadnezzar*, the terrible king of the Bible who went beyond his capabilities.

It was only a short step from here to putting on our own end of year performances. The theme could be slavery and the fate of the returnees. It could be something from the Bible such as the story of Moses, the plight of Pharaoh or the wisdom of Solomon. From the theatres performed on these streets we moved to dining halls where dining tables are hurriedly put end to end and mats spread on them to form the performing stage. Town hall, school hall, court hall, open field, street corners – these were the places of these various and varied rituals, festivals, demonstrations and performances.

The streets also accommodated family performances such as funerals, with drumming and dancing to the place of burial at home or at church. There were chieftaincy titles to be inaugurated and the family would follow the chief-to-be to the place of placing the akoko leaves (the traditional mark of endurance and long life) on his head and accompany him home singing:

The chieftain's brow admits of no sweat.
Arriving home to reap the good is your star!

Later still, on Sundays and at Christmas and New Year there would be purely secular bands travelling from place to place making music, entertaining any and all who would listen to them.

What about the theatre of politics? The main roads and the small lanes of the town were the sites for the contentious party politics of pre-independence days, as well as of the violently divisive ethnic politics of the post-independence period, dominated as it was by party thugs, the drunk and drugged hero of instant carpet-crossing. It was on these streets that Odunni Oluwole dramatised the coming enslavement of all who had voted for the Awolowos and Sardaunas and Azikiwes and refused to accept her advice that the British should not be permitted to depart from Nigeria as yet! It was from these streets that the thugs of a rival political party invaded our house and smashed everything after we had fled. Our life on these streets was not only a show, it was for show! The curtain dropped when we went inside our houses!

After my ordinary level examinations in 1961, I went out of the boarding-house at night to go and watch a play by Hubert Ogunde and his Travelling Theatre at the Court Hall near the Oba's palace. I do not remember the title of the play. A hundred or so other students, who claimed that I had permitted them to go and watch the play, also went. I was a house prefect. The school did not take kindly to this kind of behaviour, but that is another story!

The following January I left Akure for Lagos and Kings' College Lagos, and from there went on to the University of Ibadan and then to the University of Edinburgh. After leaving Akure, the rest is merely filling in the details and comparing the samples with what that town had taught me about our history, our theatre, our performance, our rituals and festivals and our understanding of the life that supports these various expressions of theatre consciousness. The rest of this chapter attempts to do the same thing.

It is important to note that the narrative of the above experience in the streets of a Nigerian city is not unique to me. Both Wole Soyinka and Femi Osofisan have given testimonies of their awakenings into the magic world of performance on the streets of their home-towns. The third chapter of *Ake – The Years of Childhood* (1981) is a detailed description of a 4.5-year-old Wole Soyinka following a police band around the streets of Abeokuta. In one important respect, such experiences as these must be the equivalent of going to the circus in Europe and North America. These were the initial exposures of young ones to performance. Thereafter, it would be the exposure to scripted plays, plays read from books, play words learnt and rehearsed and then performed in front of an audience. For this reason, it is useful that some African theatre and drama critics and academics have written about performance types such as *commedia dell'arte* and the work of strolling players.

It can be said, then, that the earliest and longest encounter with theatre in African countries is theatre and performance in the indigenous languages and in the indigenous environment. Against this background, it would seem rather inadequate to speak of Francophone theatre or Anglophone theatre when speaking of the totality of theatre and performance experiences of the African peoples of French colonial experience in west and central Africa, of the African peoples of English colonial Africa in west, east and southern Africa and of the African peoples of Portuguese colonial experience in west, east and southern Africa. Not only have these African peoples lived the greater part of their lives outside of the cultural concern and care of these colonizing languages and cultures, they have also since the 1960s regained their political and cultural if not their economic independence.

This is not to say that there are no African plays written and performed in French, English and Portuguese. The point is that these do not exhaust the totality of theatre writing and performance in all parts of Africa. It is necessary to search and locate the bulk of the theatre and performance that exists in African languages.

The link between language and performance begins with the daily and seasonal rituals of life. While these continue in the indigenous languages as well as the European languages brought to the continent through Christianity and western education, a language such as Arabic has totally replaced the indigenous languages in north Africa.

Various rituals in Africa linked to birth, the coming of age, marriage and death are carried out through traditional cultural practices as well as through Christian practices. It is not unusual to have a child among the Yoruba baptized in a church and then given another ceremony of traditional Yoruba naming. This also happens with marriages, which include a third ritual, the legal one in front of a magistrate! The dramas and performances linked to these rituals have become aspects of the cultures of many African countries and peoples. It is impossible, though, to achieve this in the Arabic language and Islamic religion. This situation is not unconnected to the fact that the Arabs themselves do not have any elaborate religious ritual and so do not have a tradition of theatrical performances similar to what exists in the rest of the world. All the same, it is not an easy research task to write about the performance inheritance of the people who lived in north Africa before the Arab conquest except among the Berber, during the ninth and tenth centuries. The same comment applies to writing about theatre, drama and performance in the contemporary situation in Africa.

The life of the European in areas of Africa where there were no settler Europeans seemed somehow incomplete. Europeans arrived in West Africa as travellers looking for geographical features to discover and name after their kings and queens, or else they came as missionaries, learning the local language and then using it to sell their own religion to the natives. They came as administrators, teachers and engineers into the space of the native, ready-made. Their histories, their antecedents, their ancient backgrounds of primitivism and pre-Christianity did not accompany them. They came as if they had always been Christians, as if they were always teachers, as if they were always the way they appeared in our towns and forests. This situation must have been a handicap to the Yoruba Ifa priests, who had to argue with the missionaries of Abeokuta and other Yoruba centres of the Church Missionary Society.

Against this background, it is not difficult to understand the inability of many of us to see the connection between the dialogue play text we read in secondary school and our theatre and drama performances. Texts such as those of William Shakespeare and George Bernard Shaw were examination textbooks for ordinary and advanced levels of the Cambridge examinations and later the West African Certificate examinations. It was only later, at university level, that the lucky student began to learn about theatre performances in England during the time of Shakespeare, about contemporary theatre life in 1950s and 1960s London and about the work of English playwrights contemporary with Wole Soyinka. It is at this level, when the student has left behind all connections with the critical language of indigenous performance styles, for the simple reason that he does not have to master it to continue to enjoy such plays, that he becomes familiar with the language of theatre, drama and performance of Europe and, perhaps, North America.

Encounters with different personalities and differing innovations in these performance styles begin to sound familiar to him. Performance poetry, storytelling sessions, street and marketplace performances begin to tell him that he was hearing of quite familiar issues.

It is at this point that the Nigerian undergraduate confronts the limitations of undomesticated and therefore foreign ideas and knowledge. In whatever area of studies the student might be – science, medicine, the arts, social sciences – he is informed that his culture has no philosophy, his people no history, no tradition of healing and no political structures because it is an unwritten culture of oral tradition. University education in Nigeria and in other parts of Africa still faces this issue of needing to domesticate foreign knowledge and foreign ideas through translating them into African languages. This is the way in which the African can begin to make genuine contributions to world knowledge and ideas. This domestication can only take place when African languages are the medium of encounter between student and the known world. Indeed, this is the only means by which the knowledge contained in his language and the knowledge brought by the European languages of colonial experience can co-mingle and cross-fertilise one another.

The street theatres and performances of my youth came from carefully articulated artistic choices. The performances came after long and arduous rehearsals. They came from a tradition of beauty seen in balance – *iwontunwosi* – a judicious measure of the left and of the right.

Amos Tutuola, in his novel *Feather Woman of the Jungle*, describes a woman thus: 'She was indeed a beautiful woman. She was not too tall and not too short; she was not too black and not too yellow.' Here is a quote from Ifa Divination poetry as recorded by Ulli Beier and Gbadamosi:

> Anybody who meets beauty and does not look at it will soon be poor.
> The red feathers are the pride of the parrot.
> The palm fronds are the pride of the palm tree.
> The white flowers are the pride of leaves.
> The well-swept verandah is the pride of the landlord.
> The straight tree is the pride of the forest.
> The fast deer is the pride of the bush.
> The rainbow is the pride of the skies.
> The beautiful woman is the pride of her husband.
> Children are the pride of their mother.
> The moon and the stars are the pride of the sun.
> Ifa says: beauty and all sorts of good fortune arrive.
> (from *Yoruba Poetry*, Lagos: Black Orpheus, 1959, page 30)

The Yoruba word *ewa* (beauty) describes both the physical and the abstract. The search for beauty might end at the door of the physically attractive as well as the house of the morally upright. Hence the simple saying 'Iwa l'ewa' rendered as 'Character is beauty'.

As documented in Bower's *Grammar and Dictionary of the Yoruba Language* published in 1858, *amewa* (one who is a judge of beauty) and *mewa* (to be a judge of beauty) demonstrate a consciousness of that which would be adjudged beautiful in the Yoruba environment. Robert Farris Thompson's 'Yoruba Artistic Criticism', the first chapter in *The Traditional Artist in African Societies* edited by Warren L. d'Azevedo and published by Indiana University Press in 1973, documents Yoruba criticism of their carvers and sculptors. Writing about the encounter of indigenous performance styles with western theatre styles of writing and performance becomes meaningful in terms of an existing indigenous performance critique. Both Professors J. A. Adedeji and Oyin Ogunba have written extensively on Yoruba theatre in English and in

Yoruba. Adedeji's *Nigerian Theatre: Dynamics of a Movement* (edited by Hyginus Ekwuazi and published by Caltop Publications Nigeria Ltd in 1998) sees Nigerian theatre as comprising two main movements: the theatre in Yoruba and the theatre in English. His *The Theatre in Yoruba* definitely makes one look forward, with hope, to a second volume, *The Theatre in English*.[1]

Out of the various readings and opinions about the theatre in Yoruba that have found expression, three fundamental formal issues make themselves quite clear: Yoruba theatre does not aspire to represent reality, rather it attempts to interpret and reinterpret reality. In this regard for instance, what Thompson has referred to as 'emotional proportion' comes into play. In the essay by Thompson mentioned above, he states:

> Yoruba notions of proportion form a dialogue between the permissive and the prescribed. Critics countenance certain dimensional liberties when they are charged with traditional sanction of aesthetic expression. Critics approve sculptural compositions set in 'social perspective' where the sculptor indicates seniority by gradations of scale. At all times, however, critics rank sculpture upon a theory of relative proportion. The members of a king's entourage must be carved in proportion to one another, regardless of their scale in relation to the monarch. (42)

For me, the issue is even more rigid than I could accept some years ago. After a performance of Ola Rotimi's *The Gods Are Not to Blame*, an adaptation of *Oedipus Rex* into nineteenth century Yorubaland, I objected to the implacable fate of King Odewale within a solution-seeking Yoruba culture. I had no problem as long as the play was seen and performed within the Greek cultural environment in which it came into being. But to bill it as a Yoruba thing as Ola Rotimi insisted on doing, seemed to me to be wrongheaded. I was speaking to Ola Rotimi against the background of translations into Yoruba of Greek classical plays by Olanipekun Esan, who was, in my undergraduate years at the University of Ibadan, a senior lecturer in the classics department. He had translated *Mercator* by Plautus as *Orekelewa, Aya Ninalowo*, Sophocles' *Oedipus* as *Teledalase*, and Plato's *Krito* as *K'a s'ooto k'a ku*. I had played a part in *Orekelewa*, although I do not now recall the part I played. I was also arguing with Ola Rotimi in terms of a long Yoruba narrative poem, *Olorun Esan* (Vengeance is God's), in which a man whose kolanut tree is maliciously cut down avenges himself by getting the daughter of the offender beheaded. In my thinking, knowing as I thought I did the

Yoruba penchant for solution seeking with the help of the *babalawo*, something would have been done to avert such terrible tragedies as that of King Odewale (Oedipus) and the owner of the kolanut tree. It is a measure of Ola Rotimi's deeper understanding of Yoruba culture that he based his argument solely on the Yoruba distinction between the world of art and the world of everyday life. These two worlds do not operate in the same parameters, with the same value systems. One does not and cannot replicate or represent the other. The moral finality that operates in the world of art might be impossible to impose on the world of everyday life. Is the Yoruba world of art, then, the world of the moral absolute? In my final year at Kings' College those of us who were doing advanced level literature were asked to work with the Nottingham Playhouse, which was visiting Lagos, Nigeria, with two Shakespeare plays, one of them *Macbeth*, one of our set books for that year, 1963. Judi Dench played Lady Macbeth. At the point where Macbeth puts out his hand and talks about how 'this my hand will the multitudinous seas incarnadine, making the green one red' the Lagos audience would burst into laughter. The actors and actresses wanted us to explain that peculiar reaction. All we could say was that as far as the audience was concerned, the person playing Macbeth was taking the whole thing too seriously. 'After all, it is only a play!'

The second fundamental formal issue is the fact that actors and actresses in a Yoruba performance do not play roles; rather, they play with their roles. The words *efe* (indulgent enjoyment more akin to *jol* in Afrikaans) and *ere* (play) highlight this formal issue.

The third fundamental formal issue has to do with the fact that the performance is a celebration to be enjoyed by both the audience and the performers in a unified encounter of participants, rather than by players and onlookers in isolation.

Whether these characteristics can be called African and can be generalised into the theatre performances of other parts of the continent is another matter all together. Professor Adedeji quotes Hubert Ogunde as saying, 'African theatre is a *celebration*. At the end of it, ensure that your audience show appreciation for the encounter and its experience with relish' (*Nigerian Theatre: Dynamics of a Movement*, 64).

Johannes Birringer observes in the preface of his *Theatre, Theory, Postmodernism* (Indiana University Press, 1993): 'Among actors, directors, and writers there is very little discussion about what a "postmodern theatre" might be, and we notice that same reluctance among drama critics and scholars who continue to write about a world of texts and performances that seems largely untouched by the debates on the politics of postmodernism or on the technological transformation of the late modern culture' (xi). Based on what has happened in the area of prose narratives and poetry, a post-modernist theatre would be one which 'technologised and edited out history – the erasure of specific histories, traditions and cultural differences promoted by the globalizing spectacles of postmodern capitalism'. But this seems quite difficult if not impossible. It would seem that there is an absolute dependence of theatre on the past – on the history of drama, on cultural history mediated by techniques of acting and a structural dependence on current institutions and conventions of representation.

Whilst critics of African literature have not been shy about applying deconstructionist, modernist, colonial, post-modernist and post-colonial theories to African prose writing and poetry, these same critics have been wary about corralling theatre, drama and performance from Africa into a theory that denies the relevance of history to artistic endeavours. It is obvious that we do not partake enough of the rationalities that made it possible for western artists and critics to consider themselves outside of the history of the horrors of the wars of the twentieth century. If anything, we were some of the victims of these wars and their horrors. Yet, we do have our own problems with our own history *vis-à-vis* the history of the western world.

We do not share enough of the post-colonial to think ourselves part of the post-colonial world. We are not modern beyond the crude levels of our consumerism to think ourselves post-modern. As for deconstruction, our daily existence demonstrates it. What else can describe our socio-economic condition of a few winners in a home full of losers, a few western-educated Africans in homes full of illiterates and unemployables, other than a situation of deconstruction? How do we make sense of a history of enslavement, colonization and continuing exploitation? How do we make sense of a continuous line of disastrous political leadership – Mobutu, Bukassa, Idi Amin, Sani Abacha, Eyadema, Ngoassou – placed against one or two worthies, such as Mandela and Nyerere? We seem to inhabit the designated sites of violence, sites of profit and exploitation, sites of disease and ignorance, sites of expendable people. At my last visit to Akure in June 2001 the streets were grid (greed)-locked and there was no longer space for those communal performances that have enlivened the people of that town for decades.

The *post* that is relevant to our situation and our history is the *post-tribal* state. The post-tribal state can be said to have been inaugurated at the Berlin Conference of 1884–5. Africa was delimited and mapped as a place of modern states with no consideration of tribal borders and cultural differences. Some 'nation-states' have as many as two hundred and fifty tribes while others have one or two. Whatever the number of tribes in each modern African nation-state, Africa has arrived at the post-tribal condition in which tribal differences are deemed dangerous and even unmentionable. At the inception of the Organization of African Unity in 1964, African heads of state agreed to accept the African borders delimited by European powers at the Berlin Conference. This acceptance of the post-tribal state confirmed a continuity of European colonial order into the period of paper independence. As the period of independence comes to an end, with either globalization or retribalization (à la Eritrea), we need to examine the failure of the post-tribal state.

European colonizing powers were ignorant of the complexity of the tribal compositions of Africa. They dealt with each tribe in the same way that the World Bank and the International Monetary Fund has dealt with African countries in the latter half of the twentieth century – one cap fits all, one medicine cures all. At the same time, the African political process – from W. E. B. Du Bois and Marcus Garvey to Kwame Nkrumah and Jomo Kenyatta – ignored the tribe in the name of a pan-African unity against Euro-American imperialism, colonialism and neo-colonialism. In this way the African political process of the post-tribal state of the colonial powers has continued under independent political leadership. Much needed political unity has eluded every African country, multi-tribal or uni-tribal. Theatre, drama and performance have been the instruments of the undermining of the post-tribal state or *status quo ante*.

The term *post-tribal state* can go behind the Berlin Conference, however. The long period between the initial contact between Europeans and Africans in the fourteenth century up to the nineteenth century can be seen as a period of the invention of the available African, never mind his tribal designation, living in sites of exploitation and profit.

The unedited acceptance of the political agenda of pan-Africanism was always going to be problematic, if not for the Caribbean or the African-American political activist, then definitely for the African. While the Caribbean and the African-American shed the linguistic and cultural specifics of the African, the African returning to Nigeria, Ghana or Kenya was returning to his people, his language and his culture. At the capital of the newly independent African country, he might play the game of the post-tribal state, but back in his own area he would have to speak the local language, not the colonial language, if he was to be understood. Juggling two identities – post-tribal African state and a tribe-specific – where does his loyalty lie? His loyalty is a lie! Whilst the political agenda for independence and liberation needed the input of all the tribes of the particular countries, the cultural agenda of Africa is dependent on the particular cultures of each African tribe. To ignore, deplore and even aspire to destroy the cultures of these tribes in the name of a non-tribal African political agenda has been the most damaging action of the post-tribal state. That we are now at the point of the failure of that post-tribal state is made obvious by the fact of two contradictory actions – globalization and the creation recently of the African Union. Both actions attempt to continue the reign of the post-tribal state. Unfortunately, its failure is so massive that nothing can save it.

In the meantime, theatre, drama and performance will continue to assert that the holy places of African peoples are not in Jerusalem, not in Mecca and Medina, not in the consumer emporiums of London, Paris, New York and Tokyo. Rather, our performance traditions will continue to assert that our holy places are next door to us, in the affirmation of our tribal identity within the embrace of our modern African country's identity, and that our everyday sacred and secular rituals continue in our indigenous languages.

Note

1. Professor Adedeji died in 2001, so sadly this volume will not appear.

2 North Africa

Egypt

AHMED ZAKI

Theatre in the form of written, staged and acted drama is a comparatively modern construct in Egypt. However, the roots that have nurtured and helped the Egyptian theatre to develop its own unique style lie in the performing arts that appeared over five thousand years ago. The palimpsest of modern Egypt is, in effect, the result of its long history, different religious traditions, the influence of diverse occupying powers, an Islamic heritage and modern pan-Arab affiliations.

Even today, local or national celebrations or inaugurations bear witness to the age, diversity and strength of the performing arts, displaying both their origins in folk or historical or long-forgotten religious traditions and incorporating new elements from local sources or abroad to make a vibrant synthesis typical of a very Egyptian approach.

The ancient land of Egypt in the north-east of Africa had boundaries that were also clearly defined barriers: the Mediterranean in the north, the first Nile cataract in the south, the Red Sea and the Arabian Desert to the east, and the Sahara Desert and the Libyan mountains in the west. However, as the Egyptians say, Egypt is the gift of the Nile. The river rises in Lake Victoria (White Nile) and is fed by the melting snows and monsoons from the Ethiopian highlands (Blue Nile), which causes annual floods in the late summer, with the waters receding in autumn leaving rich deposits of silt. The Nile was the source of life, movement and settlement for the early Egyptians, who arrived as hunters from the south, followed by various migrations from Asia in the east and other peoples arriving from the rapid desertification of the western grasslands. The Nile valley was known as the Black Land (Kemt), while the desert was the Red Land. Egypt was also divided between the south (Upper Egypt) and the more fertile delta land in the north (Lower Egypt). The Two Lands, as they were known, developed separately until they were united under Narmer (Mena) from the south in 3100 BC. This union also united the two major religions: the sun worship of the south, Amon Ra, and the nature worship of the delta, Ptah.

13

Pharaonic period

The intricacies of the varied cults and their presiding gods and goddesses are too many to present here. However, it is clear that a belief in rebirth was central to ancient Egypt: the rebirth of the sun – Ra – and the regeneration of the land – Osiris – and, as an extension, the rebirth of man. This belief was of crucial importance to an agricultural society and applied to both men and women. It was believed that certain ceremonies had to be carried out. They required specialist knowledge, skills, objects, dedication, spaces and wealth. This led to the rise of the priestly caste, who were originally intermediaries between Pharaoh and the god and who acquired enormous power, lands, wealth, temples and associated workers while handing down, adjudicating and embellishing the traditions during the thirty dynasties of pharaonic rulers, roughly divided into the Old Kingdom, the Middle Kingdom and the New Kingdom.

At first religious and ceremonial occasions dominated the calendar. An example of the grand ceremonial religious drama first appeared in written form on the Shabako Stone, which is a late copy of probably the first drama in history, the Memphite Drama, indicating the rivalry between the cities of Heliopolis (On), the centre of the worship of the sun god Amon Ra, and Memphis, the Nile port city situated on the border between the two lands, which had been chosen as the capital of the newly united country and whose god was nature, Ptah.

The earliest appearance of mortuary literature, believed to stem from very early oral traditions enacted by the priests, is the carved Pyramid Texts in the pyramid of Unas (Old Kingdom, fifth Dynasty, 2494–2345 BC) in Sakkara. The texts are hymns, rituals, prayers for the release of the soul from the body and a list of offerings. However, much later non-royal provincial rulers adapted these texts for their own coffins and the final version, 'The Book of the Dead' was a roll of papyrus incorporating all the modified and revised magical incantations and resurrection texts with their prayers, ceremonies and traditions.

The annual enactment of the Abydos Osiris Passion Play attracted thousands of pilgrims as well as the court. The fertility god Osiris had been betrayed, killed and dismembered by the evil Seth and his body parts scattered up and down the Nile, from where they were rescued by his consort Isis and his son Horus, who reassembled them, and Osiris returned to life. Osiris's head was supposed to have been buried in Abydos, which became a holy place for the burial of the pharaohs. The Passion play of the life, death and triumph of Osiris was a re-enactment by the priests and priestesses. The holy boat (*barque*) on which the mummified Osiris sat was carried from his shrine through the courts of the temple and stopped at various stations in the surrounding town, returning in triumph to the temple and culminating in the raising of the Djed pillar (a prehistoric pillar-like fetish). In the Old Kingdom only royalty and the aristocracy participated. However, in the Middle Kingdom ordinary people participated in sharing Isis's sorrow, singing hymns, making offerings and enjoying the mock battle with Seth, then following the mummified figure of Osiris in the joyful triumphant procession back to the temple.

The Opet festival was held annually at the height of the flooding of the Nile. The two temples of Thebes were Luxor and Karnak, which were dedicated to the trinity of Amon, his consort Mut and their son Khonsu. Thousands of pilgrims in Thebes joined the procession, as the sacred barges of Amon were carried from Karnak to Luxor, where the god would visit his harem accompanied by sacrifices and offerings. After twenty-four days of celebration the procession returned to Karnak, where it was welcomed with rejoicing and sacrifices. In the paintings of the Opet festival on the walls of Luxor temple the scenes include people clapping rhythmically, dancers, Nubian slaves, acrobats, people kneeling in adoration, and priestesses with *sistras* (rattles made of metal or faience, often topped with the head of the goddess Hathor).

Modern echoes of this ancient ceremony still take place in the month of Shabaan, the month before the fasting month of Ramadan, in Luxor, when, during the *moulid* or birthday celebrations of Abul Hagag, there is a procession from his mosque, built in the thirteenth century in the medieval Fatimid village. This procession of floats is paraded through the city, which is full of people enjoying the moulid.

The daily rituals of the temples, beginning with purification in the sacred lakes, usually took place out of sight and within the sanctuaries, but are depicted on the walls of the temples.

The living pharaohs were celebrated by coronation festival plays and, more importantly, by the Heb Sed. This celebrates the jubilee of the coronation and the renewal of the vigour of the pharaoh, and is a re-enactment of the unification of Upper Egypt and Lower Egypt.

Many visual and recorded depictions of this ceremony are extant, showing the rituals of running the double course, the shooting of four arrows, libations ceremonially carried by young princesses, female dancers, jugglers and participants. These scenes are depicted in the Luxor tomb of Kheru-ef, steward of Queen Tiy (Eighth Dynasty, 1567 BC) and in the Great Festival Temple of Thutmose III (1504–1450 BC), built in honour of Amon Ra in the temple complex of Karnak.

Most of the festivals were governed by the calendar, such as the celebrations of New Year (dating from the calendar compiled in Heliopolis (On) in 4241 BC), the beginning of the seasons and their associated agricultural events, namely sowing, harvesting and inundation. Many towns had their own calendar of processions, appearances of the local god or goddess and mysteries. However, river festivals attracted enormous crowds of pilgrims and sightseers, particularly that of Hathor of Dendera, who journeyed by boat to spend a fortnight in Edfu with her husband Horus – a festival joyously celebrated at every town at which they halted after coming together in mid-stream.

The festival of Bast at Bubastis in the Delta attracted up to 700,000 pilgrims: men and women ready to laugh, drink and enjoy themselves, recorded Herodotus. The modern feast of St George at Mit Damsis, celebrated nearby, echoes the old waterborne festival.

The importance of death as the beginning of the journey to rebirth is indicated by the elaborate funeral ceremonies of both royalty and rich men and women which took place after the ceremonial embalming of seventy days and the preparation of the mummy case. In Thebes funeral ceremonies involved professional mourners joining the family at a dead man's house; a procession carrying the deceased and his belongings to the Nile to transport the lamenting family to the tomb, where the priests led the ritual chants and rites of burial; the farewell to the dead as the coffin was lowered into the vault, and finally the return to the home for the funerary banquet. These scenes of mourning were re-enacted spontaneously by the peasants from Upper Egypt in 1881, when the women wailed in mourning and ran with dishevelled hair as the royal mummies were transported by steamer down the Nile from Luxor to Cairo to be placed in the museum.

Music was an art form that touched all people. It was a sacred art in the temples, performed by royalty (Queen Nefertari is portrayed shaking two sistra in Luxor Temple) and gods and goddesses: the goddess Hathor has her sistra, and her son is known as the sistra player; Bast has her sistra, and Bes uses his grimaces and tambourine to chase away the demons. There are papyri showing priestess-musicians; both royal and aristocratic ladies played instruments in the great religious ceremonies. Music was said to delight the gods, cheer men's hearts, soothe women in childbirth and drive away evil.

Secular musical performances in great houses and palaces were led by blind harpists or by troupes of young women musicians. The main instruments were sistra, harp, lute, lyre (imported from Asia in the New Kingdom), trumpet (used ritually but mostly as a military signal), wind instruments such as flute, double pipes and double clarinet, drums, round or rectangular tambourines, magical clappers made of wood or ivory and bead rattles, as well as the clicking of fingers and the clapping of hands.

Songs, sung by choirs, were many and various. There were elaborate hymns to the gods, the best known of which is the hymn to Aten, composed by Akhenaten, the worshipper of the one god, Aten; there were songs performed during the rituals and ceremonies of the gods, the pharaohs and the queens. There were songs of praise and funerary dirges; field songs to be sung by the harvesters and at seed-time; work songs to be sung by fishermen, boatmen on the Nile, builders and craftsmen; love songs and drinking songs sung in the beerhouses in the towns and villages or recited and sung at banquets to the accompaniment of music.

For the ancient Egyptians the word *dance* meant 'rejoice'. It was an integral part of religious ritual: 'the pharaoh comes to dance – he comes to sing'. There were many ritual dances and choreographed processions. Dance was performed as part of the festivals, Heb Sed, and at funerals. In the Old Kingdom, pygmies greeted the sun god with their acrobatics. Dance developed a complete choreography with complex rhythms, and it can be seen in the graceful movements of the dancing girls entertaining the guests at the elaborate banquets of the New Kingdom. In the Middle Kingdom young girls would dance the Song of the Four Winds. Acrobatic dancers also entertained. Sacred dancers made up part of the temple complex.

There were other kinds of entertainment, such as bullfights and gymnastic games, as well as forms of sport linked to military prowess, including mock fights with sticks, which are still popular.

Storytelling was part of the oral tradition, using simple language and a repetitive style. From the small number that were written down, we know that they dealt with mythology, everyday life and the supernatural, sometimes consisting of a linked sequence of stories.

Over the long stretch of recorded history there was naturally a great deal of cultural exchange, diffusion and incorporation, with Mesopotamia, Assyria, Palestine and Syria to the east, Libya to the west, Crete and the

Aegean to the north and Nubia in the south. Nubia was reached by the great highway of the Nile or by the route across the desert which was the predecessor of the Forty Days' March used later for bringing slaves from Darfur into Egypt.

The ancient Egyptians knew Nubia as the 'daughter of the sun'. The orientation of Egypt was south (thus putting west on the right hand), towards the source of the Nile, from where the original settlers had come. Aswan was the southernmost city. Nubia was divided from Egypt by narrow cataracts. In reality, the countries were independent but were linked. In the Old Kingdom Nubians were recruited to fight in the army and acted as border police. In the Middle Kingdom Nubia lost its independence and was much influenced by Egyptian culture and religion – the Nubian and Kushite nobility took part in Egyptian ceremonial processions, and Egyptian soldiers settled in Nubia. Later the Kush (Sudanese) and Meroe empires spread northwards to control the southern part of Egypt during the New Kingdom period (750–656 BC).

The importance of Nubia to Egypt was as a gateway to the south: to Kush (Sudan), to Punt (Eritrea and Somalia) and to Ethiopia – a source of gold, ivory and slaves. The fighting tribes of Nubia remained a problem to Rome, who signed a treaty with the Meroite kingdom limiting them to the area of Lower Nubia. Coptic Christianity, which became the national religion of Egypt in AD 451, spread through Nubia to Sudan and Ethiopia. (Hundreds of long-abandoned, ruined churches and monasteries were sunk beneath the artificial Lake Nasser, formed when the High Dam was built across the Nile at Aswan in 1971). After the Arab conquest (640) the Christian Nubians paid tribute (*gizya*) to their Islamic conquerors, but later the entire Nubian people converted to Islam.

The building of the High Dam meant the destruction of much of Nubia. The Nubian population was moved to higher ground, but most of the history and ancient monuments of Nubia were drowned beneath the lake, with the notable exceptions of Abu Simbel, Philae and a few other monuments, which were saved with the help of UNESCO.

Graeco-Roman period

During the pharaonic period the Egyptian empire had stretched to many parts of the Mediterranean and north Africa, as well as east to Palestine and Syria. There had long been links between the Aegean and Egypt. Greeks had arrived in Egypt as mercenaries, traders and pilgrims to various cults (see Aeschylus and *Helen* by Euripides) or as interested visitors, such as

Herodotus. The Macedonian king, Alexander the Great, entered Egypt from the east across Sinai after his conquest of Persia and Syria (Egypt was then ruled by Persian satraps as part of the now defeated Persian empire). He took over the capital city of Memphis, then moved north to the Mediterranean, where he chose the site of the new city of Alexandria. The Greek occupation, known as the Ptolemaic Period, lasted for three centuries. Memphis remained the official capital, where the Ptolemies were crowned as pharaohs, buried, deified and worshipped. However, the spiritual and intellectual centre of Egypt moved to Alexandria, which became a Greek centre of culture and a Greek city-state, the most powerful and lively among the other Greek city-states of the Mediterranean. Outside Alexandria there were many other Greek settlements and cities settled by Greek and Macedonian veterans and traders, who often adopted Egyptian customs and gods. The cities in Fayoum had theatres, gymnasia, baths and Greek chapels alongside Egyptian temples. Fayoum has produced a vast amount of Greek papyri – including the only extant copy of a lost satyr play of Sophocles, *The Trackers*, whose discovery inspired *The Trackers of Oxyrhynchus* by Tony Harrison.

Alexandria was a Greek city, built of white marble with Egyptian features that had often been removed from Egyptian temples. Ptolemy Soter built the famous Mouseion, 'a Temple to the Muses', consisting of colleges, laboratories, observatoria, a teaching hospital and a library containing Aristotle's private library, original dramas of Euripides and Aeschylus, and works of Sophocles. The official language became Greek. Public records of the activities of the pharaohs and details of national and religious feasts, both Greek and Egyptian, were kept.

Although previously during the Saite (southern Egyptian, sixth century) period the priests had made a list of all the traditions that had been observed before the country had been affected by outside influence, the Greeks misunderstood the religious culture and tradition of the country they now ruled. Their first step was to create hybrid gods, the chief of which was Serapis (Osir-Apis) who combined the characteristics of Osiris and the bull god Apis of Memphis with the Hellenistic attributes of Zeus, Aesculapius and Dionysos. The existing temple was renamed the Serapeum and rebuilt to accommodate the Graeco-Egyptian worshippers and the colossal statue of the new god brought from Asia Minor. Isis, Osiris's consort, absorbed the identity of Demeter. Horus, their son, was identified with Apollo/Harpocrates. Their cults spread throughout the Hellenized world. The beliefs and traditions of the existing Egyptian settlement of Rakhotis were still celebrated, such as cutting the canal at the time of the flood. Although the city was cosmopolitan, with areas for Levantines and Jews, there was little intercourse with the local Egyptians, apart from the Hellenized priestly class. Cleopatra VII was the first Ptolemy to learn hieroglyphics and to speak Egyptian.

The Alexandrian scholars at the Mouseion recorded the theatre practices of the early Hellenistic age. Pollux's list of tragic masks uses this source – the masks of the fat men are explained as deriving from Egyptian prototypes. Many terracotta and faience Greek masks, and copies of musical instruments, can be seen in the Graeco-Roman Museum in Alexandria. Alexandria had its own group of tragic poets and its own Guild of Artists of Dionysos, who, apart from acting in the many theatres, took part in the great processions organised by the Ptolemies, and performed in competition with actors from all over the world at the many Mediterranean Greek drama festivals. Theocritus wrote a lively dialogue for two contemporary Greek ladies attending a festival in the city.

With the death of Cleopatra VII in 30 BC the Romans took control of the eastern Mediterranean. Although the Roman rule of Egypt was a continuation of the Greek, the main change was that Egypt was no longer an independent nation with its own capital city and kings, but became the personal property of Augustus, a granary to feed Rome and a source of taxed tribute. Greek was still the official language of the administration. Greek culture remained dominant in Alexandria and in the Hellenized cities on the coast and inland. Egyptians continued to worship their traditional gods, but the financial affairs of the priesthood were controlled by a Roman official. To break the power of the priests of Abydos the cult of Osiris was moved near Aswan. The beautiful temples to Isis were completed in Philae to become the centres of the dominant cult and of pilgrimage and festivities. There is practically no trace of Roman deities in Egypt, although the emperors recorded their tours up the Nile to the various temples.

The Romans continued to build public baths and forums – such as the odeum of Kom El Dikka in Alexandria – as well as extending Pelusium on the eastern road in Sinai with fortresses, an amphitheatre and baths, and continuing the picnics and visits to Canopus at the Mediterranean mouth of the Canopic branch of the Nile (now extant). The Romans' love of what has been described as decadent entertainment, riches and luxury appears in a mosaic of a dancing girl performing for a rich family's picnic (now in the Graeco–Roman Museum in Alexandria).

Christian era

The Gospel according to Matthew records the flight to Egypt of Mary, Joseph and Jesus to escape Herod's persecution, and their return to Palestine. After the death of Jesus the early Jewish fathers of the new religion travelled throughout the Hellenized world to propagate the message of Christianity. Saint Mark arrived in Alexandria, the second most important city after Rome, in about AD 40. The Egyptians, whose ancient religion was in decline, had an educated Hellenized class of high officials who were familiar with a mixture of Greek and oriental philosophy and in whose Mouseion the Old Testament had been translated in 250 BC (The Septuagent). They, as well as a large Jewish population in the city, began to convert to Christianity. In the face of cruel Roman persecution many converts fled to the desert and to Upper Egypt, where they created the hermitage movement, often occupying deserted tombs, chapels and temples. The monastic movement was a purely Egyptian innovation developing rapidly after the persecution of the Emperor Diocletian between AD 284 and 305. The Coptic calendar dates from AD 284, the Year of the Martyrs. These Coptic establishments later took on the force of a nationalist resistance movement against the Roman occupation, which intensified when Constantine the Great (324–37) appointed the Bishop of Alexandria from Rome. Finally, the Emperor Theodosius (d. 395) made Christianity the official religion of Egypt, which became part of the Eastern Roman Empire (Byzantine). After many violent schisms the monophysite (belief in the one nature in the person of Jesus) Coptic Church of Egypt was established in 451, with a Coptic Pope and Patriarch in Alexandria and a nominal authority over the Ethiopian Church.

Inevitably, during the long-drawn-out process of the establishment of Christianity, many elements of earlier ways of life and of religion were retained, modified or transformed. The three ancient Egyptian dialects of Lower Egypt (Borhairic), Middle Egypt (Oxyrhynchus) and Upper Egypt (Sahidic) were used for sacred writing in the vernacular, which contained some Greek words that were later eliminated as being the language of the invader and the tax collector. It was written in the Greek alphabet with the addition of seven extra demotic characters. The spoken and written language was widely used until the thirteenth century and still survives in the Coptic liturgy. It is in the liturgy and music of the Coptic Church that the echoes of an ancient Egyptian past are most enduring. In the Book of Psalms, many psalms are clearly derived from the ancient Egyptian hymns of praise and worship of the old gods and pharaohs. The early Coptic monks learnt by heart parts of the Book of Psalms in Egyptian in order to qualify for the priesthood. The earliest complete Book of Psalms ever found, dating from about AD 400, was in the tomb of a young girl in the Fayoum.

Dr Ragheb Mofta, a prominent scholar of the Coptic Church liturgy who spent years working on the Oral History Project for the US Library of Congress, states that apart from the use of the ancient words of praise, pharaonic elements are clear in the process of handing down the chant orally by blind master cantors and also in the techniques of drawing out the sound. In keeping with the ascetic beginning of the early church, the only music used was the harp (Greek lyre); later it was augmented by cymbals, drums, flutes, clarinets and the sistrum. Completely new musical instruments were added, such as the *naqus* – a kind of bell struck with an iron rod. Modern liturgies are accompanied by hand cymbals, *sagat*, and a metal triangle, *muthalleth*. The highly decorated churches with the iconostasis dividing the congregation from the altar, the hanging ostrich eggs, candles, incense and elaborate vestments of the clergy, are all rich symbolic elements of the celebration of the rituals of the Coptic liturgy.

Under the Byzantine rulers and the promptings of the newly independent church, there was a systematic destruction of many of the old temples and statues. However, mass pilgrimages continued to the sites newly associated with the wanderings of the Holy Family, or with Christian martyrs and holy men or women such as Saint Catherine, whose Greek Orthodox monastery is in Sinai. Saint Menas, an Egyptian soldier with the Roman army who was martyred for refusing to pray to the Roman gods, was venerated in a vast church in the western desert which attracted pilgrims from all over the Mediterranean. There were also annual pilgrimages from Egypt to spend Easter in Jerusalem and to bathe in the River Jordan.

The main festivals of the Coptic Church are the Nativity, the Baptism of Christ, the Annunciation, Palm Sunday, Easter, Ascension and Whitsun. As late as the early nineteenth century Edward Lane described how at the Feast of Baptism men would plunge into the river and the feast would take on the elements of a river festival, with festive barges, music and picnics. Even today the old pharaonic festival of Shem Il Nessim ('smell the breezes') is celebrated by Copts and Muslims alike on Easter Monday, when families go out early to picnic in green spaces: gardens, fields and on the banks of the Nile.

Although there is very little evidence, many of the folk traditions of singing, music and dancing obviously continued. For example, there is a

Coptic tapestry from Bawit, an oasis in Upper Egypt, showing singers, musicians and dancers

Islamic period

In AD 640 the city of Alexandria was captured by an Arab Islamic army sent by Caliph Omar. The commander Amr ibn al-As described the white marble city as having 4,000 palaces, 4,000 baths and 400 theatres. (So far, only the remains of three theatres have been found.) He then turned south up the Nile to the apex of the delta to take the old Roman fortress that was also the seat of an important Coptic bishopric. Egypt became a military province of the caliphate ruled from Mecca. The conquerors built their new Islamic military base and centre of government at Fustat, now part of Cairo.

From this point on and for more than 1,200 years Egypt's fate was linked to the constant rise and fall of the different dynasties and peoples controlling part or all of the Islamic Empire or Umma. To Egypt the Arabs brought their new religion, Islam, a new administrative official language and script, Arabic, and an allegiance to the rapidly developing new Islamic Empire that was eventually to spread from north-west Africa and Spain to central Asia.

The changes took time. For the following two centuries the dominant national religion remained Coptic Christianity, with non-Muslims paying a tax (*gisya*). Whilst Islam and Arabic spread through the rest of Egypt, in Upper Egypt Christianity and Egyptian remained until the fourteenth century.

The first Islamic building in Egypt was the mosque of Amr ibn al-As in Fustat. This was used for congregational prayer and later for teaching men and women preachers; it was also where the judge (*Qadi*) heard both religious and civil cases.

The most important Islamic ruling dynasties in Egypt were as follows. From AD 640 Egypt was ruled by the Caliph Omar and from Mecca in the Higaz until 658–750, when the Omayyads ruled from Damascus. This was followed by the Abbasid Dynasty ruling from Baghdad until 805, when Ahmed Ibn Tulun, a Circassian soldier, set up an independent caliphate in Egypt. The Shiite Fatimid Dynasty from Cairoun in the Maghreb (modern Morocco/Tunis), who were descendants of the Prophet Mohammed's daughter Fatma, moved their capital to Cairo in 972. The Fatimid Caliph Muizz had built Cairo (Qahira) in 969 as a fortified centre for the new caliphate. He also built the mosque of Al-Azhar as a state mosque for congregational purposes and to be one of the world's greatest centres of Islamic studies, which became a pattern for universities throughout the world. For two hundred years Cairo flourished as a centre of Shiite learning and culture. Salah el Din el Ayyubi (Saladin), a Kurd, restored the Sunni Muslim caliphate during his 24-year rule (1169–1193), known as the Ayyubid Dynasty. When he gained control of Egypt he built his own fortified citadel dominating the old developments that he enclosed, and so created the core of the city of Cairo familiar from the stories of *The Thousand and One Nights*.

From 1250 the Mamluks, a military slave corps, overthrew the Ayyubids and established their own ruling dynasty, ushering in a turbulent period of violence and intrigue as well as a period of culture, trade, wealth and artistic and architectural development. The beginning of the sixteenth century saw Egypt once again demoted to a provincial capital, this time as part of the Ottoman Empire, but still ruled by Mamluks loyal to the Turkish Ottoman sultans.

Under the Fatimids' two hundred years of luxurious rule, the people of the city were encouraged to participate in public festivities. They continued the old customs of the ancient seasonal celebrations and the ceremonies of the agricultural year, such as the solar New Year festival, the Nile festivals of the flood (Wafa al-Nil) and the ceremonial cutting of the dam on the *khalig* (canal) with the throwing of a doll into the waters. The Fatimids also illuminated the city at the great Christian feasts. Most importantly, they added new Islamic celebrations to the calendar: the Muslim lunar New Year, Ashura, the celebrations of the nights of the fasting month of Ramadan, and, in addition to the Birthday of the Prophet (Moulid el Nabi), they celebrated the birthdays (*moulids*) of Fatma el Zahra and of Al Husayn, the Prophet's grandson who was slain at Karbala and whose head is buried in his mosque in Cairo – he, the Shiite believe, was the rightful heir to the caliphate after the Prophet died. The Fatimids added about fifty religious occasions, including moulids, to the calendar and also brought Sufi traditions with them as part of their Shiite beliefs.

Visitors to Egypt, and especially to Cairo, left descriptions of the taverns that lined the Khalij, and of the many seasonal lakes and gardens in the city filled with pleasure boats and music. They describe the entertainers: geomancers, astrologers, shadow puppeteers, storytellers, acrobats, tightrope walkers and dancers, as well as performing animals such as fleas, donkeys, camels and dancing Arab Bedouin horses held on a tight rein.

Shadow puppets had originated in the Far East, but took on a specifically Cairene character upon their arrival. Ibn Daniyal in the thirteenth century wrote the first Arab shadow play, *Ajib wa Gharib*, a humorous sketch on the entertainers and commen of his time Later shadow puppets were used to ingratiate the players with the new Ottoman conqueror in 1517, re-enacting the capture and execution of the last Mameluk Sultan of Cairo. Other performances were based on the Crusades and Salah el Din. They remained popular until the coming of the cinema.

The public also enjoyed performances of military prowess, especially those of the Mameluks, including archery and horse-riding in the large parade ground squares within and outside the city, where games and other ceremonial parades also took place. There were elaborate public ceremonies at the start and return of the annual overland and sea pilgrimage to Mecca (the Hajj). These were preceded by the procession of the caravan conveying the heavily embroidered cover for the Kaaba in Mecca (the Mahmal) that continued until 1926. However, the tradition was renewed by King Farouk in 1936, although the Mahmal was only allowed to go as far as Jeddah, and was finally discontinued in 1962.

When the Englishman Edward Lane visited and described Cairo in the early nineteenth century, it had not changed very much from the life of the medieval city. Apart from the previously mentioned entertainers and ceremonies, there were the Karagöz, the Turkish glove puppets who had also acquired a very Egyptian local character, the belligerent Aragouz.

The only acting group he describes are the Mohabbazeen, who were players of low farces at festivals, at the houses of the great and in public places. The actors were men and boys impersonating women when necessary, who got their laughs from vulgar gestures and sexually indecent actions. Sometimes the performance might take a contemporary critical or political turn.

Lane also describes the performances that accompanied domestic or social celebrations, such as birth, circumcision, marriage, the return from pilgrimage, joining a guild, the entertainment of friends, or, finally, the presence of the *naddada*, the professional wailing women and eulogists, at funerals.

Music was vital to all these entertainments. The musical terminology and some of the instruments that were not of Egyptian origin, being derived from Andalusia, Baghdad, Persia and Turkey, were adapted to the Egyptian style. Music of the highly sophisticated courts and wealthy upper classes had been written about since Fatimid times. However, the folk rhymes and music of the people were a constant accompaniment to everyday rural and city life:

builders and those involved in the physical activities of sailing and fishing, as well as street criers, all had distinctive rhythms, pitches and melodies.

The guild system was highly developed in Cairo, as befitted a city that was an international market. Singers, musicians and dancers all had their own guilds and lived in their own separate quarters of the city. Most of the public dancing girls and men came from a tribe called Ghawazee; they usually married within their own tribe, although some of the women doubled as prostitutes.

In the great houses and palaces singers, *almahs* – the name signifies they were trained and could instruct – and musicians often performed behind a screen or in a separate room divided from the courtyard or grand hall, and were watched from behind screens on the floor above by the women of the house. They would be hired to entertain at domestic festivities, to entertain a party of men, or to perform in front of a house as part of wedding festivities. They would also entertain at all the great events and at the moulids, when they would perform in the streets or in tents. Very often in the houses of rulers and the very wealthy, among the slaves from all over Asia, Africa and parts of Europe who had been purchased from the slave market were people who had been trained in the arts of music, singing or dancing in the courts of Constantinople. Ethiopian (Galla) or Sudanese female slaves of the eighteenth century were supposed to have introduced the ceremony of the Zar, when physical and mental illnesses are cured by a female leader of a group driving its participants into a frenzy of movement with the beating of drums and the tinkling bells of amulets to exorcise and drive away evil.

Often singers, musicians, dancers and street entertainers would have a regular circuit and calendar of events that would take them up and down the country. These were linked to the enormous movements of pilgrims celebrating local and national moulids – festivals commemorating the birthday of a holy man or woman centred on their relics, tombs, mausoleums or mosques. Moulids were first introduced by the Fatimids but later took on an atmosphere of their own and are still widely celebrated, though with not quite the same elaboration and classless participation as in the past. During many of the moulids, as well as during the Ramadan nights, culminating in the Great Night (Layla Kebeera), public Sufi religious rituals, with many variations, would take place. Groups of the Sufi brotherhood (*Tariq*), each with their own distinctive banners and sometimes accompanied by musicians, would join the opening parade (*zeffa*), often led by a khalifa on horseback, to an illuminated tomb or mosque. The ceremony may have begun with a congregational invocation (*hudra*) then, if the dervishes were present, a highly symbolic spiritual whirling dance (*samaa*). Sufis would then join into a swaying circle, bowing to the right and moving with increasing speed to the rhythmic chant of 'Allah' (*zikr*). The religious ceremony might also include religious singers (*munshideen*) encouraged by onlookers' cries, and also Koranic reciters (*fikees*).

The oral skills of oratory, eulogy (*maddh*) and the art of rhetoric (*fann il khataba*) have always been greatly valued and appreciated by the Egyptian people. Preaching, the rhetoric of lawyers, judges and religious instructors, reached an extremely refined, high level of skill. The reading or recitation of the Koran, with many variations in the manner of recitation, and ways of maintaining the cadence and modulations of the voice, has been developed over the centuries by expert Koran reciters. Those present at a reading of the Koran, whether it is at a domestic ceremony, a funeral, during Ramadan nights, at moulids or other religious or state events, are also participants who, as they are moved by the spirituality of the words or the technique of the reader, take part with spontaneous and ritualised responses – praising God, not the reader! Poetry was recited at the great courts and palaces, among educated gatherings, in street recitals of epic poetry (*rawi*), outside coffee houses and at moulids, by itinerant poetry reciters (*shawa'ra*) accompanied by their musicians and encouraged by the onlookers expressing their emotional responses to the work or the skill of the reciter in dramatising the different characters.

A rich panoply of performing arts was available for the inhabitants of Cairo and some of the principal towns, whereas the folk arts and traditions were an intrinsic part of the life of the Saidi in Upper Egypt, the *fellahin* of the Delta, the Nubians, the fishermen of the coast, the Bedouins and the people of the oases. In the countryside at gatherings after the day's work was done, entertainment often took the form of the *Samer*, where those present mocked local dignitaries by mimicking them, or debating nationalistic or religious subjects using the skills of rhetoric or by epic recitation.

Modern: from Mohamed Aly and Napoleon

The traditional way of life, however, was beginning to undergo a complete change. Under the Ottomans, Egypt had reverted to being a province of Turkey, ruled for them by the slave caste of Mameluks. In 1798 Napoleon broke the military power of the Mameluks and took control of Egypt for the following four years. His revolutionary army was accompanied by artists, historians and scholars who carried out a detailed study of Egypt, illustrated in *Description d'Egypte* (20 vols., Paris: Imprimerie Impériale 1890; selected reprints by the American University of Cairo). He also sent for theatre troupes to perform in French for the French community.

Mohamed Aly arrived from Albania in 1805, wrested power from the weakened Mameluks, broke with Constantinople and created an independent Egypt within the Ottoman Empire. In his determination to create a powerful modern state he used forced labour and forcible recruitment for his modern army and navy and moved into Sudan, Greece, Syria and Arabia to form an empire that he later shared with Istanbul. He used the same principles, forcing taxes from the people to fund vast building and early industrialising projects. This attracted an influx of foreigners of all nationalities, both to participate in the projects and as tourists. However, Aly also sent Egyptian scholars abroad to study, principally to France and Italy. Among them was Sheikh Rifaa al Tahtawi, who admired the French theatre and translated classic French dramas into classical Arabic. Arabic itself had changed: the old Ottoman style and diction were being replaced by a modern Arabic which was better adapted to the new ideas. The first European-style Arabic productions were translated and adapted European classics acted in colloquial Arabic by Yacoub Sannu's National Theatre Company in 1870. Sannu (1839–1912), a Jewish Cairene journalist, later fell out of favour with the Khedive, who closed him down for political criticism.

The new dramas attracted audiences from the upper and upper-middle classes. New concepts of living inevitably accompanied the enormous social and infrastructural changes. Foreign capital was attracted to the building of new roads, railways, telegraph, factories and the Suez Canal. The Suez Canal debt led to the British taking control of Egypt when Khedive Ismail was unable to pay his dues. However, before he left, and as part of the celebrations of the opening of the canal, Ismail built the Cairo Opera House in 1869 and commissioned Verdi to write the opera *Aida* for the occasion, although it was not actually performed until later. In the 1870s there were three theatres in the Ezbekia area, which had been drained and planted as pleasure gardens: the Opera House (hosting foreign companies with elaborate sets), the Ezbekieh Theatre and a comedy theatre.

At its outset, the new phenomenon of theatre not only persuaded many local and provincial groups to form theatre companies, but also attracted foreign troupes from Damascus and Beirut, most importantly Salim al-Naqqash,

Soliman al-Qardahi and al-Qabbani, who was the first producer to use Arab and Islamic historical sources for his dramas. After the failure of the Orabi Revolution of 1882 to overthrow the Khedive, who was backed by the British, more nationalistic plays appeared on stage as part of a movement spearheaded by intellectuals, journalists, writers and scholars.

On a popular level musical shows, revues, comedy and farces were attracting new audiences. The Nile-side Rod el Farag area was the centre of comedy, with its many open-air theatres. Singers, dancers and comedians, who went on to become cinema and stage stars all over the Arab world, began there in the atmosphere of improvised acts and enthusiastic audience participation.

In the musical field Salama Higazi (1852–1917) combined traditional songs with operatic techniques to create a lyric opera style. Sayyid Darwish (1892–1923) wrote operettas based on nationalistic themes and people's everyday lives. The break with the Ottoman Empire came in World War One, although the British remained the occupying power. The growth of a more wealthy and educated Egyptian middle class increased the demand for culture and entertainment, especially the theatre.

George Abyad (1880–1959), who had remained in Cairo after a tour with a company from his native Beirut, formed his own company in 1910 and dominated the theatre scene in Cairo for the next twenty years, performing translated work and original Arabic plays, both tragedies and comedies, some of which he acted with his wife, Dawlet Abyad. He was joined by Salama Higazi, who wrote music for the productions, which travelled round the Arab world and which became the inspiration for forming companies both in Egypt and in other Arab countries, notably Tunisia.

Other notable troupes formed in this period included those of Abdullah Okasha (1880–1942), who encouraged Egyptian playwrights such as Tewfik el Hakim to write for him. Among the most influential comedy troupes were the Najib al-Rihani Comic Troupe (founded in 1916), who used comedy as social criticism. Al-Rihani specialised in parts in which he played the 'little man': the employee, the worker, the underling or the teacher struggling with authority figures. His early plays were often adapted from French farces. Later, in plays written by the great comic writer Badie Khairi (1893–1966), his comedies took on a more political, socially critical slant in the face of changes brought about by the new materialism. Ali al-Kassar founded his troupe in 1918. He established the trend for creating recognisable stock characters when he created the lovable innocent trickster Nubian dealing with various unsavoury big city types. The singer Munira al-Mahdiya founded her troupe in 1915, becoming the first Egyptian star singer/actress. Later Fatma Rushdie was the first serious dramatic actress/singer to set up her own company, in 1927.

Yousef Wahby (1898–1982) was an enormously popular actor-manager who came from an aristocratic background. He headed the most admired and popular troupe in the 1930s, performing social dramas and popular melodramas in Egyptian Arabic. Egyptian playwrights became established. Tewfik el Hakim (1898–1987) is considered to be the founding father of modern Egyptian drama. His long career spanned most of the modern period of Egyptian history. He began writing while studying in France and returned home to become a circuit judge, which brought him into contact with the personalities and problems of the provinces and countryside. His themes covered the need for modernisation, government and its problems and the conflict between spirit and matter. Altogether he wrote about sixty plays, some of which are more suitable for reading than for performance, in different styles encompassing symbolism, realism and even the absurd. He is also notable for attempting to create a new Arabic for the theatre, which he called a third language: a combination of classical and modern colloquial Arabic, but it was not considered successful.

Ahmed Shawky (1868–1932), known as the Prince of Poets, was the founder of Arabic poetic drama. He wrote five historical tragedies and two comedies in verse, adapting the style of verse to individual characters.

In 1935 the state founded the National Troupe at the Ezbekia Theatre, which opened with a play by Tewfik el Hakim, *Ahl el Kaf* (People of the Cave). This troupe's repertoire consisted of translations of Shakespeare, Shaw, Racine, Corneille and other major European playwrights. However, in the commercial theatre comedy and lyric-musical plays dominated, and seven years later the National Troupe was reformed under the title of the Egyptian Troupe for Acting and Music, managed by Zaki Tulaymat (1895–1982), who had graduated from the Paris Conservatoire and was an inspiring director and teacher.

In the early days of the Egyptian theatre actors had been trained by the companies they joined. However, due in great part to the efforts of Zaki Tulaymat, the Higher Institute of Dramatic Art was established in 1944, with Tulaymat as the Dean. This raised the status of the actors themselves, as well as the quality of their performances. The new graduates formed theatre groups, taught in schools and made theatre an important factor in education. Their influence was also felt in the developing media of radio and cinema, in addition to the theatre itself In 1929 the Higher Institute for Arabic Music was founded.

There is no doubt that the great singer Um Kalthoum (1898–1975) was the most adulated performer in the entire Arab world from the 1930s until her death. Born in a small village, she came from a family tradition of religious singers who performed at moulids and weddings. She began singing as a young girl, dressed as an Arab boy, then, moving to Cairo, she gave solo concerts, ranging from religious songs to poetic love songs written by the best poets and musicians of the period. She also expressed nationalistic aspirations and gave voice to revolutionary fervour and hope. Mohamed Abdul Wahab (1902–91) was a protégé of the poet Ahmed Shawky; he later became Egypt's most influential modern musician, composer and singer. He was followed by Abdel Halim Hafiz (1929–77), who, as a representative of the new generation, had studied the oboe at the Institute of Music, but whose singing skills made him enormously popular both in live concert and cinema.

After the revolution of 1952 when the monarchy and the British influence were removed from Egypt, the leaders of the newly independent socialist state, the intellectuals and performers who had long been calling for the overthrow of the old régime, came together in a new flourishing of the theatre. A new generation of writers, actors, directors and critics all contributed to this new wave, backed by state support in setting up new theatre companies and providing new playhouses that were often converted cinemas.

The post-revolutionary drama brought into prominence many highly skilled, excellent writers, some of whom had already been working in the theatre before the revolution such as Ali Ahmed Bakathir (1910–69). The generation of the late 1950s and 1960s was socially and artistically committed. Their work covered Egypt's historical past, its present and its role within the Arab world. They aimed not only at portraying reality, but also at reshaping it using a variety of styles ranging from realism, folk art, symbolism, naturalism and expressionism, very often with European influences from Ibsen, Chekhov, Pirandello, Brecht, Ionesco and Beckett. The most important of these writers are: Nu'man Ashur (1918–87), Yusef Idris (1927–91), Alfred Farag (b. 1929), Rashad Rushdi (1912–83), Fat'hi Radwan (1911–88), Lutfi al-Khuli (b. 1929), Sa'ad al-Din Wahba (1925–97), Abdul Rahman al-Sharqawy (1920–87), Mikhail Ruman (1927–83), Najib Surur (1932–78), Mahmud Diyab (1932–83), Salah Abd al-Sabur (1930–81), Ali Salem (b. 1936), Mustafa Bahjat (1934–80).

This was an enormously exciting and creative period when the theatre was on the cutting edge of politics and society. A plethora of ideas expressing social and intellectual conflicts and exciting new talent took it to the forefront of the arts. Indeed, the period is nostalgically looked back on as the golden age of the theatre. The new, very often political plays written in different styles ranging from verse, symbolic, naturalistic, expressionistic to black comedy and the absurd required a different type of actor, and, for the first time in the Egyptian theatre, the importance of the director became evident. Early directors had often either been actor-managers themselves or little more than stage managers, although Zaki Tulaymat had brought his own individual approach to directing on his return from France, followed by Nabil el Alfi, Hamdy Rizq and Abdel Rahim el Zirkany, who taught at the Higher Institute of Drama and who were well established when the first wave of young directors returned from studying abroad, having seen and taken part in a multiplicity of theatrical events. Saad Ardache and Karam Metawa returned from Rome, Galal Sharkawy from Paris, Ahmed Zaki and Ahmed Abdel Halim from London. They were actors as well as directors and all had the enthusiasm to produce innovative works of a very high standard. The state policy was to encourage audiences and make theatre available for everyone, especially greatly increased educated audiences.

By the 1960s many of the itinerant performers at the moulids and their families had joined the State Circus. In 1959 the Reda Folklore Troupe was founded by Mahmoud Reda and his brother Aly. They collected folk dancing traditions from all round Egypt and adapted the dances for performances in Egypt and abroad. Later they were joined by the National Folk Dance Troupe. The Balloon Theatre was their main venue, which they shared with the Lyric Operetta Musical Theatre. A new ballet company and Higher Institute had been formed with the help of the Russians, whereas the Rumanians helped to train the operators of the new Children's Puppet Theatre, which built its repertoire on Egyptian and Arab traditions and folklore; it later shared its space with the Children's Theatre first instituted in 1968. In addition to all the activity in Cairo, a vast system of 'cultural palaces' on the lines of the French model were opened in all the most important towns of the country. They formed their own local amateur dramatic companies and fostered local folk and performance artists. During the early part of the nineteenth century some of the old street entertainers had been displaced. Dancing had been banned for twenty years under Mohamed Aly, then returned to the moulids, celebrations, parties and weddings; some of the dancers were even taken to world expositions in Europe and America. In the early part of the twentieth century western style cabarets opened in Cairo, and from the 1920s the most famous dancers began to open their own clubs (*salas*). The cinema began to influence the presentation of dancers such as Tahia Karioka and Samia Gamal in the 1940s, whose presentation became more spectacular. The revolution brought a more conservative approach to their costumes, but the 1970s saw a growth in the number of dancers as people splashed out on elaborate weddings and public entertainment. Tahia Karioka later acted in the political plays of her husband Fayez Halawa in the 1960s. Many of the other dancers turned actresses and producers in the 1970s. The private commercial theatres, television and cinema also benefited from an increase in the pool of talented writers, actors and directors.

The year of Egypt's totally unexpected and devastating defeat in the war with Israel, 1967, was a political, social and cultural turning point. Direct criticism of the military, or politicians, or apportioning responsibility for the defeat, or the pervading feelings of disillusion and despair and oppression were all expressed indirectly in purely theatrical terms. Playwrights used symbolist forms, folk arts, verse, historical parallels and realism. Audiences related to this new sombre, often angry and critical mood, written and performed with the same intellectual fervour against a backdrop of an increasingly intrusive censorship and a state policy that felt that theatre should be providing entertainment rather than making people more politically and socially aware.

This inward-looking period was interrupted by the October War in 1973, when Egypt regained Sinai by a Peace Treaty with Israel under President Sadat, followed by a complete change of politics, economics and society. The newly oil-rich Arab countries employed Egyptians as educators, administrators and labourers. Meanwhile Egypt, under the Open Door policy, was busily transforming itself from a socialist semi-industrial society into a private-sector-led society that was being showered with imported consumer goods. Newly rich classes demanded new stars and entertainment: revues, comedy, singing and dancing in shows that went on into the early hours of the morning, as entertainers improvised around very slight plots, sometimes taking crude potshots at the more obvious political or social faults to the delight of often rather unsophisticated audiences.

Many of the comedians and actors who had been nurtured by the state theatre sector and the special companies formed to provide live theatre for television moved into the private sector, setting up their own companies and becoming big international Arab world stars through the medium of television and cinema. This was led by such comedians as Adel Imam, George Sidhom and Samir Ghanem, followed later by Mohamed Sobhy who, working with the writer Lenin el Ramly, provided a more politically and socially aware approach to comedy.

By the late 1970s and 1980s the state theatre, once the pride of the socialist/revolutionary-inspired cultural renaissance, had neither the money nor the will to compete with the private companies, television's vast output of soap operas or the cinema making films for video. However, the serious (state) theatre was still writer-led, attracting new writers who explored the problems arising from the materialism caused by the Open Door economic policy established after the October War victory of 1973. This policy created conflict and contradiction in the changing values of all levels of Egyptian society. In addition, writers attacked the destructive effects of the bureaucratic monolith and focussed on specific social problems and phenomena within the country, such as the rise of religious fundamentalism, migration to the rich oil states, increasing western and foreign influence, as well as solidarity with the Palestinians in their fight against the seizure of their land by Israel. Writers approached these various themes in styles that varied from rural, folkloric, historical or legendary (often involving indirect criticisms of contemporary problems in a time of heavy censorship) to absurd, farce, musical or realistic late twentieth-century urban. The writers of this period who have had the most impact are Mohamed Salmawy, Samir Sarhan, Fawzy Fahmi, Lenin el Ramly, Mohamed Enany, Mohamed al-Salamony and Yousry el Guindy, in their creation of original work or in adapting foreign work to the contemporary situation. With the steady drain of talented performers from state theatre companies and the loss of consistency mitigated by occasional outstanding work or star performances, audiences rapidly declined. However, in 1988 with the inauguration of the annual Cairo International Festival of Experimental Theatre the policy changed to promote experimental small groups of urban-centred young people's theatre, including establishing a modern dance troupe. Nevertheless, the ephemeral nature of many of the groups means that discussion among theatre people on how best to nurture the present and future theatre in Egypt continues.

References and further reading
Abdel-Hamid, Raafat. *Al-fikr al-misri fil asr al-massihi* (in Arabic). Cairo: General Egyptian Book Organisation, 2001.

Armbrust, Walter. *Mass Culture and Modernism in Egypt.* Cambridge: Cambridge University Press, 1996

Egyptian Mythology. London: Paul Hamlyn, 1965.

Empereur, J.-Y. *Alexandria Rediscovered.* London: British Museum Press, 1998.

Empereur, J.-Y. *A Guide to the Alexandrian Museum.* London: British Museum Press, n.d.

Erman, Adolf. *Life in Ancient Egypt.* New York: Dover, 1971.

Fagan, Brian. *The Rape of the Nile.* London: MacDonald & Jane's, 1977.

Fakhri, Ahmed. *Al Wahat.* 5 vols. (in Arabic).

Forster, E. M. *Alexandria: A History and a Guide.* London: Michael Haag, 1982.

Fraser, P. M. *Ptolemaic Alexandria.* 1972.

Freedley, George and Reeves, John. *A History of the Theatre.* New York: Crown Publishers, 1964.

Haas, C. *Alexandria in Late Antiquity.* Baltimore: Johns Hopkins University Press, 1997.

Hassan, Selim. *Pharaonic Egypt.* 15 vols. (in Arabic). Cairo: General Egyptian Book Organisation, 2000.

Hölbl, G. *A History of the Ptolemaic Empire.* London and New York: Routledge, 2001.

Kamil, Jill. *Sakkara and Memphis.* Harlow: Longman, 1985.

Kamil, Jill. *Upper Egypt.* Harlow: Longman, 1989.

Lane, Edward. *The Manners and Customs of the Modern Egyptians.* London: J. M. Dent, 1963.

Lane, Edward William. *Description of Egypt.* Cairo: American University of Cairo Press, 2000.

Mallakh, Kamal. *Treasures of the Nile.* New York: Newsweek, 1980.

Meinardus, Otto. *Christian Egypt: Ancient and Modern.* Cairo: American University of Cairo Press, 1977.

Ministry of Culture. *The Life Story of 1000 Years.* Leipzig: Egyptian Publishing Organisation, 1969.

Nelson, Christine. *Koran Readers.* Cairo: American University of Cairo Press, 2001.

Nieuwkerk, Karin van. *A Trade like any Other: Female Singers and Dancers in Egypt.* Austin: University of Texas Press, 1995.

Posener, Georges. *A Dictionary of Egyptian Civilisation.* London: Methuen, 1962.

Rai, Aly. *Comedy* (in Arabic). Cairo: Dar El Hilal.

Riad, Henri. *Alexandria: An Archaeological Guide to the City.* Cairo: Balagh Press, 1960.

Rodenback, Max. *Cairo: The City Victorious.* Cairo: American University of Cairo Press, 1999.

Rubin, Don, ed. *World Encyclopaedia of Contemporary Theatre,* vol. IV, *The Arab World.* London and New York: Routledge, 1999.

Sharkawi, F. *The Egyptians in Greek Tragedy.* Cairo: International Association of Egyptologists, 2000.

Shashan, Boaz. *Popular Culture in Medieval Cairo*. Cambridge: Cambridge
   University Press, 1993.
Shinnie, P. L. *Ancient Nubia*. London: Kegan Paul, 1996.
Somers Clark. *Al-Assar al-qibtiya fi wadi al-Nil*. (in Arabic; trans. Ibrahim Salam)
   Cairo: General Egyptian Book Organisation, 2001.
Walker, Susan and Higgs, Peter, eds. *Cleopatra of Egypt*. London: British Museum
   Press, 2001.
Wallis Budge, E. A. *The Dwellers on the Nile*. New York: Dover, 1977.
Webster, T. B. L. *Greek Theatre Production*. London: Methuen, 1956.

   Newspapers and magazines
Al Ahram (in Arabic)
Al Ahram (in English): weekly@ahram.org.eg
Al Ahram Hebdo (in French): www.ahram.org.eg/hebdo
Egypt Today, Mohendiseen, Cairo: www.egypttoday.com
Theatre Magazine (*Megalat el-Masra*), published by the General Egyptian Book
   Organisation.
Publications of the Cairo International Festival of Experimental Theatre,
   c/o Dr Fawzy Fahmy, Academy of Arts, Pyramids Road, Cairo.
Publications of the Theatre Research Centre, c/o Dr Osama Abdel Talib, 9 Hassan
   Sabry Street, Zamalek, Cairo.

Morocco, Algeria and Tunisia

KAMAL SALHI

This section considers the significant developments in the evolution of theatre in Morocco, Algeria and Tunisia from the early cultural invasions to
the present day. It focusses on how this theatre came into existence and the
challenges it sustained. It examines the particular conception of theatre in
this region, assesses the legacy of Arab and French experiences, explores influences and experimentation, and discusses the imperatives of post-colonial
theatre activity.

The antagonist theory

Here I offer a reflective response to the argument that theatre did not exist
in north Africa because of Islam. I offer evidence for a complex source of
theatre in north African tradition as an ideological yet anticipative act of
performance firmly grounded in Islam and secular indigenous culture.

Morocco, Algeria and Tunisia may be said to have quite different customs
and traditional beliefs from those of most of the rest of Africa. They have
been influenced by the Arab countries, but since Islam is antagonistic to
drama this has not led to the same intensity of theatrical developments as in
the rest of the continent. When we speak of theatre in these three countries
we are definitely looking at a genre to which their peoples had remained
strangers through the ages. Their culture had reluctantly accepted what
was habitually designated as *theatre*. The wealth of ingenious fabulations in
their imaginary world has never given birth to a text that could be thought
to have been written for performance, implying as this does dramaturges,
actors, directors, producers, theatre groups and stage designers: a complex
productive apparatus oriented towards a public that consumes its products.
It was not until the nineteenth century and contacts with the West that these
peoples sought to introduce theatre and the novel, as we know them, into
their culture. There are numerous explanations for the fact that theatre was
missing from these three countries, which had a strong tradition of the arts

and oral literature. The most plausible explanations are historical, cultural and sociological in nature. For example, in general theatre was an urban phenomenon and could not have appeared in a Berber civilisation. This civilisation was originally pastoral, and the great Greek myths that provided the substance of ancient theatre were unknown to the north African world, particularly following the establishment of the Arab-Islamic hegemony for many centuries. Although other opinions[1] have been supported by academic work on medieval philosophers such as Averroes, whose work has been interpreted to support the view that the Arabs had no idea whatsoever about drama, genuine and artistic forms of popular expression did exist. Michael Habart argues for the existence of a theatrical tradition particular to Islam.[2] He identifies this in certain pre-theatrical forms: farce, mime and other forms of popular expression. Although western scholars accept that the legacy of classical Greece was translated and transmitted to the West by Arab scholars, they claim that the Arab translators did not understand tragic and comic works. It may be that Averroes, who was an interpreter of Aristotle, made a paradoxical mistake in his translation of *The Poetics* when he rendered 'comedy' as 'satire' and 'tragedy' as 'panegyric'. Furthermore, the Arab philosophers who influenced these three originally Berber countries unfortunately ignored the poetry of those whose ideas they admired so much and whose concepts they to a large extent adopted.[3] Some more generous authors have found the germ of theatre in numerous literary works from across the centuries. This is possibly why the *Maqamat*[4] were considered brief theatrical sketches that proved the existence of farce as a genre.

Academic consensus that the theatrical arts did not exist in north Africa is now so widespread and deeply rooted that it has acquired the status of received wisdom and is no longer questioned. In fact, this consensus is so strong that a sceptical observer must question the underlying purpose of the arguments that have been used to define it. Historical evidence suggests that the early converts to Islam abandoned their cultural past, accepting instead the values of the new religion. However, this does not mean that no theatrical tradition had ever existed amongst them. The thesis that north African theatre does not exist is often maintained by an argument characterising any element of that cultural past which did not relate to the performing arts in general and to drama in particular as pre-theatrical. It is argued that even if some spontaneous forms of drama did exist, they did not develop into a genuine form of theatre because they were smothered by Islam. All this seems excessive. Even if it is true that Islam was inimical to theatre, there is no evidence that its introduction could have immediately wiped the slate clean. A new order could not be established in a society without adapting itself to that society. Any reader who accepts these arguments uncritically would need to have a doomed vision of history and social order that envisaged the complete destruction of a society and its immediate resurrection into a new order as a result of the encounter with Islam.

The work by the medieval writer al-Ma'arri, *Risalat al-Ghufran*, had a structure and contained elements that distinguish it as belonging to the genre of the literary tale of the era and made it a comedy that did not really acknowledge its own nature. This work was adapted in 1977 by the Tunisian Madani puppet theatre under the title *al-Ghufran*.[5] However, there was no theatre as it is known today in the West, and even the refined art of calligraphy practised in the Arab schools, *Madaris*,[6] of north Africa did not take in figurative painting. The prohibition of representations of the human form until the nineteenth century must have contributed to this concept of the prohibition of all displays of the self and personal feelings. The absence of a strong theatre tradition during this period in Morocco, Algeria and Tunisia cannot be explained by the fact that it is not allowed by Islam. Nor can the prohibition of the image as representation be a convincing argument, as it is not the Koran that forbids human figuration, or *Taswir*, but rather the Islamic tradition or *Sunna* (orthodoxy) as expressed in the *Hadith* (the sayings of the Prophet). This distinction is important because it strengthens the hypothesis that this situation is a social/historical reality rather than a dogma. The prohibition of pictorial representation was a way of affirming the new religion as against the pre-Islamic era. The prohibition does not have a basis in fundamental Islamic principles, but rather is of a more superficial, ideological nature. One of the impulses behind the early artistic movement in Morocco, Algeria and Tunisia was the pioneers' conviction that north African dramatic practice from the late nineteenth century to the present represented a significant response to this critical debate.

In reality, the societies of Morocco, Algeria and Tunisia have long traditions of the performing arts. These traditions have been dismissed because they do not comply with western norms. It is important to note that the only forms of theatrical expression that are accepted by academic critics[7] of north African theatre as genuine are those that orthodox Muslims would consider heretical, such as the Shiite *Ta'zyeh*. Among the Shiites we find a mimetic drama that can be compared to western Gothic art as an extraordinary celebration of passion. Ta'zyeh is a unique theatrical form in Islam, an annual celebration that depicts the murder of Hussain, the Prophet's grandson, and all the tragic events to which this gave rise.[8] This theatrical production is a mystic halo in which formalism transcends itself as a result of the total commitment of an entire Muslim community of spectators that makes this act of passion a true act of prayer. The reason this is considered heretical seems to be that these performances express revolt and rebellion against established political and religious authorities. Theatre is not simply born from revolt and conflict. Such approaches would merely confirm implicitly the long-established cultural traditions of north Africa that extend back far beyond the advent of Islam and which also form part of a cultural continuum that stretches forward to the modern day. Jacques Berque explains the total lack of any influence from traditional forms of performance when theatre was introduced to the region by the fact that this period was one of aggression directed against a traditional culture on the part of modernity.[9] Eventually north Africans may develop a way of describing pre-colonial performing arts in Morocco, Algeria and Tunisia by reference to indigenous aesthetic terms. Until those terms are researched, agreed upon and widely understood, we have to make do with European terms.

Indigenous para-dramatic performance

This subsection comprises a discussion of pre-colonial performing arts. By scrutinising the particular forms of theatre performance and their durability over the sequential colonial hegemonies, it aims to demonstrate the ways in which practices and ceremonies, rituals and festivals, popular characters and word play, directly connect aspects of north African culture to theatre as genre.

Almost the same situation can be found in Morocco, Algeria and Tunisia respectively, with a few local particularities inherited from before the arrival of Islam. Numerous traditional forms of performance, game and ceremony were practised for centuries, and some are again being practised today, such as the *Halqa* (circle), which is undoubtedly the most celebrated and popular form of performance, particularly in Morocco. Public places, open-air markets and the outskirts of towns are the favoured locations for these performances, one location particularly famous in this respect being Jama al-Fna at Marrakesh. A Halqa is usually performed by storytellers, magicians, jugglers or artists commanding a variety of different street performance techniques. The best known are storytellers, men with a gift for narrative and mime. There are singer-storytellers who tell stories in sung verse, accompanying themselves with a musical instrument, and there are storytellers who simply tell stories in prose without music. The stories are generally myths, religious legends and fairy folk tales. The storyteller himself decides the space where he will perform by means of an imaginary circle, from which derives the name for the genre. The audience gather around this circle, which attracts passers-by interested by what they hear. The storyteller is known by a variety of names, *gawwal, meddah, rawi, muqallid, berrah, hakiya, fdawi*, depending on the country or region in question.

The storyteller has a few props – in most cases a carpet and a stick – that he is able to transform into all sorts of objects by the force of his imagination: the stick becomes an arm, a pen, a horse, an opponent, a tree and so on. The small carpet can be transformed in the storyteller's imagination into a house, a small boat, a wall, an animal or a bed. When the storyteller needs another actor, he invites a member of the audience to perform a part of the show with him. Here the storyteller also becomes a director, for he directs the audience member and gives him precise instructions on how to move and what to say. Audience participation, which is very common in this form, is also organised quite often by inviting the audience to collectively invoke the name of the Prophet, which helps to maintain an excited atmosphere. At an important moment in the narration the storyteller will stop suddenly to ask for some money before continuing his rhythmic story with movements of his stick and miming. This is one of the few theatres in the world where the audience pay after having seen the performance, and not before, a theatre so free that the audience can watch without any obligation to pay. Popular arts, if they are to be true to the reality of popular culture, must reserve the right to be independent and unrestricted and above all to maintain a sense of life. A willingness to experiment with the material available and a pride in the validity of experience are living elements in the north African popular tradition, along with a sense of humour. There is no need for artists to apologise for introducing concerns of form and argument. New forms are no more foreign than those of the French bourgeois tradition or Arab hegemonic culture. The test is whether or not they make sense of reality for participants and observers.

In locating it in north African societies influenced by Islamic culture, one is led to inscribe the art of storytelling in the context of this culture, which sometimes clashes with the indigenous secular traditions of the north African Berbers. No civilisation has cultivated the art of storytelling with greater passion than the Muslims of the Middle Ages. Storytellers had just as much prestige as modern novelists and actors. They constituted a prosperous, important class in society. Installed in a public place or even in the enclosures of mosques, they talked for hours before an attentive public, telling tales that, in the tenth and eleventh centuries were generally humorous, but tended to be mainly obscene in the twelfth and thirteenth centuries. The tale is a sophisticated, profound popular form, diverse and institutionalised in the collective mind. In these countries the story is an organised bursting forth of the imagination. Storytellers joined together for performances in groups of two or three and the public transformed itself into a chorus that punctuated and acclaimed the refrains and turns of the story. The real alternative in the end is to interpret and report clearly as an artist what you see from where you are. That of course implies a responsibility to see, to be involved, to be in a place from which things can be seen, and to give voice in a way that can be heard. The question becomes one of choosing one's ground. North Africans would normally have that choice had they not been subjected to alternative cultural histories. What is important is the vantage point from which they describe themselves, how they document and pass culture on and how their knowledge of their multi-layered history affects the picture of the present and their power to act in the future. The shape of history and who owns its public version becomes the subject of political as well as artistic conflicts.

Essentials of the traditional theatre form
It was at gatherings called either *Majlis* (seated public assembly) or *Maqama* (standing public assembly) where the storytellers gathered. These words are found today in a political context, for example parliamentary assemblies, and those of tribes or villages are also called *majlis*. Originally, puppets might accompany long stories and the storyteller's dialogue with the audience would then become a total collective entertainment. There is a wide range of classifications of stories, according to their nature and function that they play in the life of society: *nadira* (anecdote), *hikaya* (tale), *qisa* or *ustura* (legend), *hurafa* (story). The nadira is a flash of wit, a fitting remark, a sign of spiritedness, a coarse or refined pleasantry. The nadira is above all a pleasure of the mind that encompasses a certain escapism from the problems of everyday life. In north African culture one meets this genre grouped in cycles unified by the central character of Djeha (Jha, Goha), a greedy, coarse, cunning person, and incomparable scoundrel and trickster.[10] His altruism is

a genuine egotism that gives the audience the opportunity for easy, pleasur-able identification. In Djeha's simplistic philosophy, any sophistry is worth trying. For the most part, earlier plays performed in the first half of the twentieth century defended social, political theses. Djeha departed from this tradition as a grotesque farce in colloquial Arabic and Berber.

The myth of Djeha, with all the opportunities it offers, has haunted authors and provided them with material ever since. During the period between the two World Wars, this theatre was dominated by actors like Allalou, Dahmoune, and, in particular, Kaki[11] and Ksentini,[12] who excelled in a genre similar to the *commedia dell'arte*. Their performances were either caricatures of the daily life of the indigenous people of north Africa or poetic plays containing elements of burlesque. The two happened to be combined in performance. These plays sought to set problems in the political context of contemporary, colonial north Africa. The themes dealt with included colonisation, the rivalry between European settlers and Muslim landowners, the increasing poverty of the farmers and the rise of a bourgeois class of civil servants. These subjects attest to the authors' anguish at the social conditions, particularly in Algeria and Tunisia, as well as to the feelings of the public. The episodes in the plays contained elements that curiously foreshadowed the future of Europeans in their contact with north African performing arts. Most notable was their admiration for the Djeha character,[13] vitiated by condescension and ignorance. Less noticeable was the use of humour and anecdote as a mechanism of psychic release and vicarious euphoria. But the temporary cooperation of Algerians, Moroccans and Tunisians in this artistic experience was almost poignantly untypical of later developments.

In post-independent Algeria new experiments led by dramatists such as Abdelkader Alloula and Kateb Yacine[14] based on these popular, tradi-tional theatrical elements led to a proliferation of new groups in factories, villages, universities and youth clubs. The collective creations that resulted coincided with the socialist cultural revolution of the 1970s. They were intended to contribute to the education of the masses and the raising of cul-tural standards. A community theatre using Halqa, dance and music emerged and almost gained a monopoly position as popular theatre. This gave the post-independent national theatre, the official cultural institution that until then had been thoroughly mainstream and which relied on adaptations and translations of foreign classics, unexpected competition. A strident young nationalism reasserted itself in socially relevant plays by Algerian authors that were being performed in greater numbers, particularly in the Regional

Theatres of Anaba, Sidi bel Abbes, Constantine and Oran.[15] Some of the older plays by the pioneers of Djeha and Halqa theatre were rediscovered and staged. Older artists such as Kaki and Allalou were invited back into the profession. It was a time of intense political and cultural change, theories about alternative lifestyles, and artistic experimentation combining to create a bewildering diversity of new ideas about the part taken by theatre in public life. Amongst national influences, books by contemporary, avant-garde dramatists were widely read and offered insights into new experimental, political and community-based ways of working in the theatre that were imitated in the general push towards 'innovation' in style, form (compared with the national theatre), subject matter and performance venue. Ample evidence of the national theatre's malaise is provided by its perpetuation of the tradition of adapting and translating European and Arab classics. It has failed to develop and encourage original texts and forms.

The popular theatre troupes took the challenge of performing in a popular style for audiences that included many people who would not normally consider entering a formal theatre: industrial workers, prisoners, soldiers, pensioners and long-term hospital patients. Aldekader Alloula continued this approach, touring hospitals with Djeha and Meddah-like theatre. His work was perceived by Muslim fundamentalists as threatening their social basis, and he was assassinated on 10 March 1994. At the same time, rapid changes in Algerian society since the 1980s, particularly the introduction of popular monologues in the form of one-man shows, and a new sensitivity about secular Berber culture, were encouraging topical theatre and winning it greater appreciation and support. Fellag, a Berber comedian-dramatist in exile, is the most prominent figure in this new genre, which is reminiscent of the work of storytellers, Meddah and, stylistically, Djeha. His textually varying performance, *Djurdjurassique Bled*,[16] won the Grand Prix de la Critique Théâtrale et Musicale in 1997/8. His traditionally inspired theatre is highly ironic. He tells the history of the Berber people through the colonial and post-colonial periods within a framework of the political and cultural contradictions of Algeria. Throughout this brilliant, original performance humour flirts with emotion. Fellag examines the agonies, foolishnesses and humanity of the Algerian people with poetry and a pointed sense of self-mockery. As Peter Brook puts it,

> Theatre is the art of the present. We go there to experience something with other people. In a room there are people who are all different from one another, like fish in a pond. How can we bring

them all together, make them breathe like a single being? To do this, one needs an artist capable of stroking the audience as one strokes a cat, tickling it as one tickles a child, making it laugh as one makes a drunkard laugh, of whispering in its ear just as poets do, of giving it the attention and tenderness that one gives to one's brothers and sisters, and even of shaking it as one shakes a dreamer. Fellag has developed this art very well. At the Bouffes du Nord, he was always the same man. This was his real secret, the man on stage is always the man in life.[17]

This theatre thus reflected the demands and hopes of the popular masses. In Tunisia, for example, in the most recent theatrical performances in colloquial Arabic,[18] tirades are integrated, whereby a text that refers to Djeha is understood in its totality as a *Mhall-Shahed*, a typical proverb, an ineluctable truth based on experience, one that people know and have lived. This is a typical means of theatrical communication in which the public becomes the ideal audience for a lesson and meditation. Typical Djeha stories are inserted into the dialogue between the characters – with an excess of scathing irony – emphasising with a laugh the approach of a mirror theatre to the ideal receiver that is its audience. This method has a long tradition in north Africa, particularly with the Arab influence, and goes back to the Middle Ages. Even in the tale, the procedure of inserting formulas belonging to other stories presupposes (above all of the teller) the ability to attract the listener in the act of conveying the content before plunging him or her into the imaginary through the memory of their own experiences. However, the success of this kind of work did bring the pioneers serious harassment from the French administration. They were criticised severely in the newspapers, censored and even banned from the stage. The problems of censorship faced by artists in these countries point to a fundamental issue of indigenous theatre, namely its uneasy relationship with colonial hegemony. This is why in post-colonial governing systems, for example, the insecurity felt by post-independent régimes, arising from an inadequate infrastructural inheritance from the former colonial power, and from stark underdevelopment within the world economy, has led most north African ruling parties to seek ways of mobilising cultural techniques in order to reinforce a national consensus.

Pre-colonial or syncretic theatrical forms have been transformed for instrumental purposes. The roots of indigenous ideological theatre lie in the anti-colonial struggle for independence, when many nationalist groups created a political vehicle out of the indigenous performing traditions. In

Morocco, where the post-independence régime was based on the traditional feudal kingdom of the *Makhzen*, the praise and community celebration in such ceremonies as the Halqa have simply continued in a somewhat modified fashion after independence. In the 1960s popular theatre based on Moroccan traditions was performed on the stage at the Théâtre des Nations in Paris. Some performances based on the country's heritage of dance, music and poetry were appreciated strongly by the Europeans who experienced them as a living form of theatrical spectacle. This has come to be known as 'total theatre', in view of the fact that dance, music and poetry are related arts with common roots. But, even for those republics (Algeria and Tunisia) which were not based on a homogeneous pre-colonial nation-state, it was not too difficult for the performing traditions to make the transition from ritual to politicised function.[19]

There is another form less well known to the general public in Europe and the West, the *Baste*, which is often referred to as a pre-theatrical form or a form that approaches theatre. The Baste enjoyed its high point and may have first been performed under King Mohammed ben Abdellah of Morocco (1757–90). It was sometimes used as a disguised way of communicating to the king of complaints, troubles and injustices committed by local officials. The king was informed in order to encourage him to intervene in favour of the victims. The Baste or carpet is a place where the dramatic action occurs, but it is also the person who performs. This explains the name given to this traditional performance genre, which was performed for the entertainment of the Moroccan kings. The performances were short, amusing farces in which the central character was called the *buhu*, in the north of Morocco, and *al M'siyyah*, in the south of the country. This kind of court theatre has often been called an aborted form because it never succeeded in developing outside the royal courts and addressing the people, and it was never able to become a recognised theatrical form. This sociological, political circumstance prevented it from developing in Morocco. In consequence, Morocco, which was relatively isolated as the only one of the three countries to have escaped incorporation into the Ottoman Empire, lagged behind in the theatrical field. It was not until troupes from the Middle East arrived on tour that this country was introduced to western theatre and began to practise it as well.

Western domination of north Africa through colonialism and cultural influence has resulted in the establishment of western theatrical traditions associated with the proscenium arch theatre. This is a form alien to north

African cultural patterns. Nonetheless, western drama has become accepted, has attracted an audience and has produced playwrights, actors and directors. It has become the norm of drama in north Africa and elsewhere. From the late nineteenth century until the present day, Morocco, Algeria and Tunisia have produced playwrights, many with worldwide reputations. This situation has persuaded scholars that they can date the birth of theatre in that region precisely, the most quoted date being in the early years of the twentieth century. On the other hand, any form of expression, any art form, that does not comply with the norm embodied in the aesthetics associated with western views of the performing arts is not considered theatre or a proper theatrical form of expression. These assumptions are so rooted in the north African mind today or, rather, in the consciousness of westernised élites, that any authentic and genuine form of theatre, such as the Meddah or Halqa, is considered cheap and decadent. In fact, theatre is experienced in a physical setting derived from a western tradition and is still dominated by names such as Molière and Shakespeare. This does not mean that this tradition is lacking in relevance or value for Morocco, Algeria and Tunisia. However, insofar as it has implied the partial destruction of indigenous art forms, its effects have to be seen in a negative light.

Several artistic elements, such as painting, calligraphy and architecture, are combined in the context of the Arabic influence, and represent an imaginary world projected into the material world. In effect, they are the forms of creation that encourage the incorporation of material things into a dreamy exaltation. However, the imaginary cannot be separated from its religious dimension. In the view of the Arab-Muslim world, theatre as it is known in Europe and the West cuts this close link between the spiritual and the imaginary. In orthodox Islam (Sunni Islam), ritual practices, such as prayer, fasting and purification, that are done in imitation of the Prophet Mohammed, are always a form of mime. In the pilgrimage to Mecca this becomes an expression of the essence of faith. Here, theatricality is combined with eschatalogical representation, demonstrating the implication contained in transcendentalism that the oneiric life has a power that no rationalisation of Islamic eschatology can destroy.

Nevertheless, the Bedouins, the people of the pre-Islamic period, al-jahiliya, possessed a belligerent sense of humour. Far removed from theatre of any kind, and constrained by the arid environment they lived in, they were submerged in a nearly absolute realism that can only be expressed in art by prose and poetry. These people, despite the hardships of an impossible way of life, were simply incapable of anguish, of heartbreak, in essence, of tragic situations, which are the basis of all drama. In the desert the Bedouins felt nothing but the ascendancy of the forces of nature that bore down on them and deprived them of any notion of drama and struggle because a fatalism quite different from that of the Greeks bound them to the wounds of the desert.[20] It is impossible to discover within these limited intellectual horizons a form of creation like the epic, the novel or the theatre, for the Arab poem is no more than a collection of verses. The music of the period is also no more than a collection of fragments that do not express clearly defined themes. On the other hand, we know that Greek drama was born with the cult of Dionysus, that is to say, with a mythology of fertility. At the same time, if Greek mythology is truly rich with the weight of hope and belief, the religious thought of the nomads of the pre-Islamic period is surprising in its mediocrity, even though it was in constant contact with the forms and facts of nature. In consequence, Greek theatre had a religious essence, while Islam, which gave the north Africans a sense of religious transcendence in the poetic, aesthetic world, with a sublimated and sublimating movement, could have been celebrated in drama that glorified it.

Cult festival as performing art

The nature and force of the material that comes from north African religious ceremonies and festivals should prompt fundamental interest in the potential effectiveness of popular performance. It is not enough to understand the popular culture or street performance of a people, but it has been necessary for the theatre of Moroccans, Algerians and Tunisians to adapt it. Like cult festivals, post-independence community theatre was created outside established theatre buildings. Therefore, every aspect of performance had to be constructed in contexts that were largely foreign to the theatre, thus making it easier to perceive the ideological nature of particular projects. The audiences were not ones ready made for conventional theatre buildings. They had to be drawn in from remote, rural areas, becoming part of the different constituencies that the activity chose to address. The post-colonial work of the rural theatre in Morocco, amateur theatre in Algeria and student theatre in Tunisia were all about the ways in which, in a given historical period and in a given place, theatre-makers were trying to change not just the future actions of their audiences, but also the politics and the structure of the performance and community. For several decades it was customary to study local communities in the culture of these countries as if they were isolated units. In recent years the limitations of such an approach have come to be more generally recognised: that important contextual phenomena remain largely unrecognised, and that the changing nature of the social reality receives insufficient attention. The whole secret is, however, to translate a general and abstract insight into a study of a dramatic performance that can be applied to concrete situations.

In the past few years increased attention has been focussed on saints, shrines and rural celebrations in north African history, though most scholarship on this topic has generally been confined to architectural and anthropological analysis, with only slight reference to other dimensions. To widen the perspective and gain a better understanding of the cultural history of north Africa, it is useful to look at the rituals and kinds of pilgrimage that are part of traditional festivals and the vital role that these forms could have played in the shaping of modern-day outdoor performance.[21] As a popular cult *Marabouts* (or *Shurafā*) are a typical unorthodox feature of Islam in Morocco, Algeria and Tunisia.[22] Beliefs about Marabouts are to be found in local legends that often refer to religious personages of all kinds,[23] to their descendants, to burial monuments, and even to trees, caves, springs, mountains or other material signs of the presence of supernatural forces. A Marabout is a person, alive or dead, who is thought to have a special relationship with God, characterised by a tight and enduring bond. A Marabout is close to God, he or she is God's friend. In this context, *Baraka* is the native term used to designate the potential capacities of this bond. It can be vaguely translated as 'grace'. It is predominantly a benevolent power, being present in all things, plants, animals and humans in different degrees. The philosophy and principles of such practices offer a basic understanding of modern community theatre. If they had been explored further by earlier critics who rejected the idea that theatre had ever existed in north Africa, they would have provided a true sense of the ingredients of the region's indigenous theatre. The easy contempt that characterised the reactions and arguments of these critics was tainted by ignorance of the goals of the Maraboutic community.

North African Maraboutic devotion is especially oriented towards deceased Marabouts who are immanent beings. They live in human society and manifest themselves in the real world. In most cases, their worship is institutionalised in cult ceremonies. In unorthodox Maraboutic rituals, the festival represents an intensification of social intercourse. Women go unveiled and mingle relatively freely in the crowd. In fact, even today, this is one of the few opportunities when young people can meet their contemporaries of the other sex. Spirituality, sex, relaxation and entertainment are elements of psychodrama present in the festival. This would not occur if the activity had to take place indoors in a space restrictively defined by the limitations of concrete. Contact with nature in an open space has a dramatic effect on the psychological intensity of group interaction and interrelation. The ritual activity is the recitation of *Dhikrs* known as *Hadra*. A Dhikr is a maxim that is to be repeated continually at an ever-increasing rate. Dhikrs are performed by the *Meddah* or group of Meddah (the *Meddahin*), and have been incorporated into modern north African theatre by many contemporary dramatists in Morocco and Algeria. This popular form unites a large number of people sharing a single acoustic space where common preoccupations can be expressed.

The tombs of deceased Marabouts are the centres of the cult. In this respect, modern north African theatre, particularly when it uses the Halqa form discussed above, has followed the same pattern.[24] A clearly demarcated area, the *Hurma*, surrounds every shrine. Religious activities not only incorporate those things that believers actually do, but also what they refrain from at the same time. Hurma refers to the second category. All who enter this area must behave with proper respect to the Marabout. In this way the Halqa performance and modern outdoor performances in Morocco, Algeria and Tunisia show the importance of the delimitation of the performing space, within which all the actors and the whole audience are involved in the drama being staged. Many shrines are small and simple in construction. Most of them are located in the open, rude piles of loose stones in the shape of a horseshoe or circle. Shrines can consist of a little niche inside a house. There are also a number of much larger shrines built around the tomb of a Marabout. Most of them are situated in the centre of the burial-grounds. The idea of the centre has been a key conceptual element in the structural composition of the performance of dramatists such as the Moroccan Tayeb Saddiki, the Tunisian Moncef Souisi and the Algerians Abderahmane Kaki, Kateb Yacine and Abdelkader Alloula. Outside the official structure of their respective post-colonial National or Regional Theatres, they have made extensive use of the art of the Halqa, the Meddah and most of the other traditional performing arts. The difference between this work and western/European theatre is exemplified by the example of Tayeb Saddiki in Morocco, who draws huge crowds to stadiums to watch and participate in his plays, and Abdelkader Alloula, who gathers villagers in village squares to make drama out of local people's concerns. Encouraging attempts have been made to revive indigenous theatrical traditions, mainly based on the storyteller Meddah and the Halqa 'festival', reaching beyond the boundaries of north Africa. They have been seen in Paris, Rome and New York. This represents an important breakthrough in establishing the credentials of indigenous north African theatre in the wider world and, no doubt, has shown how much western culture could gain from this culture.

On the footprint of the Halqa performance

In Morocco there was a traditional form of theatre for the entertainment of high state personages, on the one hand, and for the people, on the other. The popular *al-Bsat* performances were originally short tableaux and developed gradually. The Arabic word *al-Bsat* comes from *al-bast*, meaning 'laughter or humour without timidity'. This genre evolved, and theatrical troupes were formed to entertain notables during festivals, recreating the celebrations linked with local saints and sometimes presenting daring social satires and scenes that implicitly or explicitly criticised well-known persons. The sultans were tolerant towards the members of these troupes and encouraged them by giving them gifts and offerings, just as they did with singers and musicians. These performers sometimes took local celebrities as their targets. In their performances they allowed themselves flights of fantasy, but always sought to make the audience laugh. The overall effect was to recreate the querulous participatory attitudes of a village audience in the pre-colonial Halqa. The problem is that the participation of the audience in a performance of al-Bsat is somewhat contrived, in that it is a calculatedly rehearsed effect: the real audience, unlike in pre-colonial Halqa narrative performance, cannot interfere to improve or embellish the story. This dazzling theatrical form may sometimes have served to divert attention from content that was fundamentally irrelevant to the preoccupations of the Moroccan masses.

Al-Bsat originated in Marrakesh and was adopted in the city of Fez. In these two places performers were recruited from among the various guilds of craftsmen. During the celebrations for Moroccan independence, such artists went to Rabat, making contact with their friends in the royal city and obtaining donations for their large popular performances. On the day of the performance, they performed *Dar-al-Makhzen* (The Sultan's Palace) in an atmosphere of laughter and gaiety, surrounded by onlookers old and young. This was a real 'carnival'. The performers wore clothes of varied colours and forms. The main figure had a mask that allowed him to come out with all sorts of audacious fantasies in front of the sultan without the slightest reserve. The procession of other performers, who were dressed in sheepskins, said prayers with the aid of strings of beads made of dried figs. Musicians accompanied the procession, striking their instruments to the *ad-daqqa* rhythm of Marrakesh. When they arrived at the sultan's palace, the excitement was at its height and the performers were immersed in their roles.[25] This kind of performance has a resemblance to the Athenian festivals in honour of Dionysus discussed above, in which a great troupe did a tour of a city before arriving on stage. The amusing Moroccan actors sang as they processed in a practice similar to that of the Greeks' dithyrambic chanting. The main actor stopped to say occasional words, serious or comic and sometimes followed by dancing. It should be noted that during the 1920s and 1930s a troupe from Fez, for example, moved its performances towards social and patriotic comedy, influencing Algerian groups. Alloula recognised the influence of Greek theatre when he recalled that 'in spite of the original contradiction of which it was the bearer, the Aristotelian art of theatre in Arabic, from the first years of its existence in Algeria, united with the secular struggle of our people in its aspirations to recover its liberty, its territory, its identity and its legitimate access to peace and social progress.'[26]

The al-Bsat spectacle is by no means the only theatrical tradition in Morocco. Among the other traditions that show the religious and popular features of Berber culture, there is the Sidi al-Katfi, the Ceremony of Grace, the Festival of the Sultan of the Learners. The Sidi al-Katfi originated at a religious brotherhood under Sultan Moulay Youssef (1912–27). The troupes that performed Sidi al-Katfi or the Taifa were mystical sects such as the Aissawa, the Hmadsha and the Darqawa that had a legendary philosophy of theatre, which consisted of the belief that it 'begins as religious and becomes social before being cosmic'. The theatre where they met was the house of the *Pasha* or a host from noble circles. They engaged in a special ritual that was repeated at each meeting, that is to say at each theatrical performance. A single leader, the *Muqaddam*, systematically controls this drama. The Ceremony of Grace for a bride was a theatrical festival full of action and movement celebrated exclusively by women, particularly at Fez. The Festival of the Sultan of Learners was a spring spectacle put on by students who chased each other during the day and swarmed to take part in all kinds of entertainment.

However, the introduction of western theatre in north Africa had counter-effects. This theatre was a foreign art form. From its very introduction, both the colonists and the indigenous notables knew that it had no place in the social texture of Morocco, Algeria and Tunisia. It was then necessary to make a great effort to impose it in order to substitute it for all north African dramatic performances. All other performances than those associated with the theatre would be relegated to the sphere of folklore. The colonists felt that it was essential to substitute the western theatre for Halqa or Meddah, for example, because these were too free in content and form. They were felt to be of no use to society. They diverted people from any possibility of modernising and actualising these forms. The Arabic-Muslim élite, the *Ulema*, joined with western opinion in eliminating them since they were too regionally oriented, to the extent that they played havoc with Arab-Islamic ideology, which preached national union within the larger context of the Arab world. The maintenance of these popular festivals would encourage the use of dialects and non-Arabic languages such as Berber, with the 'unacceptable' result that Morocco, Algeria and Tunisia would be isolated from the Arab world by their specific culture and traditions. It is only necessary to review the historical situation surrounding the Berber cultural movement[27] and the involvement of the Ulema of the Qarawiyin in Morocco, or the *Jama Zituna* in Tunisia, and Constantine in Algeria, to understand the delicacy of the Berber question. Even the Ulema and élite of other Arabic-speaking countries (especially Egypt, Lebanon, Syria and Iraq) made indignant calls for the Arab union to be safeguarded, arguing for a modicum of harmony to be achieved with the colonists by replacing popular and traditional elements of the local culture with the colonists' theatre performed in Arabic. The relation of the indigenous north African audience to the theatre can be said to have been a relation of substitution.

Enriching or impoverishing influences

As the section above has shown, in the societies of north Africa that were destabilised by internal contradictions, theatrical forms expressed more open cultural diversity. The examples chosen deal with traditional performance from Halqa to cult festival. The discussion of these pre-colonial theatre forms has been built up partly by contemplation of the way these forms survived into the colonial period. This section looks at the influences that have had a clearly identifiable Arab and Turkish heritage. The shadow play of Garagöz, when it blends with the Arab tradition of Meddah, gives way to political satire. While the Egyptians toured with an adapted European theatre in the beginning of the twentieth century, Moroccans, Algerians and

Tunisians explored the sophisticated system of satirical caricature inherent in the merrymaking and masquerade of north African carnival.

Under Arab influence, the Moroccans, Algerians and Tunisians had not adapted the drama of the Greeks, whose architecture had influenced them so much, because Greek tragedy was not considered a literary *œuvre* to be read. It was only written to be performed. It was the stage that created the *œuvre* and not the *œuvre* that formed the origins of the stage. Theatre, which requires a fixed point of reference, could never become established among a nomadic people. But pre-Islamic poetry was considered as the ideal and archetype of the genre for many centuries. This confident conception had led the Arab people to believe that its literature was the best and that it had no need of foreign literatures. Until the first theatrical performances in Egypt during Napoleon's expedition, north Africans had only been interested in works from abroad reputed to be of practical use and edifying effect, such as philosophy and the sciences. The French took actors and musicians with them to entertain and comfort their officers. A large hall called the Théâtre de la République et des Arts was constructed for the occasion. However, it was in Lebanon, where Christian and Muslim traditions live side by side, that the first theatrical experiments in Arabic were carried out. Marun al-Naqqash (1817–55) was the first author to write a comedy in classical Arabic completely based on Molière's *The Miser*, a play that has been exploited in a thousand different ways by adapters and translators. Al-Naqqash's version was performed in 1848 and marked the birth of Arabic theatre. In the second half of the nineteenth century, during which Morocco, Algeria and Tunisia were in the throes of political disintegration, exposed to the rivalry and greed of European diplomats and private companies, the only living form of drama was the puppet theatre or *Garagöz*.[28]

The themes explored by Garagöz, a kind of shadow theatre originating in Turkey, are well established in north African culture. Garagöz appeared in Arab countries in the fourteenth century and had taken root in north Africa, particularly in Fez, Tangiers, Constantine, Algiers and Tunis, establishing itself as a popular art form well before the French invasion. In Turkish *Garagöz* means 'black eyes'. According to legend, Kara Geuz, after whom the genre is named, and Hadji Eivaz, who also played a part in its development, were two women humorists. The art form reached north Africa in the seventeenth century. More is known about it in the nineteenth century, during which Garagöz performances often included obscene conversations with the 'God of fecundity'. The mockery of Garagöz plays was used as an instrument of political satire. The French authorities did not appreciate the obscene nature of the performances and banned them in 1843. They were also banned in Egypt in 1908, when the Egyptian people were using Garagöz as a means to vent their hatred of the British occupiers. Likewise, the Meddah, who had also condemned and attacked the French occupation, found himself harassed and often arrested. North Africans performed Garagöz in a more elaborate style that permitted diatribes against the upper classes and collaborators with the French. Here is more proof that the history of theatre in Morocco, Algeria and Tunisia started well before the early twentieth century. Egyptian and Lebanese touring companies of the first years of the twentieth century were effective in creating enthusiasm for the idea of a new, modern north African theatre as opposed to a French one. However, it is only in the late 1960s that north African scholars, mainly those connected with the theatre, started to point out that the popular art forms of the shadow theatre and the storyteller were, in reality, genuine theatrical forms that corresponded to the artistic needs of Arabic society and its understanding of the universe. Although the shadow theatre has not survived the onslaught of the colonial and post-colonial experience, the storyteller is a symbol in north African theatre of universal significance and is thoroughly embedded in the modern north African tradition.

As a distinct genre designed to be performed by actors on stage and according to certain theatrical conventions, drama would have no historical roots in this part of Africa. Despite the popularity of the shadow play and the storyteller over the centuries, they did not contribute to the rise of drama in Morocco, Algeria and Tunisia. The founders of the region's modern theatre wrote plays in a western vein. Tunisia was the scene of considerable theatrical activity during the Carthaginian and Roman periods. The country had two hundred Roman towns and cities. The Roman theatres in Carthage and Dougga are now used for summer festivals and even a week of theatre in November. The sources of real Tunisian theatre, however, are to be found in European theatre, which preceded it by more than one hundred and fifty years, though differences of mentality certainly caused enormous difficulties for the acceptance of the genre. In the region the influence of French drama on Tunisian theatre proper goes back to its first introduction, particularly the first translations and adaptations made for Tunisian Francophones. The earliest records go back to 1741.[29] A group of French actors were captured by Corsairs and taken to Tunis during the reign of Ali Bey (1735–56). The actors performed pantomimes on the theme of Harlequin and the Parrot, which earned them imprisonment and the death sentence, though this was not carried out because the prince and his courtisans were struck with terror at the sight of the masked Harlequin, who they took to be the Devil. It was only with difficulty that it was explained to the Bey that this was theatre.

While popular traditional festivals gave Moroccans and Algerians the opportunity to gain an acquaintance with the art of performance, and the visits paid by Arab troupes helped them to learn about theatrical representation, it has to be recognised that it was the western practice of theatre that provided Moroccan and Algerian performers with their formal initiation into the art form. During this stage, in the latter part of the eighteenth century, these countries were under the domination of the French and the Spanish, which explains the presence there of touring European theatre groups as well as Arab troupes. However, the Europeans performed in places that were not frequented by Moroccans and Algerians, who were known as the 'indigenous' people. By the time direct contact was made, thanks to the intervention of the French colonial authorities in theatrical activities later in the twentieth century, there had been a great movement under Arabic influence. Beginning in 1907, Egyptian troupes began to visit Morocco, Algeria and Tunisia.[30]

The basic nature of carnival

The theatre that the Egyptians promoted in the three countries allowed for the integration of orality in the form of mythical, hagiographic or humorous tales, fables, jokes, proverbs, songs and stories relating to the life of the community. A conception of theatre of this kind reflected the collective ethos of these societies. It is only through a reading of the mirror effect, and the disentangling of the symbols, that we can understand how this theatre explores the beliefs, perceptions and visions of north African society. The following example, which is an extract from a poetic narrative of marital infidelity and which we find integrated in plays, illustrates this model.

> The story of
> a married man surprised with
> a married woman
> in the village of beni-Sidal
> in the tribe of the Galîyens.[31]

On the narrative plane, this is a tale of vengeance or a fearsome, exemplary collective punishment. The story contains a limited, interdependent group of motifs such as 'adultery', 'deception', 'temptation', 'vengeance', 'punishment' and 'female cunning'. This passage, in its general configuration, is developed poetically on the basic strophes. These strophes constitute narrative micro-sequences held together by metaphoric and metonymic images. The style is sombre, as the lexical items used come from the terminology of warfare. Furthermore, the text is rich in descriptive scenes marked by an unusual violence that cast the acts of cruelty and torture committed into stark relief. This is a particular universe of discourse that springs from the cultural referents of the community in question, which is dominated by tribal and clan wars, and the struggle against the European occupiers. The code of honour is a central element for the comprehension of this community's cultural referents. Therefore, a failure to consider the context and the cultural referents may lead to the formulation of mistaken conclusions.[32] Mouliéras gives the following subjective commentary, which reveals the theatrical and symbolic dimensions of the tale: 'this atrocity was committed many times by the Rifains[33] during the recent events in Miliya. The bodies of Spanish soldiers were mutilated in this shocking manner each time the shepherds and other Berber gangsters were able to grab them.'[34] This is a *mise en scène*, in the pictorial sense of the expression, of an exemplary punishment. The educational dimension or moral is part of the social theme grasped here. The author continues his comments: 'In view of these dreadful agonies, there are few, very few Rifains tempted to be unfaithful. Their parents will be the first to tear them to pieces: if they do not do this, they are exposing themselves to atrocious reprisals.'[35]

In addition to the cultural inter-textuality that shows itself to be dominant here, and can be used to elucidate areas of difficulty, there are religious aspects present in this vision of the world, which draws nourishment from ancient mythical sources of the Rifain land, where pagan myths are mingled haphazardly with the hagiographies of Muslim saints, as discussed above, agricultural and pastoral rituals with tales of war or *jihad* (e.g. the Shiite sacrifice). It is between these intermingling aspects of the religious and the pagan that theatrical performance springs out in the form of carnival. In his account of carnival, Mouliéras explains it as follows:

> the modern Rifain carnival perpetuates a secular tradition with origins lost in the night of time. A grotesque spectacle takes place three times a year: the Muslim new year, which takes place at Al-'id-al-kabir (great festival) and Al-'id-es-sghir (small festival following

Ramadan). From the moment the sun rises the crowd invades the streets, awaiting the appearance of the five persons who make up the unique masquerade found in the locality.[36]

The terms *carnival* and *masquerade* refer to a dramatic scene, which signifies action, performed with masks and special equipment, a theatrical game and a stage work. At the same time, this carnival is an original tradition with deep roots in the Rif. It has inspired many contemporary playwrights,[37] who have made use of it in recent plays. They show a burlesque performance dominated by the principle roles of Ba-Cheikh (the Wiseman) and his Wife, the *Cadi* (the Judge), Ba-Cheikh's Jew and Ba-Cheikh's Donkey. Other secondary roles are included, such as those of the complainants, and the equipment includes Ba-Cheikh's props and the masks. These kinds of characters and props are found in the post-colonial theatre of Kateb Yacine, in which, for example, the *Mufti* (religious preacher) is turned into a figure of fun in a way that echoes the mockery of established authority in the traditions of carnival, which has always been an important custom in north Africa. In his study of the Shiite festival of *Ashura*,[38] Edmond Doutté describes 'satirical and often humorous sketches', involving a judge presiding over a 'mock trial'.[39] These sketches ridicule religion, authority and the unjust vagaries of the law, just as Kateb's theatre derides the judgements given by the *Cadi*. The burlesque participates actively in the demythication of ceremonial, which becomes accessible to all. It is a matter for social play. Humour, even if coarse, and derision are artistic and educational means that allow a society to see the truth without complacency, and to overcome its problems and contradictions. The function of burlesque is cathartic, because it makes it possible to set free the old demons inhabiting the social individual in order to master them better. An illustration of this is found in the post-colonial theatre of Kateb Yacine, in his use of the Mufti figure. The Mufti is persuaded to defile his social and religious position. He finds himself in a dung heap as a result of the Djeha figure's trickery, humiliated by a coarse joke. The mechanism of farcical representation has allowed Kateb and many other north African dramatists the kind of subversive liberation that carnival once provided from established norms. Playful irreverence and gay satire have furnished the playwright with ideal weapons against political oppression.

One can draw parallels between this narrative carnival genre and the Roman festivals celebrated in honour of Saturn, and, on a more general level, the agricultural rituals of the Mediterranean. The Saturnalia came to a close with human offerings. Much later, their playful aspects replaced their tragic content, before giving way to true burlesque. As regards agricultural festivals, the ceremonies evolved in a subtle way: from a primitive agricultural initiation rite to a 'dramatic' substitute with a social focus in which, in spite of everything, it is possible to discern traces of 'ritual murder'. In any event, the story of Ba-Cheikh and the spectacle in which he appears, along with numerous variants, is still a living tradition in other regions of Morocco, Algeria and Tunisia. Along with the oral signification of the Halqa and the plays and performances put on by troupes such as Ulad Sidi Musa and Bidat Ar-rma, it constitutes the original breeding ground of Moroccan theatre. The equivalent of Ba-Cheikh in Kabylie, the Berber region of Algeria, is *Amghar azemni*, an old man 'rigged out in a sheepskin mask together with a great beard and a white moustache' who acts as 'guide, counsellor and judge'.[40] The other characters in this masquerade include the *Aklan*, slaves played by the strongest men in the village, *Aghyul*, the slaves' donkey, *Imeddah'en* (Kabyle plural for *Meddah*) and a group of peasants who sing in praise when the people give them gifts of food.[41] In essence, these characters form the core of Kateb Yacine's later work. As described above, the Meddah sets the scene for the performance, but also takes part in the main body of the play. Kateb's Meddah and that of the carnival share many features: 'This motley crew wanders from house to house, making everyone laugh with their disguises, gestures and words, and *Amghar*'s unexpected speeches.'[42] It is common for Berber festivals to include sequences that act out the beating of famous people. In the context of cultural inter-textuality, it is useful to draw a parallel between the secular ritual of Ba-Cheikh, the Shiite festival of Ashura and the Festival of the Sultan of the Learners. It is this culturally symbolic intersection that gives insights into the possibilities for an experimental theatre that could represent the cultural patrimony of north Africa.

Modern experimentation

Whilst the colonial intrusion is an attempt to devalue indigenous culture, the history of popular theatre in north Africa is one of struggle by the people to gain control over their own culture. This is a complex dialectic in which cultural and political control by hegemonic forces has been opposed by the people's own cultural resistance. This section looks at the significant experiences of the popular performing aesthetic during the period between the two World Wars and discusses the instrumental use of drama in the national cause and for the independence movement.

Experimental theatre in Morocco, Algeria and Tunisia expresses an identification with north African culture, and thus responds to people's needs
and expectations. Unlike typical western experimental drama, the appeal
of which is limited to a particular section within the intellectual élite, it
reaches wider audiences and appeals more to the popular taste. This borrowed western form has been through different stages of imitation, translation, adaptation and experimentation in the three countries, but has often
failed to achieve its aims because it represents an attempt to absorb several
centuries of theatrical experience all at the same time, which could not have
acted as a stimulant to dramatic innovation. What actually happened was
that many of these countries' pioneers put local dramatic content into a borrowed form. Until recently, the essence of the problem was not necessarily
that of borrowed form and local content but, rather, essentially a question
of content itself. In fact, the problem is not to find contents that fit the
borrowed form, but whether such contents can give rise to their own form.
This situation is best expressed in the conclusion of Abdelkader Alloula, one
of the pioneers of this genre of popular theatre:

> There is a major element of blockage: it is the design of the the-
> atre and the settings in which we evolve. The architecture of these
> settings, of these setting-cages conceived exactly with the aims of
> identification illusion that embarrass us again and again. We are
> working very seriously to set up a space for our drama that is dif-
> ferent from Italian theatres, where everything is done to ensure that
> the viewer is a passive consumer of the illusion . . . We intend to set
> up a *Halqa* theatre.[43]

It should not be assumed that this form of theatre, in the present day, is
uniform throughout the three countries, nor does its widespread use imply
that their culture is unitary. Each country has its own specific features marked
by its individual historical and cultural evolution.

The advent of theatre as an art form in these countries is usually dated
from the early twentieth century. But by the beginning of the First World
War the renewed interest in theatre for the people in the three countries
under French rule had given way to disappointment. The early enthusiasm
for colloquial Arabic theatre differed from the enthusiasm for the theatre
of the Enlightenment: the first was concerned with the mass attainment of
national indigenous identity, the latter with rationality and civility. Furthermore, the role and status of the dramatic text became the subject of debate at

this time. Some pioneers such as Mahiedine Bachetarzi, Mohamed Abaza-kour and others maintained faith in the power of the classics they adapted to edify and unify, while others such as Rachid Ksentini and Abdelkader Allalou insisted that theatre required fresh works to stimulate reflection on contemporary political and economic issues. In a diverse society the uniform achievement of insight no longer seemed supremely desirable. Nonetheless, theatre still appeared capable of stimulating civic vitality. French theatres sometimes set out to facilitate access to the classics, augmenting dramatic fragments with anything at all that might stimulate the audiences' sense of their own identity. The Egyptian company of George Abiad toured north Africa in the early 1920s and triggered off the creation of Moroccan, Algerian and Tunisian theatre. This is partly true because the visit was met with great enthusiasm by Moroccans, Algerians and Tunisians, who, given the exclusive control of French theatre over drama in most of north Africa hitherto, took pride in the idea of 'Arab' theatre. The Egyptians, however, came with a borrowed form of drama – a form that already existed in French in the rest of north Africa. However, since they were an Arab company performing in Arabic, they acquired added appeal because of the sense of Arab nation-alism then prevailing, particularly in Algeria and Morocco. The question still remains, however, as to why an Egyptian company and not an already well-established French theatre should have initiated the idea of a specific Algerian or Moroccan theatre, even though both types of theatre were using the same forms. The reason might well be that, as mentioned above, the core of indigenous theatre already existed in the substantial pre-theatrical forms that had and still have a strong influence on popular drama. In fact, this the-atre owes its existence to a tradition of struggle and opposition developed during the recent history of the countries.

Theatre as an instrument of resistance and political commitment is also found in Morocco. Moroccan theatre took place at the limits of legality. It was never authorised and, at best, was barely tolerated by the colonial authorities during the 1920s and 1930s. In consequence, it had never ben-efited from special structures and did not function as a cultural, artistic activity, since it was in fact illicit in nature and represented a form of na-tionalist resistance. The first pioneers of this theatre of resistance (1920–40), such as Mohamed al-Yazid, Mohamed al-Kouri, Mehdi Mniai, Abdelouahed Chaoui and Mohamed Bencheikh, did not recognise theatre as an art and never practised it as a profession. For them, theatrical activities were no more than a form of political defiance directed against colonial oppression and insurrection organised in spite of all sorts of restrictions. This theatre was rather naïve, tackling its themes primarily without any artistic vision or concept. It was based on nothing but the declamation of the Arabic language without any artistic consistency other than the prerequisite of direct opposition to the existing situation of domination. The themes and references used drew on legends symbolising the grandeur of Islam, tales of historic battles in which the Islamic armies were victorious, and the sometime-mythical heroes of Islam. These activities of the theatre of resistance, which also marked the birth of dramatic expression in Morocco, made no reference to the traditional forms discussed above. However, this did not in the least bother the public, who enjoyed the inspiration offered by the subjects of these performances and who liked listening to actors forcefully declaiming classical Arabic, the language of the Koran, of combat and confrontation with the occupying languages, French and Spanish. Since it was taking place at a time of combat, the theatre of resistance was organised like a wartime activity. The stage could be set anywhere, even inside houses, as if it was a clandestine activity. The sets might be made out of painted sheets or boxes, or there might be no set at all. It was enough for an actor to advance towards the audience and declare, 'I am Saladin al-Ayyubi',[44] for the audience to believe in the role, whatever clothes or make-up he was wearing. This was a theatre of total communion between the stage and the auditorium; all the hearts present were thrilled by the slogans shouted by the actors and were sometimes repeated by the public outside the hall and in the street. This was the subversive side of nationalist theatre that the colonial authorities were afraid of, because, in their eyes, it disrupted public order.

During this period of colonisation there was a great deal of political agitation and excitement. The people of Morocco, Algeria and Tunisia, sensitised to the political climate, reacted in unforeseen ways, seeing allusions where there were none and responding strongly to apparently uninteresting details. In such an atmosphere anything could become subversive. The political tension exacerbated the authorities' sensitivity and they searched out provocation everywhere. This phase in the development of popular theatre ended shortly before the start of the Second World War. The pace of theatrical life was becoming much less intense. The French administration interfered in all indigenous affairs and a faction of the extreme right that was hostile to the nationalist organisations provoked trouble whenever the administration was criticised. In addition to these obstacles, the theatre suffered from considerable financial problems. Hence the restriction of this theatre to its basic vocation of propaganda. It was a product of its historical, political and social environment, and was developed by a large number of theatre groups. The *Saisons Arabes* of theatre productions and public shows were conceived during this period. This development saw the genuine popular theatre of the three countries forced to abandon the spontaneity and improvisation that had helped it to escape French restrictions and take on a more formal, institutional status. This new situation imposed obligations on the theatre groups. The French administration supervised their programmes and was able to influence productions. Some work continued exceptionally to enjoy prominence despite the paradoxical demands placed upon it by the colonial administration and the nationalist factions within the populations. The French wanted plays to conform to their wishes; north Africans wanted them to play an educational role, contributing to their nations' political awakening and, in some way, satisfying indigenous tastes.

The period between the two World Wars was marked by attempts to merge different troupes and organisations.[45] Following on from the large number of Egyptian companies that had never ceased touring, and benefitting from the European and Arabic classics that had influenced them, the Moroccans, Algerians and Tunisians rapidly tried to create a local popular theatre that was more in line with their tastes and customs. It is therefore possible to make a useful distinction between those popular theatre forms that emerged within the colonial hegemony and mediated nationalist tendencies in an oblique way, and those that were self-conscious expressions of the nationalist struggle. In practice, however, the line between the two approaches was often blurred. The complex relationship between the liberation movements of Morocco, Algeria and Tunisia and wider movements of cultural resistance to colonialism can be illuminated by looking at prominent trends. Throughout these countries political nationalism was usually preceded by spontaneous movements of cultural nationalism in which pre-colonial theatrical musical, dance and theatrical forms were revived as forms of protest against colonialism. Nationalist parties such as the Tunisian Dustur, the Algerian National Liberation Front (FLN) and the Moroccan Istiqlal were not slow to see the advantages of such theatre for creating popular solidarity against colonial rule.

In Tunisia, for example, the al-Shahama company had begun their activities by putting on social plays, such as *as-Samaw'al* with Bourguiba in the principal role and Bannan as the singer, *Salah al-Din* with a cast composed of the Jewish Habiba Messika in the role of Julie, Salama al-Dufani as Saladin,

Bourguiba as Richard Lionheart, Bannan as William and Muhammad al-Agrebi as Montséra. Al-Shahama also excelled in adaptations and translations of the European repertoire,[46] before moving radically towards nationalistic theatre. In the late 1920s and early 1930s there was disagreement between the actors and the company's managing committee concerning the choice of plays to be performed. The actors, Muhamad Bourguiba in particular, wanted to perform engagé theatre in the service of nationalism. By contrast, the managing committee, which was chaired by M. Charletti, who was also the Director of Public Education, sought to deal tactfully with the authorities in the Protectorate. It was forced to resign and another committee was elected under the chairmanship of Ahmad al-Safi, the secretary-general of the executive committee of the nationalist Dustur party. Having grasped the importance of theatre as a means of political expression and popular mobilisation, the Moroccan national movement set about giving assistance and at the same time using it in its political activities. The nationalist Mohamed al-Yazid gathered a number of theatre groups in Rabat during the 1920s and 1930s. The nationalist leader in northern Morocco, Abdelkhalek Torrès, also participated in these activities as a playwright, and his play Intissar al haq (The Victory of Right), published in 1934, is still considered the first published Moroccan play. Faced with the danger presented by the new weapon in the hands of the nationalists, the colonial administration was not slow to react with force. The public's attachment to this new means of expression, which was received more like an instrument of protest than a simple form of entertainment, did nothing to calm the occupiers' concerns. Many performances were banned, theatre groups were broken up, and their leaders were forced to leave their home regions or arrested and sometimes tortured, as in the case of Mohamed al-Kouri, who died while being tortured by representatives of the French administration in 1937, after having been sentenced to forced labour for life.[47] After the Second World War the revolutionaries engaged in the struggle for Algerian independence saw theatre as a weapon that could, and should, be used on behalf of their political ideology. The Algerian FLN used it for agitprop work rather than as théâtre aux armées.[48] Communists and socialists within the FLN took this notion and developed it still further, to the extent of denying that any art could be divorced from politics or have any non-political content. Roselyne Baffet describes how actors associated with the FLN became the mainstays of the Algerian Theatre after independence: 'It is in this theatre that we find revolutionary militancy, at this point still unarmed, but working for the cause of socialism.'[49] The socialist approach follows the traditional one of the Ulema[50] in its treatment of art as a serious matter: 'A work signed by an Algerian can interest us only from one point of view; the cause it serves and its position in the struggle against the colonialist movement.'[51]

Post-colonial developments

Until independence dramatists worked within a specific problematic framed by a high degree of colonial French control over artistic expression and an overt politicisation of cultural questions. On one hand the work of the pioneers of north African theatre had to be sufficiently acceptable to the French administration and the privately owned cultural companies. On the other hand it had to be sufficiently distanced to gain credibility within the indigenous population. This final section discusses the challenges of working in theatre within a post-colonial, authoritarian state structure.

Community or amateur theatre has been the alternative successor to the national theatre[52] put in place by the post-independence governments. Some of the more recently founded independent community and amateur theatre groups were to eschew the establishment approach of much of the earlier work of the national theatre. The important difference is that in the 1980s both mainstream and independent theatre companies tended to reject amateur involvement in their work as an anachronism and to argue that professionalism was necessary if they were to maintain and improve artistic standards, although there was little agreement as to what those standards were. In general, the post-independence movement in theatre was close to community values regarding the internally self-determined practices, ethics and aesthetics of a profession. Community artists are much less concerned about their work being tainted by association with amateurs, and often involve themselves with projects where there is little scope for artistic excellence in an orthodox sense. Whilst there is recognisable value in the work of several dramatists and theatre-makers, the theatrical tradition has been obliged to develop largely outside and in opposition to the state-sponsored national theatres because these institutions have systematically failed to promote the development of a truly national theatre that might be an authentic expression of the three countries' national identities and an enrichment of their cultures. Preferring instead to rely mainly on the staging of translations of foreign plays, the behaviour of these national theatres reflects the survival of the outlook that underlay the mainstream north African theatre during the later colonial period, when, for example, there was a refusal to work in the language spoken by the majority of the population and when the works promoted reflected the debased image of native north African society that the theatre's colonial supporters required. It thereby established a tacit tradition of anti-national theatrical activity that, given a new lease of life by the cultural commissars of the post-colonial states, has persisted to the present day.

The rational organisation of cultural life in Morocco, Algeria and Tunisia was a major concern in the period immediately following independence. The 1963 decree establishing the Algerian National Theatre was intended to set out official doctrine in a formal way. It envisaged increased state control and paid little attention to the opportunities offered by the touring companies. It minimised the role of these companies, most of which were amateur and which travel round the whole country with the aim of moulding sensibilities, finding sources of inspiration and asserting an Algerian identity. The national theatre was marked for a long period by a centralising ideology. In Morocco, people who worked in the theatre welcomed the Dahir establishing the Moroccan National Theatre with a mixture of euphoria and ambiguity. Although they felt that it was a gain for the profession as a whole, the practice unfortunately disproved this favourable a priori judgement. During the study days organised by the Minister for Cultural and Religious Affairs, one of the commissions was charged to put forward a reading of the Dahir, as if the text had already begun to be the subject of controversy, and it was necessary to agree as quickly as possible on a common interpretation for it. The participants in these study days had their own ideas about the national definition given by the Dahir to the theatre in its entirety and felt that the idea of the TNM might consist of setting up a national company with a programme at three levels: local for the city of Rabat, national for the other cities and towns, and international for work at festivals abroad. Shortly after the study days came to an end, the TNM became the responsibility of a different minister, and all the recommendations have been forgotten ever since. The aim set for the Tunisian National Theatre was the imitation of French drama. This decision was no great visionary act but rather the result of a request by the authorities at the Ministries of Cultural Affairs and Youth and Sports to merge the existing TNT company with groups run by French dramatists. It has remained the recipient of the largest government subsidy of any Tunisian theatre and has provided a sense of French-Arabic cultural continuity. The TNT is appreciated by privileged groups and does not command the popularity commanded, for example, by the independent Gafsa company or the intellectual audience that attends the Théâtre Phou. The TNT has not played a national role since independence.[53]

Naturally national theatres have existed in countries that enjoy a strong political identity, in the age of the great courts of Europe, for example, but not in countries where identity has remained problematic, such as Morocco, Algeria and Tunisia, although the pre-colonial traditions of these countries discussed above made attempts to constitute the basis for a theatre that would have enjoyed such a strong identity as in Europe. Theoretically, anything called 'national' must be a product or service that is financed by the state and is therefore at the disposal of the citizens of that state. This interpretation may apply perfectly well to a nationalised industry, but less happily to a theatre. A theatre building can be owned and financed by the state, but a single building can hardly be run for the benefit of the people of that state. A theatre building, as a place that hosts performances, is of little benefit to those who live in the remoter regions of the country. 'National' is therefore an epithet with wide and not always fortunate connotations. The national theatres did not encourage community, amateur or other independent movements because they held to their stereotypical forms, their commercial and professional ambitions and their conservative ideology. The survival and prevalence of the particular traditions of the Meddah, Halqa, Djeha, Garagöz, religious rituals and festivals depend ultimately upon the interaction of culture with historical and political conditions. Yet people may take action to change these conditions, and the decision to seek change depends, perhaps more than anything else, on a realisation that the dominant traditions are the only possible ones. That is why the colonial administration censored arts and the ruling authorities in independent north Africa both administer and control education, printing and cultural production. It is also why the exploitation of a variety of artistic forms and changing styles and genres are politically significant. Contemporary north African companies review their work constantly, altering their performances in often radical ways. The official discourse tends to represent those changes as stylistic improvements. However, when these troupes[54] alter material emblematic of power relations and human possibilities, they are working politically, making and remaking their own culture.

Throughout the long period that commercial managements have dominated the institutions of the theatre, many erudite and sophisticated people, mainly Arabic-educated admirers[55] of north African Arab culture and Middle

Eastern literary drama, have argued that the professional stage of the national theatres was debased by the popular taste for thrills and sensations – the same argument, in fact, that had been put forward about tastes and styles in the colonial and post-independence periods among the Ulema and pro-Middle Eastern scholars. Ultimately, it was this group of people who agitated for non-commercial, subsidised performing arts institutions in the 1960s and 1970s, when they began infiltrating the political apparatus, especially the Ministries of Education. There was at the same time another group of more practical, professional men and women of the theatre, whose objection to the mainstream was more nationalistic than intellectual or élitist. They felt that north African actors and playwrights were greatly disadvantaged by the mainstream's reliance on proven overseas successes. They too sought to promote an alternative, but they probably had more in common with the mainstream they were attacking than with the intellectual minority concerned with 'Arab culture'. Their plays proved extremely popular with working-class and rural audiences.[56] They eventually came to be considered the lower, less respectable end of the market by the theatre professionals of the National Theatres, and were anathema to the advocates of Arab literary theatre.

Whatever the thinking underlying post-colonial theatre in north Africa, whether popular performance, élitist literary drama or the work of national theatres, it is still possible for this theatre to reach popular audiences. Given its multi-cultural roots in colonial drama and popular traditions, and the influence of élite Arabic forms, much of the history of the art of theatre in post-independence north Africa concerns the three countries' attempts to decolonise the theatre by searching for alternative indigenous structures and dramatic forms. The constant pouring forth of artistic work in all forms bears witness to the dynamism of past and current developments. The emphasis has shifted from works that described political and colonial injustice to performances that address post-colonial issues. Theatre may be described as having a transformative power that can become a call to action. The development of theatre as a mode of expression is reflected in the ways each particular company has contributed to the debate. There are obviously many distinctions between the various north African theatres, distinctions that derive in large part from specific cultural and political differences. However, north Africans reflect a sensibility that, in its urgency, is undeniably post-colonial and rooted in the situation of north Africa following independence.

Moroccan, Algerian and Tunisian dramatists emphasise different dimensions of the multi-cultural elements in their work, and certain among them often alter their position from play to play, from performance to performance and from one place to another. Indeed, they appear to home in on the transformational aspects of their form of expression and its capacity to contribute to the powerful dynamic that constitutes cultural change. Their artistic corpus reflects the relationship between a sense of community and the individual's passion for the homeland. Other dramatists, often in exile, have achieved international standing and experience that strengthen their ability to communicate their ideas to the wider world and play a part in a new cultural movement made up of a multiplicity of voices. Their passionate relationship with their homeland has prompted them to make rich use of the expressive artistic resources available to them. These are interwoven to form new aesthetic patterns, which generate a fusion of two or more cultures. North Africans participate in the cosmos of their original world and the images of a culture informed by Tamazight (the Berber language) and influenced by Arabic and French. Their work represents the merging of these cultures, as well as the symbiosis between their creativity and the reality in which they live.

Cultural space, for most north African dramatists, is therefore a mythical realm of political commitment and playwriting strategies, since that is where one may aspire to appropriate the myths of earlier generations. Cultural space is not separable from a dramatist's audience. Where, and for whom, north African dramatists work is probably as important as how they try to write and perform, and, indeed, has a strong influence on how they operate. That is why it is so important to account for the particular situation of each dramatist when dealing with north African theatre. Playwrights have developed their own styles and strategies for the production of experimental theatre. North African culture is highly flexible. It evolves in a space that provokes responses and allows many opportunities for audiences to judge art without limiting preconceptions. Hence the ability of north African dramatists to effectively dissect the malaise of their respective countries from colonial times to the present on the stage, even though they are working in a form that only began to be performed in the region in the early twentieth century.

Notes
1. See Roselyne Baffet, *Tradition théâtrale et modernité en Algérie* (Paris: l'Harmattan, 1985).

2. See Michael Habart in his preface to Henri Krea's play, *Le Séisme* (Paris: P. J. Oswald, 1958).

3. Especially with regard to the writings of Ibn Khaldun (1332–1406). See *al Muqaddimah*.

4. The word *maqama* literally means a public assembly where a storyteller (*Rawi*) tells a story to an audience. In the tenth century Badi' al-Zaman al-Hamadhani invented the *maqama* as a new literary genre, in the form of a story of tricksters and beggers. For further details on *maqama* see the *Cambridge History of Arabic Literature* (Cambridge University Press).

5. Cf. *Dialogue*, n. 137, 17–4–1977, pp. 58–62. For further information, see George Zaydan's *Tarikh Adab al-Lugha al-'Arabiya* (Cairo: Dar al-'ilm li al-malayin, 1958), vol. IV, p. 138.

6. Singular: *Madrassa*.

7. Cf. Mohamed Aziza, *Le Théâtre et l'Islam* (Tunis and Algiers: SNED, 1970); Jacob Landau, *Studies in the Arab Theatre and Cinema* (Philadelphia: University of Pennsylvania Press, 1958); Cherif Khaznadar, 'Pour la "recréation" d'une expression dramatique arabe', in *Le Théâtre arabe* (Paris: UNESCO, 1969).

8. The prohibition of pictorial or plastic representations was one way of affirming the new religion by distancing it from the beliefs of the pre-Islamic era. God had to be imposed as pure spirit. In consequence, a Muslim cannot oppose himself to the will of God, the logic of fate and history. These ideological motives certainly do not suffice by way of explanation, but they exercise a certain degree of pressure in modern Islam. The only exception is the *Ta'zyeh*, a unique Islamic theatrical form. When it first developed, the Ta'zyeh developed as a form of religious theatre written in verse and was often anonymous. It is performed either in an open air place or in a closed hall called a *Ta'kiya* to commemorate the death of Hussain. Most Ta'zyeh dramas are concerned with the fight for the succession that took place on the death of the Prophet Mohammed between the Shiites (who believed that the Prophet's family should inherit his authority) and the Sunnis (who were determined to elect a caliph from among the Muslims capable of taking on such a responsibility). From a theatrical point of view, Ta'zyeh is interesting as a genre, with similarities to the mystery plays of the European Middle Ages. The audience takes part in exalted, tragic lamentations that sometimes last for days. For more detail see Peter J. Chelkowski (ed.), *Ta'ziyeh: Ritual and Drama in Iran* (New York: New York University Press and Soroush Press, 1979), p. 15.

9. Jacques Berque, 'Les Arts du spectacle dans le monde arabe depuis cent ans', in *Théâtre arabe* (Paris: UNESCO, 1969), p. 17.

10. The character of Djeha is similar to that of Harlequin, Sapcin, Sganarelle and Pantalon.

11. Abdelkader Ould Abderrahmane was known as Kaki. He is one of the most original of the few contemporary Algerian dramatists. His interest in theatre dates back to the 1940s. His conception of theatre is based on Djeha, the Meddah and Halqa.

12. Real name Rachid Billakhdar. He is often associated with Villon, Molière and Verlaine. His taste for drama led him to work as a stage hand and extra in several theatres in Paris. In 1926 he went back to Algeria and embarked on a successful but short-lived experiment in popular theatre, working alongside Mahiedine Bachetarzi and Allalou (Ali Sellal).

13. A popular figure who has had a strong influence on north African literature in Arabic and French. Many authors have dedicated works to him. Cf. Jean Dejeux, *Djoh'a. Héros de la tradition arabo-berber* (Sherbrooke, Canada: Naaman, 1982; 1st edn, 1978).

14. See Kateb Yacine, *La Poudre d'intelligence* in *Le Cercle des représailles* (Paris: Seuil, 1959). This play was performed in north Africa and France several times during the 1960s, 1970s and 1980s and was always highly successful. Other plays by Kateb Yacine, *Mohamed prends ta valise, La guerre de 2000 ans, Le roi de l'Ouest*, in *Boucherie de l'espérance* (Paris: Seuil, 1999), have met with similar success.

15. Theatre buildings dating from the colonial period can be found in a number of main cities. These are also subsidised and function along the same lines as the National Theatre. There is a theatre of this type in Anaba, the TRA (Regional Theatre of Anaba), which was founded on 16 April 1973 and which has the status of a national theatre. The TRC (Regional Theatre of Constantine) was opened in 1973 in a building dating from the early nineteenth century. It is controlled by the state, which appoints its manager/director. It is required to stage a minimum number of performances each year and to perform, encourage and promote dramatic works by Algerian authors. The oldest theatre in Oran is now the home of a relatively popular theatre. The TRO was opened on 24 April 1973 and has been led for most of its history by Alloula, a well-known dramatist. In Sidi Bel Abbes, the TRSB was created at a time (1976) when the very concept of national theatre had become something of an anachronism. Its history has been idiosyncratic and is closely entwined with the career of Kateb Yacine, who by 1976 was well on the way to being accepted as a 'national' and 'nationalist' dramatist.

16. Fellag, *Djurdjurassique Bled* (Algiers: Casbah Editions, 2000).

17. Ibid., Preface, pp. 9–10.

18. Majid El Houssi, *Le Récit de la voix: un essai sur le conte tunisien dans 'Il banchetto Maghrebino'* (Padavo: Francisci Editore, 1981).

19. Examples of this political transition are widely discussed in recent scholarship.

20. Greek tragedy is related to the phenomenon described here. It showed the powerlessness of man in the face of fate, which is determined by the gods. There was no way for the heroes of ancient Greece to escape the curses of the gods. They struggled to turn back their destinies, and though condemned by the gods, they refused to resign themselves to their lot. They fought because they wanted to live, love and hope in spite of the relentlessness of fate.

21. Examples of recent outdoor performances are analysed in Kamal Salhi's *The Politics and Aesthetics of Kateb Yacine* (New York and Lampeter: Mellen Press, 1999). See chapters 6 and 7.

22. And also in many other parts of Africa.

23. Teachers, mystics, wonder-workers, preachers, healers.

24. Surprisingly, Algerian national television recently (1991) promoted a long series of programmes produced in conjunction with theatre troupes, mainly from the west of the country. The performances were open air, following the 'stage' form of the cult festivals and the Halqa. The television channels of the three countries also show elaborate programmes about cult festivals. These are no doubt intended to revive popular traditions and religious ceremonies that contradict/oppose the fundamentalist perception of religious culture, which has grown stronger following the political and social unrest of the 1990s. This represents a considerable move on the part of the authorities towards a return to the popular arts and the north African cultural realities of the past.

25. For further descriptions of this festival performance, see Abdelkrim Berrechid, *Les Limites du présent et du possible dans le théâtre de la fête* (Casablanca: Dar Takkafa, 1985).

26. Abdelkader Alloula, *Les Généreux* (Arles: Actes Sud – Papiers, 1995), p. 8.

27. Kamal Salhi:

MCB (Mouvement Culturel Berbère). A cultural movement that seeks to defend the specificity of Berber culture, language and history. Its aims include official recognition of the Berber language and restoration of rights to Berber-speakers by the Algerian authorities, full integration of the Berber language into the education system and the use of the language in public life. The MCB's social programme is opposed to the Arabic-Islamist agenda, most notably on language, culture, history, and its views on political power, modernity and religion. The movement lays claim to territory that encompasses Algeria, Morocco, Tunisia, Libya and Mauritania, extending into the northern regions of Mali and Niger. Intellectuals supported it during the 1940s and working classes, university teachers and students in the aftermath of Independence. Since 1980 it has enjoyed the support of the entire Kabyle population.
In Margaret Majumdar, ed., *Francophone Studies (The Essential Glossary* (London: Edward Arnold, 2002))

28. Many peoples have told stories about characters who are wily and cunning, play tricks on others, mock social conventions and usually come out on top. Arlecchino, Garagöz, Punch, and Till Eulenspiegel are known around the world. These figures may play the fool, but they know how to make use of ridiculous situations to make the powerful and dignified look ridiculous.

29. See Moncef Charfeddine, 'Deux siècles de théâtre à Tunis', *L'Action*, 8 March 1969.

30. For the major events that occurred in the first sixty years of the twentieth century, the reader may refer to Mahieddine Bachetarzi's three-volume *Mémoires* (Algiers: SNED, 1968; ENAL, 1984; ENAL, 1986); Abdellah Chekroune's *L'Aube du théâtre arabe au Maroc* (Tunis: Editions de l'Union des

Radios des Pays Arabes, 1988); Mohamed Azzam, *Le Théâtre marocain* (Damascus: Editions de l'Union des Ecrivains Arabes, 1987); Hamdi Ben Halima, *Un demi siècle de théâtre en Tunisie, 1907–1957* (Tunis: Publications de l'Université de Tunis, 1974).

31. This story was recorded in Auguste Mouliéras's important book, *Le Maroc inconnu* (Paris: Librairie Coloniale et Africaine/Challamel, 1895/1899), vol. II, p. 159.

32. Ibid., pp. 161–70.

33. The Berber population of the Rif region of Morocco.

34. Mouliéras, *Le Maroc inconnu*, p. 161.

35. Ibid., p. 162.

36. Ibid., p. 107.

37. As is the case in Kateb Yacine's *La Poudre d'intelligence*. See also 'Mohamed prends ta valise', in Kateb Yacine's *La Boucherie de l'espérance* (Paris: Seuil, 1999).

38. *Ashura* is a religious day celebrated mainly by Shiites. Sunnis are not keen on this spectacular celebration, which involves the singing of devotional songs, dancing and gatherings at unorthodox 'holy' places and the shrines of local saints. Ashura is the tenth day of the Muharam (Islamic calendar). This is the day when Imam Hussain was slaughtered and killed by the Sunni Mu'awiya Ibn Sofian and is a major celebration. The Ashura celebration, with all its anti-Sunnism, is widely spread in the Berber regions of north Africa and in places where religious rituals and superstitions are an important part of everyday life.

39. Edmond Doutté, *Magie et Religion* (Paris: Jourdan, 1909), p. 507.

40. H. Marchand, *Masques carnavalesques et carnaval en Kabylie* (Algiers: Société Historique Algérienne, 1956), p. 2.

41. Ibid., p. 3.

42. Ibid., p. 2.

43. Abdelkader Alloula, 'Le Théâtre de la *Halqa*', in *En mémoire du futur. Pour Abdelkader Alloula* (Paris: Sindbad/Actes Sud, 1997), p. 161.

44. Saladin (1137–93), a Kurd who was Sultan of Egypt and Syria. He was the commander of the expeditions to Egypt in 1167. After constituting himself sovereign of Egypt and Syria, he received the homage of the Seljuk princes of Asia Minor. Subsequently, he waged war with the Christians, consolidating his dominions. In 1187 he defeated King Guy of Jerusalem and a united Christian army at Hattin. He captured Jerusalem and many fortified areas on the Syrian coast.

45. In Tunisia: al-jawq at-Tunisi al-Misri, Ibrahim Hijazi, al-Adab al-'Arabiya, as-Sahama al-'Arabyia, al-Hilal, at-tamtil al-'Arabi, Jawq at-Taraqqi al-Isra'ili, al-Jawq al-Fukahi at-Tunisi, Le Théâtre Ben Kamla, as-Sa'ada, al-Mustaqbal at-Tamtili, al-Masrah, Troupe Fadila Khimi, Troupe Ibrahim al-Akhudi, at-Taqaddum et an-Najah al-Masrahi, al-Kawkab at-Tamtili. In Morocco: Compagnie Fassie, Compagnie de la renaissance arabe, Le Théâtre de Rabat,

Troupe de Salé, L'Association al-Hilal sportif, L'Association des anciens élèves du Collège musulman de Fès/Rabat, Troupe de Fatima Rochdi. In Algeria: Al-Mutribiya, Troupe Municipale, Troupe Arabe, al-Djazairya, al-Andalusya, al-Mussilya, al-Muhadiba.

46. During the period between the two World Wars al-Shahama produced an ambitious programme of adaptations, such as *Othello*, *Le Médecin malgré lui*, *Esther*, *Cléopâtre*, *Hamlet*, *L'Avare*, *Tartuffe*, *Le Malade imaginaire*, *Les Femmes savantes*.

47. See Abib Salaoui, 'Mohamed al-Kouri, les premières tentatives du théâtre politique', *al-Alam attakafi*, 669, 22 October 1983 (an Arabic weekly published in Rabat).

48. Arlette Roth, *Le Théâtre algérien de langue dialectale (1926–1954)* (Paris: Maspero, 1967), p. 36.

49. Roselyne Baffet, *Tradition théâtrale et modernité en Algérie* (Paris: l'Harmattan, 1985), p. 47.

50. Like the Ulema of Morocco, a Muslim- and Arabic-educated élite, also known as the intelligentsia. They put forward a programme of Islamic reform that extended to literature and the music of religious devotion. Members were associated with the Cheikh Abdelhamid Ibn Badis. They promoted the Association des Oulemas Musulmans from the 1920s onwards.

51. Mohamed Cherif Sahli, *Le Jeune Musulman, journal officiel* of the Ulema in French (2 January 1953), p. 12.

52. The Tunisian National Theatre (TNT) was established by Law no. 113–83 of 30 December 1983, implementing the budgetary resources for 1984 (Article 73). It is a public cultural institution granted with legal personality and financial autonomy. The birth of the TNT coincided with the setting up of the Theatrical Days festival at Carthage. The Tunisian National Theatre publishes a review, *Espace théâtral* (*Fadhaat masrahiya*). The Algerian National Theatre was created by Decree no. 63.12 of 8 January 1963. The decree explains the considerations that have guided the theatre in Algeria. Article 1: The Algerian Theatre is a national public service. Article 2: The Algerian Theatre is under the authority of the Ministry of Cultural Affairs and the Ministry of National Education. Article 3: A theatrical company is to be established, to be known as the Algerian National Theatre, the TNA, under the authority of the head office of the Ministry of Cultural Affairs and the Ministry of National Education. The King of Morocco signed the Dahir implementing Law no. 1.72.293 of 22 February 1973 concerning the creation of the Mohamed V National Theatre (TNM). This law instituted the TNM as a public institution granted with moral personality and financial autonomy, subject to the administrative guidance of the government authority charged with cultural affairs. The TNM's aims are: the promotion of all cultural activities contributing to the development of theatre; support for theatrical research and creativity; the provision of artistic training; the coordination of performance programmes in collaboration with

municipal theatres, associations and national and international organisations; participation in theatrical events abroad; the constitution of a centre for theatrical documentation.

53. The status of the TNT is explored in the unpublished thesis, 'Le Rôle du théâtre national dans la mobilisation du large public' by Faouzia Bel Hadj Mezzi (Tunis University, 1988).

54. A good example among many others is the university theatre led by Mohamed Driss. This new style of theatre developed in the context of the thinking and forms of theatrical expression established by Brecht, but has similarities with traditional forms and uses the language of the people.

55. The Algerians Tahar Ouatar and Ben Hadouga, the Moroccan Mohamed Zefzaf, the Tunisians Sheikh Fadel Ben Achour, Mohamed Mzali, Abdelkader Mhiri and Ben Youcef.

56. An example of this situation in Algeria is analysed in greater detail in Kamal Salhi's *The Politics and Aesthetics of Kateb Yacine* (1999), in chapters 4 and 5.

References and further reading

Alloula, Abdelkader. *Les Généreux*. Arles: Actes Sud – Papiers, 1995.

Alloula, Abdelkader. *En Mémoire du futur. Pour Abdelkader Alloula*. Paris: Sindbad/Actes Sud, 1997.

Aziza, Mohamed. *Regards sur le théâtre arabe contemporain*. Tunis: MTE, 1962.

Aziza, Mohamed. *Le Théâtre et l'Islam*. Algiers and Tunis: SNED, 1970.

Azzam, Mohamed. *Le Théâtre marocain*. Damascus: Editions de l'Union des Ecrivains Arabes, 1987.

Bachetarzi, Mahieddine. *Mémoires*, vol. I, Algiers: SNED, 1968; vol. II, ENAL, 1984; vol. III, ENAL, 1986.

Baffet, Roselyne. *Tradition théâtrale et modernité en Algérie*. Paris: l'Harmattan, 1985.

Bel Hadj Mezzi, Faouzia. 'Le Rôle du théâtre national dans la mobilisation du large public'. Unpublished thesis, Tunis University, 1988.

Ben Halima, Hamdi. *Les Principaux thèmes du théâtre arabe contemporain*. Tunis: STAG, 1969.

Ben Halima, Hamdi. *Un Demi siècle de théâtre en Tunisie, 1907–1957*. Tunis: Publications de l'Université de Tunis, 1974.

Berque, Jacques. 'Les Arts du spectacle dans le monde arabe depuis cent ans', in *Le Théâtre arabe*, Paris: UNESCO, 1969.

Berrechid, Abdelkrim. *Les Limites du présent et du possible dans le théâtre de la fête*. Casablanca: Dar Takkafa, 1985.

Brett, Michael. *Ibn Khaldun and the Medieval Maghrib*. Aldershot: Ashgate, 1999.

Charfeddine, Moncef. 'Deux siècles de théâtre à Tunis'. *L'Action*, 8 March 1969.

Chekroune, Abdellah. *L'Aube du théâtre arabe au Maroc*. Tunis: Editions de l'Union des Radios des Pays Arabes, 1988.

Chelkowski, Peter J., ed. *Ta'ziyeh: Ritual and Drama in Iran*. New York: New York University Press and Soroush Press, 1979.

Dejeux, Jean. *Djoh'a. Héros de la tradition arabo-berber.* Sherbrooke, Canada: Naaman, 1978/1982.

Doutté, Edmond. *Magie et religion.* Paris: Jourdan, 1909.

Duvignaud, Jean. *L'Acteur, esquisse d'une sociologie du comédien.* Paris: Gallimard, 1965.

El Houssi, Majid. *Le Récit de la voix: un essai sur le conte tunisien dans 'Il banchetto Maghrebino'.* Padavo: Francisci Editore, 1981.

Fellag. *Djurdjurassique Bled.* Algiers: Casbah Editions, 2000.

Ibn Khaldun, Abd al-Rahman. *Muqaddimat Ibn Kalhdun.* Beirut: Dar al Kutyub al 'ilmiya, 1993.

Kateb, Yacine. *Boucherie de l'espérance.* Paris: Seuil, 1999.

Kateb, Yacine. *Le Cercle des représailles.* Paris: Seuil, 1959.

Kershaw, Baz. *The Politics of Performance: Radical Theatre as Cultural Intervention.* London: Routledge, 1992.

Khaznadar, Cherif. 'Pour la "recréation" d'une expression dramatique arabe', in *Le Théâtre arabe,* Paris: UNESCO, 1969.

Landau, Jacob. *Studies in the Arab Theatre and Cinema.* Philadelphia: University of Pennsylvania Press, 1958.

Marchand Henri. *Masques carnavalesques et carnaval en Kabylie.* Algiers: Société Historique Algérienne, 1956.

Mniai, Hassan. *Le Théâtre et l'improvisation.* Casablanca: Ouyoun, 1992.

Mouliéras, Auguste. *Le Maroc inconnu.* Paris: Librairie Coloniale et Africaine/Challamel, 1895/1899.

Najib, Al Oufi. *Dialectique de la lecture: observations sur la création marocaine contemporaine.* Casablanca: Edima, 1983.

Najm, Mohamed. *La Pièce de théâtre dans la littérature arabe contemporaine.* Beirut: Editions Dar al-Takafa, 1967.

Roth, Arlette. *Le Théâtre algérien de langue dialectale (1926–1954).* Paris: Maspero, 1967.

Saddiki, Tayeb. *Diwan Sidi Abderrahmane al-Majdub.* Rabat: Editions Stouky, 1979.

Saddiki, Tayeb. *Nous sommes faits pour nous entendre.* Casablanca: Eddif, 1997.

Sahli, Mohamed Cherif. *Le Jeune Musulman, Journal Officiel.* 2 January 1953.

Salaoui, Abib. 'Mohamed al Kouri, les premières tentatives du théâtre politique', *al Alam attakafi,* 669 (22 October 1983).

Salhi, Kamal. *The Politics and Aesthetics of Kateb Yacine.* New York and Lampeter: Mellen Press, 1999.

Sayeh, Hassan. *Réflexions au sujet du roman et du texte dramatique marocains.* Beirut: Dar al-Kitab al-Arabia, 1968.

Schmidt, Nathaniel. *Ibn Khaldun: Historian, Sociologist and Philosopher.* New York: Columbia University Press, 1930.

Table ronde – La Presse: le théâtre tunisien dans ses états. République Tunisienne, Secrétariat d'Etat à l'Information: Centre de Documentation National. 29 November 1993.

Zaydan, George. *Tarikh Adab al-Lugha al-'Arabiya.* Cairo: Dar al-'ilm li al-malayin, 1958.

Sudan

KHALID ALMUBARAK MUSTAFA

Theatre in the western sense of the word has a short history in Sudan, beginning only after the reconquest of the country and the subsequent Condominium rule (1889–1955) in which Britain was the senior partner with Egypt. If the term is defined to include performance rituals, Sudan, with its vast size (1 million square miles – almost a quarter of the area of Europe) has a cornucopia of theatrical heritage. Pre-Islamic rituals include the trance/possession Zar[1] that the country shares with several other African countries (e.g. Ethiopia, Egypt). Initiation (Sufi) rituals, linked to the Islamic period which began in 652 but which reached full state power in 1605 (with variations among different sects and orders), played very significant social as well as religious roles. Rituals of the animist southern Sudanese ethnic groups are arguably among the finest and most effective group festivities involving whole communities. They also represent links in a chain of influences traceable to ancient Nubian and Egyptian religious ceremonies.[2]

The civil wars that bedevilled the country (1955–72 and 1983 onwards) and other factors, such as an imbalance in development and education, meant that the flowering of the British and Egyptian transplantation of the western Aristotelian form of theatre took place mainly in the cities and urban centres of northern Sudan, where approximately two-thirds of the circa 30 million population of Sudan live, people who are Muslim but who are culturally Arab.

This section will offer a brief delineation of these various theatrical strands, traditions and activities with a concern for both regional and national features. Both the African and Arab-Islamic features of Sudanese heritage have left their mark on Sudanese drama. The investiture of Shilluk Reth, Nuba wrestling contests, the Azande 'stylised invective' and the Zar are examples of African (non-Islamic) communal performances. Sufi ceremonies are Arab-Islamic, but they are virulently denounced by fanatical adherents of Sunni Islam, who recognise prayer only as a means of communication with or worship of Allah.

Reth investiture

A unique theatrical ritual that involves the whole Shilluk ethnic group in southern Sudan is still observed when the occasion arises. When the *Reth* (king) dies his spirit is preserved in a sacred effigy. In order to pass on the spirit to the Reth-elect (who is chosen from a number of noble families) priests take the effigy out and engage the army of the Reth-elect in several mock battles until the effigy is victorious. The 'captured' Reth-elect then sits on a stool immediately after the effigy is removed from it. He enters a trance as the spirit is transferred into his body. The effigy is then taken back to its shrine and kept for the next investiture. The ceremony ends with a democratic open gathering, in which all members of the Shilluk group have a chance to criticise, advise, blame or praise the new Reth before he assumes full power.[3] (Television records of this ceremony have been made by the BBC and Deutsche Welle, and several local plays are based on it, including the present writer's *The Reth*, 1978.)

War of words

Another fascinating southern Sudanese ritual is that of the 'stylised invective' used by the Azande ethnic group during the intervals between real clashes or battles. According to Peter Bicknell, '[t]he voice is considered to be a weapon of some power, particularly in singing when it was used to lampoon enemies' in order to demoralise them.[4] The unwritten code of the ritual dictates that combatants are never interrupted by the other side until they complete their vocal barrage and prepare themselves for the response. The Azande live in the southern tip of Sudan, split by the border from the majority of Azande who live in the Congo. Their war-related rituals were recorded during the colonial era.

Sufi ceremonies

The Sufis are Muslim innovators and dissidents who reject worldly glory (including money and power) and sometimes claim to perform miracles. They organise themselves in 'orders' and include music, dancing (whirling) and colourful costumes in their communal *Zikr* (*Dhikr*) events. Many Sufis have been hanged under Islamic rule. The Sufi tolerance of local African (non-Islamic) traditions enabled them to spread their version of Islam in west Africa and Sudan. Neophytes undergo a highly stylised initiation with their sheikh. In Zikr (literally, rememberance) the Sufis sit or stand in a circle, swaying and chanting verses in praise of Allah. The different orders have different verses and costumes. Zikr usually takes place in the order's centre or near the tomb of a revered founder (significantly, not in a mosque). In a sense Zikr is an alternative form of worship within the faith. In the orthodox Zikr, a worshipper repeats the name of Allah (with or without a rosary) on his own after prayers. There is an account of the way in which a sheikh, Taguddin Al Bihari, staged a 'play' in the process of recruiting novices to his path. He stood in front of a crowd having built a shelter in which he hid two rams. He then asked would-be disciples to enter the shelter for initiation, which would be followed by self-sacrifice. After some hesitation two men entered. The sheikh then killed one of the rams in the shelter and the audience were alarmed to see blood trickling out. He then opened the shelter and the two men emerged safely! Since the Qadiriya order to which the sheikh belonged is the most widespread in Sudan, the sixteenth-century play-ceremony recorded above, and similar actions, must have been repeated over and over in many localities.[5]

The initiation ceremony of the Qadiriya (which differs little from that of other orders) is highly dramatic. Inclusion as a full member and the right to wear the distinctive costume (*Khirqa*) is only allowed after the sheikh/neophyte initiation, in which the aspirant performs ablution, prays two *rakaas* and sits opposite the sheikh, 'thighs pressed together and hands clasped'. He repeats a prayer, sentence by sentence, after the sheikh. As a token of accepting him 'as a son', the sheikh offers the new disciple a cup of water followed by a coded personal Zikr.[6]

Theatrical wrestling

Another non-Islamic ritual, from the Nuba mountain area of central Sudan, is the wrestling rite of passage and harvest festival for young men. The wrestlers wear colourful costumes, paint their faces and bodies (in the manner that has been photographed and filmed by Leni Riefenstahl) and 'play to the gallery' in a ritual that combines aspects of sport with theatrical spectacle and ancient animist rites. It is now a favourite tourist attraction in Omdurman, with a director/umpire and hundreds of fans.[7]

Zar

This non-Islamic theatrical ritual was outlawed after the 'bearded coup' of 30 June 1989. Zar is a therapeutic 'safety valve' for middle-aged Muslim women from northern Sudan. It has all the trappings of a staged performance. It is a 'women only' ritual in which, after dancing to percussion instruments, a woman goes into a trance. During her altered state of consciousness she is possessed by a certain spirit. The organiser of the event (which takes place in private homes) keeps costumes ready and helps the woman to put them on. Her wishes – in her adopted character – are met even if they are reprehensible in social life – such as a glass of whisky or wine.[8] A historic shift in the Zar ritual happened in the 1980s when a charismatic Zar sheikh, Mohammed Wad Hulla, managed to move the ritual from the secretive closed-door environment to open-air performances at the National Council of Arts and Letters in Khartoum. What happened was in some ways parallel to the emergence of drama out of ritual in ancient Greece. Sheikh Mohammed was open-minded about scripted roles, but his innovations were short-lived and a tide of religious intolerance forced him underground.

British and Egyptian influences

In 1902 the British established the Gordon Memorial College in Khartoum. The teaching of Shakespeare and other playwrights there, and in other schools, went hand in hand with amateur performances, both for civilians and troops. In 1934 the Bakht Ar Ruda Teacher Training Institute was established. Teachers exposed to and participating in performances spread their skills and interests wherever they were stationed.

The direct influence of these two educational institutions is epitomised by the contribution of four men, all of whom bestowed 'respectability' on the theatre because they came from well-known families. Siddiq Faried (who tragically died in a car accident while still a young man) combined theatre with politics and in 1938 was elected to the 'committee of sixty' of the Graduates' Congress – the antecedent of political parties. As a director he concentrated solely on adaptations and translations of British, Egyptian and Lebanese plays. Hassan Abdul Majeed wrote and directed plays until his death in 1980. His *Ar rafd* (Rejection) 1972, dealt with the generation gap and changing values. Ahmed At Tayeb (the first Sudanese to be awarded a Ph.D. in Drama) returned from Britain in the mid-1950s and devoted a great deal of his time to the adaptation of Shakespeare's plays, rewriting and directing them in Sudanese dialect with remarkable success. However, the most successful of the four was Abdallah At Tayeb (1921–2003), who returned to the Sudan with his British painter wife Grizelda and took over part of the former British army barracks in Khartoum, converting it into a theatre. Professor At Tayeb produced many of his poetic plays – written in classical Arabic – with rich costumes and a great deal of singing and dancing.

The gradual rise of religious fanaticism amongst university students reached a climax when religious zealots disrupted a folk dance event at the university examination hall in 1968. A student died in the clashes. That stifled what remained of the theatre, which is now a furniture store.

The Egyptians, junior partners in the administration, also performed plays at their clubs and, not handicapped by a language barrier, cooperated with the home-grown Sudanese theatre. The first amateur dramatic society (1916–24) was formed by Sudanese employees in Port Sudan. The unpublished documents of this theatrical company show that its members were both Christians and Muslims and that it used its performances to raise funds for both the mosque and the (Coptic) church in Port Sudan. The 'Acting Benevolent Literary Society' headed by Hussein Mallasi was an example of the tolerant spirit engendered by the arts. In 1933 Kahlid Abu Rous wrote and produced the first full-length play in the Sudanese dialect (as opposed to classical Arabic) and on a Sudanese theme – the fate of the legendary beauty Tajouj. In 1937 Ibrahim Al Abbadi (d. 1987), a talented songwriter, wrote *Al Mak Nimir* about love and 'tribal' conflict. In it he called for the rejection of narrow parochial loyalties and ethnic animosities in favour of an all-embracing Sudanese identity. The same call soon resonated in the resolutions of the Graduates' Congress.

The first military government (1958–64) built an open air theatre in 1959 and invited several companies from abroad to perform. When democracy was restored in 1964 the same building was renovated and became, in 1967, the National Theatre, under the leadership of AlFaki Abdur Rahman (1933–2002) (a graduate of Bakht Ar Ruda Teachers' Training Institute who took further courses in drama in London before independence). Regular seasons were organised and a very popular playwright, Hamadnallah Abdul Qadir, emerged. He was a civil servant who was influenced by Shaw and Ibsen and who had been exposed to theatre in Britain. Director Makki Sinada (b. 1944), a talented teacher who studied stage design in Egypt, produced well-written plays and provided a 'golden age' of Sudanese theatre. Makki Sinada's production of a double bill by the present writer was banned from representing Sudan at the Damascus Festival, five days before the departure of the actors in 1978.

An important aspect of the success of Hamadnallah Abdul Qadir (b. 1928) was his involvement with radio drama. Almost all his National Theatre plays were either written originally for radio or adapted by him for broadcasting. This – in a country where more than half the population is illiterate – took theatre to nomads and villagers in the remote countryside. By contrast to Abdallah At Tayeb (whose influence was confined to the university and those who liked his published plays in classical Arabic), Hamadnallah Abdul Qadir took theatre to the common people in their daily dialect. The penalty he paid was that his plays are virtually unknown outside Sudan, whilst less popular playwrights writing in classical Arabic can be performed in other Arabic-speaking countries.

In 1972 the play *Napata Habibati* (My Beloved Napata), which was based on a historical theme, was so successful that it was followed by demonstrations. The playwright, Hashim Siddiq, a talented poet and dissident, was accused by the authorities of inciting defiance to President Numeiry's régime.

The democratic era witnessed the establishment, in 1968, of the National Folklore Company. Professor and Mrs Ramazin, both Soviet citizens, toured the country and selected dances and dancers for the new company, which became a great success in Sudan and abroad. The third pillar of this positive period was the Institute of Music and Drama, founded in 1969, which provided training in all aspects of dramatic art and which ensured the flow of talent into the National Theatre and private companies which continues to this day. In the wake of the military coup of 1989 the institute lost its autonomy and became an appendix of Sudan University. The Islamisation of the Arts policy meant that the most talented lecturers and teaching assistants were forced to leave the country or work elsewhere within it.

During the second military rule (1969–85) a great deal of emphasis was laid on bi-annual cultural festivals that included theatrical performances. The Acrobatic Company was formed in 1971. Most of the seventy-one acrobats were trained as children in Sudan and China by Chinese experts. A puppet company was formed in 1976, with Rumanian help.

Theatre, the arts and sport in general suffered a setback when religious extremists took over power in a *coup d'état* on 30 June 1989. They were, and remain, openly inimical to theatre (except as a mobilisation tool). Non-Islamic rituals are frowned upon and even Islamic Sufi rituals are seen as aberrations because they have no basis in 'orthodox Sunni Islam'.

Any comment on Sudanese theatre would be deficient if it did not mention the risks taken by pioneering actresses such as Aasia Abdul Majid, Fathia Mohammed Ahmed, Rabiha Mohammed Mahmoud, Nimat Hammad and Tahia Zarroug. (Nimat Hammad formed and headed a theatre company bearing her name in 1987. She played the role of Tajouj in a new interpretation of the famous legend. The company collapsed when religious fanatics usurped power in 1989 and were openly inimical to the arts and to women in public life. Nimat Hammad sought refuge in Britain.) It would also be incomplete without reference to playwrights such as Badr Uddin Hashim, Yusuf Khalil, Yusuf Aaidabi, Unmar Al Hamidi, Fidaili Jamma Abdullahi Ali Ibrahim, Attayeb AlMahdi and others, as well as directors such as Omar Al Khidir and the actor-director 'AlFadil Saeed', who to this day still leads his eponymous company, lashing out at society's ills and pretensions and staying clear of government sponsorship. Uthman Nusairi, a talented director who, in the 1960s, revived University of Khartoum theatrical traditions and staged 'absurdist' plays, directed his latest play, *Mahmoud*, in London on 18 January 2002 – in Arabic – on the anniversary of the hanging in 1985 of the philosopher Mahmoud Mohamed Taha, who was convicted of apostasy by a sharia judge. Talented actors, mostly sidelined now, include Yahia Al Haj, Ibrahim Higazi, Izzudin Hilali, Uthman Ali Al Faki, Uthman Jamalludin, Nasser Ash Sheikh and Ali Mahdi. All are young and capable of resurrecting their careers and reinventing Sudanese theatre when the political situation alters. Hopes are rising for an end of civil war and the country is witnessing a great deal of liberalisation which augurs well for theatre.

Notes

1. *Zar*, which probably originates in Ethiopia, is a trance and possession ritual, mainly for women. The host provides food and drink enough for several days. The *Sheikha* (leader) or *Sheikh* (if he is a man) directs the ceremonies. Each participant has a 'signature tune'; when it is played she starts to dance. The Sheikha helps the dancer with the costume accessories before and during the dance (e.g., the Khawaja, British colonial officer, would require a hat, a pipe, a moustache, and wear a short-sleeved shirt and shorts). When the dancer goes into a trance she makes requests in line with her impersonated *Zar* character and adopts a matching body language. She speaks in tongues. Women claim that they have no recollection of what they did or said when possessed.

   Women, who face suffocating lifelong restrictions in society, find in the Zar a space where they have licence to flout and openly break religious and social control. Symptoms of various ailments often disappear (temporarily) after Zar sessions.

2. See Henry Frankfort, *Kingship and Gods* (Chicago: Chicago University Press, 1958), p. 198.

3. See E. E. Evans-Pritchard, *Social Anthropology and Other Essays* (London: Faber and Faber, 1962), pp. 69–70.

84 | KHALID ALMUBARAK MUSTAFA

4. Peter Bicknell, 'Zande Savagery', in Andre Singer and Brian Street, ed., *Zande Themes* (Oxford: Blackwell, 1971), pp. 41–63.

5. The Qadiriya is an Islamic order that bears the name of its founder, Abdul Qadir Al Jailani (d. 1167, Baghdad). Adherent missionaries crossed the Red Sea to Africa to preach, teach and convert. They intermarried with the indigenous population to gain protection and influence. As a result of their 'give and take' approach, they spread a version of Islam which is more tolerant than that which was the result of military conquest.

6. See J. S. Trimmingham, *The Sufi Orders in Islam* (Oxford: Oxford University Press, 1971), p. 186.

7. See Sulaiman Rahhal, 'Wrestling in the Nuba Mountains. Past and Present', *Nuba Survival*, 1.2 (October 2001), pp. 8–9.

8. See Janice Boddy, *Wombs and Alien Spirits* (Madison: University of Wisconsin Press, 1989).

3 Francophone Africa south of the Sahara
JOHN CONTEH-MORGAN

Francophone Africa: a contested term

The adjective *Francophone* as applied to sub-Saharan Africa refers to a territorial unit of twenty-one French-speaking countries. These include Senegal, the Ivory Coast and Mali in west Africa, the Republic of Congo and the Democratic Republic of Congo, formerly Zaire, in central Africa, Rwanda and Burundi in the Great Lakes region, Djibouti in the Horn of Africa, and the Comores Islands and Madagascar, both in the Indian Ocean off east Africa.

But the word *Francophone* is not just a neutral geographical entity. It is also an emotionally charged notion that has been strongly contested, at least since the mid-1970s (Louis-Calvet, 1974). It is a word with 'suspect connotations', according to the Benin scholar Guy Ossito Midiohouan (1994: 28). With its emphasis on French and its place in Africa, and the new, French-derived culture to which this language has given rise, the word, it is claimed, marginalizes the numerous African languages and non-Francophone, that is non-French-derived, cultures in these countries. At the very least, it gives a misleading, exaggerated picture of the place of French in them; exaggerated because French is only one of two official languages in a number of 'Francophone' African countries: Mauritania, where it shares that privilege with Arabic; Rwanda and Burundi, where Kinyarwanda and Kirundi respectively are also official languages, and Madagascar where Malagasy is one of the country's two official languages. These countries cannot therefore be said to be 'Francophone' in the same way that the Ivory Coast is, a country where French is the sole official language. But even in the more typical case of the Ivory Coast, only a small percentage of the population can be said to use the language with any degree of oral, let alone written, proficiency. Also, the number of French speakers varies widely between Francophone countries, from about 30 per cent of the population among those with the highest literacy rates – Ivory Coast, Gabon, Congo – to between 3 per cent and 5 per cent among the least alphabetized – Chad, Niger, Burkina Faso (Ager, 1996: 195–7).

It is facts such as these that have led critics such as Midiohouan to conclude that the idea of a French-speaking sub-Saharan Africa community is a myth, and that it corresponds more to a will to impose French and thus entrench France's influence, than to an accurate description of its place in that community (Midiohouan, 1994). To Soyinka, the 'Francophone' idea inhibits in the countries concerned, in a way that its Anglophone equivalent apparently does not, the emergence of a literary consciousness and sensibility that is above all home-nourished. He explains:

> L'une des tâches à laquelle je me suis attaché a été d'arracher les francophones à leur déférence envers la France métropolitaine, et d'essayer de les persuader que nous sommes avant tout et fondamentalement Africains.   (Soyinka, 1993: 31)
>
> One of the tasks I set myself was to tear Francophones away from their deference towards metropolitan France, and to try to convince them that we are, above all, first and foremost African.[1]

Now, French may be a minority language in 'Francophone' countries, but it would be an error to reject (or indeed uphold)[2] the notion of a Francophone Africa on the *sole* basis of linguistic criterion. Whilst a necessary condition, French is by no means a sufficient one for 'Francophone-ness'. There are equally important and unifying factors, including the historical reality, for countries of the region, of a common colonial past under France and Belgium between the late 1880s and the early 1960s, and membership, for most of them, of an integrated system of economic, cultural and political institutions: for example, the franc zone, the Community of (French) West African States (CEAO), the African and Malagasy Commission for Higher Education (CAMES), and 'La Francophonie', a geo-political organisation of French-speaking states, complete with specialised agencies, founded in 1986 along the lines of the British Commonwealth (Manning, 1988; Kirk-Greene and Bach, 1995).

But even the question of the position of the French language cannot be disposed of easily by a simple game of numbers. Numerically in the minority, its French-educated speakers nonetheless constitute the dominant cultural formation. They not only control the apparatus of the modern states – educational, legal and administrative – their cultural production has come to define the identity of their nations in a way that those nations' indigenous cultures, with all their acknowledged vitality, have not. Mediated through print culture and backed by its authority, and inspired by French literary and artistic conventions even when the latter are contested, this 'Francophone' cultural production represents the contemporary official, and by implication 'élite', culture. The others, expressed in African languages and through the medium of 'primary orality', are associated, in a typical case of cultural diglossia, with the 'unofficial', the 'popular', the 'ethnic', even if they constitute a fund of technical and thematic resources for the constitution of official 'national' cultures.

Nowhere, perhaps, is this dichotomy more obvious than in the area of 'theatre', where the very term has come to be identified with French-inspired dialogue drama, a form which, in strict typological terms, is nothing more than a type within the general sub-class of 'theatre', which, itself, is only *one* sub-class within the larger class of 'performance'. But like the French language in which it is written, this (relatively recent) drama of texts is sociologically powerful, with its plays (by such writers as Séydou Badian, Bernard Dadié and Sony Labou Tansi) studied in schools and universities in Africa and elsewhere, performed in national and continental theatre festivals such as the Marché des Arts du Spectacle Africain (MASA) in Abidjan, the Festival International du Théâtre des Marionnettes (FITMO) in Ouagadougou, as well as in French ones, especially the Festival International des Francophonies in Limoges, and benefitting from the sponsorship and professional assistance of foreign, and occasionally national, governments.

Indigenous traditions of theatre and other sub-classes of performance in the Francophone region cannot be said, in contrast, to enjoy the same recognition. When they gain access to official media or performance spaces at all, it is in the form of the exoticised displays of national dance troupes. In critical studies, these traditions tend, with the rare exception, to be indiscriminately lumped together as 'ritual' or 'pre-theatre' (Béart, 1936–7; Laude, 1954; Leloup, 1983), and as representing the infancy of what has later become *true* theatre, namely the French-inspired drama of texts.

No such evolutionary perspective will be adopted in this chapter. The plurality of theatre forms *in* Francophone Africa (as distinct from Francophone theatre) – indigenous, urban-popular and literary – will be discussed on their own terms (their contexts of performance, form and function), and not as constituting points of origin or arrival. Whilst areas of difference and overlap between them will occasionally be highlighted, the literary theatre will not be erected into the norm in relation to which all others will be judged. Of greater interest will be the transactions between them.

Indigenous traditions of performance: definitions and classifications

The region of Africa now commonly described as 'Francophone' is home to some of the most vital cultures of performance in Africa. Jean Duvignaud's characterisation of medieval European societies as 'des sociétés visuelles' (visual societies), and Balandier's observation about them that 'tout s'y montre et tout s'y joue, les pratiques sociales s'y jouent dans une dramatization permanante' (everything in them is displayed and performed, social practices are in a state of permanent dramatization) (Balandier, 1980: 44) can be applied with equal, if not greater, validity to the 'traditional' societies of Africa. In these societies every 'social ceremonial', secular or sacred, gives rise to colourful and elaborate performances that sometimes last days or weeks, which showcase the finest of the verbal, plastic and performing arts of the community. Examples (from the Francophone space) abound. The septennial *kamabolon* festival of the Mande people, for example, a five-day ceremony of social regeneration that attracts Mande both from inside and outside Mali, and whose high point is the restoration of the walls and roof of the kamabolon sanctuary (see below, 107–8), is accompanied by the performance of what the Mande consider to be the canonical version of their founding text: the epic of Sunjata (Meillassoux, 1968; Jensen, 2001). Among the Malagasy of the Madagascar Highlands, the popular feast of the 'the second burial', or *famadihana*, during which an esteemed clan ancestor is honoured and celebrated, and his or her remains exhumed and reburied, is the occasion, especially among the rural population, for the staging of a *hira gasy* performance (Edkvist, 1997). Among the Idaasha people of Benin, to give one more example, the *iru*, a festival of sacred kinship during which the power of the ruling Omojagun dynasty is displayed and confirmed, is celebrated every July or August (Akpaki, 1999).

But performances are not just reserved for exceptional social or religious occasions. More routine ones such as births, deaths, puberty or even activities such as hunting or harvesting are commemorated with a variety of ceremonies that take on the character of theatre by the very circumstances of their performance.

Two broad categories of indigenous performance can be distinguished: the recreational and the devotional. Within each of these are a variety of overlapping genres, such as masquerade theatre, spoken drama, dance and puppet theatre, dramatised narratives, recitations and civic or sacred rituals. I use the word '*overlapping*' to point to the porous nature of generic boundaries in African performance forms. Thus while, say, speech might be the predominant medium in a given performance, accounting for that performance's overall generic classification in European languages[3] as 'spoken drama', such speech rarely, if ever, stands alone. Other communicative media, such as music and dance, invariably complement it, lending to the form in question the multi-generic, Gesamtkunstwerk texture that has become a critical commonplace about African indigenous performances.

But irrespective of the category to which they belong – recreational or devotional – the genres listed above, like all performances, share a number of basic features. They are forms of conscious, framed activity as distinct from the unreflexive performed behaviour of everyday social life. They involve, in other words, what Huizinga calls in his theory of 'play', 'a stepping out of "real" life into a temporary sphere of activity with a disposition all of its own' (Huizinga, 1955: 8). This apartness from the flow of daily life characteristic of performances is illustrated by a number of features, among which is their spatial and temporal boundedness. They take place, in other words, in specially designated areas – theatre buildings, the enclosed yards of private houses, riverbanks, shrines, public squares or streets. They have a recognisable temporal beginning and ending (which can last a few moments, days or months), and exhibit a clear structure of events. Also, they use costumed performers, who draw on a range of gestures, facial expressions and body movements. Finally, the main body of their activity consists of the enactment with, or in front of, an audience, and in varying combinations of speech, song, music and dance, of an action, event or situation (allegorical, archetypal or realistic).

Where recreational and devotional genres differ is in their respective functions. The purpose of recreational genres is to entertain and sometimes instruct, while that of devotional ones is action-oriented. Their objective is instrumental – to heal afflicted bodies and souls or to act on the natural and social worlds. Translating the worthy deceased into ancestors, neophytes into initiates or ensuring a plentiful harvest are among the many transformations that these forms are supposed to accomplish.

But no genre, within either category, is inherently and rigidly recreational or sacred. It is the context of their performance rather than some innate function or properties of form that ultimately determines their class. Whilst some genres have always been associated with entertainment or worship, others like the Sunjata epic seem to have had a dual role from the outset, fulfilling a recreational function when performed at an evening of storytelling meant to regale and instruct the community, but assuming the character of a sacred text in the context of, say, the kamabolon festival. Others still, such as the *bobongo* dance theatre of the Ekondo people of the former Belgian Congo (Iyandza-Lopoloko, 1961) have evolved, under the impact of Christianity and modern secular values, from religion to pure entertainment. The *awa* of the Dogon (Imperato, 1970) and the *tyi wara* of the Bamana (Imperato, 1971; see below, 101–2), both of Mali, have increasingly become popular forms of entertainment – dating back to the late nineteenth century in the case of the tyi wara – all the while fulfilling, albeit less frequently and in a changed form, their original ceremonial functions. How much longer even this residual religious function will last, given the modernising processes at work in Mali, is an open question.

Recreational performances: some examples

Among the most popular recreational performances in Francophone countries are the oral narratives (folk-tales, myths and epics) that are part of the heritage of the indigenous cultures in those countries. A repository of the ideals and values of those cultures, these narratives also function as sites of social and moral education. In the case of epics, of which societies in Francophone Africa are richly endowed – twenty-six of the twenty-eight from which Kesteloot and Dieng selected extracts for their monumental *Les Epopées d'afrique noire* (1998) are from societies within Francophone countries – they also serve as archives of historical memory.

But beyond the purely historical or sociological, some of the narratives are symbolic explorations of philosophical issues. A good example is the *mvet, Moneblum ou l'homme bleu* (Belinga, 1978) of the Beti, Bulu and Fang peoples of Cameroon, Gabon and Equatorial Guinea. *Moneblum* narrates a battle of supernatural proportions between two mythical peoples – the immortal Ekan, the People of Iron, and the mortal Oku – subsequent upon the efforts of the latter to wrest the secrets of immortality from the former. In spite of their heroic efforts, the Oku are no match for the Ekan, whose leader, Angone Endong, ends up cornering his Oku counterpart, Zong Midzi, in the entrails of the earth, where the latter had rushed to seek armoured protection and thus immortality from his ancestors, the Phantoms. There, he puts the Oku warrior to death by forcing him to swallow a lump of molten iron. Central to this fabulous narrative is the theme of humanity's revolt against death, its quest for immortality.

But beyond their utilitarian value, be it practical or philosophical, oral narratives are also works of art designed to provide pleasure. 'The art of eloquence' and the ability 'by the spoken word to bring to life the deeds and exploits of kings' (Niane, 1960: 1) – qualities which the narrator in Niane's *Sundiata: An Epic of Old Mali* claims as a specialty of people of his craft – are some of the means used to create such pleasure. But equally important are the performance techniques of the bard. His success does not only depend on his use of language to describe setting and action, evoke emotion or depict character. It also hinges on his ability to become the characters of his narrative; to concretise their actions – for example, the scenes of ravenous and frenzied eating by the hero Nkok-Ntyama-Ngini and his guests in *Monenblum* (111–14); to transmit their emotions through voice modulations, demeanour and facial expression. When these qualities are combined with his skills as musician and dancer, it is easy to see why the performance of an oral narrative, however short, and in spite of the fact that it is done by a lone actor, takes on the character of a theatrical event, and why French-language African dramatists should have used its many genres to provide the structural basis of some of their plays: for example, the folk-tale in *L'Os de Mor Lam* (1977), *La Tortue qui chante* (1987) and *Héros d'eau* (1994) by Birago Diop, Senouvo Zinsou and Werewere Liking respectively; the mvet in *Un Touareg s'est marié à une pygmée* (1992) by Liking; the Bambara epic of Ségou in *La Reine scélérate* (1968), by Eugène Dervain, and the Sunjata epic in *Soundjata le lion du Manding* (1979), *Le Grand destin de Soundjata* (1973), *Une si belle leçon de patience* (1972) by Laurent Gbagbo, Sory Konaké and Massa Makan Diabaté respectively.

But even when the play is not the dramatisation of an oral text, some playwrights, such as Cheikh Ndao in *L'Exil d'Albouri*, Maxime Ndébéka in *Equatorium* and Tchicaya U'Tamsi in *Le Maréchal Nninkon Nniku*, have integrated into it the figure of the *griot* and his performance techniques, techniques that gave rise in the Ivory Coast, between 1970 and 1974, to an influential acting style known as *griotisation* (Kotchy, 1984b: 240–4), and defined by its leading practitioners, Niangoret Porquet and Aboubacar Touré, as

> Une nouvelle expression dramatique dans laquelle s'intègrent de manière méthodique et harmonieuse, le verbe, le chant, le mimétisme et la gestuelle, la musique et la danse. (Porquet, 1978: 46)

> A new dramatic form that methodically and harmoniously integrates speech, song, mime and gestures, music and dance.

An interesting and relatively recent development in this storytelling performance mode is its incorporation into the theatrical practice of the

Teatro delle Albe Company in Ravenna, Italy, a troupe which since 1987 has brought together Italian and Senegalese actors (the latter recruited from the large Senegalese immigrant community in Italy) to promote what it calls 'inter-ethnic theatre' (Picarazzi, 2000: 224–45). Not only are some Teatro productions conducted in Wolof and the Italian dialect, Romagnola, but a number of its subjects and performance techniques are also inspired by Wolof folk performance traditions. Picarazzi gives the examples of two productions by Mandiaye N'Diaye, one of the troupe's key members: *Le Due calebasse* (1990) and *Griot-Fuler* (1993). The first is based on the well-known Senegalese folk-tale 'Leuk-le-lièvre et Bouki-l'hyène' (Leuk-the-Hare and Bouki-the-Hyena), while the latter explores the figure of the Senegalese *griot* and his ancient Romagnola equivalent, the *fuler* (Picarazzi, 2000: 234–42).

But solo performances in the Francophone region are not limited to oral narratives. Other genres involving a lone actor include the taaxuraan and the mbandd of the Wolof of Senegal. The work of an itinerant performer, the taaxuraan is a spectacle of music and satirical song that stigmatises cupidity and stinginess. Alioune Diop (1990: 13–14) traces its origins to the tradition of hired farmhands in rural communities led in their labour by a team leader who doubles as a principal singer of work songs. But the team leader does more than intone songs. If he feels that he has not been sufficiently paid for his work, he will compose satirical songs against the offending, stingy farmer that he will then take on tour to different villages. Diop gives a short example of one such song:

> [Your] rough trousers have the feel of a donkey's droppings
> [Your] eye is as red as a bowl of palm oil
> If you do not pay me, I'll not let you go, I'll destroy you.
>
> (Diop, 1990: 14)

With time, however, the taaxuraan became an autonomous travelling entertainment genre staged by a performer dressed in baggy trousers, a sleeveless shirt and a bobble hat.

The mbandd, another comic spectacle in the tradition of the taaxuraan, combines aspects of the art of the buffoon and the griot. Gags, comic gestures and clowning characterise the performances of the *mbandaankatt* (the performer of the mbandd); but also like a griot he is a praise singer and an itinerant performer distinguishable by what Diop describes as his 'extravagant costume: a huge baggy pair of trousers that falls to his ankles, a sleeveless shirt . . . decorated with mirrors and bells . . . a head decorated with braids or a tuft of hair studded with pearls or cowries'. The object of his improvised praise songs, however, are not celebrated warrior chiefs or rich patrons, but, exclusively, beautiful girls and their families, on whom he would have collected prior information from local informants.

But theatre in the indigenous societies of Francophone Africa is more than just the work of a solo artist (stand-up comic) who plays multiple roles in an action that is part narrated, part dramatised. It also consists of idioms with several actors, in which the entire action is dramatised. Four examples of such idioms will be successively examined: the kotèba, the *sounougounou*, the *hira gasy* and the *tyi wara*.

The kotèba or *kote koma nyaga* is a rural, satirical theatre of the Bambara and (to a lesser extent) Bambarised Peul and Senufo peoples of Mali (Meillas-soux, 1964; see also Brink, 1978). Writing early in the last century, Labouret and Travélé (1928: 24), among its earliest observers, carefully distinguished this performance from '[des] exhibitions banales de marionnettes, de pres-tidigitateurs, de magiciens, de charmeurs d'animaux' (banal puppet shows and the tricks of conjurers, magicians and snake charmers). It consists, they explained, of 'de véritables pièces parfaitement ordonnées et reglées' (perfectly structured and organized plays), with 'une intrigue déterminée', (a clear plot) and 'des acteurs humains' (human actors) – a discovery that led them to conclude, almost against their expectations, 'qu'il existe bien un théâtre soudanais' (that a Sudanese [i.e. Malian] theatre truly exists).

Although Labouret and Travélé (1928: 74) render the word kotèba as 'moqueries des choses de l'association (du marriage)' (satire directed at things pertaining to the institution of marriage), the term, made up of a prefix 'kote' or 'kore' (depending on the dialect), and a suffix 'ba', carries many more meanings, all of which are related to performance. Delafosse listed some of these in the first volume of his dictionary, *La Langue mandingue et ses dialectes* (1929): 'kote', 'troupe de comédiens' (a band of actors); 'kote-de', 'un comédien' (an actor); 'kote-ko', 'une comédie' (a comedy); 'kore-dyuga', 'un bouffon' (a buffoon); 'kore ko-ma', 'jouer la comédie' (to act). The Malian theatre scholar Diawara, working from another set of meanings of 'kote', a 'snail', and 'ba', 'giant', provides an interesting translation of the kotèba as 'giant snail' (1981: 20; also Delafosse, 1929: 458).

Unrelated as this rendering might seem to theatre, it is only so at first sight. For what it describes, according to Diawara, are the spires of a giant snail shell that the kotèba is said to resemble in performance; an appear-ance caused by the swirling movement of dancers arranged in concentric circles (these can vary from three to five), and moving in counter-clockwise direction. The spinning movement of the masked dancer, the *kono*, with which a kotèba show opens and closes – the kono mask depicts 'a large multi-colored [mythical] bird four meters in diameter', and is the emblem of the association of kotèba performers – is also said by Diawara (1981: 20) to create the visual impression of a snail shell.

The membership of the kotèba, the cultural association of comedians (as distinct from their show), is made up of young unmarried men and women who are themselves part of a *ton*, a youth labour organisation of domestic and farm workers. The backbone of this cultural club is made up of initiates of the all-male *do* sacred society in which, for seven years, Bamana youth undergo rigorous physical training (in the arts of warfare) but also receive a moral and artistic education in the values of the community and its performing arts that prepares them for leadership roles in their society (Diawara 1981: 13–17). Each kotèba cultural association has a male and female patron (a *kotefa* and *kotema* respectively) to whom a pledge of allegiance of good conduct is sworn, and who are present at performances.

Like a variety show, a kotèba performance is made up of different types of entertainment that include plays. Staged in the evenings in the village square, it falls into three distinct sections. The first, the *kote-do* (the '*kote* dance') has been described by Labouret and Travélé as an 'Opening Ballet', and consists of rings of dancers (women, men, children), arranged in concentric circles with drummers constituting the innermost circle. The interplay of the rhythms made by handclapping, drum music and the ankle bells worn by some dancers is what creates the unique musical atmosphere of this phase of the performance, while the circular movement of the dancers creates the snail-like appearance referred to earlier. The dance, which starts at a slow pace but which gathers momentum as it develops, is the occasion for somersaulting, jumping and the general display of acrobatic skills. One of the functions of the opening dance is not just to allow the audience to settle in, and to create the right atmosphere, it also gives the actors (in the wings) time to put on their costumes. These take the form of tattered clothes, clay or ash-covered faces, eyelids or the upper body.

The opening sequence is followed by a prologue whose details can vary from one show to another. The one described by Brink (1978: 387–9) contains a number of danced skits by young men depicting, in a burlesque and satirical mode, the behaviour and antics of such social figures as the 'blacksmith' or the 'buffoon'. The function of these skits, according to Brink, is twofold: to set the tone of the rest of the show and to remind the spectators that disrespectful, obscene and satirical as the dramas to come might be, they are works of fiction and should thus be seen as such.

Labouret and Travélé describe a somewhat different type of prologue (1928: 77–9). Here, the action consists of a lead actor scampering round the performance space after the 'opening ballet' in a vain search for his fellow-actors. On the advice of the orchestra, which he accuses of having lured him on to the stage with its music, and thus made him lose contact with his friends, he makes several loud and pathetic appeals, imploring them, wherever they may be, to join him. They eventually emerge (from the 'wings' where they had been all along) and process fully costumed on to the stage – but not before the 'abandoned' actor has had the opportunity to entertain the audience with his fretting, panic and the elaborate poses he strikes in calling out to his friends.

The third and longest section of a kotèba show, the *nyogolon*, is devoted to the staging of skits, twenty of which can be performed in any given evening. Their subjects are based on scenes of family, domestic and sometimes economic life. The Koran-sporting but licentious Muslim cleric, the bullying but cuckolded husband, the corrupt tax collector, the boastful and yet incompetent hunter, are among the many social figures whose vicissitudes are dramatised. There is a great deal of preoccupation with sex and in some of the skits collected by Brink (1978: 390–2) there are unvarnished references to genitalia that have been attributed to a certain frustration on the part of performers whose sexual desire is repressed in a society where its free expression is the monopoly of old men. The tone of the playlets ranges from the mildly comic and entertaining, through the ribald to the fiercely satirical. The marabout-diviner, for example, in the skit of the same name (Meillassoux, 1964: 43–53), is not only portrayed as a figure of ridicule, with his macaronic Arabic and his ostentatious display of insignia of devotion (the ever-present prayer mat, rosary and woollen cap), but also as a danger to society. Fooled by Fatima, one of his clients, into believing that she is experiencing marital problems, he tries to extract sexual favours from her under the pretext of helping her. He is caught by her husband in a scene worthy of Molière's *Tartuffe*, and is beaten out of town.

In spite of its criticism of respected authority figures of Bamana society, the social vision offered by the kotèba is conservative. The spectacle does not target the basic order of society – the power of the old, gender roles, the place of religion, and so on – but rather deviations from that order.

This explains the kotèba's focus on marginality, on outsideness to Bamana standards, be they ethical, ethnic, social or even physical. The infirm, in their blindness or crippled state, are not spared ridicule any more than are ethnic outsiders such as the Bobo or Somono, who are forever depicted as idiotic in the case of the former, or lazy in the latter. In this focus on otherness-as-deviation lies an important ideological function of the kotèba: that of affirming and stabilising a normative idea of Bamananess.

Reference to character depiction signals an important feature of the kotèba, and beyond it, to all forms of African oral theatre forms – a reliance on stock figures. Each actor embodies a human type who is identifiable through a number of conventional traits: the tattered clothes and gun-symbolising pestle of the hunter; the huge bracelets and hair pearls of the coquette (a role acted by a male performer); the bow-legged Bobo peasant, and the watch- and paper-carrying French administrator. It is in the stage representation of these characters and their actions that the entertainment value of the show resides.

Of the many skills expected of the ideal performer, a command of the Bamana language is one of the most essential. This is because a lot of the humour derives from the play on words, semantic ambiguity and the ability (for the figure of the cleric) to sprinkle speech with Arabic expressions. Equally important, especially for the hunter character and the cultivation of silence that goes with the role, is the ability to mime both action and emotions. A third and no less important skill is that of the dancer. The kotèba is above all dance drama, which is why the question asked of potential recruits to its ranks is whether they can *dance* the kotèba.

If I have spent some time discussing the kotèba, it is because of its importance to contemporary theatrical life not just in Mali, where urban forms of the genre have emerged and where some of its procedures have been appropriated by French-language theatre practitioners, as shall be shown, but also in the Ivory Coast. By 1937 three urban troupes had been formed in Mali, the most important of which, the Zangué, founded by a policeman (Meillassoux, 1964: 30), was still functioning in 1963. Important differences exist between this form and its village predecessor and contemporary. Unlike the latter, it is not an age-grade association of young agricultural workers, but rather what Meillassoux calls an 'amateur (theatrical) group'. Its membership is drawn from a broad spectrum of individuals: adults and not just the young, craftsmen, artisans and policemen and not farm workers, and Malians of different ethnicities, as opposed to just Bamanas, recruited on the basis of their qualities or potential as performers and not their ethnicity. Very significantly, too, a fee formalised membership to the new groups.

Other troupes in Mali modelled on, or inspired by, the rural kotèba include the national troupe itself, the Kotèba National, founded in 1977 (Sinaba, 1990: 141–8), and theatre for development groups such as the Nyogolon, whose name ('mirror' in Bambara) itself refers to the satirical phase of a kotèba show. Dauchez reports an interesting experiment involving the use of this theatre form in a modern hospital setting as part of an arsenal of therapies for the mentally ill (1984: 140–1). In the Ivory Coast, the combination of satire and dance drama characteristic of the kotèba, and its variety show format, form the basis of the experiments of the Ensemble Kotèba troupe of Souleymane Koly (Boiron, 1993: 53–4).

Also in the Ivory Coast, in the Odienné region near Guinea a unique form of theatre, the *sougounougou*, existed. Originally a sacred performance, it had evolved into a recreational activity by the late 1920s, when it was encountered and first described by the French colonial administrator Prouteaux (1929: 448–75). He distinguishes between two types of the idiom: a pure dance form in which carefully choreographed group dances by young men, women or warriors alternate with solo performances, and a more theatrical version in which, like in a kotèba, spoken dialogue is punctuated by dance sequences. In the latter version, the sougounougou puts on stage three sets of performers: an orchestra, made up of a xylophonist and a drummer; a chorus consisting of half a dozen hunter characters led by a coryphaeus, who acts the role of the village head; and a large cast of actors. An integral part of the performance, the chorus, as a collective performer, not only engages in dialogue with the actors but also expresses the latter's emotions in song and comments on their actions. The actors – representing both human figures (the clown Nanzégé and his devoted and beautiful wife Niofolityté, the hunter, the genie, the imam, and so on), as well as animals – are notable for their elaborate conventional costumes. Thus old hats and ragged clothes are reserved for chorus members. Each also carries a quiver that contains arrow-symbolizing bow and reeds. Nanzégé is identifiable by his knee-length trousers and walking stick; his wife covers her head with a scarf, wears coral beads and a tight wrap-around. The various animals are depicted through a combination of features that include masks, costumes, movements and sounds. The lion, for example, covers its face with a brown piece of cloth that reveals the eyes and mouth, while the wild dog sports 'a false head in whitened wicker fences with an extended muzzle whose saw-edged mouth represents his teeth' (Prouteaux, 1929: 452).

It is clear from the care paid to costuming that this is a visual theatre whose performing style – another characteristic common to Africa's non-literary theatre forms – is intensely physical. The ability to look the part and to play it in a physical sense – miming the movements of various animals (galloping, crouching, hopping, and so forth), reproducing their grunting, hooting and roaring – are among the skills cultivated by sougounougou actors and prized by audiences. Even when a story is dramatised, the aim is not to focus attention on its meaning, but rather to showcase the various talents of the actors. Thus in the sketch 'The Islamic Teacher' (Prouteaux, 1929: 464), the audience is treated to Nanzégé the joker. He apprentices himself to an Islamic teacher and claims to be serious about learning the Koran. Yet his classes and prayer sessions are a riotous farce, as he holds his Koranic slate upside down, intersperses the verses with inanities, indulges in obscene gestures and prays facing the wrong direction.

Another example of rural theatre form is the *hira gasy* of the Central Highland region of Madagascar, home to the most powerful polity in pre-colonial Madagascar, the Merina kingdom. Ingela Edkvist estimates the number of troupes staging performances in these areas to be between 150 and 180, with 'several hundred thousand people attend[ing] one or more . . . performances each season' (Edkvist, 1997: 12). Although it is a rural theatre and its actors (the *mpihira gasy*) and audiences are drawn from the ranks of farmers and the country folk, the hira gasy is also performed in the districts of urban centres such as Antananarivo, capital of the Highland region. Here weekly contests, advertised through posters and on the radio, are organised every Sunday between troupes, to the delight of audiences of visiting farmers, recent migrants to the city, and the urban poor (Rakotoson, 1991: 9–10; Edkvist, 1997: 130–1).

The contexts of a hira gasy performance are varied. They range from religious events such as the reburial ceremonies or *famadihana* referred to earlier, to school and church occasions, weddings or circumcision ceremonies. In each of these events a troupe would perform for a fee. Accounts of the origins of hira gasy are varied, but most trace the form back to the musicians, singers and dancers who were recruited – mainly from among the Antemoro people of the east coast of Madagascar – and employed by (or, according to Rakotoson (1991: 14), forced into the employ of) Merina monarchs, in whose courts they were charged with a number of functions. In addition to celebrating and extolling the monarch and his exploits, they summoned his subjects to public meetings, where royal addresses or decrees were delivered. Not the least of their tasks was the provision of entertainment for the monarch, his guestu and courtiers, a task that was to expand greatly under the fiercely nationalistic queen, Ranavalona I (1828–61). In a bid to preserve the cultural integrity of her kingdom, to restore its founding 'moral economy' (Larson in Edkvist, 1997: 45), which she saw as being in danger of collapse from foreign, especially French and British Christian, influences, the queen adopted two important policies. She expelled those missionaries who continued to engage in proselytising in spite of their promises to the contrary and, second, instituted what could be called a policy of cultural authenticity, through which she sought to encourage the rebirth of the threatened but 'pure' Malagasy heritage of the ancestors. Her court became a centre of such cultural promotion, with the performance of pre-colonial Malagasy culture by musicians, dancers and other entertainers constituting an important component of its ceremonial and festivities (Edkvist, 1997: 45, 147).

Although the earliest hira gasy troupes and their shows are believed to have emerged from these court performers and their displays, it was not until the reign of Radama II (1861–3) and his successors that the hira gasy, as it is presently known, is thought to have taken firm root, especially with respect to its costumes and instruments (Edkvist, 1997: 146–64).

The culturally laissez-faire Radama (assassinated in 1863) moved away from the protectionism of his mother, reopened his kingdom to foreign influences, notably to missionaries, and promoted the use of Christian hymns and texts and European musical instruments, such as violins and brass bands, in official marches and parades. He created a standing army modelled on the British, and encouraged upper-class gentlemen of the court to adopt the uniforms of the British military (Rakotoson, 1991: 11; Edkvist, 1997: 148) and their female counterparts the 'long, laced dresses . . . of upper-class nineteenth-century French and English' women (Edkvist, 1997: 149). Finally, in a bizarre exercise of royal prerogative, he authorised the actors of the hira gasy (the only group of commoners to be so authorised) to don, in performance, the new costumes of the nobility:

> Je déclare que vous avez le droit de vous habiller, hommes, femmes et enfants, en costumes des hautes autorités, lorsque vous présenterez vos spectacles, car grâce à votre talent, mon peuple comprend la nécessité de s'unir, les bienfaits du progrès, l'amour de la patrie.
>
> (Rakotoson, 1991: 11)

For making my people understand, thanks to your talents, the need for unity, the advantages of progress and love of the fatherland, I grant you, men, women, and children, the privileges to dress like high-ranking authorities.

The present-day hira gasy tradition of peasant actors wearing hats, shoulder shawls and long European-style dresses (for the women), frock coats with epaulettes, stripes and ribbons (for the men), playing clarinets, violins and brass bands, as well as indigenous flutes and drums, singing Christian as well as traditional songs and using in their modes of address the style of the sermon and of traditional oratory, all this is thought to date from this period.

A hira gasy performance proper, typically consists of highly formalised indigenous speeches known as *kabary*, songs and dances. The most important section of a performance is the so-called 'Mother Song', which is made up of short stories composed by the troupe leader. It comes immediately after the opening preliminaries of music, prayer and welcome address. Led by the troupe leader, the Mother Song provides a commentary, through its sung stories and prescribed movements, on issues of immediate concern and relevance to the rural population: its economic plight and powerlessness, the indifference of the state, the exodus of the young to the cities. Politics is not altogether absent from a hira gasy performance (Saivre, 1980). Already in the eighteenth century, as has been mentioned, Merina monarchs used court entertainers (the precursors of hira gasy troupes) as vehicles for the transmission of royal edicts. After the fall of the Merina monarchy in 1895 the French successor régime also relied on this theatre, to spread the values of the new colonial order. Madagascar became independent in 1960 and from then onwards various post-colonial governments pressed it into the service of their different causes: cultural pluralism and then nationalism from the early sixties to the mid-seventies, and after Didier Ratsiraka's 'revolution' of 1975, 'Marxism-socialism' (Saivre, 1980; Edkvist, 1997: 153–8). Because the meanings of its stories and songs are couched in allusion, parable, analogy and ambiguity, the hira gasy is able to be critical and subversive of the existing social and political order, all the while feigning to serve it.

But perhaps the most important concerns of the hira gasy are moral and spiritual. In reaction to the increasing modernisation of Malagasy society and the resultant erosion of the foundations of its 'traditional' morality, of what the Malagasy call the 'way of the ancestors' (Edkvist, 1997: 12), the hira gasy has come to see itself, since the mid-nineteenth century, as the embodiment of cultural legitimacy, of 'tradition', and its task as being to provide moral direction to a society in danger of losing its identity. To say this, however, is not to imply that the hira gasy is pure conservatism, its self-understanding and discourse of authenticity notwithstanding. It remains a very modern performing art form, receptive to and, as Edkvist has shown (1997: 97–101), continuously integrating new ideas, styles and forms from the ambient culture. Among the interesting examples she gives of late twentieth-century borrowings (from films and the radio) are not just musical tunes, but also breakdancing, Kung Fu, kick-boxing and even Michael Jackson-type movements in the last two sections of the performance, known as the 'Boys Dance' and 'Child Song' respectively. That these palpably foreign elements are not considered by audiences to be in conflict with the hira gasy's claims to represent the ancestors is testimony to its ability to introduce the most radical changes into Malagasy rural society, all the while passing them off as 'tradition', as continuous with the 'way of the ancestors'.

While the three examples of oral theatre discussed so far are primarily though not exclusively speech-based, there are others that are dance-dominated (Tiérou, 1983). In the forms so-classified generically, dance – defined as a sequence of patterned body movements evolving in space and time – becomes the principal *language* (but by no means the only one) through which dramatic action is executed, and emotions are conveyed. A well-known example of such theatre is the *tyi wara* (sometimes written *twi wara* or *ciwara*) dance of the Bamana people of Mali, which is best known through the work of Zahan (1960; 2000), Imperato (1970) and Wooten (2000).

The twi wara started life as a sacred masked dance executed by initiates of the *twi wara do* society in the context of a seven-day festival in honour of the Bamana god of agriculture. According to the myth enacted by the dance, the god, part antelope and part human, and the progeny of a Bamana Eve, Mousso Koroni, and a snake revealed the secrets of agriculture to humans (Imperato, 1970: 8–9). The symbol of hard work and endurance, he was able to convert barren into fertile land and 'weeds into corn and millet' (Imperato, 1970: 8). But the resulting prosperity was not to last. Mankind took it for granted and grew complacent. Angry and disappointed, the god withdrew from their company and sought refuge in the earth. To propitiate him, orphaned humanity created the celebratory tyi wara dance in his honour.

Like the hira gasy in Madagascar, the tyi wara has evolved in tandem with various events in Mali's history. Even before the French conquest of that country in 1893, Imperato explains (1970: 13), Islam had long undermined the dance's animist basis to the point that its performance already by then had very little to do with any offerings to a fertility nature god. It had been secularised and became instead a kind of work dance performed to accompany and exhort units of labouring farm workers. Its songs and music proclaimed the qualities, real or made up, of the unit and its individual members, flattered their pride and exhorted them to emulate the virtues of the founding farmer-god himself.

Although it continues to perform this function today (Wooten, 2000: 19–20), the tyi wara – a word which today refers to a 'master farmer', the dance itself, and its pre-eminent practitioners – has also become a form of pure entertainment executed in the village square and not in the fields, and sometimes in a context of competitions.

Generally staged after the harvest, the tyi wara is performed by a man and a woman, dancing to music provided by a chorus of female singers led by a soloist. The dance, in a 1960s village performance observed by Imperato, consists of 'side to side undulations of the body and an up and down movement of the head' (1970: 77), with the dancers jumping in the air, making high-pitched sounds and moving around the circular performance space, slowly at first and much faster towards the end of the dance. The dancers are notable for their costumes, a dress made of black-coloured fibres, and especially a headdress (the *tyi wara koun*) that has been described as 'perhaps the best known of all Bamana sculpture, and one of the most distinctive art forms in African art' (Imperato, 1970: 18). Scholars (Zahan, 2000; Imperato, 1970: 72) distinguish between two main types of headdress (within which exist regional variations): the horizontally shaped, which tends towards the naturalistic, and the vertical type, where the representation is non-figurative. But naturalistic or abstract, the headdress is a representation in the form of an antelope (with features of an anteater) of the Bamana god of agriculture in whose honour it was carved. In the tyi wara dance, the antelope is not just present in the headdress, however, but also in the rhythms and movements of the dancer, whose display involves the miming of the antelope's gestures, gait and behaviour.

The destiny of indigenous dances in Francophone Africa is constantly changing in relation to the social and political climate. In the 1950s the Guinean choreographer Fodéba Keita decided to adapt for, and promote through, his newly founded Théâtre Africain (later named Ballets Africains) the dances of his country for the modern raised stage. This meant not just designing decors and new costumes, contracting the length of performances to a few hours and 'stripping the dances of a thousand details that are of interest only in the village square' (Keita, 1957: 208), but also creating new stories or updating old ones that would speak to contemporary situations. Keita, in other words, had a dynamic conception of indigenous dances and strongly rejected any suggestion, which he put down to primitivist nostalgia, that they should remain 'pure' and 'authentic'. He asked:

> Authentique par rapport à quoi? . . . Pour nous, authentique est synonyme de réalité. Dans la mesure où le folklore est un ensemble de traditions, poèmes, chansons, danses et légendes populaires d'un pays, il ne peut être que le reflet de la vie de ce pays. Et si cette vie évolue, il n'y a pas de raison pour que le folklore qui en est l'expression vivante n'évolue pas.   (Keita, 1957: 205–6)

> Authentic in relation to what? . . . For us, authentic is synonymous with reality. To the extent that folklore is the totality of the popular traditions, poems, songs, dances and legends of a country, it cannot but be a reflection of the life of that country. And if this life changes, there is no reason why the folklore, its living expression, should not change with it.

An important example of one of Keita's attempts to use indigenous dance to express a (then) contemporary (political) vision – he was writing in the 1950s – is his dance drama (or 'ballet', as he described his creations) based on the title poem, 'Aube africaine' (An African dawn) of his short volume of prose poetry (Keita, 1965: 69–80). The action of the poem, spoken by a narrator and danced by a group of actors to the accompaniment of the music of a *kora* (a twenty-one string harp-lute), is set in the Guinean countryside at a dawn that is both temporal and symbolic. It dramatises, through the life of a farmer, Naman, the infamous massacre in 1944 at Tiaroye in Senegal, where a strike by demobilised African World War Two soldiers protesting against broken promises of payment of back wages, was met with savage repression by French colonial troops. Naman is presented in the 'ballet' as a heroic figure of nationalist resistance in three ways. First, like a figure in epic narratives, his story is chanted to the accompaniment of the kora. Second, through the narrator's reference to Naman's earned privilege, for heroism in battle, to dance the *douga* – 'that dance of Mali emperors in which each step is a moment in the History of Mali' (Keita, 1965: 77) – a subtle parallel is established between the obscure twentieth-century Guinean farmer and war veteran and the founding hero of the Mandingo empire. Finally, the dying Naman is addressed by Sunjata himself (materialised as a bird): 'Naman tu n'as pas dansé cette danse sacrée qui porte mon nom! En libérant la Patrie africaine, d'autres la danseront' (Naman, you did not dance this sacred dance that carries my name! By liberating the Fatherland, others will dance it) (Keita, 1965: 80).

But Fodéba Keita's example of actualising traditional dances was not emulated, at least not immediately, in Francophone Africa. What followed, for a variety of reasons including financial gain and the rampant folklorisation of national culture, was the increasing commodification of traditional dances, now staged by enterprising local communities or state-subsidised dance companies (the Théâtre Folklorique du Mali (Decock, 1968); the Ballets Guinéens, as Fodéba Keita's troupe became known after independence; the Ensemble de Ballet du Sénégal, to name just three) for local élite or foreign consumption. The spectacular and technical aspects of the dances – movement patterns, athletic and acrobatic turns – took precedence over cultural meaning, ancient or recent.

A striking example of this shift from what Harper calls 'ethnic dance to theatrical dance' (Harper, 1967: 10), is provided by Imperato in his study of the *awa* masked dance of the Dogon people of Mali, whose culture was brought to international attention through the work of the French anthropologist Marcel Griaule (1938). Originally connected with funerals – commemorative or regular – and with the *sigui*, 'a ceremony of replacement of one generation by another', celebrated every sixty years (Imperato, 1971: 30), this dance started to mutate into an object of entertainment from the early 1930s, when it was first staged in Paris. By the 1960s it had taken a fully fledged commercial turn (although it continues, in its adapted form, to fulfil its original function), complete with a mechanism for calculating fees: 'In 1966 the price per dancer was approximately one US dollar, and in 1970 a new system was instituted in which payment [was] now made not per dancer, but per group of dancers: three thousand Malian francs (approximately six US dollars) for twelve dances' (Imperato, 1971: 29).

Another area in which traditional dances have been used in the modern culture of Francophone Africa is in the French-language literary theatre. But as with the various national dance troupes, these dances mostly perform, especially in the nationalist and early post-colonial plays of Dadié, Pliya and Oyono-Mbia, a cultural authenticating function, when they are not used for entertainment or to lend local colour to the action – the colour of what Chevrier calls 'the Africa of ancestors, tom-toms and bells and marabouts' (Chevrier, 2001: 12). Since the mid-seventies, however, a more creative, less folkloristic use has been made of these dances by such playwrights as the Cameroonian Werewere Liking, the later Tchicaya U'Tamsi, and the Madagascan Michèle Rakotoson, who conceive them as part of a total theatrical 'language' that includes, but is not limited to, speech.

Mention must be made, finally, of a unique dance experiment that has been going on since the 1970s in Dakar – originally centred around the Mudra Afrique Dance Center created by the famous Belgian choreographer Maurice Béjart, whose father, incidentally, was part Senegalese, and latterly around the Centre International de Danses Traditionnelles et Contemporaines in Dakar. The leading force of this experiment is the Franco-Senegalese choreographer Germaine Acogny, who after serving as artistic director of the Mudra between 1977 and 1982 and following a period in France where she taught African art dance at the Studio-Ecole-Ballet-Théâtre du Troisième Monde in Toulouse, founded in Dakar in 1995 the Centre International. The centrepiece of her activity, which has led to such prize-winning dances as 'Yewa, eau sublime' (1991), and which she has documented in *Danse africaine* (1988), is the creation of a modern African art dance tradition built on indigenous dance forms; a project that can be compared in this regard to that of the black American, Katherine Dunham, who working from African diaspora dance cultures of Haiti and Martinique, created a modernist African-American dance idiom in the 1930s (Clark, 1994).

But indigenous theatre in Francophone Africa is not limited to human actors. There also exist thriving traditions in which the action is dramatised by puppets (Arnoldi, 1995; Darkowska-Nidzgorski and Nidzgorski, 1998; Darkowska-Nidzgorski, 1980; Liking, 1987). As in the case of the theatre of human actors, that of puppets can either serve entertainment or religious purposes. The people in the Ségou region of Mali, for example, clearly distinguish between these two types, seeing the former (organised by youth associations) as belonging to *nyènajè*, that is public entertainment, and the latter (organised by men's associations) to *nyanfè*, sacred ceremony (Arnoldi, 1995: 21–4; Liking, 1987: 12). The puppets and other stage props (*boli*) used in the latter type of theatre are believed to have supernatural power, whereas those in the former are considered mere toys (*tulonko fen*).

A remarkable and well-researched example of recreational puppet theatre in a Francophone country is the *sogo bo* or youth association puppet masquerade theatre of the Bamana, Somono and Bozo peoples of south-central Mali (Arnoldi, 1995; Liking, 1987). The puppets, carved in wood and dressed in either cloth or grass, manipulated with rod or string, depict a wide variety of characters: human – farmers, fishermen (among whom the form is believed to have originated) and women (the young, the sexy, the matronly); animal (antelope, buffalo, birds); and spirit figures. European types from the colonial period (the missionary with his beard, the district officer with his whip and helmet) and contemporary African politicians are also part of the repertoire of the sogo bo and puppet theatre forms from other countries (Darkowska-Nidzgorski and Nidzgorski, 1998: 145–8).

In spite of their centrality to a sogo bo masquerade theatre performance, puppets are never the sole actors. Masquerades, drummers, singers and dancers always accompany them. Certain songs and dances are associated with specific puppets and function as a means of communication between audience and puppet figure. In her description of a sogo bo performance she witnessed, Liking distinguishes three phases: the announcement of the show and summoning of spectators through energetic drum music in the public square; the warming-up phase, during which the acting space is set up and the arriving audience entertained by song and dance; and the theatrical display proper (1987: 38). To ensure order throughout the show and to prevent over-enthusiastic spectators from spilling on to and obstructing the acting space is the masked figure *gon*, the baboon, who, as internal producer and master of ceremonies, also opens the show by introducing the various puppet characters to the crowd. The performance mostly consists of two types of danced action, during which the puppets (rather like in a sougounougou performance) mimic, sometimes in stylised fashion, the animal figures that they represent, imitate scenes of domestic or social life, or (in the case of the masquerades) engage in what Arnoldi labels 'shape-shifting dances' during which a masked dancer can change, for example, from 'undifferentiated haystack . . . to a whirling ball extending itself vertically and horizontally' (Arnoldi, 1995: 90). The range of topics dealt with by contemporary puppet theatres has greatly expanded to include development issues such as literacy, health, farming methods and democracy (Darkowska-Nidzgorski and Nidzgorski, 1998: 165).

In spite of its vitality in traditional cultures, puppetry does not yet have the same impact on modern theatrical activity in Francophone Africa as some of the other forms discussed above. However, some change is noticeable. Several private troupes have been founded, including the Compagnie des Marionnettes Danaye Kanlanfeï by the Togolese puppeteer of the same name, the Kabako Théâtre Troupe by the Malian Yaya Coulibaly, and the N'Solêh Troupe by the Ivorian Atou Ekaré. But perhaps the most systematic and best-known effort to promote puppet theatre and to use it as a resource for modern cultural and theatrical life is that of Werewere Liking. Her study trip to Mali between 1977 and 1978 not only led to an attractive volume on puppets, *Marionnettes du Mali*, but also to experimental productions such as *Dieu-Chose* (God-thing, 1988) and *Les cloches* (The bells, 1988). The first piece done entirely with puppet characters is an exploration of the theme of freedom and necessity, expressed through the figure of the puppeteer (God) and his puppet-object, and the second, which mixes human and puppet figures, is a satire of corruption in contemporary African social and political life. But one of her most ambitious puppet theatre pieces, perhaps, is the still unpublished initiatory tale *L'enfant Mbénè*, which she adapted for the stage and in particular for a group of actors in her company called 'les articuleurs' (articulators), whose work she defines as the performance of folk-tales using music, dance and 'articulated objects', in other words puppets.

Some effort has also been made at governmental level to encourage creativity in puppet theatre. In 1983, for example, Mali created the National Puppet Theatre Company – one of the few state-sponsored companies in existence in Francophone Africa – while in 1989, under impetus of the Burkina Faso drama critic and practitioner Jean-Pierre Guingané, the Burkina Faso Union of Drama Groups founded, in collaboration with the International Theatre Institute, a bi-annual International Festival of Puppet Theatre that now regularly attracts puppet theatre groups from Mali, Ivory Coast, Benin and Guinea.

Ceremonial performances: some examples

If the performances above are all pure theatre, non-literary to be sure, but theatre all the same – oral, physical, mixed media, or however one chooses to describe it – religious performances, while eminently theatrical, are not themselves theatre. Apart from their status as forms of social action, symbolic instruments that seek to effect real change on the world outside the performance space, the staging of and participation in these events is obligatory if, as in the case of fertility rituals, the community is to avoid a farming disaster. Also, the performers in religious ceremonies, unlike those in theatre, are not actors. They do not imitate characters or events. Theirs, in other words, is not an act of mimesis, but of methexis, that is, of making present the characters and events represented. 'The sacred performance', writes Huizinga, 'is more than an actualization in appearance only . . . In it, something invisible . . . takes beautiful, actual, holy form. The participants . . . are convinced that the action . . . effects a definite beatification, brings about an order of things higher than that in which they customarily live' (1955: 14). Nowhere is this observation borne out with greater accuracy than in the kamabolon ritual referred to earlier.

Organised by the Keita clan in the township of Kangaba in Mali every seven years for five days, the kamabolon is a ritual celebration of leadership and of incorporation of a new age grade into Mande society (Jensen, 1998). The ceremony, like most of the performances discussed above, has a tripartite structure: a separation phase on the first day, during which the old roof is taken off the kamabolon sanctuary (a small mud building), a transitional phase of gestation of a new social order during which the sanctuary remains roofless, and a reincorporation phase on the fifth and last day, when the restored sanctuary is given a new roof, symbol of a remodelled and reconstituted social order. Jensen describes the liminal phase of the ceremony as one of fear and tension, as society, caught between an earlier state of social stability (before the unroofing) and of a stability yet to come (after the reroofing), goes through a period of potential disorder.

An important moment of the ceremony is the eve of the reroofing, when various individuals, arranged into lineage and social groups, and following fixed trajectories, process at intervals into the sanctuary, against a background of drumming and dancing, and when, moments later, invited *griots* from a neighbouring township commence an all-night recital of praise songs and incantations that culminates, between the early hours of the morning and dawn, in the performance of the epic of Sunjata. The evening of recitals is followed, on the last day, by the hoisting atop the sanctuary of the new roof. In a remark about audience behaviour that underlines the instrumental nature of the kamabolon ceremony and which sets it apart from 'theatre' – indigenous African or any other – Jensen observes: 'At that moment [of reroofing in 1997 that he witnessed] many attendees crossed the hedge in order to touch the new roof, since it is believed that that brings blessings' (1998: 272; emphasis mine).

From a rite of passage, the kamabolon, I will now examine the *ndepp*, an example from the class of ceremonial performances characterised by

Victor Turner as 'rituals of affliction' (1968). Widely practised by the Lebou and Wolof of Senegal, the ndepp is an exorcism dance ceremony believed to cure individuals that are psychologically ill (Harris, 1981: 13–10, Diop, 1990: 15–19). This is an all-female event, rarely open to men, and even then only when they are dressed as women. The first phase of the ceremony is private. It consists of acts of ritual purification of the officiants, and of propitiation of the gods through animal sacrifice. This is followed the next day by the public phase during which a group of performers led by a master of ceremonies enacts – through music, dance and mime and with the support of a chorus made up of the public – an archetypal struggle between the forces of evil afflicting the patient and those of good. The acting space of the ndepp is circular and the costumes of the performers include headscarves, ankle and wrist bracelets and a short-sleeved, knee-length dress. Among the props are animal horns covered in red leather and decorated with cowries.

Another example of a sacred dance is the *ozila* of the Bulu people of south-central Cameroon. A variation on the universal theme of physical/social infirmity but spiritual power, the ozila is a dance of initiation into knowledge of the gods and their mysteries, revealed, according to legend, to two hapless children (an orphan and a leper) by the ghosts of their parents (Hourantier, 1977).

Unlike their recreational counterparts, which have long exercised an important influence on the modern Francophone stage, as has been observed, religious performances only began to do so in the last two decades. Among the few, but highly experimental dramatists that have engaged in this project are Werewere Liking in such plays as *La Puissance de Um* (1979), *Une Nouvelle terre* (1980), modelled on funerary rites and rites of passage respectively, the Ivorian Zadi Zaourou in *Le Secret des dieux* (1999) and *La Termitière* (1984), based on the '*didiga*', a sacred hunter performance of the Bété people, and Sony Labou Tansi in *La Parenthèse de sang* (1981), *La Rue des mouches* (1985), plays inspired by the *kingizila* healing ceremony.

Popular theatre

Popular urban theatre

Partaking in many respects of indigenous performances like those above, but also of foreign, especially western, ones, and yet constituting a class of its own, is a distinct type of tradition known as 'popular urban theatre'. The use of the word *urban* here is meant to distinguish this theatre from another type of popular theatre, the rural type. The distinction between 'popular' and 'élite' is not often made with respect to rural performances, which are *all* considered 'popular'. They may well be, but this is only true in relation to the new élite *literary drama*, and certainly not within their cultural space, where performances can be further classified into rural 'popular' and 'élite' forms. The latter are mostly associated with healing, initiation, military societies or occupational guilds, and access to them is severely restricted by considerations of age, gender, occupation and status. These societies, like the 'Do' of the Bambara of Mali, constitute the power structure that regulates the life of the community. In such a context 'popular' theatre is exemplified by the *kotèba*, a form that is not only open to every member of the public (women, children, casted individuals, non-initiates and so on), but is also sometimes critical, as was noted earlier, of the social and political order of the elders and the initiates, if only within the temporal and spatial boundaries of a show.

But the kotèba is 'popular' theatre in a number of ways that are different from its urban popular counterpart. First of all, the latter is not produced and consumed by members of an ethnic and peasant community, but of what Barber calls the 'urban "intermediate class"', consisting of wage earners, urban unemployed, artisans and school drop-outs from various ethnicities (1997: 2). Also, urban popular theatre, although rooted in indigenous performance styles, borrows massively, unlike its rural counterpart, from western dramatic forms (church drama, films, military parades, recitals, literary drama and so on), which constitute the élite forms of its own universe, and some of whose social types it ridicules. An example often given of such a theatre form in Francophone Africa is the concert party of Togo, extensively documented by Alain Ricard (1975, 1997).

Ghanaian in origin and arriving in Togo around 1940, the concert party is a spectacle of music, dance and skits that lasts several hours. Its venues are the school, church, or community hall, the courtyard of private houses or hotels, and not, like indigenous performances, the shrine or village square. Because its patrons are drawn from a variety of ethnic groups, its language tends to be a mixture of Mina, the urban lingua franca of the Togolese capital, Lomé, and French. Like the indigenous performances on which it is partly modelled, its characters are social types distinguishable by their costume: the houseboy (who in minstrel fashion paints his lips white and his face black), the prostitute (usually Yoruba or Ghanaian, who wears bright red lipstick and an Afro wig), the old man, and so on.

The phases of a show include an opening musical prologue consisting of guitar music, a session of gags and knockabouts by clowns, and a play-acting section consisting of short skits. The issues addressed in these skits are varied. Prominent among them, according to Ricard and his co-authors, Karin Barber and John Collins (1997: 29), are 'family stories': of sons, such as Atemklo in *Mister Tameklor*, or daughters, who in affirmation of their new-found sense of self, defy parental advice in their choice of domestic partner. Sometimes it is wives, Mary, in *Francis the Parisian*, who abandon their sick and impoverished spouses for sleeker, and ostensibly wealthier, city gents. But none of these or other concert party social 'rebels' ever succeeds. The urban lifestyles and characters (or what passes for them) to which they are attracted rapidly turn out to be a mirage, as their partners – rogues in sun-glasses, in bright red lipstick or sporting briefcases, and speaking borrowed French – invariably end up fleecing them. In staging skits in which devia-tion from what is considered 'traditional' conduct is greeted with failure and suffering, the concert party performs the function of moral guide for that sec-tion of the population, the appropriately named 'intermediate class', caught between the often conflicting demands and moral codes of rural and urban life.

Moral guidance through entertainment is also what was provided by the famous Mufwankolo popular theatre of Elizabethville (present-day Lubum-bashi) in the Shaba (ex-Katanga) region of Congo. This theatre, whose pop-ularity was at its peak in the mid-1970s, was best known first for its radio plays and then, from 1971, for its television drama programme entitled *Zaire of Tomorrow*, in which plays were presented in weekly instalments (Fabian, 1990). Fabian traces its origins to the 1930s culture of mining towns such as Elizabethville/Lubumbashi, where the copper conglomerate Union Minière du Haut-Katanga in concert with the Catholic church fostered the cre-ation of cultural movements, for example the Boy Scouts and various sports clubs, to meet the leisure needs of a growing youth population. As part of its cultural activities, the Boy Scouts were encouraged to compose Bible-inspired sketches that could be performed during campfire outings and on feast days. With time, however, these groups became more autonomous and started staging plays in the local lingua franca, Swahili, which emphasised entertainment values without at the same time jettisoning their moralising function. Local tunes sung to guitar music and modern, especially Latin American, rhythms became part of the spectacle. One of the earliest popular theatres to emerge in this context was La Voix de la Jeunesse Kantangaise, followed in 1952 by the Jeunes Acteurs du Katanga, which later took the stage name, Mufwankolo, of its carpenter-founder, Kyembe.

Mufwankolo plays draw their inspiration from scenes of domestic and everyday life in Katanga, but also, in highly coded manner, from the political landscape. As is common with all popular theatre, these plays do not consist of fixed texts but rather of scenarios around which dialogues are creatively improvised. Because it developed mostly as radio drama, the Mufwankolo is a language-based theatre in which the comic resides more in such things as the mockery of ethnic accents and the use of double-meanings and understatement, especially in the treatment of sensitive political issues (Fabian, 1990: 51–2), than in the physical appearance or movements of the performers.

Théâtre d'animation politique

A second type of popular theatre in Francophone Africa is what has been called the 'théâtre d'animation politique', a theatre of political cheerleading. Widely practised in many African countries, especially those with charismatic leaders who sought to build mass political organisations – for example, Guinea and Togo, under Sékou Touré and Gnassingbe Eyadema respectively – it reached an unrivalled level of organisation in the Zaire of Mobutu. Here, an entire administrative division – the General Secretariat for Mobilisation and Propaganda, complete with an assortment of civil servants from national to village level – was created within the Ministry of Information solely for mass performance spectacles (Sang'Amin, 1989). Mobutu himself is said to have got the idea for such events from watching similar ones during visits to North Korea and Communist China.

The functions of these spectacles vary, from the innocuous – entertaining visiting dignitaries or national political élites – to the more ideological, especially in comprehensively authoritarian régimes such as those mentioned above: adulating the leader, his party and the state (which are all indistinguishable), rallying the crowds and producing a heady atmosphere if not exactly of mass hysteria, of intense emotion during public events, and not least, indoctrinating the mass of the population in the political values of the régime. That the qualifications expected of the 'animateur' or lead conductor and organiser of these spectacles in Zaire, for example, is 'knowledge of crowd psychology and the ability to control it' as well as mastery of 'almost all the [party's] slogans and revolutionary songs' (Sang'Amin, 1989: 100), is a measure of the importance that a régime like that of Mobutu placed on this type of performance as an instrument of political education and thus of social control.

Though the combinations to which they are put vary depending on the troupe (and in Zaire there were salaried, semi-professional national troupes for important state occasions and many other amateur ones), the basic ingredients of a performance are the same: paeans to the leader composed around his policy slogans, miming, marching band, traditional or Soukouss, music – the whole interspersed with chanted slogans in call-and-response mode and carefully choreographed modern and traditional dances whose performers sometimes fall into formations that reproduce the colours of the national flag or name of the president-father of the nation. With the demise, in the last few years, of many of the continent's charismatic leaders and their authoritarian single-party régimes, this theatre seems to be losing its importance as an instrument of political propaganda.

Community development theatre

A third and final example of popular theatre in Francophone Africa, especially in Mali, Burkina Faso and Niger, is community development theatre or theatre of social intervention. As its name suggests, the aim of this practice is educational: to intervene in the social transformation of rural communities, especially, by using their languages and performance traditions as a means of communicating practical knowledge on such issues as family planning, health, agriculture and so on (Guingané, 1988; Morrison, 1991; Desffontaines, 1990). Its approach is to involve the target communities in the diagnosis and resolution of their problems, to perform with and not to them, to avoid presenting them with ready-made analyses and solutions generated by well-intentioned but sometimes ill-informed local or foreign bureaucrats.

Among the examples of this practice are the Atelier Théâtral Burkinabé and the Théâtre de la Fraternité, both of Burkina Faso (Desffontaines, 1990; Guingané, 1988), and the Samariya youth associations of Niger (Beik, 1987). The first, created in 1978 by the theatre academic and practitioner Prosper Kampaoré, is notable for its annual theatre 'campaigns' to the countryside. Two of its most successful pieces, first staged in 1989 at a development theatre festival in Burkina Faso that also saw the participation of the leading theorist of development theatre, Augusto Boal, are *Fatouma ou La Machine à créer des enfants* (Fatouma or the breeding Machine), on the importance of family planning, and *Halte à la diarrhée* (Stop the diarrhoea). The Théâtre de la Fraternité for its part concentrates on civic education, with such plays as *Je ne paie pas* (1996), on the issue of taxes, and *Le Bonheur dans l'urne* (1999) on elections. Other important troupes are the Nyogolon of Mali, whose play *Timinandia*, commissioned by a non-governmental organisation and staged at the same festival, deals with the importance of having infants vaccinated.

Reference above to non-governmental agencies and academics points to an important difference between 'community development' and 'urban popular' theatre. Although both are rooted in indigenous performance traditions, the latter is a commercial activity generated, organised and controlled from within the ranks of the ordinary people, for ordinary people, even if its concerns and approaches to social issues are not necessarily emancipatory. The former, on the other hand, is a theatre for the economic and social welfare of the people but is initiated and organised not by them – even when they act in its plays or collaborate in their making – but by radical intellectuals or socially progressive and reform-minded governments. In respect of its impetus from without, community development theatre is similar to the théâtre d'animation politique – also the initiative of an outside force (the state), planned with and executed by the people using their cultural traditions, not for the benefit of the people, however, as is the case with development theatre, but of the state and its supreme leader.

French-language theatre: the colonial period

Expatriate theatre

In spite of their vitality and relevance to the majority of the population, the performance forms above are eclipsed in terms of sheer social and cultural power and prestige by what has become the hegemonic form in Francophone Africa, literary drama. Although it only emerged in the 1930s in the French colonies, and in the 1950s in the Belgian ones, metropolitan French theatre itself was introduced into Africa before World War One. It took the form of performances by visiting French and Belgian troupes. Conceived mostly for the entertainment of the large European populations of such cities as Dakar and Leopoldville, the shows put on by these troupes do not seem to have been restricted to the expatriate community. According to the Belgian critic and Congo resident, Jadot, some troupes sought to increase their appeal to African audiences by involving them in the music and dance sequences of their shows. About these troupes Jadot observed:

Il arriva que leurs représentations . . . fussent rendues plus ou moins accessibles aux Africains des grandes villes. Il arriva même que certaines troupes fissent appel à des figurants de couleur et que des Noirs dansassent sur musique de J.-B. Lulli, les ballets louis-quatorziens d'une comédie de Molière. (Jadot, 1959: 64)

It happened that their shows were made more or less accessible to the Africans in the big cities. It even happened that certain troupes called upon coloured stage hands, and that Blacks danced to the music of J.[ean]-B.[aptiste] Lulli accompanying the Louis XIV ballets in Molière's comedies.

Missionary theatre

But it was through the medium of the school – the parochial and later the state school – that French drama was to take firm root in Africa. Aware of the importance of performance in indigenous societies, missionaries were quick to seize on it as a medium for the propagation of Christianity and its values. Missionaries regularly organised dramatic sketches around religious themes to mark feasts, such as Easter or Joan of Arc Day, or end of year school activities. A particularly popular story in Dahomey was the Journey of the Three Wise Men. In a modest concession to local Dahomean custom, the three magi, depicted as chiefs with large retinues, were dressed in what a French member of the audience described as 'superb traditional cloth' (pagnes superbes) (Cornevin, 1970: 47). Myrrh – meaningless to the local population, according to one of the performers – was replaced with its Dahomean symbolic equivalent, water. In Cameroon, missionaries additionally introduced French miracle plays, such as the Miracle de Théophile which was translated into the local Bassa language, while in Togo they introduced a new performance genre: the cantata (in its Togolese version), a sung and danced religious drama set to piano music that subsequently became a source of the concert party.

But it was perhaps in the Belgian Congo that religious school theatre was most influential in laying the foundations of the new drama.[4] This is partly because, unlike west Africa where education became a matter for the French state as far back as 1903, with the creation of a training college in Senegal for the entire West African Federation, it remained a church monopoly in the Belgian colonies until 1955.[5] Also, the practice of religious theatre in those colonies, especially Belgian Congo, went beyond parochial schools to the many socially influential church-sponsored youth organisations – Boy Scouts, Girl Guides, Chiro and so on – or adult organisations such as the Jaama.[6]

But Belgian missionary theatre, as practised in the Congo, differed significantly from its French counterpart in west Africa. After a period of implacable hostility to and imprecation against their 'paganism', the former turned to and embraced indigenous performance genres as the new basis of its religious theatre. The Zairian critic Sang'Amin (1989) gives two reasons for this turnabout: the Catholic Church's desire to recapture the converts it had been losing to the growing African church of the Congolese 'prophet' Simon Kimbangui, and its desire to win new ones. The strategy it adopted, after some investigation of Kimbangui's methods, was to embrace indigenous performances. Not to endorse their 'pagan' worldview, naturally, but to use their *form* and *communicative techniques*, to undermine that very world and substitute in its place the new Christian message and its 'civilising' values.[7] Sang'Amin gives as an example of a characteristic play of the period, *Katikiro*, performed between 1925 and 1926 at the St Joseph Institute in Kinshasa, in which the very costumes and physical appearance of the title character, the *katikiro* ('chief minister' of the monarch of Buganda), his insignia of office and his court rituals were used against him as proof of his brutality and role in the massacre of what had become known as the Ugandan martyrs.[8] Belgian missionary theatre then borrowed not just the *form* of African performances, but also, on occasion and unlike its French west African counterpart, whose topics were Bible history and religious legend, their subject matter, even when the use made of the latter was critical and satiric.

The most important troupes to emerge from the missionary activity were the generically named 'petits chanteurs et danseurs' (young singers and dancers). Initially established to provide spiritual uplift for audiences at public gatherings with their songs (Christian lyrics set to Congolese tunes), these troupes, made up of young converts, progressively incorporated traditional dance and mime routines into their singing. The songs themselves became less religious, stage action acquired more importance and sketches were introduced into the show. The latter took a variety show format consisting of opening introductory songs followed by various dance routines and finally dramatic sketches. The young singers had moved from religion to recreation and, in the process, had created what Sang'Amin describes in connection with the Kenge Young Singers troupe as 'a new genre'.

En fusionnant chants et danses, mime et jeu théâtral, la troupe Kenge venait de créer un nouveau genre qui renouait avec le spectacle traditionnel profane. (1989: 77)

By fusing song, and dance, mime and acting, the Kenge Troupe had just created a new genre whose roots go back to traditional secular performance.

Known in Congo as *spectacle populaire* ('popular show'), this genre, of which the Mufwankolo discussed earlier is a good example, has since been an abiding feature of that country's theatrical scene.

School theatre
The next important element after the church, in the development of theatre in Francophone Africa, was the state school. In France itself and in its colonies, where education, as already noted, was in the anti-clerical tradition of the (Third) Republic, a matter for the *école laïque*, the latter played a crucial role in the spread of modern theatre. In addition to plays by Molière and dramatic monologues, the school introduced, according to one of the region's most influential educators, Charles Béart, 'les chansons françaises . . . les fables de La Fontaine, les fanfares' (French songs . . . Fables by La Fontaine . . . and brass bands) (Béart 1936–7: 9–10). Indeed, it is in one of them, L'Ecole William Ponty, that the first play in French by a west African was written.

William Ponty's role in shaping early Francophone theatre cannot be exaggerated. Founded in 1903 in Senegal, it drew its students, who came from all over the French West African Federation (AOF) from a special social background – in the words of the French Inspector of Education, George Hardy:

Ceux dont la famille a toujours secondé avec honneur notre œuvre civilisatrice et mis son prestige héréditaire au service de nos intentions. (Vincileoni, 1986: 25)

those whose families have always supported our civilizing mission with honour, and put their hereditary prestige in the service of our objectives.

But French educational authorities were faced with something of a dilemma. How could they both impart a modern education to their subjects and yet prevent them from using the methods and ideals of that education

to talk and 'write back' to empire, from becoming disloyal subjects? The solution envisaged, and one crucial to the rise of French-language theatre, involved the creation of what French educators called 'a Franco-African culture'.[9] William Ponty, charged with creating that culture, would do two things. First, it would provide a rudimentary education to its students that would be enough to produce 'colonial auxiliaries', but not good enough for them to question the colonial project. In the words of the governor, Camille Guy:

> Les bons programmes ne s'obtiennent qu'en élaguant, non en ajoutant. Enseignement du français et des sciences élémentaires, des travaux techniques et enseignement professionnel approprié au milieu. C'est suffisant. (Vincileoni, 1986: 25)

Good syllabi can only be made by pruning, and not by adding. French, elementary science, technical studies and a vocational education relevant to the environment – that is enough.

To give any more, he continued, is not to 'prepare French citizens', but to produce what he preferred to describe, in a classic gesture of exclusion and pathologisation of dissent, as 'des déclassés, des vaniteux, des désaxés qui perdent leur qualité native et n'acquièrent que des vices des éducateurs' (outcasts, vain and deranged individuals who lose their native intelligence, and acquire nothing but the vices of their teachers) (Vincileoni, 1986: 25–6). Among such 'outcasts' – in reality, nationalists or quite simply colonial subjects critical of empire – he singles out, quite tellingly, the black French colonial administrator-novelist from Guyana, René Maran,[10] whose prize-winning novel, *Batouala*, especially the preface, is a searing critique of French rule in Oubangui-Chari, the present-day Central African Republic.

Second, William Ponty would prevent its students from being estranged from their indigenous traditions as a result of their new French education by having them research these traditions and, in their final year of training college, write up their findings as part of their course requirements. The best of these exercises – 'où la pensée française a pu se mêler intimement à la pensée indigène' (where French thought has been able to mix intimately with indigenous thought, Béart, 1936–7: 12) – were dramatised at end-of-year school ceremonies, a practice that gave rise in 1933 to the first dramatic composition in French by a west African, *L'Entrevue de Béhanzin et de Bayol* (1933). Between 1935 and 1945 William Ponty became a centre of

intense dramatic activity that culminated in the annual student Fête d'Art Indigène (Festival of Indigenous Art), during which plays were performed to large public audiences in Dakar, and (in 1937) in Paris at the International Exhibition.

What are the characteristics of William Ponty theatre? Its subjects were essentially drawn from traditional lore and custom. When plays were not dramatising marriage ceremonies (*Un Mariage chez les mandégnis*, 1937; *Un Mariage au Dahomey*, 1934), coming-of-age and various initiation rituals (*Trois scènes sérères*, 1937), they were staging legends (*Sokamé*, 1937) or coronation practices (*L'Election d'un roi au Dahomey*, 1936).[11] Their approach, determined largely by the paternalism of their French audiences, was folkloristic and documentary. The programme notes to the 1936 Feast reveal this aspect of French audience reactions:

> Tous étaient heureux de constater que ces noirs ne manquent ni de bon sens . . . ni d'esprit ni même de sens artistique . . . Tous ont été à même de remarquer que ces jeunes gens instruits et éduqués n'étaient nullement des déracinés et qu'ils associaient étroitement l'école et la vie indigène. Ils aiment l'Afrique, ils aiment la France.
>
> (Compte-Rendu de la Fête de l'Ecole William Ponty, *L'Education Africaine*, 1936: 180)

All were happy to note that these Africans lacked neither common sense, nor wit or art. They were all in a position to note that these young educated men were not rootless and that they closely associated school and native life. They like Africa, they like France.

Although rare, events or figures from African history were not absent from the Ponty stage. African rulers such as Béhanzin, Sunjata, Samory and Assémien were the subject of collective compositions such as *La Rencontre de Béhanzin et de Bayol* (1933), *[L']Entrevue de Samory et du Capitaine Péroz* (1936), *La Ruse du Diégué* (1937), by students from Dahomey, Guinea and Mali respectively, and *Assémien Déhylé* (1934) by Bernard Dadié. But interestingly, here again the approach tended towards the ethnographic. The sketches dwell on, or show off, aspects of culture – 'griots', seers and the arts and practice of their trades, court ceremonial, the performing arts (in *Assémien Déhylé*, especially) – with little regard to their dramatic relevance. When a composition involves an encounter between an African ruler and the French, the former, in keeping with the prevailing colonial ideology is always presented

as an obstacle to France's mission. In the Samory–Péroz sketch, for example, the Guinean ruler comes across as a big-mouth who speaks the language of courage and resistance, only to be seen – in the climactic meeting with the French captain, Péroz – behaving obsequiously, and capitulating to his demands (for access to trade routes) without as much as a protest:

PÉROZ: Tu insultes la France, prends garde.
SAMORY: J'avoue m'être laissé emporter par une colère indigne de moi.
PÉROZ: Retractes-tu tes paroles emportées?
SAMORY: Soit, je les retire . . . Chef, tu as raison, je signerai le traité d'amitié car tu es fort et bon.
         ([L']Entrevue, L'Education Africaine, 1936: 45–6)

PÉROZ: Be careful, you are insulting France.
SAMORY: I must confess to having let myself be carried away by anger unworthy of me.
PÉROZ: Do you withdraw your angry words?
SAMORY: Yes, I do . . . Boss you are right; I'll sign the friendship Treaty because you are strong and a good man.

French authorities, clearly satisfied with this portrayal of events, describe the composition as 'an accurate and fine piece of historical reconstruction' (R.D., L'Education Africaine, 1936: 17) – a reaction that echoes their reviews of the 1933 piece (now lost) – about a similar encounter between the Dahomean ruler, Behanzin, and the French colonel, Bayol; reviews that refer to 'the proud and haughty attitude of the brutal despot' (see Cornevin, 1970: 56).

When a Ponty history play is set outside the historical period of French expansion in Africa, as is the case with La Ruse de Diégué, on the thirteenth-century emperor of Mali, Sunjata, it prefers not to concentrate on the achievements for which Sunjata is best remembered: freeing his (Malinké) people from (Susu) dominion and forging one of the most celebrated polities in medieval west Africa. It focusses, rather, on what has been dubbed the 'Samson and Delila' episode in his career, in which Diégué, Sunjata's sister and wife of his enemy, Soumangourou, learns the secrets of her husband's invincibility only to betray them to her brother, Sunjata. No doubt worthy of a play, one wonders, however, the extent to which the choice of this episode was not an act of self-censorship on the part of the students, concerned as they were about depicting the dramatically unrepresentable or unsayable – acts

of ancient valour and resistance to foreign rule – preferring instead harmless episodes of female betrayal, mystery and magic.

But whether the topic of Ponty sketches was from lore or legend, their form, composed of a series of episodes loosely linked by song and dance (in African languages), remained essentially the same. The dialogue is in French, a French richly infused with African imagery and proverbs, although in the hands of such characters as Moriba, Péroz's interpreter, or Le Pêcheur (the Fisherman) in *Les Prétendants rivaux* (The rival suitors), it is quite simply pidginised.

Theatre of cultural centres and social clubs

In 1945, as a result of curricular changes at William Ponty, school theatre went into decline. As a result, dramatic activity shifted to cultural centres and to social clubs and associations. According to Cornevin (1970: 109–18), cultural centres were a French idea that had been imported to west Africa from the French Equatorial Federation, where they had proved successful. The idea consisted in establishing centres with library, film and theatre facilities in district headquarters in all the countries of the federation. Their objective, according to the governor, Bernard Cornut-Gentille, was to foster contacts and cooperation between the new élites and the mass of the population: 'Les centres culturels ne sont pas un "tabernacle" qui ne s'ouvrent qu'à quelques-uns et l'élite qui les dirigent doit en chercher l'épanouissement au profit du plus grand nombre' (The cultural centres are not a 'tabernacle' open only to a few; the élites who run them must work in the interests of the majority) (Cornevin, 1970: 109). A feature of these centres and an important factor in the development of French-language theatre were the keenly contested drama competitions they organised between various national centres (in the first round) and (in the second, in the federal capital, Dakar) between the winners of the national competitions. Entries could be original creations, as long as they were in French, or productions of French plays.

If cultural centres were a French idea and creation, social clubs or cultural associations such as the Amicale des fonctionnaires de Niamey in Niger, the Tréteaux of Mali, the Cercle Amical in Burkina Faso, the Théâtre Indigène and the Cercle Culturel et Folklorique, both of the Ivory Coast, were the fruit of private, local initiatives. By the late 1940s, when these clubs were being founded, several generations of French west Africans had graduated from Ponty and other institutions. They had acquired enough social capital and prestige in their countries to constitute the kernel of a new élite known

as the 'évolués'. The practice of modern theatre became a symbol of their modernity, new status and aspirations (Jezequel, 1999).

But social clubs were not just a French west African idea. In the Belgian Congo, évolués also established cultural associations – on the model of expatriate Belgian ones – that regularly organised lectures, recitals and concerts and that undertook grand fundraising and cultural activities under the patronage of the expatriate and especially the religious establishment (Nkashama, 1993: 262–72; Sang'Amin, 1989: 89–95). Theatre was an important aspect of their activities. When they were not trying to stage Labiche comedies (Sang'Amin, 1989: 90) or not involved in 'des imitations vraisemblables du répertoire classique' (decent imitations of plays from the classical repertory), they were producing works by one of their own, such as Albert Mongita's Soki Stanley, La Quinzaine (1957), Ngombe, or L. S. Bondekwe's Athanase, le professeur de lumière. Scripted plays in Congolese languages, Ciluba, Lingala and Kiswahili, and directed at an audience of mine workers were an important and unique form of the theatre of this period. Its notable practitioners, whose works were in part entries for a literary competition organised by La Voix du Congolais (which also published the prize-winning plays), included Justin Disasi, Albert Mongita and Christophe Tshimanga.

An interesting aspect of the théâtre des évolués (Belgian or French) worth noting is not so much its imitation of western models, as the new consciousness or cultural values that animate it. Whether it was produced in French-sponsored cultural centres or private social clubs, this theatre was no longer a mere retailing or exhibition of native customs and practices, as was the case in the Ponty sketches. Rather, it had become a critical presentation of them as ethically or socially incompatible with 'progress'. In other words, clearer contours of a modern, and in the Belgian case especially, Catholic viewpoint from which these customs were now judged, had emerged. It is this viewpoint, and the need to promote it (even if ambiguously sometimes), that authorized the Ivorian F. J. Amon d'Aby, for example, to speak out against inheritance laws in matriarchal societies in Kwao Adjoba (1953), or the extended family in Entraves (1955); that leads Dadié to poke fun at diviners in Siddi, maître escroc (Siddi, Master Swindler, 1960), and to satirise laws of succession in Min Adja-O (1955). Theatre, then, had become an instrument of social modernisation that the élites could use, in the words of the Ivorian dramatist of the period, Amon d'Aby, 'to stimulate their compatriots to

reflect deeply on their common heritage in the light of the needs of a world undergoing rapid change' (1988: 62).

But in spite of its defensible objectives, évolué social theatre has been criticised on several grounds. In addition to its formal imitativeness, its approach to so-called 'traditional' customs and practices, it has been observed, is unbalanced, clearly exhibiting an anxiety for change not for change's relevance to society, but for its own sake (Nkashama, 1993: 262–71; Sang'Amin, 1989: 93–5). When this feature is combined with the theatre's silence on the colonial project – with the rare exception of the Ivorian Gadeau's *Les Recrutés de Monsieur Maurice* (Mr Maurice's recruits, 1942), on forced labour, or the Belgian Congolese Bondekwe's *Professeur de lumière*, a satire of the 'enlightened' élite – it is easy to see how the charge of complicity with that project can be made (Nkashama, 1993: 270). A headlong address of that project was to come later – in the fourth, and what could be called 'mature', phase of Francophone theatre.

French-language theatre: the post-colonial period

Enabling factors
A number of factors contributed to this theatre's development during the period under discussion. The first was the continued assistance, in material and human resources, provided the young theatre by the French government. In addition to contributing to the creation of theatre arts institutes in such countries as the Ivory Coast and Senegal, France sponsored several visits, between 1963 and 1968, by theatre critics and directors to various French-speaking countries. Their mission was to organise workshops and stage productions with aspiring dramatists, and even read manuscripts of their plays (Schérer, 1992). This type of assistance has continued well into the post-colonial period, with much of France's attention focussed in the 1980s, however, on one country, Congo-Brazzaville, and within it, on one private troupe, the Rocado Zulu theatre of Sony Labou Tansi. Between 1984 and 1987 France sent five theatre directors, including Daniel Mesguich, Pierre Vial and Michel Rostain, to work with him and his colleague, Pascal Nzonzi, and had a French academic, Jacqueline Leloup, appointed to Congo's National Theatre (Baños-Robles, 1990: 134–9).

Another factor in the development of Francophone theatre after 1960 was the Concours Théâtral Interafricain, the radio drama competition

established in 1966 by the French Overseas Radio Service in collaboration with African broadcasting services. Publication facilities, a listening audience and tours of various Francophone capitals guaranteed that the best entries greatly stimulated, as had been hoped, the writing of plays. A study conducted in the late 1970s indicated that 80 per cent of all Francophone plays were competition entries (Ligier, 1983; also Ligier, 1993), a percentage that does not seem to have changed much if one looks at the names of post-1970s competition winners – Togolese writers Agbota Zinsou and Kossi Effoui, the Madagascan Michèle Rakotoson, the Malian Moussa Diagana and Cameroonian Werewere Liking. In 1993 the competition, renamed Radio France Internationale Théâtre, was thrown open to playwrights from the global Francophone community.

A third source of stimulation for dramatists are the various continental and international theatre festivals organised to encourage and promote new talent and foster cooperation among dramatists, stage designers, directors and performers, not just from Africa but also Europe (France, Belgium, Switzerland) and North America (Quebec and the Caribbean). The most important and regular of these events include the Festival International des Francophonies in Limoges, France, founded in 1984 to celebrate world French-language theatre, the Festival Africain de Théâtre Francophone (FATF) and the Marché des Arts du Spectacle Africain (MASA), founded in 1992 and 1993 respectively in the Ivory Coast and jointly sponsored by that country and international Francophone cultural agencies, the Festival International du Théâtre pour le Développement (FITD) and the Festival International du Théâtre des Marionnettes (FITMO), both in Burkina Faso and founded in 1989 and 1993 respectively. In addition to performances, some of these gatherings, like FITMO and Limoges, organise seminars and workshops for participants. A feature unique to Limoges, and one in which several Francophone dramatists (Sylvain Bemba and Yoka Mudaba, and Moussa Konaté) have participated, is the three-month playwright-in-residence programme, and the publishing possibilities to which it had led for some of them.

But before this raft of important current festivals there was the earliest of them all, the Festival of Negro Arts, which saw, in its very first year in 1966 in Dakar, Senegal, the triumph of Aimé Césaire's *La Tragédie du roi Christophe* (1963), a play that revealed to French-speaking African playwrights the possibilities of theatre as a medium for national self-refashioning, and which inspired the Ivorian Bernard Dadié, according to his own testimony, to write

the first widely acclaimed African play in French in the post-colonial period, *Béatrice du Congo* (1970), which premiered in the Avignon festival that same year by Jean-Marie Serreau.

Theatre and history

A classification of plays of this period by theme would yield three broad categories: historical, social and political. Although these categories have been present at any given time in the drama produced since independence, it remains true that plays devoted to the staged recreation of figures and events from history, legend or myth, especially among west African playwrights, dominated the output in the immediate pre- and post-colonial period up to the mid-1970s. The Chaka cycle of plays on the nineteenth-century Zulu warrior of the same name – Leopold Senghor's *Chaka* (1956), Séydou Badian's *La Mort de Chaka* (1962), Condetto Nénékhaly-Camara's *Amazoulou* (1967), Abdou Anta Ka's *Les Amazoulous* (1970), Djibril Tamsir Niane's *Chaka* (1971), and Marouba Fall's *Chaka ou Le Roi visionnaire* (1984) among others; André Salifou's *Tainimoune* (1973), Cheikh Ndao's *L'Exil d'Albouri* (1979), Amadou Cissé Dia's *Les Derniers jours de Lat Dior* (1965), Jean Pliya's *Kondo le requin* (1966); Massan Makan Diabaté's *Une si belle leçon de patience* (1972), Laurent Gbagbo's *Soundjata le lion du Manding* (1976) and Sory Konaké's *Le Grand destin de Soundjata* (1973), the last three, all on the Mandingo *mansa*, or emperor, Sunjata; Ola Balogun's *Shango* (1968); the group of plays on the female founder of the Ashanti/Baoule peoples of present-day Ivory Coast and Ghana, Abraha Pokou – for example Virgile Adiko's *L'Epopée de la reine Abla Pokou* (1971), Charles Nokan's *Abraha Pokou ou La Grande africaine* (1970) and Eugène Dervain's *Abra Pokou* (n.d.) are among the many examples of this type of drama. Whilst most of them are set in the nineteenth century and portray rulers who resisted French colonial conquest, some, like the Sunjata plays, are set in the thirteenth century, well before any contact with France, while others still, the Shango and Abraha Pokou plays, deal with mythological figures.

Of course, the redeployment of history on the Francophone stage has served different purposes since the 1960s. These include the well-known nationalist project, pursued well into independence, of collective self-definition in the face of self-serving imperial representations of the African past; a project that involved the staging of real or sometimes glamorised records of past achievement. Of course, the nationalist version of that past is no more or less exempt from simplification and myth-making than is its imperial predecessor and contemporary. Both arise from contexts of power relations – for colonial domination in the case of one, and national liberation in the other – which they both reflect and shape.

But the invocation of history on the Francophone stage served more than anti-colonial purposes. It also provided models of ideal conduct and symbols of unity for the young states, which, with independence and the absence of a common external adversary, faced the threat of disintegration through the reassertion of micro-nationalisms. In such dramatic pieces as Senghor's *Chaka* and Badian's *Mort de Chaka*, history served yet another purpose, namely to give legitimacy to the new political leadership by presenting it as continuous with that of a revered ancestor – in this case, Chaka's.

But if the celebratory dimension of Francophone historical drama is understandable in the context of nationalist assertion, it also remains deeply flawed in many respects. Peopled with monarchs and empire builders, the new nation that this drama imagines and calls into being is caught in a nineteenth-century French imperial, or Napoleonic, paradigm of national achievement; a paradigm whose criteria – centralised and hierarchical systems of government – it does not subvert, but paradoxically seeks to satisfy by its focus on pre-colonial African empires, to the exclusion of all other, possibly more democratic but non-centralized political formations. Since the mid-1970s, however, this history-based, heroic conception of the nation has gone into decline. The ideal that it celebrates – of the all-powerful state and charismatic leader that demand total loyalty of the citizen in the name of national unity – has gone bankrupt in the post-nationalist era, where the pursuit of national unity has often served as a pretext for the repression of dissent and the confiscation of power by self-proclaimed fathers of the nations.

Theatre and politics

Like history, politics is no less a major concern of the Francophone stage. The anti-colonial struggle has continued to inspire, years after it ended, such plays as Boubacar Boris Diop's *Thiaroye terre rouge* (1981), Pierre Dabiré's *Sansoa* (1969) and Alexandre Kum'a N'dumbe's *Amilcar Cabral ou La Tempête en Guinée-Bissao* (1976) and *Kafra-Biatanga* (1973). But it is the political situation in contemporary Africa, with its civil wars, predatory states and rulers, military and civilian despots, ethnic and national rivalries, that has given rise to many political farces, satires and tragicomedies, such as Tchicaya U'Tamsi's *Le Maréchal Nnikon Nniku prince qu'on sort* (1979) and *Le Bal de Ndinga* (1987),

Williams Sassine's *Indépendan-tristes* (1997), Moustapha Amadou Wade's *La Tragédie de l'indépendance* (1987), Maxime Ndébéka's *Le Président* (1970), most of Sony Labou Tansi's plays, including *Parenthèse de sang, Je, soussigné cardiaque* (1981), *Une Chouette petite vie bien osée* (1992) and *Qui a mangé Madame d'Avoine Bergotha* (1995), Michèle Rakotoson's *La Maison morte* (1990), Zadi Zaourou's *L'Œil* (1983), interrupted in performance by the police as an incitement to class hatred and a threat to public order, Ngandu Nkashama's *L'Empire des ombres vivants* (1991) and *Bonjour monsieur le ministre* (1983), the latter published under his pseudonym, Elimane Bakel, Jean Mba Evina's *Politicos* (1974) and Werewere Liking's *Un Touareg s'est marié à une Pygmée: épopée mvet pour une Afrique présente* (1992), among so many others.

Theatre and society

Although history and politics have hugged the attention of Francophone drama since independence they have not been among its earliest preoccupations. As was observed earlier, most of the school drama produced in the 1930s at William Ponty in Senegal, and later in the cultural centres and social clubs of the so-called 'évolués' sectors of the Francophone population, was exclusively devoted to the dramatisation of social manners and custom – documenting them, almost ethnologically in the case of the William Ponty pieces, and criticising them in the name of progress or Christian morality in the theatre of the emerging middle class. Even if perhaps less visible, this concern with social custom continued into the post-colonial years, producing, from a strictly theatrical point of view, some of the best works by Francophone dramatists. Unlike the historical or political dramas, which in their earnestness tend towards the preachy and the bombastic in sentiment and language, the social comedies are livelier and less oppressive. They pay closer attention to dramatic language and situation, to the construction of suspenseful plots, to the incongruous in human behaviour. Their characters are not exalted humourless figures, but conmen, corrupt civil servants and businessmen, sleek city gents, superstitious country folk, pretentious 'have-been-tos' and charlatan traditional doctors. Plays in this category include Guillaume Oyono-Mbia's *Trois prétendants . . . un mari* (1964), *Notre fille ne se mariera pas* (1973) and *Le Train spécial de son excellence* (1979), Jean Pliya's *La Secrétaire particulière* (1973), Protais Asseng's *Trop c'est trop* (1986), Guy Menga's *La Marmite de Koka-Mbala* (1966) and *L'oracle* (1969), Bernard Dadié's *Monsieur Thogo-Gnini* (1970) and *Papassidi maître-escroc* (1975) and Senouvo Zinsou's *On joue la comédie* and *La Tortue qui chante* (1984). Other social dramas deal not so much with custom and conduct, but with the pressing social issues of poverty, disease, gender inequality and economic exploitation. Among these works are Moussa Konaté's *L'or du diable* (1985) and *Le Cercle au féminin* (1985), David Jaomanoro's *La Retraite* (1990), Sylvain Bemba's *Une Eau dormante* (1975), Koulsky Lamko's *Comme des flèches* (1996) and Werewere Liking's *Puissance de Um* (1979) and *Singué Mura* (1990).

Francophone theatre and the search for a new poetics
In an interview in 1989 Werewere Liking observed about the dominant French-inspired theatre of her colleagues:

> C'était trop occidental! . . . [O]n aurait dit que leur créativité était bloquée: ils n'osaient pas ajouter un iota – sauf peut-être quelques chansons et un peu de danse. Sur le plan purement théâtral, il n'y avait pas une réflexion basée sur un apport personnel, ou un apport de notre culture d'origine . . . Je me suis mis en tête d'essayer de voir s'il n'y avait pas des expressions qui pouvaient correspondre à ce que c'était que le théâtre dans nos traditions . . . Je commençais à observer les rituels . . . je cherchais la théâtralité à l'intérieur.
>
> (Hawkins, 1992: 235–6)

> It was too Western! It was as if their creativity was blocked: they did not dare add an iota – except perhaps some songs and the odd dance. From the point of view of pure theatre, it contained nothing by way of a personal contribution or a contribution from our traditions . . . I set myself the task of finding out whether no idioms existed that could be equivalent to what was theatre in our traditions . . . I began to observe rituals . . . to search for the theatrical in them.

The search to which Liking refers is arguably the single most important development in Francophone African theatre since the 1980s. Whilst the earlier French-inspired tradition was content to borrow *aspects* of these traditions, the odd dance and song – mostly for reasons of local colour and (misconceived) cultural authenticity – the new theatre seeks to integrate them *organically* into its plays. Thus it systematically appropriates not just the structure, function and theatricality of the various examples of the various forms previously discussed, but also their physical acting style, with its emphasis on the actors' bodies, their improvisational style, collective creation and audience participation techniques, their integrated use of the plastic and performing arts and their non-illusionistic techniques. In other words, a play from the new theatre, such as Liking's *Une Nouvelle terre* (1980), Zadi Zaourou's *Le Secret des dieux* (1999) or Sonouvo Zinsou's *On joue la comédie* (1975), does not just borrow features from the *Ngué* initiation ritual of the Bassa of Cameroon, in the case of the former, the *didiga* hunter-narrative performance of the Bete of the Ivory Coast, of the second, and the Togolese concert party of the third. They *are* an ngué, a didiga, a concert party in modern French dress, or at least aspire to the condition of those forms.

The shift to a performance-based as opposed to a text-based, theatre has also seen the emergence of a new figure on the Francophone scene, that of the playwright-director. Whilst most of the notable dramatists of the early period were just that, authors, many of those of the post-1980s theatre are also directors, whose private troupes, in spite of material problems, have been more than ephemeral entities. Examples of such playwright-directors and their troupes include Zadi Zaourou (Didiga Theatre), Werewere Liking (Ki-Yi Mbock), Sony Labou Tansi (Rocado Zulu theatre), Souleymane Koly (the Kotèba Ensemble), Prosper Kampaoré (Atelier théâtre Burkinabé) and Jean-Pierre Guingané (Théâtre de la Fraternité).

But what, it may be asked, is the significance of this return to theatrical roots by the above practitioners and, additionally, the likes of the Ivorian Niangoran Porquet (Kotchy, 1984: 241–3), or the Mauritanian Moussa Diagana of the *Légende du Wagadou vue par Sia Yatebere* (1990)? It is certainly not, in my view, a mere exercise in formal experimentation by playwrights in search of novelty or in the grip of nativist nostalgia. It is, among many things, the keen expression of a resistant cultural politics. By privileging hitherto marginalised forms of performance, the new drama is in fact promoting those forms, and by extension their custodians, the folk, as the repositories of 'authentic' African theatrical cultures. Central to the political project of the new Francophone theatre, then, is a contestation of the dominant culture of the westernised élites, seen as inauthentic because of its dependence on French culture.

African languages literary theatre

There exists in some Francophone countries, and distinct from African languages 'traditional', 'popular' and 'development' theatre, a *literary* theatre in African languages. In addition to that practised in ex-Belgian Congo and cited earlier, there is the example of Madagascar. Between 1922 and 1945, according to Rakotoson (1998), a scripted theatre in the Malagasy language flourished, complete with a varied repertoire and troupes, some of which, like Jeannette (named after its star actress), survived for seventy-five years. A mixture of the missionary-sponsored *konserta masina*, dramatised Bible stories interspersed with speeches and song, and the tradition of the French operette – a major early twentieth-century European entertainment activity in Madagascar – the theatre in Malagasy, a language reduced to writing by the London Missionary Society, 'produced over a thousand plays'. Set in the days of the by then overthrown monarchy, these plays, some of which continue to be performed, mostly dealt with the theme of 'forbidden love and wars' (Rakotoson, 1998: 50–1).

Whilst its production may not have been as abundant as that of Madagascar, Togo (a German colony until 1917) is the second of three former Francophone territories most often associated with an African-language literary theatre. According to Amégbléamé (1990) and Gbanou (1998), a religious literature in one of the country's languages, Ewe, was produced by local pastors as far back as 1849, but it was not until 1926, with the founding in London of the International Africa Institute, and the literature-in-African-languages competition that it organised, that a secular literature in Ewe was born (Gbanou, 1998: 63–4). The 1933 competition drew twenty-eight entries in Ewe alone, not to mention works in Ibo (Nigeria), Bulu (Cameroon) and Zulu (South Africa). The first prize went to a tragedy in Ewe, *Toko Atolia*, by Kwasi Fiawoo, who also became that language's most celebrated writer, with two more dramatic works in that language and two in English (Gbanou, 1998: 65). His prize-winning play was later translated, first into German and then in 1943 into English as *The Fifth Landing Stage*.

Problems and prospects

It is pointless to speculate on the long-term prospects of a self-sustaining French-language theatre in Africa. One major problem that this theatre faces is its near total dependence on foreign, especially French, assistance for almost all its needs: from acting spaces, actor training and festival participation to even faithful audiences – a situation that has led the French critic Françoise Ligier to raise the alarm that unless France readjusts its support, to 'focus on the theatrical activity undertaken in Africa for Africa', as opposed to that existing only for the French festival market, it will have contributed, ironically, to the conversion of the work of the most promising practitioners into tourist art, thereby making it irrelevant to their society. She observes: 'Le théâtre naît de la société qui le crée. Il y grandit, s'y enracine, y acquiert . . . sa spécificité. L'artiste et le public dialoguent librement, chacun créant l'imaginaire de l'autre' (The theatre springs from the society of which it is a part. It grows, sinks roots, and acquires its specificity from that society. The artist and the public enter into dialogue freely, each shaping the imagination of the other) (Ligier, 1993: 12).

The case of Sony Labou Tansi, examined in detail by Devésa (1996), is illustrative in this regard. In return for the help he received over a five-year period (1985–9), Labou Tansi was not only expected to write a play a year specifically for the Limoges festival; the play had, as part of the agreement with the French authorities, to be co-produced with a French director (see Baños-Robles, 1990: 137 on the agreements). Besides a certain loss of artistic freedom that came with the sponsorship he enjoyed and his elevation by French authorities as the successful face of France's cultural cooperation with Africa, Labou Tansi came to be perceived by his fellow Congolese as 'writing a theatre for the French, for Europeans' (Devésa, 1996: 192). Proof of the validity of this observation swiftly came when he fell out of favour with his French sponsors, who were disappointed that he did not conform to their expectations in his 1993 play *Monologue d'or et noces d'argent pour douze personnages* and roundly criticised him for being too political (Devésa, 1996: 193).

But beyond France, it is Francophone African governments that should shoulder the burden of supporting their theatre and its practitioners. For unless they do, the valiant efforts of a Jean-Pierre Guingané, who in 1996 built the Espace Culturel Gambidi in Burkina Faso, a private facility that includes a 600-seat theatre and actor-training facilities, or of a Werewere Liking, whose Villa Ki-Yi artists' commune in Abidjan – complete with a theatre building, weaving and tie-dyeing facilities, was founded in 1983 – will remain just that: efforts. And Francophone theatre will become, like the material economies of most African countries, an 'extraverted' activity: 'one entirely oriented towards the outside, subordinated to it, and organized to satisfy its needs' (Conteh-Morgan, 2001: 24).

Notes

1. Unless otherwise stated, translations from the original French are mine.
2. See, for example, Fiangor, who writes: 'la plupart des états africains aujourd'hui francophones le sont parce que la langue française demeure, tel un cordon ombilical jamais coupé ou du moins, mal coupé entre eux et la France' (1998: 31). Most Francophone African states are so described because the French language, like an umbilical cord, remains either uncut or badly cut.

3. I have italicised 'in European languages' to draw attention to the difficulties involved in using English-language genre terms such as 'spoken drama', 'dance theatre', and 'music theatre' to describe artistic phenomena that are differently apprehended and classified in the languages of the indigenous African cultures from which they spring. For an important theoretical consideration of this issue, see Yaï, 1999.

4. For a study of Congolese theatre see Nkashama, 1993 and Sang'Amin, 1989.

5. As a result of a convention between the Vatican and the Congo signed in 1906, education was 'entrusted mainly to the Missions' (Jadot, 1959: 16). The number of state schools in 1921 was 9, with 1,861 enrollees, as against 120 religious schools with 20,311 students. By 1940 the figure for mission schools had shot up to 5,156, with 246,404 pupils, as against only 15 for government schools with 4,188 pupils (Jadot, 1959: 16, 30).

6. *Jaama*, an Arabic word for social 'family' organizations, were founded in the mining areas to cater for the spiritual, social and leisure needs of migrant miners (Sang'Amin, 1989: 94).

7. This strategy partly explains the emergence in the Congo of the earliest Africanised Catholic mass, the 'Missa Luba', which (long before Vatican 2) used local languages and instruments in the celebration of the mass.

8. Historically, this massacre, preceded by that of Bagandan converts to Islam, took place in 1886 during the reign of Kabaka Mwanga. For fascinating details on religion and politics in the Buganda kingdom from the 1840s to the early 1900s, see Gikandi, 1998.

9. For a detailed exposition of this policy, see Béart, 1936–7: 11–14 and Warner, 1976.

10. A French Guyanese and colonial civil servant in Oubangui-Chari, René Maran won the Goncourt prize for his novel *Batouala* (1921), whose preface is a biting denunciation of colonial rule.

11. For published versions of these pieces, see the journal *L'Education Africaine* 1934, 1935, 1936 and 1937.

References and further reading

Acogny, Germaine. 1988. *Danse africaine*. Frankfurt-on-Main: Verlag Fricke.

Ager, Dennis. 1996. *'Francophonie' in the 1990s: Problems and Opportunities*. Clevedon: Multilingual Matters.

Akpaki, Roger. 1999. 'Regards croisés des pouvoirs et des populations: la fête annuelle dite Iru chez les Idaashas (République du Bénin)' in Odile Goerg, ed., *Fêtes urbaines en afrique: espaces, identités, pouvoirs*, Paris: Karthala.

Amégbléamé, Simon. 1990. 'L'Influence biblique dans la littérature ewe' in Janos Riesz and Alain Ricard, eds., *Semper Aliquid Novi. Littérature comparée et littératures d'afrique: mélanges offerts à Albert Gérard*, Tübingen: Gunter Narr Verlag.

Arnoldi, Mary, J. 1995. *Playing with Time: Art and Performance in Central Mali.* Bloomington: Indiana University Press.

Balandier, Georges. 1980. *Le Pouvoir sur scène.* Paris: Balland.

Banham, Martin, ed. 1998. *The Cambridge Guide to Theatre.* Cambridge: Cambridge University Press.

Banham, Martin and Wake, Clive. 1976. *African Theatre Today.* London: Pitman.

Baños-Robles, Bernard. 1990. 'Huit années de coopération au Congo'. *Notre Librairie,* 102.

Barber, K., Collins, John and Ricard, Alain, eds. 1997. *West African Popular Theatre.* Bloomington and Oxford: Indiana University Press and James Currey.

Beaumarchais, J.-P., Couty, D., and Rey, A., eds. 1994. *Dictionnaire des littératures de langue française.* 4 vols. Paris: Bordas.

Béart, Charles. 1936–7. 'Le Théâtre indigène et la culture franco-africaine'. *Education Africaine.*

Béart, Charles. 1960. *Recherche des éléments d'une sociologie des peuples africains à partir de leurs jeux.* Paris: Présence Africaine.

Béart, Charles. 1962. 'Les Origines du théâtre dans le monde; position actuelle du théâtre africain'. *Académie des Sciences d'Outre-Mer.*

Beik, Janet. 1987. *Hausa Theatre in Niger.* New York: Garland.

Belinga, Eno. 1978. *L'Epopée camerounaise: Mvet Moneblum ou l'Homme Bleu.* Yaoundé: Université de Yaoundé.

Blair, Dorothy. 1976. *African Literature in French.* Cambridge: Cambridge University Press.

Boiron, Chantal. 1993. 'L'Auteur et l'interprète, Souleymane Koly'. *Notre Librairie.*

Bonn, Charles and Garnier, Xavier, eds. 1999. *Littérature francophone: récits courts, poésies, théâtre.* Paris: Hatier.

Brink, J. 1978. 'Communicating Ideology in Bamana Rural Theatre Performance'. *Research in African Literatures.*

Calvet, Louis-Jean. 1974. *Linguistique et colonialisme: petit traité de glottophagie.* Paris: Payot.

Chemain, R. A. 1979. *Panorama critique de la littérature congolaise contemporaine.* Paris: Présence Africaine.

Chevrier, Jacques. 1984. *La Littérature nègre.* Paris: Nathan.

Chevrier, Jacques. 2001. 'Preface' in *L'Afrique noire et son théâtre au tournant du XXe siècle.* Paris: l'Harmattan.

Clark, Vévé. 1994. 'Performing the Memory of Difference in Afro-Caribbean Dance: Katherine Dunham's Choreography, 1938–87' in Geneviève Fabre and Robert O'Meally, eds., *History and Memory in African-American Culture,* Oxford: Oxford University Press.

Conteh-Morgan, John. 1994. *Theatre and Drama in Francophone Africa.* Cambridge: Cambridge University Press.

Conteh-Morgan, John. 2001. 'French Critics and Francophone African Theatre'. *Oeuvres & Critiques,* 26.1.

Cornevin, Robert. 1970. *Le Théâtre en Afrique noire et à Madagascar*. Paris: le Livre Africain.

Coulon, Virginie. 1994. *Bibliographie francophone de littérature africaine*. Vanves: EDICEF-AUPELF.

Coulon, Virginie. 1998. 'Le Théâtre de langue française de l'afrique noire'. *Palabres*, 2.

D'Aby, Amon. 1988. *Le Théâtre en Côte d'Ivoire*. Abidjan: CEDA.

Darkowska-Nidzgorski, Olenka. 1980. *Théâtre populaire des marionnettes en afrique sud-saharienne*. Bandundu, Zaire: Centre d'Etudes Ethnologiques.

Darkowska-Nidzgorski, Olenka and Darkowska-Nidzgorski, Denis. 1998. *Marionnettes et masques au coeur du théâtre africain*. Saint-Maur: Sepia.

Dauchez, Philippe. 1984. 'Une expérience en cours: le Kotéba thérapeutique'. *Notre Librairie*, 75–6.

Decock, Jean. 1968. "The *Théâtre Folklorique* du Mali'. *Arts Africains/African Arts* 1–3.

Delafosse, Maurice. 1916. 'Contribution à l'étude du théâtre chez les noirs'. *Annales et mémoires du comité d'études historiques et scientifiques de l'AOF*.

Delafosse, Maurice. 1929. *La langue mandingue et ses dialectes*. Vol. 1. Paris: Paul Geuthner.

Démougin, Jacques, ed. 1987. *Dictionnaire de la littérature française et francophone*. 3 vols. Paris: Larousse.

Desffontaines, T.-M. 1990. 'Théâtre-Forum au Burkina Faso et au Mali'. *Notre Librairie*, 102.

Devésa, Jean-Michel. 1996. *Sony Labou Tansi*. Paris: l'Harmattan.

Diawara, G. 1981. *Panorama critique du théâtre malien dans son évolution*. Senegal: Sankore.

Diop, Alioune. 1990. *Le Théâtre traditionnel sénégalais*. Dakar: Nouvelles Editions Africaines du Sénégal.

Edkvist, Ingela. 1997. *The Performance of Tradition: An Ethnography of Hira Gasy Popular Theatre in Madagascar*. Uppsala: Acta Universitatis Upsaliensis 23.

Fabian, Johannes. 1990. *Power and Performance: Ethnographic Exploration Through Proverbial Wisdom and Theater in Shaba, Zaire*. Madison: University of Wisconsin Press.

Fiangor, Roger. 1998. 'Ainsi naquit une dramaturgie africaine intellectuelle en afrique noire francophone'. *Palabres* (Théâtres d'Afrique et des Caraibes), 11.1–2 June.

Gbanou, Selom. 1998. 'Entre Aristote et la Bible: Toko Atolia, un exemple de tragédie en langue africaine'. *Palabres*, 11.1–2 June.

Gikandi, Simon. 1998. *Uganda's Katikiro in England*. Manchester: Manchester University Press.

Griaule, Marcel. 1938. *Masques Dogons*. Paris: Institut d'Ethnologie.

Guingané, Jean-Pierre. 1988. 'Théâtre et développement au Burkina Faso'. *Revue de la société d'histoire du théâtre*, 160.

Harper, Peggy. 1967. 'Dance in a Changing Society'. *Arts Africains/African Arts*, 1.1: 10–13, 76–7, 79–80.

Harris, Jessica. 1981. 'Toward a New Senegalese Theatre'. *Drama Review*, 25.4.

Hawkins, Peter. 1992. 'Un "néo-primitivisme" africain? L'exemple de Werewere Liking'. *Revue des Sciences Humaines*, 227.

Hourantier, Marie-José. 1977. 'La Danse initiatique Ozila'. *Présence Africaine*, 103.

Hourantier, Marie-José. 1984. *Du rituel au théâtre rituel*. Paris: l'Harmattan.

Hourantier, Marie-José, Schérer, Jacques, and Liking, Werewere, eds. 1979. *Du rituel à la scène chez les bassa du Cameroun*. Paris: Nizet.

Huizinga, J. 1955. *Homo Ludens. A Study of the Play-Element in Culture*. Boston: Beacon Press.

Imperato, Pascal J. 1970. 'The Dance of the Tyi Wara'. *Arts Africains/African Arts*, 4.1.

Imperato, Pascal J. 1971. 'Contemporary Adapted Dances of the Dogon'. *Arts Africains/African Arts*, 5.1.

Imperato, Pascal J. 2000. 'Two Worlds of Ciwara'. *Arts Africains/African Arts*, 33.2.

Iyandza-Lopoloko, Joseph. 1961. 'Bobongo: danse renommée des Ekonda'. *Musée Royal de l'Afrique Centrale*, 4.

Jadot, J. M. 1959. *Les Ecrivains africains du Congo-Belge et du Ruanda-Urundi*. Brussels: Académie Royale des Sciences Coloniales.

Jensen, Jan. 1998. 'Hot Issues: The 1997 Kamabolon Ceremony in Kangaba (Mali)'. *International Journal of African Historical Studies*, 31.2.

Jensen, Jan. 2001. 'The Sunjata Epic – The Ultimate Version'. *Research in African Literatures*, 32.1.

Jezequel, Jean-Hervé. 1999. 'Le "théâtre des instituteurs" en afrique occidentale française (1930–1950): pratique socio-culturelle et vecteur de cristallisation de nouvelles identités', in Odile Goerg, ed, *Fêtes urbaines en afrique: espaces, identités et pouvoirs*, Paris: Karthala.

Kazadi, Ntole. 1991. *L'Afrique afro-francophone*. Provence: Institut d'Etudes Créoles et Francophones, Université de Provence.

Keita, Fodéba. 1957. 'La Danse africaine et la scène'. *Présence Africaine*, 14–15.

Keita, Fodéba. 1965. *Aube africaine*. Paris: Seghers.

Kesteloot, Lilyan and Dieng, Bassirou, eds. 1998. *Les Epopées d'afrique noire*. Paris: Karthala.

Kirk-Greene, Anthony and Bach, Daniel, 1995. *State and Society in Francophone Africa since Independence*. New York: St Martin's Press.

Kotchy, Barthélémy. 1984a. *La Critique sociale dans l'œuvre de Bernard Dadié*. Paris: l'Harmattan.

Kotchy, Barthélémy. 1984b. 'New Trends in the Theatre of the Ivory Coast (1972–83)'. *Theatre Research International*, 9.3.

Kwahulé, Koffi. 1996. *Pour une critique du théâtre ivoirien contemporain*. Paris: l'Harmattan.

Labouret, Henri. 1927. 'Sur le théâtre soudanais'. *Anthropologie*, 37.

Labouret, Henri and Travélé, Moussa. 1928. 'Le Théâtre mandingue (Soudan français)'. *Africa.*

. 1941. *Paysans d'afrique occidentale.* Paris: Gallimard.

Laude, Jean. 1954. 'A l'origine du drame: fêtes magiques et religieuses en afrique'. *Théâtre Populaire,* 6.

Leloup, Jacqueline. 1983. 'La Naissance du théâtre en afrique: théâtre traditionnel ou pré-théâtre?'. *Recherche, Pédagogie et Culture,* 61 special issue, *Théâtres et contacts de cultures.*

Ligier, Françoise. 1983. 'La Politique de la stimulation. Théâtre et radio: une collaboration positive'. *Recherche, Pédagogie et Culture,* 61, special issue, *Théâtres et contacts de cultures.*

Ligier, Françoise. 1993. 'Lettre ouverte à Monique Blin'. *Notre Librairie.*

Liking, Werewere. 1987. *Marionnettes du Mali.* Paris: NEA-ARHIS.

Mabana, Kahiudi. 2002. *Des transpositions francophones du mythe de Chaka.* Bern: Peter Lang.

Manning, Patrick. 1988. *Francophone Africa 1880–1985.* Cambridge: Cambridge University Press.

Maran, René. 1921. *Batouala. Véritable roman nègre.* Paris: Albin Michel.

Meillassoux, Claude. 1964. 'The "koteba" of Bamako'. *Présence Africaine,* 52 (English edition).

Meillassoux, Claude. 1968. 'Les Cérémonies septennales du Kamabolon de Kaaba'. *Journal de la Société des Africanistes,* 38.

Midiohouan, Guy Ossito. 1994. *Du bon usage de la francophonie.* Porto-Novo: CNPMS.

Midiohouan, Guy Ossito. 1987/1988. 'Portée idéologique et fondements politiques de la Francophonie (vue d'afrique)'. *Peuples Noirs, Peuples Africains,* 59–62.

Morrison, J. 1991. 'Forum Theatre in West Africa: An Alternative Medium of Information Exchange'. *Research in African Literatures,* 22.3.

Niane, Djibril Tansir. 1960. *Soundjata, ou l'épopée mandingue.* Paris: Présence Africaine.

Nkashama, Pius Ngandu. 1993. *Théâtres et scènes de spectacle: études sur les dramaturgies et les arts gestuels.* Paris: l'Harmattan.

Picarazzi, Teresa. 2000. 'Italian African *meticciato artistico* in the Teatro delle Albe'. *Italica,* 77.2.

Porquet, Niangoret. 1978. *Mariam et griopoèmes.*

Prouteaux. 1929. 'Premiers essais de théâtre chez les indigènes de Côte d'Ivoire'. *Bulletin du Comité d'Etudes Historiques et Scientifiques de l'Afrique Occidentale Française.*

Rakotoson, Michèle. 1991. 'Le Hira Gasy: discours paysan ou ritual des rois?' *Théâtre-Sud,* 3.

Rakotoson, Michèle. 1998. 'Les Ancêtres du théâtre malgache'. *Palabres,* 2.1–2.

R.D. 1936. 'Fête d'art scolaire donnée par les élèves de l'école William Ponty', *Education Africaine.*

Ricard, Alain. 1975. 'Théâtre scolaire et théâtre populaire au Togo'. *Revue d'Histoire Littéraire de la France*, 1

Ricard, Alain. 1986. *L'Invention du théâtre. Le théâtre et les comédiens en Afrique*. Lausanne: L'Age d'Homme.

Saivre, Denise de. 1980. 'De Madagascar, un théâtre populaire: l'Hira-Gasy'. *Recherche, Pédagogie et Culture*, 49.

Sang'Amin, Kapalanga. 1989. *Les Spectacles d'animation politique en République du Zaire*. Ferme de Blocry: Cahiers Théâtre Louvain.

Schérer, Colette, ed. 1996. *Catalogue des pièces de théâtre africain en langue française*. Paris: Presses de la Sorbonne Nouvelle.

Schérer, Jacques. 1992. *Le Théâtre d'afrique noire francophone*. Paris: Presses Universitaires de France.

Schipper, Mineke. 1984. *Théâtre et société en afrique*. Abidjan-Dakar: NEA.

Sinaba, Fadjigi. 1990. 'Théâtre moderne et Kotéba: une interview collective des comédiens du Théâtre National du Mali'. *Théâtre-Sud*, 1.

Soyinka, Wole. 1993. 'Sur la langue française, sur la francophonie, sur Limoges et sur le théâtre'. *Notre Librairie* (Créateurs africains à Limoges).

Thiérou, Alphonse. 1983. *La Danse africaine, c'est la vie*. Paris: Maisonneuve & Larose.

Traoré, Bakary. 1958. *Le Théâtre négro-africain et ses fonctions sociales*. Paris: Présence Africaine.

Turner, Victor. 1968. *The Drums of Affliction*. Oxford: Clarendon Press.

Vincileoni, Nicole. 1986. *L'Œuvre de B. B. Dadié*, Issy les Moulineaux: Classiques Africains.

Warner, Gary. 1976. 'Education coloniale et genèse du théâtre néo-africain d'expression française'. *Présence Africaine*, 97.

Waters, Harold. 1988. *Théâtre noir: encyclopédie des pièces écrites en français par des auteurs noirs*. Washington, DC: Three Continents Press.

Wooten, Stephen. 2000. 'Antelope Headdresses and Champion Farmers: Negotiating Meaning and Identity through the Bamana *Ciwara* Complex'. *Arts Africains/African Arts*, 33.2.

Wurtz, Jean-Pierre and Thfoin, Valérie. 1996. *Guide du théâtre en afrique et dans l'Océan indien*. Paris: Afrique en Créatios.

Yaï, Olabiyi. 1999. 'Tradition and the Yoruba Artist' *Arts Africains/African Arts*, 32.1.

Zahan, Dominique. 1960. *Sociétés d'initiation Bambara, Le N'Domo, le Koré*. Paris: Mouton.

Zahan, Dominique. 2000. 'The Two Worlds of Ciwara'. *Arts Africains/African Arts*, 33.2.

Zimmer, Wolfgang. 1995. *Catalogue des pièces de théâtre africain en langue française*. Paris: Presses de la Sorbonne Nouvelle.

4 Anglophone West Africa

Nigeria

DAPO ADELUGBA AND OLU OBAFEMI, WITH
ADDITIONAL MATERIAL BY SOLA ADEYEMI

Nigeria has a long theatre history, reaching back to the numerous ceremonies, religious rituals and community festivals that define the existence of the people. The cycle of human life is marked by a succession of these events, from domestic occasions to the elaborate procession of ritual forms. The tradition of theatrical performances, in both form and substance, evolved from these festivals and rituals. To study the development of Nigerian theatre over the years, therefore, requires an understanding of the nature of the Nigerian societies, the customs, the social phenomena, structures and values that characterise the societies, and the various cultural identities of the people. However, because the cultural manifestations and the theatrical forms and substance are so involved, tracing the historical development of Nigerian theatre is bound to be complex. Nevertheless, an authentic historical study of Nigerian arts and of Nigerian theatre from the pre-colonial periods is a feasible project.

Nigeria is the most populous country in Africa, with one of the largest land areas. It is a country of great diversity because of the many ethnic, linguistic and religious groups that live within its borders. Oral traditions, archaeological surveys and written documentation establish the existence of dynamic societies with advanced social systems in the present Nigeria dating back to the dawn of modern history. A number of ancient kingdoms developed in the area that is now Nigeria, many of them important cultural and trading centres. In parts of Nigeria, archaeologists have found stone tools, human skeletons, rock paintings and other remains of prehistoric settlements that are 40,000 years old. The clay figures produced by the Nok civilisation (about 500 BC to AD 200) that flourished in what is now central Nigeria are among the oldest known examples of African sculpture. There were early kingdoms, such as Kanem, which developed in the Chad area during the AD 700s. By the 1300s, Bornu (now called Borno) had become the political centre of the kingdom. The Kanem–Bornu kingdom traded with countries in Africa, Asia and Europe. In the south, the Yoruba people had established an important cultural centre at Ife as early as AD 1000. The Yoruba from Ife later founded states in various parts of the surrounding territory. The most important of these was the kingdom of Oyo, which extended into what is now the country of Benin during the 1700s.[1] The importance of this kingdom is reflected in its highly evolved social and political systems, which included the promotion of cultural performances, some of which are documented in the diaries of explorers Richard Lander and Hugh Clapperton.[2]

The Nigerian economy is chiefly agrarian, though the country is a major producer and exporter of petroleum products. It is a leading producer of cocoa, groundnuts, palm oil and cotton. Like most African states, Nigeria was a colony (with some areas designated as 'protectorates') of Britain from the late nineteenth century until gaining independence in 1960.

Claims can fairly be made for an ancient ancestry for Nigeria's fine and performing arts. However, the rest of this discussion will concentrate on the more recent history, where evidence is more secure.

Nigeria's performance spaces are a *mélange* of traditional and modern heritages, architecturally and in terms of content, styles, genres and forms. There are proscenium theatres, arena theatres, thrust theatres and theatres-in-the-round. Whilst there are indoor theatres in large numbers, open air performances are feasible during most of the dry season and parts of the rainy season in a two-season climate such as Nigeria enjoys. There are musical dramas, dance dramas, acrobatic and other displays, and both indigenous and foreign plays are regularly produced. Nigerian theatre is informed by a complex integration of form and function.

Traditional Nigerian theatre

An unending debate continues over what is the essential Nigerian drama. Beyond the understanding of the existence in most Nigerian societies and communities of a theatrical tradition, whose auto-chthonous roots are found in numerous sacred rituals and festivals, there is no definitive canon of the Nigerian theatre. Even from the perspectives of the more known, being documented, of the indigenous, traditional theatres in Nigeria, there are no consistent or uniform modes of description for a 'Nigerian theatre'. However, it has been established that a popular theatre tradition existed before colonial intervention on the Nigerian artistic scene. Such a popular tradition was found by Yemi Ogunbiyi as separate from the European popular theatre concept, where the popular theatre such as vaudeville, burlesque, circus and musical comedy is distinguished from what is considered high artistic theatre, unlike the 'complex' Nigerian form 'that involves an expression of physical pleasure and joy' (Ogunbiyi, 1981: 11). The popular traditional theatre includes the Ekpe festival as a religious festival and dance drama, the Bori spirit mediumship as ritual drama, the Alarinjo as traditional travelling theatre, the Adimu-Orisa (Eyo) funeral rites, the Gelede, the Kwagh-hir theatre, the Bornu puppet show, the Yankamanci Hausa comedy, the Ikaki Tortoise Masquerade, Ezeinogbe: Igbo masquerade play, the Okun-Okura Masquerade Ensemble, the Urhobo Udje Dance Performance and the Ozidi Saga. Invariably, the emerging scenario is the absence of a stable aesthetic criterion for placing or defining traditional theatre in Nigeria.

Perhaps the most conspicuous area of controversy is in the determination and classification of these performances as ritual or as drama. These debates have been articulated in the annals of theatre scholarship in Nigeria and require only an informative summary here. The most canvassed evolutionary deduction for Nigerian traditional theatre is that it originated out of ritual performances, that is, as a transmutation of ritual into entertainment. Using the seven-day-long Edi festival of Ile-Ife as a benchmark, Ola Rotimi draws a distinction between the ritual aspect and the dramatic displays, while highlighting the gradual metamorphosis that takes place in the process. Echeruo, writing on the dramatic limits of Igbo ritual, lends credibility to this deduction by outlining the clear sequence of dramatic events in Igbo myth, ritual and drama that incorporates 'elements of song, dance, and costuming which in various combinations have resulted . . . as heroic drama, burlesque, satire and ribald comedy' (Echeruo, 1981: 137). Yoruba traditional travelling theatre (also known as *Alarinjo* or *Eegun Alare*) is one of the most reliable aesthetic formats of the Nigerian theatre – one which perceives theatre as growing out of and along with ritual (Adedeji, 1971: 375). The Alarinjo itinerant professional theatre exhibits three developmental stages of ritual, festival and theatre – espousing the above evolutionary trend – from about the fourteenth century, when Sango, the deified Alaafin of Oyo, according to oral history, founded the ancestor worship (*Egungun*) festival to honour his departed father. The festival was formalised two centuries later into a seasonal lineage festival of specialised dance displays. These were then refined into purely entertainment guilds, as professional Yoruba theatre. The transformation, which is regarded as the quintessential evolution of Nigerian traditional theatre, needs expanding upon.

When Alaafin Ogbolu became king of Oyo in 1590, the capital city had been removed from Katunga to Oyo Ighoho due to successful incessant attacks by a predatory army. Ogbolu resolved to move the seat of government back to Katunga, but most of the people did not support the idea – most had been born in exile and some still remembered the anguish suffered from the attacks. Another reason why the people did not want to leave Igboho – and perhaps the most convincing reason advanced – is that Igboho was by then well settled and securely fortified. More so, it is not too distant from the banks of the River Niger and the people had developed good trading links with the Borgu and Nupe tribes further north. Leading the vanguard of the opposition was the king's council in chamber, the six high-ranking chiefs known as the Oyo Mesi, led by the Alapinni, who was also the representative of the Egungun cult. Customarily, emissaries would have to be sent to the old site of the capital city for reconnaissance, but the Oyo Mesi sent, ahead of the king's emissaries, six ghost-mummers to frighten them off the site, effectively convincing the king that the ancestors and the gods were not in support of the relocation. The ghost-mummers sent by the Oyo Mesi each represented a councillor – the albino (Alapinni), the leper (Asipa), the hunchback (Basorun), the prognathous (Samu), the cripple (Akiniku) and the dwarf (Laguna). These stock characters succeeded in frightening away the king's advance party (Smith, 1988: 33). The royal cymbalist, Ologbin Ologbojo, himself a member of the Egungun cult, advised the king to send six famous and trustworthy hunters to investigate the situation at Katunga. The hunters captured the ghost-mummers, who were brought to the palace where they became entertainers under Ologbin Ologbojo. It is related that the first public performance they had, with the Oyo Mesi present, was the enactment of the story of the Ghost Catcher (Adedeji, 1981: 223).

Adedeji records that Katunga was reoccupied in about 1610, and by the middle of the seventeenth century the ghost mummers had become well established at the king's court. The group also took part in the annual Egungun festival and became variously known as 'Oje' or 'Egungun apidan' (magic-performing masquerade). Nevertheless, the graduation to Alarinjo performers did not occur until Ologbin Ologbojo's son, who was born half-ape, half-human, sought to disguise his features. This son, Olugbere Agan, with the costume and wooden facemask built for him, made a career as a costumed actor and a strolling player (Adedeji, 1981: 224). Thus began the Alarinjo theatre.

Gradually, several new troupes developed outside the lineage of Olog-bojo, after the fashion of Alarinjo. By the first half of nineteenth century there already existed such troupes as Aiyelabola, Agbegijo, Ajangila, and Ajofeebo (those who dance for white men), the troupe that entertained Clapperton and Lander in 1826, according to oral history. By this time also, the repertoire of the troupes had increased and improved to the level of professionalism. They still participated in the annual Egungun festival, but their performances now became increasingly structured towards entertaining people on non-festival days, particularly at secular ceremonies such as child-naming, funerals and weddings. They also became itinerant. With this development, Alarinjo became a theatrical art and the increased professionalism improved the troupes' performances. Their method of presentation in the first half of the nineteenth century became defined. A performance usually started with songs and drumming and acrobatic displays, which heralded the troupe to a town. On the day of a performance, the drummers, singing and chanting, accompanied the actors around the town. They ended up at the market square, where performances were usually staged. The performances were generally more spectacle than sketches, because the main intention of a troupe was to entertain first before making social or political comments.

A performance usually started with the ritualistic *ijuba* or a sort of opening glee that also recited the *oriki* of the troupe and which 'apart from clarifying the role of the dramatist in society, reveals the relationship between the performer's art and the import of what he communicates' (Adedeji, 1969: 52). This was followed by the dance, divided into two parts – a ritual dance to honour the notable deities and divinities worshipped in the town, and a social dance which was invariably the dance steps in current fashion – and lastly, the drama, which consisted of two genres – spectacle and revue. Adedeji, commenting on the genres, states: 'The dramatic spectacles are designed to meet religious objectives and are based on Yoruba myths and totems. The revues are sketched out as components on the state of, or happenings in, Yoruba society. In both types satire is a theatrical element' (52). The ending of the performance, the finale, consisted of a valedictory song and dance.

The conclusion here is that the masque-dramaturge as a courtly and then popular theatrical form comprising song, dance, music, costume and spectacle emerged in a stage-by-stage process from ritual, festival and theatre. This kind of metamorphosis is likely to hold true for the other ethnic theatres if and when their histories are properly researched and documented. In essence, the varying categorisations of indigenous theatres into dramatic phenomena, pre-theatrical modes, emerging drama when expanded into a story and endowed with mimetic impulse, underscore the essence that ritual, as a universal phenomenon, shares the dynamic attribute of drama as essentially communal performance.

In sum, the dominant informing aesthetic of Nigerian traditional theatre, long established in the pre-literate, pre-colonial indigenous tradition, and one which summarises the basic taxonomic propositions in modern scholarship of Nigerian theatre, is the concept of *total theatre*. In many of the Nigerian ethnic theatres, dialogue or dramatic narrative has evolved. Studies of Ikaki of the Kalabari, Alarinjo and Eegun Okura of the Okun-Yoruba, Kwagh-hir of the Tiv and, especially strikingly, the Ekong of the Ibibio, reveal that from the preparatory stage of mask-sculpting, through rigorous and painstaking rehearsals to staging, an aesthetic of robust, fully-fledged theatre evolved from the people's tradition, and this has been recreated, transposed and crystallised on the contemporary Nigerian stage. The traditional theatre remained dominant in this form until the advent of the colonial period in the late nineteenth century.

The cultural nationalist phase (1860–1944)

Cultural nationalism emerged with the resistance to the performance modes of the European churches, whose firm ideological and utilitarian purpose was to use the theatre, in this case European concerts and Christian cantatas, as an entertainment medium to 'humanise' and Christianise the educated native élite. This was achieved through the rejection of African cultural mores, values and beliefs, including every form of entertainment. British colonialism and the Church Missionary Society (CMS) introduced a policy of producing an élite class of leaders for the Church and for the social and commercial scenes. The first batch of leaders was drawn essentially from the settler-population and comprised the offspring of repatriated slaves, immigrants from the freed slave colony of Sierra Leone, later to be joined by Brazilian immigrants. They had received western education and thus the majority of them uncritically absorbed the paternalistic notion of the inviolability of the tenets and models of western culture and civilisation as represented by Christianity. They were, in the memorable words of E. A. Ayandele, 'mentally, religiously and culturally part of the British Empire . . . as they had all originally accepted without questioning the western version of Christianity, had adopted European names in favour of African ones, [and] donned European dress' (Ayandele, 1974: 19). Thus, the CMS,

Wesleyans, Baptists, the Catholic Mission and the Methodist Missionary Society equated western civilisation with Christianity and morality with spirituality according to Christian tenets, all of which formed the project of the educational programme of the emergent African élite. On 24 October 1866 the first concert programme was organised by members of a 'social and cultural centre for public enlightenment, dedicated to the promotion of the arts, science and culture', the Academy, whose object was to modernise Lagos society (Ogunbiyi, 1981: 17). The concert was organised under the patronage of influential Lagos élites Bishop Samuel Ajayi Crowther, J. P. L. Davies, J. A. Otunba-Payne, Charles Foresythe, Robert Campbell and others. The model of the concert was European and the audience was drawn significantly from the emigrant élite community of Sierra-Leoneans, Brazilians, Europeans and a minority, unlettered indigenous Lagosians. Other concerts mounted by various other groups and modelled after the Victorian music hall of songs, revues, sketches, recitations and glees, followed in rapid succession.

One outcome of these largely mission-owned concerts and musicals was the unwitting development of a cultural nationalist programme by the emerging black élite in Lagos. In the last decades of the nineteenth century and the first decades of the twentieth century the proliferation of groups and the organisation of concerts led to a rivalry among the various groups and church missions, since the concerts were central to both the doctrinal and convert-seeking aspirations of the churches. To win converts, each group started pandering to the traditional theatrical taste of the public. The Protestant Mission of West Africa actively encouraged the inclusion of items of West African life – indigenous songs and language, drums and gongs, native dances and gestures, and experimentation with indigenous materials. Other missions found these, according to the *Lagos Observer*, a detestable exhibition of low forms of heathenism and thus sermonised against them. As Gbileka observed, the conscious infusion of indigenous materials from the Ogboni cult[3] by the 'secessionist churches', especially the performances by the Ake Church Choir of the Ake Mission, amounted to a 'belligerent brand of cultural nationalism (which) encouraged native drama and gave it a purposeful sense of direction' (Gbileka, 1997: 10). Such was the seriousness of the indigenisation performance programme of the Ake School of Entertainment in 1894 that a critical observer noted that the drama 'showed the real state of the town at present and one would fancy himself as if he really were in a true Ogboni Assembly' (cited in Leonard, 1967: 2). This growing cultural nationalism found a more vigorous expression with the

emergence of the small, well-educated and cultural élite after the establishment of indigenous churches, starting with the successful breakaway of the
native Baptist Church from its parent body in Europe in 1888. The new
churches promoted the culture of the African race. The Brazilian Dramatic
Company, with members of the Lagos élite such as Herbert Macaulay, also
took an active and acknowledged role in the growth of the entertainment
industry at this stage.

In 1889 schoolteachers from various denominations held meetings, demanding the development of Yoruba literature in standard Yoruba orthography, the shedding of European garments in Lagos and the adoption of
native costumes, even as they furthered the cause of Christianity and western
education (Ayandele, 1974). They gently criticised the habit of the uncritical
imitation of western values and codes and advocated the essence of indigenous modes of thought and conduct. This immediately raised the question
of self-reliance – the provision of public staging arenas where indigenous
performances could take place without hindrance or foreign censure. Unfortunately, for decades, this demand for community performance structures
remained unheeded, as the government evaded the expressed need to provide
for the cultural and intellectual requisites of Lagos.

Of scenography, theatre structure, stage lighting, set and other theatre
resources, there was nothing but makeshift staging. At the close of the
nineteenth century there was no electricity in Lagos. Performances were held
with hanging lanterns and Chinese lamps. Apart from productions such as the
annual Coker concerts produced by Robert A. Coker, which were reported
as being well lit with variegated lamps, most productions during this period
were staged with limited accessories and effects. Indeed, because of the
government's lukewarm attitude to the entertainment requirements of the
city, only the concert tradition initiated and executed by the tiny bourgeois
élite, the Victorian Lagosians, provided any form of audience relaxation and
amusement for the rapidly emerging cosmopolis. It was through the efforts
of this élite class and a handful of Europeans that the Glover Memorial
Hall was built and declared open by Governor McGregor and his wife in
1899. The concerts and entertainments that blossomed in the 1880s were
performed in other public buildings such as the Phoenix at Tinubu Square,
the Lagos Club House, the European Club House and the Academy on
Awolola Street, Lagos. Eventually, the concerts, as the main manifestation
of colonial theatre in Nigeria, declined, as they were unable to evolve an
authentic Nigerian character. The élites such as Herbert Macaulay and his

peers, hitherto the supporters of these concerts, became more politically and economically committed, and the concerts ended until the emergence of the Yoruba Travelling Theatre in the mid-1940s.

The demise of colonial theatre and the emergence of the renascent, otherwise described as native, Nigerian drama coincided with the intensification of racial discrimination in the Breadfruit CMS Church in Lagos and the eventual secessionist movements resulting from the combative brand of cultural nationalism among African élite Christians. The direct outcome of this radical development was the establishment of the Bethel African Church in 1901. Secessionist churches and, more pertinently, the Abeokuta Mission, which actively encouraged the syncretic dimension of the theatre, gave form and purpose to the rise of the native drama tradition in Nigeria. They also, in a significant way, began the active cultivation of an indigenous theatre audience, as they mobilised Muslims and practitioners of African religion to find meaning, purpose and educational value in a brand of concerts that were heavily indigenised. Yoruba farces built around the concept of the Ogboni cults were being staged by the Ake School of Entertainment by 1894. This awareness, followed by a proliferation of secessionist churches in Lagos, numbering some fourteen by 1917, emboldened the growth of an authentic, firmly rooted Yoruba native drama in the early decades of the twentieth century. African songs, chants, dance and music became regular service components of the Protestant churches. This is arguably the beginning of the syncretic theatre aesthetic that has characterised not only the popular Yoruba theatre tradition of the forties, fifties, sixties and seventies, but also the succeeding literary theatre of contemporary Nigeria largely established by Wole Soyinka, J. P. Clark and later Ola Rotimi, Wale Ogunyemi and the subsequent second generation of Nigerian dramatists of the emergent radical tradition.

From 1894, when the Egbe Ife Drama Group produced *King Elejigbo and Prince Abeje of Kontagora* written by D. A. Oloyede, one of the first examples of truly Nigerian drama, native drama gained an appreciable foothold. The production was sponsored by the Bethel African Church and first performed at the church's schoolroom, before receiving a more public staging at the newly opened Glover Memorial Hall in 1904. The group went on to stage other plays such as *The Jealous Queen of Oyo* (1905) and *Penelope* (1908), all at the Glover Memorial Hall. These productions acquired the form and structure of the contemporary well-made play – being divided into scenes and acts, with themes derived from Yoruba folklore and oral narrative motifs.

By 1912 the secularisation of theatrical entertainment in southern Nigeria was sufficiently advanced for the colonial government to gazette a 'Theatre and Public Performance Regulations Ordinance', which required that performing groups obtain a licence before going public (Soyinka, 2002: 429). The climax of the achievement of popular native drama came in the thirties and forties, with productions by celebrated composers led by A. B. Davies, who was later joined by other skilled composers such as G. T. Onimole, A. A. Layeni and H. A. Olutoye. With the arrival of Chief Hubert Ogunde in 1944, with the richness and virtuosity of his stagecraft and the popularity of his early plays, such as *The Garden of Eden and The Throne of God*, indigenous drama, generally referred to as Yoruba operatic (travelling) theatre, became a veritable and established theatre tradition in Nigeria. This was in spite of the ravaging impact of the First World War in the intervening years, which destabilised both the fervour and the spirit of black cultural nationalism and essence.

Modern Nigerian theatre: travelling theatre (1944 onwards)
From the premise of total theatre aesthetics described above, we go to the specifics of the Yoruba operatic theatre, which scholars such as J. A. Adedeji (1968), Biodun Jeyifo (1984), Olu Obafemi (1996) and Karin Barber (1997) have extensively researched. These include its part chant, part song, part dialogue nature, its closeness to its Renaissance-derived European 'ancestry', with its librettos, arias and scores, its spectacle, dramatic and theatrical flavour, and robust audience participation. There is also its informal/improvisational nature and its evolution as an art form. However, more important is the sociology and economics of its emergence. Karin Barber states that the Yoruba travelling theatre 'open[s] a window onto popular consciousness that is unique in its detail and clarity', revealing 'the anxieties, preoccupations and convictions that underpin ordinary people's daily experience' (Barber, 1986: 6). The totality of the character and consciousness of travelling theatre can best be summarised through a brief survey of the vista of its major practitioners, led by its proponent, Hubert Ogunde, and his colleagues/successors, Duro Ladipo, Kola Ogunmola, Moses Olaiya, Oyin Adejobi, Ade Afolayan (Ade Love), Lere Paimo, Ishola Ogunsola and more than two hundred practitioners of the fast-eclipsing Yoruba travelling theatre between 1944 and the mid-eighties.[4] We have earlier identified its formative inheritance of Christian/western educational values and theatrical models, as well as the indigenous folkloric performance tradition and worldview of

the Yoruba. All these aspects have influenced the essential content, arts and design of the theatre. The second formative factor is bread-and-butter motivation – the need to run a professional theatre that is economically viable, a professional theatre which supports the extended family. The demand for a theatre which reaches and appeals to the taste of its intended audience necessitates copious borrowing from the Yoruba tradition in terms of subject matter and form, in order to sustain a professional theatre distinguished by the personality and entrepreneurial flair of the individual artist.

The initial aesthetic format of this theatre as composed by Hubert Ogunde from 1944 was a syncretisation of the Native Air Theatre's disposition of employing Yoruba cultural adjuncts with Yoruba music and dances. The Aladura movement, one of the secessionist churches that grew out of the cultural Renaissance of the late nineteenth century, used theatre to propagate its doctrines, 'basing church plays on stories taken from the Bible and setting them to music and dance' with a uniquely innovative Yoruba cultural influence (Ogunbiyi, 1981: 22). This was the beginning of the Native Air Opera in 1933, a movement that had a significant impact on the development of the Yoruba travelling theatre pioneered by Hubert Ogunde. The Yoruba travelling theatre, in structure, is very close to the Alarinjo theatre. As in the latter, a performance consists of an opening glee, a spectacular parade of dance and songs by chorus dancers led by a lead singer, who ultimately is the troupe's leader, followed by a more elaborate dance, often indistinguishable from the opening glee, and lastly, the drama. A closing glee usually concludes a performance. The dramaturgy assimilated the Alarinjo masque festival form and anticipates the total theatre aesthetics of the future drama of Nigeria. It consists of a dynamic interplay of the visual, verbal and kinetic elements of music, dance, poetry and songs, with invited audience participation, as in the traditional festival theatre. The structure of the traditional travelling theatre – the opening glee, the play proper and the closing glee – is the major aesthetic plank of Ogunde's theatre. This has been greatly emulated by the other proponents of the Yoruba operatic (travelling) theatre.

Ogunde's earliest plays, such as *The Garden of Eden and The Throne of God* (1944), exemplify this Yoruba travelling theatre structure. The plays were initially sedentary in performance, staged as they were in the Church of the Lord in Lagos and officially premièred in the Glover Memorial Hall under the chairmanship of Nnamdi Azikiwe (who went on to become the first president of independent Nigeria). Following remarkable and serious research into the indigenous Yoruba culture, especially dance, music, folklore and

folk-tales, Ogunde's Africa Music Research Party crystallised oral performance forms into plays and revues to be produced on the conventional
stage. Beyond the aesthetic evolution is the socio-political dimension of the
plays, which were a conscious response to the growing nationalist struggle
for self-determination and independence at the time. Ogunde's theatre
immediately provided the cultural perspective of the National Youth Movement's cultural nationalism. *Africa and God* (1944), for instance, was the
answer to that movement's demand for African renascent mobilisation. *Strike
and Hunger* (1945) and *Worse than Crime* (1945) represented and were deeply
committed to the wave of cultural consciousness and political nationalism
immediately after the Second World War. *Strike and Hunger* pointedly exposed and satirised through theatre the tyranny and exploitation of foreign
domination in colonial Nigeria.

Ogunde acknowledged that his plays gained the mass appeal of the
indigenous Lagos population and created a pain in the hearts of the colonial
overlords, who read incitement into them (Lindfors, 1976: 246). Ebun Clark's
seminal study reveals numerous instances in which the politics and popularity
of Ogunde's theatre attracted discomfort, harassment and intimidation from
the agents of the colonial establishment, even immigration officers refusing
to issue him with a passport to go to England (Clark, 1979). Duro Ladipo,
who started his own theatre company in 1960, advanced on the tradition
Ogunde set and evolved a theatre that was more engrossed in oral traditions,
oral history and indigenous performance modes than the former. Indigenous
music with drums and flutes formed the major idiom of his theatre, while
oral poetry, such as chants and incantations embodying mythical, legendary
and historical materials provided the ideological and aesthetic constituent
of the drama. Popular examples from his *œuvre* are *Oba Ko So* and *Moremi*,
two plays from the 1960s.

Moses Olaiya, perhaps the sole survivor of the earlier travelling theatre
generation, used the medium of farcical comedy to engage his audience.
With materials derived from the socio-political scene, Olaiya developed the
indigenous Efe or Yeye comic theatre heritage into a well-defined blend of
traditional and western forms. Other notable practitioners of the travelling
theatre include Kola Ogunmola, who collaborated with the Ibadan School of
Drama in 1962 to produce *Lanke Omuti*, a stage adaptation of Amos Tutuola's
The Palmwine Drinkard, a production generally regarded as the beginning of
the experiment to blend the travelling theatre heritage with the western
literary tradition.[5]

The populist aesthetics of Yoruba travelling theatre performances was built on loose improvisation, the spectacles of props and costume, lively and engaging musical ensemble and the socio-political and cultural relevance of its content. Whilst many of the creations have since vanished due to the impermanence of non-scripted theatre, some of the productions have been able to survive in the Yoruba language as well as in foreign languages, through audio and cinematic recordings. A few of these have been transcribed and published as texts. For instance, Duro Ladipo's trilogy, *Oba Ko So*, *Moremi* and *Oba Waja* were translated and edited into *Three Nigerian Plays* by Ulli Beier (1967), and Kola Ogunmola's *Lanke Omuti* became *The Palmwine Drinkard* (1972). By the 1980s Yoruba travelling theatre's fortunes had fallen on hard times, as the practitioners began to take advantage of modern technologies in the arts to produce their drama as home videos. A commercially vibrant medium, cinematic/filmic art has captured the imagination of the practitioners of live theatre of the vernacular mode, as a result, from the late 1970s, of contact with and under the influence of cinema artists such as Ola Balogun. The practitioners of travelling theatre initially moved cautiously into film making and home video. Some of Ogunde's more successful plays were made into films. These include *Aiye* (1980), *Jaiyesimi* (1981) and *Aropin N'Teniyan* (1982). Moses Olaiya started by projecting cinema shots in episodes into this theatre, before going on to make full-length films in 1981, with *Orun Mooru* (*Heaven is Heated*). Others, which he embarked upon independently of Ola Balogun, who he had collaborated with initially, include *Aare Agbaye* (1983), *Ore Adisa* and *Ashale Gege* (*Pamperer of Prostitutes*). The latter two were home videos for private projection. Ade Afolayan, another prolific actor/director, transferred many of his stage productions, such as *Ija Ominira* and *Kadara*, into cinema and, later, home video. This incursion into home video by these actors/directors has largely contributed to the present decline of the once vibrant Yoruba travelling theatre.

Modern Nigerian theatre: the literary theatre tradition (1956 onwards)

A small but important link between indigenous travelling theatre and literary theatre exists in what has been termed the Onitsha market popular drama, a small segment of the Onitsha market literature, which flourished from the 1940s to the start of the Nigeria–Biafran war in 1967, when the literature seemed to have died. The literature, comprising revues, pamphlets, plays and novelettes, was written by a newly educated class of traders and artisans. The themes of the plays were wide-ranging, from religious and moral pieces, family squabbles and love and biographies of African leaders to purely didactic pieces. A popular drama of this mode is Ogali Agu Ogali's *Veronica my Daughter* (1957). This entertaining drama, like other examples from the Onitsha market literature, is written in a style chiefly influenced by classic literature, the Bible and Shakespeare. In language and style the plots are simple and loosely structured, but they serve as prototypes of James Ene Henshaw's better structured and more popular plays, plays now regarded as the first examples of conscious literary drama in Nigeria. Henshaw's plays include such titles as *This is Our Chance* (1956), *A Man of Character* (1956), *Children of the Goddess* (1964), *Medicine for Love* (1965) and *Jewels of the Shrine* (1965). He explored topical, socially and politically relevant and popular themes. The plots of the plays are simple, and the characters are straightforward and non-complex.

The origin of the contemporary literary theatre tradition must be traced to the drama of Henshaw, which Yemi Ogunbiyi has also described as a more refined form of Onitsha market literature in language and style. Henshaw's contributions, argues Ogunbiyi, 'lay, ultimately, in the area of example – the example of simple plays, simple characterization, of uncomplicated plot and even predictable resolutions' (Ogunbiyi, 1981: 27). Henshaw's plays are populist and filled a lacuna, a paucity of drama texts in Nigerian schools, before the arrival of more profound and serious dramatic texts from Wole Soyinka, J. P. Clark, Ola Rotimi and Zulu Sofola, playwrights who properly typify the first-generation Nigerian playwrights and dramatists of the English literary tradition. Therefore, if we take the year 1956 as the year of the birth of Nigerian drama in English, it is merely to acknowledge the significance of Ene Henshaw to the evolution of that tradition.

However, the year 1960 is generally accepted as the starting point of serious contemporary Nigerian drama. This was the year that Wole Soyinka founded his semi-professional troupe, The 1960 Masks, to produce plays and revues. The factors that led to the formation of this troupe include, to some extent, the theatrical activities at University College, Ibadan, from 1956 onwards, which had started creating an audience for literary drama within the university. The School of Drama itself was founded in 1962 under the direction of Geoffrey Axworthy, assisted by Martin Banham, but already, as part of the English Department, the duo had produced a number of plays, including Soyinka's *The Swamp Dwellers* and *The Lion and the Jewel* (in 1958). With a background of an indigenous vibrant theatre tradition and the

influence of a largely European expatriate community, many European plays
were also performed. Plays by Bernard Shaw, André Obey, Shakespeare,
Gogol, Anouilh, Ibsen, Fry, Pinero, Miller, Dryden, Webster, Frisch,
Mortimer, Wilder, Jonson, Yeats, Dürrenmatt, Congreve, Molière, Behan,
Beckett and Pinter (Layiwola, 2000: xiii). Gaining inspiration from the
academic atmosphere, a number of dramatic entertainment groups emerged,
creating a vibrant theatre culture in Ibadan. The groups included the Arts
Theatre Production Group (ATPG) and the University College Ibadan
Dramatic Society (UCIDS), both of which predate the School of Drama
and no doubt encouraged the establishment of the school and the development of the Arts Theatre. In 1959 the Players of the Dawn was formed as an
amateur group by graduates of the university residing in Ibadan. Most of the
members later formed the nucleus of Soyinka's 1960 Masks. A simultaneous
theatrical development in the eastern part of Nigeria was taking place at the
same time, in particular John Ekwere's Ogui Players, which later became the
Eastern Nigerian Theatre Group. Amateur theatre formations thus provided
the main source of growth of a literary theatre culture for this first theatre
generation. Much later, in 1968, Ola Rotimi began the Ori Olokun Theatre
at the University of Ife, around which a strong theatre culture rose in Ile-Ife.
This theatre was the only professional English-speaking theatre company. It
was also unique in its membership composition, drawing members from all
walks of life. The ideology behind the company 'affirmed the notion that the
struggle for a meaningful cultural liberation is not the exclusive concern of
any one select group in society, but rather that of all' (Ogunbiyi, 1981: 35).

Seeking to build on the achievement of the literary theatre and to link this
kind of theatre to the nascent popular Yoruba travelling theatre, the School
of Drama invited the actor/director Kola Ogunmola to take up a residency
in 1962. The resulting production at the Arts Theatre of *Lanke Omuti*, an
adaptation of Amos Tutuola's *The Palmwine Drinkard*, was immensely successful, not only for the spectacle but also for the opportunity it provided for
a future collaboration between the university and travelling theatre troupes.
Although Kola Ogunmola left the university after his residency, another
popular actor/director, Duro Ladipo, later took up a residence at the university's African Studies Department and remained there until his death in
1975.

Between 1957 and 1965 a robust ferment of intellectual activities developed at the university and in the city of Ibadan at the Mbari Centre,
from which the first serious and significant generation of literary dramatists,

including Wole Soyinka and J. P. Clark (now Clark-Bekederemo), started. The 1960 Masks staged the première of Clark's *Song of a Goat* at the Mbari in 1961 Other dramatists who started writing around this time include Wale Ogunyemi, Zulu Sofola and Samson Amali. We can locate Ola Rotimi within this generation, even though he was not part of the Ibadan experiment. A later generation of playwrights emerging from the Ibadan school includes Femi Osofisan and Bode Sowande, who served their apprenticeships, partly, in the theatre of Wole Soyinka in the early 1970s. A binding cord of literary theatre is their being deeply rooted in indigenous performance traditions, from which the total theatre format evolved. There is also the factor of their exposure and training in the western theatrical tradition and education, from which they have inherited the dual heritage of dramaturgy and the language of expression. All of these dramatists – from Soyinka to the generation of Nigerian playwrights of the 1990s, write and produce their plays in English, through which they engage in varying degrees of theatrical experimentation to attain greater accessibility to their literate and semi-literate audiences.

In terms of thematic concerns, many of the plays of this generation of dramatists are characterised by a conspicuous metaphysical presence, conscious individualism and a certain élitist and reformist perspective. Some of the plays satirise the dysfunctional political system and the leadership in Nigeria at that time. Some of the dramatists have resorted to myth and ritual for ideological and aesthetic inspiration. Plays of the period include Soyinka's *A Dance of the Forests* (arguably the forerunner of profound and seminal Nigerian drama, originally scripted and commissioned for the Nigerian independence celebration), *The Strong Breed* and *The Swamp Dwellers*, Clark's *Song of a Goat* and *The Masquerade*, Zulu Sofola's *Wedlock of the Gods* and *King Emene*, Wale Ogunyemi's *Obaluaye* and Ola Rotimi's *The Gods are not to Blame*.

The theatre of the succeeding generation of dramatists is defined by its materialist bent. Leaders of this second generation of literary dramatists, almost all of whom were trained outside Nigeria, are influenced by more universal thematic and dramatic considerations, especially Marxism and its ideology of dialectical materialism. At varying levels of accomplishment, the plays of these dramatists are best characterised as theatre of ideology and politics, committed to social and historical reconstruction through class struggle and a proletarian consciousness. Their theatre deals, more or less consciously, with urgent and topical political and social problems largely identifiable with the realities of a neo-colonial society, problems of poverty, violence, insecurity, disease, corruption and so on, with a certain idealistic proposition of alternative strategies of social transformation. The theatre therefore focusses on the plight of the people rather than the leaders, and on the underprivileged instead of the kings and princes of the society. Femi Osofisan, Bode Sowande, Kole Omotoso, Olu Obafemi, Tunde Fatunde, Tess Onwueme, Segun Oyekunle, Iyorwuese Hagher and Sam Ukala constitute the major entries here. The more notable of the plays include Femi Osofisan's *Once Upon Four Robbers*, *The Chattering and the Song*, *Morountodun* and *Tegonni: An African Antigone*, Bode Sowande's *Farewell to Babylon* and *Tornadoes Full of Dreams*, Olu Obafemi's *Nights of a Mystical Beast* and *Naira Has No Gender*, Tess Onwueme's *The Reign of Wazobia*, *Tell it to Women* and *Desert Encroaches*, Tunde Fatunde's *Oga Na Tief Man* and Sam Ukala's *Akpakaland*.

Popular theatre, or Theatre for development

The latest generation of theatre practitioners and playwrights that has emerged since the early nineties can best be described as producing protest theatre and dramas more in the line of theatre for development. This is due in part to the Samaru experiment of the Community Theatre Programme of the Ahmadu Bello University in Zaria. There is also a current worldwide developmental programme, championed by Non-Governmental Organisations (NGOs) and the various organs of the United Nations. Part of the historical context for this may be the collapse of the socialist world at the opening of the 1990s and the domination of world economies by the globalisation phenomenon. The new writing is not limited to the younger generation alone, however, as older writers including Wole Soyinka and John Pepper Clark-Bekederemo have continued to produce theatrical works that thematise the current developmental problems in Nigeria. Soyinka's *Opera Wonyosi* (1981), *The Beatification of Area Boy* (1995) and the more recent *King Baabu* (2002) and Clark-Bekederemo's *Bikoroa Plays*, *The Wives Revolt* (1985) and *All For Oil* (2001) are examples of some of the plays being produced by the older generation of dramatists. Although most of the new dramatists may have been influenced by recent events on the world stage, dramatists such as Soyinka had in fact used the Mbari Centre to produce the *Before the Blackout* revues in the 1960s and the University of Ife in the *Before the Blow Out* revues of the 1970s to protest against the irresponsibility of the then Nigerian political system. The new Nigerian dramas include Felix Okolo's *Mekunnu Melody* and *Walking Stick Evil* and Ben Tomoloju's *Jankariwo*.

In the 1970s and 1980s popular theatre developed around Ahmadu Bello University in Samaru, Zaria, and the popular theatre experiment took place with the rural, agrarian communities, addressing among other issues the problems of political awareness, land speculation and usurpation, health and medical matters. The community play-making projects, Wasan Maska, Wasan Samaru and Wasan Borno, were essential community theatre experimentations in Hausa land in the 1970s, 1980s and 1990s. These experiments spread into Benue State via the same Zaria scholars, namely Oga Steve Abah, Harry Iyovwuese Hagher, Salihu Bappa, John Sanni Illah and the students involved in the Samaru projects and Tar Ahura's significant efforts. In the 1990s major theatre for development projects were embarked upon in the south-west and south-east of the country, through the combined and individual efforts of the Nigerian Popular Theatre Alliance of Steve Abbah, Chuck Mike's Performance Studio Workshop (PSW) and Collective Artists, as well as the UNESCO/ University of Ibadan collaborative research projects based at the Theatre Arts Department of the University of Ibadan. Efforts continue to popularise community-specific theatre as an instrument of social mobilisation and conscientisation, via initiatives such as theatre for development, community theatre and theatre for integrated development.

Conclusion

Nigerian theatre is still developing towards being a people's theatre. However, the theatre is vibrant and eclectic. Although the proliferation of modern reproductive technology has focussed current theatre towards video production, and the myriad social problems may be preventing people from going to the theatre, theatre is still as popular as ever. The popular theatre – mainly unwritten, urban, improvised vernacular travelling theatre – is gradually merging with the literary theatre, in video productions and in the works of Femi Osofisan and younger university-trained dramatists such as Felix Okolo and Ben Tomoloju. The entrepreneurial theatre of the travelling troupes and the director's theatre of literary drama in essence has given rise to a new genre of theatre in the last two decades or so (in Nigeria since 1975, to be precise). This new mediatory, action theatre aims to offer an alternative approach and medium by which theatre can be of direct service to the marginalised urban and rural peasant masses. This tradition, which sees theatre as a forum of democratic struggle and which emphasises community, inter-personal participation in self-realisation has begun to gain a slow ascendancy in a large number of communities in Nigeria. It uses the existing and familiar performance forms of the various communities, such as songs, dances, music, storytelling, puppetry and mime, to both validate those cultural forms and to serve as an adequate instrument to bring about social change within these communities.

Notes

1. In formulating these ideas, we have been assisted by the research of an art historian, Professor Cornelius Oyeleke Adepegba of the University of Ibadan Institute of African Studies, who died in 2002. His chapter, 'Yoruba Art and Art History', in Deji Ogunremi and Biodun Adediran's edited work, *Culture and Society in Yorubaland* (1998) has been particularly useful. We have used *The World Book Encyclopaedia* (International) (1995), vol. XIV, N – O, page 206 advantageously in preparing this overview. Yemi Ogunbiyi's seminal treatise on Nigerian theatre, *Drama and Theatre in Nigeria: A Critical Source Book* (1981) has also proved invaluable.

2. The *Alaafin* (king) of Oyo sponsored a command performance on 22 February 1826 for the entertainment of British explorers Hugh Clapperton and Richard Lander and their party, to mark their seven-week stay in Old Oyo, the capital of the kingdom. See Clapperton, 1829: 53–6 and Lander, 1830: 115–21.

3. Ogboni is a secret society that recognises the earth as the 'mother' of all human beings. Members pledge solidarity to one another and to the earth, and support one another under *any* circumstances. The premise is that we are all going to 'sleep' in the earth.

4. For more on the rise and decline of the Yoruba travelling theatre, see Jeyifo, 1984.

5. For more on the experiment by the Ibadan School of Drama, now University of Ibadan Department of Theatre Arts, see below.

References and further reading

Adedeji, J. A. 1969. 'The Alarinjo Theatre: The Study of a Yoruba Theatrical Art from its earliest Beginnings to the Present Times'. Unpublished Ph.D. thesis, University of Ibadan.

Adedeji, J. A. 1971. 'Oral Tradition and the Contemporary Theatre in Nigeria', *Research in African Literatures*, 2.2.

Adedeji, J. A. 1981. 'Alarinjo: The Traditional Yoruba Travelling Theatre', in *Drama and Theatre in Nigeria: A Critical Source Book*, ed. Yemi Ogunbiyi, Lagos: Nigeria Magazine.

Adepegba, Cornelius Oyeleke. 2002. *African Art Forms Across 'Tribes' and Times*, Inaugural Lecture, 2002. Ibadan: Ibadan University Press.

Ayandele, E. A. 1966. *The Missionary Impact on Modern Nigeria 1842–1914: A Political and Social Analysis*. Harlow: Longman.

Ayandele, E. A. 1974. *The Educated Elite in Nigerian Society*. Ibadan: Ibadan University Press.

Banham, Martin and Wake, Clive. 1976. *African Theatre Today*. London: Pitman.

Banham, Martin, Hill, Errol and Woodyard, George, eds. 1994. *The Cambridge Guide to African and Caribbean Theatre.* Cambridge: Cambridge University Press.

Barber, Karin. 1986. 'Radical Conservation in Yoruba Popular Plays', *Drama and Theatre in Africa,* Bayreuth African Studies 7.

Barber, Karin, Collins, John and Ricard, Alain. 1997. *West African Popular Theatre.* Bloomington and Oxford: Indiana University Press and James Currey.

Beier, Ulli. 1967. *Three Nigerian Plays: Oba Ko So, Oba Waja and Oba Moro.* Ibadan: Mbari Publications.

Clapperton, Hugh. 1829. *Journal of a Second Expedition into the Interior of Africa,* London.

Clark, Ebun. 1979. *Hubert Ogunde: The Making of Nigerian Theatre.* Oxford: Oxford University Press.

Drewal, Henry J. and M. A. 1983. *Gelede: Art and Female Power among the Yoruba.* Bloomington: Indiana University Press.

Dunton, Chris. 1992. *Make Man Talk True: Nigerian Drama in English since 1970.* Munich: Hans Zell.

Echeruo, M. J. C. 1981. 'The Dramatic Limits of Igbo Ritual', in Yemi Ogunbiyi, ed., *Drama and Theatre in Nigeria: A Critical Source Book,* Lagos: Nigeria Magazine.

Ekeh, Peter P. and Ashiwaju, Garba. 1989. *Nigeria Since Independence: The First 25 Years.* vol. VII, *Culture.* Ibadan: Heinemann Educational Books (Nigeria).

Enekwe, Ossie. 1981. 'Myth, Ritual and Drama in Igboland', in Yemi Ogunbiyi ed., *Drama and Theatre in Nigeria: A Critical Source Book,* Lagos: Nigeria Magazine.

Etherton, Michael. 1982. *The Development of African Drama.* London: Hutchinson University Library for Africa.

Gbilekaa, Saint E. T. 1997. *Radical Theatre in Nigeria.* Ibadan: Caltop Publications.

Jeyifo, Biodun. 1984. *The Yoruba Travelling Theatre of Nigeria.* Lagos: Nigeria Magazine.

Jeyifo, Biodun, ed. 2002. *Modern African Drama.* New York: W. W. Norton.

Ladipo, Duro. 1967. *Moremi.* Lagos and Ibadan: Macmillan.

Ladipo, Duro. 1970. *Oba Kòso (pèlú Ìtumò ní Èdè Gèési).* Lagos and Ibadan: Macmillan.

Lander, Richard. 1830. *Records of Clapperton's Last Expedition to Africa.* Vol. 1. London.

Layiwola, Dele, ed. 2000. *African Theatre in Performance: A Festschrift in Honour of Martin Banham.* Amsterdam: Harwood Academic Press.

Lemard, Lynn. 1967. 'The Growth of Entertainment of Non-African Origin in Lagos from 1866 to 1920'. M.A. thesis, University of Ibadan.

Lindfors, Bernth, ed. 1974. *Dem Say: Interviews with Eight Nigerian Writers.* Austin: University of Texas Press.

Lindfors, Bernth, ed. 1976. *Critical Perspectives on Nigerian Literature.* Washington, DC: Three Continents Press.

Lindfors, Bernth. 1977. *Forms of Folklore in Africa: Narrative, Poetic, Gnomic, Dramatic.* Austin. University of Texas Press.

Losambe, Lokangaka and Sarinjeive, Devi, eds. 2001. *Pre-Colonial and Post-Colonial Drama and Theatre in Africa.* Trenton, NJ and Asmara, Eritrea: Africa World Press.

Malomo, Jide and Gbilekaa, Saint, eds. 1993. *Theatre and Politics in Nigeria.* Ibadan: Caltop Publications.

Obafemi, Olu. 1981. 'Cultural Heritage and Social Vision in Contemporary Nigerian Theatre'. Ph.D. thesis, University of Leeds.

Obafemi, Olu. 1996. *Contemporary Nigerian Theatre: Cultural Heritage and Social Vision.* Bayreuth: Bayreuth African Studies.

Obiechina, Emmanuel. 1973. *An African Popular Literature: A Study of Onitsha Market Pamphlets.* Cambridge: Cambridge University Press.

Ogunba, Oyin and Irele, Abiola, eds. 1978. *Theatre in Africa.* Ibadan: Ibadan University Press.

Ogunbiyi, Yemi, ed. 1981. *Drama and Theatre in Nigeria: A Critical Source Book.* Lagos: Nigeria Magazine.

Ogunbiyi, Yemi, ed. 1988. *Perspectives on Nigerian Literature.* Lagos: Guardian Books.

Ogunremi, Deji and Adediran, Biodun, eds. 1998. *Culture and Society in Yorubaland.* Ibadan: Rex Charles Publications in association with Connel Publications.

Oni, Duro and Ododo, Sunday Enessi. 2000. *Larger than his Frame: Critical Studies and Reflections on Olu Obafemi.* Lagos: Centre for Black African Arts and Civilisation (CBAAC).

Òsófisan, Fémi. 2001a. *Insidious Treasons: Drama in a Postcolonial State (Essays).* Ibadan: Opon Ifa Publishers.

Òsófisan, Fémi. 2001b. *The Nostalgic Drum: Essays on Literature, Drama and Culture.* Trenton, NJ and Asmara, Eritrea: Africa World Press.

Parrott, Fred J. 1972. *Introduction to African Arts of Kenya, Zaire and Nigeria.* New York: Arco Publishing.

Rotimi, Ola. 1981. 'The Drama in African Ritual Display', in Yemi Ogunbiyi, ed., *Drama and Theatre in Nigeria: A Critical Source Book,* Lagos: Nigeria Magazine.

Smith, Robert S. 1988. *Kingdoms of the Yoruba.* Oxford: James Currey.

Soyinka, Wole. 1973. *Collected Plays I.* Oxford: Oxford University Press.

Soyinka, Wole. 1976. *Myth, Literature and the African World.* Cambridge: Cambridge University Press.

Soyinka, Wole. 2002. 'Theatre in African Traditional Cultures: Survival Patterns', in Biodun Jeyifo, ed., *Modern African Drama,* New York: W. W. Norton.

Traore, Bakary. 1972. *The Black African Theatre and its Social Functions.* Trans. Dapo Adelugba. Ibadan: Ibadan University Press.

Ghana

JAMES GIBBS

J. H. Kwabena Nketia (1965) and A. A. Opoku (1970) have produced authoritative accounts of festivals and rituals that provide a guide to Ghana's theatrical, pre-theatrical and proto-theatrical conventions. The ceremonies they describe, together with other cultural practices, such as rites of passage and children's games, incorporate impersonation and performance elements that ensure they should be considered in any survey of dramatic traditions. More specialised studies, such as those by J. K. E. Agovi (1979) and Sophia Lokko (1980), have shown how annual community gatherings incorporate specific elements of drama. The work of such scholars, taken with the contributions of archaeologists, historians, and linguists, has begun to produce authoritative accounts of theatrical traditions in what is now Ghana.

Annual festivals, which bear the freight of the past while reflecting contemporary influences, provide a focus for enquiry. Nowadays such occasions are recorded in detail by returning indigines and by visitors but, as a result of this desire to record and in a fascinating interplay between impulses to preserve and alter, changes have been made. For example, the Aboakyer Deer-Catching Festival celebrated by the Efutu of Winneba now begins only after the sun has risen so that there is enough light for those with cameras. Visitors wishing to take photographs during the Odwira Festival of the Akuapem are put under intense pressure to purchase 'press cards' and, once they have them, become privileged recorders of events. In addition to intense pressure from photographers, the influence of government policies and the manoeuvring of commercial forces have also affected the way festivals are celebrated. For example, during the last years of the twentieth century, the National Commission on Culture began promoting festivals as part of its policy of fostering a 'festival culture'. This worked at various levels, from local and district to regional, national and international. At around the same time breweries aligned their advertising strategies with the same celebratory occasions. As a result, the décor for festivals has come to include bunting bearing brewers' logos, and the proceedings now incorporate presentations, at key moments in the proceedings, of crates of beer. From these instances it can be seen that festivals provide an ever-changing link with the past through performance, spectatorship and procedure.

The examples given in the previous paragraph are all from the south, reflecting a bias that is impossible to shake off given the present state of scholarly analysis of Ghanaian culture. Readers should be aware that there is a tendency among those who survey the situation in Ghana to concentrate on the most widely spoken languages and on the most populous or most easily accessible ethnic groups. The south and Asante receive a disproportionate amount of attention. For a succinct account of the diversity of language groups embraced by the arbitrarily drawn borders of Ghana, the reader is directed to James Anquandah's comments on the 'two main language groups' in the country. He writes about 'the Kwa group of southern and middle Ghana, and the Gur group of northern Ghana', which contain numerous mutually unintelligible languages. In 1980 he estimated that 45 per cent of the population of Ghana were Akans; he put the Mole-Dagbani at 16 per cent, the Ewe at 13 per cent and the Ga-Dangame at 9 per cent (Anquandah, 1982: 38–9). This leaves a substantial 17 per cent who are speakers of other languages and creates the impression, misleading given the impact of urbanisation, the effect of population movements and the extent of intermarriage, that linguistic-ethnic affiliation is unambiguous and unchanging. In Ghana, as in other countries, migrant groups cultivate their distinct identities by meeting to sing, tell stories and dance in the manner of their 'home towns'. Such performances are in some ways more open and in other ways more closed to innovation than the convention 'back home'.

The (ever-changing) elements that have contributed to the development of a distinctive theatre tradition in Ghana include dances, rhetorical forms, symbols and symbolic acts. But perhaps most important, and certainly the easiest to identify, has been the impact of the cycle of tales associated with the trickster figure of Ananse the spider. Primarily associated with the Akan language group, Ananse stories have long attracted folklorists, who have reduced them to writing. 'Reduced' is an appropriate term, since the process often involved stripping them of the gestures and musical elements that flesh out the performance. Dramatists have reversed this process.

Ananse has inspired several local dramatists, both Akan and non-Akan, who have transformed the tales (*anansesem*) into plays (*anansegro*), which have become part of a national tradition of narrative theatre. In this national tradition of narrative drama can be found the work of Efua Sutherland (1927–96), who was passionately concerned about the traditions and conventions of the nation-state, Ghana, that came into being as she turned 30 years of age (in 1937). Her privileged upbringing and education, initially in Cape Coast, had led her away from the villagers, who, in her words, had 'minded the culture'. Having recognised her distance from her people's roots, she sought to create a theatrical tradition that combined elements of distinctive local conventions with experiences of world theatre that included, for example, Greek tragedy, Irish dramatists, Bertolt Brecht, and *Lady Precious Stream*. Her thinking found expression in a series of texts and in two important buildings: the Drama Studio in Accra and the Kodzidan or Storytelling House in Atwia Ekumfi, Central Region.

The reference to Greek tragedy prompts the recognition that some of the energy driving developments in theatre came from the interaction of west Africa with the wider world. While there were trade routes across the Sahara, and while important Islamic influences were felt, the growth points were along the coast where Africa made contact most directly with Europe. The name given to the first fort the Portuguese established on the coast, El Mina, indicates the source of the riches that attracted seafarers to what became known as the 'Gold Coast'. The European forts and castles near the shore draw attention to the nature of the early contact, and the presence of dungeons where captured Africans were held until the slave traders' ships dropped anchor indicate another reason for interaction. With the traders came Christianity and eventually missionaries, some of whom established schools as well as churches. Once again, the complexity of the situation should be appreciated and the following dates are worth noting: 1683 arrival of French Catholic missionaries, Axim; 1828 arrival of Basle missionaries, Christianborg; 1835 arrival of Wesleyan Methodists, Cape Coast; 1847 arrival of Bremen missionaries, Transvolta. Over the decades, churches, both those representing 'main-stream denominations' and those set up by local separatist groups, established their own traditions of performance and their own annual festivals. With the establishment of a European community, churches and schools, the circumstances that would eventually lead to a theatre tradition that involved scheduled performances, paying audiences, playscripts and other elements of 'European theatre' were put in place.

Secondary schools, such as Mfantsipim (1876) and Achimota (1927), came to play important roles in the broadening of theatrical experience in the country. In 1918 the London publication *West Africa* reported the performance of *The Blinkards* written by one of the foundation pupils at

Mfantsipim, Kobina Sekyi. Episodic in form and composed in a mixture of English and Fanti, the play communicates Sekyi's scorn for those of his countrymen and women who uncritically aped English manners. His lively satire is of a piece with his own determined Ethiopianism, which also found expression in *Ethiopia Unbound* by his fellow countryman, Joseph Casley-Hayford. Sekyi's demanding play was put on by a group, the Cosmopolitan Club of Cape Coast, that itself came in for a healthy dose of Sekyi's satire. The text of *The Blinkards* lay, largely forgotten, in an archive until 1974, but since then it has been produced a number of times, both in Ghana and beyond.

Within the sometimes Shavian satire of *The Blinkards*, a robust, free-wheeling, local humour can occasionally be glimpsed. Though a graduate of London University, playwright Sekyi was sufficiently in touch with his own community to sound notes that subsequently burst forth in a popular syncretistic tradition of the concert party. This hybrid emerged in Sekondi/Takoradi out of a fusion of local and imported traditions, including trickster stories (Ananse again), Empire Day entertainments, church cantatas, American black-face minstrelsy, the silent cinema and expatriate entertainment. A short, tightly focussed study of the origins of the concert party by Efua Sutherland (1969) has been followed by K. N. Bame, John Collins and Catherine Cole, whose works are listed in the bibliography. They provide accounts of the economic and artistic foundations for the professional and semi-professional 'trios' that flourished, mostly along the coast, but who toured inland, arranging their itineraries to coincide with the payment of labourers. Patterns of concert party performance have varied, but shows frequently include a musical prelude, a series of comic turns, the main 'concert' or moralising musical drama and a concluding music session.

Over the last seventy years the 'concert party' has been synonymous with 'theatre' for hundreds of thousands of Ghanaians. Inevitably, and appropriately, the form has responded to changing economic and political circumstances. For example, shortly after Ghana became independent, the prime minister, Kwame Nkrumah, encouraged Haitian-born man-of-the-theatre Felix Morisseau-LeRoy to bring together the best concert party actors and to work with gifted women – the actors had hitherto all been male. Training was rigorous and was linked to the policy of retaining existing styles while preparing performers to use scripts written by Morisseau-LeRoy but 'Ghanaianised' by veteran 'partymen' Bob Johnson and Bob Thompson. Within a short time, it was claimed, a fully professional company 'run on socialist theory' was ready to perform and did so hundreds of times, a striking, if short-lived, example of linking political ideology with a popular theatrical convention. One lasting effect of this work was the establishment of women in the Ghanaian acting professions. The careers of Araba Stamp and Adeline Buabeng show the transforming impact of Nkrumah's initiative.

John Collins, writing out of first-hand experience with the Jaguar Jokers Concert Party, has described the trials experienced by touring performers, the variety of venues they perform in and the demanding audiences they encounter. Collins has also drawn attention to the themes to which concert parties return, in such productions as *Orphan do not Glance*, and the extraordinary variety of music that enriches the performances. Recent developments that are shaping audiences' expectations include the accommodation of concert parties in television slots and in the weekend matinee programmes at the National Theatre in Accra known as the Key Soap Concert Party. These influences are, it should be noted, only the most recent of a succession of factors that have affected the concert party tradition.

As a general rule, concert parties work from ideas generated within the company and shaped by group improvisation and performance. Only at the behest of researchers were the performances recorded and transcribed. However, the 'Sekyi tradition' of playwriting has run parallel with this 'improvised convention' for many years. In tracing the development of the literary drama in Ghana, two texts from the 1930s deserve comment: *The Third Woman* by J. B. Danquah (1939) and *The Fifth Landing Stage* (1937) by F. K. Fiawoo. The former draws on a story found in R. S. Rattray's *Akan-Ashanti Folk-Tales* entitled 'In a Tribe there is no Person Wholly Devoid of Sense' and on *Prehistoric Man in Genesis* by the Revd F. de P. Castells. Philosophical and not without entertainment value, the play was published in 1943, but, perhaps because of the tortuous, imitative and obscure manner in which it is written, it has only rarely been produced.

The Fifth Landing Stage has fared better in performance, particularly in Ewe. Its author, F. K. Fiawoo, who was born in Wusutu, near Kpandu, in 1891, did not have the opportunity to begin higher education until he reached the United States in 1928, but during the next five years he obtained three degrees and an educational qualification. Through his writing, he engaged in a vigorous cultural debate, and his play *Toko Atolia*, translated under the title *The Fifth Landing Stage* (published 1943), was part of this exchange. The title is a reference to the place of execution for malefactors among the Anlo-Ewe, and directs attention to the fact that justice and compassion were known in Africa before the Europeans arrived. The villain of the piece, Agbebada, seems invincible but is finally exposed and condemned to be buried up to his neck in the mud below the high tide mark. However, Kumasi, the embodiment of social virtues who has cause to want him dead, rescues him. From beginning to end, this episodic drama engages in a dialogue with Europe, specifically with the condescension of missionaries towards African society, but also with Aristotelian or neo-classicist and Shakespearean ideas of the theatre. According to Kofi Awoonor, the original text catches the 'cadences of spoken Ewe' and sticks 'very faithfully to the speech patterns of an older language' (Awoonor, 1975: 136). A landmark work of Ewe literature, *The Fifth Landing Stage* has been fairly regularly produced in Ewe in eastern Ghana, and has very occasionally been performed in English elsewhere.

The post-war period, and particularly the 1950s, saw the theatre in Ghana caught up in the Cold War and the struggle for independence. The expansion of the British Council, and its promotion of theatre in English, dates from this period, and, as one might expect, prompted a nationalist response. Nkrumah's influence on the concert party has already been referred to. His brand of centralised government, passionate Pan-Africanism and support of the 'African personality' all came to have great significance. He encouraged Efua Sutherland in the first phase of the Ghana National Theatre Movement. Sutherland, who became both the principal historian of the movement and its leading light, set up the pioneering Ghana Drama Studio Players in 1958. The following year the Ghana Experimental Theatre Players were ready to put on an *anansegoro*, or 'spider play', in Akropong. The performance, for which a text was meticulously rehearsed and a set constructed, incorporated formalised exchanges between a storyteller and the (paying) 'audience', and songs (*mboguo*) which were performed by both the cast and by members of the audience. The experiment showed that Sutherland was beginning to realise her dream of bringing together indigenous traditions, particularly those linked with Ananse stories, with relevant imported conventions.

From the late 1950s until her death in 1996, Sutherland was an influential, sometimes a dominating, figure in the Ghanaian theatre. The experiments already referred to led eventually to *The Marriage of Anansewa* (extract published 1975) that has become a classic of African theatre. She wrote a play entitled *Foriwa* that brought together ideas of festival drama with theatre for community development (it premièred in 1962) and another, *Edufa* (1967), that explored the parallels between Ghanaian and classical drama. Her short biography of Bob Johnson referred to above constitutes a succinct account of the origins of the concert party. Sutherland also stimulated the development of a writers' group encouraged local publishing, created a literary journal, helped to establish the study of African performance traditions at university level, and was the moving force behind a professional theatre group (Kusum Agoromba) that performed in English and Akan. Furthermore, she was the driving force behind the construction of the Drama Studio. Financed partly by the CIA (though Sutherland probably did not know the precise source), the shape of the Drama Studio was inspired by the courtyards or compounds that are focal points for much creative activity in Ghana. It was built, Sutherland later wrote, 'as a cultural symbol of our people's awakening to the necessity to endeavour determinedly to assert our cultural rights in all respects' (Sutherland, 1987: 1.) Revealingly, it incorporated a modest proscenium arch stage on one side; also significantly, it was demolished in the early 1990s.

In her work at the Drama Studio and at the University of Ghana, Sutherland was supported by Joe de Graft, who had initially contributed to the development of drama in the country through school productions of Shakespeare, of his own work and of plays by James Ene Henshaw. Remarkable progress was made during the years following independence and by 1962 the theatre in Ghana was flourishing. In that year there were numerous concert party groups touring the country, the Workers Brigade Concert Party had begun to work with socialist themes, the Drama Studio was open and productions there included two plays by Nigerians (one by Henshaw, one by Wole Soyinka), two by J. C. de Graft (*Sons and Daughters* and *Visitor from the Past*, later retitled *Through a Film Darkly*) and two by Sutherland (*Foruwa*, more often spelt *Foriwa*, and *Edufa*). Performances encouraged by the Arts Council of Ghana for the same year included *Antigone in Haiti* and *Doguicimi* by Morisseau-LeRoy, and preparations were being made for performances of *The Fifth Landing Stage*.

To sketch in other parts of the picture, one should note that there were drama groups based in local communities, such as the Osu Youngsters' Society, and in churches, including the Good Samaritan Society. Ga 'folk opera' companies, concentrated in Accra, such as the Dumas Choir that was later involved in putting on Saka Acquaye's *The Lost Fisherman*, had developed a fairly distinctive style, and there were also productions by educational institutions, such as Winneba Secondary School, which received government support for its production of *The King and I*. At the University of Ghana, a short-lived students' theatre scored a remarkable success with *The Dilemma of a Ghost*, written by a student who then called herself 'Christina Ata Aidoo'. In it can be recognised the subtlety of stagecraft, stringency of comment, and strength of dialogue that have made Ata Aidoo such a significant Ghanaian dramatist. At this time, there was also considerable encouragement given to puppet theatre, where European patterns were followed but local musical and dance styles dominated the presentation.

In the mid-sixties, however, circumstances altered as financial constraints were felt and as the personality cult surrounding the Head of State became stifling. After Nkrumah was overthrown by a *coup d'état* on 24 February 1966, some, such as the Workers Brigade Concert Party, found themselves somewhat isolated, while others, the versatile and gifted Acquaye among them, felt released from ideological pressures. In the remaining years of the decade, Acquaye's *The Lost Fishermen* was regularly revived and the Freelance Players, many of whom were graduates of drama courses at the University of Ghana, established themselves as a significant group. At this time, Soyinka's influence was strongly felt through productions, some by George Andoh-Wilson, of *The Trials of Brother Jero*, *The Lion and the Jewel* and *Kongi's Harvest*, which drew attention to the harder edge that the Nigerian brought to thinking about African theatre.

Seeds that Sutherland had sown began to bear fruit in the 1970s, as Martin Owusu (born Agona Kwaman, 1943) and Mohammed Ben-Abdallah (born in Kumasi in 1944), both of whom had studied at the University of Ghana, had work performed (see Owusu, 1970, 1973; Ben-Abdallah, 1987, 1989, 1993). Whilst building on conventions of narrative drama and acutely aware of the importance of writing for children, both turned to historical topics. Ben-Abdallah, as can be seen from plays such as *The Trial of Mallam Ilya*, incorporated masks, puppets and dance into his adventurous dramaturgy.

After the young flight lieutenant, J. J. Rawlings, seized power on 4 June 1979, and after his 'second coming' following a coup on 31 December 1981, politics and the arts became entwined once more. Playwrights Asiedu Yirenkyi (born 1946, Akropong), Ama Ata Aidoo (no longer 'Christina') and Ben-Abdallah all held high office, often in Information, Education or Culture. This period saw the promotion of festivals at various levels, leading up to Panafest and the construction of the National Theatre (see below). Panafest and the National Theatre take the 'story' of Ghanaian drama into the 1990s and beyond, showing the interaction of a younger generation with ideas Sutherland had espoused.

Under the terms of an agreement partly negotiated by Ben-Abdallah, signed with the government of China in 1985, the Drama Studio was razed to the ground and 'rebuilt' on the university campus at Legon. On the cleared site near the centre of Accra, Chinese engineers constructed a massive, some would say monstrous, National Theatre: the foundation stone was laid in June 1990 and the building opened in January 1993. The facilities are dominated by a vast proscenium stage with a huge auditorium in which capacious seats mean that many members of the audience are a great distance from the stage. The design of the building means that there is a huge expenditure on air-conditioning – a cost that has made the hiring of the hall prohibitively expensive for many groups. The symbolism of this sequence of events should not be missed, nor should the force of the lines from one of Aidoo's poems, in which she writes to a friend: 'But the Drama Studio is gone, Robert, / razed to the ground: / to make way for someone's notion of / the kind of theatre / I / should / want' (1992: 19). In the years that remained to her, Sutherland never visited either the new National Theatre or the 'Efua Sutherland Drama Studio', the 'rebuilt' studio at Legon.

The National Theatre is now a fact of theatrical life in Ghana. It was opened with a production that brought together the National Dance Ensemble, the National Symphony Orchestra and the performance company Abibigromma. Over the years, directors, scenic artists and lighting designers have taken on the challenge presented by the building. For example, during 1994, Anton Phillips (director) and Larry Coker (lighting) were flown in by the British Council to work on *Old Story Time* by Trevor Rhone. In the same year, Femi Osofisan mounted his own script *Nkrumah Ni . . . Africa Ni!*, and Steven Gerald (University of Texas at Austin) directed Mustapha Matura's *The Playboy of the West Indies*. However, only the National Dance Ensemble, choreographed by Nii Yartey, has managed to come to terms with the wide open spaces of the stage and the scale of the auditorium.

Whilst steering away from the template provided by Sutherland regarding theatre buildings, the Rawlings years saw the celebration of the 'First Festival of Historical Drama' in Cape Coast, which promoters were at pains to point out had its origins in a proposal Sutherland had made in 1980. The first international or Pan-African festival was held in December 1992, and since then a wide variety of performing groups from Africa and the

African diaspora have been brought together in the name of Panafest. There have been fruitful meetings and exchanges, but all too often there have been organisational disasters. Audiences have been pitifully small for the artistic events, though a football match between Ghana and Jamaica (1996) attracted great interest. The match, justified in the press on the grounds that soccer was introduced in colonial, that is historical, times, showed how far the festival had moved from that envisaged by Sutherland.

During the 1990s drama was increasingly used for community development. There were precedents for this, for example in the mass education and social welfare programmes of the 1930s, but a new impetus was given to the work by contact with the international theatre for development movement and by donor agency support. Sandy Arkhurst, who has served the Ghanaian theatre faithfully in many capacities in the course of a distinguished career, ran relevant courses at Legon, and animators from outside have conducted practical sessions. One of these was Chuck Mike, best known for his work with the Nigerian Performance Studio Workshop. Performers based at the National Theatre have also been involved, and some influence has been felt from Augusto Boal and other innovators.

The end of the millennium has seen warnings, based on poor attendances at the National Theatre, that the theatre in Ghana is dying. However, during September 2000 there were signs of health, with revivals of classic Ghanaian texts and productions of new work by younger writers, including Yao Asare, who was born in Nkonya-Tayi, Volta Region (1953). Groups such as Audience Awareness, GIPAS (Ghana International Performing Arts Society), Living Echoes, Pacesetters and Theatre Mirrors have soldiered on, sometimes, as with Joris Wartenberg's *King Lion's Law*, undertaking very ambitious productions. Students at educational institutions, particularly the School of Performing Arts in Legon, and professionals attached to the school and the National Theatre, have continued to defy the prophets of doom. Non-Governmental Organisations have used a variety of theatrical means to raise awareness and stimulate discussion (see Arkhurst, 1994; Dogbe, 2002). In open air cinemas, compounds and cocoa storage sheds, as well as at the National Theatre in weekend Key Soap Concert Party slots, the remaining concert parties continue to perform. The use of the name 'Key Soap' points to the disturbing extent to which Ghanaian theatre had become dependent on sponsorship of one sort or another. Productions of *Amen Corner* and *All My Sons*, supported by American dollars, adaptations of Molière, with French assistance, and the continued involvement of the British Arts Council

(*Yaa Asantewa* was 'shipped' from Britain to Ghana in 2001) provide further evidence of this dimension.

At the beginning of 2001, to mark the fifth anniversary of Sutherland's passing, productions of her plays were put on and a double-issue of *Matatu*, entitled *FonTomFrom*, dedicated to her appeared. Subtitled 'Contemporary Ghanaian Literature, Theatre and Film', *FonTomFrom* brought together academic articles, interviews with practising playwrights, reviews of plays and an attempt to chronicle the emergence of the video industry. Appropriately the volume included a previously unpublished Sutherland play, *Children of the Man-made Lake*, and her important essay 'The Second Phase of the National Theatre Movement in Ghana'. Although the Accra Drama Studio had been demolished at the beginning of the 1990s, and although she died in 1996, Sutherland continues to exert a powerful influence over theatre in Ghana. The national tradition of narrative drama to which she contributed continues, most obviously in the work of younger playwrights such as Asare, whose *Ananse in the Land of Idiots* makes explicit reference to her. Sutherland's influence can also be seen in a fascinating recent interview conducted by Esi Sutherland Addy with Adeline Buabeng, someone who has lived and worked in the Ghanaian theatre for the last forty years.

References and further reading

Agovi, J. K. E. 1979. 'Kundum Festival Drama among the Ahanta-Nzema of South-West Ghana'. Ph.D. Thesis, Legon: Institute of African Studies.

Aidoo, Ama Ata. 1965. *The Dilemma of a Ghost*. Harlow: Longman.

Aidoo, Ama Ata. 1970. *Anowa*. Harlow: Longman.

Aidoo, Ama Ata. 1992. *An Angry Letter in January*. Coventry: Dangaroo.

Anquandah, James. 1982. *Rediscovering Ghana's Past*. Accra and Harlow: Sedeco and Longman.

Anyidoho, Kofi and Gibbs, James, eds. 2000. *FonTomFrom: Contemporary Ghanaian Literature and Film, Matatu 21/22*. Amsterdam: Rodopi. (Includes historic documents, creative writing by Sutherland, critical/bibliographical material, and interviews with Ben-Abdallah, Ansah, and Marshall.)

Arkhurst, Sandy. 1994. 'The Community Theatre Project: A Rethink'. *SPA Newsletter* (Legon), 2 (April–June).

Asare, Yaw. 1991. *Ananse in the Land of Idiots*. (Produced but not published.)

Asare, Yaw. 1999. *Desert Dreams*. (Produced but not published.)

Awoonor, Kofi. 1975. *The Breast of the Earth*. Garden City, NY: Anchor Press/Doubleday.

Bame, Kwabena N. 1985. *Come to Laugh: African Traditional Theatre in Ghana*. New York: Lilian Barber.

Banham, Martin, Gibbs, James and Osofisan, Femi. 2001. *African Theatre Playwrights and Politics*. Oxford: James Currey. (Articles on de Graft and Ben-Abdallah, interview with the latter by Awo Asiedu, and report on Ghanaian theatre in 'Noticeboard'.)

Ben-Abdallah, M. 1987. *The Trial of Mallam Ilya and Other Plays*. Accra: Woeli.

Ben-Abdallah, M. 1989. *The Fall of Kumbi and Other Plays*. Accra: Woeli.

Ben-Abdallah, M. 1993. *The Land of a Million Magicians*. Accra: Woeli.

Collins, John. 1994. *Highlife Time*. Accra: Anansesem Publications.

Dogbe, Esi. 2002. 'Visibility, Eloquence and Silence: Women and Theatre for Development in Ghana', in *African Theatre: Women*, ed. Jane Plastow, Oxford: James Currey.

Lokko, Sophia. 1980. 'Theatre Space: A Historical Overview of the Theatre Movement in Ghana'. *Modern Drama*, 23.

Nketia, J. H. Kwabena. 1965. *Ghana – Music, Dance and Drama*. Legon and Accra: Institute of African Studies and Ministry of Information. (Major work of documentation that investigates the indigenous matrix from which the theatre emerged.)

Opoku, A. A. 1970. *Festivals of Ghana*. Accra: Ghana Publishing. (Includes accounts of Adae, Odwira, Akwambo, Homowo and other festivals.)

Owusu, Martin. 1970. *The Story Ananse Told*. London: Heinemann.

Owusu, Martin. 1973. *The Sudden Return and Other Plays*. London: Heinemann.

Sutherland, Efua. 1965. *The Second Phase of the National Theatre Movement in Ghana*. Legon: Institute of African Studies. Reprinted Anyidoho and Gibbs, 2000, 45–76.

Sutherland, Efua. 1967. *Edufa*. Harlow: Longman.

Sutherland, Efua. 1968. *Vulture! Vulture! Two Rhythm Plays*. Accra: Ghana Publishing.

Sutherland, Efua. 1969. 'Theatre in Ghana', in *Ghana Welcomes You*, ed. Janice Nebill, Accra: Orientation to Ghana Committee.

Sutherland, Efua. 1971. *Foriwa*. Accra: Ghana Publishing.

Sutherland, Efua. 1975. *The Marriage of Anansewa*. Harlow: Longman.

Sutherland, Efua. 1979. *The Story of Bob Johnson: Ghana's Ace Comedian*. Accra: Anowuo. (Intended to be the first in a series about the makers of Ghanaian theatre. In the event, the only title.)

Sutherland, Efua. 1980. 'Proposals for a Historical Drama Festival in Cape Coast'. Unpublished article.

Sutherland, Efua. 1987. 'Memorandum to the Chairman and Members of the PNDC on the subject of future action for the development of Ghana's potential in dramatic art'. Unpublished report, 21 March.

Sutherland-Addy, Esi. 2002. 'Drama in her Life: Interview with Adeline Ama Buabeng', in *African Theatre Women*, ed. Jane Plastow, Oxford: James Currey.

Sierra Leone

MOHAMED SHERIFF

A history of theatre in Sierra Leone begins with the traditional theatre, which today coexists with a western-style African theatre that has evolved as a result of the country's contact with European culture in the colonial era. There are three stages in this historical development. The first is theatre in the pre-colonial era dating far back in time when the country's own pure theatrical forms evolved. The second stage is the colonial era, which saw in the capital, Freetown, the establishment of a European theatre which all but replaced her traditional theatrical forms, leading to the birth of a hybrid western-style African theatre as a result of both the influence of European culture and a reaction by indigenous Sierra Leoneans to the dominance of British plays. Lastly, the post-independence era has seen an acceleration in the pace of the movement away from a purely western theatre and the further development of western-style African theatre and a revival of Sierra Leone's traditional theatrical forms in the capital.

Traditional theatre

As in other parts of Africa, traditional theatre from the pre-colonial era is as old as Sierra Leone's existence itself. This theatre differs in both its form and purpose from western theatre or the western-style theatre that evolved as a result of colonialism. This is an important factor in any study of the early history of theatre in Sierra Leone, as in the African context theatre is a broad term covering various kinds of performances, including even some kinds of storytelling.

There are no known records of theatrical activities in pre-colonial times in Sierra Leone, but by tracing the evolution of theatre through its cultural heritage and oral traditions a broad historical development can be determined. Drama is an integral part of the socio-cultural life of Sierra Leone. It features in every form of social interaction. In festivals and celebrations, religious and cultic rites, in storytelling sessions and even in day-to-day interactions, the elements of being in a state of possession, of role-playing and impersonation and various little functional dramas are so evident that their theatricality is often taken for granted. Therefore it is essential to examine some of these traditional socio-cultural practices and their inherent dramatic elements in order to trace the evolution and early history of Sierra Leone theatre. Many of these activities or practices are not in themselves drama in the artistic theatrical sense of the word, but they do give an insight into how theatre or performance evolved.

Activities surrounding deaths and funerals provide interesting examples. In a newly bereaved home, the most obvious way people, especially the women and female sympathisers, pour out their grief is by wailing, sometimes with agonising thrashing of their bodies in the intensity of their grief. Failure by, for instance, a close female relative to express grief in this manner may portray her as cold-hearted and unsympathetic. So, whether one is genuinely moved or not, one has to put up a convincing performance of being grief-stricken to fulfill the expectations of society.

A more developed form of this kind of drama is to be seen among certain Temne communities. When a chief dies, no one is supposed to express public grief or even discuss his death until the news is formally broken. Everyone has to pretend not to have heard the news. At a specified time people gather in the compound of the chief and one of his attendants stands on the roof of the house, from where he smashes an earthen cooking pot. The crowd then erupts into wailing and the public mourning or performance begins, depending on whether one is genuinely moved or not. But these are simple forms that merely show the dramatic nature of Sierra Leone's socio-cultural activities and can best be described as simply theatrical. There is, however, no doubt that it is out of these simple forms that more complex, creative and developed performances have evolved. Though not originally from what is today Sierra Leone, the Kru dance of death, celebrating the invincibility of death as described by John Peterson in 1969, is a good example.

> Death dressed in extravagant attire highlighted by rough goatskins sang low and monotonously as he played on a gunbay, producing a simple sound made by a bead string striking the side of a calabash. Two Kru dancers, each with a knife, first approached death, individually intent on mortally wounding him: each backed away as the crouching, singing figure took a quick step towards them; they returned together trembling before the persistent unending power

that the singer held, and when he stepped unafraid towards them again, their daggers crossed above his head and instead of shattering his skull, they framed a never-ending conquest of death over them.[1]

This is a short but well-developed dance drama, with costume and mask, incorporating mime, music, song and dance.

The examples so far are taken from death and death-related activities, which are naturally unpleasant experiences. If out of death and the activities surrounding it theatre of entertainment or performance can evolve, how much more so can it be for activities such as harvests, festivals, marriages and births, which are desirable experiences.

At a mystical level, the dramatic elements of role-playing and impersonation are evident in rituals of possession. In investigating a witch or witchcraft, the witch-doctor of a witch-finding cult like the *Ariogbo*, dressed in costume from head to toe, is possessed by a powerful force that guides his thoughts and actions until he accomplishes his task. There is such spectacle involved in these ritualistic performances, which are often accompanied by some form of music or drumming and dancing, that the audience finds it both awesome and amusing.

Over the years because of the spectacular nature or the performative quality of such rituals they have gradually been freed from their immediate task or function and occasionally presented to a wider audience for entertainment. It is at this stage that the creative powers of the artists in society are employed to refine these presentations and develop them into performance or theatre for entertainment. The original ritualistic performances would still be maintained, however, for their specific functions.

The example of the *Soko* performer of the Poro society is noteworthy and deserves some attention. Dressed in elaborate headgears, smoked raffia skirts and clothes decorated with cowry shells, Sokos present a very awesome and bloody spectacle in a performance whose main features include, among others, the slashing of their bodies and tongues with razor-blades or sharp knives, the plucking out of their eyes and returning them to their sockets and driving swords into their bellies and out through their backs – all this with a substantial shedding of blood. There are eye-witness reports of a Soko performer being shot dead and buried in public view only to reappear later from back stage very much alive; of a performer cutting a little girl in two, placing her body parts in a tub and carrying it back stage – later the girl would appear dancing a sprightly dance amidst cheering from an awe-struck audience. Certainly magic is involved in all this and the performers must, no doubt, be in some state of possession. They execute simple dance steps which go with soft, simple but eerie music created by drumming some small hard objects against tortoise shells. Such performances have their origins in rituals that were exclusive to their members. Significantly, although the Sokos are members of the Temne Poro society of Bombali, Tonkolili and the Port Loko districts in the Northern Province, those features of their rituals that are permissible as performance for a public audience have been exported to other places such as Freetown in the west, where some of their members have chosen to settle. They can be seen performing on street corners or in large open spaces such as football fields or parks. But even at this public stage such a performance still retains some aspects of its functionality. The display epitomises the healing powers of the Soko, their ability to heal the physical, psychological and social wounds of society. It is meant to both entertain and instil awe in an audience.

The Kru dance of death described earlier, the dramas or performances of secret society masquerades such as the *Bundo, Falui, Egugu, Oje* and Gelede, amongst others, fall into this category of secret rituals that have some aspects of them evolving into public performance.[2]

Evident from all this is the operation of traditional theatre as mainly a functional activity that doubles as a form of entertainment in some cases and at certain stages of its evolution. Also the above account gives an insight into the roots and evolution of traditional theatre in Sierra Leone. A broad movement can be identified, from little dramas of everyday life to ritualistic performances to theatre of entertainment, but with other dramatic develop-ments within and alongside this broad movement. As has been stated earlier, no specific dates can be determined for the development of pre-colonial the-atre, but there is no doubt that the rituals, festivals and ceremonies, both religious and secular, the masquerades and other performative events form an integral part of the Sierra Leonean culture and have been performing important functions in the lives of the people over the centuries. Alongside these functional theatrical events is age-old traditional storytelling, which is not merely a narration but also a highly theatrical presentation requiring strong audience participation, with singing of refrains, clapping, drumming, dancing and miming. There are also other forms, such as the Tehtehmuteh puppet show and the Yamama, Gongoli and Kakadebul masquerades, whose origins are not in any secret rituals and whose main function is entertainment.

This, then, is the nature and evolution of theatre in Sierra Leone before it came in contact with western culture.

Theatre in the colonial era

In the eighteenth and nineteenth centuries the British made Freetown a sanctuary for freed west African slaves from the West Indies, North America and England, as well as those recaptured on the high seas before they could be taken away to slavery.

The first settlers were brought by the British in 1787. The Sierra Leone Company, which was formed in 1791, administered the settlement until 1808, when it became a crown colony. The British gradually extended their influence over the rest of the country in the face of resistance from the north and in 1896 Great Britain set up a protectorate over the hinterland. From then on Sierra Leone was ruled as a British colony under a British governor, until 1961 when it gained independence.

As is often the case, apart from their government, the British also brought along their language, religion and education and considerably influenced the way of life of the indigenous people and the liberated slaves, particularly in Freetown. In addition to the existing cultural and traditional practices in Freetown and its surrounding areas, the freed slaves, as should be expected, brought with them their own forms of entertainment, based on their culture, which easily became part of the cultural life of the community. The Kru dance of death described earlier, and the Egugu, Oje and Gelede masquerades are typical examples.

But by the end of the nineteenth century such was the power and influence of European culture in Freetown that liberated slaves gradually began adopting European ways and lost their own traditional lifestyle, especially certain kinds of folk entertainment and practices that were considered 'heathen and barbaric' secret society activities, from a European Christian point of view.

As a result, performances of secret societies, along with various masquerades and traditional theatrical forms, were considerably scaled down and all but replaced by a formal western-style spoken theatre and musical performances in Freetown. This new theatre had its origin in the dramatisation of biblical stories by Christian religious organisations, as a way of propagating Christianity and winning adherents to the faith. Such organisations also

performed established British plays with Christian themes. These performances, which normally took place on Sunday afternoons, became the most
popular form of entertainment for a long time. Up until the 1960s plays
such as *Everyman, The Bishop's Candlesticks* and *Murder in the Cathedral* were
still being produced. A more secular drama evolved alongside these religious
Sunday afternoon plays. Such drama was performed first by schools and then
later by social groups that drew their memberships from the European community and which included members of the *Krio* élite.[3] This drama featured
prominently in the social life of Freetown from the 1930s to the 1950s. The
plays produced were mainly European classics, with an occasional original
play by members of the European community. An example was *The Downfall
of Zachariah Fee*, written and directed by the then governor of Sierra Leone,
Sir Arnold Hudson, in March 1934. The most notable performing group
was the British Council Dramatic Society, formed in 1948 with a largely
British membership and a sprinkling of educated Sierra Leonean élite, who
were very much at home in British culture. This society was to set the pace
for theatrical development in Freetown, producing only British plays and
inspiring the formation of similar British-oriented groups.

The dominance of British plays was to continue until the late 1950s.
Then, in 1957, at a time when the campaign for independence, with its
concomitant black consciousness movement, was gaining momentum, the
first Sierra Leone Festival of Arts was held. The festival inspired the writing
of Sierra Leonean plays and provided an opportunity for the production of
a number of them, including John Akar's plays, *Valley Without Echo* (1954),
performed in 1959, and *Cry Tamba* (1961), performed in 1963.

Post-independence theatre

The attainment of independence in 1961 saw a further movement towards
a more Sierra Leonean-oriented theatre and the emergence of another notable Sierra Leonean playwright, Raymond Sarif Easmon, whose first play,
Dear Parent and Ogre (published 1964) won first prize in a drama competition organised as part of the independence celebrations in 1961. It was the
first African play to be produced by the British Council Dramatic Society.
Another significant boost to Sierra Leonean theatre came about in 1963,
when John Akar set up the National Dance Troupe upon the request of the
Sierra Leone government. In setting up the dance troupe his aim was, as he
put it, 'to present a flawlessly authentic indigenous show . . . everything was
to be authentic, an inseparable part of our rich folklore'.[4] The successes of

Akar and Easmon encouraged the writing of more Sierra Leonean plays and were no doubt part of the inspiration behind the establishment, in 1964, of the National Theatre League, which comprised most of the amateur dramatic societies. There was by now a growing indigenous cultural consciousness and self-confidence among the people, manifested in theatrical circles by a change of attitude towards the British Council Dramatic Society, with its British plays and British-oriented audience. There was a widespread consensus that theatre should be for ordinary people, about ordinary people and in the language of ordinary people.

Certain determining factors lent force to this trend. The first was the emergence, on the theatrical scene, of a young school-leaver, Oladipo Robin Mason, with his plays, *His Father's Will* (1963), followed by *Country Boy* (1964), *Dr Margai* (1965) and *Love and Crime* (1966). Mason established his own drama group, the Western Dramatic Society, and made it a policy to perform only Sierra Leonean plays.

Perhaps more significant still was Yulisa Amadu Maddy, whose change of name from Pat Maddy reflected his African consciousness. Maddy had a special pride in identifying himself with the grass-roots. The lead characters in his plays were all drawn from school drop-outs, layabouts, prostitutes, criminals and even murderers. He studied drama in England, produced African plays for Danish radio and trained the Zambian National Dance Troupe. With his more professional background and African consciousness he was able to explore the possibilities of using indigenous theatrical elements to create plays that were distinctly African. Notable among them are *Big Berin* (Great Funeral), *Obasai* (Over Yonder), *Yon-Kon* (Clever Thief), *Alla Gbah* (The Big Man) and *Gbana Bendu* (The Tough Guy), all written in the late 1960s and the early 1970s.

A third factor in determining the shape of Sierra Leonean drama was Thomas Decker's translation of Shakespeare's *Julius Caesar* into Krio in 1964. This was a remarkable development for theatre in Sierra Leone as it freed writers and would-be writers from the shackles of writing plays only in English. Decker then provided the impetus for the fourth determining factor, the writing and production of Sierra Leonean plays in Krio. The first to do this was Juliana John (now Mrs Rowe), who was, incidentally, a member of the cast of the Krio version of *Julius Caesar*. She first wrote and directed *Na Mami Bohn Am* (1968), followed soon after by *I Dey I Nor Du* (1969). These two plays were the first really popular plays, attracting very large audiences from all walks of life.

The contributions of Thomas Decker, followed by Juliana John, showed clearly that Krio and other indigenous languages could be used to make theatre more accessible to the people.

Conclusion

This remarkable development in Sierra Leone's cultural history, which started in the 1960s and continued right through the 1970s, gathered pace in the 1980s and has survived the bloody ten-year civil war of the 1990s. Initially new groups sprang up everywhere, producing plays mainly in the vernacular, and by the mid-1980s there were well over thirty drama groups in Freetown alone. Whilst some of these groups have ceased to operate for various reasons, new ones are still being formed. Notable groups include Tabule Experimental Theatre, now Tabule Theatre, founded in 1968 by one of Sierra Leone's best-known dramatists, Raymond Ayodele Charley (1948–94), and Adeyemi Meheux; Gbakandia Tiata, dormant now for several years, founded by Yulisa Amadu Maddy in 1968; the Shegureh Players, founded by Clifford Shefumi Garber in 1973; and Ronko Theatre, founded by Abu Bakarr Sankoh, Foday M. Kamara and three others in 1979.

Several other noteworthy groups were founded in the 1980s and 1990s, all of which continue to shape the history of theatre in Sierra Leone. Amongst those that need some mention here are the Freetong Players, which specialises in a cappella-style music, founded by Charlie Haffner in 1985; Spence Productions, founded by Julius Spencer in 1989; and Pampana Communications Drama Company, founded by Mohamed Sheriff and Oumarr Farauk Sesay in 1993. Freetong Players has the distinction of becoming, in 1990, the first full-time professional folk-style theatre group. Spence Productions and Pampana Communications Drama Company also stand apart from other groups in that they have a more professional approach to theatre and are both recognised for the high artistic quality of their presentations. Unlike other groups with standing casts of amateur actors given occasional honorarium, both these companies contract and pay artists professional fees for each of their productions. This approach has the advantage of a wider and better choice of artists and therefore puts on higher-quality productions. It cannot be but fair to mention a few more notable groups of this era, namely Kailondo Tiata, Kontikiti Theatre, Preachers Theatre and Kakua Players.

A distinction must be made between the western-style Sierra Leonean theatre, which evolved as a result of the influence of British/European theatre, and the traditional theatrical forms that survived the onslaught of

European civilisation and culture. 'Folk' theatre throughout the colonial period thrived in the provinces, but was very much localised and out of the
attention of the wider public until the establishment of the Sierra Leone
Dance Troupe, which began to expose some of its forms to the public. A
new development took place with folk theatre from the mid-1980s, picking
up pace in the 1990s. It now started to function as a means of raising the
level of awareness of the people and educating them on a diverse range of
issues, such as health and sanitation, breast-feeding, voter registration and
election procedures and peace-building. In the 1990s in particular the demand for these kinds of services from drama groups became so high that
some groups all but ceased to do public performances for entertainment
and commercial purposes. Folk theatre is now being used as an effective
tool for development. Two groups that deserve mention here are Freetong
Players, though its activities appeared to have been scaled down until recently when leader Charlie Haffner, who was absent for a few years, returned,
and Pampana Communications, which is fully engaged in awareness-raising
theatrical activities throughout the country. A significant development of the
1990s was an upsurge of religious singing and acting groups within both
Muslim and Christian organisations, particularly in Freetown. These amateur performing art groups perform for the public for the dual purposes of
fund-raising and propagation. The Islamic groups have, however, attracted
an amount of criticism from other Muslims for staging plays which the latter
consider irreligious from an Islamic point of view.

Western-style theatre never really made much impact outside Freetown.
To date, there are just a handful of theatre groups doing western-style African
theatre outside Freetown, but there are many cultural traditional performing
groups all over the country, despite the devastation and instability caused
by war.

In the capital the attainment of independence saw the revival of secret
society performances and masquerades, as well as the formation of new
masks and cultural dance groups, all of which, alongside the western-style
African theatre, provides a rich variety of performances for the people of
Sierra Leone today.

Notes

1. John Peterson, *Province of Freedom* (London: Faber and Faber, 1969), p. 282.
2. Although now well-known components of Sierra Leone's repertory of
masquerades, the Egugu, Gelede and Oje masquerades were originally from

Yorubaland in Nigeria, brought to Sierra Leone by the liberated slaves or
recaptives. Some of their apparently cryptic public utterances are easily
recognised as some form of Yoruba by speakers of that language. They
operate mainly in the capital, Freetown, home of the descendants of the
liberated slaves.

3. The Krios are widely known to be the descendants of freed slaves from
England, the West Indies, North America and of those recaptured on the
high seas before they could be taken away to slavery.

4. John Akar, 'The Arts in Sierra Leone', *African Forum*, 1 (1965), pp. 86–91.

References and further reading

Becker, M. E. L. 'Modern West African Drama'. B. A. thesis, University of Durham,
Sierra Leone, 1969.

Consentino, Donald John. 'Patterns in Domesia: The Dialectics of Mende
Narrative Performance'. Ph.D. thesis, Graduate School of the University
of Wisconsin-Madison, 1976.

De Graft, J. C. 'Roots in African Drama and Theatre'. *African Literature Today*, 8
(1976).

James, Frederick. *Borbor Theatre: How Can it be Used as a Strategy for Rural Development
in Sierra Leone?* Freetown: Institute of Adult Education in Sierra Leone,
1987.

Jones, Eldred. 'Freetown – The Contemporary Cultural Scene'. Freetown a
symposium, unpublished essay, pp. 200–208.

Kamlongera, Christopher. *Theatre for Development in African with Case Studies from
Malawi and Zambia.* Bonn: German Foundation for International
Development, n.d.

Palmer, Eustace. 'The Development of Sierra Leone Writing', in *A Celebration of
Black and African Writing,* ed. Bruce King and K. Ogungbesan, Oxford
and Ahmadu: Oxford University Press and Bello University Press, 1975.

Palmer, Eustace and De Souza George, Raymond. 'Sierra Leone', in *The World
Encyclopedia of Contemporary Theatre,* vol. III, *Africa,* ed. Don Rubin,
London and New York: Routledge, 1997.

Sheriff, Mohamed, 'Against the Odds', in *Sierra Leone: Theatrical Seasons, 1996–1997,
1997–1998, 1998–1999,* World of Theatre series, London and New York:
Routledge and International Theatre Institute, 2000.

Sheriff Mohamed. 'Recent Trends in Sierra Leonean Theatre'. B. A. thesis, Fourah
Bay College, University of Sierra Leone, 1984.

Spencer, Julius. 'A Historical Background to the Contemporary Theatre'.
International Journal of Sierra Leone Studies, 1 (1988).

A note on recent Anglophone Cameroonian theatre

ASHERI KILO

Anglophone Cameroon refers to the English-speaking provinces of the Republic of Cameroon. Two out of the ten administrative provinces, namely the North West and the South West Provinces, constitute what can be referred to as Anglophone Cameroon.

After the First World War, German Kamerun was handed over to Britain and France by the League of Nations as mandated territory on 20 July 1922. By this act, French Cameroun and British Cameroons were born, the latter ruled from Lagos as part of Eastern Nigeria. In a United Nations plebiscite on 11 February 1961, Southern Cameroons voted to join La République du Cameroun, which had become independent on 1 January 1960, and the Federal Republic of Cameroon came into being as an officially bi-lingual (English and French) country on 1 October 1961. The country changed its name to the United Republic of Cameroon after a national referendum in 1972 and later on to the Republic of Cameroon in 1984, maintaining its official bi-lingual character.

Anglophone dramatists and theatre practitioners have responded to the conditions of their history and their minority status. Emmanuel Fru Doh explains in *Anglophone Cameroon Writing* the reason why Anglophone theatre practitioners and dramatists feel concern for their community: 'The Anglophone Cameroonian, earlier colonized by the white man, is once again a victim of "colonization" but, this time, his colonizer is his former partner with whom he served, and were together tormented and exploited by the colonialists.'[1]

Compared to other Anglophone theatres in Africa and to the Francophone theatre in Cameroon itself, Anglophone theatre is under-published in terms of texts and under-performed, since the artists in western Cameroon find themselves in a disadvantaged minority position.

Several attempts have been made to take stock of Anglophone drama and theatre. Hansel Ndumbe Eyoh has given a historical account of Cameroon

drama and argued that it has evolved from the dramatic tradition of Cameroonian folklore.[2] Asheri Kilo has written a bibliographical account of theatrical
activities in the country, discussing both published and unpublished drama
texts.[3] Bate Besong's doctoral thesis entitled 'Politics and Historicity in
Anglophone Cameroon Drama'[4] is based on a textual analysis of Anglophone plays and provides a historical and critical perspective on selected
literary texts. Bole Butake and Gilbert Doho have published a collection of
critical essays on theatrical activities in Cameroon in general entitled *Théâtre
camerounais/Cameroonian Theatre*.[5] This is a particularly valuable source of information on aspects of indigenous theatre throughout Cameroon. A workshop on Anglophone Cameroonian writing took place in Yaounde in 1993,
giving rise to the publication *Anglophone Cameroon Writing* referred to above.

Theatre expressed in forms of religious and civic ritual, popular entertainment and political protest is familiar to virtually every culture. Theatre
for Cameroonians has become the cultural arena representing the struggles,
desires, frustrations and aspirations of their various communities. Cameroon
being a complex society, containing many subcultures, many forms of theatre
have developed to cater for the different tastes of the audiences. Whilst traditional communal theatre and performance – often based on storytelling –
continues to thrive in rural areas, in the major urban areas, from the 1960s,
a 'mainstream' theatre has created a more radical theatre culture, especially
among Anglophone Cameroonians. Even here playwrights remain responsive to their culture and to traditional practices. Anglophone Cameroonians
have came to realise the potential of theatre, particularly its role in education and social change. New kinds of theatrical forms have emerged, a 'total
theatre' utilising western forms as well as traditional art forms.

The emergence of the broadcast media as an alternative form of entertainment has had a bearing on the theatre. The introduction of film, television
and video contributes to the decrease in attendance at play productions.
Paradoxically, however, television and radio have played a vital role in pop-
ularising Cameroonian theatre, making it accessible to many people who
watch plays on television and listen to radio broadcasts. Over two hundred theatre troupes are registered with the Ministry of Culture in Yaounde,
but in the Anglophone sector of Cameroon only a handful are active. In
Buea, records from the Delegation of Culture show that only fifteen theatre groups were ever registered. In Bamenda, in the North-West Province,
only five theatre groups have ever been registered. In these two provinces
theatre performances are centred on college campuses, and are created and

performed by students and teachers basically because of a lack of theatre infrastructure.

In Yaounde three Anglophone theatre troupes the Yaounde University Theatre, the Yaounde Children's Theatre Collective and the Flame Players, have promoted the performance of Anglophone plays. The Yaounde University Theatre is one of the troupes that has made a significant contribution to the growth of theatre practice in Cameroon as a whole. One of its major achievements has been the sensitisation of the English-speaking audience, making it more responsive to theatre of a serious nature. The troupe has performed several plays from Anglophone Africans, including Wole Soyinka's *The Trials of Brother Jero* (1979, Yaounde), *The Lion and the Jewel* (1982, Yaounde), *The Swamp Dwellers* (1980, Yaounde), Athol Fugard's *The Island* (1980, Yaounde, Buea, Limbe, Kumba) and *Sizwe Bansi is Dead* (1983, Yaounde). It has also performed Bole Butake's plays, including *The Rape of Michelle* (1985, Yaounde), *Lake God* (1986, Yaounde, Bamenda), *The Survivors* (1988), *And Palm Wine Will Flow* (1990, Yaounde) – Butake has emerged as one of the major Cameroonian playwrights. Hansel Eyoh's *The Inheritance* was performed in 1991 in Yaounde. The troupe produced Ola Rotimi's *The Gods are not to Blame* (1990, Yaounde) and *Our Husband has Gone Mad Again* (1992, Yaounde), Bate Besong's *Beasts of No Nation* (1991, Yaounde) and Babila Mutia's *Before this Time Yesterday* (1993, Yaounde).

During the early years of its creation the troupe contacted Anglophones in the North-West and South-West Provinces. In 1982 a tour lasting five weeks played two performances in each of the towns of Buea, Limbe, Kumba and Bamenda. At the time, secondary and high school students were the target audiences, the aim being to kindle their interest towards a theatre culture, but financial constraints stifled this ambitious project. When *The Rape of Michelle*, a topical play critical of government, was staged at the Yaounde Conference Centre in 1985, the troupe's attempt to tour the play in Anglophone Cameroon was prohibited. *Lake God*, which Butake wrote with the Lake Nyos gas disaster in the background, was allowed to tour the North-West Province in 1987. The electrifying effect of a performance of *And Palm Wine Will Flow* in 1990 at the University of Yaounde campus confirmed Butake as a prominent political satirist.

Amongst the unpublished plays staged by this troupe are Robert Ekukole's *Love on Credit* (1989 for television), Thomas Gwangwa'a's *Seminal Dregs* (1988), Patricia Nkweteyim's *The Family* (1990) and Joseph Banavti's *The Reapers* (1993). So far the Yaounde University Theatre has succeeded in providing an alternative form of entertainment for the Anglophone population, and Anglophones and Cameroonians as a whole have come to realise that theatre can play a vital role in nation-building. Yaounde University Theatre performed Bate Besong's *Beasts of No Nation*, directed by Bole Butake on 26 March 1991, at the Amphitheatre 700 of the University of Yaounde. Jean Stephane Biatcha, a government official and the chief of service for clubs and associations at the university, walked out of the hall in protest, castigating Besong for writing provocative and subversive literature. Reports reached the government and Bate Besong was detained and maltreated. For a long time his plays were not performed. Referring to Besong's play, S. A. Ambanasom, in 'Pedagogy of the Deprived: A Study of the Plays of Victor Epie Ngome, Bole Butake and Bate Besong',[6] writes that 'Physical torture of political enemies is a common theme in Bate Besong's works . . . the shit imagery in *Beasts of No Nation* is a strong and significant symbol of the putrescence that has overwhelmed the society'.

The Yaounde Children's Theatre Collective was founded by H. N. Eyoh in 1988. This troupe comprised twenty-four members, ranging from ages 13 to 15. The troupe started off as a workshop of the Yaounde University Theatre, with a selection of children from Anglophone schools in Yaounde. Eyoh worked closely with Bole Butake, Patricia Nkweteyim and Joseph Banavti. This troupe performed Hansel Eyoh's *Munyenge*, an adaptation of a traditional tale in which a princess turns down her parents' choice of eligible suitors in pursuit of her own choice, a stranger who to her great consternation turns out to be a devil (a familiar African folk-tale). The first performance of this play was at the Goethe Institute in Yaounde on 17 March 1990. The troupe visited Lingen in Germany on 14 April 1990 to attend a one-week theatre festival. In 1991 it staged *The Magic Fruit* by Hansel Eyoh in Yaounde. In time the children who were the foundation members of the troupe dispersed to colleges outside Yaounde, making work difficult for the very young children who stayed on. The group went quiet in 1992 and later dissolved.

The Flame Players are amongst the theatre troupes that kept theatre alive in the mid-1980s and early 1990s. This Anglophone university-based theatre troupe was founded in 1987 by a group of theatre enthusiasts as a launch pad for a meaningful and enduring creative contribution to the intellectual and cultural development of Cameroon. Under the leadership of Dr Godfrey Tangwa, the troupe produced J. C. de Graft's *Through a Film Darkly*, directed by Bole Butake in 1987 in Yaounde and which subsequently toured to Bamenda, Mbengwi, Buea and Limbe. A television adaptation was later scripted in 1989 by Thomas Gwangwa'a and directed by Robert Ekukole, both working at the Cameroon Radio and Television Corporation in Yaounde. The Flame Players have also performed *Our Cousin* by Thomas Gwangwa'a in 1989, Sankie Maimo's *Retributive Justice* in 1993 and Ola Rotimi's devised work *Grip'am* in 1995 in Yaounde. *Shoes and Four Men in Arms* by Bole Butake was performed in Yaounde in 1996 and later that year at the University of Buea. This play was later taken to Germany at the end of 1996 as part of a theatre festival.

In 1997 the Flame Players performed Judith Bi Suh's *None is All Honey* at the University of Buea, after having performed it in Yaounde. The company has been rather inactive since 1997. They face administrative problems, which almost led to their disintegration, but are currently trying to rebuild themselves.

As far as Anglophone Cameroon is concerned, most drama and theatre activities take place on college campuses. Bamenda's Delegation of Culture found no trace of any active theatre group. The chief of service in charge of cultural activities mentioned the existence of Palace Productions Association, which was directed by a Mr Tangyie Suh Nfor but whose activities had long since dwindled.

In Buea, the South-West provincial headquarters, Victor Musinga's Drama Group has remained the only active group amongst those registered for nearly thirty years. Formed in the 1970s, the Musinga Drama Group has performed only Musinga's own plays, two of which have been published. Eckhard Breitinger sees Musinga's theatrical style as 'that of the author/director/manager perhaps comparable in organization to the set-up of the Yoruba popular theatre of Ogunde, Duro Ladipo or Baba Sala'.[7]

Musinga has toured his plays in the South-West Province and has had tremendous support from the management of Alliance Franco-Camerounaise in Buea. His last public performance was in December 2000 during the National Festival of Arts and Culture (FENAC) that took place in Limbe, where he won first prize in the provincial competition. His choice of themes attracts the Cameroonian masses. His audiences are civil servants and clerks, the class that constitutes the body of his theatrical group.

Breitinger (see above, note) has observed that over the years Musinga has developed his dramatic techniques but that the essence of his melodramatic plots has remained the same. Good and evil are neatly separated and the moral messages that Musinga puts forward are clear, serious and never muddled: they are presented and made credible with a fair amount of comedy and farce.

The University of Buea Theatre Arts Unit is a rich source of theatrical activity in Buea. Since its creation, in 1993, the unit has produced over thirty plays, ranging from Greek tragedies to scripts written by staff and students of the university. A recent production was on 18 May 2001 and was Bate Besong's *Once Upon Great Lepers*, directed by the playwright. The play is Besong's rejection and denunciation of a political dictatorship that dehumanises and oppresses the ordinary Cameroonian.

The Ministry of Higher Education has instituted a Festival of Arts and Culture for state universities in Cameroon. This certainly is a vibrant way of reviving the theatre spirit in the country. The first University Festival of Arts and Culture (UNIFAC) took place at the University of Ngaoundere in December 1999. The second was at the University of Dschang in December 2001, during which Asheri Kilo's play *Caught in the Loop* (2001) was staged. This play deals with the ravaging impact of HIV/AIDS and the cultural implications of this disease on students and the community at large. The third festival took place in December 2002 at the University of Buea.

In the North-West provincial headquarters of Bamenda, the situation is bleak. Palace Productions Association remained the only active theatre troupe in the early 1980s and 1990s. Today they are extinct. Palace Productions Association started as the Mutual Dra-poets in 1980, with David Chuye Bunyui and Peter Suh-Nfor Tangyie as its directors. The troupe wrote and toured sketches such as *Funny Happy* and *Pa Atungshiri* in 1984, in both the North-West and the South-West Provinces. They also performed Athol Fugard's *The Island* in 1986 and Soyinka's *The Swamp Dwellers* in 1986. They produced Bate Besong's *Requiem for the Last Kaiser* in 1995. In the same year they staged Protus Tah's *The Ordeal of the Eighth Day* and John Menget's *Fruit of the Flesh*. Suh-Nfor's *Bedroom Magic* was the last play they staged in Bamenda in 1990, before they slowly disintegrated. Their director was promoted to a demanding administrative position as principal of Government High School Bafut, and as such he could not find enough time for Palace Productions. Campus productions do take place on his college campus. As is the case in Buea and the South-West Province, college-based plays only emerge on special national celebrations, when inter-college competitions are launched. On Radio Bamenda, there is a series of broadcasts of drama sketches produced by Elizabeth Achu, an animator of the Cameroon Radio and Television Corporation in Bamenda. Her radio programme, entitled

Awareness, broadcasts plays written and directed by herself. Some of her over twenty-five titles handle themes such as sexual promiscuity, caring for AIDS patients, water preservation, empowerment of women, abortion and other social issues. Although mainstream theatre practice is on the decline in Bamenda extensive work is being undertaken by Butake and Emelda Ngufor in the North-West Province in the sphere of theatre of conscientisation and theatre for development.

Theatre for development

The experience with mainstream theatre practice has shown that the impact of such theatre performances remains within the urban centres. Television and radio as forms of communication are still linked to a few élite groups. Some of these forms of communication leave out illiterates and the rural people who, more than any other group, are targets for development programmes.

The concept of the use of theatre as a vehicle for development was first introduced in Cameroon by H. N. Eyoh after his participation in the Theatre for Development workshop in Murewa, Zimbabwe, in August 1983, at which Kumba, Cameroon, was adopted as the venue for the follow-up workshop. The Kumba workshop took place in 1984, with participants from Nigeria, Ghana, Mauritius, Zaire, Tanzania, Zimbabwe, Ethiopia, Ivory Coast, Sweden and Cameroon. In *Hammocks to Bridges*[8] we read that the Kumba workshop had as its objectives the following items:

1. To initiate theatre people, development agents and village communities into the practice of theatre for conscientization and mobilization.
2. To demonstrate the process with the view of enabling the Cameroonian authorities to evaluate its potential as a means of development.
3. To contribute to the search for new methodologies in the practice of theatre for integrated rural development.
4. To hold a practical experience in village-based theatre involving villagers in analysing data and in the drama-making process.
5. To assess the effectiveness of the methodology, both in its immediate feasibility and long term impact.

The Kumba workshop was carried out in Kake, Kurume and Konye, where problems had been identified amongst the villagers. The inside-out method-ology of involving the participation of villagers in improvising plays that reveal their problems was the preferred technique that experts used in Kumba in 1984. Eyoh observed through his experience with popular travelling theatre troupes taking plays to the people that this method of working had shortcomings, in that rural masses could hardly voice their own concerns and that their cultural values were scarcely highlighted. Through the Kumba workshop, the Konye, Kake and Kurume villagers were able to perceive their reality and their environment from their own point of view. The community got involved in different levels of discussion, analysis, dialogue improvisation and enactment, encouraging the sharing of ideas and information. But there was no follow-up and the hopes raised in the villages fizzled out.

In 1998 Bole Butake and Doho Gilbert conducted a series of theatre for development workshops in Ndop, North-West Province, from June 22nd to 28th. They worked in three villages in the province, namely Baba I, Bamunka, Babanki, and had as spectators about 6,000 people of all age groups. From August 26th to September 1st, Butake and Doho worked in Garoua, the North Province of Cameroon, specifically in Tokasco, Pitoa, Garoua and Gashiga, with about 6,500 spectators. In Yaounde from October 12th to 18th they worked in Biyem-Assi Efoulan and Oyomabang, with 2,500 spectators.

In all the theatre for development workshops, Butake and Doho, along with the participants, created a number of plays. In Ndop, the play was entitled *Man No Rest Party* and was a satire on the repressive attitude of the forces of law and order and the misconception of democracy as practised in society. In Garoua, the play was entitled *Mariage Forcé* and was a satire on the anti-democratic practice of traditional rulers and their lust for more wives. In Yaounde, the play entitled *Meetings des Partis Politiques* revealed the corruption in political campaigns and the consequences of tribalism and popular justice.

The workshops were carried out via an organisation called ASTRAC (Association pour la Sauvegarde des Traditions et Cultures du Cameroun). The main objective of the project was to select at random from specific localities around the country, men and women, young and old, and to train them in the techniques of using popular theatre methodologies in informal education on the themes of democracy and human rights.

Butake and Doho have stated in an unpublished report on the project that

> The *raison d'être* of our project was the concern of the American Government through the Democracy and Human Rights Fund of the United States Embassy in Yaounde, to build up a culture of

democracy and respect of human rights in Africa in general and Cameroon in particular, especially since 1990, when multi-party politics was reintroduced on the Cameroonian political landscape with a lot of hesitation as witnessed by the conduct of elections, which tended to be characterized by undemocratic practices and the gross violation of human rights.[9]

In the project, some sixty people were trained in the methodology and techniques of the practice of popular theatre. These participants had the obligation to carry on with the process in their localities.

In February and March 1999, Butake and Emelda Ngufor Samba carried out another project aimed at testing skills in social drama for research and extension work in the area of human rights and citizenship, socio-cultural development and gender orientation among Mbororo communities in Donga-Mantung Division. The objectives of the project as stated in the report that followed were:

1. To identify which language members of each community wish to generate their literacy in.
2. To mobilise and sensitise the communities involved in the Ballotiral project in the direction of understanding and valuing literacy and the power of generating it for themselves.[10]

Most of Butake's work in theatre for development has been in the area of theatre for democratisation and human rights. However, he has done extensive work with children. In April 1999 he ran a children's theatre for environment education workshop in Bamendankwe in the North-West Province.

In April 2001 Butake conducted another workshop on children's theatre for environmental education with children from Bamendankwe and Awing. This workshop took place at the pastoral centre in Bamendankwe. In June 2001 he was in Nkor, his native village, giving children environmental education through the use of theatre.

In this same context, Asheri Kilo has worked with Buea women through drama of conscientisation. Each year during the week building up to 8 March, the International Day of the Woman, the students of the Drama and Theatre Unit of the University of Buea carry out workshops with women's groups in Buea. During discussions of the theme of the year, problems are raised by the women and a play is improvised on the subject of the discourse. In 1997 the result was a play entitled *The Divorce*, which was later on scripted and directed by Asheri Kilo and staged on campus for University of Buea students while the première production took place in a community field at the Youth and Animation Centre in Buea Town. *The Divorce* is a play that encourages women to stand their ground in the marital homes. It informs women about legislation on matrimony and, ironically, discourages divorce.

The following year, women in the Tole Tea Estate were participants of a workshop which had as its objective the encouragement of women to be more politically alert, to run for positions in Parliament and to expose fraud and other malpractices during elections. *Potopotoh* was the resulting play. It was later scripted and a repeat performance given on 6 March 1998 at the Women's Empowerment Centre in Buea in the presence of the governor of the South-West Province and the Delegate of Women's Affairs.

In 1999 *The Empty Sack* was performed, and, in March and June 2000, *Matrimonial Tears. The Cornerstone* was rehearsed and performed in the University of Buea by students of the Department of Gender and Women's Studies in March 2001. These plays were later scripted by Asheri Kilo after successful participatory workshops with Buea rural and urban women, and toured schools in Fako Division as part of a project on 'Education for Development and Democracy' carried out by the Department of Women and Gender Studies of the University of Buea.

Problems encountered

Although there seems to have been enormous progress in Anglophone Cameroon drama within the last three decades, one must acknowledge the fact that, at a time when African theatre, music and dance are in ever-increasing demand and receiving even greater public recognition on the international scene, there remain difficulties for the Anglophone Cameroonian artist wishing to perform in this country. At best, observed from the dates of most of the performances recorded in this discussion, it is clear that performances are limited to National Cultural Weeks in March, April and May each year, mainly because of the near-total absence of performance spaces.

Exchanges with other African countries at international theatre festivals, concerts and meetings are extremely limited. National tours have been few due to a lack of financial support from public authorities, the absence of private sponsors and the high cost of transportation in Cameroon.

Cameroon has very few purpose-built theatres. Anglophone Cameroon has none. In the North-West Province, shows take place in the Congress Hall or the Community Hall, both of which are designed for political meetings and rallies. It is worse in Buea, where the University of Buea's biggest lecture theatre, Amphi 250, has become the home of theatre shows. The Alliance Franco-Camerounaise serves as the best theatre space in Buea, but this has a capacity of only one hundred seats. In Limbe, the Urban Council Hall is the only venue available, but it is completely lacking in theatrical atmosphere or technical equipment.

Notes

1. Emmanuel Fru Doh, 'Anglophone Cameroon Literature. Is there any such Thing?', in Navola Lyonga, Eckhard Breitinger and Bole Butake, ed., *Anglophone Cameroon Writing*, WEKA 1 (Bayreuth: Bayreuth University Press, 1993), pp. 77–8.
2. Hansel Ndumbe Eyoh, unpublished Ph.D. thesis ('The Development of Drama in Cameroon: 1959–79'), University of Leeds, 1979.
3. Asheri Kilo, unpublished Ph.D. thesis ('Anglophone Cameroonian Drama 1969–91'), University of Leeds, 1992.
4. Bate Besong, unpublished Ph.D. thesis, University of Calabar, 1996.
5. Bole Butake and Gilbert Doho, eds., *Théâtre camerounais/Cameroonian theatre* (Yaounde: BET Publishers, 1988).
6. In *Epasa Moto*, vol. 1, no. 3 (Limbe: Pressbook Printing Press, 1996), pp. 222–3.
7. Eckhard Breitinger, 'Masquerades of Tradition: Recent Anglophone Drama in Cameroon', in *Shades of the Empire in Colonial and Post-Colonial Literatures* (Amsterdam: Rodopi, 1993), pp. 146–7.
8. Ed. Hansel Ndumbe Eyoh, with Etienne Ze Amvela, Bole Butake and Paul Mbangwana (Yaounde: BET Publishers, 1984), p. 17.
9. ASTRAC project report entitled 'Theatre, Democracy and Human Rights', 1998, p. 3.
10. Project Report of Ballotiral field trip on 'Social Drama as a Tool for Catalysing Community Research and Analysis for Reflect', 1999, p. 5.

5 East Africa

Ethiopia and Eritrea

JANE PLASTOW

References to Æthiopia, Ethiopia and Abyssinia litter works of literature dating back to the Bible, and are in no way reliable guides to the ancient history of the nations currently called Ethiopia or Eritrea. Æthiopia simply meant the land of black people and was therefore a reference by ancient Greeks to the African continent. The first empire we know of existing in the region was the land of Punt or Sheba, which was converted from animism to Judaism consequent to a visit by Makeda, the Queen of Sheba, to King Solomon in the tenth century BC.

Legend in Ethiopia says that the queen had a son by Solomon, and that when this boy, Menelik, visited his father he returned to his homeland with not only Judaic priests but also with the Ark of the Covenant, which he had taken by a trick. Although there are scarcely any Jews in Ethiopia today, the last remnants of their descendants only left the country during the great famine of 1984, when they were evacuated to Israel, and many aspects of Ethiopian church practice reflect a Judaic inheritance. Perhaps most notable in performance terms are the dancing priests of the Ethiopian Orthodox Church. Using great drums and sistrum the priests perform a religious dance or *shibsheba* in full vestments on holy days.

Punt was succeeded by the Axumite empire, which had its heartlands in the highland regions of what is now northern Ethiopia and southern Eritrea. Axum was a trading nation dealing with Arab, European and African partners. The intricately carved stealae of Axum are its greatest historical monument, but at its height in the sixth century AD Axum controlled large parts of the area currently known as the Horn of Africa and extended across the Red Sea into Arabia.

Axum converted to Christianity in the fourth century AD, when Christian missionaries reached the court of the Emperor Ezana. The impact of this Orthodox Coptic Christianity on the development of Ethiopia, both politically and culturally, can hardly be over-estimated. The church has always been closely linked to the monarchy and quickly became part of the mechanism of social control, so that the history and power of church and state have been closely intertwined for sixteen centuries.

An early reference I have found to performance neatly demonstrates the power of state and church, and their wish to control the populace. In the sixth century one Bishop Grigentius issued a law in Axum's South Arabian domains that 'public singers, harp-players, actors and dancers were all suppressed, and anyone found practising these arts was punished by whipping and a year's hard labour'.[1]

The church quickly became the dominant patron of high arts in the empire. Church rituals are elaborate, often requiring a considerable number of richly costumed priests. Churches themselves are often elaborately and richly painted, and the symbolic style of icon painting promoted by the church has subsequently influenced contemporary Ethiopian-Eritrean art and theatre worlds. Importantly, the church was for many years dominant as the centre for literacy. The only schools were church schools, teaching literacy in the church language of Ge'ez. Ge'ez had originally been the common tongue of the highland peoples, but by the ninth century spoken forms were splitting off amongst the various ethnic groups, with Ge'ez retaining its status as the language of the church and the only language with a written form.

Specialist church performance forms further developed in the sixth century, when an Ethiopian priest, Saint Yared, is credited with having developed both a unique form of musical notation and the *qene* poetry beloved of the Ethiopian intelligentsia. Important Ethiopian playwrights such as Kebede Mikael, Endalkachew Makonnen and Mengistu Lemma have all acknowledged qene as a formative influence over their writing style.

Over the centuries specialist church schools developed for the study of religious dance – *aquaquam* – music – *zema* – and poetry – qene. By the eighteenth century the *aquaquam beit* (dance house) in the imperial capital of Gondar had 276 masters, and students might study the intricacies and strict rules of their discipline for up to eight years.

These were all élite art forms, designed to impress and differentiate the ruling classes from the mass of the peasantry. Feudal Ethiopian-Eritrean society was extremely hierarchical. The ideal for the upper classes was to move as little as possible. Physical labour except in the areas of farming or making war was seen as degrading. There were also rigidly enforced symbolic dress codes for different classes. For example, red was an imperial colour, and in times of war or on the emperor's regular progresses around the empire only his tent would be red. This symbolism of colour and means of differentiating rank has persisted into many plays. Heroes and leaders are often fairly static and appear in rich dark colours, whereas fools rush around, may be physically deformed, and speak doggerel or prose as opposed to the poetry which heroic characters commonly used in early theatre.

As has been the case in many cultures, it is far more difficult to find information on peasant art forms, especially before the twentieth century. The only accessible information found in modern Ethiopia relates primarily to the Amhara ethnic group, who currently make up around 25 per cent of the Ethiopian population, and who controlled the nation from 1270 right up until the collapse of the Marxist régime of Mengistu Haile Mariam in 1991. This is despite the fact that contemporary Ethiopia and Eritrea have more than seventy distinct ethnic groups, many of whom were only incorporated into those countries in the nineteenth century.

The most commonly referred to performers are the *azmaris*. An azmari can be male or female, and has usually been seen as a praise-singer, most commonly playing an instrument and/or singing. Azmaris have often taken on a role analogous to that of a jester, and female azmaris in particular might also dance. They can work alone or in small groups. The earliest reference to such performers comes from the Portuguese traveller Francisco Alvares, who wrote about a visit to the imperial court in 1520, when he was entertained by musicians playing the flute and *masinko* – a kind of one-string violin. In later centuries we know that great nobles commonly employed azmaris as part of their retinue. A few azmaris rose to high positions in such lordly service, but commonly these entertainers would sing praises to any who would pay for their services. To be an azmari was to be part of a caste grouping, and was a vocation often, though not necessarily, passed down through families. Azmaris even developed their own language, *yeazmari quenqua*. They usually lived on the edge of settlements, and though their skills were highly valued – they could act as conduits of public opinion in voicing normally unthinkable criticism of the ruling classes, and would often be employed for weddings or other celebrations – no respectable person would consider admitting an outcast azmari into their family.

Information on other performance forms in the empire is meagre. Only the highland peoples had a written language, and this was controlled by the church and state, so we have few records of peasant activities. Moreover, from the seventh century Axum ceased to be an outward-looking, dynamic society. The Christian highlands were progressively isolated as Islam became the dominant religion in the surrounding lands. Coptic Orthodox Christianity cut itself off from the main streams of the Orthodox and Catholic faiths by holding to a monophysite belief which divorced it from the other Christian churches, and the core peoples of the empire developed a conservative siege mentality, fearing the introduction of new ideas as an erosion of their identity and status as *Dakika Israel* – the Children of Israel, and the chosen ones of God. Periods of expansion to the south did take place in the fifteenth and nineteenth centuries, and about half modern Ethiopia's peoples are Muslim rather than Christian, but the Amhara and Christian power base remained intact, and in order to gain power and influence it was necessary to embrace Christianity, to speak Amharinya – the language of the Amhara – and to conform to Amhara cultural mores.

Ethiopia

Modern drama was brought to Ethiopia by an Amhara nobleman, Tekle Hawariat. By this time, it should be noted, Eritrea had become a distinct and separate entity; an Italian colony with borders delineated in 1890. Tekle Hawariat was an unusually well-travelled man who lived for many years in Russia, France and England. When he returned to Ethiopia in 1912 he was horrified by the Byzantine nature of the Ethiopian court, which was then convulsed by a struggle for the succession. He was also concerned by what he saw as the backwardness of Ethiopia. He therefore wrote a play to show the élite what proper drama was, and to use as a vehicle for criticism of the court.

Tekle Hawariat's play, *Fabula: Yawreoch Commedia* (Fable: The Comedy of Animals), was a satire based on the fables of La Fontaine. In its preface the playwright bemoans the absence of drama in Ethiopia. His characters were thinly disguised as animals, but the performance *circa* 1916 was witnessed by the Empress Zauditu, who clearly and rightly saw the piece as an attack on her and promptly banned all theatre from the court. There were a number of interesting aspects to this performance. Firstly, the new form was attacking the hierarchy, when élite art forms had been used to buttress the state. Secondly, the characters were animals. This fits in with common folk-story patterns, where anthropomorphic animal stories were used to teach social values. Thirdly, the playwright had attempted, however thinly, to disguise his meaning. This conforms with Amhara linguistic conventions. To speak openly is often seen as foolish in traditional society, and a man would be admired for his ability to speak obliquely. Ethiopia's most famous poetic

196 | JANE PLASTOW

form is called *samena worq* (wax and gold), and consists of writing where the apparent outer meaning disguises a very different inner message. This ability to dissemble and use *double entendres* was highly admired and would be important to future playwrights using theatre to give disguised messages to their audiences. Fourthly, the actors were press-ganged children, who were not expected to act well but to deliver the lines of their simplistically and crudely delineated characters in order to convey the playwright's message. In Ethiopian theatre it has traditionally been the playwright who is admired and the ability to use fine language that has been valued. The actor has been seen as a necessary tool for the delivery of the lines, and performance ability has been secondary. Therefore, until recently playwrights came from the élite and were highly honoured and well rewarded for their mastery of language, but actors were seen as the lowest of the low; modern-day azmaris, and indeed many of the early actors were azmaris because no respectable person would be seen on stage.

The development of drama now passed over to the few modern schools in Addis Ababa. These had been set up by Emperor Menelik and were largely European-staffed. However, Amharic was taught as a subject and new plays were written by Ethiopian staff members for their pupils to perform in Amharic. This development has been crucial to the growth of Ethiopian drama, which has been seen as an import from Europe and a predominantly literary form utterly divorced from the music and dance traditions of the people. But because it has always been in the hands of Ethiopians – and very few foreigners have ever spoken Ethiopian languages – this drama has been mediated through an Ethiopian sensibility from its beginning in a way that was not possible in colonised African nations.

When Haile Selassie came to the throne in 1930 he was anxious to be seen as a modernising monarch and he supported the reinstatement of drama at court. The two dominant figures in the theatre of the 1930s were the schoolmaster-playwrights Yoftahe Negussie and Malaku Baggosaw. Haile Selassie ensured that the new court drama would be supportive of his rule, and theatre's role was to glorify imperial and church history. Malaku Baggosaw's *Talaku Dagna* (The Great Judge) of 1934 was the most successful of these plays, and indicates the kind of theatre the emperor supported. *Talaku Dagna* was a retelling of the Solomon story, legitimating Haile Selassie's semi-divine status as Solomon's descendant. It was performed by schoolboys in Ethiopia's first theatre, a zinc shed attached to the prestigious Menelik School. Interestingly, the play was so popular that it was performed to a paying public twice a week for four months. The practice set a precedent in Ethiopia and ever since plays have been performed once, twice or even three times a week, but never in a continuous run.

In 1936 Ethiopia was invaded by Italy. Prior to the invasion Malaku Baggosaw set up the country's first national cultural group, Ye Ethiopia Hizb Ager Fikir Mahber (Ethiopian National Patriotic Association), formed to perform music, dance and short propaganda plays in the central square. Under Italian rule all Ethiopian cultural activity was suppressed, but by 1941 the emperor was back and drama began to move beyond the court and school.

Most influential was the reformed Ager Fikir theatre, now under Makonnen Hapte-Wold, who specifically saw his mission as preserving and developing the culture of the nation. His performers were professionals, usually azmaris, and they were all male, for no woman appeared on the Ethiopian stage until the 1950s. There were no actors but rather skilled performers of *kinet*. The term kinet may be loosely translated as art or culture, but it usually refers to performances of traditional dance, music and song. As Ethiopian theatre developed, kinet would be seen as the traditional indigenous performance form related to ordinary people, and drama as an import identified much more closely with the élite.

The first Ager Fikir Theatre had been an Italian officers' club. Performances took place every Sunday, and musicians lured the audience inside by playing fanfares at the doors. The show was essentially a variety performance consisting of traditional music and dance, and including a short play that was usually shown early, as people came for the kinet and paid little attention to the drama.

Most particularly, this audience was not interested in the serious subjects of school and court drama. They wanted comedy. The comedies were usually written out in scenario form, increasingly by the Ager Fikir's premier dramaturg, Iyoel Yohannes (said to be responsible for over seventy plays). They relied on improvisation by usually illiterate actors, who used a lot of physical humour and often featured a fool as the central butt of the piece. So up until the 1960s comedy was identified with popular theatre and tragedy or serious drama with the court and the educated élite.

In 1946 Yoftahe Negussie set up a rival theatre in the Addis Ababa municipal buildings. He advertised for sixty male performers of dance and music, and the emperor promised a yearly budget for the enterprise – though like many of Haile Selassie's monetary promises, this never materialised.

Actors were paid a pittance and had to work privately as azmaris in order to survive. A third, short-lived professional company, Yeandnet Theater Kifil (United Theatre Company), was set up by Mathewos Bekele in 1953, and this was the first company both to employ women and to go on tour. It travelled to Ethiopia's major cities down appalling roads in an open truck that also carried its makeshift stage and folding chairs for the audience.

Because they were usually only written in scenario form, we have few records of the popular plays. The élite theatre is much better documented. Men such as Kebede Mikael and Daniachew Worku were highly educated and experimented with a range of literary forms. Perhaps the prime example of élite writers is Ras-Bitwodded (Prince-Beloved) Makonnen Endalkachew. He was Ethiopia's first prime minister, and in the 1950s he wrote a series of heavily moralising, didactic plays, usually based on church or imperial history. *Salisawi Dawit* (King David III) is a good example. The story centres around an eighteenth-century king who incurs the scorn of his subjects by building a folk music hall in Gondar. His son, Prince Jacob, is so distressed by his father's love of secular music that, after a series of long discussions on morality, government and religion, the Prince pines and dies, while the King and Queen 'came to hate music, regarding it as the principle cause of the untimely death of their beloved son'.[2] This period also sees the first – and still very rare – women playwrights. Seneddu Gebru was the headmistress of Ethiopia's first high school for girls, and Romana Worq Kasahun was a broadcaster and campaigner on women's issues.

Many of the élite writers had little notion of dramatic form. In these early plays stage directions are often indistinguishable from the dramatic script, many are in verse form, and some, like Te'ezagu Haylu's *Haile Mariam Mamo* about a famous patriotic hero of the same name, were simply unperformable, being made up of thirteen acts and an accompanying historical essay. Performance was not what was important. These plays were literary exercises in the didactic tradition of church writing by a generation who were experimenting with modern imported literary forms, but who saw them as both an extension of church writing and a new way of developing traditionally highly valued rhetorical skills. This unique drama tradition was strictly controlled by the emperor. Haile Selassie was an autocrat *par excellence*. He personally censored many publications and performances and ensured that for many years nothing would emerge which was in any way critical of his authority.

Modern Ethiopia theatre possibly begins with the construction of the Haile Selassie I Theatre (now the National Theatre) in 1955. The Emperor spent a fortune on the construction of this 1,400-seat auditorium, complete with modern lighting and sound systems and with European technicians brought in to run the place. Although the theatres have often struggled financially, they have subsequently been joined by three other, state-funded buildings, showing films throughout most of the week and drama or kinet shows two or three times a week. They employ permanent companies of dancers, musicians and actors, with the National having a permanent staff of over one hundred. For the bourgeois of the capital, drama has therefore been an accepted part of Amhara culture and entertainment for some fifty years. What was to happen in the 1960s was that it would become increasingly a popular and influential voice calling for reform.

Three men in particular were responsible for this change. In the late 1950s Mengistu Lemma, Tesfaye Gessesse and Tsegaye Gebre-Medhin were all given scholarships by the Emperor to study in the West. When they returned to Ethiopia in the early 1960s they were to transform and galvanise the theatres. All these men were to varying degrees influenced by the socialist ideas they had encountered in the West and advocated social and political reform. Their western theatrical influences were Shakespeare, but also Shaw, Wesker, John Osborne and J. B. Priestley; influences they combined with a reverence for Amhara poetic forms and the Amharic language, to begin to create a still poetically expressed vision of the world, but one where for the first time ordinary people could take centre stage.

Not only the Emperor but also the actors were at first resistant to these changes. Actors were still paid appallingly low wages and they organised a number of strikes in the 1960s. They preferred the popular kinet-style performances, and an actor might be sent to join the drama rather than the kinet troupe as a punishment. Above all there was still a huge gulf between actors and playwrights/directors. A playwright received 50 per cent of box office takings for his work, an actor only a few Ethiopian dollars. It took time before Tsegaye's gritty and more realist dramas, often centring on the plight of the poor, such as *Ye kermsasow* (A Man of the Future), would appeal to actors used to playing great heroes. But gradually this theatre did gain in popularity. Tsegaye's plays and translations of Shakespeare and Molière make up half the output of the Haile Selassie Theatre in the 1960s, while Mengistu became Ethiopia's prime comic and satirical playwright, poking fun at the young élite in plays such as *Yelecha Gebecha* (Marriage of Unequals) and *Telfso Bekisse* (Marriage by Abduction).

Throughout the 1960s Haile Selassie played a cat and mouse game with the new generation of playwrights. Some material was sent back with demands for heavy cuts, sometimes the emperor walked out of performances he found distasteful, and gradually life became more and more dangerous for those using theatre to criticise the ruling class.

However, in early 1974 Ethiopia was beginning to rise in 'the creeping coup' that would finally overthrow the imperial régime. Members of the armed forces, students, teachers and taxi drivers all went on strike over pay and conditions. The actors joined in, demanding the removal of the government-appointed theatre supremo, Captain Atnafu, and his replacement with men who knew something about theatre. They won and Tsegaye became director of the Haile Selassie Theatre while Tesfaye took over the Ager Fikir. As Ethiopia underwent the turmoil of revolution, the theatre became a truly popular centre for the debate of new ideas amongst the intelligentsia and the bourgeoisie.

By September 1974 the Emperor had been replaced by the military Dergue, but for a while it was unclear what direction and affiliations the new government would make. The Ethiopian public had been shielded from political ideology and from critical aspects of their own society. The theatre was well placed to become a centre for political debate, and between 1974 and 1977 a host of plays by Tsegaye, Tesfaye and Mengistu, but also by others such as Abe Gubegna, Berhanu Zerihun and Taddele Gebre-Hiwot, debated political alternatives and attracted audiences longing for information on the changing Ethiopian order. There were also experimentations in style, ranging from the first musicals, such as Taddele Gebre-Hiwot's *Man Now Etiopiawe?* (Who is the Ethiopian?) investigating alternative political systems, to Tesfaye Gessesse's absurdist *Iqaw* (Iqaw) and Tsegaye's epic on the beginnings of revolution, *Ha Hu Ba Sidist Wore* (ABC in Six Months).

The freedom was only short-lived. As early as 1975 Tesfaye Gessesse was detained without trial for three months for *Iqaw's* criticisms of state terrorism. In April 1976 theatre performers protested about pay and conditions and about their disappointment with Tsegaye's autocratic rule. A musician was shot dead and eighty artists were arrested. Interestingly, the performers did win their fight to become state employees with proper wages and pension rights. But as the Dergue instituted its 'Red Terror' the theatres came under the strict control of the new Ministry of Sports and Culture, and critical voices were gradually silenced.

The Dergue, under the increasingly absolutist control of Mengistu Haile Mariam, ruled Ethiopia from 1974 to 1991. Throughout most of that time the authorities maintained a stranglehold over the content of the theatre. It lost its position at the cutting edge of political debate, though it retained a strong hold on the affections of the Amhara bourgeoisie and remained a popular place for youth and family entertainment, with the city's 1,000-plus seater theatres often full.

The Dergue was responsible for a number of important measures in developing theatre. They set up compulsory peasants and youth associations throughout the country, and many of these established their own kinet groups. At first such groups concentrated on music and dance, but by the late 1970s agitprop theatre was spreading fast. The form also hit the professional theatres, with titles such as *Becommunistoch And Enat* (By the Unity of the Communists) and *Tiglachin* (Our Struggle), and the evidence is that at first such productions were popular as they were seen as a source of information. The Dergue established three new professional companies in the capital, including a children's theatre, and supported yearly tours to major cities. They also established theatre studies as a degree subject at the university.

This was an interesting development because university-trained actors would gradually challenge the hierarchical status quo. Old-style actors were often uneducated and under the control of much better paid and educated directors and playwrights. Actors were commonly typecast. An actor might become known for playing maids and be given that role time after time over twenty or so years. Accusations of favouritism were rife and women performers were commonly seen as little better than prostitutes right up until the 1990s.

Censorship meant that after audiences tired of agitprop the diet became increasingly one of romantic comedies, translations of anodyne European plays and a few classics, but under the dynamic influence of the university's first foreign theatre arts department chairman, Robert McLaren – a dissident white South African Communist – Ethiopia's only theatre-training establishment looked much more to international socialist practice, peoples' theatre, and attempted to integrate some Ethiopian dance and music into productions. There was also real concentration on the skills of acting, which gradually impacted on the theatres.

The Dergue was overthrown in 1991 by northern Tigrayan-led forces. Some of the old guard identified with Amhara hegemony lost their jobs, but there has been no renaissance of relevant theatre. Most playwrights are Amharas who dislike the new government, and most still remember the price paid for dissent under the 'Red Terror'. International exposure remains limited, and though the theatre houses are still popular places of entertainment, Amharic video-making is growing rather than the theatre, and there are few works dealing with the realities of life or questioning and engaging with contemporary Ethiopian society.

Eritrea

Via a mixture of treaties and conquest the borders of present-day Eritrea were established in 1890, when the country was created as an Italian colony. Within Eritrea were nine ethnic groups roughly equally split between Christians and Muslims, with the exception of the largely animist Kunama; widely renowned within Eritrea as possessing the richest variety of indigenous cultural and performance forms. As throughout Africa, music, dance and storytelling were the prime modes of performance. Christian society was dominated by the Ethiopian Orthodox Church and followed many cultural patterns described in Ethiopia. The Muslim peoples – the Hidareb, Rashida and Afar and Nara – were known as warriors and traders, and many of their performance forms celebrated warrior skills with elaborate sinuous swordplay and richly dressed, veiled women providing an accompaniment. However, the richness of the country's performative heritage was of little interest to the colonisers, and as in so many parts of Africa, the written record is minimal when it comes to historical cultural practices.

What the Italians were interested in was introducing their own performance forms to the growing population of colonisers. They established cinemas, dance clubs, bars and an opera house complete with tiered balconies and dancing nymphs painted on the ceiling in the capital of Asmara. In the early days of the colony there was significant contact between Italians and Eritreans, but as Mussolini's fascist régime gained power an apartheid segregation of African and European areas was established, and Eritreans were barred from attending performances at the opera house for either amateur or imported shows.

Nonetheless, the father of modern Eritrean theatre, Alemeyhu Khasay, gained his inspiration from performances he saw at the opera house when he was employed in the box office in the late 1930s. Alemeyhu was particularly attracted to the slapstick comedians. His natural talent was spotted by an Italian director, who applied for permission for him to replace a sick white actor. When this request was turned down for race reasons Alemeyhu resigned his job and became a lawyer's messenger.

The British took over as a caretaker administration in 1941, during the Second World War, and it is at this point that we see the first indigenous theatre groups emerging. Shakespeare was taught in schools, and a number of schools and churches set up drama groups. The first professional singers emerged, working in bars and clubs. More cinemas were opened to Eritreans, and in 1944 Alemeyhu Khasay set up the Mahber Theatre Dekabet – Ma.Te.De. (Indigenous Theatre Association) – with sixteen members, most of them teachers.

It is interesting that from the beginning this association saw itself as having a role in the political process. Association members were singers, musicians and actors, and they fought to promote Eritrean cultural forms as well as putting on propaganda plays. Drama and music were always seen as separate forms, and, as in Ethiopia, there was a significant divide between slapstick comedy and dialogue-dominated 'serious' drama. Again as in Ethiopia, there were many variety-style performances, and a number of groups travelled and performed between the two countries, cross-fertilising each other in terms of performance initiatives. Ma.Te.De. produced a number of plays calling for unification with Ethiopia, as well as works such as the 1951 production *Ali in Asmara* by Gebremeskel Gebregzibher, which called for a rejection of Arab influences in the capital. It should be noted that nearly all theatre in Eritrea has been produced in Tigrinya, the language of the main Christian ethnic group in the region of Asmara and also the people with most access to modern education. As in Ethiopia, the first plays had all-male casts and women were only gradually enticed on to the stage, many of them bar-women who had no reputation to lose.

Eritrea was contentiously united with Ethiopia in 1952 by the United Nations. In 1961 Alemeyhu Khasay set up a new organisation, the Asmara Theatre Association (ATA), which operated until 1974. The performers were all amateurs who again put on variety-style shows, usually running from around 8 p.m. to 1 a.m. in cinemas after the last film showing. They also toured to the large Eritrean communities in Ethiopia, where their work, especially the comedy sketches, was immensely popular and attracted audiences of over a thousand.

All this theatre work was subject to censorship and had been from the early days of the British administration. However, during the 1960s Eritrea came under increasingly close scrutiny from Ethiopia. Haile Selassie had manoeuvred the removal of Eritrea's federal rights to internal self-government and a liberation war began in 1961 which lasted for thirty years, with more and more Eritreans joining the struggle for independence. All play scripts had to be submitted for approval, and Eritrean writers increasingly turned to allusive writing and symbolism to make their coded messages in support of the liberation struggle.

After the Dergue took over in 1974 Ethiopian control became ever more intensive. In that year Eritrean guerrilla fighters attacked an Ethiopian base. In revenge soldiers surrounded the opera house, now known as Cinema Asmara, and threatened the entire audience of over two thousand. The actor and playwright, Solomon Gebregzhier, was taken out and shot twenty-four times before being left for dead, though he in fact survived his ordeal. The ATA was shut down and performers were forced to make propaganda for the Dergue and to train amateur groups in the regions.

In response, the liberation movements set up their own cultural propaganda networks. In the 1970s there were two liberation fronts, the Eritrean Liberation Front (ELF) – largely identified with an Islamic leadership – and the Eritrean People's Liberation Front (EPLF) – a more Christian/socialist organisation. The ELF attracted a number of leading musicians to join its ranks, but by the 1980s it was the EPLF which was using the cultural tool in the most innovative way. In 1978 the EPLF was forced into a 'strategic retreat' into the northern mountainous region of Sahel. From here they set up a whole network of cultural troupes, not only amongst the fighters but also amongst the women, children, the disabled and even prisoners of war. The groups were intended to have multiple purposes: to promote unity amongst all Eritrean ethnic groups, to provide education on social topics such as women's rights, to boost morale and to provide nationalist propaganda. The troupes put on variety shows, comprising song and dance from all the ethnic groups, both modern and traditional and, increasingly, short plays. The most notable playwrights, such as Alemseged Tesfai, put considerable research into developing relevant naturalist drama, and the premier groups toured both the front lines and liberated areas, carrying their own stage, performing at night to avoid fighter plane attack, and travelling abroad to the diaspora to raise support for their cause. Notably, the EPLF commissioned extensive research into the performance traditions of the various ethnic groups in order to resist Amharisation and to promote the philosophy of 'Unity in Diversity'.

Since independence the government has fostered international links, especially with groups in the UK and Norway. The National Youth Association has been particularly active in supporting the nation-wide growth of amateur performance groups, and the People's Front for Democracy and Justice, the ruling party, supports both acting and traditional music and dance groups.

There has been interest in promoting a community theatre that discusses social issues, and the first translations of plays from other African nations have recently been published and performed

Notes

1. Sergew Hable Selassie, *Ancient and Medieval Ethiopian History to 1270* (Addis Ababa, 1972), p. 156.
2. Makonnen Endalkachew, *Selaswi Dawit*, in *Three Plays* (Addis Ababa, 1955).

References and further reading

Matzke, Christine. 'Of *Suwa* Houses and Singing Contests: Early Urban Women Performers in Eritrea', in Jane Plastow, ed., *African Theatre: Women*, Oxford: James Currey, 2001.

Matzke, Christine, 'Trying to Find the Stepping-Stones: Writing Tigre and Bilen Dancing in Eritrea. An Impressionistic Choreography within a Theatre Context', in Eckhard Breitinger and Yvette Hutchison, ed., *History and Theatre in Africa*, Bayreuth: Bayreuth African Studies/South African Theatre Journal, 2000.

Molvaer, Reidulf K. *Black Lions: The Creative Lives of Modern Ethiopia's Literary Giants and Pioneers*. Asmara: Red Sea Press, 1997.

Plastow, Jane. *African Theatre and Politics: The Evolution of Theatre in Ethiopia, Tanzania and Zimbabwe*, Amsterdam: Rodopi, 1996.

Plastow, Jane. 'Alemseged Tesfai: A Playwright in Service to Eritrean Liberation', in Martin Banham, James Gibbs and Femi Osofisan, ed., *African Theatre in Development*, Oxford: James Currey, 1999.

Plastow, Jane. 'Theatre of Conflict in the Eritrean Independence Struggle', *New Theatre Quarterly*, 50 (1997).

Plastow, Jane. 'Uses and Abuses of Theatre for Development. A Case Study Focusing on the Relationships Between Political Struggle and Development Theatre in the Ethiopia–Eritrea War, 1961–91', in Kamal Salhi, ed., *African Theatre for Development*, Exeter: Intellect Books, 1998.

Plastow, Jane and Tsehaye, Solomon. 'Making Theatre for a Change: Two Plays of the Eritrean Liberation Struggle', in Richard Boon and Jane Plastow, ed., *Theatre Matters: Performance and Culture on the World Stage*, Cambridge: Cambridge University Press, 1998.

Warwick, Paul. 'Eritrean Theatre in the Liberation Struggle', *New Theatre Quarterly*, 51 (1997).

Kenya

CIARUNJI CHESAINA AND EVAN MWANGI

Indigenous traditional roots of contemporary Kenyan drama

Contemporary Kenyan drama is deeply rooted in the people's indigenous traditional dramatic forms. In order to understand modern Kenyan drama, therefore, it is important to appreciate not only the origins of indigenous traditional drama but also the social context of the dominant forms.

Kenyan traditional drama owes its origins to the beliefs and worldview of the people about the relationship between human beings and the cosmos, as well as the relationship between the human world and the supernatural. Drama came to be used as a tool for survival, interwoven with the whole social fabric.

In an untamed geographical environment, it was believed that evil lurked in the atmosphere and it was necessary to find ways and means of arresting the hostile forces of nature. The dramatisation of a myth about the origin of an impenetrable forest or a huge river would serve to demystify the landmark's enigmatic nature, dissolving the fear it instilled in the people.

Just as drama forged smooth communication between humans and nature, it was found to be a most useful tool for facilitating communication between the human world and the supernatural. Catastrophes such as earthquakes, droughts, famines and disease needed the intervention of the gods. It was believed that such misfortunes did not just descend on the people without a reason. Their basis could be traced to some human error of commission or omission. Incantation or dramatisation of religious poetry was used to invoke super-human power to help combat catastrophes and to ward off evil powers. These dramatic forms were also used to placate the gods and supplicate for better times.

But it was neither desirable nor necessary to wait until disaster struck in order to communicate with the supernatural. To guarantee security and a kind of equilibrium, humans had to maintain good relations with the supernatural world at all times. Acknowledgement of the existence and power of the supernatural world over the human had to be a continuous process. Drama was the major tool for ingraining the consciousness of this in the psyche of the people. Hence before a journey, a hunting expedition or a war adventure a religious oago would direct a ritualistic dramatic episode for the community. The sacrificial proceeding would be accompanied by dramatic performances. In the case of preparation for war, actual dramatised war gymnastics would be performed as the warriors proved their readiness for the imminent encounter with the enemy.

Kenyan people's philosophy on death and mortality contributed significantly to the development of drama. As evidenced by various myths in the people's oral tradition, death was recognised as an inevitable companion to life. However, it was not seen as an end to life. Rather, death was seen as part of the growth of the living, particularly in the case of the demise of the elderly. It was an avenue through which the dead joined the ancestors. Elaborate drama therefore developed to enable the living to come to terms with the phenomenon of death and to help them usher the new ancestor into his new elevated world.

Just as on a day-to-day basis human beings communicated with the supernatural powers for survival through various hardships, it was necessary to maintain a good rapport with the ancestors in order to guarantee their support. Hence, belief in the omnipresence of the ancestors was reflected in certain dramatic episodes, depending on the occasion. Before apportioning meat from a newly slaughtered animal, for instance, the ancestors' share had to be 'delivered'. Before eating food or taking a drink, a person fed the ancestors with their rightful share. Over the ages, the appropriate traditional mimes for the feeding of the ancestors were established and passed on from generation to generation.

A most interesting element of the origins of drama in Kenya was the philosophy behind the relationship between the forces in the cosmos. Kenyan people recognised the intricate relationship between the supernatural world, the human world and the natural environment. It was believed that while nature was at the disposal of human beings and the latter could survive through appropriate exploitation of natural resources, reverence to the supernatural forces was mandatory for this relationship to be sustained. The utilisation of herbs for medicinal purposes illustrates this point.

The medicine-man or the medicine-woman did not pluck medicinal leaves in a hurry or mechanically, the way we pluck cabbages today. Nor did these medicine-people cut medicinal barks or twigs of trees in today's matter-of-fact style of tree pruning. Appropriate movements and incantations were used, in recognition of the fact that healing was a religious process. During the actual administration of medication to the patient, the medicine-person had to invoke supernatural powers for success. Such invocation was achieved through dramatic performance, whose participants included not only the doctor and his patient but also the medicine assistants, the patient's relatives and so on. The performance facilitated a psychological fusion of three forces: the human, the superhuman and the natural.

Lastly, climatic changes provided a basis for the development of traditional drama in Kenya. Traditionally, people were fascinated by climatic shifts from one extreme to another. It was observed that sometimes it was warm or hot and at other times cold. Sometimes it was dry and vegetation looked sad, while at other times it was wet making the fauna and flora smile. Since these changes affected people's existence, it was deemed necessary to find ways of acknowledging and coming to terms with them. Drama filled this need. Hence, when climatic changes culminated in a bumper harvest the people had to celebrate the season by giving thanks to the deities and the ancestors. This was done through masquerades impersonating the deities and ancestors, as well as through song and dance. Indeed, celebration of seasons of plenty can be traced as one of the major origins of dance drama in Kenya.

The above is a sketch of some of the origins of indigenous Kenyan drama. We now turn to an overview of the dominant traditional forms in their social context.

The social context of dominant traditional forms
Kenyan traditional drama was utilitarian in nature; it had specific social functions to serve within various cultural parameters.

The drama took diverse forms, but it could be categorised under the following umbrellas: role-play and children's games; the arts of storytelling and folk-tale; impersonation; improvisation; ritual-related drama; and dance drama. One factor that must be emphasised, as seen in the previous section, is the strong interlacing of traditional drama with the life of the particular community. With this aspect in mind, it would be a futile exercise to attempt a discussion based on rigid categorisations. There are of course overlaps in the social contexts, and some of the forms intermingle to strengthen one another. It is for this reason that this overview follows a holistic approach.

We start with a look at the traditional young child's social environment and how drama facilitated in developing his or her cultural identity. The arts of storytelling and folk-tale are incorporated here because it was indeed aimed at teaching the young child about the social environment and their place within it. The discussion then moves to the role of drama in Kenyan communities' rites of passage from adolescence, adulthood and death. Ritual-related drama, improvisation and impersonation are discussed within the parameters of these rites. Although dance drama figures prominently here, special attention is given to song and dance as a form that entertained while facilitating day-to-day living, in addition to strengthening communal cohesion.

The traditional Kenyan child was introduced to drama at birth. It was drama that assisted to usher him into the world. Amongst the Miji Kenda of the coast of Kenya, for instance, song and dance played a significant part in easing the pregnant woman's labour. The birth attendants and those women assisting the delivery would treat the labouring mother to a performance whose movements were related to the whole process of procreation. They would tease her and urge her to be brave, hence giving her psychological strength to deliver her baby safely. Among many Kenyan communities, women's innermost joy for the safe delivery was expressed through dance drama. Women would dance with the baby, teasing him and telling him he belongs to the whole clan, as a way of welcoming him into their culture.

Later, the choice of the cultural name of the growing child was facilitated by drama. Among the Kalenjin, for example, an elder would dramatise the names of the ancestors in a bid to tickle the child to reveal which ancestor had been reborn through him. As the names were uttered, the child's reaction would be monitored. The name that resulted in calm after a child's tantrum, for instance, would clearly indicate that the particular ancestor had been reborn. Of course, the climax of the naming ceremony was celebrated by the community through dance drama.

As children grew up, they learnt that drama was part and parcel of life. It helped them to learn and simultaneously entertained them. Among very young, pre-adolescent children, drama was performed in the context of play and relaxation. The forms included dramatised games, dramatised riddling, performance of simple satirical skits and imitation of nature. Hence, the children would learn about their communities' cultures and discover the natural environment as they socialised with each other and entertained themselves. Humour was an outstanding characteristic of children's drama. The young ones specialised especially in the absurd, as illustrated by the following Gikuyu children's skit:

CHILD ONE: (*imitates a monkey's walk*)
What is that oh!
What is that oh!
OTHERS: (*pointing at Child Two's bottom*)
On your bottom
Flashing in all its redness?
CHILD TWO: Monkey (*in a pleading voice*)
It is just a small scar
A thorn scratched me
While we were picking berries
Berries from the forest
OTHERS: (*laughing in unison and imitating the monkey's limp*)
CHILD TWO: Monkey (*in a harsh voice*)
Whoever repeats that question
Will hear the whole forest tumble down
All the trees will turn to powder!

This skit enables children to socialise with one another, while at the same time entertaining them with the absurdity of the little monkey's red bottom. In addition, they learn to communicate with nature: the animals (represented by the monkey) and the plants (represented by the trees in the forest). This communication subsequently enables children to dissolve some of their fear and to find their place in the natural environment.

It will be noticed, however, that children often choose to express themselves through animals, with which they can identify. In this skit, they tease monkey's child rather than, for instance, the child of lion or leopard. In other dramatised games, children will imitate doves rather than eagles and hawks, while in the human world they will tease old women rather than warriors.

Still at the pre-adolescent stage, drama played a significant part in children's growth when they engaged in role-play. In role-play the girls dramatised various roles observed as belonging to the mothers while the boys would imitate various roles played by the males within their community. One point to note is that role-play was extremely culture-specific. In a Maasai community, for instance, where the responsibility of building houses fell on the shoulders of women, girls would role-play the task of building houses. Among the less nomadic peoples such as the Abagusii, on the other hand, it would be unthinkable and almost a taboo for a girl to play the process of house construction.

The importance of children's role-play in traditional Kenyan communities cannot be ignored. The people's subsistence depended to a great extent on a division of labour, which was stratified along age and gender lines. Role-play therefore assisted in gender stereotyping and relevant socialisation into cultures in which an individual's role was clearly defined.

For the older children, drama was performed either for relaxation during restful periods (such as evenings or after harvests) or in the course of carrying out various chores. Dance drama and storytelling were the most popular forms for evening relaxation. The type of drama performed during various jobs depended on the nature of the particular responsibility. Herdsboys would, for instance, weave dramatic performance around practising hunting or warfare skills. This was performed out in the grazing fields when the animals had eaten their fill and were resting chewing the cud. The boys would then amuse themselves while sharpening skills that would prove useful in their future social roles.

Cultural taboos controlled the type of drama that might interfere with children's responsibilities. Among many Kenyan communities, it was taboo for anyone to engage in storytelling during the day. Concentration and involvement in the art was likely to divert a child's attention from the task at hand.

The art of storytelling in Kenya is as old as the human race, acting as the record or expression of the people's history, accepted norms and values. The art of storytelling was the creative arm of folklore, which was used to socialise the youth while teaching them about their cultural heritage and their place within it.

Storytelling found its vibrance and effectiveness through dramatic performance. It was dramatic performance that enhanced the involvement of all and broke the distinction between the narrator and the audience, making everybody present a participant. This approach underlined the fact that storytelling was essentially a communal art.

The most effective starting style was for the narrator to throw a number of riddles at the audience, choosing those members observed to be distracted. The trick would amuse the rest and inspire alertness. Since stories were 'written' in the memory of the people and not on paper, it was of paramount importance that they were dramatised in order for the message to come through. The dramatisation also helped bring out the humour, which entertained the audience as messages were imparted to them.

Dramatisation was done mainly via voice variation, facial expression and gesture on the part of the narrator. In addition, the young participants were treated to further images through being invited to imitate the animal characters in the stories. As noted above, this dramatisation kept the art alive as it assisted the crystallisation of the message.

Lastly, drama facilitated interaction of various artistic aspects of folklore, bringing everybody on board. Where there was a song in a particular story, the audience would participate, making the storytelling session a kind of musical. A seasoned narrator would unexpectedly summarise the moral of a story using an appropriate proverb, hence giving the whole performance a kind of elaborate grand finale.

A major source of Kenyan drama were the artistic performances supporting ceremonies related to rites of passage and to initiation into various stages of social strata. Besides dance drama, aspects of improvisation and impersonation or masquerade figured prominently in these performances. However, the point to note here is that these performances were serious elements of the ceremonies. They were integral to the rites and not mere spectacles for entertainment.

Among the Kalenjin, elaborate circumcision ceremonies were held to mark adolescents' movement or graduation from childhood to adulthood. White-ochre body masks distinguished a youth as an initiate. Since the circumcision season was a communal celebration, everyone took advantage to adorn themselves with the most interesting garb one would not wear ordinarily. It was an occasion for showing off. Participants draped themselves in animal skins of all colours. Ostrich feathers and colobus monkey hats crowned heads. It was an occasion to practise various disguises.

Drama facilitated the circumcision ceremonies. Dance drama provided a vehicle through which the community escorted the initiates on the journey to a new social horizon. Dancing together helped cement social cohesion by enabling participants to shed old tensions and renew relationships with their neighbours, kith and kin. It was a season for castigating social misfits through satirical songs.

But to the new initiates, drama played a most significant role during the education sessions. It must be noted here that the actual operation would have been empty if taken in isolation from the education imparted to the new adults. Therefore, during these sessions it was necessary to create an atmosphere that inspired the seriousness of the maturity phase the initiates were entering into. Instructors disguised themselves and masqueraded as the ancestors they represented. Costumes, dramatic demonstrations, gesticulation and voice disguises enabled the instructors to play their role effectively.

A most interesting utilisation of drama in the instruction of male Kalenjin initiates was the use of background noise and 'off-stage' voices. This was used in the instruction and warnings against sexual immorality. Promiscuity was considered immoral and therefore in order to curb the tendency, it was important to imprint the cultural expectations at initiation. Owing to the taboo associated with sexual matters, people never discussed the subject overtly but had to use discreet language. Hence at initiation the instructors conformed but attained their aim through using background noises sugges-tive of sexual intercourse, then used austere 'off-stage' voices to ask questions and warn the initiates about the consequences of sexual immorality.

The key to participation in sexual intercourse was given at the mar-riage rites, which formed the next stage after initiation. This is an area in which drama figured prominently in traditional Kenyan communities. Drama started manifesting itself from the courtship stage, then wove itself through the dowry negotiations and other wedding preparations. The climax of the marriage rite, the wedding itself, was a melting pot of drama in which the entire community participated.

Among the Meru, the Embu and Mbeere of eastern Kenya a young man going to woo a girl took with him one or two friends. Evening was preferred, not for dubious reasons, but rather to allow everyone to complete their daily chores. Outside the girl's hut, the young men would not knock at the door the way we do today. The suitor would blow his nose loudly. This was a tradition that had survived the test of time to such an extent that courtship had acquired the euphemism 'blowing the nose'. If the young lady did not like the young man, then she would fake deafness to the nose sound. The mother would also join in the drama. She would, for instance, ask the girl to go check 'who is making noise outside'.

Listening was very important, as it was through sensitive listening that a young lady could tell, from the tone utilised, whether her mother approved of the suitor or not. If the mother's disapproval was detected, then the young lady could pretend not to have heard even the mother's voice. Even when everything was positive and the girl was ready to respond to the suitor, the response could not be expressed overtly. Etiquette demanded caution and moderation in expressing emotions of love.

The actual courtship among many Kenyan communities was a kind of dance of hide and seek, mock fight and so on. The drama was so intense that a young lady might take some time to know who was the actual suitor among three friends. The dowry negotiation was an opportunity for the elders to show off their powers of oratory as well as prowess in performance. In order to avoid possible misinterpretation that the bride-to-be was being regarded as a commodity on sale, everything would be couched in drama. Euphemisms were used to refer to the girl and to the forthcoming union. Props such as sticks were used to represent the number of goats, cattle and other commodities to be given as symbolic presents to the girl's family.

Just as dowry negotiation sessions provided the opportunity for the elders to show off their oratorical powers, the task of taking the bride to her marital home provided the occasion for the bridegroom's age mates to practise their theatrics and other performing skills. The occasion was created by the tradition whereby brides were not expected to go to their marital homes willingly or to show that they were overjoyed to wed.

It was feared that if a bride was too enthusiastic, she and her family would be misjudged as being desperate and this would undermine her worth among her in-laws. Performance assisted brides to show their worth. Apart from adornment and an affected walk, a bride would act out a kind of mourning as if a big tragedy had struck. Among the Gikuyu of central Kenya, this act of the bride had become so institutionalised that it had acquired the name 'a bride's wailing'.

In contrast to a bride's wailing and feigned reluctance to set off to the marital home, a vivacious drama was enacted by the young men who carried her off. Among the Luo of western Kenya, the whole thing looked like a war. The bridegroom's friends arrived unannounced at the bride's home. In order to incite their male counterparts on the bride's side, each shouted his praise name in a terror-inspiring tone. These were not single-word names but rather whole verses, such as

> I am Odhiambo
> Lion Killer
> Come from Oyimbo
> Open the gates!
>
> I, grandson of the great
> Warrior Lwanda Magere
> A lion in my hands
> Feels like a rat
> Open the gates!

War theatrics would then ensue. The bride's side would put up resistance with equal force and the two groups of young men would engage in what appeared to be a real combat. Onlookers who did not fully understand the culture might be frightened, seeing it as a real full-scale war, but the participants were cognisant of the mission at hand. Eventually, the bride would be carried shoulder-high in spite of her kicking, scratching, screaming and pretended opposition to the rite of marriage.

But marriage ceremonies were not all tough negotiations and feigned combat. They also provided occasions for enjoyment and the expression of deeply felt emotions. Song and dance drama provided this opportunity. The genre, for instance, gave women the poetic licence to protest against their low social status and to demand their rights as mothers of their communities. The following Embu women's popular wedding dance song illustrates this point. As they swing their hips and rub their thighs in a somewhat erotic dance, the age mates of the bride's mother sing the following:

Kanyanya let me push you along
Kanyanya let me push you along
So that you can deliver a message for me
To my son-in-law
Tell him to bring me a hairy he-goat
A hairy he-goat which can produce fat
To rub on my thighs
They are painful
While I was delivering this child
You men were hiding
To avoid hearing my groaning
Hmn! Hmn! Hmn! Hmn!

As the women utter the idiophones signifying groaning, they beat their thighs. The thighs are symbolic of the whole child delivery process. It will be noticed that drama and the poetic genre enable the women to convey a difficult message while respecting the boundaries of expression set by the culture. The bride's mother is not allowed to talk directly to her son-in-law, hence she sends her counterpart 'Kanyanya', mother of the bridegroom. More importantly, the culture takes women's contributions for granted and does not expect them to complain. Yet here, they go as far as demanding a share of the bride-price from whose negotiation and benefit they have been so far excluded. Hence drama provides a tool for protest and self-expression.

Apart from the initiation and marriage rites, funeral rites contributed significantly to the development of drama in Kenya. It must be acknowledged

that not all Kenyan communities held ceremonies at burial. However, those
that did made full use of drama to attain various aims.

The death of an individual in traditional Kenya was not an affair exclusively for the family of the deceased, it was an event which affected
the whole community. Drama provided a channel through which a bereaved
community could come to terms with the loss of a beloved one. As intimated
above, drama was used to usher an elder into the world of the ancestors. In
addition, drama was used to cleanse the immediate relatives of the deceased
and prepare them for life in his or her absence. Death ceremonies varied
from community to community. Whereas some communities such as the
Kamba and Kalenjin minimised drama at bereavement, communities such as
the Luhya and Luo held elaborate ceremonies involving all affected.

Drama facilitated the ceremony known as *Ter Bur* among the Luo. This
was a ceremony at which the widow was inherited by an appropriate relative
of the deceased. It must be mentioned in passing that ceremonies such as
Ter Bur are now dying out owing to certain historical developments such
as the spread of HIV-AIDS.

Dance drama was a most popular performing art. It was through dance
drama that a community came to terms with the phenomenon of death.
Dance drama facilitated mutual support at these tragic moments. The song
and the accompanying movements assisted the affected family and the community at large to undergo psychological therapy for the tensions brought
about by death. Some communities had professional mourners who performed appropriate dirges. Furthermore, the song provided an expressive
channel through which the bereaved could mourn and gain confidence for
life thereafter in the absence of the deceased.

The foregoing is an overview of the indigenous traditional roots of
Kenyan drama. It will be seen that the beliefs and worldview of Kenyan
people have contributed tremendously to the foundations of contemporary
Kenyan drama. The performing art draws closely not only from the cultures
of the people, but also from the dramatic forms which gave these cultures'
expression in the traditional setting.

The colonial era and subsequent neo-colonial phase are significant foundations, a second pillar in the development of modern Kenyan drama. Where
the traditional forms were communal performances and closely linked to
ritual, the forms introduced in the colonial era were more for the stage.
In the traditional forms, the line between the so-called performer and the
audience was very thin, but the forms introduced during the colonial era
were predominantly aimed at a specific audience.

The next section examines the history of post-colonial Kenyan theatre. It is built on the premise that artistic development cannot be divorced from historical development. History provides a people with experiences that affect their worldview, making them search for appropriate means of survival. Drama as a performing art, then, provides an imaginative expression through which a society learns to adapt to its changing historical circumstances.

History of post-colonial Kenyan theatre

Kenya gained independence from Britain on 12 December 1963. By this time theatre had established itself as a tool of entertainment among the settler community and as an agent of anti-colonial struggle among indigenous Kengans. These two strands developed side by side in post-colonial Kenya. Made up of over fifty ethnic communities, the country enjoys theatre in a variety of indigenous languages, although there is an attempt to forge a national theatre, especially through the Kenya Schools and Colleges Drama Festival, which brings together performances from different parts of the republic. Kenya's post-colonial theatre remained a site of exchange between local cultures and myriad other foreign value systems, with Kenya's place in the evolving global dispensation exercising the mind of both established and nascent artists.

The 1940s had seen a rise in comedies ridiculing the Swahili spoken by colonialists. Swahili is the country's national language and the comedy went on after independence, with slapstick comedies being shown on national television to a range of enthusiastic audiences. A case in point is *Vitimbi*, a television programme which since its inception in the early 1980s used drama's potent techniques, humour and empathy, to treat social themes.

The Kenya National Theatre, opened on 6 November 1952, became the hub of theatre activities, and the history of Kenyan theatre is closely tied to the politics surrounding this institution. The other influential instrument in shaping the development of Kenyan theatre is the Kenya Schools Drama Festival, an initiative of the British Council and the East African Theatre Guild. The first national festival was held in 1959 at the Kenya National Theatre. The event was hosted annually by the theatre until 1982, when the festival started being hosted by the eight provinces of the country on a rotational basis. The festival was initially run by the British Council. The Kenyan Ministry of Education took over the festival in 1969. Although as early as 1965 teachers were expressing the need to incorporate performance into the English curriculum to enhance theatre, the sentiments were never put into practice. Despite criticism of published dramatic texts remaining core to language studies in secondary schools, theatre remains an activity outside compulsory schoolwork.

The Kenya National Theatre is under the aegis of the Kenya Cultural Centre established on 27 December 1950 to provide a theatrical and literary forum to Kenyans without distinction of race or creed. Funding for the theatre came from government grants and financial assistance by Nairobi City Council. People associated with the establishment of the theatre were the Governor of Kenya, Sir Phillip Mitchel, Brian Figgis, Kathleen Robinson, Sir Richard Woodley and James Master.

Theatre developments in the country revolve around the perceived failure of the Kenya National Theatre as a space and facility to foster national interests. Established by the colonialists and located in an exclusive area in the upper part of Nairobi, it is not accessible to the majority of Kenyans. The performance fee of Ksh 15,000 in a country where half of the population lives below the poverty line is too high for theatre groups to access the space. The stage was initially reserved for professional and semi-professional groups that excluded African performances. The situation was allowed to continue after independence (Mumma, 1994: 135). African theatre of the early 1960s reflected the social relations between the British colonialists and the African Kenyan. The plays used African symbols such as the shield and the spear in their background, a contradiction to crown emblems. Negative characters in the plays were made to wear imperialist designs as a strategy of ridiculing them. However, even years after independence, such theatre could not be dramatised in a national space that was still in the grip of foreigners.

The Kenya National Theatre was so unpopular with the local population that in the late 1960s the Kenya Cultural Council decided to erect community halls in other parts of Nairobi. In 1968 recreational complexes were built in Kariokor, Kaloleni, Shauri Moyo, Uhuru, Majengo and Dagoretti by the Nairobi City Council, 'to cater for the recreation of the people in these areas' (Mumma, 1994: 140). The populations in these parts of the city comprised the poor and the working class, as opposed to the élite that could access the national theatre. At the Schools Drama Festival, African students were given a raw deal, as they 'had to compete with white and Asian students in the rendition in performance of plays from Shakespeare, Miller, Ibsen and Molière' (Mumma, 1994: 214).

The year 1968 saw the appointment of an African Kenyan, Seth Adagala, as director of the Kenya National Theatre. He mooted the idea of a theatre school to teach movement, stage management, acting, scriptwriting, directing and play production. The move was largely to integrate Africans into the European-dominated Kenya National Theatre. The curriculum was Eurocentric and ignored African aesthetics under the pretext that it was only practical, according to a Kenya Cultural Centre report published in 1969, to start from the known disciplines in the theatre. The report is silent as to why European modes would be seen as the 'known', but implicit in the clause is that the theatre was European in orientation. The initial promises that the school would 'gradually move into the rather unknown realms of the African theatre' were not fulfilled.

The school, which started its operations in 1968, produced the major personalities of Kenyan theatre today – Paul Onsongo, Edwin Nyutho, Alex Dindi, Tirus Gathwe, Allan Konya and Ann Wanjugu. The performances by the school were in English and were modelled on conventional European theatre, leading Ngugi wa Thiong'o to complain pointedly that Kenya National Theatre, despite the insertion of Kenyan voices courtesy of the Kenya Theatre Company, remained an élitist space (Ngugi wa Thiong'o, 1986: 39). The school closed in 1975, officially because of lack of funds but in reality because of apathy on the part of the government (Mumma, 1994: 148). The year 1968 also witnessed the appointment of Seth Adagala as the first African adjudicator, a process that was celebrated as a first step towards the decolonisation of theatre in Kenyan schools.

A number of plays were written and produced in the 1960s. *The Black Hermit* by Ngugi wa Thiong'o is one of the earliest Kenyan post-colonial plays. The play was written to mark Uganda's independence from Britain in September 1962, but was acted a few months later because the script was not ready at the time of the celebrations. At play's première the dramatic community of Makerere University, where Ngugi was a student at the time, took the parts. Though not a theatrical masterpiece – it is hardly performed in Kenya – the play is important because it captures the tensions between traditional life and modernity ushered in by colonialism.

Ngugi's *This Time Tomorrow*, the first sound version of the play, was broadcast on the BBC African Service in 1967. This short play gives its title to the collection of two other scripts, *The Wound in the Heart* and *The Rebels*, together with which it is published. Set in a ramshackle shack at the Uhuru slum market, it is a statement on the problems of urbanisation in Africa. The main conflict emerges from the opposition between the poor populace and the local authorities who want to evict them from their market without offering a substitute. The City Council are engaged in a clean-up exercise in which they want to demolish the dwellings of the have-nots because they are an eye-sore to 'tourists from America, Britain and West Germany' (41).

The Rebels, like *The Black Hermit*, revolves around a young man with a western education who rebels against the tribe. Charles, a young man for whom the village elders have chosen a wife, the chief's daughter, comes home with a foreign fiancée. Charles does not believe in the primacy of the tribe, but the rest of the community thinks it is their duty to preserve the traditions. Ngugi makes Charles voice the collective dilemma of the educated in Kenya: 'Torn between two worlds. I wish I were not myself. Then I would not have to choose between a father's curse, a tribe's anger, and the anguish of a betrayed heart' (13).

The changes initiated in the late 1960s started bearing fruits in the 1970s. Expatriate teachers started leaving and Africans had a chance to produce plays with students. At the Schools Drama Festival in 1971, *Olkirkenyi*, a play in the Maasai language by Olkejuado Secondary School students, won in the national finals. In 1975 teacher training colleges and polytechnics were incorporated into the festival, a measure 'to get drama well established in schools' (Mumma, 1997: 37). The Colleges Drama Festival witnessed emergence of talented thespians such as Felix Osodo and Otumba Ouko.

It is in this decade that major Kenyan dramatists emerged. Francis Imbuga (1947–), rated Kenya's leading playwright, started his career at this time. Like Ngugi's plays of the 1960s, Imbuga's early writings dramatise the tensions between rural and urban Kenya, a recurrent motif in his writing. *The Married Bachelor*, written in 1971, portrays the escapades of a university lecturer of culture called Denis. Revolving around the circumcision of Denis's son, Yohana, the play dramatises the conflict between modernity and tradition. Imbuga's *Kisses of Fate*, also written in 1971, dramatises the story of two youths who unwittingly fall in incestuous love. *The Fourth Trial* (1971) is a humorous play telling the story of a childless couple, Musa and Helen. Each is blaming the other, with Helen saying that Musa has contracted a venereal disease from a city prostitute, while he insists that she is to blame because she is deformed. Back in the village they call Mukembo, the witch doctor, to their aid. His tricks work, but towards the end it is revealed he is nothing but a charlatan. His was just a confidence trick.

It was *Betrayal in the City* (1975) that put Imbuga on the national map. He had written his earlier plays as an undergraduate student at the University of Nairobi; at that time his style had not matured and his organisation of ideas was still fuzzy. Whilst the earlier plays are more or less melodramatic, and do not resolve conflicts without resorting to coincidences, *Betrayal in the City* is a sophisticated dramatic gem. The play and its sequel, *Man of Kafira*

(1982), satirise the corruption which defines post-colonial Africa. *Betrayal in the City* was chosen as one of the two plays to represent Kenya in the Second World Black and African Festival of Arts and Culture (FESTAC) in 1975; the other play was Ngugi wa Thiong'o and Micere Githae-Mugo's *Trial of Dedan Kimathi*. Imbuga's play, like Ngugi and Mugo's, was popular and 'performed to capacity crowds at the Kenya National Theatre' (Makini, 1985: 29). Without directly attacking the powers that be, Imbuga gives a candid picture of what ordinary people have to go through at the hands of autocratic African dictators. Imbuga finished *Game of Silence* in 1977, and it premièred at the Kenya National Theatre. In this play, Imbuga creates comic figures to satirise the intolerance of neo-colonial régimes.

Despite the agony the Kenya National Theatre was going through in the 1970s, the period saw the emergence of alternative theatre spaces. In 1974 the University of Nairobi launched the Free Travelling Theatre, an interdisciplinary outfit made up of students and staff. It started performing plays in local languages, Kiswahili and English. It took theatrical pieces to rural areas, performing in halls, churches and the marketplace. Its objective, according to the 1975 programme, was 'to take theatre to the spaces it rightfully belongs; these are the people's theatres and we shall all perform together' (quoted in Mumma, 1994: 150). Other groups that sprang up in the period include the Tamaduni Players, the University Players and the Mshido Players of Kenyatta University, an institution that until the late 1990s enjoyed the most vibrant theatre activities. Kenyatta University's theatre success depended on the presence of Ghanaian Joe de Graft, Ugandans John Ruganda and Austin Bukenya, and Kenyans David Mulwa, Francis Imbuga, Wasambo Were and Arthur Kimoli.

There was a setback when Seth Adagala was replaced by James Falkland in 1975. According to Nairobi's *Daily Nation* of 6 July 1975, there was fear that Kenyan theatre was being given back to the colonialists. Mumma (1994) notes that in 1976 Falkland was reluctant to allow Ngugi and Mugo's *Trial of Dedan Kimathi* and Imbuga's *Betrayal in the City* performance space in the Kenya National Theatre. Both plays were to enter the canon of Kenyan drama.

The 1970s witnessed the resuscitation of traditional dramatic forms and a vigorous critique of colonialism and neo-colonialism. Ngugi wa Thiong'o's campaigns in that period undoubtedly gave impetus to community and political theatre, which both remain vibrant to this day. Gikandi has noted that 'Ngugi cannot be considered a major African playwright' (2000: 160). But it is in the theatre that arguably the most revered African theorist comes close to deconstructing the problem of the dichotomy between a work of art and the public viewing of it. Although Gikandi seems to see theatre, as Chidi Amuta does, as a collaborative art that explodes the barrier of literacy that shackles other forms in their written expression (Amuta, 1989: 167), most of Ngugi's plays are not performed in Kenya, and are thus reduced to the status of the passive novel. However, his impact on Kenyan theatre via his theoretical statements, and the formative influence he has had on younger generations of dramatists such as Wahome Mutahi (1954–2003) and Opiyo Mumma (1957–2000), cannot be gainsaid.

Ngugi co-wrote *The Trial of Dedan Kimathi* with Micere Githae-Mugo, and the Gikuyu-language play *Ngaahika Ndeenda* (I Will Marry When I Want) with Ngugi wa Mirii. The peasants' unity of purpose in the fight for a better Kenya free of foreign domination provides the material for the two plays. Both plays celebrate the peasant struggles in a world dominated by western capital. Revolving around Dedan Kimathi, the legendary leader of the Kenyan war for independence against the British, *The Trial of Dedan Kimathi* eulogises the freedom fighter's resilience in his rejection of colonialists' and capitalists' offers to sell out the fight for Kenya's self-determination. The playwrights were interested not only in debunking colonial myths that portray Kimathi and the Mau Mau movement as a group of terrorists, but also in offering what they saw as a corrective image of the freedom fighter to the one drawn by Kenyan playwright Kenneth Watene, who portrays Kimathi as a weak, brutal, jealous and murderous womaniser. The play's performance in the Kenya National Theatre challenged in a fundamental way the European domination of the national facility (Cook and Okenimkpe, 1997: 220).

Ngaahika Ndeenda marked a major shift in Kenyan theatre practice. The playwrights, working along the same lines as Brazilian theatre artist Augusto Boal and educationalist Paulo Freire, created a theatre enterprise that incorporated the people as stakeholders in the performance. The play was first performed in the open theatre at the Kamiriithu Community Cultural and Educational Centre. Kamiriithu comprised a 2,000-seat open air theatre that had been constructed by the community. The dramatists lament the exploitation and marginalisation of the peasants who fought for Kenya's liberation by a new group of leaders and financiers who have taken over the country's economy.

The peasants' and workers' fight against their oppressors forms the background of the play. For the first time peasants had inputs into a major theatre production. Ngugi and Ngugi only created the plot, the peasants provided the songs and made changes to the work to suit their aesthetic tastes. The resulting product was a text that was at once revolutionary and popular, incorporating local theatre forms and treating thematic issues with which the community could identify. Pundits connect Ngugi's detention in 1977 to the popularity of, and revolutionary message in, *Ngaahika Ndeenda*. The government of Jomo Kenyatta, the founder president, detained Ngugi on 30 December. He was released on 12 December 1978 by Kenyatta's successor, Daniel arap Moi. But the fact that the government incarcerated only one of the authors indicates that there was seen to be more than meets the eye in Ngugi's campaigns. Ngugi was viewed by the local powers-that-be as a formidable source of challenge to their leadership. The Kamiriithu debacle was more of an assault on Ngugi as a politically leaning individual than on theatre practice. But it had a far-reaching effect on the Kenyan theatre community, with Ngugi's detention shaking artists off balance.

Ngugi regrouped Kamiriithu. From November 1981 the group prepared to perform *Maitu Njugira* (Mother Sing for Me) a Gikuyu musical by Ngugi that depicts the anxieties of postcolonial Kenya using indigenous theatrical forms. The expectations of the anti-colonial struggles are contrasted sharply with the current realities to express the people's disillusionment with the new order and to justify a replacement of the system of government. After more than two months of rehearsal the play was ready for performance at the Kenya National Theatre, on 19 February 1982. The group, whose purpose was to reclaim the Kenya National Theatre as a space for drama in local languages by the local people, was denied a licence to perform. On 11 March the government outlawed the Kamiriithu Community Cultural and Educational Centre. The following day, the open air theatre was razed to the ground. The event profoundly affected theatre practice in the country. According to Wasambo Were, after the Kamiriithu saga 'dramatists developed cold feet and refrained from producing plays with similar themes' (1991: ix).

The 1980s witnessed a flurry of political theatre, a trend that was to continue unabated, albeit with different political foci and nuances. Particularly striking because of its public appeal was Alamin Mazrui's Swahili play, *Kilio cha Haki* (The Cry for Justice). This play, published in 1981, depicts peasant workers fighting for justice against a colonial farmer. The text uses the colonial situation to comment on parallels with the neo-colonialism plaguing the Third World as a whole. It calls for rebellion against laws that do not respect basic human rights. In a combative move against Kamiriithu, similar projects to Ngugi's thrived in other parts of the country, in particular outside central Kenya. The most vibrant was the Vihiga Cultural Festival in western Kenya. Unlike Kamiriithu, this festival had the blessing of the government and the country's head of state would grace it.

It is in the 1980s that gender started inserting itself formidably as an analytic category. Although plays such as *Ngaahika Ndeenda* touched on gender issues, the representation of women in drama was not a major concern. Imbuga's *Aminata* was specifically written for the Second World Women's Conference held in Nairobi in 1985. This drama revolves around Aminata, a young woman lawyer with a bright legal career before her. Her father leaves her a piece of land in his will. This is a great cause of conflict between the protagonist and her brothers because, according to tradition, a woman should not inherit land. Whilst the topical issue makes this a popular work, it is the technique Imbuga uses to capture the link between rural and urban Kenya that makes it compelling theatrically. The dramatist incorporates song and dance and introduces characters such as Agege and Babio, who require humorous improvisation on stage.

Theatrical performances celebrating African values were staged. Okoiti Omtata's *Lwanda Magere* is a good example. This play is a dramatisation of the tragic end of a legendary warrior from Luo, a community living around Lake Victoria in western Kenya. Lwanda Magere has a mysterious body that cannot be harmed physically. In battles with the enemy Lango community, the Luo are always victorious because of Lwanda Magere's prowess. This is so until he falls into the hands of a Lango seductress, who digs out the warrior's secret weapon and relays the information to her people. During the next battle, Magere is felled with the first spear throw. Drawing on Luo folklore, this play uses local idioms to construct the legendary figure. Through the play Omtata demonstrates the tension between fate and free will in charting human destiny. Magere is also portrayed in the short play 'There were Strings on Magere's Shield' by Ochieng-Konyango.

In the 1980s the Primary Schools Drama Festival was introduced to address the neglect of theatre for and by children. With the festival incorporating under its umbrella a wide range of items, the feasibility of the Kenya National Theatre as the venue for the annual activity came under scrutiny. In 1981 Wasambo Were, the festival's organising secretary, arranged for winning items to tour different parts of the country. It was also decided that the Schools/Colleges Drama Festival would be hosted on a rotational basis by Kenya's eight provinces. This festival adopted a utilitarian perspective of art. The artists were not expected to hanker after a remote past or present innovations without social relevance. As pointedly noted by Wasambo Were, 'beside the provision of entertainment, drama was gradually being seen as a tool to express the aspirations of the real and living rather than the dead, removed or fictitious' (1991: vii).

Major texts such as Khaemba Ongeti's Swahili-language play *Visiki* (1984) and Barnabas Kasigwa's *Wishful Thinking* are products of the festival. Worth mention is the 1981 *Makwekwe*, a play in the Swahili language by Kapsabet Girls High School, which dramatised the plight and dreams of down-trodden slum dwellers. Symbolised as the *makwekwe* (weeds), the slum dwellers enact a dream to choke the rich. The play, like *Majitu* (Ogres), *Kilio* (Crying) and *Visiki* (Troubles), is in Kiswahili, the country's national language. The Swahili drama in the festival complements a host of other plays in the language, injecting Kenyan theatre with elements of Arabic-Islamic expression. Major dramatists creating in Swahili include Jay Kitsao, Rocha Chimera, Chacha-Nyaigoti Chacha, Kyallo Wadi Wamitila and Kithaka wa Mberia.

To create variety in the festival, and to incorporate Kenyan oral traditions in the national activity, dance drama was introduced in 1982. The dances performed in Kenyan languages revolve around cultural themes such as marriage, circumcision and wedding. In 1987 dramatised verse, both solo and choral, was introduced. To further inject Kenyan traditional sensibilities, oral narrative was introduced in 1999.

The 1990s brought theatrical forms of the 1980s to a new height. In 1991, Theatre Workshop Productions produced *Drumbeats on Kirinyaga*, a dance drama that used popular forms to fight for artists' freedom of expression. Whilst *Ngaahika Ndeenda* (I Will Marry When I Want) drew its themes and characters from the Gikuyu community, *Drumbeats on Kirinyaga* was a cultural montage that incorporated characters from various ethnic communities. Despite foregrounding Mount Kenya in its title (Kirinyaga is a more authentic name for the mountain, Kenya being a colonial corruption) the play diffused the limelight from the mountain as a mythical symbol of the populous and economically and politically dominant Kikuyu community of central Kenya, to other marginalised spaces in independent Kenya. The play draws on historical resistance moments such as the 1912 Mumbo cult in Luoland; the colonial administration's shooting of 160 people demonstrating for the release of nationalist Harry Thuku in 1922; the rebellion spearheaded by woman nationalist Mekatilili against British colonialists in 1918; and the uprising led by arap Manyei against the British in 1923.

In the 1980s and early 1990s there was a clampdown on activities that seemed to oppose the government. Peter Wanyande notes that the restriction of political activity extended to cultural production (1995: 55). Gichingiri Ndigirigi notes that between 1989 and 1993 a number of Kenyan productions were denied licences for public performances, 'the worst year [being] 1991, when a total of eight plays were denied performance licenses' (Ndigirigi, 1999: 77). However, with the repeal of Section 2(A) of Kenya's constitution in December 1991, a move that led to the reinstitution of multi-party politics, theatre space expanded immensely. Plays that had been denied a licence, such as Henrik Ibsen's *An Enemy of the People*, Dario Fo's *Can't Pay, Won't Pay* and Tewfik al-Hakim's *The Fate of Cockroach*, received them. In 1993 the Miujiza Players, whose founding chairman was a lawyer, challenged the government over the denial of a licence to perform *The Master and the Frauds*; the judge ruled in Miujiza's favour (Ndigirigi, 1999: 77).

Following the example set by Ngugi and his Kamiriithu theatre, but without the confrontational grammar in Ngugi's theatre production, many groups exploited the popular theatre to depict problems affecting society. The decade shows a marked shift from the little theatre to a bolder aesthetic that is public-driven. The aim of people's popular theatre is to nurture commitment to the use of popular modes of communication in order to stimulate and initiate social change. The movement aims to use theatre as a teaching methodology, an awareness tool on issues affecting the community, a form of cultural self-assertion. To achieve these, it employs African artistic modes as its central theatrical form. It seems to heed Wole Soyinka's warning in *Myth, Literature and the African World*. For Soyinka, African drama avoids the

> compartmentalising habit of thought which periodically selects aspects of human emotion, phenomenal observations, metaphysical institutions, and even scientific deductions and turns them into separatist myths (or 'truths') sustained by a proliferating superstructure of presentation idioms, analogies and analytical modes.
>
> (Soyinka, 1976: 37)

If this habit was seen as Eurocentric, it was avoided even when privileging so-called African modes of self-expression. 'African modes' have been influenced by cultural practices from different parts of the world: the continent had become a multicultural space where different cultures negotiate for recognition. Practised by artists brought up with both modern theatre techniques and traditional storytelling modes, the strategies of the people's popular theatre involve a fusion of diverse techniques whose Africanness is not circumscribed by racial nativism or cultural essentialism, but by the fact that African actors and audiences enjoy themselves in the enactment of their desires.

It was through the popular theatre that Ngugi wa Thiong'o's Kamiriithu phenomenon lived on in similar theatre projects. Although without the op- positional politics of Kamiriithu, Ngugi's idea continued to be felt on the Kenyan theatre scene. Theatre based on people's perception of self became vibrant in different sections of the country. It was used as a methodology of teaching and communication about urgent issues facing society. An example is the Sigoti Teachers Group. This group came into being in March 1994. It brought together secondary and primary teachers in Nyakach Division, Kisumu District, in western Kenya. The first topic the group dealt with was the AIDS epidemic in the region. The shows were informal, and although scripts were written, members were not supposed to cram the lines. The ed- ucational issue the performance wanted to put across required memorising certain lines, but rigid conformity to the script was unnecessary. The audi- ence was encouraged to participate, and the 'responses and questions from the spectators make every program depend on improvisation' (Reisinger, 1995: 54).

Another example of a community theatre group from the same area is the Sigoti Ramogi Dramatic Community. Initially made up of seventy women community health workers, it was formed in 1987. It drew its member- ship from the community. The group was scaled down to a membership of twenty to enhance cohesion among the members. It disseminated ideas discussed in workshops through improvisations staged in the marketplace and at community meetings. Themes ranged from domestic hygiene to nu- trition and sanitation (Reisinger, 1995: 61). The Kama Kazi (Kiswahili for 'as if it were work') Players was founded in 1991. It was composed mainly of school-leavers with informal training in drama. The youths perform plays with themes touching on sexually transmitted diseases and AIDS. Using participatory theatre, older plays were reworked to dismantle the actor– spectator dichotomy. Ngugi notes in *Penpoints, Gunpoints and Dreams* (1998) that ideal African theatre is participatory: democratic values are expressed through action in which the audience and the actor participate actively in the theatrical production. Adopting a similar methodology, the theatre of the 1990s presented plays in a new light, in which a play shorn of politics was politicised by the audience and narrators. Imbuga's *Aminata* is an excellent case in point. Between 1995 and 1997 the Kenya Drama/Theatre Education Association and the Free Travelling Theatre reworked the script of the play to enable the participation of the audience. The audience was involved in speaking and listening, discussing and role-playing in both small groups and as a whole unit (Mumma, 1999: 37–40). Participatory theatre drama practices continued to be used by Non-Governmental Organisations and government ministries as agents to change attitudes in communities.

Another group that developed during the 1990s is the Mizizi Creative Centre. This is a self-supporting group formed by leading artists George Otiu Kidenda, Fred Owuor Ouko, Hilda Adhiambo Obyerodhyambo and Oby Obyerodhyambo. Launched in 1996, the group asserts popular African culture in the face of the neo-colonial western culture which globalisation has brought in its wake. The centre is intimately connected to its evolution of *sigana*, an interactive participatory storytelling form which is used in performance, research and research dissemination. Taking the form of a traditional storytelling session, the structure of Mizizi's *sigana* performance weaves together acting, narration, music and other expressive techniques in the form of traditional call and response, chants, role-play, banter and communal dilemma resolution (Obyerodhyambo, online).

The 1990s also saw the emergence of playwrights whose talents had come to maturity. David Mulwa (1947–) is one of the vibrant theatre practitioners in independent Kenya. A senior lecturer in Theatre Arts, Drama and Creative Writing at Kenyatta University, Mulwa has penned several plays that engage with the realities of post-colonial Kenya. The play *Glasshouses* (first published in 2000) was originally written and performed on Voice of Kenya television in 1985. Exploring the theme of child abuse, it has been expanded to cover other social issues such as the gap between poor city slum dwellers and the rich owners of opulent mansions. In 1987 it was performed at the National Drama Festival to great success, and was one of the attractions for participants of the year's All Africa Games held in Nairobi. The play tells the story of Kito Makato and his wife Kawira. Their marriage of twelve years is in the throes of collapse because the couple have not been open with each other. Makato takes himself to be the custodian of his wife's morality and behaviour and is quick to find fault in her. She responds with silence, persuasion, threats, wit and sarcasm in turns to subdue her husband and show him he should not judge others before he has judged himself. Eventually,

Kawira reasserts her dignity as the real home-builder when Makato sheds the privileges he has earned at the family pedestal.

Mulwa was one of the dramatists to confront taboo topics head on. In the late 1990s and early twenty-first century, at a time when conservative estimates indicated that one in every seven people was HIV positive and that 500 people were succumbing to AIDS daily, it became urgent to deal with the malady which was declared a national disaster in 1999. Although not accepted officially, the condition had claimed several lives in the Kenyan theatre community. Theatre practitioners being some of the most worshipped entertainment idols, fall easily prey to alcohol, drugs and sexual temptations. Mulwa's *Clean Hands* portrays the AIDS problem in a language and style that is deliberately kept simple so that the message is delivered with directness and point. Written in 1990 on the invitation of World Vision, it premièred at the Kenya Cultural Centre and had subsequent runs at the Kenya National Theatre in 1991, when it was videotaped by the Kenya Institute of Education for dissemination in Kenyan schools and colleges.

Mulwa's earlier play, *Redemption* (published 1990), is equally moralistic, but is also a heart-warming aesthetic marathon of truth about post-colonial Kenya. Using church splinter groups as its organising principle, the play confronts the audience with evils thriving even in places thought to be the holiest of all. Although revolving around religion, it portrays secular problems that also affect people outside the church. *Redemption* was commissioned by the National Council of Churches in Kenya to, according to the council's secretary-general, the Revd Samuel Kobia, writing in the preface of the published edition of the play, 'speak to the church, family and the nation' through theatre as a traditional medium of communication. When the play was performed before more than 600 church leaders towards the end of 1989, it was felt that its message should be spread to the rest of the population. It was staged in Nairobi in the same year and in February 1990 before travelling to Nakuru, Machakos and Meru towns.

The 1990s also witnessed efforts to Africanise spaces associated with European theatre in Kenya. Beginning in 1990, James Falkland of the Phoenix Theatre began to Africanise western musicals and theatrical classics. One of the most compelling was *Too Good to be True* (1995). This was an adaptation of William Shakespeare's *The Two Gentlemen of Verona*. In 1992 members of the Phoenix Players helped create Miujiza Theatre, an African repertory group, with Falkland as a co-founder and Steve Mwenesi, a regular actor on the Phoenix stage, as chairman.

The twenty-first century has ushered in a renewed commitment to socially relevant theatre. The plays performed talk openly about AIDS, discussing topics traditionally regarded as taboo. Waigwa Wachira's *Gift from a Stranger*, a comedy addressing the theme of the HIV-AIDS epidemic, was shown around schools and colleges in 2001. Overtly political themes in the Kenya Schools and Colleges Drama Festival remained unofficially banned, with a play entitled *Coup d'etat* suffering disqualification in the 2000 festival. However, even the disqualified plays were performed without much ado in other spaces, such as the Kenya National Theatre, the French Cultural Centre and the British Council auditoriums. Outside the schools and colleges context, political theatre has thrived unabated, exploiting the freedom of expression afforded by political pluralism. Wahome Mutahi's Gikuyu-language plays *Mugathe Mubogothi* (His Excellency Mubogothi) and *Makaririra Kioro* (They'll cry in the toilet) are satires that openly lampoon the political leadership, using regalia and symbols associated with prominent people in government circles. Apart from employing in its background symbols associated with Daniel arap Moi's government, *Makaririra Kioro* gives characters names, traits, and even attires that immediately recall real personalities and contemporary political developments in the country. The openness of the caricatures, without censorship from the lampooned power wielders, was testimony to the widening space and potential for theatre in Kenya. The plays have not been shown in confined theatre spaces, but rather in hotels and on the streets.

The history of Kenyan theatre spans pre-colonial, colonial, neo-colonial and post-colonial trajectories. Throughout, theatre has remained an arena for confronting colonial attitudes in order to re-establish the values of pre-colonial theatre, which is deemed more participatory and democratic. However, the influence of other cultures, such as Islamic traditions and European and American values, have not been rejected wholesale. They have been reworked to enable the actors and spectators to engage in a theatre that is developmental.

References and further reading

Amuta, Chidi. 1989. *The Theory of African Literature: Implications for Practical Criticism.* London: Zed Books.

Cook, David and Okenimkpe, Michael. 1997. *Ngugi Wa Thiong'o: An Exploration of his Writings.* Oxford: James Currey.

Eyoh, Hansel Ndumbe. 1987. 'Theatre and Community Education: The African Experience'. *African Media Review*, 1.3.

Gikandi, S. 2000. *Ngugi wa Thiong'o.* Cambridge: Cambridge University Press.

Imbuga, Francis. 1972. *The Fourth Trial: Two Plays.* Nairobi: East African Literature Bureau.

Imbuga, Francis. 1973. *The Married Bachelor.* Nairobi: East African Publishing House.

Imbuga, Francis. 1977. *Betrayal in the City.* Nairobi: East African Educational Publishers.

Imbuga, Francis. 1979. *Burning of Rags.* Nairobi: East African Educational Publishers.

Imbuga, Francis. 1979. *Game of Silence.* Nairobi: East African Educational Publishers.

Imbuga, Francis. 1980. *The Successor.* Nairobi: East African Educational Publishers.

Imbuga, Francis. 1984. *Man of Kafira.* Nairobi: East African Educational Publishers.

Imbuga, Francis. 1988. *Aminata.* Nairobi: East African Educational Publishers.

Makini, Gachugu. 1985. 'The Drama of Francis Imbuga'. MA thesis, University of Nairobi.

Mulwa, David. 1990. *Redemption.* Nairobi: Longman, Kenya.

Mulwa, David. 2000a. *Clean Hands.* Oxford: Oxford University Press.

Mulwa, David. 2000b. *Glasshouses.* Oxford: Oxford University Press.

Mumma, Opiyo John. 1994. 'In Search of a Kenyan Theatre: The Theory and Practice of Educational Drama and its Potential for Kenya'. Ph.D. thesis, University of Manchester.

Mumma, Opiyo John. 1997. 'The Drama Festival Movement: Practices and Practitioners in Western Kenya', in *Drama and Theatre Communication in Development,* ed. Conkie Levert and Opiyo Mumma, Nairobi: Kenya Drama/Theatre Education Association.

Mumma, Opiyo John. 1999. 'Drama and Theatre as Modes of Creative Learning', in *Emerging Patterns for the Third Millennium: Drama/Theatre at the Equator Crossroads,* ed. Evan Mwangi, Tobias Otieno and Opiyo Mumma, Nairobi: Kenya Drama/Theatre Education Association.

Ndigirigi, Gichingiri. 1999. 'Kenyan Theatre after Kamiriithu'. *Drama Review,* 43.2.

Ngugi wa Thiong'o. 1981. *Writers in Politics.* London: Heinemann.

Ngugi wa Thiong'o. 1983. *Barrel of a Pen: Resistance to Repression in Neo-Colonial Kenya.* Trenton, NJ: African World Press.

Ngugi wa Thiong'o. 1986. *Decolonising the Mind.* London: Heinemann.

Ngugi wa Thiong'o. 1998. *Penpoints, Gunpoints and Dreams: Towards a Critical Theory of the Arts and the State in Africa.* Oxford: Oxford University Press.

Nkosi, Lewis. 1981. *Tasks and Masks: Themes and Style of African Literature.* Harlow: Longman.

Obyerodhiambo, Oby. 1991. 'The Drumbeats on Kirinyaga'. Unpublished play.

Obyerodhiambo, Oby. Online. *Sigana: Re-engaging Contemporary Cultural Reality.* http://www.swaraj.org/shikshantar/ls3.oby.htm

Ochieng-Konyango. 1997. 'There were Strings on Magere's Shield', in Chris Wanjala, ed., *The Debtors: Plays from East Africa*. Kampala, Nairobi and Dar-es-Salaam: East African Literature Bureau.

Omtata, Okoiti. 1987. *Lwanda Magere*. Nairobi: East African Educational Publishers.

Ongeti, Khaemba. 1984. *Visiki*. Nairobi: East African Educational Publishers.

Reisinger, Marieke. 1995. *Struggling for the Stage: Research in the Sustainability of Theatre Groups and the Role of Facilitators*. Kisumu-Nijmegen: Vakgroep Ontwikkelingscommunicatie.

Soyinka, Wole. 1976. *Myth, Literature and the African World*. Cambridge: Cambridge University Press.

Wanyande, Peter. 1995. 'Mass Media–State Relations in Postcolonial Kenya'. *African Media Review*, 9.3.

Were, Wasambo. 1991. 'Foreword', in Kasigwa N. Barnabas, *An Anthology of East African Plays*, Nairobi: Longman, Kenya.

Tanzania
AMANDINA LIHAMBA

The history of theatre in Tanzania is a history of the inter-relationships between the environment, societies and peoples, their modes of production, the cultural practices and aesthetics that have supported these, inputs brought about by technological developments, population and social movements from within and outside the continent of Africa, as well as the creativity, dynamism and ingenuity of the people as they respond to developments and changes individually and collectively. The history of Tanzania is so intimately connected with that of the rest of East Africa that sometimes it is difficult to speak only of a Tanzanian cultural history.

Geographically, Tanzania is dissected by one arm of the Great Rift Valley, resulting in plateaus that roll towards the Indian Ocean in the east and towards Lake Victoria in the west. In the north and south-west there are mountains and highlands, while in the south and the west there are woodland savannahs. Hugging the mainland are several islands in the Indian Ocean, including Zanzibar and Pemba, whose union with the mainland in 1964 created the Tanzania of today. The geography is important, because its features have informed performances and their content. Water and dry land, mountain and valley, the coast and the hinterland, the grassland and the forest have always provided contrasting social and aesthetic elements.

200 BC to AD 1800
Recent studies have shown that a Bantu-speaking people populated the coast of Tanzania by the year 200 BC. They became part of the Swahili-speaking communities that expanded to the whole of the coastal area between the Limpopo River in the south and the Horn of Africa in the north, known as Azania. These communities have been credited with having evolved a cosmopolitan Swahili culture whose later characteristics included the performed poetry and dances of the various indigenous peoples. Between 200 BC and AD 700, coastal communities traded not only with the people of the hinterland but also with Mediterranean countries and those around the Red

233

Sea, the Middle East and India. These were the communities of Kilwa Kisi-wani, Kilwa Masoko, Zanzibar and Bagamoyo that Arabs and Persians found when they arrived on the coast to trade and settle between the tenth and eleventh centuries, as Islam rose in the Middle East. The Swahili communities incorporated the music and language of the newcomers into their culture. Following Vasco da Gama, the Portuguese interrupted this commerce in the fifteenth century in order to divert the Indian Ocean trade to Europe. Their efforts were defeated at Fort Jesus in Mombasa in 1799.

The coastal communities were made up of peoples who had populated the hinterland through successive migrations from the north, north-west and west. These included the Nilotic pastoralists, the Cushitic herders, the Khoisan hunters and iron-making (and majority) Bantu agriculturalists. The different communities that were part of these groups evolved cultural practices that were part of and supported the relevant political and eco-nomic systems. Whilst some of these communities, such as the Waluguru and Wamwera, continued to have a communitarian social system organised around kinship, by the beginning of the sixteenth century other commu-nities such as the Wahaya and the Wahehe had developed into stratified societies of kingdoms and chieftainships as a response to territorial and trade expansion, religious needs and technological developments in iron-making. The groups, however, were never static and intermingled constantly as they came in contact with each other. With the Wahaya and other strat-ified societies, specialised groups for court performances were not unusual. Court poets composed and performed heroic recitations extolling the virtues of the rulers and their families, kept historical records and mobilised for war while elders sang, accompanying themselves with the *enanga*, a seven-stringed zither. Performers were, in turn, rewarded and protected by their rulers. In all societies, storytelling, dance and music not only entertained but variously underlined accepted social norms, criticised ideas that were against conformity and confirmed the myths and rituals of society. In the Usambara mountains the story of Mbegha was narrated as both a legend of origins and of the political power struggles of certain families. By the eighteenth century specialised performances related to specific functions and crafts for hunters of various animals had developed in Ukerewe Is-land and amongst the Wasukuma and Wanyamwezi peoples. Amongst these were the dances of the porcupine hunters and snake dancers. Just as there were cult performances, there were also performances specific to gender and age groups. The Maasai in the north, the Wagogo in central Tanzania and the coastal Waswahili are but a few examples of those peoples who evolved such practices.

The theatre, 1800 to 1960

1800 to 1918

After the Portuguese were defeated in East Africa in 1799, other European countries continued to trade in the area. The British and the French had commercial interests in Zanzibar and the coast. Even though Germany was engaged in commerce, especially with Zanzibar since 1847, it was the fear of being eclipsed by other European countries such as Britain and France in the establishment of African spheres of influence, as well as the need to control some east African trade routes, that determined the German colonisation of Tanganyika that took place from 1884 and accelerated after the Berlin Conference ended in 1885. Besides the Germans, Greeks, Italians and some Afrikaners from South Africa established themselves in the highlands of Usambara, Meru and Kilimanjaro, while people from the Indian sub-continent increased and settled everywhere. German labour policy engendered massive movements of people from their native areas to urban and plantation centres to seek employment, so that they could pay the imposed taxes. The cultural practices of the various ethnic groups in the country thus came together. By 1894 such urban areas as Dar-es-Salaam drew in many of Tanzania's one hundred and twenty ethnic groups, who settled either in their own enclaves or in mixed areas. In 1914, fifty-two different ethnic groups were recorded as living in Pangani, south of Tanga Region. Many of these groups brought with them the performances of their places of origin and displayed them partly as an expression of their identity and unity and partly to share them with others. The snake dances of the Wasukuma and Wanyamwezi peoples from western Tanzania and the mask dances of the Wamakonde from the south of the country were popular performances amongst immigrants. Besides the performances of specific ethnic groups, there developed performances of a multi-ethnic nature. Some of these dances were new creations that sprang up as part of the political and economic changes, while others were adopted from specific groups. These included *robota*, a dance based on the activities of boiling sisal, *lelemama*, which was popular amongst urban women, and the *Bom*, which was related to *Beni* in its form. The *Beni ngoma*, a militaristic mime dance with contest and display central to its form, spread from Tanga and other coastal towns to areas in the hinterland at the turn of the twentieth century. Groups paraded in smart and flamboyant uniforms and competed the songs and their synchronised movements. This dance gained more popularity later, during British colonialism, especially between 1920 and 1950. Another form that became quite popular from the turn of the twentieth century was *vichekesho*. Vichekesho were comedic skits that were at times performed as interludes for *Taarab*, an East African musical form informed by African, Asian and Arabic musical motifs. Taarab exemplifies a coastal aesthetic and convention that calls for the indirect expression of conflict, confrontation and emotions through third parties.

Unlike the British that followed them, German colonialists were more interested in imposing economic and political structures than theatre aesthetics. They introduced no theatre institutions and were not known to be interested in inculcating their aesthetics in the local population. Because of ignorance and because for the most part it suited them, they denigrated local performances as 'uncivilised' activities. In spite of the German incursion, however, societies in Tanzania continued the performance traditions that had existed before German colonialism, but, as earlier discussed, they made adjustments as necessity demanded. The various revolts and resistances against German colonial rule found expression in ritual performances, ceremonials and the content of dance dramas. Three such were the 1888/9 resistance by coastal peoples led by Abushiri bin Salim, the Wahehe resistance led by Mkwawa which was waged from 1891 until Mkwawa's death in 1894, and the Maji Maji wars of 1905–7 led by Kinjeketile. The latter two inspired important theatre works after independence.

1920 to 1960

The theatre scene in Tanzania changed considerably after the First World War, when Germany was defeated and its colonial territories divided amongst the victors. Tanzania was given to Britain to be administered as a trust territory. A period of aggressive introduction of western theatre thus began. Western theatre introduced new theatrical elements and aesthetics, such as the proscenium stage and its conventions, which called for different performer–audience relationships. There were also different demands for communicating the fictional world of the drama and its characters. Claims were made for theatre's non-political status and entertainment became the final purpose of theatre performance. These factors were at times complementary and at other times antagonistic to existing traditional performance aesthetics. The institutionalisation of western theatre was facilitated through two major channels, schools and expatriate drama clubs. By 1920, European drama had been introduced in racially segregated schools and by 1922 Victorian drawing-room drama such as *The Ugly Duckling*, *The Birds of a Feather* and *The Sheriff's Kitchen* could be seen in Dar-es-Salaam schools. There was a lull between 1922 and the 1940s, but the momentum picked up again between 1949 and 1952 when most schools became active in dramatics. In the repertoires of schools were the works of William Shakespeare, George Bernard Shaw and Gilbert and Sullivan. To encourage active participation, the British Council inaugurated the Schools Drama Competition in 1957 and, when this was withdrawn in 1963, the event was picked up as a youth festival in 1966 by the Dar-es-Salaam-based Youth Drama Association. The entries were primarily plays by European writers and it was not until 1967 that Wole Soyinka's *The Trials of Brother Jero* and J. Henshaw's *Medicine for Love* became the first African entries. The competitions and festivals relied heavily on the participation of Dar-es-Salaam schools and neighbouring Morogoro. Schools from up-country were thus excluded. Drama in schools, competitions and festivals all had a great impact on local theatre production and theatre writing in later years. Moreover, the competitions provided a model that was later copied by the ministry responsible for culture.

The second venue for western drama was the expatriate clubs established to promote an 'appreciation' of the dramatic and musical arts as well as to provide facilities for the same. The major function of these theatres, however, was to give colonialists a sense of identity and consolidate their myth of superiority. In Tanzania, the two major clubs were the Dar-es-Salaam Players and the Arusha Little Theatre, established in 1947 and 1953 respectively. These theatres drew their repertoire from what was popular in the theatres of Britain and America. The theatre buildings were for the exclusive use of members and rarely were other, non-European groups invited to perform until after independence.

Whilst in rural areas traditional performances continued, some formal organisations grew up amongst the Africans in the urban areas, whose functions included the performance of dances and dramas from the members' places of origin. In Dar-es-Salaam there were, for example, the Southern Tanganyika People's Union of the Wanyasa and Wamatengo, the Ulanga Association of Wapogoro, the Ukami Union of the Wazigua, Wakwere, Waluguru and Wakwami. Some organisations performed short plays and skits that they had created themselves. Taarab grew in popularity. This was

due to Siti Binti Saad, who rose from the 1920s to become an eminent performer who travelled widely in eastern Africa and the Indian sub-continent.
By the 1950s there were Taarab groups in Tanga, Dar-es-Salaam, Dodoma
and Zanzibar. Vichekesho also grew to become more popular due to the
efforts of such individuals as Bakari Abedi, who in 1954 founded his own
club in Zanzibar. The colonialists encouraged humour that denigrated the
African but, left alone, the African performers satirised everyone in their
human foibles and stupidities. Besides traditional and western theatre elements, another important factor for the development of vichekesho was
film, which was introduced in the country in 1922. Thereafter the colonial
administration supported the showing of Charlie Chaplin and Harold Lloyd
comedies. Interest was further generated through local production, which
began in 1953, and the participation of local performers in such films as
The Post Office, *The Tax*, *Muhogo Mchungu* (A bitter cassava), *Chalo Amerudi*
(Chalo has returned) and *The Chief*. These were informed by local slapstick
comedies, and they in turn informed vichekesho.

Beni performances, whose movements, costuming and music was influenced not only by African motifs but also by colonial military bands and
organisation, continued to be popular during the 1930s. The imitation of European dress and drills, especially by the African civil servants, teachers and
soldiers, was seen as a civilising process for the local people. Later, however,
when Beni's broader social function was understood, both the missionaries
and the government either banned or discouraged people from participating
in what was seen as a 'Communist' society. By the mid-1930s, specific bans
existed in Tabora, Ukerewe, Masasi and what is now Sumbawanga area. As
a counter-measure to Beni multi-ethnic orientation, the colonialists prop-
agated 'African traditionalism' and this became policy by 1948. By then,
however, Beni's popularity was not at its peak, although its variants continue to exist today in the form of such syncretic mimes as *Mganda*, *Kalela*
and *Malipenga*, which are practised by communities from the south and
southern highland regions of Tanzania. Many cultural groups in both urban
and rural areas have also incorporated mime dances into their repertoire.

Independence and after, 1961 to 2000

Theatre groups and writing for the theatre: 1961 to the end of the 1970s
The hopes that were generated by the creation of a ministry responsible for
culture immediately after independence diminished quickly, as the ministry

lacked the resources to spearhead the development of such cultural areas as the theatre. However, inspired by what Guinea and Senegal had accomplished in the area of performance, the ministry did manage to establish national cultural troupes in dance (1963), acrobatics (1968) and drama (1974). For the first time there were training programmes in these sectors carried out either internally, as was the case for drama and dance, or externally, as was the case for acrobatics. It was also the first time that artists were guaranteed a regular income and were seen as part of the national workforce. The repertoire had both a regional tone and an international tone. For the drama troupe, these included *Kinjeketile* by Ebrahim Hussein (1977), *Everyman* by Obotunde Ijimere (1978), *Harakati Za Ukombozi* (The struggle for liberation) by Amandina Lihamba and others (1978), *Mabatini* (Iron Sheets) by Godwin Kaduma (1982) and *Heshima Yangu* (My honour) by Penina Muhando (1983). The troupe performed many more plays, such as *The Exodus* (1975), *Mwenyekiti* (The chairman, 1876), *Jiwe la Kwanza* (The first stone, 1977), *Buriani* (Farewell, 1978), *Tunda* (Fruit, 1980) and *The Challenge and the Gap* (1981), which were created through improvisations. Because the troupe failed to achieve its aim of being a model national theatre, the ministry turned it into a College of the Arts. Inaugurated in Bagamoyo in 1981, this college has also conducted training programmes and is host to one of the three annual theatre festivals, which have attracted both national and international participants. (The other two are facilitated by the University of Dar-es-Salaam.)

Because of the nationalistic fervour that prevailed immediately after independence, theatre performances portrayed issues that dealt with anti-colonialism, nationalism, liberation and development. This was especially so after the Arusha Declaration of 1967 that gave Tanzania its blueprint for a socialist direction in development, locally known as *Ujamaa* (familyhood or kinship). The tenets of Arusha called for the eradication of all forms of exploitation, discrimination, corruption, poverty, ignorance and disease, as well as the safeguarding of human rights and democracy. These found favour with theatre practitioners, who translated them in plays, skits and musical compositions. Hussein's *Kinjeketile*, *Tambueni Haki Zetu* (Recognize our rights) by Penina Muhando (1973), *Mukwava wa Wahehe* by M. Mulokozi (first performed in 1968) and *The Vulture* by Herbert Shore (1969) are a few examples. Hussein, Mulokozi and Muhando took their inspiration from Tanzanian history, while Shore adapted his from E. Schwartz's *The Dragon* but with a similar theme of liberation. Problems of neo-colonialism, élitism and privilege were treated in such plays as Hussein's *Mashetani* (Devils, 1971), D. E. Hauli's *Dunia Iliyofarakana* (The world in conflict, 1968), Penina Muhando's *Hatia* (Guilt, 1972) and *Pambo* (Ornament, 1975), and Hassan Lyoka's *Dunia Imeharibika* (The world in ruins, 1978). Ngalimecha Ngahyoma's *Huka* (1975) and *Kijiji Chetu* (Our village, 1975), Emmanuel Mbogo's *Giza Limeingia* (The dawn of darkness, 1977), Mukotani Rugyendo's *The Contest* (1977) and Godwin Kaduma's *The Canker* (1970) all took as their themes issues of socialism and cultural change, Ujamaa living, leadership and development. Some of the plays began to display an experimentation with elements of traditional African theatre, such as storytelling, heroic recitations, music and dance, while moving away from realism. Besides Hussein, the leading Tanzanian and east African playwright, others include Penina Muhando and Emmanuel Mbogo, who have continued to experiment with forms and the content of theatre. From the late 1960s, there was also a growing interest in the theatrical notions of Germany's Bertolt Brecht. Brecht's *The Measures Taken* was translated into Kiswahili and performed at the University of Dar-es-Salaam in 1974, but it is in the works of Hussein that Brecht's influence on Tanzanian theatre is most evident. Attempts to create a popular movement through the theatre manifested themselves also in the travelling theatres that involved groups from both the university and organised cultural troupes. These attempts aimed at undermining élitism and creating linkages that spurned class divisions. They were also supposed to highlight the culture of the people through the use of their own theatrical forms. These plays, which were for the most part written in Kiswahili, were only one area where post-independence issues were tackled in theatre. The others were the work of organised theatre groups and radio theatre.

Two organised theatre groups were operating in Dar-es-Salaam prior to 1964 and these were the Utamaduni Urafiki or the Friendship Textile Drama Club and the Tanganyika Textile Drama Group. By the early 1980s, Dar-es-Salaam alone had over forty performance groups, while other urban areas, such as Dodoma, had five, Korogwe had three and Mwanza had five groups. There were many more groups that performed traditional dances, music and Taarab, which at some point in time opted to show skits or short plays. Many of these groups were initially organised by such government-related institutions as banks, textile industries, army and other defence units, as well as educational institutions. Later on they were organised by Non-Governmental Organisations and individuals. Besides traditional dances, Taarab and acrobatics, most of these groups used Vichekesho as their major dramatic form.

Instead of the African ignorant of European practices, the form satirised and took to task individuals and groups that were not in line with nationalistic and Ujamaa notions. Using farce and comedy, characters with anti-social and anti-Ujamaa tendencies were set up as being fools and their goals not achievable unless they repented or assumed different ideological beliefs. Even when the groups treated social issues with indirect political comment, they invariably concluded with a social moral, thus continuing the practice from traditional theatre. Continuing another traditional theatre practice were groups that used praise singing as a major form in their performance. Groups such as those in Dodoma led by Makongoro and Ng'winamila adapted the traditional praise singing art of the Wanyamwezi and the Wasukuma of western Tanzania to praise political leaders and their policies.

Radio theatre, 1961 to 1980
Radio theatre was another venue where social behaviour, political attitudes and economic activities that work against Ujamaa were vigorously condemned. Radio broadcasting started in Tanzania in 1951 and by 1954 radio plays were part of the programmes. At independence in 1961, such issues as love and jealousy were portrayed in such plays as *Ndui* (Plague, 1954), *Hadithi na Mauaji* (The tale of murders, 1958) and *Mapenzi ni Hasara* (Love has no benefits, 1961). Independence brought in problems of alienation and cultural and economic disruption, and the trauma brought on by colonialism became a relevant preamble to the Arusha Declaration. Support for the official propaganda for Arusha was reflected in such plays as *Makazi Mapya* (New settlement, 1967) and *Kijiji cha Urithi* (The inherited village, 1972). These were weekly half-hour radio plays, but it was the longer plays that were serialised or presented in soap opera fashion which became very popular. One of these was *Pwagu na Pwaguzi*, inaugurated around 1974. This was a two-character comedy act. In all the episodes, each of which is complete in itself, the characters start out with grand schemes that they then invariably bungle. Because they dream of making quick riches without working hard or through the swindling of others, *Pwagu* and his friend *Pwaguzi* never achieve success. Besides the fact that the two possess neither the skills nor the organising capabilities, they have to fail because their actions are unproductive and sometimes exploitative of others from a socialist point of view. The subject matter was presented in a Vichekesho style, with broad comedy and satire. It was not unusual to find versions of stage Vichekesho adapted for radio and vice versa. There were also adaptations of stage plays such

as Hussein's *Kinjeketile*, Julius K. Nyerere's translations of Shakespeare's *The Merchant of Venice* (1968) and *Julius Caesar* (1969) as well as Okot p'Bitek's *Song of Lawino* (1972). More often than not, the same performers moved from stage to radio. This both enriched and brought confusion to some aspects of each medium. Even though there has been an expansion of radio stations, radio drama is still limited in its resources, in spite of its popularity. The content of radio, however, has expanded, as is evidenced in the currently popular and long-playing *Twende na Wakati* (Let's move with the times) and *Zinduka* (Wake up), which raise social issues while being conscious of entertainment values.

Ngonjera

No other theatrical form has been as intimately identified with the Arusha Declaration as *Ngonjera*. Even though Mathias Mnyampala began to pop-ularise it in 1964 and he picked up momentum after the Arusha Decla-ration, this dialogue verse drama owes its existence to the traditional and Kiswahili poetic dramatic dialogues and songs exchanged between poets and singers. By 1968, Mnyampala had published *Diwani ya Mnyampala* and *Ngonjera za Ukuta 1 and 2*, which spearheaded Ngonjera as an official the-atrical mouthpiece of the ruling party and its government. Besides the sym-bolism in its verse dialogues, Ngonjera is developed through an argument or a question-and-answer technique between those who have the knowl-edge of an issue and those who do not. Ngonjera delivered its propaganda unambiguously. While Mnyampala's Ngonjera hinted at a sense of conflict and characterisation, these aspects were much more developed by his fol-lowers, as Ngonjera responded to demands for more dramatisation, songs, music, narrations, settings, costumes, comedic elements and such visual aids as photographs, posters and charts. These elements slowly became part of the form and by the early 1980s they were the norm rather than the exception. Ngonjera was created not only by the cultural troupes that also performed Vichekesho, but also by well-known writers such as E. Kezilahabi (*Fifteen Minutes of Patriotism*, 1973), Martin Mhando (*Unity is Strength*, 1973), S. Mbunda (*Ujamaa Villages*, 1974) as well as schoolteachers, university students and many others. As early as the mid-1970s, Ngonjera also began to feature as a poetic device in plays and can be found in Penina Muhando's *Lina Ubani* (There is a Panacea, 1985) and Paukwa's *Ayubu* (Job, 1982). Whilst its popularity as an official propagandistic form waned in the 1990s, the form is still being used in schools and within cultural groups.

Theatre groups and theatre writing: mid-1970s to 2000
The promises of the Arusha Declaration, however, began to appear hollow by the mid-1970s and disillusionment settled in. This was reflected in theatre through the writings and productions of some cultural groups. Written earlier than their publication dates indicate, the plays included *Lina Ubani* (1985), *Nguzo Mama* (The Mother Pillar, 1982) and *Mitumba Ndui* (The Pox, 1989) by Penina Muhando, *Jogoo Kijijini / Ngao ya Jadi* (The Village Cock/ The Shield of Tradition, 1976), *Arusi* (Wedding, 1980) by Ibrahim Hussein, *Kaputula la Marx* (The Shorts of Marx, 1979) by E. Kezilahabi, *Ayubu* (first performed in 1982) and *Mafuta* (Oil, 1986) by the Paukwa Theatre Group and *Mkutano wa Pili wa Ndege* (The Second Conference of Birds, 1991) by A. Lihamba. The plays portrayed the contradictions, conflicts and obstacles for development, democracy and aspirations that set in because of or in spite of the Arusha Declaration. Political corruption, hunger for political power and a focus on individual social and economic profits are shown to have perpetuated poverty, ill health and ignorance for the majority of the people. The portrayal of these issues was done through forms that incorporated such elements as mime, acrobatics, dance and musical motifs, including Taarab, heroic praise poems and their inversions, poetic narratives, extended metaphors and symbolism.

As the economic crisis of the late 1970s intensified in the 1980s, the country responded to the pressure exerted by the World Bank and the International Monetary Fund by implementing the Structural Adjustment Programme (SAP). Throughout the country, government-owned institutions were either scrapped, had to curtail their activities or were later privatised. Cultural troupes owned by such organisations ceased to function. Multi-party politics challenged the ideology and the hegemony of the ruling party and there were demands for more diversity of representation and freedom of expression from the various media and cultural forms, including the theatre. Most groups that exist today are privately organised, except for one that is owned by the ruling party. Even though they are not as numerous as they were in the 1970s and 1980s, these groups have injected new elements in theatre practice. With the exception of such groups as the Paukwa Theatre Group, and to a limited extent the Mandela Theatre Group, most groups organised in the 1970s and 1980s did not include people who had formal theatre training. Such groups as Parapanda Arts, The Lighters and Womyn that were organised in the 1990s have members who are alumni of the University of Dar-es-Salaam, Bagamoyo College of Arts and Butimba. These groups produce their own creations and continue to experiment. Parapanda Arts, for example, has produced a number of dance, musical dramas and poetic dramatisations based on poetry created by its members or on the poetry of such writers as Shaaban Robert. Experimentation is also taking place with emerging writers who are moving from Kiswahili to the medium of English. Frowin Nyoni's *A Vigil at my Mother's Bedside* (1999) and *The Wedding* (2000) exemplify this new trend, but it is too early to gauge its popularity.

Another major trend of the 1990s has been the emergence of competitiveness between performance groups and especially between two groups, Tanzania One Theatre (TOT) and Muungano (Union), both based in Dares-Salaam but claiming a following from all over the country. Even though the repertoires of these groups include Vichekesho, traditional dances and choir music, they compete mainly through Taarab, whose popularity has overtaken the other forms. Taarab's ability to express issues and emotions with *double entendres* has made it a useful medium for competition. Competitions are not new to Tanzanian theatrical practice, as evidenced in the traditional dance competitions popular amongst the southern Wamatengo and Wangoni as well as the western Wasukuma. As stated earlier, Kiswahili poets and *Taarab* groups have always competed with each other, especially along the coastal urban areas. The new competitions are occurring at a time when Taarab has developed into a more dramatic, movement-oriented, visual, confrontational and less subtle form than the form that previously depended upon its lyricism and poetic ambiguity. For the first time since Siti Binti Saad, Taarab has created star performers and the groups compete to lure away the best performers from each other. Khadija Kopa, for example, has become a household name and her changes of allegiance from one group to another have also become well known. Many groups that perform similar activities, such as TOT and Muungano, have not been able to keep pace with the competition due to their limited financial base and the resources that are needed to satisfy the stars and to maintain a large ensemble that includes a chorus and instrumentalists as well as the costumes required. To ensure unflagging audience interest, the groups are forced to change their repertoire and performance routines often and tour the country regularly. Taarab traditionalists are not happy with this new Taarab, known as *Mipasho* (heated talks), as it is deemed crude and less poetic. Mipasho, however, has its defenders, who see the changes as historically inevitable, especially at a time when audience sensibilities have been affected by television, film and music videos and are therefore demanding more visual effects, more movement and more acting.

Theatre for development, 1979 to 2000
Even though there have always been aspects of theatre and community development in which the theatre was harnessed to facilitate social and political issues, its contemporary version can be traced to the end of the 1970s. Tanzanians participated in theatre for development workshops in Botswana in 1978 and Chalimbana, Zambia in 1979, where the Laedza Batanani work in Botswana in which theatre facilitated adult education was discussed and developed. It was from these two events that Tanzanian workshop participants returned to organise similar activities within the country. There were several reasons why theatre for development became very attractive in Tanzania. The failure of developmental efforts after independence urged some Tanzanians to look at theatre as a possible partner in addressing serious socio-political and economic problems. The intensification of poverty and the problem of corruption, and, in spite of the Arusha Declaration, the inability of the state and its organs to build up and sustain an infrastructure that would be responsive to the needs of the majority, became some of motivating factors for theatre for development. Moreover, the people and their arts had been ignored.

In 1980, Eberhard Chambulikazi, Penina Mlama and Amandina Lihamba embarked on what was to become the first of a series of theatre for development programmes in the country. Between 1980 and 1990 work was done with communities in Malya in Mwanza region, Bagamoyo and Msoga in the coast region, six villages in Tanga region, Mkambalani in Morogoro region, Newala in Mtwara region and in Mtwara. Many more communities were involved during the 1990s as more individuals, institutions and cultural troupes were trained and became involved in the theatre for development process. Both the University of Dar-es-Salaam and the Bagamoyo College of Art developed courses related to the process of theatre for development, with on-site training taking place during workshops and theatre for development events.

Even though there have been attempts at using a holistic rather than a one-issue oriented approach to the process of theatre for development, during the 1990s there has been much use of the process for issues of health, especially for HIV/AIDS, malaria, for civic and legal education, elections and issues of the environment and gender. Like their counterparts elsewhere in Africa, theatre for development practitioners in Tanzania have had to face issues that make the process both challenging and problematic – such as the relationship between the theatre as process and as product; the role of the participant outsider in a community; institutionalisation of the process; sustainability and ownership; the relationship with government organs and individuals; aims of the process; and the tensions that arise from sponsorship and funding issues. Theatre for development continues to grow in spite of and because of these challenges. The challenge, however, is also coming from outside theatre for development specifically and the theatre practice generally in the form of electronic media and television. Although limited to a small percentage of the population, television is making inroads in aesthetic expectations and theatrical needs. Local cultural media has little support to enable it to compete in the cultural globalisation dictated by America.

References and further reading

Bakari, J. A. and Materego, G. R. *Sanaa kwa Maendeleo*. Dar-es-Salaam: Amana, 1995.

Chami, Felix A. 'Graeco-Roman Trade Links and the Bantu Migration Theory'. *Anthropos*, 94 (1999).

Gunderson, Frank and Barz G. *Mashindano*. Dar-es-Salaam: Mkuki na Nyota, 2000.

Hussein, Ebrahim N. 'On the Development of Theatre in East Africa', Ph.D. thesis, Humbolt University, 1975.

Iliffe, John. *A Modern History of Tanganyika*. Cambridge: Cambridge University Press, 1979.

Kerr, David. *African Popular Theatre*. Oxford: James Currey, 1995.

Lihamba, A. 'Politics and Theatre in Tanzania after the Arusha Declaration, 1967–1984'. Ph.D. thesis, University of Leeds, 1985.

Makoye, H. 'Tanzanian Traditional Dances: Choreography and Communication in Urban Dar-es-Salaam'. M.A. thesis, University of Dar-es-Salaam, 1996.

Mlama, Penina Muhando. *Culture and Development: The Popular Theatre Approach in Africa*. Uppsala: Scandinavian Institute of African Studies, 1991.

Muhando P. O. 'African Traditional Theatre as a Pedagogical Institution'. Ph.D. thesis, University of Dar-es-Salaam, 1983.

Mwaifuge, Eliah S. 'Beliefs and Human Behaviour in the Theatre of Ebrahim Hussein'. M.A. thesis, University of Dar-es-Salaam, 2001.

Ranger, T. S. *Dance and Society in Eastern Africa: 1890–1970: The Beni Ngoma*. London: Heinemann, 1975.

Ricard, Alain. *Ebrahim Hussein: Swahili Theatre and Individualism*. Dar-es-Salaam: Mkuki na Nyota, 2000.

Uganda

ECKHARD BREITINGER

ROBERT SERUMAGA: . . . theatre in Uganda should not start from the National Theatre in the city and then spread outwards, but should start from the villages, and build up to the National Theatre in the city.

OKOT P'BITEK: . . . I like to see the National Theatre as a kind of workshop, where we do a lot of experimental work . . . in the countryside, we don't have artificial drama and artificial music . . . and by 'artificial' I mean things taken out of their context. In the village you have death dances and marriage dances and poetry . . . that are very real . . . I would like to see that in the National Theatre, we take this very real thing, this very real drama from the countryside, experiment on it and see how we can project this.[1]

The above interview, between Robert Serumaga, Uganda's first internationally renowned dramatist, and Okot p'Bitek, the Oxford-trained anthropologist-cum-religious studies scholar and first Ugandan director of the National Theatre in Kampala, discusses the cultural base and the objectives of theatre in Uganda. As such, it answers one pertinent question that has plagued the debate on African theatre: whether theatre existed in Africa before the colonial powers introduced formal western theatre, performed in purpose-built theatre houses, on proscenium arch stages to paying audiences. Okot p'Bitek refers to the tradition of ritual performance as the base from which a truly Ugandan art theatre should be developed. He mentions rural performance traditions of his Acholi home area, in northern Uganda. Robert Serumaga, the Buganda royalist, could refer to the rich performance traditions at the royal court of the *kabaka* (king) of Buganda in south/central Uganda. Neither of them questions the existence and validity of pre-colonial theatrical traditions. Both of them see the national theatre as a representation of the 'other' theatrical tradition, that of colonial cultural imposition. This interview thus touches on two sets of crucial issues in the history of theatre in Uganda; on the relationship between traditional, colonial and post-colonial/modern theatre on the one hand, and the co-existence or mutually supportive role of theatre in Luganda (or other Ugandan languages) and theatre in English. These issues do, of course, overlap, but they reside predominantly in different organisational structures, with their own specific histories, namely the Christian churches with their missions and their plays, the schools, the Makerere University campus, and civic organisations and public administration.

Cultural institutions

Since urban theatre, as Okot and Serumaga rightly remark, was a result of British colonial intervention, it had to rely on structures and institutions that were created by the British. Drama in performance became an essential part of the study of literature (that is, texts of the 'great tradition') in the secondary school curricula. Prestigious boarding schools such as King's College Budo (for boys) and Gayaza High School (for girls) that catered for students from all the east African colonies, invited students from the day schools in the city to their theatrical performances. Aggrey Memorial School and Lubiri Secondary School followed that model. The attitude towards theatre was ambiguous, however, as far as language was concerned. On the one hand, the educational system clearly favoured the performance of scripted classic texts, that is, the production of culturally alien European plays. On the other hand, some schools encouraged the performance of improvised and unscripted playlets in Ugandan languages. These plays mostly dramatised local folk-tales, that is, topics and motives gleaned from the immediate, indigenous cultural environment. As a rule, the use of the mother tongue in the school compound was strictly forbidden, punishable with menial and manual labour, such as weeding the school garden, cutting grass or washing up in the kitchen. Colonial educators obviously attributed a culturally upgrading effect to theatre that could even compensate for the otherwise undesirable use of African languages.

Yasmin Alibhai-Brown, a student of Kololo Secondary School, which taught Indian dance and music to its purely Indian students, describes the impact of theatrical activities.[2] After independence, in 1962, the school had to enroll African students. A progressive English literature teacher made the school participate in the All Africa Drama Competition with a production of *Romeo and Juliet*, the idea being to address the latent racial tension between Africans and Asians with the confrontation of the Capulets and Montagues.

An African Romeo kissing an Asian Juliet on stage – in public – caused an uproar far beyond the school compound. This episode illustrates two other important aspects of the British colonial project: the important role attributed to drama competitions in the colonial educational system; and the separation and sub-division of colonial society into distinct racial and ethnic groups – a kind of cultural apartheid.

In the early 1950s Margaret Macpherson and David Cook had started the Inter-Hall Drama Competitions at Makerere University, a contest for original one-act plays, written, directed and performed by students of one particular hall of residence. In 1957, Byron Kawadwa started the School Drama Festival; in 1960, the Ugandan National Cultural Centre (that also ran the National Theatre) initiated the Annual Drama Festival for theatre groups outside school and university campuses. In the 1980s, when this competition was revived, it was at the same time extended to offer prizes for best plays in Ugandan languages, as well as for plays in English. The Mengo Cultural Centre, next door to the kabaka's palace, regularly organised 'concerts' for artists performing in Luganda; the Namirembe Festival was another competitive festival for Luganda performers.

The drama competition strategy continues to the present day. The National Resistance Movement cultural desk organises its own 'party' drama competitions, the Mothers' Union (of the Anglican Church) has competitions, and AIDS drama competitions prevailed during the 1990s, with separate categories for primary schools, secondary schools and community theatre or commercial/professional theatre groups. Critics seem to agree that the pressures of the drama competition system do not necessarily enhance the aesthetic or dramatic quality of the productions. Taking first or second place in a competition – that is, performing for the adjudicators – gains priority over an original or group-specific artistic profile or performance style.[3]

The Inter-Hall Competitions of the 1950s had a different effect, because they encouraged a number of promising young writers to present their work in public. Elvania Namukway Zirimu, Erisa Kironde, Tom Omara, David Rubadiri, Nuwa Sentongo, Sam Turya-Muhika, whose plays moved from the university's main hall to the National Theatre, generated a real boom of plays in English. Some of these plays were anthologised in the Heinemann African Writers Series and in David Cook's *Origin East Africa*. Ngugi wa Thiongo's *This Time Tomorrow* also originated as an Inter-Hall Competition entry. It is certainly debatable how effective and appropriate the drama competition method can be for the sustainable and artistically solid development of a theatrical tradition, but the method firmly established itself as a filter and a monitoring process that controls, for instance, access to the National Theatre and its audience. The drama competition is a decisive and shaping force in the theatrical landscape of Uganda.

The segregationist structure of colonial society is also revealed in the organisational set-up of theatrical groups before and after independence. Each racial or ethnic group ran its own theatrical group that catered specifically for the tastes and demands of its own constituency. The theatre group catering for the expatriate (white British) community was the Kampala Amateur Theatre. Although the theatre in Kampala, at the time the only purpose-built theatre house in Africa, was called 'National', access was strictly limited to white theatre groups. After independence, Asian groups were also admitted, but it was only in 1967/8, after Okot p'Bitek had become the first Ugandan director of the National Theatre, that the house was really opened to all groups, including those representing the majority population in the country. Asians were divided mainly along religious lines. Indian theatre groups – both Muslim and Hindu – favoured traditional dancing and music; the Goans – a Catholic minority within the Asian minority – had their own Goan cultural centres and cultural groups. African theatre groups were also organised along ethnic lines. The northerners – mostly members of the army and the police force – kept to themselves and concentrated more on sports. The Baganda groups dominated the cultural scenery in Kampala. They gathered around charismatic playwright-directors representing different social groupings: Wycliffe Kiyingi's African Artists Association stood for the culturally dedicated professionals in Kampala; Byron Kawadwa's Kampala City Players were mostly recruited from the schools; the Ngoma Players was a Makerere students' group; Robert Serumaga organised his own Abafumi Company, which he hoped to develop into a fully professional theatre troupe, similar to Derek Walcott with his Trinidad Theatre Workshop. The different cultural groups mounted theatre and musical shows that catered specifically for their own ethnic/racial constituency. The National Theatre became a meeting point after 1967, but when Idi Amin declared his 'Economic War' in 1971, when Asians were expelled and their goods expropriated, when the white expatriates rapidly withdrew from Uganda, this multi-cultural co-habitation abruptly ended. The period from the late 1960s (Obote's first presidency), the dictatorship of Idi Amin, and Obote's second presidency up until 1986 was characterised by political persecution, censorship, anti-intellectualism and killings that isolated Uganda from the rest of Africa and the world. It was only after 1986, when a new expatriate community came to Uganda, that different ethnic cultural groups cooperated again and generated a new multi-ethnic and multicultural atmosphere.

Taking theatre to the people

In 1947 the Social Welfare Department of the colonial administration started a campaign to mobilise people towards government programmes and to improve the economic performance of the protectorate. Cultural officers, heading community centres, were posted in each district to organise theatre shows with prefabricated plays that educated the village communities about hygiene, crop management, soil erosion and agricultural techniques. The cultural centres were equipped with communal radio sets and regular gatherings were arranged to listen to agricultural broadcasts in the form of radio drama. The plays created for the Social Welfare Department followed the usual pattern of didactic theatre, contrasting a positive role model with negative behaviour. Whilst the positive role model changed from play to play, the negative role was represented by the character of Kapere, the funny man. The crucial point about the Kapere playlets was that the hero was not purely negative. Kapere might get everything wrong, he might behave like the boisterous village clown in his checkered black-and-white shirt, he might represent urban aspirations that are far beyond his capacities, but he also represented a potential for development, because of his ambitions and unlimited optimism to be able to improve his social standing and to engage in all kinds of income-generating activities. Kapere as played by James Mpagi in the first Luganda radio serial gained the popularity of a modern folk hero. The social welfare plays thus initiated the idea of a travelling theatre in Uganda, and Kapere's capriciousness, his adventures, his misfortunes and his exaggerations shaped the audience's taste for farce. After independence, the original objectives of this community theatre initiative eroded under the increasing economic and political instability of Obote and Idi Amin. The role of cultural officers was reduced to organising local dance performances for the entertainment of visiting government officials. Folklore was hijacked for political purposes – enhancing acceptance of the régime internally and projecting images of popular support to the outside world. Independent of later abuses, the community theatre initiative of the 1950s had created a viable model for later educational theatre projects in local languages, although activists of theatre for development from the

1980s onwards were more oriented towards participatory theatre and the grass-roots approaches of Augusto Boal, Paolo Freire and their African followers.

Betty Baker and David Cook were fully aware of the social welfare drama when they started the Makerere Free Travelling Theatre in 1964. Their motivation was didactic in the sense of creating an awareness and appreciation of theatre outside school and university campuses, but it was not utilitarian in the sense of trying to improve the productivity and economic performance of the people. After nine months of preparation and rehearsals a troupe of a dozen students and staff started their first three-week tour, with about ten one-act plays, early in 1965. The Makerere Travelling Theatre staged two performances every day (a total of forty-six shows on their first tour), performing in such different venues as schools, church or community centres, on sports grounds or open air boxing rings, in factories and even at the Kilembe copper mines. The repertoire consisted of new African plays in English, plays in Kiswahili and plays in Ugandan languages mostly written by group members. Favourites with the various audiences were Nyerere's Kiswahili translation of *Julius Caesar*, Chekhov's *The Bear* and Obotunde Ijimere's *Eda/Everyman*. Key personalities of the first tours were John Ruganda, Rose Mbowa and Tom Omara, who all later made their names in their own rights as playwrights, directors and actors. The Makerere Free Travelling Theatre operated for a total of ten years, beginning with hardly any financial support – just a Landrover from the British Council for transport. Later Coca Cola became a regular sponsor and the university provided a bus for transport.[4]

When John Ruganda had to leave Uganda, he took the travelling theatre idea to Kenya and from 1974 successfully ran the Nairobi University Free Travelling Theatre. Other travelling theatres operated at Moi University, Eldoret, but also in Malawi and Zambia. The Makerere Travelling Theatre as an 'experimental model', in David Cook's own assessment, 'can claim to have proved all the points it set out to prove'; it gained wide popularity in rural Uganda and it created a theatrical style on which the theatre for development activists could build.

Theatre in Luganda

To appreciate the theatrical representations of customs, culture and events in Uganda, an understanding of the historical developments since the 1880s and the political turmoil since independence is essential. In the

1880s Christian missions, the Protestant Church Missionary Society and the Catholic White Fathers were fighting for spheres of influence, particularly for control over the Kabaka's court. When Islamic military pressure from Equatoria Province (today Sudan, then nominally part of the Osman empire) added to the power struggle, the British decreed in 1890 their protectorate contract. The country was then politically divided by party politics, with the Catholic Democratic Party controlling central and southern Uganda, the Protestant, later socialist UPDC controlling the north, and the royalist Kabaka Yekka Party rallying around the king of Buganda (also king of Bunyoro, Butoro, Bukiga). At independence the British thought that they could establish a political structure to mediate the ethnic tensions they had themselves created by making Kabaka Mutesa II head of state and president of Uganda, and Milton Obote from the Acholi/Langi north head of government and prime minister. Instead of a democratic structure for conflict mediation through checks and balances, the British planted a time bomb. Two historical events ingrained themselves into the historical consciousness of the Baganda population: first, the killing of twelve newly converted Christians by the pro-Islamic Kabaka Mwanga in 1886, and second, Obote's Kabaka coup in 1966, when he deposed the president, declared Uganda a republic and banned the four traditional kingdoms. Both events are of high symbolic importance for the Baganda population.

Theatre in the Ugandan languages and Luganda in particular, was promoted by the missions and, at the time of cultural nationalism before and after independence, by cultural associations such as the Luganda Language Association and cultural 'combatants' including Wycliffe Kiyingi and Byron Kawadwa.

The attitude of the missions to theatre had always been ambiguous. Missionaries strongly objected to traditional performances, festivities and rituals as being heathenish. Particularly the Ndongo-mbaga wedding dance, because of its 'pornographic' suggestiveness, was strictly banned and church members were threatened with excommunication for participating in heathenish rituals. On the other hand, all churches realised, just as in medieval Europe, that theatre could serve as a tool for evangelism. Passion plays and nativity plays helped to explain the Gospel to the newly converted. Later, when Obote/Amin mounted political repression, dramatists such as Kiyingi and Kawadwa used religious topics to camouflage the political agenda of their plays before the censorship board. In the 1980s, charismatic churches used theatre to evangelise their missionary campaigns.

In 1950 the music teacher Mbabi Katana composed an opera, *Para Sayuni* (Zion). Students from Mukono Theological College under Bishop Tucker dramatised stories from the Bible and took them to the villages, with choral music from Moses Serwaddwa. The passion play *Gwe Waliyo* (Were You There?) transferred the Passion to a Ugandan setting. The Mutundwe village congregation produced a naturalistic nativity play, *Amazaalibwa*, that embedded the biblical story into the Buganda village context, with real cows and real dung. What made these plays popular was the fact that they spoke about biblical events in the words and images of Ugandan everyday life.

Independent churches of the 1980s and 1990s have used theatre to enhance the group identity of 'born again Christians', but because they operate mostly in the slum areas of cities or in poorer rural areas, they also address social issues. Primrose Szozi's *Lwaki Sekukulu* (Why Christmas?), performed by the Soul Winning and Deliverance Church in the slum area of Bwaise in 1993, revealed how the realities of slum life dominate the evangelistic effort of these plays. Mary and Joseph, to reach their hometown of Beserekemu to register for the population census, hire a *boda-boda* (bicycle taxi) in Bwaise, but run out of money before they reach their destination. Mary's pregnancy is seen as a typical teenage pregnancy. *Lwaki Sekukulu* strongly advances its religious message, but at the same time mirrors the social and economic plight of the most underprivileged section of Ugandan society. The most successful religious play has been *Heavensgate*, which was performed for three weeks each from 1992 to 1994, with four performances a day, each attended by 1,000 spectators, at the Kampala Pentecostal Church. In the style of a morality play, *Heavensgate* speaks about a mother and her 8-year-old daughter, who are killed in a road accident. When they reach heaven, the innocent daughter is snatched from her mother's arms, a devil dragging the mother into Hell. The production exploited melodramatic situations, and presented drastic but stereotypical images of the horrors of Hell through sophisticated stage devices. Sensationalism and sentimentalism constitute the obvious attraction of this play, which preys on the same cheap emotionalism as the social farces of the commercial theatre.[5]

The development of art theatre in Luganda, beginning with religious plays, folk operas and then progressing to cultural nationalist plays and eventually post-independence plays of disillusionment, parallels the development in Nigeria. There dramatists such as Hubert Ogunde, Duro Ladipo,

Baba Sala and Kola Ogunmola began with church cantatas, from which they developed Yoruba folk operas that celebrated Yoruba history, attacked the colonial government and satirised the new political élite.

Wycliffe Kiyingi, the doyen of Luganda theatre, pursued the same goals for his Baganda constituency, as did Okot p'Bitek for the Luo speakers in the Acholi north. Both intended to de-emphasise expatriate colonial culture and to centralise majority culture. His African Artists Association, which Kiyingi founded in 1954, aimed at promoting indigenous drama, 'written and performed by Ugandan artists . . . in Luganda for Ugandan audiences'.[6] In Kiyingi's own assessment, his greatest achievement, morally and artistically, is the passion play *Omwana W'omuntu* (The Son of Man, 1969): 'Christ's Passion contains all the grand emotions and political stratagems that dominate our lives today, from Judas' treacherous kiss, Pilate's pretended innocence, Peter's betrayal at cock crow.' When set in a modern Ugandan context, they make for a politically relevant contemporary play. Kiyingi refers to the racist implications of the mission play, which denigrate 'pagan' cultural traditions, but he also conceives Christ's passion as an allegory for the betrayal of the Ugandan people by its political leaders and the ensuing sufferings. Under the pretext of a purely religious play, Kiyingi formulates his criticism of Milton Obote's ethnicist policies.

With his first full-length play, *St Langwa*, performed at the Pope's visit to Uganda in 1969, Byron Kawadwa adopted a similar strategy of hiding political topicality behind the façade of a historico-religious theme. This play deals with the killing of the Ugandan Martyrs by King Mwanga in 1886. The protagonist, Langwa, a courtier, wrestling champion and protégé of the *katikkiro* (prime minister), adheres strictly to the newly aquired Christian principles that are presented here as the essence of the Bugandan ethos. Langwa and his fellow Christians fall victim to court intrigues and tactical diplomatic moves, but mainly to King Mangwa's lack of moral integrity. Lord Lugard (the first governor of Uganda) had at the time condemned King Mwanga as 'a murderer, a public sodomite', while modern historians highlight Mwanga's diplomatic abilities when dealing with the onslaught of British imperialism. Mwanga's persistent reputation as the killer of Bishop Hannington, his sexual extravagances and his unpredictability could easily be projected to current political leaders. Kawadwa's *St Langwa* should therefore be read not so much as a revision of the Christian/colonial version of the history of Uganda in transition, around 1900, but rather as an indictment of the political situation under Obote. The political visions which Kawadwa expounds in the debates between Langwa and his mentor the katikkiro contrast with King Mwanga's – and Milton Obote's – dictatorial politics of violence and ethnic repression. The historical Mwanga ended in exile, just as did Mutesa II, whom Obote had recently dethroned. Kabaka Mwanga represents in the eyes of Baganda traditionalists (and Kawadwa is one of them), the king who sowed the seeds for the destruction, by Milton Obote, of the monarchy sixty-five years later. Byron Kawadwa is a revisionist in the sense that he rejects the British colonialist version of history, but he also ascribes the decline and fall of the Buganda monarchy then and now to the failure of African political leadership. Kiyingi and Kawadwa used religious issues to express their pro-Bugandan convictions against the régime of Obote and later Idi Amin, but their reputations in the history of Ugandan theatre rest more on their secular plays.

Kiyingi and his African Artists Association were the first African theatre group to perform at the National Theatre in 1961, with their play *Wokulira* (By the Time You Have Grown Up, You Will Have Seen Many Things). *Wokulira* dealt with the life of the catechist Katumbula in peri-urban Kampala. Kiyingi was commissioned to transform his play into a radio serial, and this ran successfully until 1966. On the very night that Obote overthrew the kabaka as head of state, Kiyingi and his entire cast were arrested and the play was banned. The episode of the radio serial that enraged Obote and the censorship board – written and recorded weeks before – spoke about a power struggle in the suburban community and how the village chief 'grabbed the power'. In 1986, when Yoweri Museveni came to power, *Wokulira* was revived as a radio serial with the same 1960s cast. The serial now centred on the Resistance Council (RC) in Muduma, Katumbula being the RC chairman, supported or antagonised by Dominico – the Secretary for Mass Mobilisation – the Women's Secretary and a changing set of supporting characters. Dealing with the ideological darling child of the new government – the Resistance Councils as grass-roots democratic institutions – may appear to be politically accommodating. But behind the generally supportive presentation of the new system, Kiyingi immediately satirised the malpractices and the personal shortcomings of the new political class. *Wokulira* now dealt with rigged RC elections, lack of accountability and responsibility and diverted funds. As in his first play, *Mberenge Kamulali* (1954), Kiyingi satirizes Katumbula's son-in-law Kinene as the westernised 'monkey man', oblivious of his own Ganda culture, just as Okot p'Bitek's hero Ocol negates his Acholi culture. Again, we see that Kiyingi assumes the same role of supporter of Ganda culture against unwarranted modernism that Okot p'Bitek had played for the Acholi.

In 1976, Kiyingi staged the play *Muduma bne Kwaffe* about the Africanisation of the economy. Kasumai, an East African Rifles veteran, was the first African shopkeeper to compete with the Indian Dukawhallas. When Amin declares his 'economic war' that promises a new dispensation, Kasumai is politically harrassed while his simpleton neighbour, Khamadi – as a Muslim closer to the powers that be – is rewarded with a confiscated textile factory, which he runs into bankruptcy in no time. Different from Ngugi wa Thiongo's class analytic treatment of the same issue, Kiyingi locates the source of the conflict in the long-standing religious rivalries within Ganda society. Kiyingi claimed that he was always writing about 'what is happening around me', but he is concerned with 'the funny little things in life', not with the bigger issues of national politics or political figureheads. He describes how the small people – the 'Common Man' of Obote's charter – pursue their own little goals and try to accommodate or even subvert the high-flown goals of national politics.

Byron Kawadwa, Kiyingi's junior colleague, surpassed his mentor by raising Ganda culture and theatre to international critical attention. He was the first African artistic director at the National Theatre and represented Uganda at the Festival of Black and African Arts (FESTAC) in Lagos in 1977 with the successful opera, *Oluyimba Lwa Wankoko* (Song of the Cock).[7] On his return from Nigeria, Kawadwa was arrested during rehearsals and murdered by Idi Amin's henchmen. Wole Soyinka dedicated *A Play of Giants*, about the most atrocious African dictators, to the memory of Byron Kawadwa and commemorated him in his essay 'Climate of the Arts' (in *Art, Dialogue and Outrage*, 1988) as 'the first martyr of theatre under Idi Amin'. Kawadwa's *Oluyimba Lwa Wankoko* deals with the same issue as Soyinka's *Dance of the Forests*: the false idealisation of the pre-colonial past for propaganda purposes in the period of cultural nationalism. While Soyinka focusses on the corruption of political élites then and now, Kawadwa concentrates on the fickleness of the masses and institutionalised court intrigue. Wankoko arrives at the kabaka's court as the 'new man' from up-country, without political backing from the clan chiefs – just like Milton Obote. But he is a talented schemer and mass mobiliser. He wins the confidence of Prince Suuna, who entrusts him with the delicate task of wooing Princess Barungi of neighbouring Toro for the prince. Needless to say, Wankoko betrays the prince, proposes himself to the princess and establishes himself as leader of the palace workers. He thus gains full control over the royal court and tilts the political system of the entire monarchy. Kawadwa chose for his play the historical situation of the mid-nineteenth century, when the Baganda and Bunyoro kingdoms forged a dynastic alliance. The figures through which he unfolds his historical scenario, particularly the style in which issues are handled by the characters of the play, point directly to the political situation in Uganda immediately after independence. Kawadwa paid special attention to painting the historical atmosphere with accuracy by first performing on a public stage the songs of the Palace Guards (*Ffe basajia ba Kabaka* – We are the Kabaka's men, we eat from his hand) and other elements of ritual court performance. These performances were considered sacred, restricted to the kabaka's palace, to be performed only by initiated court artists such as Muyinbda Evaristo or Sekinomu Namale, to the exclusive audience of the king, and his courtiers, but never to be performed in public to commoners. Wassanyi Serukenya, who wrote the musical score, used eighteen *entenga* royal drums in his orchestra – *entenga* drums also being strictly forbidden to the uninitiated. The string instruments were similarly restricted to court performance, as was the *amaggunju* dance of the Mushroom Clan that frames the play in the opening and closing scenes. Kawadwa, as a staunch royalist, was fully aware that he was breaking one of the most cherished taboos in Ganda culture. Kawadwa's theatrical idiom seems to treat the tradition of sacred court performance as disrespectfully as his protagonist Wankoko treats court etiquette. In doing so, Kawadwa must have had very strong reasons that can only be explained in terms of the new political situation after Milton Obote had ousted the kabaka, banned the four kingdoms and driven Mutesa II into exile. Presenting royal court music and dances in public became in itself a political statement against that commoner from the north – Milton Obote – who had destroyed what the Baganda cherished most. Kawadwa the royalist breaks the taboos of the kabaka's court to expose the breach of taboos committed by Obote. Kawadwa/Serukenya's use of traditional music and dance performance must therefore not be seen as a traditionalist or folkloristic pose, but as an indictment of the new class of politicians: Wankoko, the upstart, who came from nowhere, represents the Obote – or Kongi – type of politician who plays with traditional culture without respecting it, who mobilises the masses but despises them, who talks about national aims, common efforts and sacrifices, but who means only personal enrichment.

Kiyingi asserted the visibility and validity of Ganda culture and theatre as against the hegemonic colonial culture. Kawada reshaped traditional

Ganda performance into a modern and politically relevant form that gained international recognition and could well have filled the gap when expatriate cultural groups withdrew and theatre in English became a purely academic affair. Due to Kawadwa's murder and the persecution of artists and intellectuals, few writers in Luganda followed his model. Escapist farce without any political stand became the rule for the surviving artists up to 1986.

Theatre in English[8]

The Inter-Hall Drama Competitions and the experience of the Makerere Free Travelling Theatre brought a number of writer-cum-director-cum-actors to the fore, such as Elvania Naukwaya Zirimu, Erisa Kironde, Tom Omara, David Rubadiri, Nuwa Sentogo and Austin Bukenya, whose plays moved from the university's main hall to the National Theatre in Kampala. Whilst dramatic talent and productivity seemed to abound in the late 1960s, political repression quickly brought the development of art theatre to a standstill in the 1970s. To escape the murderers of the Special Branch, playwrights resorted to allegorical expression and figurative allusions and thus lost the popular audience.

Erisa Kironde's *Kintu* (Inter-Hall prize 1959) set the tone with a folkloric drama about the Baganda creation myth of the original couple, Kintu and Nambi. The God Gulu has taken Kintu's only possession, his cow, so that Kintu has to negotiate the release. He also asks that Gulu's daughter Nambi be given to him as his wife. On their return from Heaven, Nambi's brother Walumbe follows them – he brings death into the world. Looking back to the origins of Ganda culture when Uganda is striving for independence means a valorisation of indigenous culture. But Kintu's negotiations with Gulu about his cow also refer to the negotiations for independence at Lancaster House.

Robert Serumaga was the only Ugandan playwright of international reputation in the 1970s. He had trained as an economist in Ireland, where he was exposed to the theatre of the absurd. Back in Uganda, Serumaga first teamed up with the Makerere theatre activists Rubadiri, Ruganda and Mbowa to form the Theatre Limited group in 1966. His ambition was to create a new African theatre style, which he hoped to achieve with his Abafumi Group (1971). Serumaga submitted his actors to rigorous Stanislavski training that emphasised the actor's body, the movement and the voice as the essential theatrical elements. With *A Play*, Serumaga relocates Strindberg's *Dream Play* in a Ugandan setting, where Mutimukulu confronts Rose with his nightmares. His second play, *Majangwa* (1971), deals with the one-time successful performers Majangwa and Nakirijja who now perform pornographic shows at the roadside to earn a few shillings. This sixty-minute play consists of a single scene in which the two characters speak about their betrayed expectations, their illusions and frustrations, of 'setting out for new horizens beyond the reaches of small minds' or performing a sex act as 'a promise of rain'. At the last minute, a car passes by and a dead body is dumped by the roadside, thus bringing an explosion of Ugandan political reality into the short absurdist play, in the style of Beckett's *Waiting for Godot*. Suddenly, the existentialist qualms of these two artists transform into a documentation of moral degradation: the artistic degradation from serious performer at public functions to peep show dancers, but also the moral degradation to become 'willing executioners' of the régime, when Majangwa immediately volunteers to burn the dead body to destroy the evidence. Nakirijja assesses their degeneration mercilessly: 'Shadows of ourselves, that's what we are. A mockery of the past.' Serumaga merged existentialist ennui, absurdist verbosity without stage action and the impact of the political environment. With *Renga Moi* (1972), he relocated a legend from the Acholi north to the 'village of the seven hills' (Kampala), a story of rival loyalties and moral obligations. Renga Moi as chief commander is caught in a dilemma: he has to undergo a cleansing ritual for his newly born twins; during the cleansing, he has to abstain from all public activities. When his town is invaded by enemy troops, Renga Moi can either observe the ritual obligations and betray the nation, or do his patriotic duty and risk bringing the wrath of the gods onto his family and the entire community. He victoriously leads his troops into battle, only to find on his return that his children have been killed by the chief priest because of the sacrilegious behaviour of their father. Again, Serumaga merges ritual performance, traditional legend and the political realities of the day – random killings under Amin – into a single play. In his last 45-minute play, *Amayirikiti* (1974), only seventeen words are spoken, and that by a dumb coffin-maker. The title refers to the Luganda proverbial phrase, 'where dead dogs are thrown under the flame tree'. Enforced deadly silence is the pervasive image created by the title and the few words of the play. The rest of the play consists of dance and movement, freezing action before a scaffold backdrop on which lifeless bodies are hung. Serumaga experimented with a theatrical idiom that could carry the weight of the horror of his message that is beyond words, but also for an idiom which the censors and Amin's killers could not grasp. He certainly managed to fool

Amin, who invited him to perform the play before the African heads of state on the occasion of the Organisation of African Unity meeting in Kampala in 1975.

Robert Serumaga had changed his theatre style rapidly from the purely verbal absurdist dialogue without action to a purely physical theatre without words and bodily action only. The Ugandan audience was unfamiliar with both forms and did not give credit to Serumaga's artistic achievement as did festival audiences in Europe. Within Uganda Serumaga's innovative theatrical style found hardly any followers, but the concept of physical theatre was picked up in Southern Africa. Nor did Serumaga's idea of a professional troupe running its own training academy fall on fertile ground inside his country. Alex Mukulu operated for a while on the same model of the hand-picked and self-trained actors and artists' commune. Actors who trained under Serumaga are, however, still be seen in international productions, for example, a 2001 co-production of the Stockholm Stadtsteater and the South African Market Theatre of Jean Genet's *The Blacks*.

Andrew Horn labelled the period of Ugandan theatre after independence a 'golden age',[9] referring both to the quantity and quality of theatrical productions in the 1960s. With the murder of Kawadwa and the mysterious death of Serumaga in Nairobi, two international figures of Ugandan theatre in Luganda and English were silenced. Two representatives of English theatre, John Rugyendo with his Marxist agitprop plays such as *The Barbed Wire*, retreated to neighbouring socialist Tanzania, while John Ruganda in Kenyan exile changed his style in the direction of social satire. The political punch that characterised Ruganda's earlier plays (*The Burdens*, *The Floods*, *Black Mamba*) had softened considerably in *Echoes of Silence*.[10]

Activists of Luganda theatre such as Christopher Mukibi, who continued to work inside Uganda during 'the years of trouble', could barely keep the doors of the theatres open. This interregnum period in which Ugandan theatre and Ugandan culture in general became practically invisible on the international plane and which remained hardly visible inside the country, ended in 1986 with the takeover by Yoweri Museveni and his Resistance Movement government. Within no time, more than four hundred theatrical groups were registered as members of the Ugandan Theatrical Groups Association. Some of the groups had been lying dormant and now revived their activities. Others were newly created, often short-lived groups that still testify to the optimism with which cultural activists perceived this new era of unprecedented freedom of expression.

Rose Mbowa's *Mother Uganda and her Children* (1986) marked a new beginning for theatre in Uganda, one that combined the experiences of the 'golden age' with new political and theatrical visions. This play attempts to merge the dramatic forms of folk performance with Brechtian parable structures. *Mother Uganda* was originally commissioned by the Africa Centre in London as a 'folklore show'. Mbowa revived the most prestigious interdisciplinary project at Makerere University in the 1960s, the Imbalu Project. Just as university dons of the 1960s had gone out to the field to research the circumcision/initiation rituals, Mbowa's students and co-authors were sent out to their villages to study and record the performance traditions of their home cultures. Their findings were edited and reproduced in a style of documentary accuracy and then mounted into a collage that revealed the rich diversity of ethnic cultures in Uganda. Thus, the first impression of *Mother Uganda* is that of a folklore pageant that takes the spectator on an ethnographic tour through the country. Circumcision and initiation rites of the Bugiso, wedding rituals among the Acholi, planting season and harvest celebrations, each are presented in authentic style and in the language of the region of origin. But the play not only marks different cultural spaces and regions in Uganda, it also marks the stations in the life of an ordinary Ugandan through initiation, marriage, child-bearing, seasonal and routine rituals. Diversity and specificity is thus summarised in a life experience of a typical Ugandan beyond the divisions of ethnicity. Mbowa welded the diverse ethnic performances together via a superimposed political plot (in English), with Tabusana (Swahili for 'troublemaker') as the protagonist. Tabusana abuses traditional rituals performed to fortify ethnic harmony and identity, sows discord among his neighbours and benefits from their conflicts to his own enrichment. He represents the ethnocentric Ugandan politician that has plagued the country in the past. In the end, Mother Uganda succeeds in converting Tabusana into a responsible citizen who enjoys digging the earth on his *shamba*. A political parable about national unity derived from a pride in ethnic diversity requires a dramatic idiom that transgresses ethnic and linguistic division. Mbowa achieved this by de-emphasising the verbal component of the performance text and instead highlighting the visual, dynamic and physical components. The ethnic scenes communicate more through song, dance and mime than through dialogue, and the English parable text is reduced to basic political key messages. Mbowa thus succeeded in allying ritual performance, folk tradition and a contemporary political plot with an inclusive theatrical idiom that allowed space for Ugandan languages within the framework of a common language of national unity, thus fulfilling the major requirements postulated by Serumaga and Okot for a Ugandan theatre of the future.[11]

The model set by *Mother Uganda* was followed by other dramatists of the 1990s. Stephen Rwangyezi further developed the dance theatre but disregarded the political component. His Ndere Troupe limited itself to folkloristic productions. Alex Mukulu gave priority to the modernist component. *Thirty Years of Bananas, The Wounds of Africa* and *The Guest of Honour* deal with Uganda's recent history – the plight of the post-colony, the racial issue of Africans and Asians – in a similar theatrical idiom. Alex Mukulu, however, changes the linguistic conduct from a juxtaposition of several languages to a code-switching from one language to the other. He also changes dance, song and mime performances from traditional styles to modern disco or show dance performance, obviously influenced by South African musicals such as *Sarafina*. Charles Mulekwa (*Times of War*) has reverted again to a format of dialogue drama.

In terms of quantity, popular commercial theatre in the urban and periurban areas has become the most common feature of Ugandan theatre since 1986. On the other hand, theatre for development, both in rural areas and in the impoverished slum areas of Kampala, has gained prominence. Again, it was Rose Mbowa who shaped the major approaches to theatre for development, both as an indefatigable activist and as the teacher/instructor who introduced theatre for development in the curriculum at the Department of Music, Dance and Drama at Makerere University.[12]

Notes

1. 'Interview with Okot p'Bitek by Robert Serumaga', in Dennis Duerden and Cosmo Pieterse, eds., *African Writers Talking* (London: Heinemann, 1972), pp. 149–56, here p. 153.
2. *No Place like Home* (London: Virago Press, 1995), p. 128.
3. Rose Mbowa, 'Cultural Dualism in Ugandan Theatre since Colonialism', in B. Reitz, ed., *Contemporary Drama in English: Centres and Margins* (Trier: Wissenschaftlicher Verlag, 1994), pp. 163–73.
4. David Cook, 'The Makerere Free Travelling Theatre: An Experimental Model', in Eckhard Breitinger, ed., *Uganda: The Cultural Landscape* (Bayreuth: Bayreuth African Studies, 39, 1999), pp. 47–61. Quote in main text at page 60.
5. Rose Mbowa, 'Luganda Theatre and its Audience', in Breitinger, *Uganda*, pp. 227–46.
6. Interview with Wycliffe Kiyingi, 1992, cited in Breitinger, *Uganda*, p. 237. Quote in main text is from this source.

7. Mercy Miremebe Ntangaara, 'Democracy and the Proletariat's Dream in Byron Kawadwa's *The Song of Wankoko*', in Charles Bodunde, ed., *African Languages Literature in the Political Context of the 1990s* (Bayreuth: Bayreuth African Studies, 2001), pp. 63–89.

8. Mercy Mirembe Ntangaara and Eckhard Breitinger, 'Ugandan Drama in English', in Breitinger, *Uganda*, pp. 247–72.

9. Andrew Horn, 'The Golden Age in Ugandan Drama', *Literary Half Yearly*, 19.1 (1978), pp. 22–49.

10. Francis Imbuga, 'An Introduction to John Ruganda the Playwright', in Breitinger, *Uganda*, pp. 273–84.

11. Eckhard Breitinger, 'Designing a Multi-Ethnic Theatrical Idiom: Rose Mbowa's *Mother Uganda and her Children*', in Eckhard Breitinger, ed., *Theatre and Performance in Africa*, 2nd edn (Bayreuth: Bayreuth African Studies, 31, 2003), pp. 21–9.

12. Rose Mbowa and Eckhard Breitinger, *Theatre for Development* (Bayreuth 1996); Jessica Kaahwa, Geoffrey Wadulo *et al.*, 'Theatre for Development in Uganda – Strategies for Democratisation and Conscientisation', in Breitinger, *Uganda*, pp. 207–25.

6 Southern Africa

DAVID KERR WITH STEPHEN CHIFUNYISE

Indigenous para-dramatic performance

Any history of theatre in an African region must stumble against the conceptual boulder of indigenous performing arts. These arts form the bedrock of attitudes and practices on which modern theatre is built, and yet in most accounts of African theatre, analysts give only a passing genuflection to indigenous performance before passing on with relief to colonial and post-colonial theatre. Moreover, terms such as *indigenous* and *pre-colonial* are themselves ludicrously inadequate, ranging historically from Paleolithic times to the late nineteenth century. The category *pre-colonial* also gives the colonial incursion into southern Africa a centrality, which is probably disproportionate to its actual impact.

This chapter cannot pretend to provide an adequate counterweight to this unbalanced perspective. That could only be achieved if students of African performing arts (ourselves included) had done the painstaking research into the oral, archeological, artistic and written evidence about pre-colonial performance similar to that which academics have achieved for pre-colonial religion and economic history. In the absence of that body of research, we offer some tentative indicators to what a history of southern African pre-colonial theatre might look like, and some important issues raised by it, before moving on, with lingering self-doubts, as well as relief, to a survey of theatre in the colonial and independence periods.

Naturally, the most speculative period of all is the earliest, which, for want of better terms, we could call the Khoisan or pre-Bantu period. Bantu, of course, is itself a problematic term, given its misuse by the engineers of apartheid, including anthropologists. Nonetheless, there seems to be a move to restore it to a scientific, ethnographic meaning, stripped of ideology. Even in that context, however, pre-Bantu is an unsatisfactory term, given that Bantu migration into and within southern Africa was a complex process from about second century AD to modern times, and given the speculation that some immigrants may have had Nilotic rather than Bantu origins.

The indigenous peoples of southern Africa, a linguistically diverse but culturally similar group of hunter-gatherers, are normally given the term *San*. Some academics prefer the colonial term *bushman*, on the grounds that there are no indigenous generic names, and all others (the Khoi term *San*, the Tswana *Basarwa* or the Afrikaaner *boschjesman* from which *bushman* is derived) had their origins in insults. The Khoi people, who migrated into southern Africa in about the fourth century and ethnically rather similar to the San, but developing a pastoral economy much earlier, are sometimes grouped together with them in the term *Khoisan*.

The main evidence of San performing arts of both the 'pre-Bantu' and 'post-Bantu' periods comes from the extraordinarily rich artistic heritage of cave paintings and engravings, which are found almost throughout southern Africa, including what is now South Africa. The oldest cave paintings (in southern Namibia) date from over 20,000 BC, the most recent (in South Africa, depicting colonial women and soldiers) from the 1880s. Most surviving art probably derives from the last millennium. Even within this more recent period, after San groups had experienced Bantu incursions, there are very few changes in the stylistic features. This does not mean, of course, that the culture to which they referred, and the dances, which often appear in the paintings, did not change, but there are no written or oral accounts providing evidence of such developments.

Early European art criticism that identified San rock art as displaying a primitive and childlike simplicity is now recognised to be a total misreading. Art historians and archeologists recognise that the stylisation of the paintings and engravings expresses a complex spirituality, which is closely associated with a state of trance.[1] This analysis has been achieved not only through study of the art, but through extrapolation from anthropological studies of Kgalagadi peoples of eastern Namibia and western Botswana, expecially the Ju/'hoasi (sometimes referred to as the !Kung). Although the Ju/'hoasi do not themselves have a tradition of rock art, their explanations of the function of their trance dances give much insight into the rock art of the San people from a much earlier period, and thus, to some extent, of their performances.

Anthropological evidence suggests that the dances of the San played a crucial role in creating a state of trance that allowed dancers, under the guidance of an experienced shaman (who could be male or female) to connect them with their inner spiritual power (n/um in Ju/'hoasi), which helped cleanse society of physical or spiritual maladies. The state of trance was physically quite dangerous, producing headaches, nose-bleeding and faint-ing. The trance 'traveller' went through various stages, first a sensation of the world spinning, an echo of the spinning motions of the dancers, secondly a passage into a terrifying underground spirit world in which the dancer turned into an animal, where he or she became aware of other spirits living in God's house, and thirdly a return to the physical body, which had been tended through massage by other dancers. Some of the rock art shows the externals of trance dance, 'performers', who wear the ankle rattles which are still a necessary, percussive feature of Ju/'hoasi dance, gyrating with knees bent and arms held back, or lying on the floor in the third stage of trance. Others used stylised techniques to show the inner visions of trance, such as *theranthropoi* (half-human, half-animal characters), and depictions of bloated, circular figures or emaciated figures with liquid streaming from noses or genitals. It is likely that the paintings or engravings were created in a state remembering the 'dreamscapes' created by the trance and the stylisation was an attempt to depict the spiritual power it unleashed.[2]

Since wild animals (such as eland, lion or bush-pig) are cited as forms favoured by spirit travellers during their trance, it is hardly surprising that dancers often imitated animals. There is little evidence, however, that they used animal masks or other animal paraphernalia to take on their person-alities; the mimicry was achieved through techniques of dance mime. In later periods, however, such equipment was used. Isaac Schapera describes a 'gemsbok dance' in Bechuanaland in which dancers wore horns and skin hats to represent the gemsbok, with other dancers playing dogs and hunters.[3]

The striking continuity of motifs and artistic techniques in rock art may have given support to stereotypes of San society as totally timeless, a throw-back to Stone Age culture. Archeological and oral evidence, however, indi-cates that many San groups changed from a predominantly hunter-gatherer economy to that of pastoralism, and by the mid-nineteenth century most San had become articulated with Bantu groups, such as the Tswana or Herero, through a system of pastoral vassalage. Nevertheless, there are very few de-pictions of domestic animals in the rock art, and wild animals predominate in the mimed iconography of contemporary San dances. In other words, the major function of the dance seems not to have been to imitate contemporary reality, but to maintain social harmony through spiritual forces released by the state of trance.

This is a phenomenon that, in modified forms, is found not only in San trance dance, but also in pre-colonial Bantu performance culture. It is a kind of retroactive, iconographic spirituality whereby artistic and cultural markers (paintings, dance mimes, masks, ritual paraphernalia or song texts) refer back to earlier historical periods or economic modes of production, in order to retain a community's links with its spiritual source of power and self-authentication.

The San themselves as well as their culture have played a role in the spiritual framework of many Bantu peoples. Despite the marginalised socio-economic position of the San in the economic formations of Bantu polities, at a spiritual level Bantu rainmakers and spirit mediums have always acknowledged the San's chthonic power, owing to their original ownership of the land. For example, the numerous San rock art sites in Zimbabwe's Matopos Hills were venerated as rain shrines by both Shona and Ndebele spirit mediums. Victor Turner has described the political implications of such ritual potency.

> [I]ndigenous people . . . are held to have a mystical power over the fertility of the earth and of all upon it. These autochthonous people have religious power of the strong, and represent the undivided land itself as against the political system with its internal segmentation and hierarchies of authority.[4]

A whole network of Bantu territorial spirit mediums and rain cults are linked to this mythical potency and became particularly influential at times of political insecurity. This thread of ritual/aesthetic resistance to political control runs throughout the history of southern Africa's performing arts.

The tendency towards retroactive iconographic spirituality is very noticeable in that complex of ritual community therapy and performance commonly called *Ngoma*.[5] Whilst literally meaning 'a drum' in many southern African languages, the term has a much wider set of associations, which can be summed up as 'an indigenous ritual of healing, dance rhythm and rhyme . . . at the heart of the social effort of turning tables for ailing and deprived individuals and communities so that their well-being is restored'.[6] Ngoma thus refers to most southern African therapeutic rituals, such as spirit possession, rainmaking, ancestral masquerades, first-fruit ceremonies, funerals, initiations and the installation of chiefs.

The most spectacular and obviously 'theatrical' of such performances are the ancestral masquerades. Of these, the most thoroughly researched, and the one on which we expend some space, is the *Gule wa Mkulu* (Big Dance) of the *Nyau* cult found among the Chewa and Manganja people. Its origins can be traced back to at least the fourteenth century and almost certainly much earlier; it is probably associated with the transition from a hunter-gatherer to an agricultural mode of production.[7] Much of its aesthetic iconography may have been influenced by San trance performance. Although it is impossible to provide precise dates for historical developments of the masquerade, its performance features contain layers of economic, social and political development within the dense symbolism of its aesthetic. Birch de Aguilar provides a speculative four-part periodisation of the cult, associated with certain mask types: 1. the *kasiyamaliro* phase during the first millennium AD, which includes the groups' migration from their ancestral Luba homeland in the Congo basin, from which they broke away in about the fourteenth century; 2. the *Chadzunda* phase from the sixteenth to the eighteenth century, when the cult came under the impact of Zimba raids unleashed by Portuguese mercantile imperialism; 3. a mimetic phase from about the beginning of the nineteenth century, when the Chewa and Manganja became more closely articulated with the slave trade and other manifestations of imperialism; 4. the twentieth century, when colonial rule, independence and urbanisation made syncretism even more wide-ranging.[8]

Nyau is an all-male secret society, which has a complex set of spiritual and secular functions. The *Gule wa Mkulu* masquerade was performed at initiation ceremonies, the funeral of chiefs and on other important ritual occasions. The masks were of two major varieties: sacred zoomorphic characters, such as *mkango* (lion), *njovu* (elephant) and, most sacred of all, *kasiyamaliro* (a metaphorical name for the antelope); and comic anthropomorphic masks, such as *nkhalamba* (old man) and *thamu thamu* (drunkard). The masks represented ancestral spirits and were arranged in a rough hierarchy: zoomorphic masks representing sacred spirits (of which wild animals were of higher status than domestic); anthropomorphic masks, though still representing spirits, tended to have a more secular orientation. Some of the zoomorphic masks, such as *njovu* or *nsato* (python), were very complex structures, requiring more than one man to manipulate them. The masks were created in a secret part of the forest, the *dambwe*, and were only brought out into the public domain of the *bwalo* (village arena) for the Gule wa Mkulu performance in the latter stages of the ritual. At the end of the ritual the zoomorphic structures were taken down to the river and ceremonially burned.

The whole cycle of the ritual, described by Schoffeleers as a 'mystery play',[9] encapsulated the spiritual and ecological factors that gave rise to it during the break-away from the Luba empire. It provided a choreographic parable for the mythic origins of the Chewa/ Manganja peoples, representing 'a reconciliation of all the natural, spiritual and human forces of life and death'.[10] The dancing together of zoomorphic and anthropomorphic incarnations of spirits represents a belief in a prehistoric, prelapsarian golden age in which spirits, humans and animals lived in harmony before human beings committed the original sin of inventing fire, which caused the animals to stampede and God to flee to heaven. The animals split into the wild species living in the forest and the domestic species living with humans in the villages. In ecological terms, the myth referred to humanity's technological conquest of nature, the invention of fire, hunting and eventually the establishment of permanent villages and an economy dominated by agriculture and animal husbandry.

Other layers of social and political history are also reflected in Gule wa Mkulu. Aggressive behaviour of young males and the suspension of some sexual taboos probably indicated a ritualised rebellion against *chikamwini*, the matrilineal kinship system and its associated rules. This might also explain oral traditions that state the masquerade was originally a female dance stolen by men from women. At a political level, the dances may, in some areas, have developed into a ritualised expression of local village commonality, opposing the centralised authority of the eighteenth-century Phiri paramount chieftainship.[11] At the level of social control, the satirical stereotypes of the anthropomorphic characters (such as the tumbling of *thamu thamu*, the drunkard) served as a set of moral guidelines both to the newly initiated adolescent boys and to society in general. These, too, were linked to the kinship system.

Although the retroactive spirituality of *Nyau* was deeply conservative, it was capable of absorbing new influences when society was feeling the impact of sudden historical change. The system of satirical stereotyping allowed the Chewa and Manganja peoples to preserve their identities by lampooning aggressive intruders, such as the Zimba in the early eighteenth century or Swahili and Arab slave traders in the mid-nineteenth century. Similarly, the ritual rebellion against chikamwini helped preserve the matrilineal kinship system in the mid-nineteenth century, when it was coming under attack from patrilineal Ngoni invaders. This capacity for absorbing and resisting change would be useful during the colonial period.

An equally impressive form of masquerade theatre, *Makishi*, had its origins probably in the sixteenth century. According to Gerard Kubik, Makishi, Gule wa Mkulu and the Nkonde masquerade form of *Mapiko* (from

Mozambique and Tanzania) are all related through their common Congo ancestry.[12] Makishi refers to the masked spirits who dance at the *Mukanda* rituals of the Mbunda/Luvale people in order to protect young male initiates during the circumcision ritual.

Makishi had many similarities to Gule wa Mkulu. As with Nyau, Mukanda provided a polysemic *Gestalt*, with not only spiritual functions relating to the central myths of the Mbunda/Luvale, but also more secular ones relating to moral education, especially in the field of sexuality. In another similarity with Gule wa Mkulu, Makishi contained a mixture of zoomorphic masks, such as *mtunguli* (hyena) and *kanyenenyenge* (pelican), and anthropomorphic, such as *chizaluka*, the fool or the mischievous *ndondo*. Turner describes the purpose of the characters, particularly for the newly circumcised:

> Animal masks, bird plumage, grass fibers, garments of leaves swathe and enshroud the human neophytes and priests. Thus symbolically, their structural life is snuffed out by animality and nature, even as it is being regenerated by these very same forces. One dies *into* nature in order to be reborn *from* it.[13]

The elaborate masks, made mostly of sisal and covering the whole body, performed more than an aesthetic function; they linked spiritual and ecological forces essential for the survival of the Mbunda people.

A major difference between Nyau and Mukanda was that some of the most sacred Lunda/Luvale masks represented specific, historically identifiable ancestors, including the 'ruling' *likishi*, *mupata-lyandengandenga*, the spirit of an eighteenth-century king.[14] Although the choreographed movements of some masked characters were very aggressive towards women, interestingly, in another difference from Nyau, Mukanda had not only the male version of *Makishi Avemula*, but also a less sacred female version (*Makishi Awampwero*), whereby women were able to exact revenge on men. In the female version women did not normally wear sisal masks, but elaborate face and body painting.[15]

Although masquerade performances may have been the most spectacular form of initiation Ngoma, there were many others which contained theatrical elements. A good example is found among the Tswana people, who had a male initiation ceremony, *Bogwera*, and a female version, *Bojale*. In Bogwera, adolescent initiates were circumcised and taught the duties of male adulthood. Some instructions, particularly for the arts of warfare and hunting, were done through a type of dance mime. Probably the most famous of these was the 'Lion Dance', in which the young initiates 'hunted' down one or more dancers dressed in lion-skins. Thulaganyo Mogobe describes the whole performance as a mixture of choreographed military precision, ferocity and humour in 'a well-structured piece of theatre'.[16]

Female initiation ceremonies were equally capable of theatrical elements. For example, in what is now Zambia and Malawi a whole nexus of female initiation rites, variously called *Chisungu* (chiBemba) or *Chinamwali* (chiNyanja) provided pubescent girls with instruction in sexuality and social etiquette, often through songs, dance mimes or even short dramatic sketches. Lucy Mair described one mime in which *namkhungwi* (mature female instructors) 'appeared to be simulating decrepitude – hobbling with hands held against their backs, dancing with stiff legs'.[17] Annette Drews gives the translation of a whole text in a recent Kunda Chinamwali ceremony, a densely textured dialogue between *namwali* (initiate) and *phungu* (instructor) with copious participation from other women present at the *mwambo* (instruction).[18] Although containing many syncretic elements from Christianity and modernity, these examples probably give some indication of the type of performance associated with female initiation during the pre-colonial period.

In addition to the domestic issues of gender role demarcation and sex education, some southern African rituals took on a public form and blatantly ideological function. This is particularly true of the historical re-enactments and fertility cults associated with kingship. The eighteenth-century Lunda empire of Mwata Kazembe, for example, in the Luapula Valley, was celebrated in the *Umutomboko* ceremony, which re-enacted the crossing of the Luapula River and celebrated the power of the king through dances and praise songs.[19]

A rather different form of ideologically charged royal ritual is found in the Swazi *Incwala* ceremony. Incwala probably emerged in the eighteenth century with the rise of kingship among the Swazi people. Its function was the symbolic expression of mutual rights and duties pertaining to the king, princes and commoners. It was also, according to B. A. Marwick, a 'pageant in which the early life of the Swazi is re-enacted in dramatized form'.[20] The ceremony was divided into the little Incwala (which lasted for two days), and the big Incwala, lasting for six days. The fourth day (*kuluma*) was the most theatrical. Helen Kuper has described the version of this ceremony in the late 1930s and early 1940s with respect to King Sobhuza. 'The king appears in a mysterious, awe-inspiring costume and enacting in drama his ambivalent position vis a vis the people and the princes.'[21] He 'executes a crazy elusive dance with knees flexed and swaying body . . . a dance that no ordinary man knows and that the king was never taught.'[22] The king's position was ambiguous because although the ritual 'strengthens the king and the earth',[23] this was achieved through a ritual humiliation of the ruler, at which commoners, especially women, performed 'sacred songs expressing hatred of the king'.[24] The ceremony, of course, did not diminish the king's authority, but rather served to release tensions between the princes and king, and to remind the monarchy of its duties to the common people, in a ceremony which ultimately had a 'nationalising value'.[25]

The reaction of indigenous theatre forms to colonialism
Kuper's description of Incwala is from the colonial period. Although colonial accounts of indigenous dances, mimes, dramas and rituals form one of our most useful areas of evidence concerning pre-colonial performance, it is necessary to realise that those performances sometimes underwent radical transformation in the process of responding to imperialism. With respect to Incwala, Leroy Vail and Landeg White emphasise that the ritual, far from being a totally sacred 'tradition' passed down unchanged from generation to generation, had almost died out towards the end of the nineteenth century under the rule of kings Mbandzeni (1875–89) and Bhunu (1890–9).[26] It was revived as a reinvented tradition in 1921, when the young Sobhuza came to the throne to help in the power struggles the Swazi had with the British and with South Africa. It played a major part in Swaziland's national struggle leading to independence in 1967.

Such a diachronic view is essential for analysing the functions and practice of indigenous southern African performing arts during the early twentieth century, as they interacted dialectically with the complex cultural influences consciously or unconsciously extended by colonial agencies. In general, we identify a rough spectrum ranging from those that reacted with an aggressive assertion of indigenous power and identity to those that appeared to identify with the power of the alien colonising authority. These distinctions, however, are very ambiguous, since they changed their emphases and local functions as they evolved in response to new historical developments.

One example of theatrical resistance is provided by Nyau. The symbolism and system of stereotyping in Gule wa Mkulu, which helped the Chewa and Manganja to preserve their identities in the face of immigration by Zimba, Ngoni, Swahili and Yao peoples, played a similar role in resistance to colonialism. Masqueraders lampooned the iconography of Christianity (particularly Catholicism) through the creation of white masks representing characters such as Simon Petulo, Yosefe and Maliya (Simon Peter, Joseph and Maria). Throughout the 1920s there was a major struggle between the missionaries and the Nyau cults in northern Rhodesia and Nyasaland. Masqueraders also created satires about such colonial military or administrative figures as *sajeni* (sergeant), *mjoni* (Johannesburg mine foreman), *disi* (DC or district commissioner) and *mzungu* (white man). *Sajeni* was a very tall character, using the same mask technology as the indigenous stilt dance figure, *makanja*; he wielded a *sjambok* (whip) in what Mapopa Mtonga describes as 'a caricature of the colonial police in Rhodesia, terrorizing the inhabitants of Harare'.[27] Likewise, Chris Kamlongera and colleagues describe *mjoni* as wearing 'a white plastic mask, dressed in sackcloth with a hood and a whip'.[28] Not surprisingly, the colonial authorities attempted to restrict the Nyau cult, but with little success.[29]

At the other extreme one might place syncretic forms of theatre, which tried to imitate aspects of colonial life and ritual. Prominent among these were the militaristic mimes of *Mbeni*, *Muganda*, *Malipenga*, *Kalela* and *Fwemba*, which might have been associated with earlier Tanganyikan dances but which grew to prominence in northern Rhodesia and Nyasaland in the period following the First World War. These mimes combined indigenous competitive war dance elements with an imitation of colonial army marching steps and uniforms. John Mitchell noted the smart European costumes and straightened hair with a parting, and emphasised the compensatory element in the psychology of the mime dancers, participating through vicarious fantasy in 'social relationships from which they were normally excluded'.[30]

However, mimes had a far more complex relationship with colonialism than mere compensatory mimesis. David Kerr explains the increased sense of administrative and aesthetic ownership, which Malipenga dancers exercised over the mime on Likoma Island, using its choreography and the poetry of its songs to mediate modern issues such as labour migration and the cash nexus.[31] In urban areas, militaristic mime took on an even more radical form. Mtonga suggests that Mbeni songs satirised 'racial discrimination [and] the superiority of the white man'.[32] After the strikes by miners on the Copperbelt in northern Rhodesia in 1935, one of the tasks of the Russel Report was to investigate the role of Mbeni groups in the cultural support of the strikers.[33] At a later stage many of the militaristic mimes' songs and dances identified with the struggle for national independence. The Fwemba dance, for example, developed a stone-throwing mime reflecting the anger of young nationalist militants. Albert Matongo quotes a Kalela song from 1955 that spelt out such commitment:

> Our friends let me give you a message
> Those of you in the Congress
> Unite with those in the trade unions.[34]

Thus, a cultural form which had seemed almost abjectly imitative of colonial life in its early stages, had, by the period of late colonialism, developed some variants that were militantly opposed to imperialism.

A totally different type of militaristic mime, almost certainly unrelated to the east African variants, also offered resistance to colonialism in early twentieth-century Namibia. The Nama people celebrated the exploits of the Khoi leader Hendrik Witbooi in his 1889 defeat of the Afrikaaner commando, Jan Jonker, in an elaborate dance mime re-enactment of the events, using quite realistic costuming and props.[35]

The indigenous form, which was perhaps the most ambiguous in its attitude to colonialism, was spirit possession. Obviously, the masquerade theatre forms we have already examined were a type of spirit possession, but there were many other types often associated with territorial cults, such as the Mwari rain-making cult of the Shona. Spirit possession rituals used a mixture of musical, choreographic, liturgical, linguistic and medicinal ritual to provide therapy for physical and psychological ailments, especially during times of rapid social transformation. When a doctor or patient became possessed, he or she incorporated the 'power' either of an ancestral or an alien spirit, a process which entailed 'acting' out the role of the possessing spirit. Ria Reis, for example, describes how a female *sangoma* (healer) of the Swazi *Ukuvumisa* cult, with the assistance of feathered headdress, spear and cowhide whip, made 'her gentle appearance change into that of a severe looking man . . . a wild warrior'.[36]

The disguise offered by spirit possession created a space for licensed criticism of abuses in society, and since possessing spirits are nearly always alien, the forms provide what Steven Friedson calls 'a living history' of the troubles faced by ordinary people.[37] Vail and White have given an extensive history of *Vimbuza* spirit possession among Tumbuka women from the mid-nineteenth to the mid-twentieth century, showing how it provided them with a medium for protesting against increased marginalisation.[38] They explain that the prophetic Vimbuza associated with rain-shrines in the early nineteenth century changed after the invasion of the Ngoni under Mbelwa in the 1850s. The Ngoni introduced a form of domestic slavery and began to replace the matrilineal, matrilocal kinship system with a patrilineal kinship system based on bride-price. Tumbuka women, the main victims of this system, began to be possessed by Ngoni spirits, through whom they were able to express their frustration.

The arrival of Christian missionaries in the 1870s, the gradual conversion of most Ngoni in the subsequent four decades, and the hardships created by the colonial economy made women's situation even worse. After studying numerous Vimbuza songs, Vail and White suggest that 'the central themes are the collapse of the matrilineal extended family, the weakness of village life, and the resulting marginalisation of women', as contrasted with an earlier 'time when stable and harmonious relationships, freedom from poverty and a degree of personal happiness . . . were all guaranteed by the stability of the matrilineal extended family'.[39] Unsurprisingly, several Ngoni elders collaborated with colonial authorities during the 1920s in an unsuccessful attempt to suppress Vimbuza.

The poetic licence which spirit possession allowed meant that its songs and dances could reflect an astonishing variety of phenomena associated with the process of modernisation brought about by colonialism. European spirits began to possess the doctors and patients and refer to modern artifacts like java print cloth or cooking pots.[40] Schoffeleers gives an interesting example of Mai Menala, a woman serially possessed by several spirits in the Sena madzoka ritual. One of these was the spirit of a British colonial military officer, who demanded to drink bread and tea. Schoffeleers describes one scene of the performance: 'The drummer suddenly burst into a blood-curdling imitation of a machine gun. Menala aimed her rifle, shouted commands at an invisible platoon, and started a military drill that brought her audience to shrieks of delight. It was nothing less than first-rate theatre.'[41] This performance probably had several functions, but one of the most important was likely to have been a protest by Mai Menala against perceived neglect from her husband.

Thus spirit possession exercised several possible reactions to colonialism and modernity, ranging from absorption or even admiration of its power to resistance. As will be seen later, spirit possession's potential for resistance proved particularly important during the cultural and military struggle for the independence of Zimbabwe. In this, it was reprising a tactic used by many earlier organisations struggling for independence in the 1960s, the leaders of which adapted songs and dances from indigenous performance for overtly political conscientisation.

The ambiguous reaction of spirit possession to the modernising aspects of colonialism was matched by the way indigenous performance reacted to Christianity. Although some types of Ngoma, such as Nyau and Vimbuza, offered resistance to Christianity, many adapted to it. Syncretic forms began to emerge, such as the African independent churches with their own type of Pentecostal spirit possession. Indigenous entertainment dances were forced to make concessions to Christianity. For example, after Christian missionaries banned the Mashonaland dance, *Mbende*, in 1910, a sanitised Christian version called *Jerusarema* emerged, until missionaries tried to condemn this version too, after sexual dance motifs began to reappear.[42] Likewise, girls' initiation cults throughout the region began to be replaced by Christian 'kitchen parties'.

This is not to say that indigenous forms began to wither away, but rather that they found countless ways to adapt to innovation and modernity. Jantzen says of pre-colonial ngoma organisation that it represents 'an "uncaptured" power base where leaders and resources, decentralized as they are, resist co-optation by the nation state'.[43] There is a sense in which this tradition of localised aesthetic independence continued in a transformed way after the arrival of colonialism and even in the post-independence nation-state.

Colonial theatre

Attempts by colonialists to introduce theatre into southern Africa can crudely be divided into those designed to provide psychological support to white settlers and colonial officers by linking them to European culture, and those that aimed to educate 'natives' into western 'civilisation' or related modernising ideologies. These two projects, however, were riddled with as many contradictions as the broader 'civilising mission' of colonialism itself.

The earliest European inhabitants of Anglophone southern Africa outside of South Africa, who formed small settlements in the mid-nineteenth century, before the imposition of formal colonialism, were missionaries or entrepreneurial adventurers involved in hunting or prospecting. Both groups were too isolated to sustain meaningful theatre activities. However, the Lochner Concession of 1888 and the royal charter allowing Cecil Rhodes's British South African Company to establish an administration in southern Rhodesia paved the way for an influx of white farmers and later mine workers. A viable theatre culture began to emerge among these settlers.

At first the main theatrical activity was the extension of South African visiting troupes from Europe, to include Bulawayo and Salisbury into the circuit. As early as 1892 the popular vaudeville of Madame Blanché performed in Bulawayo.[44] Some early individual theatres were built, the Palace in 1911 and the Electraceum in 1912, providing an almost exclusive diet of vaudeville.[45] As settlers continued to arrive, however, it became possible to build more substantial whites-only clubs for sports, drama and socialising. Theatre, far more than in Europe, tended to be integrated into these wider recreational activities. By the 1930s most white settlements had such clubs, and the Salisbury Repertory Players (REPS, founded in 1931) provided a network of plays and/or support for local amateur groups. At about the same time, after the discovery of copper in northern Rhodesia, large settlements of whites in Lusaka and the Copperbelt led to more theatres there. Scattered clubs could also be found in Nyasaland. Theatre clubs on the Copperbelt played an important role in the *embourgeoisement* process, by which white miners were integrated into the élitist roles demanded by colonial mores.

The theatrical style associated with these theatres of social solidarity was one that emphasised traditional nineteenth-century conventions. Elaborate illusionistic sets were almost *de rigueur* and the repertory tended to consist of 'European and American musicals, reviews, comedies or farces, with a traditional pantomime put on at Christmas time'.[46] There was very little reflection of anti-illusionistic experimental or avant-garde European theatre. The emphasis was on what Stephen Chifunyise and Robert Kavanagh call 'ego-boosting attempts at cultural regeneration',[47] a nostalgic recuperation of an idealised and cosy Englishness, with a good-humoured tolerance for Gaelic or other non-English varieties of European culture. This creation of white solidarity in the midst of a perceived alien and savage primitiveness accounts for the glamour with which theatrical performances were surrounded. Anne Davidson, the wife of a Nyasaland colonial officer, describes in her memoir of the 1950s the extraordinary formality of audience dress code for performances at the Zomba Gymkhana Club.[48] She also comments with satisfaction on the plays' in-jokes aimed at the close-knit élite audience, since it produced 'the feeling of being one of a large and familiar gathering'.[49]

The function of social identity in colonial theatre explains the long and almost unremitting policy of excluding black Africans from theatre clubs, even after many 'natives' achieved advanced educational qualifications and 'western' skills. A few liberal clubs, such as the Waddington Players in northern Rhodesia in the late 1950s, attempted inter-racial membership, but most of the large clubs retained a rigid colour bar until independence. The excuse given was that of 'maintaining standards'. Associations such as the Northern Rhodesia Drama Association (NRDA, founded 1952) and the Association of Rhodesian Theatrical Societies (ARTS, founded 1958) helped to police theatrical 'standards' by inviting academic or professional British theatre experts to adjudicate drama competitions and give drama workshops. These associations (with changed names) and the policy of imported European expertise continued even into the 1970s.

Owing to its reliance on imported plays and theatre conventions, southern African white colonial theatre did not give rise to a vigorous play-writing tradition. In Southern Rhodesia, however, some playwrights did emerge. Jane Plastow has examined examples of plays, ranging in time from 1911 to 1964, by such authors as Howard Gott and Jack Watson, exposing their tendency to racist melodrama, with white female victims threatened by black, gratuitously violent villains.[50] Another common stereotype was the soft aristocratic or liberal Englishman out of touch with the tough pioneer spirit of white Rhodesia. The plays' archaic forms and the narrow ethnic constituency to which they appealed aptly reflect the restrictive, inward-looking nature of such nostalgic colonial theatre.

Theatre designed by white educators or entrepreneurs aimed at black audiences had a rather more complex project. One significant strand was the need to create an image of the African 'other', both for projection to the imperial centre in Europe, and, by an ambiguous process of internal reflexivity, back to the Africans themselves. During the nineteenth and early twentieth centuries vaudeville impresarios forged a convenient partnership with the emergent academic discipline of anthropology to create a theatre of spectacle, which was halfway between freak show and the ethnographic celebration of European imperial conquest. Southern African performers, like the San dancer Franz 'Clicko' Tanibisch, whose one-man displays of 'primitive' bushman culture were performed in Europe, Cuba and the United States between 1913 and 1940, became very popular.[51] Such exoticism purveyed to European audiences an image of savage alterity, which not only satisfied prurient curiosity but also helped justify imperialism's 'civilising mission'.

More influential in Africa itself were the displays of military power, which formed part of the Empire Day celebrations (held annually throughout the British Empire on 24 May). In addition to military parades and manoeuvres by the colonial army to impress African audiences with the might of empire, there were also African 'traditional' dances and small improvised plays designed to reconfigure indigenous culture within a colonial paradigm of 'cooperation' and 'progress'. These expanded to beyond Empire Day itself during the Second World War, when colonial departments of information used multimedia events to drum up support among Africans for the Allied war effort.[52] Africans were encouraged to express pride in selected aspects of their culture, provided they avoided such vices as promiscuity or idolatry.

Closely associated were plays created through improvisation to present African audiences informal education in 'modern' methods of agriculture, hygiene and savings. Such drama became particularly common after the spread of Phelps-Stokes methods of education through the Jeannes school in the late 1930s, designed to provide practical industrial and agricultural training. These performances sometimes provided fertile breeding grounds for the 'reinvention' of African traditions through alliances between new African élites and colonial missionaries or administrators. Kerr gives an example of Ngoni Christian men scapegoating African women for their laziness at a play performed for the opening of a Nyasaland clinic in 1935.[53]

More formal education for Africans in primary and secondary schools led to the rise of literary drama. The staple form of drama for Africans attending such élite schools as Munali (Lusaka, northern Rhodesia) and Dedza (Nyasaland) was Shakespeare, though end of term concerts provided the opportunity for more popular fare. In addition, missionary presses and colonial educators from the 1930s onwards encouraged carefully supervised play-writing in local languages. The Catholic Mission at Mazenod and the French Evangelical Mission at Morija (both in Lesotho) were particularly active. Plays, however, were written in most of the major languages of southern Africa. In addition, from the 1950s onwards the colonial governments contributed to this process with the establishment of 'Literature Bureaux'. As with the local language informal theatre, this was all part of the British project of indirect rule, whereby Africans were encouraged to rule themselves within the wider parameters of British sovereignty, and the development of local languages was an important prop for supporting such decentralised local culture.

The plays were more for literary purposes than for performance, and were tightly circumscribed by theme. Shakespeare was a dominant model. Michael Seboni from Bechuanaland translated several Shakespeare plays into seTswana, following the example of South African seTswana translator, Solomon Plaatje. Another popular genre with Shakespearean dimensions was the historical play, such as Leetsile Raditladi's seTswana chronicle,

Motsatsele II (1937) and R. M. Khaketla's 1947 seSotho play *Moshoeshoe ke Baruti* (Moshoeshoe and the missionaries). Comic plays include Twenyman Mofokong's *Seb'ona sa Jaalu* (The calabash of Beer, 1939) and in a different vein, Mrs N. M. Khaketla wrote a pioneering psychological romance, *Mosali Eo U Neileng Eena* (The woman you gave me) in 1957, about a shell-shocked seminarian returning to Lesotho from the First World War. Her career continued well after Lesotho's independence in 1968; she was still writing innovative plays in the 1980s.[54]

Film and radio provided colonial communicators with other forms of entertainment, which could sugar the didactic pill intended to induce African acceptance of changes brought about by imperialism. The earliest examples of instructional films were those shown as part of the British Educational Kinema Experiment (BEKE). This brief experiment (1935–7) in making silent local short films to educate and entertain Africans was based in Tanganyika's Usambara Mountains, but films were toured around Nyasaland and northern Rhodesia with a mobile projection unit.[55]

During the Second World War the British Central Film Unit (successor to the Empire Marketing Film Unit) showed films intended to promote loyalty in the empire to the Allied cause. After the war, several locally based film-makers pushed for a film unit geared to southern African conditions. In 1948 the Central African Council, with jurisdiction over Nyasaland and the Rhodesias, established the Central African Film Unit (CAFU) under its Public Relations Committee, with headquarters in Salisbury. Film-makers such as Louis Nell, Stephen Peet and Alan Izod found appropriate technical solutions to the problems of making numerous films in a short space of time and under difficult conditions.[56] Mobile cinema vans helped solve the problem of film distribution to a scattered, mostly rural population.

Some films were documentaries, but many were didactic story films, such as *Zimbani*, a Mr Wise and Mr Foolish story of two brothers, Washona and Pengela, who take up tobacco farming, with Washona succeeding since he listens to the colonial agricultural officer while Pengela, who doesn't, fails. The heavy-handed moralising of the films was mitigated by their reliance on narrators (since the films were shot mute or with only a musical soundtrack). These local language mediators often overlaid a scurrilous or even anti-colonial message onto the visuals.[57] CAFU was disbanded in 1964 when Zambia and Malawi won their independence.

Public service radio broadcasting was initiated in southern Rhodesia in 1934. This service, which eventually became Southern Rhodesia

Broadcasting Services, was exclusively geared to whites, and the only plays consisted of radio drama imported from the British Broadcasting Corporation. In northern Rhodesia, government information officer Harry Franklin, dissatisfied with the Eurocentric orientation of the British propaganda broadcast during World War Two, successfully initiated Central African Broadcasting Services (CABS) in 1948, geared to African listeners not only in northern Rhodesia and Nyasaland but also in southern Rhodesia. The development of the cheap 'Saucepan Special' radio in 1949 supplemented the rather unsatisfactory reception conditions at community listening points. Some CABS achievements even survived its takeover by Federal Broadcasting Services in 1953.

CABS, with its headquarters in Lusaka, had a carefully worked out language policy, with relatively autonomous separate sections for English, chiBemba, chiNyanja, siTonga, siLozi and the other main African languages in the region. Broadcasters Harry Kittermaster and Peter Fraenkel trained young Africans such as Andreya Masiye, Alex Nkhata, Edwin Mlongoti, Stephen Mpashi and Edward Mungoni in radio techniques. It was left to the broadcasters themselves to develop a drama policy. Masiye was interested in writing plays in English, and the 1957 production of his play, *Kazembe and the Portuguese*, was a landmark in African broadcasting.[58]

Far more widespread, however, were improvised plays in local languages, based on indigenous traditions of oral narrative. As early as 1947 Edward Mungoni initiated a regular play in siTonga, *Malikopo*; instead of scripts there was an ensemble system of improvised dialogue based on an agreed narrative framework. Another popular series, *Mwa Shimwamba Kopolo*, produced by Stephen Mpashi and roughly based on the didactic agriculture-based British series *The Archers*, achieved great popularity in chiBemba, using a similar system of ensemble improvisation within a scenario worked out by an inter-racial committee. This radio drama technique, almost unique to Africa, became very popular after independence, not only in Zambia but also throughout southern Africa.

Thus mediated forms of colonial theatre, as with unmediated varieties, may have had an initial function of comforting the colonial settlers and administrators, but they soon became involved in the modernisation process as it affected a wide variety of African communities. It is not always easy to describe African involvement in performance modes introduced by colonialists as totally dependent and demeaning. Individual artists were able to adapt European forms and styles to an African aesthetic and to progressive ends. Veit Eulmann comments that even such an apparently reactionary form as exoticist dance, 'not only enabled whites to fantasize about blacks, but in turn also helped blacks to define themselves in opposition to whites'.[59] In very different ways, then, the whole spectrum of colonial performance provided models which influenced through imitation, negative renunciation, or very often both, the development of theatre in the post-colonial period.

Theatre in the post-colonial period

As with the colonial period, there is some problem in dealing with theatre in neat historical phases, owing to the late independence of Zimbabwe and Namibia, and to the uneven development of specific theatre tendencies throughout the region. This has entailed giving Zimbabwe and Namibia 'special case' subsections.

One of the significant features of post-colonial southern African theatre is the continuation of some aspects of colonial theatre structures, now catering for the large expatriate enclaves. For the first decade after Zambia's independence in 1964, the former white playhouses, such as those in Lusaka, Chingola, Ndola and Kitwe, continued to be almost exclusively expatriate theatres, showing mostly former West End London hits or pantomimes as entertainment for the large numbers of white miners in the Copperbelt or the civil servants and artisans in Lusaka. A similar version of the same phenomenon could be found in Malawi at the Zomba Gymkhana Club and Blantyre and Limbe Sports Clubs.

This Indian summer of 'nostalgia theatre' was doomed to extinction as expatriates left the region. Moreover, among the African majority, independence ushered in strong movements of nationalist patriotism, which sought autonomous cultural expression.

Perhaps the most important of the patriotic forms was dance, since it had played such a crucial, consciousness-raising role during the struggle for independence. Several southern African governments tried to mobilise this spirit of choreographic nationalism in order to help build a pan-ethnic consensus. Soon after independence, Zambia's Department of Cultural Services created the National Dance Troupe under Edwin Manda, which performed prominent dances of the various Zambian ethnic groups. These were often performed for tourists, but also to urbanised Zambians, who found in them a choreographic metaphor for the ruling party's slogan 'One Zambia, one nation'. When, due to shortage of funds, the National Dance Troupe went into decline in the early 1980s, the Pamodzi Cultural Dance troupe, based at a major Lusaka hotel, continued the trend.

In Malawi, there was a rather different use of 'traditional' dance. Kamuzu Banda, the president-for-life in what by 1970 had become a one-party dictatorship, built a traditional dance system called *Gule la Chipani*. This was a series of transformed local women's dances (such as *chimtali, mbotosha, chioda* and *chitelele*) which were performed at mass public rallies in venues like Kamuzu Stadium in Blantyre, by thousands of women wearing MCP *zirundu* (brightly coloured national dress made from java-print cotton and showing a portrait of the president). The dances were highly politicised in that the original words were changed to glorify President Banda or to denounce his enemies, and there was a large element of coercion, which went into assuring compliance with the dances' technique of mass mobilisation. Their basic function was similar to the Zambian National Dance Troupe, to provide public rituals of national unity.[60]

In those countries that had a more homogenous ethnic and linguistic culture, namely Lesotho, Swaziland and Botswana, there was less need for major manipulations of traditional dance for ideological purposes, but traditional dance groups as vehicles for national pride did emerge, particularly in some of the schools. A related nationalist phenomenon was the renewed interest in major pre-colonial political rituals. The most spectacular examples of these occurred in Swaziland, where the monarchy retained powerful control over the organs of state. Two pre-colonial rituals, the Reed Dance (*Umhlanga*) and the *Incwala* ceremony, took on major dramatic and political significance in bolstering the role of the post-colonial monarchy. At the Umhlanga, performed every year in August/September, bare-breasted young women express their allegiance to the *ndlovukati* (queen mother) and are, in Matt Mogekwu's words 'made to display their chastity to the nation and the world'.[61] Usually, the king chooses one of the women as a *liphovela* (fiancée) and possibly a wife later. The dance is a major tourist attraction, but its political importance can be gauged by the arrest of a journalist, Bheki Makhubu, when he cast doubts on the suitability of the liphovela chosen by King Swati at the 1999 Umhlanga.[62] The Incwala ceremony is perhaps of even greater national importance; as we have already seen, it acquired major symbolic nationalist value during the struggle for independence in the 1950s. After the death of King Sobhuza in 1982 it assumed importance again, as councillors for the new young king, Swati, sought cultural ways to stem the rising tide of republicanism.

A quite different role was played by the revival of indigenous community rituals in Zambia. Whilst troupes like the National Dance Troupe fostered national unity, various regional festivals served to provide a focus for local pride. In some cases, as with the Lozi *Kuobmoka* ceremony, when the *Litunga* (king) transfers by barge from his wet season palace at Lealui to his dry season palace at Limilunga, this was partly a tourist spectacle. It was also a political symbol, providing legitimate and controlled expression for Bulozi nationalism within a Federal Zambian hegemony. In other parts of Zambia, ceremonies such as *Umutomboko* among the Lunda people, *Shimunenga* among the Ila, *Malaita* among the Kunda and *Kulamba* among the Chewa were less obviously part of the tourist calendar. Commenting on Malaita, Annette Drews gives these local ceremonies a political interpretation: 'The gaiety of the masks, the beer, the colours and the drums . . . symbolize power . . . which is perceived to be enveloped and supervised by the state.'[63] So important were these regional ceremonies deemed to be by the UNIP government, as outlets for regional pride, that it encouraged the Ngoni people to revive the Incwala ceremony in 1980, with advice from Swazi cultural experts, seventy years after it had been last performed in the province. Moreover, training schools, such as the Likumbi lya Mize Cultural Association (Makishi) and the Kulamba Cultural Association (Gule wa Mkulu) were set up in the 1990s to revive pre-colonial theatre skills.

One feature which all the versions of politicised dance had in common was the use of national media to promulgate them to the whole nation. In Zambia, 'traditional dance' was featured in a thirty-minute Television Zambia programme, entitled *ZAMARTS*, produced by Wesley Kawonga. This programme, popular during the late 1970s and early 1980s, featured praise poetry, music and short dramatic sketches as well as dance.

In other countries in the region, radio provided the main outlet for traditional song and dance. Most of the major neo-traditional rituals expressing nationalist unity or the political hegemony of ruling parties and families were covered by state broadcasting networks. During the MCP régime in Malawi, the various rituals at which women were forced to dance, the republic celebrations, the state opening of Parliament and President Banda's airport arrivals or departures, were religiously covered by the Malawi Broadcasting Corporation. The same is true of the Reed Dance and Incwala in Swaziland, and the politicised dances associated with President Mugabe in Zimbabwe and President Nujoma in Namibia.

In addition to dance performances, independence brought a demand for dialogue drama for the stage. There was a strong feeling that just as the emergent nations needed national airlines, sports teams and broadcasting services, there was also need for styles of drama, which could help foster a national identity. Young dramatists were intensely aware of the theatrical achievements already made in West and to a lesser extent East Africa; they wanted to build a rival dramatic tradition in southern Africa. This process, however, was more ambiguous than the attempts to mould traditional dance into a vehicle of national consciousness, since it was less subject to the ideological policing provided by organs of state power. The main vehicles for this early post-colonial theatre were schools and universities.

The pioneering institution in the region for developing drama was the University of Zambia. The theatre movement emerging there in the late 1960s had a strong populist orientation. Expatriate lecturers in the English department, Michael Etherton and Andrew Horn, cooperated with students such as Mapopa Mtonga and Masautso Phiri to plan a theatre process appropriate to the newly independent Zambia. They built Chikwakwa Theatre, an open air structure made of wood, grass and clay, with a strong African ambience. They initiated a travelling theatre run by the students (Unzadrams), aimed not only at taking theatre to the people but also stimulating and researching indigenous performing arts. Early productions at the Chikwakwa Theatre were Mario Fratti's *Che Guevara* and *The Lands of Kazembe*, a version of Masiye's 1957 radio play. The Travelling Theatre toured plays in Chinyanja and English around Eastern Province in 1969.

In 1971 Etherton and Horn were deported for their involvement in student demonstrations. Chikwakwa Theatre activities, however, continued under the artistic directorship of Fay Chung, David Kerr, Mapopa Mtonga and others. In the late 1970s Travelling Theatre increasingly concentrated on training workshops and devised productions in local languages.

In Malawi, the Chancellor College Travelling Theatre, which started in 1970, took on a rather different orientation. From the outset the Censorship Board in Malawi (established by the 1968 Censorship and Control of Entertainment Act) tended to discourage radical attempts at theatrical mobilisation of popular causes, and the circuit was mostly restricted to educational institutions. Many of the early plays were adaptations of classics from Europe or other parts of Africa. Even in Malawi, however, playwrights emerged during the 1970s, writing almost exclusively English-language plays for the Travelling Theatre. It was only in 1982 that artists began performing plays in chiChewa and the other Malawian languages. In the same year a new Department of Fine and Performing Arts allowed for the production of plays within a formal academic context.

At the University of Botswana, a travelling theatre was initiated in 1981 by the head of the English department, Felix Mnthali, a Malawian professor who had been impressed by the achievements of Chancellor College Travelling Theatre. The chairman of the secretariat that ran the Botswana group was Victor Ntubani, a Zimbabwean Shakespeare scholar. All the early plays were in English, but after Motswana lecturer Thulaganyo Mogobe took over the chairmanship of the theatre, in 1998, plays began to be introduced in seTswana. The group travelled not only to different parts of Botswana, but also to Zimbabwe and Namibia. The climax of the year's activities was normally a 'command performance' for the state president and several other dignitaries, a sharp contrast with the tense relationship the Zambian and Malawian University Travelling Theatres had with their respective governments. Mogobe complained that the 'cordial relations which the theatre enjoys with the Establishment . . . could serve as a limiting factor'.[64] By contrast a drama course, UBE 423, introduced by the English department in 1992, tended to adopt a position more critical of the establishment, with students devising plays in English and seTswana on topical, social or political issues such as sexism, racism or class conflict.

Expatriates also made significant contributions to university drama at the Universities of Lesotho and Swaziland. South African exiles Zakes Mda and Masitha Hoeane played an important role in Lesotho. Mda's play, *The Hill*, and Hoeane's *Cry the Whistle* and *Bridge of Destiny* were performed in the 1980s.[65] At the University of Swaziland, Ugandan playwright and director John Ruganda encouraged Swazi students to perform their scripted, English-language plays in the mid-1990s.

Another important source for an embryonic African drama could be found in secondary schools. All southern African Anglophone countries had a vastly increased secondary schools programme after independence, and although none of the ministries of education granted drama an official place on the school syllabus, most of them encouraged drama as an extra-curricular activity.

An important vehicle for promoting educational theatre was the schools drama festival. Their organisation differed from country to country, but each had rather paternalistic origins. In Zambia the organisation came under the umbrella of the Theatre Association of Zambia (TAZ), a white-dominated successor to the colonial Northern Rhodesia Drama Association. Schools, whether predominantly black or white, entered the annual amateur section of the TAZ annual festival, judged by a British drama expert flown in for the occasion.

In Malawi the Schools Drama Festival started in 1973, organised by the Association of Teachers of English in Malawi and funded by the British Council. The competition, which was restricted to schools, started at district level on a knock-out basis, moving to regional eliminations and culminating in a frenzied national final, more reminiscent of a football cup than a drama competition. Rules were very tight, with plays only allowed in English and with strict regulations about length, decor and size of casts. Despite these restrictions, skilled teacher playwright/directors emerged from this process, such as Owen Mbilizi in the 1980s and Smith Likongwe in the 1990s.

Schools drama in Botswana was similar to the Malawian model. The Botswana English Teachers Association started a schools drama festival in the northern region in 1984. This spread to other regions and by 1991 there was a national drama festival on a knock-out basis. Unlike in Malawi, however, plays were not restricted to English; seTswana plays were even more popular, an indication of seTswana's strength as a lingua franca. Most plays consisted of fairly static dialogue drama interspersed by choral dance interludes, a form probably derived from the university travelling theatre.

Schools drama was less geared to large-scale competitive festivals in Swaziland and Lesotho. Several Swazi schools organised themselves into a movement called PODRASO (Poetry and Drama Society), promoting drama and oral verse derived from the *izimbongi* tradition. This provided a seedbed for some of the troupes which emerged there in the 1990s. In Lesotho, drama tended to be left to the enthusiasm of individual schools, the most active of which was the private Machabeng International High School in Maseru.

Although the drama emanating from educational institutions took on variant forms in different southern African countries, according to local culture and ideology, there were some common features. Far more than the 'traditional' dance troupes, the literary drama of schools and universities offered an ambiguous attitude to the nationalist project of the newly independent African states. The crux of this ambiguity was the contradiction between artists' desires to celebrate the anti-colonial indigenous roots of the new nations and the dissatisfaction they often felt with the dictatorial tendencies of the ruling parties which established their power base in the late 1960s and early 1970s.

The contradiction was particularly visible in the predilection playwrights had for historical or mythical themes. The nationalist imperative drew young playwrights to explore the mythic roots of their pre-colonial heritage. Some were conscious (from university courses) of the role historical/folk drama played in the cultural nationalism of European states such as Norway and Ireland. In Zambia, Masiye's *The Lands of Kazembe* (1971), with its tale of the Lunda king's denial of Portuguese attempts to create an empire stretching from the Indian Ocean to the Atlantic Ocean, was a key early text. Kasoma's *Black Mamba* (about 1973)[66] and Chifunyise's dance dramas, *Mwaziona* and *Slave Caravan* (1975), played a similar recuperative role.

In Malawi, Chimombo's *The Rainmaker* delved even further into the past to celebrate the life of Mbona, a mythic religious hero who defied secular authority to start a popular rain cult. Other plays such as N'gombe's *The Banana Tree* and *The King's Pillow* and Kamlongera's *Chauta's Wrath* also exploited a similar vein.[67] In Botswana, *A Kind of Justice* by Mtubani and Janie explored more recent history, a critical moment of Bechuanaland's colonial history in 1933.[68]

These productions, however, rarely gave naïve endorsement of the régimes established by the newly independent states. Some plays, such as Kasoma's *Black Mamba*, with its examination of the struggle for Zambia's independence, raised the wrath of the UNIP establishment, which tried to restrict its performance. In Malawi, where state repression was even more blatant, playwrights used the historical-mythic material as allegorical disguise for critiques of the MCP régime. For example, in *The Rainmaker*, it is not difficult to see that a seventeenth-century conflict between a young prophet, Mbona, and an older tyrant, Kamundi, served as a screen for youthful Malawian frustration with the gerontocratic rule of Kamuzu Banda. A similar trend emerged in schools drama. Stewart Crehan has commented on the proliferation of Zambian productions with a vague pre-colonial setting, which pitted young, idealistic warriors against older, manipulative, corrupt kings.[69]

Plays with a contemporary setting also tended to maintain an ambivalent attitude to the new régimes. Popular genres here were romantic melodrama and social satire on issues concerning modernisation. Examples of such Zambian plays from the 1970s include Kasoma's *The Poisoned Cultural Meat*, Chifunyise's *Blood* and *The District Governor*; from Malawi, examples are Timpunza-Mvula's *The Lizard's Tail*, Innocent Banda's *Cracks*, Ng'ombe's *The Echoing House* and Kamlongera's *The Love Potion*. Playwrights and directors of such plays were often torn between the desire to expose social problems and the need to avoid provoking the wrath of vigilant state censors.

University and schools drama had a considerable influence on another form of theatre, one which was seen as necessary for achieving national identity in southern Africa, the mediated drama of television and radio. Much of the writing talent for television and for English-language radio drama came from the educational institutions. Since governments closely controlled the broadcasting companies (even if they were nominally corporations), this sometimes led to conflict.

In Zambia the main impetus for television drama came from President Kaunda's watershed speech of 1975, in which he called for a 'cultural revolution' to replace western 'imperialist' music and film on radio and television with Zambian equivalents. The policy had little permanent impact on radio, where drama or storytelling programmes in local languages of siTonga, chiBemba and chiNyanja were already well established and where disc-jockeys tended to ignore the injunction to play more Zambian music. In television, however, there was some influence. In addition to the already mentioned *ZAMARTS*, Television Zambia introduced a new weekly, studio-bound, thirty-minute slot, *Play for Today*.

For the first two years *Play for Today*, which for policy reasons contradicting Kaunda's cultural nationalist rhetoric were in English, relied mainly on university students and lecturers. Many of the plays, which were popular in local languages on the Unzadrams tours, either had their origins in or were adapted to television performance. The two most prolific playwrights were the student Mulenga Ng'andu and the Zimbabwean lecturer Stephen Chifunyise. The latter's social satires and melodramas, such as *Blood*, *I Resign* and *I Am Not for Sale*, proved particularly popular. Where scripted plays could not be found, improvised plays filled the gaps.

Zambia and Zimbabwe, however, were the only southern African countries that had their own television stations in the period immediately following independence. The main outlet for mediated drama in the region was through radio, and here each country had its own national policy.

Zambia Broadcasting Services continued a colonial policy of maintaining eight semi-autonomous language sections, English, plus seven indigenous language. The siTonga section continued with the drama programme *Malikopo* established during the colonial period, under the guidance of the same director/actor, Edward Mungoni, right through to his death in 1988. In the chiBemba section there were various experiments in drama programmes, but the most successful were Mwansa Kapeya's series, *Shangalilwa*, in the early 1970s, *Pompelyongo* in the late 1970s and *Ifyabukaya* in the 1980s and 1990s. In English, Chinyanja and Silozi there were only sporadic attempts at drama until the 1980s, when a younger generation of dramatists emerged.

In Malawi, playwrights based at schools and university colleges played a crucial role in the development of English-language radio drama in Malawi Broadcasting Corporation's weekly *Theatre of the Air* slot, initiated by Frank Dlamini in 1971. Far more popular, however, were the didactic comedies in chiChewa, *Kapalelpale* and *Pa Majiga*, devised through improvisation by a team under the direction of former Malawi Broadcasting Corporation watchman Smart Likhaya Mbewe.[70]

The radio drama of all the southern African countries, however, owing to the tight control government ideologues maintained over broadcasting, tended to avoid the controversy which sometimes gripped stage drama.

The ideological turmoil of stage drama's early development in Zambia had an institutional dimension. During the copper boom years of the late 1960s and early 1970s, expatriates who flocked to Zambia for work gravitated to the former colonial theatre clubs, such as the Lusaka Playhouse, Roan Antelope Drama and Opera Society, Kabwe's Venus Theatre and the Mufulira Arts Society. Their organising association, TAZ (see earlier), saw itself as the natural tutelary agency to guide an emergent Zambian theatre. The young radicals of the university, however, sought inspiration in indigenous traditions of performance. In protest at expatriate arrogance they defected from TAZ and established an Afro-centric theatre organisation, the Zambian National Theatre Arts Association (ZANTAA), in 1975. The university and many schools pulled out of the TAZ competitive drama festival and arranged an annual non-competitive festival with its own theatre workshops, not only in drama but also dance and music theatre.[71]

Soon ZANTAA activists called for the establishment of a national theatre. As a step in this direction some of the most talented ex-Unzadrams artists initiated a group, Tikwiza Theatre, which saw itself as an embryonic national theatre. Their first play, a historical epic entitled *Uhuru wa Ndongo* (1977), criticised not only colonial brutality but also corruption and hypocrisy in a barely disguised post-independence Zambia. Subsequently, however, the group developed tensions, which manifested themselves in different theatre policies. Some artists, such as Masautso Phiri, Mumba Kapumpa and Haggai Chisulo, wanted to concentrate on large-scale productions condemning racist policies in South Africa or Angola (notably Phiri's *Soweto*, 1976, and *Mercenaries*, 1978).[72] Tikwiza's highlighting of these issues received government approval. Other artists, however, such as Mapopa Mtonga, Moses Kwali and Dickson Mwansa, preferred present plays focussing on Zambian issues (notably Mwansa's *The Cell*, 1982), thereby attracting strong criticism from the UNIP government.[73]

By the early 1980s the Zambian government had decided to clamp down on theatre. Chikwakwa Theatre was starved of funds and Tikwiza's search for a national theatre lost its impetus. In 1986 (by which time there were far fewer expatriates promoting and attending theatre) government forced TAZ and ZANTAA to unite as a single body, the National Theatre Arts Association of Zambia. In television too, ZANTAA were no longer given the remit to produce *Play for Today*; this responsibility was given to the ideological state paramilitary organisation the Zambian National Service under Lieutenant Craig Lungu in 1982. The diverse and often radical orientation of the ZANTAA plays changed to a more professionally polished, instrumentalist satirical genre.

The drama scene in southern Africa was transformed by a new movement emerging in the late 1970s, theatre for development. This linked performance to campaigns of economic and social amelioration in such fields as health, literacy, agriculture or social welfare. The movement expanded from its epicentre in southern Africa throughout the 1980s to most of the continent, and it made significant contributions to drama theory and practice in other continents too.[74]

Although its roots can be traced to didactic elements in both pre-colonial and colonial theatre, the immediate origins of theatre for development can be confidently traced to the Laedza Batanani project in Botswana (1975–6). Expatriate adult educators at the University of Botswana, Ross Kidd and Martin Byram, along with Batswana, Jeppe Kelepile, Frank Youngman, Martha Maplanka and Sports Moiketse, disillusioned with conventional methods of development communication, turned to theatre as a more attractive and participatory methodology. The first experiments were in the Bokalaka area of north-east Botswana in 1975. From 1976 the organisers set up a national committee to run workshops in several parts of the country. The team established a working pattern which involved researching the problems of a community and creating devised plays, performed to the villagers, who then analysed them in open debate and worked out programmes of community action based on these discussions. The process was made considerably easier owing to the existence of an indigenous community discussion forum, the *kgotla*; however, the tendency for the kgotla to discriminate against women, youths and non-Batswana created an obstacle to full community participation.

The Laedza Batanani team made links with Zambia's Chikwakwa Theatre in order to generate interest in the methodology among theatre workers. After small scale contact a major regional workshop was organised at Chalimbana in Zambia in 1979 attended by delegates from Botswana, Zambia, Tanzania, Swaziland, Lesotho and the Zimbabwean and South African liberation movements. From this point onwards the ideology and methodology of theatre for development spread rapidly. Workshops in Swaziland (Nhlangano, 1981), Malawi (Mbalachanda, 1982) Zimbabwe (Morehwa, 1983), Lesotho (Maseru, 1984) and Namibia (Rehoboth, 1991) spread the methodology throughout the region. International workshops in Germany (Berlin, 1980), Canada (Thunder Bay, 1981) and Bangladesh (Koitta, 1983) linked African theatre for development with similar movements in other continents. In the process, the originators of the movement began to critique the early practices of the movement. The theories and practice of Brazilian activist Augusto Boal had a particularly strong impact in moving African theatre for development workers to seek a more participatory, people-centred approach to the problems of cultural mobilisation.

The progress in theatre for development methodology was nowhere more eagerly pursued and documented than in Lesotho.[75] Exiled South Africans Zakes Mda and Masitha Hoeane at the University of Lesotho, along with local Basotho including Motlokoa Selinyane, Regina Chabisi and Mahluli Mngadi, built a movement called Marotholi Travelling Theatre (MTT), initially linked to the National University of Lesotho but eventually independent. The campaign, supported by the Ford Foundation, had its own regularly published newsletter and cooperated closely with appropriate social agencies and with other media (for example, through radio and comic book versions of plays). Mda has traced the way MTT developed from early agitprop plays such as *Kopano ke Motla!* (Unity is strength; a 1985 production about migrant workers) through experiments with participatory drama techniques in *Rural Sanitation Play* (1986) and *Agro-Action Play* (1988), to the much more fully participatory productions, *The Trade Union Play* (1988) and *The Alcoholism Play* (1989). One of the major achievements of Marotholi was to continue the regional networking originally initiated by Laedza Batanani through workshops and the MTT newsletter.

The theatre for development movement had a major impact on drama in the region, not only because of the campaigns themselves, but also because it offered alternative methods of play creation, dramaturgy and, above all, patronage. As Non-Government Organisations (NGOs) and even government departments became interested in the potential of drama as a communication tool, emergent theatre groups began to see potential sources of support outside educational institutions. This gave rise to a huge increase in small independent groups from the early 1980s onwards, working mostly in African languages; often they used financial support from donors for theatre for development projects as a hidden subsidy for more traditional forms of art theatre. Not a few were nakedly commercial in their approach to NGO funding.

Malawi provides an interesting example. After the Mbalachanda workshop of 1982, Chancellor College Travelling Theatre changed its policy by including ChiChewa plays in its previously all-English repertoire. One of these, *Mchira wa Buluzi*, which was created at the workshop, was a local language version of Timpunza-Mvula's play, *The Lizard's Tail*; it proved to be stunningly popular. Several independent groups sprang up in the mid-1980s, performing chiChewa plays, mostly on a commercial basis, but sometimes taking NGO commissions. Kwathu Arts Theatre, run by Charles Severe with plays like *Madzi Akatayika* (If the water is spilt), was the most popular of these. But many others, such as Umodzi, Lonjezo, Black Lass and Force Theatre, toured community halls, bars and schools throughout the late 1980s and 1990s. The only professional group to emerge through this process, Wakhumbata Educational Theatre, concentrated on plays in English under the directorship of Du Chisiza Jr, who was also its principal actor and playwright.[76]

A similar process took place in Zambia. After the Chalimbana workshop many popular theatre groups established themselves, including, among others, Bakanda Theatre, Tithandize, Fwabena Africa, Tinabadwa and Target 2000, all of them competing for donor funds as well as for paying audiences. Undoubtedly the most popular and successful of these groups was Kanyama Production Unit Theatre, which toured much of the region and throughout the late 1980s provided a model for unemployed youth to obtain some kind of living through theatre.

In Botswana, the home of Laedza Batanani, theatre for development was firmly established, there being rather poor audience attendance for commercial shows during the 1970s and 1980s. In 1985 the Reetsenang group of community theatres was created under the directorship of Zimbabwean Frank Chitikuta. This was both a theatre company and an umbrella organisation for other theatre for development groups. Reetsenang, through some of its key practitioners and workshop facilitators, such as Emmanuel Rametsi and Samson Setumo, developed a recognisable style which placed great emphasis on dance, mime and emotive songs performed over frozen action and the rhetorical delivery of dialogue. Important groups who responded to the demand for community theatre were Baramodi, Magosi Dedicated Artists, and, after they broke with Reetsenang, Rametsi's Okava Theatre Trust and Setumo's Millennium Production House. Many groups, such as Diphala Traditional Dance and Drama or Bopaganang, combined drama with traditional dance. One particularly imaginative group that flourished in the late 1980s and early 1990s was Mambo Arts Trust, which had its own offices and shops. It undertook research into a broad variety of Botswana crafts, fine art, dance and music, as well as giving performances. Another exciting group, Ghetto Artists, based in Francistown under the artistic directorship of Otukile Vuyisele, also combined theatre for development with other activities such as dance, video and educational print communication.

In Swaziland the process of building independent groups was much less developed than in other countries in the region. But by the early 1990s several troupes had emerged, which, like some of the Botswana equivalents, tended to combine song, dance and drama. These included Siphila Nje Drama Society, Peoples Educational Theatre and Bhunya Bombers.

One result of theatre for development's popularity, and that of the local language drama groups which sprang up in its wake, was the revival of local language drama publication. Plays were published in such languages as seTswana, seSotho, siSwati, chiNyanja, chiBemba, chiShona and siNdebele throughout the 1980s and 1990s, providing schools with more up-to-date texts than the colonial ones they often hitherto had to rely on for African-language literature syllabuses.

So far in this account there has been little mention of Zimbabwean and Namibian post-independence theatre. This is owing to the unusual conditions created by the late achievement of independence by these nations. This is the right point to redress this imbalance, initially by showing the theatre scene in the build up to liberation from white-dominated power, and then by showing how the newly independent nations telescoped many of the struggles and stages of theatrical development, which in other nations took two or more decades, into a few years.

In 1964 when the federation of Rhodesia and Nyasaland broke up, Zambia and Malawi obtained their independence. Southern Rhodesia, however, remained under the rule of Ian Smith's Rhodesian Front, which in 1965 made a Unilateral Declaration of Independence (UDI) from the colonial power,

Great Britain, in order to retain the white racist political system. When it became clear that Britain would not intervene militarily, and that the sanctions it imposed would not bring down Smith's government, the nationalist organisations Zimbabwe African National Union (ZANU) and Zimbabwe African People's Union (ZAPU) intensified the guerrilla war (often called the Second Chimurenga) that they had already initiated against the Rhodesian régime. Many Zimbabwean nationalists were detained and others fled into exile.

These events had implications for the development of theatre. Among white theatre audiences the most remarkable feature was a lack of substantive change, despite the alteration in 1963 of the SRDA into the Association of Rhodesian Theatrical Societies (ARTS). Sanctions meant the end of visiting British touring groups, but REPS and other ARTS groups continued performing British plays in the same escapist vein, as if the crisis of 1965 and the state of siege it had created had never happened.

Formal theatre for blacks told a similar story. Mission and state schools and the playwriting sponsored by the Rhodesian Literary Bureau (founded in 1953) continued to produce plays with safe social themes concerning the impact of modernisation.[77] The most famous of these were the plays of Paul Chidyausiku, who wrote several chiShona scripts during the 1960s.[78] The state's draconian censorship system, however, prevented black authors from dealing with nationalist issues. Comic examples of these safe plays and also adaptations of African novels found their way on to Zimbabwean television in the 1970s, notably T. K. Tsodzo's *Babumini Francis* (Uncle Francis, 1977).[79] A related phenomenon from the 1970s was the involvement of white missionaries or teachers, such as Daniel Pierce, in the creation of an equally self-censored liberal drama intended for black actors and audiences.

Another rather escapist genre was comic, improvised radio drama, particularly the farcical series *The Mukodota Family*, created in the late 1960s by Safirio Madzikatire, who played the central role of the outrageously sexist, Mukodota. In style, subject matter and manner of creation/performance the series had strong similarities to the improvised plays pioneered at CABS. After Zimbabwe's independence, *The Mukodota Family* made a successful transfer to television.

Black Zimbabweans acquired slightly more autonomy over traditional dances and plays, which were performed at Salisbury City Council's recreational facilities, organised by Basil Chidyamathamba. These events started in the 1950s and continued into the UDI period with an annual Neshamwari

Festival of Music. It was music, in fact, which provided urban Africans with their only real outlet for nationalist sentiments in the period between UDI and independence, particularly through the veiled metaphoric lyrics of such popular 'Chimurenga' singers as Thomas Mapfumo and Oliver Mtukudzi, who used indigenous traditions of poetic symbolism to obscure the revolutionary message of their songs.[80]

The most innovative theatrical reactions to the emergency in Zimbabwe took place in the rural areas. One remarkable development was the way spirit possession rituals such as *Mashabe* and *Mapira*, which had come under severe attack from Christianity from the 1920s onwards, made a revival in the 1970s. *Mhondoro* spirit mediums in the strategically sensitive Zambezi Valley, for example, became important agents for sanctioning the activities of guerrilla fighters with the blessings of ancestral heroes such as Chaminuka and Nehanda, the woman executed by the British during the first Chimurenga.[81] Smith's agents tried to counter this activity, particularly in the Marondellas area, by coopting spirit mediums to the cause of the white régime, but the strategy failed, owing to the guerrillas' more assiduous adherence to ritual procedures and owing to their assassination of a key 'sell-out' medium.[82] In addition to attaching themselves to traditional ritual forms of resistance, guerrillas also created a syncretic type of performance called *Pungwe* in chiShona and *Ukwejisa* in siNdebele. According to Ross Kidd, these all-night performances, which mixed speeches, poetry, music, song and dramatic sketches, were 'highly participatory – villagers and fighters acted out and danced their commitment and built up their morale through collective music-making'.[83] Outside of Zimbabwe a variety of performances ranging from simple dance mimes to full-length plays took place in the ZANU and ZAPU refugee camps and schools in Zambia and Mozambique, with the aim of raising morale and commitment among the refugees and Zimbabwean exiles.[84] When in 1980 the war drove the Smith régime to the Lancaster House peace talks and Zimbabwe finally became independent after the victory of Robert Mugabe's ZANU PF at the democratic elections, theatre underwent a process of rapid and radical change. Independence brushed aside the cultural exclusiveness and white domination that had existed during the UDI régime. In addition, a wave of returned exiles and richly experienced practitioners from other African countries poured into Zimbabwe with innovative ideas for building the new nation's theatrical culture.

The way radical theatre activists dealt with the split between white and black theatre modes illustrates the application of lessons learned from the

Zambian and Kenyan experiences. Rather than confronting the NTO (the 1977 successor to ARTS) head on, progressive theatre artists set up their own organisations and working methods. An alternative theatre emerged in three institutions. Stephen Chifunyise, veteran of the Zambian theatre, who returned in 1983 to Zimbabwe's Ministry of Youth, Sports and Culture, oversaw government-sponsored theatre and performance. The ministry supported community theatre, dance and music groups in the country and sponsored the annual Independence Anniversary Cultural Gala. The university's Faculty of Theatre Arts was led by Robert McLaren, a veteran of South Africa's Workshop 70 and of theatre work in the United Kingdom and Ethiopia; he promoted an anti-imperialist socialist theatre both within the university and in a satellite community theatre, Zambuko/Izibuko. Ngugi wa Mirii, an exile from Kenya's Kamiriithu Theatre, escaped to Zimbabwe in 1983 and became the first director of the Zimbabwe Foundation for Education with Production (ZIMFEP), which used theatre as one of its major communication strategies.

These three institutions formed a loose, if sometimes acrimonious alliance, trying to promote a radical, socialist theatre with its cultural roots in African villages and urban townships, and using chiShona and siNdebele as major languages, though not to the exclusion of English. The 1983 workshop at Murehwa was particularly important in that it included some theatre for development practitioners from other African countries, but tried to link their methodologies to Zimbabwe's professedly socialist national orientation. The main institutional outcome was the formation of the Zimbabwe Association of Community Theatres in 1985, under the leadership of Ngugi wa Mirii. ZACT was not only an umbrella organisation for community theatres but undertook to train theatre workers through a series of workshops and to provide logistical support for the community theatre network.

The mix of talent, enthusiasm and NGO-sourced money brewing in Zimbabwe in the early 1980s kick-started a community theatre movement with astonishingly varied styles and subject matter. These can be briefly summarised as follows:

1. Agitprop theatre. This was provided particularly at the university and by Zambuko/Izibuko, with plays about the impact of the liberation struggle in both Zimbabwe and South Africa.
2. Workers' theatre. Several groups of workers used theatre to mobilise for their rights. These include Shingayi Domestic Workers Drama Group

(Harare), Kuwirirana Theatre Group (Bulawayo) and Fambidzanai Theatre Group (Harare).

3. Women's rights theatre. These include the two Harare-based groups, Just for Women and Glen Norah Women's Theatre Group, led by Tisa Chifunyise.

4. Children's theatre. This was organised on a national scale by the NGO, Children's Performing Arts Workshop (CHIPAWO), which was affiliated to the international organisation, Association of Theatre for Children and Young People (ASSITEJ).

5. Religious theatre by Christian groups such as the Gweru-based Faithful Messengers.[85]

Although many of the activities were highly uncoordinated, ZACT's acquisition of offices at the National Stadium and a permanent theatre base in Harare's Waterfalls township in 2000 has provided a potential focus for community theatre. It has already not only made a major impact within Zimbabwe, but has also influenced the development of community theatre in Botswana and Namibia.

A slightly different set of imperatives is associated with the rise of 'traditional' dance activities in Zimbabwe. The government saw dance as an important medium for reflecting indigenous values. It created the Zimbabwe National Traditional Dance Association in 1980 and the National Dance Company in 1981, which performed a prestigious dance drama, *Mbuya Nehanda*, in the same year. After Chifunyise arrived in 1983 a series of influential workshops was initiated, showing how dance could be built into complex dance dramas to express community concerns. This in turn influenced many drama groups to incorporate dance into the texture of their performances. Outside of this community-oriented performance, a whole variety of dance styles and genres emerged, ranging from official government praise singers for President Mugabe (consciously based on Kamuzu Banda's *Gule la Chipani*) to the professional art dance company group, Tumbuka, which mixed traditional dance steps with western ballet.

Inevitably independence also had an impact on the former white theatre associated with REPS and the NTO. Many of the clubs continued with their conservative policy of performing British plays to almost exclusively white audiences. However, the administrators responsible for NTO, aware of the fate of TAZ in Zambia, realised it could not claim to be a national organisation if the majority of the population were effectively excluded. The inclusion of Ben Sibenke's *Uncle Grey Bonzo* in the 1981 NTO festival (which it won) is an indication of this shift.

When Susan Hains became chairperson in 1985, she worked very hard to make NTO inclusive of black theatre. She initiated a series of workshops for schools and community theatres, which to some extent were modelled on and rivalled ZACT's workshops. She also insisted that entries to the NTO annual competitive festival (Winterfestival) could be open to plays in any language, not just English. In 1986 the Bulawayo-based theatre group Amakhosi, under the leadership of Cont Mhlanga, won first prize at the Winterfestival with the play *Nansi le Ndoda* (Here is the man), in a mixture of English and siNdebele. Some white groups pulled out of NTO in protest, others began to make themselves more inter-racial. According to Martin Rohmer, by 1991 only 15 of the NTO's 53 member groups were still predominantly white.[86]

Amakhosi, with its unimpeachably subaltern roots in Bulawayo's high-density township of Makokoba, became the main feather in NTO's cap. *Workshop Negative* (1986), Amakhosi's phenomenally successful analysis of racial reconciliation in an industrial setting, which was also an allegory of the betrayed promises of Zimbabwean independence, became a *cause célèbre*, initiating a national debate.[87] Other Bulawayo-based groups, such as Indaba and Iluba Elimnyama, were also associated with NTO, although their main affiliation was to the independent Bulawayo Association of Drama Groups (BADG). The success of Amakhosi and of NTO's community theatre workshop (the Poor School) had an impact on several other NTO plays with inter-racial casts. These include Andrew Whaley's *Platform Five* (1987), *The Nyoka Tree* (1988) and *The Rise and Shine of Comrade Fiasco* (1990) and Jeremy Summerfield's *Mhondero* (REPS, 1993).[88]

Throughout the period a state of cold war existed between NTO and ZACT, with ZACT accusing NTO of being contaminated by its Eurocentric origins (particularly through its adherence to competitive drama competition and to foreign adjudicators), and NTO accusing ZACT of too slavishly toeing the government line on socialism. By the late 1990s, however, conditions had changed so much that some of the earlier political fault lines in theatre had also begun to change. By this time Mugabe's ZANU-led government had lost popularity. Although it clung to power in the 2002 elections partly through the violent mobilisation of pro-ZANU groups calling themselves war veterans, it was with a majority massively reduced by the Movement for Democratic Change party, some of whom, including their leader Morgan Tsvangurai, were trade unionists.

These events had a subtle but perceptible impact on theatre. Some of the community groups associated with ZACT lost their enthusiasm for the government policy of socialism, which they perceived in a contemporary Zimbabwean context to be hypocritical and self-serving. The uneasy rapprochement between ZACT and NTO already noticeable in the early 1990s became even clearer.

This ideological realignment coincided with changes in the affiliation of some of the key players. In 1996 McLaren left the university to concentrate on his work with Zambuko/Izibuko, and even more vigorously with CHIPAWO. In 1998 Hains retired as executive secretary of NTO and her place was taken by Bright Mbiriri. In 2000 Stephen Chifunyise, who had been in and out of government positions for the previous ten years, made a clear decision to concentrate on NGO work, particularly CHIPAWO. Wa Mirii remained as the leader of ZACT, and, in addition to its former roles, he tried to use the organisation as a debating arena for some of the divisive political issues about land. He, too, had become particularly interested in children's theatre. It is as if many of the radical activists, after the failure of Zimbabwe's socialist dream, had decided to invest most of their energies in building a new generation of theatre practitioners. Many of the younger generation, such as Daves Guzha of Rooftop Productions, showed scant interest in the ideological feuds of the 1980s. Thus, the general tendency has been for theatre to disengage itself from overt politics and to move towards the kind of indirect social change achievable through NGO work.

The cultural shifts of the 1990s also affected less formally organised performing arts. This was most obvious with some of the musicians who had supported the Second Chimurenga. Oliver Mtukudzi, and even more openly, Thomas Mapfumo, composed songs critical of the ZANU leadership. Even at village level there were signs of resistance through performance. Marja Spierenburg gives an example of Mhondero mediums who had, in the 1970s, supported the Chimurenga struggle, using the power of their spirit possession cult to resist the post-independence government's mid-Zambezi Rural Development Project.[89] In both formal and non-formal spheres the dashing of political expectations arising at independence led to major readjustments in Zimbabwean theatre, music and dance by the turn of the new millennium.

In 1983 when Zimbabwean post-independence theatre was taking off, Namibian theatre maintained an almost surrealistically divided nature. Lavishly well-resourced plays, supported by South African-style Performing Arts Councils, still performed with white casts for exclusively white audiences, while the beginnings of a counter-theatre for black and multi-racial audiences was just beginning to emerge in Katutura and other townships in Windhoek. At the same time, the South-West Africa People's Organisation (SWAPO), based in Lusaka, sent its cultural group on tour to many other countries, as part of SWAPO's propaganda campaign, performing patriotic songs, Namibian dances and dramatic sketches.

This polarised cultural scene could not last. By the mid-1980s the state of emergency in South Africa made the de Klerk government realise that the republic's continued administration of south-west Africa was untenable. South Africa's attempt to promote the Turnhalle Alliance as a moderate, multi-racial alternative to SWAPO necessitated a dilution of the earlier Apartheid cultural policies. The South-West Africa Performing Arts Councils tried to open up its productions to black audiences, and black or 'coloured' theatre groups performing in Afrikaans were encouraged to participate in the South African Afrikaans Taal en Kultuurvereniging (Afrikaans Language and Cultural Festival). The climax of this cultural thaw was reached in 1989, shortly before the elections, in the production of Frederick Philander's play *Katutura 59*, depicting the events of 1959 which led to the beginnings of the militant struggle against South African colonialism in the territory.[90]

At independence in 1990, the main elements of an emergent, multi-racial counter-theatre were to be found in three groups. Philander's Serpent Players (later the Windhoek Players, then Committed Artists of Namibia) continued to stage an annual youth drama festival, an important vehicle for new work, particularly the many resistance theatre pieces being developed in black schools all over the country.[91] In community theatre, Bricks, an active CBO (community-based organisation) promoting democratic communication in print, art and video, had by 1986 developed a theatre wing called Platform 2000. This group clashed with the Apartheid authorities and began developing a coherent strategy, based on the practices of other theatre groups such as Boal's Theatre of the Oppressed and ZACT's Zimbabwean programme. The School for the Arts of the Academy (later University of Namibia) which had staged (since 1987) a number of provocative satires (with multi-racial casts) by prominent leftist playwrights or directors, George Weidemann, Gerrit Schoonhover and Dorian Haarhoff, consolidated its tradition of resistance with an independence play, Haarhoff's *Guerrilla Goatherd*, depicting the resistance of the southern Bondeslwart people in 1922.[92]

After independence, the way had thus been prepared for some kind of reconciliation between the formerly opposed black and white theatre traditions. A few months before independence the Performing Arts Councils were closed down and changed into the National Theatre of Namibia, with a brief to represent all communities and ethnic groups in the new nation. Although the theatre building in Windhoek continued to host local and visiting prestige productions, a community theatre section was developed, undertaking workshops throughout Namibia in order to stimulate relevant theatre ventures. A permanent black performance troupe at the National Theatre toured the country with its productions *Stories and Legends of Namibia* and *Fast Norman and his Friends*.

Bricks and Committed Artists of Namibia also found new roles to play in the liberated nation. Bricks hosted an influential workshop in Rehoboth in 1990 with distinguished persons from almost every continent making contributions to brainstorming about the direction of Namibia's future community theatre. Partly as a result of this, Bricks changed its orientation away from resistance theatre to issues of community development, especially the growing menace of AIDS. It also built closer links with theatre organisations outside of Namibia, particularly ZACT. Committed Artists of Namibia, which had provided sharp criticism of the old régime, did not take long to find that provocative role in the new.

A clutch of post-independence groups also responded to the demands of independence. Afkawandahe, as its name suggests (an acronym referring to Afrikaaner, Kavango, Wambo, Namo, Damara and Herero) attempted for a few years in the early 1990s to address the problems of creating a unified multi-cultural, multi-lingual nation by using a variety of languages and musical/choreographic forms in its productions. Several 'traditional' dance groups also sprung up in different parts of Namibia within an ethos of resurgent district pride; these included Sunshine Kids from Gobabis, Kambundu Cultural Group from Rundu, Uukumwe from Kavango and Rossko Cultural Troupe from Ruacana. Such cultural troupes performed at national competitions organised by the Ministry of Basic Education and Culture.[93]

There are several positive developments in recent Namibian theatre. A number of actors and plays have enjoyed international exposure, including Lucky Mosalele's *Mogomotsiemang* (Botswana, Germany, Northern Ireland and Zimbabwe) and Vickson Hangula's award-winning play, *The Show Isn't Over Until . . .* (Botswana and South Africa). Theatre for Development has flourished with workshops organised by the National Theatre (under Norman Job), the Namibian Cultural Development Centre, and Community Outreach Theatre. A small film and television industry is also beginning to emerge with directors such as Bridgette Pickering, Dudley Vial, Vickson Hangula and Laurinda Olivier-Sampson. Training opportunities in theatre have also recently emerged at the University of Namibia, the College of the Arts, the Rehoboth College of the Arts and the Namibian Institute for Educational Development. This vigorous activity has given rise to vehement debates between theatre workers and the government over official support for the theatre arts.

Namibia's independence coincided with new developments in the region, which had a major impact on theatre. The most important of these was the collapse of Apartheid, leading to democratic elections in South Africa in 1994. Linked to this was the collapse of the Soviet Bloc, which contributed to a realignment of power in southern Africa and to the movement for democratic change. Former one-party states, Zambia and Malawi, changed governments in 1993 and 1994 respectively, after multi-party elections. The 2 million Mozambican refugees who had been in the region, returned to their formerly war-torn country. The demands created by the new democracy, as well as the need to repair the ravages caused by war, civil unrest and the scourge of AIDS, led to an increase in the power of NGOs, including as patrons of theatre for development. The imposition of Structural Adjustment Programmes by the IMF increased commercialisation, particularly of television and radio drama.

The consequences for theatre have been profound. The liberation of South Africa has meant that essentialist appeals to African tradition as a bulwark against colonialism and Apartheid have tended to become *passé*. The new civil rights which accompanied democracy have meant that theatre artists feel freer to criticise both the previous MCP régime and governments. In Malawi, Du Chisiza Jr wrote a play mocking some of the new shibboleths of democracy, *Democracy Boulevard* (1993). In Botswana, Magosi Dedicated Artists and the UBE 423 course created plays attacking aspects of government policy, while Amakhosi continued to lambast the régime in Zimbabwe, despite a clamp-down on civil rights. The new pluralism has also meant that political struggles formerly based on the black–white conflict now begin to widen to include global injustice, as seen in Zambuko/Izibuko's *Simuka Zimbabwe!* (Arise Zimbabwe!, 1993).

The whole region has witnessed an extraordinary proliferation of plays about AIDS, many of them funded by NGOs or the governments. Edutainment soap operas centring on AIDS/HIV issues have become popular in the electronic media. Examples are *Tinkanene* (We have been talking) and *Tikuferanji* (Why are we dying?) on Radio Malawi and *Kabanana* on Television Zambia. In stage drama, although some of the plays about HIV have achieved a degree of subtlety, most of them end up achieving only what Martin Rohmer in an analysis of *Zvakamuwanawo* (It also befell him), a 1993 AIDS play by the Zimbabwean group Indaba, calls 'a denigration of the performer's own culture'.[94] One result of the AIDS campaigns has been the opening up of sexual issues previously thought of as taboo. It has also meant a rethinking of attitudes to women and children, who were some of the main victims of the virus. Artists have begun to give much energy to addressing issues of human rights and social exclusion. With the help of donor funding, women's theatre groups were established, such as Glen Norah and Chambira Women's Theatre in Zimbabwe. Organisations promoting theatre for women and/or children have also emerged, including Zambia's Women in Theatre and Film and Zimbabwe's ASSITEJ. Women directors or playwrights seem to be finding increased confidence; these include Norah Mumba in Zambia, Tisa Chifunyise in Zimbabwe, Tania Terblanche, Maria Amakali and Laurinda Olivier-Sampson in Namibia, Zondwa Sithebe in Swaziland and Gertrude Kamkwatira, who took over the directorship of Wakhumbata in Malawi after the death of Chisiza in 1999.[95] Many other groups, such as Zimbabwe's Zambuko/Izibuko (*The Adamant Eve*, as early as 1986), Botswana's UBE 423 (*You Are Not Dead*, 1993, and *I Love My Country But . . .*, 1995) have performed plays that advocate the cause of women. Several plays also champion the cause of children. Examples of these from Botswana alone are: Ghetto Artists' *Action for Orphans* (2000) UBE 423's *Murdering the Soul* (1999) and Bopaganang's *Mangwana* (2001).[96]

Ecological issues have also begun to concern artists. The South African NGO theatre for Africa has set up theatre groups in Zimbabwe (Malilangwe Trust) and Botswana (Phutulogo Theatre) to sensitise the public about ecological issues, and has toured the whole region with a play about wildlife management, drawing upon actors from five different southern African countries.

Yet another development of the new pluralism is the increased networking both within and between countries. Several successful regional drama festivals have been established, such as Linkfest in Bulawayo, Zimbabwe, and Maitisong Festival in Gaborone, Botswana. At the organisational level, in addition to the national groups already mentioned there are several more specialised groupings. In Zambia there is a national group called the Zambian

Popular Theatre Alliance attempting to instil some regulatory order in the chaotic field of theatre for development, while CASnews provides an Internet link, catering mostly for the formerly expatriate theatre clubs, which are now run by Zambian nationals. Zimbabwe has an astonishing plethora of special interest theatre networks, an indication both of the vigour and the rather divided nature of the drama scene there. Attempts had been made since the early 1980s to provide regional or continental groupings, with little success. From 1998, however, the Southern African Theatre Alliance (SATI) operating from the Market Theatre Laboratory in Johannesburg, has begun to provide a comparatively well-resourced base for theatre networking in the whole region.

Conclusion

This rather sketchy survey of colonial and post-colonial theatre may give a blurred impression of incompatible national projects and drama practices totally deracinated from pre-colonial modes of performance. However, a close examination of the actual 'traditions' of theatre crystallising in the region indicates significant continuities as well as disjuncture.

Most of the indigenous trance dances, masquerades, spirit possession rituals and other forms of Ngoma still survive, even if, through commercial influences, their aesthetic features and some of their functions have been transformed. At the same time, the new forms emerging in the colonial period have themselves deep roots in indigenous culture. This is obvious with syncretic dances, like militaristic mimes, but can even be seen with the imported genre of drama. As Kennedy Chinyowa says of traditional Shona narrative, 'storytelling lives on in modified form such as community based theatre, children's performing arts and other theatrical modes'.[97] The tendency of southern African drama practitioners to use collaborative, devised techniques of play creation, the prominence of genres which mix dialogue, music, mime and dance and the strong imperative towards a didactic, socially relevant drama are rooted in indigenous performance practices. Even the retroactive iconic spirituality which we observed in pre-colonial performance has its parallel in the frequency of play plots and motifs, attempting to recuperate historical/mythic energies in order to vitalise or validate the struggles of the present.

We therefore see the whole history of southern African theatre displaying a sometimes clear, sometimes ambiguous, but ultimately productive dialectic between preservation of key indigenous aesthetic and symbolic markers, and their transformation/adaptation in order to mediate innovation or social change.

Notes

1. David Lewis-Williams and Thomas Dowson, *Images of Power: Understanding Bushman Rock Art* (Johannesburg: Southern Book Publications, 1989), pp. 60–70.
2. Richard Katz, Megan Biesele and Verna St Denis, *Healing Makes our Hearts Happy: Spirituality and Cultural Transformation among the Kalahari Ju/'Hoansi* (Rochester: Inner Traditions International, 1996), pp. 17–20.
3. Isaac Schapera, *The Khoisan Peoples of Southern Africa* (London and New York: Routledge and Kegan Paul, 1930), pp. 203–4.
4. Victor Turner, *Dramas, Fields and Metaphors* (New York: Cornell University Press, 1974), p. 234.
5. *Ngoma* is a term popularised by John Jantzen. See his *Ngoma: Discourses of Healing in Central and Southern Africa* (Los Angeles: University of California Press, 1992).
6. Rijk van Dijk, Ria Reis and Marja Spierenburg, eds., *The Quest for Fruition through Ngoma: The Political Aspects of Healing in Southern Africa* (Oxford: James Currey, Athens: Ohio University Press, Gweru: Mambo, Blantyre: Kachere: Bookworld, 2000), p. 4.
7. Matthew Schoffeleers, 'The Nyau Societies: Our Present Understanding', *Society of Malawi Journal*, 29.1 (1976), pp. 59–68.
8. Laurel Birch de Aguilar, *Inscribing the Mask: Interpretation of Nyau Masks and Ritual Performances among the Chewa of Central Malawi* (Sankt Augustin: Anthropos, 1996), pp. 63–5.
9. Matthew Schoffeleers, *Religion and the Dramatisation of Life: Spirit Beliefs and Rituals in Southern and Central Malawi* (Blantyre: CLAIM, 1997), p. 12.
10. Barbara Blackmun and Matthew Schoffeleers, 'Masks of Malawi', *African Arts* (1972), pp. 36–49 at p. 38.
11. De Aguilar, *Inscribing the Mask*, p. 64.
12. Gerard Kubik, *Makisi, Nyau, Mapiko: Maskentraditionen im Bantu-sprachigen Afrika* (Munich: Trickster, 1993).
13. Turner, *Drama, Fields*, p. 253.
14. William Mwondela, *Mukanda and Makishi: Traditional Education in North Western Zambia* (Lusaka: NECZAM, 1970), p. 12.
15. Gerard Kubik, *Mukanda na Makisi*, record sleeve notes (Berlin: Abteilung, 1965).
16. Thulaganyo Mogobe, 'Theatre in Botswana: A Study of Traditional and Modern Forms', unpublished Ph.D. thesis, University of Leeds, 1995, p. 47.
17. Lucy Mair, 'A Yao Girl's Initiation', *Man*, 51 (1951), pp. 98, 60–3, 61.
18. Annette Drews, 'Gender and Ngoma', in van Dijk *et al.*, *Quest for fruition*, pp. 39–60, 50–2.

19. Francis Lampi, 'The Dramatic Events of the Umutomboko Ceremony', *Chikwakwa Review* (1976), pp. 6–11.

20. B. A. Marwick, *The Swazi* (Cambridge: Cambridge University Press, 1940), p. 9.

21. Helen Kuper, *The Swazi* (London: International African Institute, 1952), p. 47.

22. Helen Kuper, *An African Aristocracy, Rank among the Swazi* (Oxford: Oxford University Press, 1947), p. 218.

23. Ibid., p. 207.

24. Kuper, *Swazi*, p. 47.

25. Kuper, *African Aristocracy*, p. 224.

26. Leroy Vail and Landeg White, *Power and the Praise Poem* (Charlottesville and Oxford: University of Virginia Press and James Currey, 1991), p. 101.

27. Mapopa Mtonga, 'The Dramatic Elements of Gule Wamkulu', unpublished M.A. thesis, University of Legon, 1980, p. 90.

28. Chris Kamlongera *et al.*, *Kubvina: An Introduction to Malawian Dance and Theatre* (Zomba: University of Malawi Press, 1992), p. 39.

29. Ian Linden and Matthew Schoffeleers, 'The Resistance of the Nyau Societies to the Roman Catholic Missions in Colonial Malawi', in T. Ranger and I. Kimambo, ed., *The Historical Study of African Religion* (London: Heinemann, 1976), p. 264.

30. John Mitchell, *The Kalela Dance*, Rhodes-Livingstone Papers 27 (Manchester: Manchester University Press, 1956), p. 12.

31. David Kerr, *Dance, Media Entertainment and Popular Theatre in South East Africa* (Bayreuth: Bayreuth University Press, 1997), pp. 47–69.

32. Mtonga, *Gule Wamkulu*, p. 173.

33. Albert Matongo, 'Popular Culture in a Colonial Society: Another Look at Mbeni and Kalela Dances on the Copperbelt, 1930–64' , in S. N. Chipunga, ed., *Guardians in their Time: Experiences of Zambians Under Colonial Rule, 1890–1964* (Basingstoke: Macmillan, 1993), pp. 180–217, 198–201.

34. Ibid., p. 204.

35. Schapera, *Khoisan Peoples*, pp. 404–5.

36. Ria Reis, 'The "wounded Healer" as ideology', in van Dijk *et al.*, *Quest for Fruition*, pp. 61–75, 66.

37. Steven M. Friedson, *Dancing Prophets: Musical Experience in Tumbuka Healing* (Chicago: University of Chicago Press, 1998), p. 65.

38. Vail and White, *Power and the Praise Poem*, pp. 237–68.

39. Ibid., pp. 247–8.

40. Elizabeth Colson, 'Spirit Possession among the Tonga', in J. Beattie and J. Middleton, ed., *Spirit Mediumship in Africa* (London: Routledge and Kegan Paul, 1969).

41. Schoffeleers, 'Nyau Societies', p. 19.

42. Kariamu Asante, *Zimbabwe Dance, Rhythm, Forms: Ancestral Forms, Aesthetic Analysis* (Trenton, NJ and Asmara: Africa World Press, 2000), pp. 41–7.

43. Jantzen, *Ngoma*, p. 177.
44. Dietland Schoerzenburger, *Community-based Theatre: Funktionalitat, Entwicklungs und Rezoptionsgerschichte der Volkshtheater in Zimbabwe*, Beitae zur Afrikanstik vol. LVIII (Vienna Institut für Afrikanistik, 1996), p. 29.
45. Jane Plastow, *African Theatre and Politics: The Evolution of Theatre in Ethiopia, Tanzania and Zimbabwe. A Comparative Study* (Amsterdam: Rodopi, 1996), p. 76.
46. Susan Hains, quoted in Schoerzenburger, *Community-based Theatre*, p. 30.
47. Stephen Chifunyise and Robert Kavanagh, eds., *Zimbabwe Theatre Report 1* (Harare: University of Zimbabwe, 1988), p. 13.
48. Anne Davidson, *The Real Paradise: Memories of Africa 1950–1963* (Edinburgh: Pentland Press, 1993), pp. 47–9.
49. Ibid., p. 274.
50. Plastow, *African Theatre*, pp. 77–81.
51. Neil Parsons, ' "Clicko": Franz Tanibosch, South African Bushman Entertainer in England, France, Cuba and the United States, 1908–1940', in Bernth Lindfors, ed., *Africans on Stage: Studies in Ethnological Show Business* (Bloomington and Cape Town: Indiana University Press and David Philip, 1999).
52. Kerr, *Dance, Media Entertainment*, pp. 90–2.
53. Ibid., p. 205.
54. For information on African-language literary drama in the colonial period see Albert Gerard, *African Language Literatures: An Introduction to the Literary History of Sub-Saharan African Languages* (Harlow: Longman, 1981).
55. Rosaleen Smyth, 'The Development of British Colonial Film Policy, 1927–1939, with Special Reference to East and Central Africa', *Journal of African History*, 20.3 (1979), pp. 437–50.
56. Louis Nell, *Images of Yesteryear: Film-making in Southern Africa* (Harare: Harper Collins, 1998).
57. Kerr, *Dance, Media Entertainment*, pp. 114–15.
58. Andreya Masiye, *The Lands of Kazembe* (Lusaka: Neczam, 1973). See also Kerr, *Dance, Media Entertainment*, pp. 121–3.
59. Veit Eulmann, ' "Spectatorial Lust": The African Choir in England, 1891–1893', in Lindfors, *Africans on Stage*, 107–34, 121.
60. For politicised dance in Malawi and Zambia, see Kerr, *Dance, Media Entertainment*, pp. 19–45.
61. Matt Mogekwu, 'The Politics of Press Freedom and the National Economy in Swaziland', paper presented at the Seminar on The 'Political Economy of the Media in Southern Africa', University of Natal, Durban, 24–29 April 2000, p. 10.
62. Ibid.
63. Annette Drews, 'Gender and Ngoma: The Power of Drums in Eastern Zambia', in van Dijk *et al.*, *Quest for Fruition*, p. 41.
64. Mogobe, *Theatre in Botswana*, p. 84.

65. See Zakes Mda, *The Plays of Zakes Mda* (Johannesburg: Ravan Press, 1990) and Masitha Hoeane, *Let My People Play: Participatory Theatre Plays* (Rome: Institute of Southern African Studies, National University of Lesotho, 1994).

66. Kabwe Kasoma, *Black Mamba* (Lusaka: Neczam, 1972).

67. See Steve Chimombo, *The Rainmaker* (Limbe: Montfort Press, 1975); James Gibbs, ed., *Nine Malawian Plays* (Limbe: Montfort Press, 1976); James N'gombe, *The King's Pillow and Other Plays* (London: Trafalgar Square Publishing, 1991).

68. Victor Mtubani and Benjamin Janie, *A Kind of Justice* (Gaborone: University of Botswana Press, 2000).

69. Stewart Crehan, 'Fathers and Sons: Politics and Myth in Recent Zambian Drama', *New Theatre Quarterly*, 3 (1987).

70. For television drama in Zambia and radio drama in Zambia and Malawi, see Kerr, *Dance, Media Entertainment*, pp. 134–98.

71. David Kerr, *African Popular Theatre in Sub-Saharan Africa from Pre-Colonial to the Present Day* (Oxford, Portsmouth, NH, Nairobi, Cape Town and Harare: James Currey, Heinemann, East African Publishers, David Philip and Baobab Books, 1995), pp. 109–11.

72. Masautso Phiri, *Soweto Flowers Will Grow* (Lusaka: Neczam, 1979).

73. Stewart Crehan, 'Patronage, the State and Ideology in Zambian Theatre', in Liz Gunner, ed., *Politics and Performance: Theatre, Poetry and Song in Southern Africa* (Johannesburg: Witwatersrand University Press, 1994), pp. 253–72.

74. For a summary see Kerr, *African Popular Theatre*, chapter 8.

75. Zakes Mda, *When People Play People: Development Communication through Theatre* (Johannesburg and London: Witwatersrand University Press and Zed Books, 1993).

76. See Du Chisiza, *Democracy Boulevard and Other Plays* (Blantyre: Wakhumbata Ensemble Theatre, 1998) and *Da Summer Blow and Other Plays* (Blantyre: Wakhumbata Ensemble Theatre, 1998).

77. See Ranganai Zinyemba, *Zimbabwean Drama: A Study of Shona and English Plays* (Gweru: Mambo Press, 1986).

78. Paul Chidyausiku, *Ndakambokuyambira* (Gweru: Mambo Press, 1968).

79. T. K. Tsodzo, *Babumini Francis* (Gweru: Mambo Press, 1977).

80. Alex Pongweni, *Songs that Won the Liberation War* (Harare: College Press, 1988).

81. See David Lan, *Guns and Rain: Guerrillas and Spirit Mediums in Zimbabwe* (Oxford: James Currey, 1985) and Terence Ranger, *Peasant Consciousness and Guerrilla War in Zimbabwe* (Oxford: James Currey, 1985).

82. Terence Ranger, 'The Death of Chaminuka: Spirit Mediums, Nationalism and Guerrilla Warfare in Zimbabwe', *African Affairs*, 81.324 (1982).

83. Ross Kidd, *From People's Theatre for Revolution to Popular Theatre for Reconstruction: Diary of a Zimbabwean Workshop* (The Hague and Toronto: CESO/ICAE, 1984), pp. 6–7.

84. Preben Kaarsholm, 'Mental Colonisation or Catharsis: Theatre Democracy and Cultural Struggle from Rhodesia to Zimbabwe', in Gunner, *Politics and Performance*, pp. 225–51.

85. Information mainly from Stephen Chifunyise, 'Trends in Zimbabwean Theatre', in Gunner, *Politics and Performance*, pp. 55–74.

86. Martin Rohmer, *Theatre and Performance in Zimbabwe* (Bayreuth: Bayreuth University Press, 1999), p. 86.

87. Cont Mhlanga, 'Workshop Negative', *African Theatre*, 4 (2003).

88. Andrew Whaley, 'The Rise and Shine of Comrade Fiasco', in Martin Banham and Jane Plastow, ed., *Contemporary African Plays* (London: Methuen, 1999).

89. Marja Spierenburg, 'Social Commentaries and the Influence of the Clientele: The Mhondoro Cult in Dende, Zimbabwe', in van Dijk *et al.*, *Quest for fruition*, pp. 76–98.

90. For publication the play's title was changed to *The Curse*. See Frederick Philander, *The Curse* (Braamfontein: Skotaville, 1990). For much of the information on Namibia in this section, I am indebted to Terence Zeeman.

91. Kubbe Rispel's *Die Droom*, the most prominent of these, is found in Terence Zeeman, ed., *New Namibian Plays*, vol. II (Windhoek: Gamsberg Macmillan/New Namibia Books, 2002).

92. Found in Terence Zeeman, ed., *Goats, Oranges and Skeletons, A Trilogy of Namibian Independence Plays* (Windhoek: Gamsberg Macmillan/New Namibia Books, 2000).

93. Andre Strauss, 'The Status of Theatre in Namibia', in Renato Matusse, ed., *Past Roles and Development of Theatre Arts in SADC* (Maputo and Gaborone: SADC, 1999), pp. 86–95.

94. Rohmer, *Theatre and Performance*, p. 222.

95. See Zodwa Sithebe, *Of Heroes and Men* (Pietermaritzburg: Shuster and Shuster, 1991) and Laurinda Olivier-Sampson, *A Moment in Our Lives*, in Zeeman, ed., *New Namibian Plays*, vol. I.

96. David Kerr, 'Drama as a Form of Action Research: The Experience of UBE423 at the University of Botswana', *Journal of Southern African Theatre*, 11.1–2 (1999), pp. 133–54.

97. Kennedy Chinyowa, 'Shona Storytelling and the Contemporary Performing Arts in Zimbabwe', *African Theatre*, 4 (forthcoming).

7 South African theatre

YVETTE HUTCHISON

South Africa, like other countries of the African continent, has a rich festival culture. However, unlike the festivals of most African countries, these have not primarily grown out of indigenous contexts, but have emerged from centuries of European and African forms interacting to provoke diverse, inter-cultural performance practices. South Africa's more than thirty annual festivals offer access to performances ranging from inter-cultural and cross-cultural dance and music productions to amateur and professional theatre in any one or a combination of South Africa's eleven official languages. This theatre activity constitutes a vast history, particularly from the colonial period, much of which has been thoroughly documented.[1] This chapter traces some of the roots and intersections that have led to these performances.

The writing of such history is controversial, especially in this decade of transition. One of the most pressing issues is terminology. As many people have pointed out, *theatre* is a European term with specific meaning. Kole Omotoso addresses some of the debates and suggests how notions of theatre can be broadened. This includes engaging with inter-cultural, syncretic performances. However, there are still profound silences: research by anthropologists, sociologists or others doing fieldwork, which has not been incorporated into mainstream theatre research or histories in any detail. In order to support the shift towards filling these gaps, this chapter foregrounds areas of performance that have not been discussed in detail in many available South African theatre histories, and suggests how the interaction of these diverse forms have defined the nature of contemporary South African theatre. This choice of focus means that there is less detail on well-published mainstream South African theatre history.

Whilst engaging with these issues, Loren Kruger traces the venues and forms of urban performance in 'concerts' and 'sketches', the Eisteddfodau, missionary choirs and township musicals because, she argues, 'theatre in South Africa is not essentially European or African; rather it takes place between and within practices, forms and institutions variously and con-tentiously associated with Europe, Africa, America, and ... African America'.[2]

This statement is a departure point for sketching the various voices that constitute South Africa's theatre history. The journey begins by outlining some of the issues related to oral literature and its recovery, starting from San stories and songs, and moving on to the stories, praise poetry, songs and dances of the indigenous peoples that migrated to South Africa. The area of oral literature is controversial, as many critics argue that it does not belong in theatre histories, but with poetry or music. However, oral performance forms cannot be ignored when tracing South Africa's theatre history for two reasons. Firstly, because of the strong element of performance which is central to these forms; and, secondly, because of the impact these forms have had on later South African theatre.

The chapter then continues by considering the development of early European theatre in the country, and finally focusses on the new syncretic forms that emerged from intersections of these various oral, popular and literary forms in the twentieth century. Because of the wide diversity of forms, languages and periods, particular forms are used to illustrate how a genre may have emerged in a specific time and place, how it illuminates an understanding of that moment, and how it may have impacted on future South African performance.

Issues related to recuperating oral performance forms

Although rock art suggests that performance has existed in southern Africa for thousands of years, most written descriptions of performance date from the early nineteenth century. Missionaries or Europeans on hunting expe-ditions wrote many of these accounts.[3] This raises two issues concerning approaches to recuperating and writing South Africa's theatre history. The first is that the history is both oral and thousands of years old, and thus not easily or reliably accessible. The second is that most accounts of indigenous South African performance were recorded by passing outsiders and were based on superficial, chance observation, greatly determined by the degree of linguistic and cultural understanding of the author, whose purpose was unclear. Such writing was aimed either for the English or German reader, or, specifically, for a church organisation. Thus, the sources, written primarily from a white western ideological perspective, make the reconstruction or recuperation of oral forms more complicated.

Ontologically, one has to assess the textual 'status' of the work in need of translation. As Duncan Brown points out, most of this work has gained currency through translation and publication in languages other than the original performance, '(usually English) by missionaries, colonial administrators, anthropologists, historians, and the like'.[4] Also, every translation is a 'reading' of a text, involving decoding and recoding. Here issues of transcription, problems of access and translation impact.[5]

Critically the western literary paradigm, which endeavours to account for, place and trace forms, often in a linear, causal manner, has predominated. The primary focus for literary histories has been texts written by English, Afrikaans or mission-trained black poets or dramatists. Much early writing on oral literature has been anthropological-classificatory in nature. It treats the text as a carrier of cultural information, with little or no attention paid to aesthetic form or elements of the performance itself. Literary studies remove forms from the contexts from which they emerged.[6] Ruth Finnegan was one of the first scholars to move from anthropological readings of literature to a more historicised reading, based on first-hand field research.

In addressing the problems related to recording and tracing a living oral tradition in a western literary history or critical tradition, Barber and de Moraes Farias refer to Olabiyi Yai's proposal that

> The way forward . . . is through the indigenous critical practices which are embedded in the process of production and performance of oral literature. This criticism is indivisible from literary production; is generative and expansive, in the sense of generating more literary production; is metamimetic and ameliorative, arousing poets to transcend their predecessors and their own past performances; and it is participatory.[7]

The problem, though, as they go on to point out, is that this can 'only arise within the ambit of indigenous oral production'. Nevertheless, tracing such forms and histories in their contexts, and as shifting rather than as universal, or static forms is important as it challenges the literary narrative that has tended to define theatrical histories in general, and South Africa in particular. Vail and White have traced in detail how nineteenth-century European scholars assumed African stasis, perceiving neither individuals nor acknowledging the dynamic nature of an African society. This reinforced ideas of these peoples as having no individual initiative and creativity.[8]

Through acknowledging the processes of reconstruction and defining context, theatre historians acknowledge their place and processes in the 'readings' given, and thus resist any attempt to treat such oral texts as 'stable' objects. In remembering Jameson's argument on the dialectical nature of reading historical texts, the historian is aware that while she or he inter-rogates the past, his or her own present social practices are in turn called into question.[9] Thus we are made critically aware of what we 'do' when presenting moments and calling them a 'history'.

Oral poetry and performance

The suppression, or omission, of oral literary histories in favour of the textual has a long history and is related to dominant critical practices. These practices were exacerbated in South Africa by the country's particular past socio-political repressions and oppressions. Oral forms have been largely associated with black societies, and thus been used as a way of controlling and separating cultural histories. It is with this awareness that the following section outlines the broad aspects of some of these oral genres; aware that their manifestations and energies differ from the printed or translated forms because both the product and context are fluid and performative in nature.

Songs and stories of the San

The term *San* as opposed to the ethnographic *Bushman* or */Xam* is used throughout. Whilst some research has revealed that San was a derogatory term for the indigenous people used by the Khoi; the colonial term Bushman signals both a race and gender bias; and /Xam or !Kung refer to specific groups of people.[10] Although in the 1980s there was a strong movement towards rejecting San, contemporary South Africans have moved back to using it in preference to other terms.

Biesele has argued that San hunter-gatherers have lived south of the Congo–Zambezi line for thousands of years.[11] Prior to the arrival of the Dutch, there were perhaps 150,000–300,000 San living throughout southern Africa (dispersal evidenced through rock paintings and engravings). Today there are about 50,000, of whom only 3,000 live permanently as hunter-gatherers. Most San now work as herders, farm labourers, game trackers or soldiers. Linguistically, the San are close to the Khoi, and some linguists regard the two languages as forming a single group, called the Khoisan, characterised chiefly by its click consonants.[12] Artistic evidence of their first contact with the colonials dates from the 1870s. Their distinctive society was destroyed by the turn of the century. Chief sources of the oral histories and stories are the /Xam of South Africa and Namibia and the !Kung of Botswana.

What knowledge we have of the San peoples in southern Africa is largely available through the German linguist W. H. I. Bleeck and his sister-in-law, Lucy C. Lloyd, who interviewed and transcribed stories and narratives of six /Xam-speaking people,[13] representing three families. They were San convicts held in Cape Town between 1870 and 1884.[14] One of the earliest recorded narratives was by //Kabbo, who had been arrested and taken to Cape Town for stealing a sheep. The transcriptions trace from the perspective of the colonised people the nomadic way of life and clashes in attitudes to the land and ways of life of the hunter-gatherers and the aggressive modernising European culture represented by the magistrate, police and the law.[15] Although the transcriptions indicate omissions in parenthesis, literal translations, recorded repetitions, and conscious syntactical strangenesses, one remains uncertain about the extent to which the narrators were understood or even told the full story to people who had the power to send them back to prison. Also, the oral nature of the text loses much of its performative aspect in the transcription, and transcribers have struggled to overcome this problem, as well as to make the stories accessible to non-San audiences.[16]

Much regarding the physical nature of the performances has been reconstructed or proposed from analyses of the wall paintings and engravings, which are numerous and found throughout southern Africa. The paintings depict abstract images, animals and people. They also trace arrivals of other peoples, shown in paintings of masts from ships, horsemen and wagon drivers.[17] Much has been written in particular about trance dances, the most important of the San's religious rituals; many of which are still performed today. It suggests the use of musical instruments, performance of shamans and the relationship and roles of the clan.

San societies are highly verbal, and all members of the community can perform variations of basic oral forms.[18] The performances include both sacred and profane stories and songs, which may be part of communal religious life or may reflect personal moods and events. Genres are defined by the manner in which an event is treated, especially in terms of textual strategies or the performance context. The focus here is on the stories and songs.

Stories San stories blur western distinctions between prose, poetry and performance by mingling the narrative aspects of plot and character with rhythm through sound patterning, pauses, abrupt breaks and fluctuations of tone and volume coherence.[19] These strategies are reminiscent of prayer or lyric poetry, and are typical of oral literature, which uses repetition as a rhetorical device to build anticipation and create narrative. The dramatic body movement, facial expression, verbal animation and climactic gesture are as important as the narrative aspects of the performance. The repetition emphasises the circular structure of many of the narratives, which reflect how the peoples' lives are defined by seasonal, solar and lunar cycles. The poem 'Habits of the Bat and Porcupine' exemplify such use of repetition.

> Mama told me about it,
> that I should watch for the porcupine,
> if I saw the bat;
> then I would know that the porcupine was coming,
> for the bat came.
> And I must not sleep:
> I must watch for the porcupine,
> for, when the porcupine approaches, I feel sleepy,
> I become sleepy, on account of the porcupine;
> for the porcupine is a thing which is used,
> when it draws near,
> to make us sleep against our will,
> as it wishes that we may not know
> the time at which it comes;
> as it wishes that it may come into its hole
> when we are asleep.[20]

Both the narrative structure and the performance of this poem would convey the struggle against sleep in the movement and repetitive patterns of 'sleep' and 'asleep' that are juxtaposed to the phrase 'I must watch'. It also expresses the day-to-day beliefs and practices of the people; in this case a hunting practice.

There is no set time for storytelling, it may occur by day or night, in the band, visiting friends or other bands. It is the province of older people, and is intrinsically bound up with a sense of personal and social identity, as an old !Kung woman affirmed:

> The old person who does not tell a story just does not exist. Our forefathers related for us the doings of the people of long ago and anyone who doesn't know them doesn't have his head on straight. And anyone whose head is on straight knows them.[21]

The choice of story depends on the audience, which is crucial to the event. For example, Guenther points out that the four narrators of the Bleek and Lloyd collection chose semi-factual, legend-like stories that could be told in a serious fashion, rather than outrageous trickster stories or stories which unabashedly refer to sex and excretion, which abound in /Xam tales today.[22] Thus in the Bleek–Lloyd collection, the bulk of the stories performed are about the doings of the Early Race, the mythological ancestors of the San people who are closely associated with animals. According to San cosmology, all animals were once people. Other stories deal with more recent history, hunting or everyday events. There are no stylistic differences between the tales, whether sacred or profane, as the San do not find any disjuncture between the profound and the humorous, and do not feel that scorn or amusement in any way diminishes the significance of the stories being told. A good storyteller is judged by his or her knowledge of the doings of the Old People and by general verbal and performative ability. /Xam and !Kung stories of the Early Race seem to mediate the major social, political and economic problems facing San society. Biesele says of !Kung narrative cycles about the Old people:

> Basic themes . . . include some of the problem points of living, such as marriage and sex, the food quest, sharing, family relationships, the division of labour, birth and death, murder, and blood vengeance. Other concerns include the creation of the present world order and the relationship of hunter-gatherers to peoples with more advanced economies.[23]

Among the most important creation stories are those involving the trickster god, referred to by the /Xam as /Kaggen and by the !Kung as Kauha (similar to the trickster god Heiseb of the Khoi). These stories are not simple episodic narrations, but performed in cycles in 'tit-for-tat' fashion, and are often bawdy and scatalogical. Among the Bleek–Lloyd records there are some twenty-one narratives involving /Kaggen and the narrator /Han=kass'o stresses the links in the cycles of the various escapades. The narratives explore the god's conduct, character and magical powers. He is usually associated with the mantis, but he can assume many other guises. He is the creator of the moon and many other creatures. The storyteller must be adept in performing, as many of the narratives include dialogue, which the storyteller signals through pitch and tone variations in his or her voice. Brown argues that these stories operate both as entertainment and as social structures through which rights and duties respecting ownership of a kill, food and support of the weak by the strong can be negotiated.[24]

Twentieth century attempts to record and make these stories more available have been pioneered by people such as Laurens van der Post (1958, 1961) and Stephen Watson (1991). Older German and Portuguese sources have aided later scholars, such as Megan Biesele, Mathias Guenther, Lewis-Williams, and Harriet Deacon – pioneers in this field of research and recovery.

Songs Songs, like narratives, may be about either the communal, specifically the religious life of the community, or may be intensely personal creations. Religious or therapeutic songs are believed to originate from a god. They are often named after animals (Giraffe, Gemsbok, Eland songs) and are performed at trance dances, at which the women clap and sing while the men dance in order to enter a trance state. The singers believe that the religious songs have power (*n/um* is the !Kung word that describes the power of trance), but the songs may be sung light-heartedly by day without n/um.[25] Many of these are still performed today.

Personal or mood songs are more individualised verbal responses to events or situations. These may range from simple songs like //Kabbo's lament at the loss of his tobacco pouch and his consequent 'tobacco hunger',[26] to complex songs which employ highly developed aesthetic and social insights, such as Dia!k-wain's 'The Broken String'. These songs are accompanied by a single-stringed bow or a four- or five-stringed instrument known as a //gwashi.

> People were those.
> Who broke for me the string.
> The place does not feel to me,
> > As the place used to feel to me,
> > On account of it.
> > For,
> The place feels as if it stood open
> > Before me,
> Because the string has broken for me.
> Therefore,
> The place does not feel pleasant to me,
> > On account of it.[27]

In the mood songs metaphor, symbol and image particularly come to the fore. In Dia!k-wain's song the broken string is the central metaphor, which is compared to a changed landscape. The footnote suggests that Dia!k-wain learnt the song from his father Xaa-ttin, who composed the lament 'after the death of his friend, the magician and rain-maker !Nuin/kui-ten, who died from the effects of a shot he received when going about in the form of a lion'.[28] The death of the shaman leaves a silence as the broken string of the instrument. It may also suggest the string of a bow, and the string used by the shaman leading the rain-bull, which if broken is a particularly bad omen.

New combinations of forms are being performed and developed by the community associated with the Kuru Development Trust at Ghanzi today. They have integrated African and western styles with their oral performance forms. This suggests dynamic, adaptive performance forms that respond to changing physical environments and socio-economic contexts.

Bantu South African oral literature

Although oral forms are often divided into genres, these are rarely performed exclusively. African oral performance includes stories, songs and dances that may be divided into praise poetry, work songs, love lyrics, wedding songs, lullabies, children's verses, stories, riddles and prayers. Dhlomo summarised these collectively in the term *izibongelo*, which for him encompassed all 'tribal dramatic art'.[29] Unlike much western poetry or storytelling, the nature of these forms in the African context is by definition performative.

This section begins by tracing some of the general characteristics of the forms, their functions, and then looks at how they in turn have influenced other emergent traditions of South African theatre.

Storytelling Storytelling is a form central to all southern African societies, called *litsomo* or *dishomo*[30] in Sesotho, *inganekwane* in Zulu, and *iintsomi* in Xhosa. It includes fables and moral tales. In almost all societies there are formulae used by both the narrator and audience for starting and ending folk-tales. Cole-Beuchat traces some of these in Tsonga and Ronga tales.[31] Naming an object may signal a particular kind of story. During the narration the narrator may sing songs, which the audience picks up in the refrain. If the songs are unknown to the audience, the narrator teaches them. The songs are often a magic formula that produces a specific occurrence. These tales are traditionally narrated at night around fires when everyone has finished their work and before they sleep. In Ronga society it is taboo to relate tales during the day. Elderly women are usually the storytellers in Tsonga or Ronga societies, but men may do so also. Riddles and proverbs, which are often included in everyday speech, are highly valued and give the narrator greater status if cleverly interwoven in the tales. Early African literature's narration is influenced by traditional storytelling in the plot, characters, moral themes and endings. It has also shaped the rich metaphoric language and imagery used in contemporary South African theatre.

Although urbanisation has adversely affected the development and passing on of storytelling traditions across the generations, it is nevertheless evident in contemporary South Africa from television soaps (see Fatima Dike's play *So What's New?* (1991) for an insight into the influence of *The Bold and the Beautiful* on South African women and culture) to Athol Fugard's plays. Fugard's early plays *Hello and Goodbye* (1965), *People are Living There* (1968) and *Boesman and Lena* (1969) tell the stories, or 'witness . . . truthfully' the stories of the 'nameless and destitute', in Fugard's terms.[32] Fugard, Barney Simon and Mbongeni Ngema draw heavily on these traditional narrative forms for their collaborative work and workshop plays. This tradition then became a pattern for many plays that would follow that tell the stories of ordinary people in fragmentary moments.

More overtly, however, people such as Gcina Mhlope have reclaimed oral storytelling forms, particularly in the urban context. In 1992 she founded Zanendaba Storyteller, which aims to reintroduce storytelling, especially with children. It is also evident in her more formal playwrighting. Her first play, *Have You Seen Zandile?* (1985), created collaboratively, draws on these storytelling traditions as she relates her own childhood: growing up with her grandmother in the Transkei and being kidnapped by her mother and taken to Durban. Later she wrote and directed *Proud to be Dark-Skinned* (*Somdaka*) after collaborating with Barney Simon on *Born in the RSA* (1985), a play comprising a collage of personal narratives. She and Janet Suzman used similar techniques in their adaptation of Brecht in *The Good Person of Sharkeville* (1995). These plays suggest how a particular Nguni storytelling tradition has been adapted and incorporated into contemporary South African theatre.

Songs and dances   Most indigenous South African communities were traditionally centred strongly on song and dance, which are difficult to separate. For example, the Zulu *amahubo* songs are usually accompanied by war dances and there is no separation between them. The rhythm establishes the requisite emotion. Other Zulu songs include the *imidunduzelo*, lullabies or nursery songs sung by mothers carrying babies on their backs to make them sleep or stop crying, and the *imilozi*, which are poems created from combinations of onomatopoeic sounds which form a vocal painting and thus evoke a corresponding emotional response. These sounds may include bird calls, animal cries or trains.[33]

Sesotho songs are called *dithoko*. Franz outlines some of the forms of Sesotho songs collated by Mangoaela in Lesotho. The Mosotho 'praiser' was a poet whose work could be spoken, chanted or sung. The poems create 'picture-talks', rich metaphors and similes linking the people to the natural world around them. Contemporary economic conditions have meant the chants have become simpler in imagery and length, and the language has given way to more 'business-like and material exactness' in usage.[34] Like all peoples of southern Africa, the Sesotho people were profoundly influenced by the coming of the missionaries, in their case by the invitation of Moshoeshoe in 1833. One demonstration of the impact the missionaries made on indigenous societies has been the adaptation of traditional songs into Christian hymns. The evolution of some of these forms in the urban, particularly mining contexts is discussed later in more detail.

The impact of colonial western education and Christianity on southern African culture is by no means limited to the Basotho people and their songs and stories. Zulu rites and ceremonies, Zionist rituals and the festival of the Nazareth Baptist Church, and folk dances are significant examples of how colonial forms have been incorporated into indigenous performance practice. Peter Larlham traces these forms and their evolution, beginning with colonial travellers' or missionaries' accounts of Zulu rituals and ceremonies. He maps how these forms have changed or disappeared because of Christianity, European education, the change of social and religious values and beliefs, economic pressure and the reduction of Zulu military training. He also shows how students and Black Consciousness artists of the 1970s returned to some of these early performance forms, particularly those of praise poetry, improvised exchange, notions of participation and litany-like response, for dramatic forms of protest.[35]

The Zionist and Nazareth Baptist Church are clear examples of the appropriation of Christianity for the redefinition and consolidation of the Zulu cultural identity. The prophets Ntsikana and Isaiah Shembe (a Zionist who broke away to form the Nazarite Baptist Church) adopted and adapted

Christianity, reinterpreting doctrine and worship by incorporating some of the pre-colonial performative modes into their contemporary Christian services. The aim was to break away from the white dominated church groups and to address the Natives Land Act of 1913, which stated that a 'Native' could only purchase or live on land in reserved areas. From 1913 independent church leaders acquired land as a strategy of survival. Isaiah Shembe purchased farms and established a church settlement at Ekhuphakameni near Durban, Natal, in 1916. The Urban Areas Act of 1923 further curbed the freedom of movement for black South Africans and forced such groups to 'adaptive structures'. They perceived the power of Christianity, which was used to justify Apartheid policy, and yet had no means to fully participate in church activities or its cultural heritage. They thus selected and adapted what was useful to their position.

These leaders looked particularly to the Old Testament for inspiration. For example, Enoch Mgijima stressed the comparison between the 'landless flock of Israelites', struggling against the Midianites and Philistines, and his own group. They parallel the Zionist prophet, central to all services, and the traditional Zulu diviner (*isangoma*). All Zionist churches emphasise ritual action with full participation of all members. The structure, content and performance conventions are a synthesis of traditional religious belief and practice and an individual leader's dynamic response to Christianity. For example, Zionists have included most of the first-fruit ceremonial observances in the purification of the king or priest, colourful dress and community singing and dancing into their services. Much of the performance includes the rhythmic stamping and shuffling characteristic of traditional Zulu and Xhosa dances.[36] The membership, the structure of the service (with its central focus on healing), the location, the use of space, particularly the circular form, and the use of sticks or staffs all suggest how the subversion and appropriation of Christianity is used to define local identity and solidarity.

Isaiah Shembe formed the Nazareth Baptist Church in 1916. His traditional Zulu perspective is evident in his maintenance of the strict Zulu divisions of gender and status, not only in performance, but also in accommodation arrangements and in the organisation of the dancing groups. The leader defines all the arrangements, including dances, according to visions he receives, and which he justifies with extensive biblical references.

Despite its conservative retention of traditional Zulu beliefs and customs, Shembe uses the traditional *imbongi* praise poetry in a particular way, in relation to modern topics. For example, when commissioned to compose and perform *izibongo* for the Prince of Wales on his visit to South Africa in 1925, his eulogy contained the following ironic comments:

> Ah Great Britain! Great Britain!
> Great Britain of the endless sunshine . . .
> She sent us the preacher: she sent us the bottle,
> She sent us the Bible, and barrels of brandy.[37]

Gunner argues that a unique characteristic of Shembe's poetry is the extent to which he uses the traditional praise poem to eulogise (and criticise) a contemporary religious leader on a scale usually reserved for Zulu royalty. Here is an early example of a traditional oral form being adapted into emergent South African performance forms.

The third area Larlham traces is that of folk dances, particularly among migrant workers living in hostels and compounds in urban areas. These men lived far from their homelands and societies, and there were no local recreational facilities. This resulted in their adapting and creating performances of folk songs and dances in the compounds, which then fed back into their homelands. The men brought, modified and recreated songs and dances from specific districts in urban contexts.

For example, in Durban most dancers are Zulu and the dance styles come under the general title of *ingoma* (song or dance). The groups either emphasised competitive dancing or they performed for unpaying, 'accidental' black audiences. This competition dancing in Durban originated in the 1920s and 1930s in male compounds in industrial areas. The large firms for whom the men worked, or tourist audiences, sponsored and organised the competitions. Participants wore identification in order to allay any fears of residents at the warlike apparel, that is, brushed woollen leg decoration, small headdress, dancing stick and small cowhide shield. The team members were called *amasoshosa* (soldiers), signalling the source of many of these dances. Paying audiences may be called upon to judge the competition, or Sunday afternoon performances were judged by the response of the audience. The scale of performances is evidenced in the venues – which at times was a large sports stadium in the city.

Performances began with dances advertising the company through gestures and formations that identified the team: striking a match (Lion Match Company), mimed drinking from milk bottles (Clover Dairies) or forming letters. The leader controlled dancers' movements with a whistle. A common identifiable feature is the high, stamping step; for example, the *IsiZulu* and *isiKhuze* styles. The *isiBhaca* style originated with the Pondo and Baca peoples of southern Natal; they swing the leg back before stamping. The most popular form is the *isiShayameni*, characterised by a light bouncing gait created by waist-high stepping sequences, with arms curved forward over the head. The teams tend to dance in one style, which may remain unchanged over long periods of time. There is a strange combination of learning by imitation, demanding absolute precision, while simultaneously greatly valuing innovation.

The accompanying songs are called *bullets* – ammunition against rival teams. The songs are subordinate to the dances and stop once the dance progresses. They are structured by the repetition of lines and words and tune variations, which establish rhythm. Themes focus on everyday life and events, including social discontent.

Exceptionally, songs dominate in the *isicathamiya* style. The best-known contemporary isicathamiya group is Ladysmith Black Mambazo. This form developed in the 1930s among male migrant workers in the Natal Midlands. Larlham traces the form's various possible sources, even suggesting the influence of the Charleston on its choreography in the 1930s. Bongari Mthethwa says that in Zulu it became known as *ukureka*, which derives from 'ragtime'.[38] Initially all groups were linked to the Dalton Road hostel in Durban, with competitions every Saturday night, judged preferably by an arbitrary white (or alternatively an Indian or coloured) person brought in after midnight, on the assumption that he would not be partisan as he knew none of the teams. By the 1940s the form was very popular in Johannesburg, where regular Saturday night competitions were organised with six to eight choirs of thirty singers each competing. There is an interesting combination of traditional formation step dances and rhythms created in the American tap mode, with foot-slides and sharp toe taps. They also include high straight-legged kicking steps. The dress competition at the end of an evening suggests how much American fashion influenced the workers, who generally wore a three-piece suit, valuing accessories such as cuff links, tie tacks, socks, ties and handkerchiefs of matching colour and design. There are interesting divisions between the songs and dances performed before the judge arrives – which are more innovative and critical – and the more western forms for competition. Both are valued and rewarded differently: the former by peer approval and respect, the latter with a prize of all the entry money of the evening.

There are many comparable examples of evolving traditional forms in the rural context. Deborah James discusses the evolution of the male form of song and dance, *kiba*, by female migrant workers in the Northern Transvaal.[39] Orkin refers to a branch of the Industrial and Commercial Union (ICU) in Durban in the late 1920s, which seems to have created a peculiar local form of culture in reaction to the political economy and exploitation. Although none of this was overtly political, it seemed to reach back to a pre-industrial past, drawing on 'a collective historical past' with particular 'military symbols and rituals' to create 'a common sense of identity amongst racially oppressed workers'.[40] These traditional forms merged in the urban context and were reinvented as new cultural forms. Contemporary cross-cultural performers include the poet Chris Zithulele Mann and popular performers such as Roger Lucey, Jennifer Ferguson, Ray Phiri (Stimela) and David Kramer. Some of these movements are discussed later in more detail.

Praise poetry Possibly the single most researched and commented on form of oral performance in South Africa is that of praise poetry. It constitutes southern Africa's most original contribution to the oral performance form, despite its relatively poor representation in surveys or syllabi in literature, drama or theatre departments. It has profoundly influenced black literary production in South Africa, from hymns to poets and 1970s plays. It has particular prominence in Zulu, Xhosa, Ndebele and Sotho societies, with many similarities between the praises performed by the different peoples.

Vilakazi argues that it is characterised by poetry charged with emotion, possessing a strong rhythm created by phrase structure and pauses[41] and a particular use of personal nouns. I shall outline the Sesotho and Zulu forms, noting that the Xhosa, Ndebele and Swazi forms are similar to the Zulu.[42]

Sesotho praises are referred to as *dirêtô* or *dithoko*. Much has been recorded and transcribed by Lekgothoane. These praises refer to past, present and future events. Lekgothoane and van Warmelo argue that they also contain prophecy, prayer and refer to tribal matters and aspects of Sesotho worship. They may praise or ridicule people, evoke emotions or promote harmony between the human community and the divine. People are personified as animals, often their totem, and as such their lives and deeds are celebrated. This serves both an historic and an evocative function.[43]

A praise poem in Zulu is referred to as *isibongo* (plural *izibongo*), derived from the Zulu word *ukubonga* meaning to thank (one). The poet is an *imbongi* (plural *izimbongi*). Bryant defines praise poetry as follows: 'To praise, extol, a person or thing; the Zulu manner of expressing one's gratitude being to 'praise' the giver or his gift – hence, give thanks . . . worship, offer sacrifice to, pray to, as to the amaDhlozi or ancestral spirits.' He goes on to show that isibongo may refer to a 'tribal or clan name, name of praise, given to a young man by his comrades . . . every native, and especially chiefs, has a number of these praise-phrases coined for him by others, and which are often added on to his name by way of a distinction.'[44] Izibongo are sung or performed on ceremonial occasions and may be about people, animals, rivers and natural objects. They may be personal praises or praises to the clan or ancestors. The praises to creatures tend to function as rituals of thanks or appeasement. The form seems primarily designed to establish cognitive maps within society. Clan praises, known as *izithalazelo*, define Zulu identity and may serve as polite forms of address. Royal izibongo are about the chief or king,[45] and are an extension of the form and function of the personal praise poem.

The first personal praise form is the lullaby (*isihlabelelo*), composed by the mother for her child. Following this is the *isithopo*, or personal praise name granted by either the parents or peers. Over time this is extended to reflect, favourably or not, on the individual's individual physical and moral characteristics. Such personal izibongo are highly inter-textual and draw on elements which are both self-composed, drawn from praises of friends, relatives, ancestors or are part of the cultural currency of the society. This type of izibongo mediates the personal and social identity that defines the individual in a community. In the case of Zulu men, these praises are performed by the imbongi while the referent dances vigorously to the recitation of his praises.[46] In the case of women, Gunner points out that the personal 'izibongo' are important for the ways in which they treat the problems faced personally.[47] Many of these performances and praises are bawdy and humorous.

The royal izibongo expand and formalise the personal izibongo. However, instead of the king collecting and collating his own praise names or accounts of his political and military prowess, it is done by an imbongi, and the royal izibongo are regarded with more seriousness as their function is more complex and far-reaching.

There is no formal class or caste from which the imbongi comes, but in southern African society it is traditionally a role reserved for men.[48] There is no system of apprenticeship, the aspirant must learn the craft of oral composition from observing and imitating other izimbongi. This involves

memorising their poems and adapting or extending them. They then have
to earn the respect of the community. A number of izimbongi may perform
for, or be attached to, a chief, but one will emerge as official imbongi, by
popular acclaim. This office is signalled by his costume – dressing in skins,
carrying two sticks, a knobkerrie or a shield and a spear. Other izimbongi
as a rule are not free to wear skins or carry spears, sticks or shield.

The performance form is built around evocative and emotive language.
Opland argues that the emphasis is on collection and perfection rather than
on creation. This distinguishes Zulu praise poetry from Xhosa poetry, whose
focus is 'primarily improvisational'.[49] He relates this to the function of the
praise form in each respective society: Zulu izimbongi, particularly from the
period from Shaka onwards, focussed largely on centralising and stabilising
the Zulu kingdom. Xhosa society, in contrast, had no monarchical chief, and
was not primarily concerned with creating or maintaining social cohesion
and national unity.

The poetry is highly dramatic in style: the izimbongi stalk up and down
before the ruler declaiming their praises as loudly as possible, with gestures
becoming more frequent and dramatic as the recitation proceeds. The imbongi may leap into the air or crouch with burning eyes until the praise is
complete.[50] Izimbongi are highly metaphorical and allusive in their manner,
bringing familiar cultural images into new contexts of meaning. Most izibongo are irregular in structure, with little or no rhyme or metre. The praises
usually begin with an opening formula – a salute to the ruler, or the recitation of his clan praises. This focusses the attention of the audience on the
performance to follow. The formal principle of the poems is that of 'naming',
using epithets, appellations or proverbs to express the attributes of the ruler.
Coplan argues that this both works as a thematic and formal structuring device, as an expansible image in the use of repetition, references and context.[51]
The poems usually conclude with a sentence like 'I disappear' or 'Finisher
off!' The audience may participate with shouts of 'Musho!' (Speak/praise
him), which punctuates the poem.[52]

Many commentators have seen the function of praise poems as primarily
that of uncritical adulation or licensed critiquing of a ruler. However, scholars
such as Vail and White have challenged such a static, simplistic view of this
poetic performative form (1991). The complexity is evident even in the structure of the poetry. For, if as Snead argues, repetition 'foreground[s] principles
of circularity', the structure itself thus challenges contemporary views of persons and events in its 'constant recreation and re-evaluation of history'.[53] Its

function is complex, encompassing political, historical and religious aspects of the community. On a political level the isibongo is a discursive means of negotiating relations of political power in a society. It articulates expectations subjects may have of their ruler, while acknowledging political and military successes. It may also criticise excesses. Like the fool in Elizabethan society, the imbongi may speak with a fair amount of impunity that which is otherwise taboo. This both allows a ruler to get a sense of the needs and thoughts of those over whom he rules, and the community a safe way of challenging a ruler.

Historically, the praises establish the lines of a ruler's legitimacy, recount his power, achievements and the majesty of his rule. This is particularly evident in the many Zulu praises of Shaka, father of the Zulu state in about 1824, and the way tracing lineage back to Shaka defines the legitimacy of later Zulu rulers. Hence Mazisi Kunene's scheme of dividing Zulu poetry into three periods around Shaka's ascendancy and rule: pre-Shakan (c. 1750 – 1800); Shakan (c. 1800–50); post-Shakan (c. 1850–1900). Vail and White similarly trace the shift in political and historic significance of Ndebele royal praises through three periods, following the migration of the Ndebele people from Natal in 1822.[54]

Thus from the examples of the Ndebele people, and the shifts in Zulu praise poetry, it is evident that the form is not fixed, but rather responds sensitively to re-evaluate and revise a shifting historical context. This form may be compared to the Yoruba *oríkì* which Karin Barber suggests may represent the 'past in the present', and thus the performances 'represent a way not just of looking at the past, but of re-experiencing it and reintegrating it into the present'.[55] This reinterpretation of the past in performance formulates new understandings of history.

Whilst the political and historic aspects of izibongo are important, Gunner argues that often they are emphasised to the detriment of the religious function, which is fundamental to the spiritual life of the society.[56] Opland links this aspect of the poetry to the importance of ancestors in Zulu praise poetry, where ancestors are believed to profoundly influence the affairs and conditions of the living. At crisis points an imbongi may enlist the help of ancestors by performing their praises. He says at such moments that the imbongi functions as a 'vestigial shaman'.[57]

Whether focussing on the historic, political or religious, one of the challenges of praise poetry for an audience is the density of references, often specific to a context and dependent on local knowledge. Another is the very dramatic nature of the performance. Transcribed texts are a small part of the overall performance, and reconstruction depends on the accuracy in recording, translation and overall attention to detail of the performance beyond the words, on the part of the transcriber, because, as Opland points out, often 'choreography supercedes poetry, for the fewer the words, the better the poet is able to represent history in action'.[58]

These forms are constantly being redefined for the contemporary context. For example, Basotho mine workers have shifted from their traditional sense of the praise poem to a new genre, *sefela*, which encodes their life experiences in the mining context. Basotho women sing and dance their experiences in their *sewelewele* (or *seoeleoele* in older orthography, poetic narrative) in black townships of the former Orange Free State, Transvaal, and Lesotho. Landeg White has shown how praise poetry has served to record shifting power in Zulu society, changing in style, imagery and theme in response to historical factors.[59] Xhosa praise poetry, which traditionally recounted exploits and failings of chiefs and war captains, moved to comment on African *indunas* (compound overseers) and shift bosses at the mines.[60] Examples of this in the trade union context are of Mi S'dumo Hlatshwayo, Mzwakhe Mbuli and Alfred Qabula.[61] Praise poetry featured at the inauguration of President Nelson Mandela and at the opening of South Africa's first democratic parliament in 1994. Poets speak in the context of funerals, trade unions or political parties to advise, criticise and praise in contemporary South African circumstances. Each performance employs old improvised verses in new combinations. This is an example of how diverse forms in South Africa have been adapted and used in new theatre contexts.

Before analysing the degree to which this is evident in twentieth-century South African theatre, the next section will outline South Africa's early European theatre history.

Recorded European theatre in South Africa, 1652 to 1910

European history in South Africa begins with the Portuguese discovery of the sea route around the Cape of Storms (later the Cape of Good Hope) in the fifteenth century. However, the Dutch only settled in the Cape in 1652. Beginning in 1657, European settlers were allotted farms by the colonial authorities in the arable regions around Cape Town. In response to the colonists' demand for labour, the VOC (Verenigde Oostindische Compagnie/Dutch East India Company) imported slaves from East Africa, Madagascar and the East Indies. These should not be confused with later indentured labour encouraged from India and China. By the early 1700s, the Europeans had begun to spread into the interior. These farmers (*trekboers*) intruded upon the land and water sources, and the indigenous inhabitants were progressively dispossessed. This provoked armed conflict, which ended when resistance was overcome in the late 1800s. Diseases such as smallpox decimated the Khoi and San peoples, which resulted in the decline of their cultures. The slave population steadily increased until by the mid-1700s there were more slaves in the Cape than there were 'free burghers' (European colonists). These Asian slaves formed an artisan class, which significantly shaped the working-class culture of the western Cape.

The British controlled the Cape from 1795 to 1802, and again from 1806 when it took over from the Batavian Republic (1803–6). Britain annexed the eastern Cape in 1814 and Natal in 1843. Subsequent colonial expansion into the interior by missionaries, traders, farmers, civil servants and military troops expanded British control throughout these areas. Simultaneously, the Zulu kingdom emerged as a highly centralised state. In the 1820s Zulu monarch Shaka controlled a considerable area of south-east Africa. Consequently, substantial states such as Moshoeshoe's Lesotho and other Sotho-Tswana chiefdoms were established, partly for reasons of defence. This period of disruption and state formation became known as the *mfecane* or *difaqane*. Simultaneously, further clashes with the indigenous residents resulted from Boer expansion northwards from the 1830s.

The discovery of diamonds in Hopetown in 1867 and gold on the Witwatersrand in 1886 accelerated urbanisation, mechanisation and the exploitation of cheap labour. These discoveries presaged the emergence of the modern South African industrial state. Labour was required on a massive scale that could only be provided by Africans. At the same time, the Europeans had to maintain control of the resources and land. They thus established closed compounds as a means of migrant labour control. By denying Africans rights within the urban areas and keeping their families and dependants on subsistence plots in the reserves they could control wages, deny labourers basic rights and maintain the fiction that they did not belong in 'white South Africa' but to 'tribal societies'. These assumptions informed the development of later Apartheid ideology and legislation.

During the Anglo-Boer War (October 1899–May 1902) many black farmers responded to the military's demand for produce, caused by the British policy of scorched-earth farm burnings, and availed themselves of employment opportunities at good wages. They also realised that they could recolonise land lost earlier. Thus, when the Treaty of Vereeniging was signed, the most important priority was to re-establish European control over the land and to force the Africans back to waged labour. This was achieved through the seminal Natives Land Act (formalised in 1913), reserving 'home-lands' for black people in South African, and the 1923 Natives (Urban Areas) Act, which introduced pass laws, entrenched urban segregation and controlled African mobility.

Simultaneously an educated élite of black clerics, teachers, business people, journalists and professionals grew. Steps towards the formation of national political organisations of Africans began around the turn of the century. The most significant of these, the African National Congress (ANC) was founded in 1912. Worker militancy emerged in the wake of the First World War and continued through the 1920s through organisations like the Industrial and Commercial Workers' Union and the Communist Party.

The Anglo-Boer–South African War was a seminal factor in the development of Afrikaner nationalist politics. Although South Africa was granted home rule as the Union of South Africa in 1910, its controversial relationship with Britain is evident in its ceding from the British Commonwealth when it became the Republic of South Africa in 1961. In 1914 the National Party (NP) was formed in a breakaway from the ruling South African Party. Many Afrikaners supported the NP because they could not reconcile themselves to the government's decision to support Britain both in the First World War and the Second World War, against Germany. The Great Depression of the 1930s, in between the wars, provided the support the NP needed to come to power in 1948, because people felt that the South African had failed them economically. The Apartheid legislation and systems that followed would define the country culturally and politically for the next forty-two years, until the unbanning of the ANC and the Communist Party and the release of key political prisoners such as Nelson Mandela in 1990. This marked the shift towards the first fully democratic election in South Africa, in 1994.

It is against this background of socio-political history that South Africa's theatre history must be understood. The following section outlines key European dramatic influences on South African theatre from the 1700s to the formation of the republic in 1910. Between about 1790 and 1880 the Dutch, French, German and British theatre provided the basis for the formal theatre which dominated South Africa until the end of the twentieth century. At times the various Europeans collaborated, at other times the British theatre was separate. The history is discussed accordingly.

Theatre from the Dutch East India Company to Afrikaans theatre

In the 1700s the Dutch East India Company (DEIC) controlled the Cape. The governor following Van Riebeeck (1652–60) was very strict, allowing a little light entertainment once a year, on the Sunday after the return of a home fleet.[62] The first governor who encouraged entertainment was Louis van Assenburgh (1701–11). The impact of various cultures is apparent from the outset in the strong Asian musical influence that the Malay slaves brought with them, which was recorded by the German physicist H. Lichtenstein.[63] Many of the wealthier settlers used slaves (from Malaysia and Indonesia) to play music at table during meals; later they formed the music groups that played at weddings, dances and at the theatre. They interacted with the local Khoi in the employ of the DEIC, who also played music and danced in the evenings. One of the earliest plays created in South Africa was written in 1740 by a Malay slave named Majiet (said to be the son of Sheik Jousuf) in Arabic script, which, when translated, sounds close to kitchen Dutch. It was about a slave girl who, having resisted the advances of her Dutch master, is assaulted by his son.

Popular forms predominated the entertainment van Assenburgh arranged, which ranged from puppet shows and dog and bull fights to firework displays. This was paralleled by early garrison theatre, which began with the Dutch soldiers' stagings of 'mummeries' in the barracks, probably short scenes remembered from amateur societies in Holland.

Despite this early Dutch entertainment, it was the French who provided the real foundation for European theatre in South Africa. They landed in Cape Town in 1780, when Britain declared war on Holland and France sent a fleet to defend the Cape. By 1781 the DEIC was weakening and Cape Town was known as 'Little Paris'. Soldiers drilled in the morning and played versions of the Comédie-Française in the evening in the barracks, with young men playing female parts, open to a public audience. This cultural moment was brief, however, and ended when Dutch ladies were forced to withdraw from supporting the theatre after a scandal; the French went home, owing to pressures of the Revolution, the declaration of the Republic and a subsequent war with Britain.

By the end of the eighteenth century a large percentage of the DEIC employees and soldiers were German, and two thousand German men arrived in 1787. In 1796, when the Dutch fleet surrendered to the British, many of the soldiers and sailors taken into English service were German. During this period German and Dutch amateurs played alongside the English at the

African Theatre in Cape Town (opened 1801). German amateurs performed in German or Dutch. The Goede Hoop Lodge was another popular venue for theatrical activities, especially German singing. The subscriber concerts, which had previously been convened in private homes, moved to the African Theatre and were performed either as part of the drama or between the plays.

In the brief period from 1802, when Britain and France signed the Treaty of Amiens and the Cape returned to Dutch rule, Charles Villet and Charles Boniface revitalised the Dutch theatre by establishing schools for drama and presenting selections of contemporary French theatre.[64] Popular theatre forms discernible in home concert parties, melodrama, comic operetta, pantomime and French comedy from the French and Dutch continued and would later develop into Afrikaans theatre.

From 1811 the amateur Dutch companies performed and developed half of the productions staged at the African Theatre. Boniface led his French and Dutch players into the new wave of Afrikaans theatre. Theatre began to move beyond Cape Town with the establishment of an amateur group, Door Ijver Vruchtbaar, in Stellenbosch in 1838, and productions at Stellenbosch's Turf Club. Grahamstown had developed its own Graham's Town Theatrical Amateur Company, performing plays by Sheridan and Rhodes (best known for *Bombastes Furioso*) in 1837. One of their most significant performances was of Andrew Geddes Bains and Frederick Rex's *Kaatje Kekkelbek*, the first theatrical piece to use Afrikaans on stage. It is a sketch in verse and prose and dealts with Grahamstown's prison, soldiers, and personalities through the eyes of a Khoi girl who has been to Dr Philip's mission school in Cape Town. The piece begins: 'Mij naam is Kaatje Kekkelbek, I come from Kat River, Daar is van water geen gebrek But scarce of wine and beer . . . Mijn ABC in Ph'lipes school I learnt a kleine beetje, But left it just as great a fool As gekke Tante Mietje.'[65] This piece is remarkable because it speaks to border audiences about their own experiences in their own, often mixed languages. It also gives a fascinating insight into colonial life from the perspective of someone twice removed from the centre: a Khoi woman. It would be a long while before such theatre re-emerges on the South African stage, but it gives a glimpse of the elements that would define theatre in the mid-twentieth century in South Africa.

From the mid-1800s the newly emergent Afrikaner community focussed on establishing their language and identity. There are many parallels between the early Afrikaans language and cultural movements and those of Zulu or

Ndebele peoples who were also establishing and defining national identities in cultural forms, particularly through praise poetry.

Collaboration between Dutch, German and French immigrants was possible because they seemed more willing and able to shift between languages than were the British. This is evident even in 1865, when Johan Combrink resuscitated the company Door Ijver Bloeit de Kunst with a production of *Adelaide van Beyeren*, a Dutch translation of a French play, and Kotzebue's *De Dronkaard* at Parry's Theatre Royal. The latter play may have been a version of William H. Smith's American play, *The Drunkard, or The Fallen Saved*, of 1844. These performances were to raise funds for the Free Staters killed in the war with the Basotho people. This group performed in Cape Town, Paarl, Stellenbosch, Robben Island and toured as far as the diamond fields by ox-wagon. Later Afrikaans theatre emerged from these diverse interactions.

Meanwhile, Dutch theatre outside of Cape Town became more critically engaged. The Anglicisation of the Cape, annexation of the Kimberley diamond fields and the Transvaal Republic, and the Jameson Raid culminated in the Anglo-Boer war in 1899. The Dutch felt themselves no longer settlers, but citizens, and their language no longer Cape-Dutch, but Afrikaans. One of the key ways in which they explored and expressed this new sense of language and culture was through the *Rederijkerskamer*. These societies were styled on Dutch guilds, a phenomenon of sixteenth- to nineteenth-century Holland, closely allied to the church and which performed morality and allegorical plays, farces and classical tragedy both locally and at the main towns and at fairs. The first two Rederijkerskamer, called Thespis and Aurora, were formed in Paarl. Aurora opened in August 1862 with a production of *Rocco* by A. Wijnstok and *Schijn Bedriegt* (Apparent Betrayal) by Neef Paul. Although initially the guild was not anti-British, after the British-Basotho pact against the Free State it became defined in Dutch and Afrikaans terms. Later it was impossible to separate its activities with those of Die Genootskap van Regte Afrikaners (the Society of Real Afrikaners), formed in 1875 to protect the nature and language of Afrikaans in response to attempts made by the English to suppress Afrikaans in South Africa, especially under Lord Charles Somerset. Although Afrikaans had been written earlier – by Malay slaves in Arabic script – Boniface in *De Nieuwe Ridderorde*, Geddes Bain in *Kaatje Kekkelbek*, Louis Meurant in a newspaper in Grahamstown – these groups instigated a more formalised, conscious approach to developing a language, culture and identity. This is evidenced by their aspiration to write a national anthem.

By the end of the century the combined efforts of the *Patriot*, the first Afrikaans newspaper (1878), and *Die Genootskap* produced the first Afrikaans play, *De Jonge Kunstschilder* (The young artist; translated from Dutch) on a farm outside Paarl. Key figures during this period were the brothers S. J. and D. F. du Toit (known as *Oom Lokomotief*), and Melt Brink. They wrote plays, poetry and translated for the Aurora, both in Paarl, Cape Town, and as far as Somerset-East. Debating societies proliferated, especially in small towns around Cape Town, where only Afrikaans was allowed. Concerts consisted of music, recitations and humorous duologues. In 1891 a Rederijkerskamer was formed in Pretoria called Onze Taal (Our language). Like Aurora, it produced short plays, interspersed with recitations and music. The Second Language Congress gathered in Paarl in 1897, where *Magrita Prinslo* was performed for the first time. It became the first published play in Afrikaans. Two years after this the Anglo-Boer–South African War was fought, causing the suspension of all cultural issues until after 1904, when consideration was given once again to establishing and developing the Afrikaans language and culture. The Aurora continued, playing in Dutch and Afrikaans until 1914. The Afrikaanse-Hollandse Toneelvereeniging (Afrikaans-Dutch Theatre Association) was formed in 1906 with Gustav Preller, editor of *Land en Volk*, as director. He had been founder of the Afrikaanse Taalgenootskap (Afrikaans Language Association). He believed theatre should be used to convince Afrikaners that Afrikaans was the language in which they ought to be educated.

It is worth noting that the fight for an identity, culture and language was largely undertaken through theatre. Even the formation of a particular history and memory is evident. Dominee S. J. Du Toit's *Magrita Prinslo* tells the story of Piet Retief's part in the Great Trek with much sympathy, even though Du Toit was opposed to the Trekkers. Attitudes to oppositional peoples were also being defined. An example of this is his melodramatic account of the slaughter of the Dutch party by the Zulu chief Dingaan, and the comic depiction of Swartland the 'medicine-man'. Such condescending attitudes to indigenous Africans would predominate through the twentieth century in South Africa.

British theatre in South Africa
Earl Macartney was the first British governor of the Cape, from 1795. His successor, Sir George Yonge, was profoundly dedicated to the arts and culture. He strongly supported the little Barracks Theatre, which followed the

tradition of garrison theatre established by Dutch and French soldiers. British officers took theatre to the remotest corners of the colony, and sustained South African amateur theatre for decades. Often garrison or barracks theatre survived periods when other amateur and professional theatre collapsed.

One of Sir George Yonge's most significant contributions to theatre was the African Theatre in Cape Town, for which he canvassed equal support from both the Dutch and English living in the Cape. He designed the theatre himself. It was situated in Boeren Plein (Farmer's Square) or Hottentot Square, where farmers outspanned their oxen. It was estimated to cost £2,500 and allowed female actresses. It opened in September 1801, eight months after Sir George Yonge was forced to leave the Cape for financial maladministration. The programmes following were many and varied, and Dutch and English shareholders and companies utilised the theatre equally.

In 1806 the Cape once again reverted to the control of Britain. Among the officers in Cape Town in 1807 was Captain W. Frazer, a Scotsman who was 'at heart a man of the theatre'.[66] He introduced Sheridan and Goldsmith to the Cape. Captain Frazer and three other officers from the 21st Light Dragoons, the Madras Cavalry and the Royal Artillery formed the group All the World's a Stage, playing comedies and farces at the African Theatre from 1807. For years these English performers played only for charity and contributed significantly to the Widows and Orphans Fund, which supported families who had lost men to shipwrecks, storms, fires, disease, wild animals and native raids, as pensions and insurance were unknown.

Puritan opposers of the theatre suggested that the earthquake in Cape Town in 1809 was an act of divine disapproval, and the theatre was forced to close down until 1811, when amateur companies again began performing popular pieces. In the meantime, Astley's Circus had appeared in full in South Africa in 1808. They developed the already strong equestrian interest that had begun among the Malay slaves.

The African Theatre revived after Lord Charles Somerset became governor in 1814. Travelling companies from England and Australia visited, 'playing Empire', impacting heavily on the physical definition of theatre spaces, organisational systems and the fundamental principles behind theatre as representational art. However, Lord Somerset's recall to England in 1826 was a grave warning to future governors of the Cape to remain distanced from the arts, and no future governor showed any interest in local theatre. With the exception of a few garrison theatres, English theatre was silenced until 1829 when the English Theatrical Amateur Company and the Cape Town Amateur Company were united by Mr H. Booth, when he revived All the World's a Stage and began performing comedies and melodramas.

In 1836 Puritanical sentiment again swept through both the Dutch and English communities in Cape Town. This culminated in the African Theatre being sold in 1838 and turned into a church, known today as St Stephen's Church, on Riebeeck Square. Only the Garrison Players escaped this assault on theatre, and they continued to perform in the Barracks Theatre until the early 1840s, by which time the Dutch had revived formal theatre with a venue in De Vos's wine store in Boom Street (1843), which later became the Roeland Street Theatre. In 1846 the African Victoria Theatre opened, and in 1848 the new Drury Lane opened and the French Dramatic Artistes from Mauritius made their first appearance in Cape Town at the Victoria Theatre. Their programme included a 'Grand Musical Interlude, a Grand Comic Ballet, a Comic Solo, a Grand and Comic Galopade and a Graceful Waltz'.[67] Similar theatres in the European tradition sprang up in Grahamstown, Port Elizabeth, Pietermaritzburg, King William's Town and Stutterheim, with amateur groups leading the way.

Previous attempts at professional companies in the Cape had been brief. Amateur theatre had created and defined early South African theatre. Then, from the appearance of Sefton Parry en route back to England from Australia in 1855, a new generation of actor-managers appeared on the South African theatre scene to build the professional theatre. Besides Parry, other key figures included Disney Roebuck, who arrived in 1873, Luscombe Searelle, who stopped in South Africa en route back to England from Australia in 1886, Leonard Rayne, who came with a company from England in 1895, Harry Stodel, who arrived in Johannesburg from England in 1890, and William Schlesinger, who had come from America to sell insurance and who built African Consolidated Theatres from 1913.

In 1855, Sefton Parry was in the Cape only two months when he converted a large room in Lord Somerset's Commercial Exchange into a room for concerts, naming it the Drawing-Room Theatre, and launched his first plays. Parry returned two years later with his actress-wife and established a new theatre and travelling companies, performing popular pantomimes and farces. At the end of his first season the pantomime Beauty and the Beast was so successful that it provoked the first tour of the Colony by a professional company. By 1860 Parry had reopened the renovated Theatre Royal with a fully professional company, whose members came from various companies in England. In the first season they performed fifty productions. Until his departure back to England in 1863, Parry and his companies travelled and performed between the Cape and Port Elizabeth

After Parry's departure activity slumped, the Theatre Royal closed, and by the time Disney Roebuck arrived in 1873 the theatre had burned down. Roebuck reinjected spirit into professional theatre in South Africa with comic productions that were well mounted and costumed and with an extensive repertoire. Like Parry, he toured the eastern Cape and extended into Natal.

At this time racial interaction was not an obvious issue in South African theatre. The *Cape Times* relates that despite being in English, the Dutch or Afrikaans-speaking Malay audience was 'to be seen every evening in the gallery, and sometimes even in the pit' of the theatre to see Roebuck's plays in Cape Town.[68] The touring companies of Roebuck, Charles du Val and others were welcomed in Kimberley, Bloemfontein, Middelburg, Senekal and Pretoria, even if the Boer community spoke Afrikaans or German and understood little or no English. The exiled Zulu chief Cetshwayo was a privileged guest at Roebuck's pantomime *The Fair One with the Golden Locks* in 1882.[69] Much of this had to do with the spectacular nature of the theatre, which by the 1880s included much Gilbert and Sullivan.

In 1886 impresario Benjamin 'the Guv'nor' Wheeler and his son Frank convinced Luscombe Searelle to postpone his return to London and conducted his operas in South Africa. These were so successful that in 1886–7 he performed an unbroken programme of opera for six months. Searelle extended his repertoire to include Gilbert and Sullivan, set up various companies and toured the country. By 1889 he controlled theatres in Kimberley, Pretoria, Pietermaritzburg and Durban; he toured Rhodesia, Delagoa Bay and Kimberley. However, Harry Stodel challenged Searelle's operas with a music hall, which opened in 1891. This challenge, together with a series of mishaps with fires at the Exhibition Theatre in Cape Town and his Royal Theatre of Varieties in Johannesburg, forced Searelle to sell Stodel the Varieties and leave South Africa in 1898. Capetonians responded to the loss of their only theatre, the Exhibition Theatre, by financial contributions that resulted in the opening of the Opera House in 1893 and the Tivoli in 1903.

Leonard Rayne was another significant name in the development of professional travelling theatre in South Africa. In 1898 his company toured to Pietermaritzburg, Port Elizabeth and Durban with plays ranging from farce to Shakespeare. His success seemed to characterise this kind of escapist colonial theatre brought from the 'mother country' and performed out of any real socio-political context. Bryant comments on this aspect of Rayne's productions:

> In Rayne's productions . . . tragedy, if it did occur, came always in the middle, never at the end. This comforting formula was the theatre's trump card at a time when few other opiates existed. It provided tuneful music, situations of high drama and romance played out by lovely virtuous women and handsome upright men, with a sprinkling of easily detected rogues, and these situations were always resolved on the basis that right – or love – would triumph and virtue be rewarded.[70]

Harry Stodel was a dynamic figure who had begun in Johannesburg but who moved to Cape Town in 1899, because of Boer hostility, as he was both English and a Jew. He bought the opposition Tivoli Theatre in 1910, which had struggled to survive financially since the Boer War. The theatre's only real success had been the launching of Stephen Black's *Love and the Hyphen* in 1908, the first play written in English by a South African, although not the first play written in South Africa. Stodel reopened the Tivoli as a music hall that hosted large, lavish companies. Patriotism was high and plays like *The Dawn of Union* by R. Musgrave were popular. The play was 'a potpourri of music, comedy and drama – a miniature pageant illustrating many of the incidents in South African history'.[71] Stodel included elaborate animal shows, including performing dogs, pigeons, snake charmers, fighting kangaroos, seals and elephants. Again one notices the escapist, extravagant nature of South African colonial theatre, which, when it touches on political or conflictual issues, does so in farcical or comic modes.

However, Stodel realised that the film industry would be the real challenge to theatre. Consequently, he built the Alhambra Cinema and showed films at the Opera House and the Tivoli, alongside his variety shows. In 1913 he met William Schlesinger, who supported his plans to centralise the distribution of films and the importation of various acts and theatrical companies to South Africa. Stodel in turn supported Schlesinger's plans to build up a cooperative of theatre owners, and buy up privately owned theatres in order to build new, better ones. He 'surrendered his cinemas and leases, together with his circuit of about twenty-six independent exhibitors' and thus African Theatres, the basis for African Consolidated Theatres, was created.[72] Rayne refused to cooperate, but dwindling audiences and casts cut by Asian influenza pressurised him into reducing his repertoire, dropping the classical plays and relying on melodrama to attract audiences. After his closure in 1924 many in his company found work with Stodel, who, with Schlesinger, continued to import dramatic, musical and pantomime companies to tour the African Theatres circuit.[73] During the 1914–18 war, Schlesinger placed all his resources at the disposal of General Smuts to raise money for the war effort. However, after the war a combination of the Great Depression and the onset of cinema proved too much of a challenge for theatre and the Tivoli was forced to close in 1931.

Ironically, despite all this early theatrical activity in South Africa, historians have tended to name Stephen Black the first English South African dramatist. Black was both an actor-manager and author of satirical comedies. He began as a journalist, but at the advice of Rudyard Kipling he developed his sketches, thereby joining Boniface, Bain and Melt Brink in writing dramatic works about local people and their culture. It is these satirical-comic sketches that mark his work as significant in South Africa's theatre history. His first play, *Love and the Hyphen* (Tivoli Theatre, 1908) commented on Cape society, particularly the social and political implications of colour. Other plays include *Helena's Hope Ltd*, based on his experiences in a Rhodesian gold mine, *Van Kalabas Does His Bit* (1916), based on his war experiences, and *The Uitlanders* (Foreigners, 1911). Black also contributed to the newspaper *Outspan* and translated French texts into English, for example *The Flapper* from *La Gamine* in 1911. His satirical plays offer a useful early record of the social mores and layers of early twentieth-century Cape society, with its complicated racial interactions and the signal issues that would be developed for the rest of the century.

1910 was a significant date in South African history. At this time South Africa became a union and began the movement towards independence from Europe. This was a moment in history when cultural initiatives are mobilised to 'invent tradition' and 'imagine a community'.[74] An actual pageant was performed in Cape Town in 1910, which was a more general allegorised performance of aspirant identity and purpose in South Africa. The pageant involved 5,000 performers and the South African navy. It presented historical sketches depicting the Europeans' (Portuguese, Dutch and British) arrival on the South African coast, the appropriation of land by treaty or conquest, and the meeting between Moshoeshoe and President Hoffman of the Orange Free State in 1854. The pageant did not reflect Britain's annexation of Lesotho, the discovery of diamonds in 1867, industrialisation or the effects of mining. Whilst a few black leaders were acknowledged (Moshoeshoe,

Sheik Yusaf), generally Africans were relegated to the Hegelian category of the 'unhistorical' and 'undeveloped'; their European counterparts were the 'historical heroes'.[75] This focus was to set the dominant focus for formal theatre in the years that followed.

Twentieth-century theatre

The European tradition established in the nineteenth century continued to flourish. However, European theatre developed alongside African performance and both traditions were profoundly influenced by the education system, particularly mission-based, and urbanisation. The impact of the intersections of these traditions on one another and in these particular contexts is evident in 1958–9 with *King Kong*.

1900 to 1960

Theatre and the educational system   All education in South Africa was linked to the church and embedded in European ideology, literature and theatre, particularly Shakespeare. The state or missions ran black schools. The missions in particular encouraged theatrical and literary production and were the only places black men and women could train to express themselves in prose fiction or performance.

One of the most significant mission schools was the Marianhill Mission, in Durban, where Father Bernard Huss produced numerous religious plays, comedies and dramatisations of Zulu narratives. Peterson argues that 'the pioneering work at the mission between 1900 and 1925 laid the patterns and concerns that were to bedevil theatre for the entire period under discussion [1900–40]',[76] and it could be argued, even beyond. Huss profoundly influenced former students such as Vilakazi and the Lucky Stars, who continued to create theatre after having left the mission school. Huss also influenced the Reverend Ray Phillips, who headed the American Mission Board on the Witwatersrand. One of his major initiatives led to the establishment of the Bantu Men's Social Centre from which the Bantu Dramatic Society and Dhlomo emerged. This theatre was collaboratively improvised, incorporating song and dance, and showed the strong influence of European education and Christianity.

The application of mission-based education and theatre was not simple. The intersection of the European and African worlds provoked tension between using theatre to promote colonial ideology and the need for recipients to express themselves critically. The differences between Mary Waters's and

Herbert Dhlomo's plays illustrate this tension. Waters's *The Light* (published in 1924) was used in the mission education context to promote a version of the conquest of the black inhabitants of South Africa as mystic and spiritual, thereby simultaneously establishing a religious history and imposing Christian ethics through theatre. It overtly argued the benefits of colonisation to the colonised.[77]

Waters's play *U-Nonqgause: A drama of the Cattle Killing of 1857*, published in the same year, was challenged by Dhlomo's first play, *The Girl Who Killed to Save* (1936), which is also important as the first English play by a black playwright to be published. Both plays explore the events surrounding the vision of the Xhosa prophetess Nongquase, which led to a mass cattle killing and consequent famine in 1857. Waters's version focusses almost entirely on the missionary perspective of the historic event. The missionary's final comment on the events suggests that the incident was actually part of a divine plan to redeem errant blacks from their rebellious course. The play is a paternalistic patriarchal vision of frontier history. Although Dhlomo's play does not significantly change the ending of the play, it formulates issues regarding the acceptability of assimilation and conversion from an African perspective. Orkin argues that it encourages the appropriation of the discourses of assimilation in the cause of liberation, rather than in a gesture of submissive acceptance.[78] The missionaries certainly do not go unchallenged in the play. The five songs included in the original manuscript emphasise the syncretic nature of the work. The last song, a hymn beginning *Nkosi kawu sikelele* (God bless you), links traditional *amakwaya*, Xhosa hymns, and the opening line of *Nkosi sikelel' iAfrika*, a song long associated with African aspirations of independence.[79]

Herbert Dhlomo (1903–56) was significant in defining South African theatre. He was a product of Adams College missionary school and entered education himself as a teacher. In 1937 he became the first African librarian-organiser at the Carnegie Bantu Library in Johannesburg. After a series of disagreements with his employees he left for Durban in 1941, where he became assistant editor of the *Natal Sun* (*Ilanga lase Natal*). Dhlomo's creative work focussed on his need to articulate the African experience. He wrote at least nine plays (collected posthumously by Couzens in *Collected Works*, 1985) and numerous poems. Unfortunately, much of his early dramatic writing has not been published, for instance *Shaka*, which was to be grouped with *Cetshwayo* (1936), *Dingana* (1937) and *Moshoeshoe* (1937). Other plays between 1939 and 1941 include *The Living Dead, Ruby, The Pass Arrested and Discharged;*

The Workers and *Malaria*. These plays address social issues with increasing bitterness. Many were not published and some, such as *Ruby*, have been lost. Dhlomo significantly formulated a black South African literary critical and artistic perspective. The plays after 1935 suggest his growing scepticism of European culture. His work both acknowledges African drama and traditions and suggests the impact his European education had had insofar as he aspired to 'graft African tradition onto the European'.[80]

Another significant example of how education used European theatre in ideological ways was the emphasis on Shakespeare in schools. The possession and knowledge of Shakespeare texts were evidences of empowerment. Dan Twala relates how in the 1930s 'Everyone thought he was great when he could quote a word or two from Shakespeare'.[81] This resulted in various productions and translations of Shakespeare texts, most often *The Merchant of Venice* and *Julius Caesar*.[82]

However, colonisation by means of European theatre did not go unchallenged. Training by missions was paralleled by the development of urban syncretic African performance.

Urban cultural development   Urbanisation was culturally significant for both the black indigenous population and Afrikaners themselves. After quelling the Bhambatha rebellion in 1906, Kavanagh argues, 'the process of defeating and subjugating the indigenous peoples of South Africa was completed. The process of transition from pre-capitalist forms of society to capitalism was accelerated.'[83] This happened most notably in the migration from rural areas to the new urban areas, which expanded rapidly as people came to sell their labour.[84] Urbanisation accelerated rural black South Africans' contact with European values, norms and cultural forms, including performance, which challenged the various cultural practices workers brought with them to the cities. Would the old ways survive, disappear or transform into something new?

Urbanisation became an issue for the Afrikaner in the 1930s with a large number of poor whites living in the cities, which provided dramatic commentary by Ampie Coetze and Andre Hugenot. The difference between urbanisation for the Afrikaner and for the black worker was that the former had access to political and economic power to express their concerns, particularly in theatre – which moved from travelling towards urban-based – while the latter did not. The English were not really affected by urbanisation, as they owned much of the industry.

Urban formal theatre   The power of emergent urban cultural forms was recognised and employed both by the aspiring urban black middle class and by white liberals to soften the increasingly repressive position of black South Africans. The Bantu Men's Social Centre was created in 1924 in Johannesburg in an attempt to define a modern African identity 'that avoided slavish imitation of Europe and the artificial revival of tradition'. It provided educational, athletic and performance opportunities for all Africans. Ironically, the most prestigious and culturally representative of the activities arranged was the annual *Eisteddfodau* (from the Welsh Eisteddfod), first in Port Elizabeth and Johannesburg in 1931.[85]

Experimentation with form is also evident in the translation and performance of European classic texts, an offshoot from mission education. By 1920 'well-made' plays were being performed in schools in Zulu and Sesotho. The first play published in an African language in South Africa was *Debeza's Baboons*, translated into Xhosa by G. B. Sinxo in 1925. At this time Dhlomo emerged as a significant playwright.

The earliest record of a published play performed by a black theatre group was a production of Oliver Goldsmith's *She Stoops to Conquer* in 1932 by the Bantu Men's Dramatic Society in Johannesburg. They performed many European plays, while consciously trying to define their own cultural context. In a pamphlet published in 1934 by the British Drama League the society asserted that while it would 'present European plays from time to time, the aim of the Bantu Dramatic Society is to encourage Bantu playwrights, and to develop African dramatic and operatic art. Bantu life is full of great and glorious incidents and figures that would form the basis of first-class drama.'[86]

Another ambitious dramatic venture was Esau Mthethwe's Lucky Stars, formed in Natal in 1929. They 'based their drama on totally indigenous themes of rural life and customs', with a repertoire of original didactic and satirical comedies in Zulu, based on traditional life, incorporating music and dance.[87] They toured *Umthakathi* (The Sorcerer), which explores the difference between witchcraft and legitimate traditional medicine and soothsaying, and *Ukuqomisa* (Courting), which explores norms associated with winning a lover with charms and the traditional taboo of marriage for a younger sister until the elder sisters are wed. Vilakazi asserts that this group 'greatly influenced Johannesburg Location productions'.[88]

The 1930s also saw the formation of the Bantu People's Players, who may or may not have been connected with the Bantu Men's Dramatic Society. This group's production of Eugene O'Neill's *The Hairy Ape* (1937) is important insofar as it begins the shift towards multi-lingual theatre in South Africa. The play was performed in Fanagalo, a hybrid mixture of English and various languages used by miners, to represent American slang. Dan Twala played the lead role and Belgian Andre van Gyseeghen directed.[89] However, Kruger asserts that this early black theatre was not radical theatre, but rather was very patronised and defined by Europeans, quoting the company's own insistence that they were 'entirely dissociated from political movements and parties'.[90] However, it is important to take into account the context – the Herzog Acts of 1936 and the strong influence of mission education – when evaluating the significance of such early theatre. Experimentation with form, mixing European texts and African performance styles, and working in multiple languages are strands that can be traced right through twentieth-century theatre in South Africa.

Popular performance forms   Cultural interaction was extended beyond Europeans to include contact with Africans from surrounding countries. Of the 85,000 mine-workers listed by the Transvaal Chamber of Mines in 1904, only 19,000 came from within the country. By 1919, 20,000 lived in the slum yards of Johannesburg, and double that figure by 1927.[91] Thus, in the 1920s and 1930s slum yards became the focus of black recreational life. With the illicit liquor trade developing, 'shebeen society' (informal pubs) became the centre for entertainment. Musical performance was traditionally essential to social drinking. Thus, municipal and domestic workers, or contract workers brought African, African-American and European (particularly Afrikaans) forms together into syncretic urban performances.

Another simultaneous influence was the rapid development of the cinema industry in the 1920s and 1930s.[92] For example, Vilakazi traces Zulu musicians he calls *abaqhafi* (s. *umqhafi*, cultural driftwood, uncouth, heavy drinker), who were not traditionalists, Christians or school-educated. They dressed and behaved like American western film characters and gained reputations as guitarists.

Semi-professional black musicians emerged as a demand for 'modern' music grew in the cities. In the 1920s they assimilated the various styles into a single urban musical style called *marabi*, which was strongly influenced by the social and economic context of the black working class. It was identified particularly with sexuality. The name may come from the Sesotho term *ho rabaraba*, 'to fly around/roam', also the meaning of *lerabi* (pl. *marabi*), or from the Marabastad area where African domestic workers (or 'roamers') lived. Coloured musicians of the Cape, known as 'Crooners', were another early influence, bringing with them the Cape Afrikaans and black American musical styles as they played banjos, guitars, tambourines and bones. Other Afrikaans influences included the *vastrap* and *tickey draai* melodies, with Xhosa instrumentalists as a link.

The rural Sesotho version of the *marabi* party was the *famo* (from *ho re famo*: to open nostrils, to raise garments, displaying the woman's genitals), a defiantly suggestive dance. It also includes lengthy recitative songs performed by women, often bewailing their position in the urban setting. These paralleled the male *dikwata* (*likoata* in old orthography, praise songs), the *difele* (or *sefela*, pl. *lifela*), which also formulated singers' urban experiences and reformulated their social values and identities as Basotho in a migrant context.[93]

The middle-class urban black South African identified more with jazz and ragtime, which was played at *itswari* (from soiree, a form consisting of three chords repeated over four or six hours). Musicians such as Meekly Matshikakaza's Big Four's jazz band typically entertained whites and middle-class Africans at these gatherings. The relatively inexpensive pedal organ was well suited to cramped shebeens. Here *itswaris*, *tula n'divile* (Xhosa folk melodies played on a keyboard) and marabi reached their height as keyboard styles. Dan Twala's descriptions of the music and its context is not unlike Harlem in the 1920s.[94]

In the 1920s and 1930s the *stokfels*,[95] cooperative women's associations, emerged. These acted as credit rings in which each member contributed a set amount each week in anticipation of receiving the combined contribution at a regular interval. The woman then organised a stokfel party (at which marabi bands played), where members and guests paid an entrance fee. Christian women ran something similar called *manyano*, gatherings with a Christian focus.

Coplan argues that the year 1936 was particularly significant in the development of black urban music and theatre, as groups gathered to perform in Johannesburg's British Empire Exhibition. These included migrant mine dancers, *ingom'ebusuku* groups, jazz orchestras, minstrels and mass choirs. This event facilitated cultural stimulation and exchange, which was then extended through subsequent tours to small towns throughout the country.[96] An example is the Pitch Black Follies, with whom Griffiths Motsielo had combined to form the Strutters and Blackbirds in 1927, when they moved beyond the minstrel format. They combined the Lucky Stars' dramatic or comic sketch format, based on cultural and historical material, with the minstrel tradition of tragicomic scenes from urban life.

> [Their] 'Grand vaudeville' performance in Johannesburg in 1938 included 'Primitive Africa', 'Recitation', 'I Quaqa' (a song about a beetle), 'Xhosa poet', 'Ntsikana's Vision', 'Tribal dance', hymns by J. K. Bokwe and Tiyo Soga, a 'Sesotho Song and Dance', a (military) 'Recruiting Sketch', a shebeen-*skokiaan* queen sketch, an Afrikaans medley, 'Die Oorlams Mense van Vrededorp', and a jazz song and dance.[97]

Whilst admitting the processes of the 'enactment of a desirable future . . . through the embodiment of ideas and ideologies in the performance of citizen-subjects' in the various pageants in South Africa, such as the 1934 Emancipation Celebration, the pro-British Pageant of South Africa in 1936, the Afrikaner equivalents in the 1938 Voortrekker Centenary, and the 1952 Tricentenary of Jan van Riebeeck's arrival at the Cape,[98] one can also see the irony of cultural forms refusing containment, as they redefine themselves in new dynamic syncretic forms and identities. This ambiguity of cultural position and autonomy continues into the 1940s and 1950s. Orkin argues that by this time theatre and performance among the oppressed classes 'suggests conflicting impulses, on the one hand, towards authentication of life at the periphery whilst, again, abrogating or displacing the colonial and imperial centre, and, on the other hand, towards affiliation with that centre'.[99]

An example of such affiliation is evident in the collaboration between the Orlando Boys' Club dramatic society, with director Griffiths Motsielo, and Jewish South African impresario Bertha Slosberg to produce *Africa*, a music-hall-style pageant at the Communal Hall, Western Native Township. Ezekiel Mphalele, the headmaster of Orlando High School in 1945, had developed a deep interest in drama while at school in Johannesburg, and so he introduced dramatics at Orlando High School, adapting various English classics (for example, Shakespeare, Dickens) and folk-tales. He later became director of AMDA (the Drama School for the Union of South African Artists). Together with Khoti Mngoma, Mphalele formed the Syndicate of African Artists in the mid-1940s, to 'bring serious music and the arts to the doorstep of our people, who are not allowed to go to white theatre or the concert halls'.[100] Despite the European focus, their engagement with issues is evidenced in their forced disbanding in 1956 due to police harassment.

Traditional European theatre European theatre continued relatively untouched by the emergent African urban performance forms. The Anglo-Boer War was the first real cultural provocation to which artists responded by indicating either a strong loyalty to Britain or their desire to develop and foster a distinctive Afrikaner nation identity. The establishment of the Union in 1910 and the subsequent discovery of minerals, which brought enormous growth in the country's economic resources, offered further possibilities of a new South African autonomous identity. These events provoked writing from within the country and financed more amateur and professional companies. By the mid-1930s there were more than thirty touring companies travelling rural areas by road and rail. The Federation of Amateur Theatrical Societies of South Africa (FATSSA, 1934–60) was established under the directorship of P. P. B. Breytenbach as a network to promote English and Afrikaans amateur theatre.

The Second World War, following the drought and depression of the 1930s, together with the rise of radio and film spelt the virtual end of professional theatre, and repertory groups dominated again. After the war professional theatre revived, although white theatre was confined almost entirely to touring British companies.

Afrikaans theatre underwent significant definition from 1930–40 with the Dertiger (Thirties) movement under the leadership of N. P. van Wyk Louw. Although most of the drama continued the social realism and naturalism of the twenties, van Wyk Louw's play *Die Dieper Reg* (The Deeper Right), produced for the 1938 Voortrekker centenary, reflected the aesthetics of poets who focussed on individual inner conflict and subjective responses to beauty and pain. Van Wyk argued that it tended to 'aestheticise politics' and that the 'new aesthetic had its counterpart in the *Purified* National Party [established 1934]', which included 'hierarchical differentiation in its intellectual response to culture and science, which focussed on differentiation between English and Afrikaners' (his italics).[101] It was only in the mid-1930s that race shifted into focus. Developing an Afrikaans literature and culture became ever more important. Thus, when the National Party came to power in 1948 it was not surprising that a definite Afrikaans theatre began to emerge. The new government established the National Theatre Organisation (NTO, 1948–62), the first bi-lingual state theatre organisation, directed by P. P. B.

Breytenbach. However, it was not truly 'national' as it served the interests of whites only, ignoring black communities. In 1962 the NTO was replaced by four regionally based Performing Arts Councils (PACs) in Natal, the Transvaal, Orange Free State and the Cape Provinces. Lavishly funded, over the next thirty years PACs gave opportunities for white writers, directors and actors who were interested in developing Eurocentric theatre, music, opera and ballet productions to experiment and create high-quality productions, which would become the foundation of formal theatre in South Africa for the next three decades. Not all of the work financed was in support of the dominant ideology, though. Writers such as Chris Barnard, André Brink and Pieter Fourie wrote controversial, contestatory plays that premièred in PAC venues. The absurdity of the application of segregation policies is evident in the situation of PACOFs production of Adam Small's *Kanna hy kô Huistoe* in Bloemfontein, where Small, as a coloured man, was not allowed to attend the performance. The segregation policy changed in the 1980s when state venues were opened up to all South Africans.

Multi-racial collaboration   Many multi-racial theatres and theatre groups sprang up between the 1950s and 1970s as alternatives to the state-funded PACs. These were usually organised by whites and supported by black African intellectuals who were resisting the growing hegemony of Afrikaner nationalism. However, this collaboration and the publication of drama by the rising black middle class were seriously hamstrung by the introduction of the Bantu education system in 1953, following the formal-ising of Apartheid from 1948. One of the key principles of Apartheid was 'separate development', which included ethnic and linguistic definition and separation. Although many writers refused to cooperate and publish in their so-called Bantu languages, there were some writers prepared to write plays on 'suitable' themes in Bantu languages, published by companies owned by Afrikaner capitalists under government auspices for prescription in schools. Many of these plays were never performed at all; others were performed to black audiences in urban areas.

Ironically, the government's use of culture to entrench Apartheid ideology provoked a clearly identifiable black popular theatre within a decade.[102] Initially this was closely related to collaboration between black and white artists who rejected the emergent policies of 'separate development'. For example, Teda de Moor promoted and supported black performances for white audiences, producing African dance dramas with students from the

Jan Hofmeyer School of Social Work in Johannesburg from 1941. In 1952 she collaborated with George Makanya to found the Bantu Theatre Company of Cape Town. It toured Hugh Tracey and K F Masinga's *Chief Above and Chief Below* through South Africa, focussing on the transition from the rural to the township context. Alf Herbert promoted township jazz shows, and Ian Bernhardt, manager and actor of the white amateur dramatic society the Dramateers, formed the all-black group, the Bareti Players (1953–5), whose first production was *A Comedy of Errors* (1955).

Collaboration was evident in the formation of various groups. In 1952–3 the Union of South African Artists was established by Bernhardt, Guy Routh, Dan Poho, Bob Leshoai, Sidney Sepamla, Meshack Mosia, musician Gwigwi Mwrebi and others to protect the professional rights of black artists. By 1958 it had become one of the most successful promotional entertainment bodies in the country. Two other significant organisations formed during this period were the African Music and Drama Association (AMDA, 1960), and the Rehearsal Room at Dorkay House in Johannesburg. The drama school at AMDA was run by Nora Taylor, Mphalele's mentor, with Bob Leshoai, who initiated the schools projects.[103] Athol Fugard, Gibson Kente and Barney Simon were among those who worked collaboratively from the Rehearsal Room.

The centrality of music in urban popular culture had been evident since the 1920s, and eclectic performances continued to develop at venues such as Aunt Babe's and Back of the Moon in Sophiatown. Performers drew on American, English, Afrikaans and African cultural traditions and comic sketches as well as jazz, singing and dancing. By the 1950s there was a clear association of African-American performance culture with urban cultural autonomy, and Sophiatown was the black cultural centre in the north. Other influential forms were *tsaba-tsaba*, a local adaptation of American jive, and *Kwela*, or penny-whistle players, which in turn fused into *mbaqanga*, the people's own jazz.

These eclectic collaborations between artists from different cultures culminated in 1959 with *King Kong*, a musical based on the rise and fall of the black South African heavyweight boxing champion Ezekiel 'King Kong' Dhlamini. Liberals saw this play as exemplifying their belief that socio-political progress could come through creative collaboration, especially in the cultural field. However, as Coplan and Orkin point out, the collaboration was not unproblematic.[104] Nevertheless, it showed both the artists, South Africans and the wider world the potential of urban black

South African artists, including Miriam Makeba, the Manhattan Brothers and Gibson Kente. This play marked the beginning of the township musical era.

The second major impact on the development of syncretic forms of theatre in South Africa was Athol Fugard's collaborative work, which he began with Lewis Nkosi, Nat Nakasa, and Bloke Modisane in 1958 with *No-Good Friday*. He went on to produce *Nongogo* (1959) and *The Blood Knot* (1961) and formed the Rehearsal Room group at the Union of South African Artists' premises in Dorkay House. Together, these artists developed the 'workshop' technique of theatre-making, which integrated African uses of imagery, physicalisation and improvisation into contemporary western theatre. Over the next twenty years Fugard played a major role in collaboration with a generation of black actors who worked outside the township variety form.

1960 to 2002

The 1960s marked a new era of growing tension with the destruction of Sophiatown, the Sharpeville massacre and the beginnings of the Black Consciousness Movement in South Africa. Apartheid legislation curtailed interracial cooperation in the arts, making even limited collaborations fraught and virtually impossible. The separate amenities and community development provisions of the 1964 Group Areas Act prohibited multi-racial performance companies and required permits for blacks to perform in or attend shows in white areas, and vice versa. Union Artists had to give up performances, although AMDA retained its teaching facilities under a black leadership. Ian Bernhardt helped to form the Phoenix Players, an all-black company at Dorkay House, initially to present Fugard's *Hello and Goodbye* to a black audience.

Township musicals   Ironically, this forced separation invigorated urban black cultural movements. Influenced by *King Kong*, Fugard's collaboration with the Serpent Players, and Alan Paton's musical *Mkumbane* (with a score by Tod Matshikiza), artists such as Gibson Kente revolutionised urban African popular theatre during the 1960s. Kente incorporated urban syncretic music styles (gospel and jazz) with straightforward melodrama to create a spectacle of township life in song and dance. *Manana, the Jazz Prophet* (1963) was his first play, written, scored, directed, produced and performed by black artists according to an emergent black urban aesthetic. *Sikalo* (Lament, 1966) followed. It dealt with central urban issues: gangsterism, inter-generational conflict, social disorganisation and physical suffering in townships. Kente then broke with Union Artists to form his own company with Sam Mhangwane, producing *Lifa* (1968) and *Zwi* (1970). Recognising that simplicity and mobility were the keys to success in township halls, he simplified sets and costumes and thus rejuvenated theatre in the black communities. By 1974 the performers in his three companies earned four times a factory worker's wage. His film *How Long?* (1974) and the plays *I Believe* and *Too Late!* (1975) were banned. Although not overtly political, Kente's plays were influenced by the Black Consciousness Movement. Later plays include *Can You Take It* (1977), *La Duma* (It Thundered, 1978) and *Mama and the Load* (1980). However, as Coplan points out, Kente paradoxically 'portray[ed] the consequences of apartheid without directly indicting the system',[105] which provoked considerable criticism from later playwrights. Despite this ambiguity, Kente contributed significantly to the synthesis of narrative, mime, movement, vocal dramatics, music and dance, combining established forms of theatre with traditional oral performance forms into township melodrama, using urban experience and culture. He also developed a mass audience for the next generation of artists.

Sam Mhangwane and the Sea Pearls Drama Society also featured in the emergent township musical arena. They produced musicals in Sowetan *Tsotsitaal* (street slang): *Crime Does Not Pay* (1963), *Unfaithful Woman* (1964, which toured for twelve years continuously), *Blame Yourself* (1966) and *Thembi* (1978). Boikie Mohlamme and Winkie Dibakwane created similar work.[106] The preoccupations of township playwrights were with social tension and reintegration. The plays, although written substantially in English, include Tsotsitaal and the urban dialects of Zulu, Xhosa and Sesotho. This was a form of resistance to the government's insistence on separate development, while simultaneously enabling performers to communicate their experience beyond themselves to international audiences.[107]

Collaborative theatre Parallel to the popular township musical, other syncretic theatre was evolving. After leaving Johannesburg, Fugard continued his collaborations with the Serpent Players in Port Elizabeth in 1963. Nomhle Nkonyeni, an early member, relates how the group began performing classic texts such as *The Caucasian Chalk Circle* and *Antigone* and then moved into improvisation. For example, *The Coat* (1966) emerged from one of the group members being arrested and his sending his coat home to his wife. *The Last Bus* (1968) came from their experience of having to catch a bus out of a white urban area before 10 p.m. The idea for *Friday's Bread on Monday* (1970) came from Zacharias Nkuigini seeing children going to buy stale bread in white areas for 5 cents on Mondays, as 'nobody buys on Sundays'.[108] In the early 1970s Fugard began to work more intensely with two of the members: John Kani and Winston Ntshona. Together they workshopped *Sizwe Bansi is Dead* (1972) and *The Island* (1973). Reports are mixed on the impact of these plays. Some critics argue that they were seminal to the consciousness of black mass audiences. Others suggest that black play-goers found the plays

> too complex in structure and expression, too 'talky', and too unmusical – in short, too Western in form – to be worth seeing more than once . . . Other African critics complain that characters representing the African 'common man' in Fugard's plays . . . are too shuffling, unintelligent, and unconscious; not proud enough or admirable enough to represent black suffering, values and aspirations.[109]

Either way, they became key plays in formulating new theatre in South Africa insofar as they brought together popular performance forms and the western literary drama tradition, while challenging politics through the individual stories of silenced, marginalised people. They also signalled the more multi-lingual nature of the emergent South African theatre.[110]

After the Black Consciousness Movement and state legislation made collaboration more difficult, Fugard shifted to a more internal focus in *A Lesson from Aloes* (1978) and *Dimetos* (1975). In 1982 he returned to race-related issues in *Master Harold and the Boys*. His later plays – *Playland* (1992), *My Life* (1994), *Valley Song* (1996), *The Captain's Tiger* (1997), and most recently *Sorrows and Rejoicings* (2001) – seem to have returned to his earlier, more personal focus; exploring how individuals negotiate relationships and memories.

The work of Workshop '71 and the Reverend Mqina's frequently banned *Give Us This Day* (1974) seem placed half way between Fugard's collaborative work and Kente's musicals. They combine direct criticism of Apartheid by fully conscious characters with the township musical style. This suggests the potential transformative power of the urban popular form to reach mass political consciousness. This was in sharp contrast to the use of traditional culture in shows such as Welcome Msomi's Zulu Macbeth, *uMabatha* (1972), and exploitative displays of black tradition by white producers, for example *Ipi Tombi* (1974) and *Meropa*.[111] It was also more multi-lingual than the

Serpent Players had been, thus extending the issue of language, and its potential for subversion in South African theatre, even further.

Workshop '71 combined western style improvisational 'workshop' drama techniques with township acting, song and dance to create plays that were satirical and which provoked socio-political consciousness. Beyond *Survival*, from the early to mid-1970s their plays include *uNosilimela* (1973), *Zzzip*, *uHlanga* (The Reed, 1975) and *Crossroads* (1976); the productions were usually directed by Robert Mshengu McLaren (Kavanagh).[112] *uNosilimela* was written by Credo Mtwa as an exploration of traditional values, performance forms and legend. It is an African romance that follows a traditional Zulu folk narrative (*inganekwane*) and traditional mimetic dramatisation (*umlinganiso*). The protagonist, a time-travelling princess, suffers and in her journey to self-realisation argues for traditional values as the way forward for urban Africans. Despite the traditional story and performance forms, it was both technically and conceptually challenging for township audiences in the ill-equipped township halls. This suggests how urban space and cultural context challenged traditional cultural forms and demanded new, appropriate reclamations of 'tradition'.

Fatima Dike's *Sacrifice of Kreli* (1976) is another collaborative project that used a traditional African tale to relate the past to the present. Based on the historical research of producer Rob Amato, the story takes place in 1885 and traces the efforts of Gcaleka Xhosa chief Kreli to revitalise his nation after their defeat by Cape colonial forces in 1877–8. Fatima Dike and Cape Town's Sechaba Theatre Company (founded by Amato) used the historic text to comment on the nature of and issues related to contemporary African leadership. It was performed in Xhosa for African audiences in the Cape, first in the Space, in the Transkei, and in Xhosa and English for urban racially mixed audiences elsewhere.

This is a good example of how inter-racial 'fringe' venues such as the Space in Cape Town (1972–9, later the People's Space), the Great Hall, the Box and the Nunnery at the University of Witwatersrand, and the Stable Theatre in Durban made collaboration and new work possible. Dike went on to produce *The First South African* and *Glasshouse* at the Space.

Dorkay House's Phoenix Players promoted exchange between townships and cities. Their play *Phiri* (1972) was an African jazz musical version of Jonson's *Volpone* in a township setting. It was the collaboration of Barney Simon (script and stage directions), Cyril Magubane and Mackay Davashe (music) and Gordon Wales (choreography) and was performed by local black artists. However, the official closing of the Bantu Men's Social Centre following *Phiri*'s last rehearsal boded ill for urban black culture. It also highlighted the uneasy compromise between black and white aesthetics and production values. The pressure of the Group Areas Act and growing racial polarisation saw the demise of Dorkay House and the Phoenix Players after *Phiri*. The combination of McLaren's departure for England, and the wake of the Soweto uprisings, meant that Workshop '71 could not sustain their work and many members joined either the Market Theatre in Johannesburg or the People's Space in Cape Town.

One of the most significant collaborative spaces was the Market Theatre, founded by Barney Simon and Mannie Manim as a non-racial venue in Johannesburg's Indian Fruit Market in 1976. Barney Simon was influenced by the collaborative work of Joan Littlewood in the 1950s and Athol Fugard in the 1960s. He worked in Zululand and the Transkei, running workshops in the 1970s, where he met Mannie Manim, who subsequently left PAC Transvaal to form the Company and to work on the Market Theatre with Simon.

The Market Theatre's history is controversial and diverse. The project was supported financially by Johannesburg City Council, various businesses and professionals. The trustees contravened the Group Areas Act from the start by agreeing to its being a multi-racial venue, although the ban on multi-racial companies was lifted in 1977. It evaded censorship mainly through its national and international visibility. It has hosted innumerable South African theatre practitioners, presenting both militant, contestatory theatre and traditional western plays. As one of the few non-Apartheid spaces in South Africa, it offered South Africa a glimpse of a socio-political and cultural alternative. Many significant South African plays by the Company, Junction Avenue Theatre Company and individual artists who have become central to South African theatre have premièred at the Market.

Some of the tensions that have affected the Market are its physical placement at the metropolitan centre as opposed to within the township, and its access to and use of capital from private white companies in Johannesburg. It has attempted to address some of these issues through the Laboratory, which facilitates training and exchange between artists and community groups in and beyond the area. Its significance as a space is evidenced in the artists it has facilitated, such as directors Francis and Alan Joseph, performers James Mthoba, Winston Ntshona, John Kani, Sam Williams, and Black Consciousness playwrights such as Manaka and Maponya.[113]

Barney Simon's own work was characterised by the workshop process. His collaborative plays include *Hey Listen!* (1974) adapted from his own *Jo'burg, Sis! stories, Cincinatti* (1979), *Woza Albert!* (1981), *Black Dog/ Inj'emnyama* (1984), *Outers* (1985), *Born in the RSA* (1985), *Score Me the Ages* (1989) and *Silent Movie* (1992). His plays focus on the singular experience of the individual and the restoration of dignity and respect for the individual on the margins, while taking a special interest in multi-lingual theatre.

Simon's collaboration with Mbongeni Ngema and Percy Mtwa in *Woza Albert!* suggests how various influences weave in and out to create ever-changing and evolving forms in South African theatre. Percy Mtwa had worked for Dunlop Industries before joining one of Gibson Kente's companies. Here workers' plays (discussed later), township musicals and western forms, particularly Grotowski's poor theatre, coalesce in the formation of the Earth Players and the production of *Woza Albert!*, which combines the stories of the ordinary township people so central to the musical form, with the more critical resistant focus of Black Consciousness writers. This play utilises fragmentary stories of ordinary people while drawing on one of the dominant underpinnings of South African Apartheid hegemony, namely Christianity, to question the validity of the ideology. The question tying the diverse stories together is: What would Christ's reaction be were he to return to Apartheid South Africa in his Second Coming? The play sets up a dynamic performance, at once critical and entertaining. Despite the criticism against the play for not moving beyond outlining the problem to encouraging more direct resistance for change, it is significant in its syncretic form, which signals the shifting paradigm of South African theatre and the use of the Black theological discourse. Ironically, the play does not include song or dance.

Ngema returned to musical elements in his later work *Asinamali!* (We Have No Money, 1985), a musical exploration of township rent strikes. He collaborated with Hugh Masekela on the music for *Sarafina* (1986), a play that celebrated the indomitable spirit of South African youth protesting against Apartheid education. Its success enabled Ngema to form the Committed Artists at the Market in December 1988. This group toured his last two plays abroad in 1989. He unsuccessfully attempted community theatre with *Sarafina 2* (1997), an AIDS play. In 1990 Ngema created and directed the musical play *Township Fever. Maria, Maria* (1997) returns to the theological paradigm, where Ngema musically fuses Christ's story with that of Steve Biko. Percy Mtwa went on to create *Bopha!* (1985). A mix of popular township musical and issue-based theatre is evident in this work.

The Junction Avenue Theatre Company is another group that is closely associated with the Market Theatre and which is collaborative in nature. The company was formed in the mid-1970s in Johannesburg. Although originally it had an almost exclusively young, university-educated white membership – Malcolm Purkey, William Kentridge, Pippa Stein, Astrid von Kotze, Ari Sitas and Patrick Fitzgerald – it broadened both its membership and focus in 1978 when several of Workshop '71's township members joined. Their first collaborative work was *Crossroads* (1976). This play was part of the resistance theatre that followed the Soweto uprising. The play uses individual narratives directed at the audience, mainly in English. The use of personal testimony, primarily in English but punctuated by vernacular, with some song, provided a framework for much of the theatre that followed in the late 1970s and 1980s, most obviously *Born in the RSA* (1985) and even the post-Apartheid *Ubu and the Truth Commission* (1997). It also evidenced the impact of the Black Consciousness Movement on black South African playwrights.

From the outset the focus of Junction Avenue was the exploration of personal and communal histories. For example, their first play, *The Fantastical History of a Useless Man* (1976), critically evaluates the place of the white liberal in South Africa's history. In 1978 they collaborated with Ramolao Makhene, Siphiwe Khumalo and Arthur Molepo to create *Randlords and Rotgut* for a history workshop at Witwatersrand University. This play critically explored the conflicting interests of the mining and liquor industries. In 1979 they began creating 'workshop' plays, which could be made and performed by workers. After *Ilanga and Security* (1979), a play about unemployment which helped to raise funds for members of the Food and Canning Workers Union who had been fired from Fattis and Monis, they worked on *Dikitsheng* (1980), a play about employment exploitation. This was performed by maids and their employers in suburban church halls. The group's collaboration with workers in *The Sun Also Shines: Ilanga Lizo Phumela Abasebenzi* (1980) led to the more formal development of worker theatre in Natal. Astrid von Kotze and Ari Sitas moved from Junction Avenue to join this movement.

Junction Avenue Theatre Company continued its multi-racial, histori-cally focussed theatre productions through the 1980s and 1990s, working primarily from the Market Theatre. Their plays include *Will of a Rebel* (1979), about Breyten Breytenbach, *Marabi* (1982), adapted from Modikwe Dikobe's *Marabi Dance*, *Sophiatown* (1986), which focusses on forced re-movals, *Tooth and Nail* (1989), which presents fragments of alternative South

African histories, and the musical *Love, Crime and Johannesburg* (1999). They have also produced children's theatre and educational projects. Most of the plays are created by the cast and are directed by Malcolm Purkey. The Market Theatre has also facilitated new female voices. For example, the adaptation of Elsa Joubert's novel *Die Swerfjare van Poppie Nongena* (The Long Journey of Poppie Nongena, 1982) was a powerful bearing witness of a twice marginalised voice – that of a black woman. Gcina Mhlope's work has moved oral storytelling from the margins to the centre and Reza de Wet has experimented with magic realism in exploring Afrikaner nationalism and mythology. Some of these moments will be discussed later in more detail.

The Black Consciousness Movement's impact on theatre Although some Black Consciousness supporters believed in cultural collaboration, others rejected collaboration in multi-racial theatre projects, and demanded a more confrontational stance by black artists. Groups who pioneered this movement from the 1970s, drawing their aims and ideology from the African-American Black Consciousness Movement, include: TECON (Theatre Council of Natal), founded in 1969, but soon thereafter banned; PET (People's Experimental Theatres) founded in Lenasia in 1973 to encourage black creativity; the MDALI (Music, Drama and Literature Institute, Cape Town) and SABTU (South African Black Theater Union, Natal), both founded in 1972; and Mihloti (Tears). These groups sought to inaugurate a national black culture movement, but often collapsed when their members or leaders were banned or detained.

A new generation of urban playwrights who supported the visions of these organisations and the wider Black Consciousness Movement emerged in the 1970s. Among them were Matsemela Manaka and Maishe Maponya. These artists began creating black resistance theatre that used black writers and performers to directly address their own socio-political realities, varying in degrees of radicalism. The imposition of Afrikaans as the official language of education, provoking the uprising in Soweto in 1976 and resulting in the death of Steve Biko in 1977, fuelled the theatre, which identified itself with 'resistance' or 'protest' drama. Plays were performed primarily at the Market, Space, and Baxter Theatres.

Maishe Maponya was and is an artist strongly committed to the Black Consciousness Movement and who was opposed to the popular musicals of Kente. He began writing plays in 1975 as a member of the Medupi Writers Association and was a founder member of the Bahumutsi Drama Group in

1977 and Allahpoets in 1978. He was frequently harassed by the authorities, who restricted performances of his work and withdrew his passport. His plays constitute a fearless criticism of the abuses and consequences of the Apartheid system. Some of these include *The Cry* (1976) and *Peace and Forgive* (1978). His best-known play is *The Hungry Earth* (1979), which looks at the lives of three miners in rural and urban settings and the exploitation of the industrial labour system. *Nurse* (*Umongikazi*, 1983) is about working conditions and racist practices in hospitals. *Gangsters* and *Dirty Work* (1984) was a diptych on the security state and its agents, and the harassment and torture of writers. In 1996–7 he wrote and performed *A Song for Biko*, which comments critically on post-Apartheid decisions. His plays are multi-lingual and use agitprop physical theatre techniques. They include song, dance and mime and call upon actors to play multiple roles, juxtapose scenes and styles (for example, poetic recitation and torture in *Gangsters*). The scripts themselves give little sense of the impact of the performance.

Matsemela Manaka's unique contribution lies in his innovative use of performance styles, music and paintings from the wider African and European contexts, which at that time were inaccessible to most black South Africans. He founded the Soyikwa African Theatre Group, which workshopped satirical plays in response to current events. Between 1977 and 1991 Manaka wrote fourteen plays in the workshop context. He also wrote the critical essays 'Theatre of the Dispossessed' and 'Theatre as a Physical Word'. His plays integrate European and African forms of dance, music and physical theatre to explore the major socio-economic issues of Apartheid and post-colonial Africa, including rural poverty and the results of urbanisation, detribalisation, the migrant labour system, forced removals, social disintegration in the townships, and crime. *Egoli: City of Gold* (1978–9), like earlier African theatre, is episodic and improvisational, using flashbacks, dream sequences and other non-naturalistic techniques reminiscent of Workshop' 71's productions.

Manaka contributed significantly to South African theatre in his incorporation of music and dance in his plays, particularly in collaboration with his wife, who is an accomplished dancer and teacher.[114] Their sense of physicality extends from the conscious use of theatrical images – from the steel chains around the two workers' necks at the start of *Egoli* to the mimes in *Pula* (1982), *Children of Asazi* (1984/6) and *Toro*. These mime images are embodied in the key figures in the plays, usually musicians or dancers, and move beyond thematic ornamentation to express the essence of the plays.

Manaka's perception of the place of the black artist in an urban, colonised context is evidenced by the way he combines European and African music and dance forms. For example, in *Gorée* (1989) he combines the African *djembe* and European violin with 'Venda, Tswana, Xhosa, Sepedi, Tsonga, Ndebele, Swazi, Ghanaian, Nigerian, Senegalese, ballet, contemporary and jazz dances'.[115] He does this to emphasise significant moments in the plays. It is this aspect of his work that most clearly illustrates his commitment to and sympathies with the visions of Black Consciousness and pan-Africa, as he relates his work to both the continent as a whole and to the wider diaspora. Manaka sees culture as both a unifying force and a political forum. All of his works have been managed, designed, lit, produced and directed by black artists. The plays are often scripted for all-black casts, and the few white characters his plots require are always negative portraits, usually of white authority mimed by black artists, with the use of pantomime noses and spectacles. These plays provide a vision of South Africa's reality and potential. Manaka's sense of music and dance beyond South Africa enriches his work, as he experiments profoundly with syncretic forms.

Another group of artists who were not necessarily Black Consciousness playwrights but who wrote from a resistant position were South African exiles such as Zakes Mda and Masitha Hoeane in Lesotho, Anthony Akerman in Tanzania[116] and Mongane Wally Serote in Botswana.

Somewhat apart from his contemporaries in style, Zakes (Zanemvula) Mda is nevertheless a significant figure in creating a sophisticated theatre which utilises concise dialogue and intellectual debate. From a position of exile, largely in Lesotho, much of his writing has focussed on the impact South Africa's policies have made on its border countries, particularly in the context of mining and issues related to migrant labour. He also looks at neo-colonial issues. For example, his first major play, *We Shall Sing for the Fatherland* (1978), considers the position of revolutionary soldiers in the post-revolutionary context. His next play, *The Hill* (1979), traces migrant labour and the impact it has on rural women, specifically in relation to prostitution. Other plays include *Dead End* (1979), *Dark Voices Ring* (1979), *The Road* (1982), *And Girls in their Sunday Dresses* (Edinburgh Festival, 1988), *Broken Dreams, Joys of War* (1989) and *The Nun's Romantic Story* (1995). He has also contributed considerably to theatre for development through plays that call for community social action, particularly with the Lesotho-based Marotholi Travelling Theatre Company.

Theatre for development was one of three types of alternative theatre that came to the fore during the latter part of the Apartheid era. The other two are workers' theatre and theatre-in-education.

Workers' theatre   Alongside emergent syncretic theatre, the South African political economy provoked experimental theatre from black miners, industrial workers and urban squatters. In 1978 Phyllis Klotz collaborated with the women of the Crossroads squatter camp to create *Imfoduso*, a play which dramatised their resistance to the police's forcible removal of them back to the homelands. It was first performed in the community, toured other black communities and was finally performed at the Market Theatre in Johannesburg. Three women, Nomvula Qosha, Thobeka Maqutyana and Poppy Tsira, went on to collaborate with Phyllis Klotz on *You Strike the Women You Strike the Rock* (1986), a play outlining issues related to migrant labour under Apartheid. These plays give the women's personal perspectives on the struggle and their positions on the fringe of a township in Cape Town, thus moving away from general politics to the specific implications of Apartheid policies for individual people.

Ilanga lizophumela abasebenzi (The Sun Will Rise for the Workers) is a workers' play that developed out of the defence of fifty-five Zulu foundrymen who were illegally arrested in 1980 in Johannesburg. For the purposes of the defence, the union lawyer Halton Cheadle had them act out the events of the strike. This led to the elaboration of their roles and performances into a full-scale play. The workers demanded accurate reconstructions of statements and events from one another until consensus was achieved. Junction Avenue Theatre Company helped them to adapt the re-enactment for the courtroom. Despite the fact that the workers lost the trial, they performed the theatre piece for co-workers at the Metal and Allied Workers Union Hall, and later at the University of the Witwatersrand. This theatre was significant as a reflexive theatre form, which combined docu-drama with more traditional African styles of direct address, with performers moving among spectators and encouraging their engagement and response. Its impact was great, as thousands of workers throughout the country saw *Ilanga* on videotape.[117]

Astrid von Kotze was particularly involved in recording the processes and effects of the Natal Workers Movement from 1983 to 1987, most notably for the Dunlop Play in 1983. These workshopped plays gave participants a forum in which to formulate their grievances and the issues relating to their working conditions and a new sense of self-worth and confidence.

Leaders emerged from the process, new social networks were created among workers and there was greater resistance to mistreatment. In her book on the movement, von Kotze suggests that another outcome of the workshops and travelling to perform was that the workers 'learnt about their common history, both in Dunlop and the wider context of South African labour history'.[118]

The Durban Workers' Cultural Local (DWCL) was formed in 1983 and existed until 1986. Key figures in this organisation were Alfred Qabula, Naftal Matiwane and Nise Malange from the Transport and General Workers Union (T&G), who were all originally involved in the Dunlop Play. They wanted culture to play a central role in union affairs, and so various projects were undertaken. In collaboration with Ari Sitas and the Culture and Working Life Project (CWLP), Elias Banda from the National Union of Textile Workers (NUTW) and later Jabu Ndlovu from PWAWU (Paper, Wood and Allied Workers Union, later Printing), created *Why Lord.* In 1984 the regional education committee of FOSATU (the Federation of South African Trade Unions) requested help for a project in Pinetown. They created *K'oze kube nini* (How Long Will We Suffer? Milner Park, Johannesburg, 1984), a play about migrancy and the labour-drafting of workers in the countryside. The group went on to work with women in the play *Kwa Mashu Streetcleaners.* Sadly, this play was never finished because of mobility issues and on-going conflicts. The women did, however, receive a pay increase in 1986. An awareness of the processes used by Fugard and Kente and of plays such as *Woza Albert!* and *Umabatha* (the Zulu *Macbeth*) fed into these plays.

May Day 1985 saw a mass workers' cultural event, with speeches, songs, dances, poetry and plays, at the Curries Fountain soccer stadium in Durban.[119] Plays performed included *Once Bitten Twice Shy*, a play on migrancy including the clash between traditional values and an urban lifestyle, particularly between generations, and *The Spar Play I*, about unfair dismissals. Performance circumstances were difficult, as the crowd was large and the performers nervous. Despite this, the event signalled the cultural aspirations of workshopped people's plays.

Other plays to emerge from the movement were *Usuku* (The Day, 1985), performed at the T&G union's AGM at the Edendale Ecumenical Centre, a play which argues that the struggle requires sacrifice. It deals with people's fear of losing a wage or pension, which results in their holding back from uniting. *Gallows for Mr Scariot* is a play about retrenchment which was re-workshopped and rehearsed in Johannesburg with William Kentridge and

Ramolao Makhene from Junction Avenue Theatre Company. It opened as *Mpimpi* (Black Manager) at the Clairwood Trade Union and Cultural Centre in October 1985. This figure would recur through later plays, as does the issue of collaboration and solidarity.

In response to the declaration of a national state of emergency, the Congress of South African Trade Unions (COSATU) was launched in King's Park Stadium, Durban, in December 1986. Here Alfred Qabula became a formidable figure as an urban imbongi. Besides helping in the creations of plays, he addressed workers in the traditional praise form, with the poem 'The Tears of a Creator'. Here one sees a clear interweaving of traditional performance forms with contemporary urban politico-economic issues and the consequent development of new forms.

Other plays performed by the Metal and Allied Workers' Union Congress (MAWU) in Johannesburg in 1986 include *You're a Failure Mr Mpimpi*, which addressed spying by the *impimpis* (black managers), and *Ithesho* (The Job), about how gangsters are not born, but are people who resort to crime because of unemployment. *Mkhumbane*, the story of the shack community of Mkumbane, and *Qonda* (Vigilantes), which looks at the clash between 'comrades' and 'vigilantes' or bodyguards to township councillors, were performed by the Natal Regional Culture Meeting at Howard College in Durban in September 1986.

By mid-1986 cultural centres had spread through Natal to Ladysmith, Hammersdale, Howick, Port Shepstone, Pinetown and Newcastle under the general auspices of COSATU. The plays set out to 'reflect workers' concerns about the workplace and home'. The role of culture was 'to forge links between workers and the township community, especially the youth'.[120] At the end of 1987 many union leaders were attacked, arrested or murdered. COSATU responded by consciously building structures for activities on an even larger scale.[121]

Workers' theatre and its blending of traditional performance forms with new socio-politically relevant urban contexts overlaps with theatre for development projects, which focus on community participation and cultural action for conscientisation,[122] and also theatre-in-education projects. Much of South Africa's early theatre for development was associated with Mda and his Marotholi Travelling Theatre in Lesotho. Other examples include Manaka's literacy play *Koma* (1986), Doreen Mazibuko's voter-education play *Moments* and Maponya's Winterveld project with unemployed squatter camp youths.

The drama departments at the Universities of Zululand and Pietermar-itzburg have done much work in theatre. Drama-in-education was very important because most plays written in African languages for schools were never performed, or were performed only on radio, thus practical projects needed encouragement.[123] Other examples of such projects are Manaka's performances of *Julius Caesar* in Setswana and English in rural areas, the Market Theatre's taking *Romeo and Juliet* to the riot-township of Sebokeng, and the on-going work of the Junction Avenue Theatre Company and the Handspring Puppet Company in education projects using theatre and film.

Contemporary text-based drama   The playwrighting tradition es-tablished by the NTO from which people such as Butler, Manson, W. A. de Klerk and Uys Krige emerged, continued through the PAC's producing P. G. du Plessis, Chris Barnard, N. P. van Wyk Louw, James Ambrose Brown and by the mid-1970s the Grahamstown Festival. Later playwrights have included Bartho Smit, Deon Opperman, Reza de Wet, Charles Fourie, Paul Slabolepszy and Pieter-Dirk Uys, whose satires trace political conditions in South Africa from the early 1970s. These satires fit into the cabaret tradition in South Africa, which draws on European political cabaret of the Weimar years, especially Brecht.[124] Throughout, Fugard has moved between scripted and collaborative work. In the mid-1990s there was a strong return to this tradition.

Reza de Wet was one of the most fascinating South Africa writers to emerge in the 1980s. Using magic realism, she writes critically about the socio-political realities of Afrikaans society from a personal, feminist per-spective. Her first play, *Deep Ground* (*Diepe Grond,* 1985) was published in *Vrystaat-Trilogie* (*Free-State Trilogy*) with *Op Dees Aarde* (On This Earth, 1986) and *Nag, Generaal* (Goodnight, General, 1988). This trilogy uses the micro-cosm of a physically and psychically sick Afrikaans family to reflect on the consequences of Calvinist religion and Apartheid politics on the individual and society as a whole. She won the Prize for Afrikaans Drama in 1994 for her second trilogy, *Trits,* which includes *Mis* (Dung/Mass, 1993), *Mirakel* (Miracle, 1992) and *Drif* (Crossings, 1994). In these plays she focusses more particularly on the repressed female figure who is freed by an ambiguous, ambivalent magician. The trilogy is consciously constructed in the genre of the Medieval play cycle, with the three episodes in three different spaces. Her sequel to Chekhov, *Drie Susters II* (Three Sisters II) premièred in 1997. It looks at a rural Afrikaans family in post-Apartheid South Africa. Her English plays include *In a Different Light* (1988) and *A Worm in the Bud* (1990). They reflect on Afrikaaners and black South Africans from an English perspective. De Wet's plays challenge South Africa both via her use of genre and politically through her feminist perspective framed by her detailed Afrikaans cultural context.

The South African Indian playwrights who refer to their work as Indic theatre (South African Indian intercultural practice) have developed a particular body of plays. In the 1960s Krishna Shah, from east India, led workshops at the Durban Academy of Theatre Arts, which people such as Muthal Naidoo[125] attended and developed into the Shah Theatre Academy in 1963. This academy focussed on Indian and local black plays. Muthal Naidoo's years as a student and lecturer in the United States from 1965 to 1972, where she developed a black theatre programme and directed plays by African authors such as Soyinka, influenced her sense of identity as a theatre practitioner in South Africa after her return to the country in 1976. She resumed work with the Shah Theatre, and identified herself with the students' protest movement in the 1980s. Her play *Of No Account* (Market, 1982) explores racism and sexism in an office; *We Three Kings* (1992) explores the South African Indian Council Elections, but *Oh God!*, whose title she changed to *Lucy's Dilemma* (short for Lucifer) was never performed. The innovative inter-cultural and feminist aspects of her work are evident in *Flight from the Mahabareth* (1995), which challenges traditional Indian gender roles through the Hindu paradigm of the holy *Mahabarata*. She exemplifies the development of approaches to race and gender discourses from the perspective of a marginalised community that has developed new theatrical forms progressively from the 1970s to the present in South Africa.

Other Indic theatre figures are Ronnie and Kessie Govender and Kriben Pillay. In 1978 Kessie Govender formed the Stable Theatre in Durban, which became the focus for Durban-based black theatre. He wrote *Working Class Hero* in 1979, which examined the effects of segregation across the racial divide; his *The Shack* (1979) was banned in Soweto. Kriben Pillay has evolved styles from traditional Indian performance and adapted these to the issues and forms of South African society and theatre in the musicals *Side by Side Masisizane* (1992) and *Coming Home* (1993) and the play *Looking for Muruga* (1991).

By the early 1990s a strange reversal had occurred in South African theatre – the margin had become the centre and state theatre became marginalised. After Apartheid ended in 1994, theatre had to redefine its artistic and political aims and focus. The cultural boycott ended, exiles returned, censorship was lifted and new challenges emerged. As the role, function and leadership of political, cultural and educational institutions were re-evaluated, so the allocation of resources shifted. As artists searched for a focus, there were many revivals of classic texts such as *Woza Albert!* and *The Island* and an increase in escapist musicals. Young playwrights began to explore the implications of change in the urban context – for example, Sue-Pam Grant's depiction of a decaying inner Johannesburg in *Curl Up and Dye* (1989), and Paul Slabolepzsy's *Mooi Street Moves* (1992), which revisits *Jim Comes to Jo'burg*. The Handspring Puppet Company, under William Kentridge, was another innovative company to emerge in the 1990s. This company evolved out of Junction Avenue Theatre Company and utilises collaborative theatre-making techniques to explore post-colonial issues framed by classic playwrights such as Büchner in *Woycek on the Highveld* (1992), Goethe in *Faustus in Africa!* (1995), and Jarry in *Ubu and the Truth Commission* (1998), and by Monteverdi in *Il Ritorno d'Ulisse* (1999). Its innovation has extended to combine multi-media animated drawings, video, puppets, actors and music in stage explorations of history and the individual's sense of 'truth'. In a significant way this is the culmination of many of the traditions of South Africa, beginning with storytelling, European popular theatre, the intervention of cinema, Fugard and previous artists 'bearing witness' to their own and other people's lives.

The extraordinary energy of post-Apartheid South African theatre is most evident in the variety of performances, styles and topics at the many festivals. As the PACs have disintegrated and so many experimental theatres folded or struggled to survive, so their role has been subsumed into a network of festivals. Their role has shifted from promoting particular forms of theatre – English at Grahamstown, Afrikaans at Oudtshoorn – to promoting performance ranging from ritual and ceremony of amateur township-based performances (for example, Brett Bailey and the Third World Bunfight's *iMumbo Jumbo and The Days of Miracle and Wonder* and *Ipi Tombi?*) to mainstream theatre and many dance productions in over thirty places. Dance has become a particularly dynamic, inter-cultural form which transcends language barriers, as can be seen in the consistently exciting and challenging cross-cultural work of Robyn Orlin's company and Jazzart in Cape Town, which combines innovative dance with effective community-based outreach programmes. Festivals are where all the factors and forms discussed in this chapter come together, where people like Kentridge and Fugard launch their new work; where in 2001 David Kramer presented his project *Karoo Kitaar Blues*, in which rural Karoo guitar players demonstrated the diversity and richness of their instruments, styles and compositions; where local pop artists play alongside *stoepstories* (verandah narratives). There has been an explosion of restaurant theatres in most city centres and all of these performers network and interact at the various festivals.

With the opening out of resources, cultural interaction and the pluralising of festivals, one hopes that South African theatre will continue evolving as a critical, subversive, paradoxical combination of multiple worlds and languages. Perhaps only cultural forms can both explore and express the complexities of the contradictory histories and identities that constitute South Africa.

Notes

1. See Bosman, Binge, and Fletcher for early histories, and Coplan, Hauptfleisch, Larlham, Kavanagh, Orkin, Steadman and Kruger for later studies. Special thanks to Professors Hauptfleisch, Zulu and Omotoso for their comments and advice on early drafts of this chapter.
2. Kruger, 1999: 17.
3. For details see Vail and White, 1991, Opland, 1983: 1–31.
4. Brown, 1998: 10.
5. For an analysis of the issues and processes involved, see Bassnett-McGuire, 1980 and Guenther, 2001.
6. See, for example, the impact of the comparative discussions of Parry and Lord regarding various oral poetries in the 1920s and 1930s. Both treat oral poetry as a universal genre, characterised by common techniques, emergent from specific and disparate historical contexts and circumstances.
7. Yai, 1989: 5.
8. Vail and White, 1991: 3–15.
9. Jameson, 1988: 175.
10. Diacritic notes such as / X, !K, //k refer to click consonants in the various San languages. Wilhelm Bleek and Lucy Lloyd began recording these languages in the nineteenth century. Their *Bushman Dictionary* was donated to the Bleek Collection at the University of Cape Town by Professor J. A. Engelbrecht in 1961. The /Xam and !Kung refer to different San peoples of southern Africa. They are as distinct as the Zulu and Xhosa people are from one another.
11. Biesele, 1993: xix.
12. Hewitt, 1985: 650.
13. Their names were /A!kumta, //Kabbo, /Han≠kass'o, Dia!kwain, ≠Kasin and !Kweiten ta //ken (Deacon, 2001: 11).
14. Jeanette Deacon and Thomas Dowson (2001) have collated papers on the Bleek and Lloyd collection, which include analysis of this work from the 1990s linguistic and archeological perspectives. These debates impact on any attempt to write a retrospective history.

15. For discussion of this see Brown, 1998: 35.
16. Biesele traces how this is being attempted in 1993: xii; 2001: 142–60.
17. Traced in Lewis-Williams, 1981, 1990; 2000; 11; Lewis-Williams and Dowson, 1989.
18. For details see Hewitt, 1985: 651; Brown, 1998: 49.
19. Brown, 1998: 50–1; Guenther, 2001: 96.
20. Adaptation Bleek and Lloyd 1911: 9; Brown, 1998: 65.
21. Quoted in Biesele 1976: 308; Brown 1998: 530.
22. Guenther, 2001: 88, 91.
23. Biesele, 2001: 303.
24. Brown 1998: 62.
25. Lewis-Williams, 1990: 28–30.
26. Transcribed in Bleek and Lloyd, 1911: 235.
27. Lewis-Williams, 1990: 86, from the Bleek and Lloyd translation; Brown gives an alternative translation, 1998: 69.
28. Bleek and Lloyd, 1911: 236.
29. Dhlomo, 1993: 202.
30. The former term refers to the orthography used in pre-1994 South Africa and Lesotho, which is still used in Lesotho. The latter is the current orthography used in South Africa. I shall refer to both throughout, with the contemporary given first.
31. Cole-Beuchat, 1993: 39–45.
32. Fugard, 1983: 172. See Walder, 1992 for an analysis of this aspect of Fugard's plays.
33. For details of these songs see Vilakazi, 1993: 69–73.
34. For a full explanation as to how and why this has happened, see Franz, 1993.
35. This section relies heavily on Larlham, 1985, which provides much more detail on forms and influences than can be discussed here. Unless otherwise signalled, this is the primary source used.
36. For details, see Vilakazi, 1993: 74; Larlham, 1985: 21–46; Brown, 1998: 119–63.
37. Quoted from various sources in Gunner, 1982: 100; she discusses the contemporising of the classic praise poem in her article, pp. 99–108.
38. Larlham, 1985: 53–4.
39. James, 1994: 80–109.
40. Quoted from ICU in Orkin, 1991: 11.
41. Vilakazi suggests that rhythm is established by the pace and style of delivery, the use of repetition and by parallelism, which is powerfully evocative. Rhythmic structure is defined by 'breath-group' of verbal units defined by the performer's regular pauses for breath (1993: 61–7). Cope traces the use of parallelism into three types, and also the use of each. For discussion, see Brown, 1998: 103–4.
42. Some of P. A. Cook's recordings and translations during a visit to Swaziland in 1929 are available in Cook, 1993: 160–75.

43. Examples may be read in Lekgothoane, 1993: 132–53, with their English transcriptions and notes.

44. See Grant 1993: 85, and pp. 86–117 for discussion of the form and transcriptions of poems by Gwebisa, who belonged to the Manhlakazi section of the Zulus in the 1920s.

45. James Stuart was the first to record Zulu praise poems, which he undertook between 1888 and 1912 during his years of service in what is now Kwa-Zulu Natal. He meticulously transcribed and annotated most of the leading oral poets in the region. Many of his informants were men old enough to provide first-hand accounts stretching back to Dingane's reign. Stuart collected and transcribed 258 poems during his travels in Natal. These were later translated by Daniel Malcolm, and were published posthumously by Cope in 1968, with further editing or 'polishing'. Each of these stages has created problems explored in detail in Brown (1998: 80–113). The manuscripts of Stuart's transcriptions and annotations are in the Campbell collection archives, and copies of Stuart's sound recordings are in the SOAS archives, University of London. Sections have been published in Webb and Wright's *James Stuart Archive*, volumes I–IV, 1976, 1979, 1982, 1986.

46. See Dhlomo on the function of such warrior *izibongo*; 1977: 48.

47. Gunner, 1989b traces contemporary women using the traditional form, particularly in urban contexts.

48. It has since been appropriated by urban women. See James, 1994 and Kashula, 2002 for details.

49. Opland, 1983: 258.

50. Cf. Grant, 1993: 86.

51. Coplan, 1987: 12. See Scheub, 1987 for detail.

52. Brown outlines the performance aspects in detail in 1998: 75–97.

53. Snead, 1984: 67; Brown, 1998: 108.

54. In the first phase, up to about 1859, the poetry accepts Mzilikazi's power as supreme, legitimates and celebrates the achievements of his leadership, criticises aspects of his leadership and allows ordinary people to present requests and comments (1991: 92). In the second phase, the poetry begins establishing a 'history' of past events. The focus is on nation-building and legitimising power (Vail and White, 1991: 95–102). The third phase of Ndebele history, dating from the 1890s, focuses on a new ethnic awareness and revival. Challenged by Xhosa and Shona speakers, Ndebele ethnic consciousness became an issue and praise poetry was revived as part of a cultural development (1991: 102–6).

55. Barber, 1989: 14.

56. Gunner, 1984: 36.

57. Opland, 1983: 72.

58. Opland, 1987: 13.

59. White, 1982.

60. Coplan, 1987: 13.
61. For discussion and examples see Von Kotze, 1988; Horn, 1996; Brown, 1998: 213–56; Kaschula, 2002.
62. Bosman, 1928, 1980 provide detailed accounts of early history of South African European theatre in Dutch. Jill Fletcher, 1994 has made key aspects of Bosman's accounts more accessible in English. These publications are the major sources for this section.
63. Bouws, 1982: 13.
64. For details see Fletcher, 1994: 43–52.
65. Original manuscripts in the Jagger Library, University of Cape Town.
66. Fletcher, 1994: 35.
67. Ibid., 73, 77.
68. *Cape Times*, 3 August 1877.
69. *Cape Argus*, 23 January 1882.
70. Fletcher, 1994: 125.
71. Ibid., 128.
72. Ibid.
73. Stodel, 1962: 175.
74. For detailed analysis of this see Merrington, 1995; Hopkins, 1997; Kruger, 1999.
75. *Historical Sketch*, 1910: 99, 95.
76. Peterson, 2000: 5. He traces the development of theatre in Durban and Johannesburg, in particular the influence of mission education, focussing on the work of Vilakazi, Dhlomo, the Bantu Dramatic Society and the British Drama League.
77. For discussion see Orkin, 1991: 7–10.
78. Orkin, 1985: 33.
79. For discussion of these songs, see e.g. Kruger, 1999: 57. There is another comparison, that can be made between this and Ogunde's use of popular culture, particularly songs in Nigerian popular theatre.
80. Dhlomo, 1977: 7.
81. Couzens, 1985: 51.
82. See Orkin 1991: 234–48; Orkin, 1987; Visser, 1998; and Johnson, 1998 for critiques of how Shakespeare has been used in cultural indoctrination in Africa, and how the texts have been used subversively in return.
83. Kavanagh, 1985: 45.
84. For details, see Coplan, 1985: 90–2.
85. Ibid., 115–21.
86. Cited in Orkin, 1991: 24.
87. See Steadman, 1985: 84ff.
88. Quoted in Kavanagh, 1985: 45.
89. Ibid., 46; Orkin, 1991: 24, 25.
90. Kruger, 1999: 58–9.

91. Coplan, 1985: 56, 60. In this section much of the information related to syncretic musical performance is drawn from Coplan, 1985.

92. See Tomaselli, 1991 and Marx, 1996 on the influence of American *film noir* on gangs and the South African black urban identity; Coplan, 1985: 93–4 for Vilakazi; and Peterson, 2000: 127–35 for Phillips's role in promoting film through BMSC to control mine workers.

93. Coplan, 1985: 98–101, 1987b. He underlines the importance of Kimberley in the development of difele/ sefela, as by 1987 180,000 Lesotho men working as migrant labourers had worked at Kimberley. This is often compared to the biblical city of Sodom in the songs, and becomes a geographic metaphor for life at the mines (Coplan, 1987: 4).

94. In Coplan, 1985: 96–7.

95. The term came from the Cape and referred to rotating cattle auctions or the stock fairs of English settlers in the nineteenth century. Later it referred to a working-class cooperative. For detail see Coplan, 1985: 102–4.

96. Coplan compares this with modern black American performances that toured in small towns in the 1920s; 1985: 126.

97. Ibid., 127–8.

98. Kruger, 1999: 10.

99. Orkin, 1991: 54.

100. Kavanagh, 1985: 47.

101. Van Wyk, 1995: 51.

102. Coplan explores the problems of definition and terminology, debates over the terms 'black', 'alternative', 'committed' and 'popular' theatre to explore theatre 'that advances the interests of the politically excluded, economically exploited, socially subordinated majority of South Africa' (1987: 6). While acknowledging the arguments for each term, he argues that the term 'black' theatre is most likely 'to stick' because of 'the implicit popular recognition of who this theatre is really for and about' (1987: 7). I have chosen to use 'black theatre' throughout.

103. For information on these organisations see Kavanagh, 1985: 49–50 and Coplan, 1985: 205.

104. Coplan explores the development and complexities of collaborations and evolving forms (1985: 143–80) and Orkin traces the representative problems and artists' grievances with management (1991: 72–80).

105. Coplan, 1987: 18.

106. Maponya, 2001: 310.

107. These plays were seldom performed outside of the townships, and western aesthetics and expectations are often hugely different from those of the township audiences, for whom the work was created.

108. Nkonyeni, July 2001.

109. Coplan, 1985: 215.

110. See Temple Hauptfleisch 1988 and 1989 on multilingual theatre in South Africa.

111. See Coplan, 1985: 217–19 for the history of and objections to *Ipi Tombi*.
112. For his article on Workshop '71, see McLaren, 1996.
113. For a detailed commentary on the complexities of this venue's history, past and present, see Kruger, 1999, chapters 7 and 8.
114. For detail on the various influences, see the introduction to Manaka's plays by Davis, 1997.
115. Victor Metsoamere quoted in Davis, 1997: 37.
116. For an outline of his theatre work in exile, particularly with reference to Fugard's plays, and his own play *Somewhere on the Border* (The Hague, 1982), see Akerman, 1996: 89–100.
117. Coplan, 1987: 23.
118. Von Kotze, 1988: 39. Unless indicated, von Kotze is the source for the detail in this section.
119. Hlongwane reflects on a similar cultural day in 1989 in his article, 1994: 199–202.
120. Von Kotze, 1988: 77.
121. For details on COSATU structure and projects from 1986 to 1992, see Sitas, 1996: 132–9, and for comments on the use of traditional performance forms by Dhlomo, Kunene, Gwala, Vilani, Zondi, Hlatswhayo and Qabula, see Sitas, 1994: 139–62. For an exploration of how this relates to the construction of identity, see Gready, 1994: 163–98.
122. For a discussion of comparative theatre for development movements, see Mda, 1993: 146ff.; 1994: 203–10.
123. See for example Dalrymple, 1987.
124. For outlines of specific work and the history of cabaret in South Africa, see the special issue of *SATJ* 8.2 (1994).
125. For information on Naidoo see her interview with Perkins, 1999: 113–15.

References and further reading

Akerman, A. 1996. 'Theatre in Exile', in G. V. Davis and A. Fuchs, eds., *Theatre and Change in South Africa*, Amsterdam: Harwood Academic Press.

Barber, K. 1989. 'Interpreting Oríkì as History and as Literature', in K. Barber and P. F. de Moraes Farias, eds., *Discourse and its Disguises: The Interpretation of African Oral Texts*, Birmingham: Birmingham University Press.

Barber, K. and de Moraes Farias, P. F., eds. 1989. *Discourse and its Disguises: The Interpretation of African Oral Texts*. Birmingham: Birmingham University Press.

Bassnett-McGuire, S. 1980. *Translation Studies*. London: Methuen.

Bhekizizwe, P. 2000. *Monarchs, Missionaries, African Intellectuals – African Theatre and the Unmaking of Colonial Marginality*. Johannesburg: Witwatersrand University Press.

Biesele, M. 1993. *Women Like Meat: The Folklore and Foraging Ideology of the Kalahari Ju/hoan*. Johannesburg and Bloomington: Witwatersrand University Press and Indiana University Press.

Biesele, M. 1995. ' "Different people just have different minds": A Personal Attempt to Understand Ju/'hoan Storytelling Aesthetics'. *Current Writing*, 7.2.

Biesele, M. 2001. ' "He stealthily lightened at his brother-in-law" and thunder echoes in San oral tradition a century later', in Jeanette Deacon and Thomas Dowson, eds., *Voices from the Past: /Xam San and the Bleek and Lloyd Collection*, Johannesburg: Witwatersrand University Press.

Binge, L. W. 1969. *Ontwikkeling van die Afrikaanse Toneel*. Pretoria: J. L. van Schaik.

Bleek, W. H. I. and Lloyd, L. C. 1911. *Specimens of San Folklore*. London: George Allen and Co.

Bosman, F. C. L. 1928. *Drama en Toneel in Suid-Afrika*, vol. I. Cape Town: J. Dusseau and Co.

Bosman, F. C. L. 1980. *Drama en Toneel in Suid-Afrika*, vol. II. Pretoria: J. L. van Schaik.

Bouws, J. 1982. *Solank daar musik is*. Cape Town: Tafelberg.

Brown, D. 1998. *Voicing the Text: South African Oral Poetry and Performance*. Oxford: Oxford University Press.

Canonici, N. 1999. 'Interplay Between Orality and Literacy in Zulu Literature', in J. Smit, ed., *The Dancing Dwarf from the Land of the Spirits*, Durban: Centre for the Study of Southern African Literature and Languages (CSSALL).

Cape Argus, 23 January 1882.

Cape Times, 3 August 1877.

Chapman, M. 1996. *Southern African Literatures*. Harlow: Longman.

Cole-Beuchat, P. D. 1993. 'Notes of Some Folklore Forms in Tsonga and Ronga', in R. H. Kaschula, ed., *Foundations in Southern African Oral Literature*, Johannesburg: Witwatersrand University Press.

Cook, P. A. W. 1993. 'History and Izibongo of the Swazi Chiefs', in R. H. Kaschula, ed., *Foundations in Southern African Oral Literature*, Johannesburg: Witwatersrand University Press.

Coplan, D. 1985. *In Township Tonight! South Africa's Black City Music and Theatre*. Johannesburg: Ravan Press.

Coplan, D. 1987a. 'Dialectics of Tradition in South African Black Popular Theatre'. *Critical Arts*, 4.3.

Coplan, D. 1987b. 'The Power of Oral Poetry: Narrative Songs of the Basotho Migrants'. *Research in African Literatures*, 18.

Couzens, T. 1985. *The New African: A Study of the Life and Work of H. I. E. Dhlomo*. Johannesburg: Ravan Press.

Dalrymple, L. 1987. 'Exploration in Drama, Theatre and Education: A Critique of Theatre Studies in Natal'. Unpublished Ph.D. thesis, University of Natal.

Davis, G., ed., 1997. *Beyond the Echoes of Soweto: Five Plays by Matsemela Manaka*. Amsterdam: Harwood Academic Press.

Davis, G. V. and Fuchs, A., eds. 1996. *Theatre and Change in South Africa*. Amsterdam: Harwood Academic Press.

Dhlomo, H. I. E. 1977. 'Drama and the African'. *Literary Criticism and the Theory of H. I. E. Dhlomo*, special issue of *English in Africa*, 4.2.

Dhlomo, H. I. E. 1993. 'Nature and Variety of Tribal Drama', in R. H. Kaschula, ed., *Foundations in Southern African Oral Literature*, Johannesburg: Witwatersrand University Press.

Fletcher, J. 1994. *The Story of Theatre in South Africa: 1780–1930*. Cape Town: Vlaeberg.

Fortune, G. 1993. 'Some Recurrent Structures in Shona Praise', in R. H. Kaschula, ed., *Foundations in Southern African Oral Literature*, Johannesburg: Witwatersrand University Press.

Franz, G. H. 1993. 'The Literature of Lesotho', in R. H. Kaschula, ed., *Foundations in Southern African Oral Literature*, Johannesburg: Witwatersrand University Press.

Fuchs, A. 1990. *Playing the Market: The Market Theatre, Johannesburg, 1976–1986*. Amsterdam: Harwood Academic Press.

Fugard, A. 1983. *Notebooks 1960–1977*. Johannesburg: Ad Donker.

Grant, E. W. 1993. 'The Izibongo of the Zulu Chiefs', in R. H. Kaschula, ed., *Foundations in Southern African Oral Literature*, Johannesburg: Witwatersrand University Press.

Gready, P. 1994. 'Political Autobiography in Search of Liberation: Working-Class Theatre, Collaboration and Construction of Identity', in L. Gunner, ed., *Politics and Performance*, Johannesburg: Witwatersrand University Press.

Guenther, M. G. 2001. 'Attempting to Recontextualise /Xam Oral Tradition', in J. Deacon and T. Dowson, eds., *Voices from the Past: /Xam Bushmen and the Bleek and Lloyd Collection*, Johannesburg: Witwatersrand University Press.

Gunner, E. 1982. 'New Wine in Old Bottles: Imagery in the Izibongo of the Zulu Zionist Prophet, Isaiah Shembe'. *Anthropological Society of Oxford Journal*, 13.

Gunner, E. 1984. 'Ukubonga Nezibongo: Zulu Praising and Praises'. D.Phil. thesis, School of Oriental and African Studies, University of London.

Gunner, E. 1989a. 'Orality and Literacy: Dialogue and Silence', in K. Barber and P. F. de Moraes Farias, eds., *Discourse and its Disguises: The Interpretation of African Oral Texts*, Birmingham: Birmingham University Press.

Gunner, E. 1989b. 'Songs of Innocence and Experience: Women as Composers and Performers of "Izibongo", Zulu Praise Poetry', in C. Clayton, ed., *Women and Writing in South Africa*, London: Heinemann.

Gunner, L. 1994. *Politics and Performance: Theatre, Poetry and Song in Southern Africa*. Johannesburg: Witwatersrand University Press.

Gunner, L. 1995. 'Remaking the Warrior? The Role of Orality in the Liberation Struggle and Post-Apartheid South Africa'. *Current Writing*, 7.2.

Hauptfleisch, T. 1988. 'Multilingual Theatre and Apartheid Society (1970–1987)'. Proceedings of the XIIth Congress of the International Comparative Literature Association, Munich, vol. IV.

Hauptfleisch, T. 1989. 'Citytalk, Theatretalk: Dialect, Dialogue and Multilingual Theatre in South Africa'. *English in Africa*, 16.1.

Hauptfleisch, T. 1997a. *Theatre and Society in South Africa*. Pretoria: J. L. van Schaik.

Hauptfleisch, T. 1997b. 'Theatre in South Africa', in *The World Encyclopaedia of Contemporary Theatre*, vol. III, *Africa*, ed. Don Rubin, London and New York: Routledge.

Hewitt, R. 1985. 'The Oral Literature of the San and Related Peoples', in B. W. Andrzejewski *et al.*, eds., *Literatures in African Languages: Theoretical Issues and Sample Surveys*, Cambridge: Cambridge University Press.

Historical Sketch and Description of the Pageant held at Cape Town on the Occasion of the Opening of the First Parliament of the Union of South Africa. 1910 Cape Town: Pageant Committee.

Hlongwane, A. K. 1994. 'Reflections on a Cultural Day of Artists and Workers on 16 April 1989', in L. Gunner, ed., *Politics and Performance*, Johannesburg: Witwatersrand University Press.

Horn, P. 1996. 'What is a Tribal Dress? The "Imbongi" (Praise Singer) and the "People's Poet." Reactivation of a Tradition in the Liberation Struggle', in *Theatre and Change in South Africa*, ed. G. V. Davis and A. Fuchs, Amsterdam: Harwood Academic Press.

James, D. 1994. '*Basadi ba baeng*/ Visiting Women: Female Migrant Performance from the Northern Transvaal', in L. Gunner, ed., *Politics and Performance*, Johannesburg: Witwatersrand University Press.

Jameson, F. 1988. 'Marxism and Historicism', in *The Ideologies of Theory: Essays 1971–1986*, vol. II, *The Syntax of Theory*, London and New York: Routledge.

Jeyifo, B. 1996. 'The Reinvention of Theatrical Tradition: Critical Discourses on Interculturalism in the African Theatre', in P. Pavis, ed., *The Intercultural Performance Reader*, London and New York: Routledge.

Johnson, D. 1998. 'From the Colonial and Post-Colonial: Shakespeare and Education in Africa', in A. Loomba and M. Orkin, ed., *Post-Colonial Shakespeares*, London and New York: Routledge.

Kaschula, R. H., ed. 1993. *Foundations in Southern African Oral Literature*. Johannesburg: Witwatersrand University Press.

Kaschula, R. H. 2002. *The Bones of the Ancestors are Shaking: Xhosa Oral Poetry in Context*. Lansdowne: Juta.

Kavanagh, R. 1985. *Theatre and Cultural Struggle in South Africa*. London: Zed Books.

Kendall, L. 1999. 'Whose Stories are These? Basotho Women's Tales as a Bridge between Orature and Literature', in J. Smit, ed., *The Dancing Dwarf from the Land of the Spirits*, Durban: CSSALL.

Kruger, L. 1999. *The Drama of South Africa: Plays, Pageants and Publics since 1910*. London and New York: Routledge.

Larlham, P. 1985. *Black Theater, Dance and Ritual in South Africa*. Ann Arbor: University of Michigan Press.

Lekhotholoane, S. N. 1993. 'Praise of Animals in Northern Sotho', in R. H. Kaschula, ed., *Foundations in Southern African Oral Literature*, Johannesburg: Witwatersrand University Press.

Lestrade, 1937. 'Traditional Literature', in I. Schapera, ed., *The Bantu-Speaking Tribes of South Africa: An Ethnographic Survey*, Cape Town: Maskew Miller, 1996.

Lewis-Williams, J. D. 1981. *Believing and Seeing: Symbolic Meaning in Southern San Rock Paintings*. New York: Academic Press.

Lewis-Williams, J. D. 1990. *Discovering Southern African Rock Art*. Cape Town and Johannesburg: David Philip.

Lewis-Williams, J. D. and Dowson, T. M. 1989. *Images of Power: Understanding San Rock Art*. Johannesburg: Southern Book Publishers.

Manaka, M. 1984. 'Some Thoughts on Black Theatre'. *English Academy Review*, 2.

Maponya, M. 2001. 'The Anatomy of Resistance in South African Theater', in O. Enwezor, ed., *The Short Century: Independence and Liberation Movements in Africa 1945–1994*. Munich: Prestel.

Marx, L. 1996. 'Underworld RSA'. *South African Theatre Journal*, 10.2.

Masilela, N. 1987. 'The White South African Writer in our National Situation'. *Matatu*, 2.3–4.

McLaren, R. 1996. ' "The Many Individual Wills." From *Crossroads* to *Survival*. The Work of Experimental Theatre Workshop '71', in G. V. Davis and A. Fuchs, ed., *Theatre and Change in South Africa*, Amsterdam: Harwood Academic Press.

Mda, Z. 1993. *When People Play People: Development Communication Through Theatre*. London: Zed Books.

Mda, Z. 1994. 'Marotholi Travelling Theatre: Towards an Alternative Perspective of Development', in L. Gunner, ed., *Politics and Performance*. Johannesburg: Witwatersrand University Press.

Merrington, P. 1995. ' "Pageantry and Primitivism": Dorothea Fairbridge and the Aesthetics of Union'. *Journal of Southern African Studies*, 21.4.

Merrington, P. 1997. 'Masques, Monuments and Masons: The 1910 Pageant of the Union of South Africa'. *Theatre Journal*, 49.

Merrington, P. n.d. 'Heritage, Genealogy, and the Inventing of Union, South Africa 1910'. Unpublished paper, 1995 conference.

Mofokeng, J. 1996. 'Theatre for Export: The Commercialization of the Black People's Struggle in South African Export Musicals', in G. V. Davis and A. Fuchs, ed., *Theatre and Change in South Africa*, Amsterdam: Harwood Academic Press.

Nkonyeni, N. 2001. Interview with D. Kerr. Unpublished.

Omer-Cooper, J. D. 1988. *History of Southern Africa*. Oxford: James Currey.

Opland, J. 1983. *Xhosa Oral Poetry: Aspects of a Black South African Tradition*. Cambridge: Cambridge University Press.

Opland, J. 1987. 'Dialectics of Tradition in South African Black Popular Theatre'. *Critical Arts*, 4.3.

378 | YVETTE HUTCHISON

Orkin, M. 1991. *Drama and the South African State.* Johannesburg: Witwatersrand University Press.
Orkin, M. 1996. 'Whose Popular Theatre and Performance?', in G. V. Davis and A. Fuchs, ed., *Theatre and Change in South Africa,* Amsterdam: Harwood Academic Press.
Orkin, M. 1997. *Shakespeare Against Apartheid.* Johannesburg: Ad Donker.
Perkins, K. A. 1999. *Black South African Women: An Anthology of Plays.* London and New York: Routledge.
Petersen, B. 1994. 'Apartheid and the Political Imagination in Black South African Theatre', in L. Gunner, ed., *Politics and Performance.* Johannesburg: Witwatersrand University Press.
Petersen, B. 2000. *Monarchs, Missionaries and African Intellectuals: African Theatre and the Unmaking of Colonial Marginality.* Johannesburg: Witwatersrand University Press.
Scheub, H. 1987. 'Oral Poetry and History'. *New Literary History,* 18.3.
Selby, J. 1975. *A Short History of South Africa.* London: NEL Books.
Sitas, A. 1994. 'Traditions of poetry in Natal', in L. Gunner, ed., *Politics and Performance,* Johannesburg: Witwatersrand University Press.
Sitas, A. 1996. 'The Workers' Theatre in Natal', in G. V. Davis and A. Fuchs, ed., *Theatre and Change in South Africa,* Amsterdam: Harwood Academic Press.
Sole, K. 1987. 'Oral Performance and Social Struggle in Contemporary Black South African Literature', in D. Bunn and J. Taylor, ed., *From South Africa: New Writing, Photographs and Art,* special issue of *Triquarterly,* 69.
Steadman, I. 1984. 'Black South African Theatre after Nationalism'. *English Academy Review,* 2.
Steadman, I. 1985. 'Drama and Social Consciousness: Themes in Black Theatre on the Witwatersrand until 1985'. Ph.D. thesis, Witwatersrand University.
Steadman, I. 1994. 'Towards Popular Theatre in South Africa', in L. Gunner, ed., *Politics and Performance,* Johannesburg: Witwatersrand University Press.
Stodel, J. 1962. *The Audience is Waiting.* Cape Town: H. Timmins.
Tomaselli, K. 1991. 'Popular Communication in South Africa: "Mapantsula" and its Context of Struggle'. *South African Theatre Journal,* 5.1.
Vail, L. and White, L. 1991. *Power and the Praise Poem: Southern African Voices in History.* Oxford: James Currey.
Van der Post, L. 1979. *The Lost World of the Kalahari.* 1958. Harmondsworth: Penguin.
Van Wyk, J. 1995. 'Social Concerns in Afrikaans Drama in the Period 1930–1940'. *Alternation,* 2.1.
Vilakazi, B. W. 1993. 'The Conception and Development of Poetry in Zulu', in R. H. Kaschula, ed., *Foundations in Southern African Oral Literature.* Johannesburg: Witwatersrand University Press.
Visser, N. 1998. 'Shakespeare and Hanekom, *King Lear* and Land: A South African Perspective', in A. Loomba and M. Orkin, ed., *Post-Colonial Shakespeares,* London and New York: Routledge.

Von Kotze, A. 1988. *Organise and Act.* Durban: Culture and Working Life Publications, University of Natal.

Walder, D. 1992. 'Resituating Fugard: South African Drama as Witness'. *New Theatre Quarterly*, 8.32.

White, L. 1982. 'Power and the Praise Poem'. *Journal of Southern African Studies*, 9.1.

White, L. 1989. 'Poetic Licence: Oral Poetry and History', in K. Barber and P. F. de Moraes Farias, ed., *Discourse and its Disguises: The Interpretation of African Oral Texts.* Birmingham: Birmingham University Press.

Wilson, M. and Thompson, L., eds. *The Oxford History of South Africa*, vol. II, *1870–1966.* Oxford: Oxford University Press.

Yai, O. 1989. 'Issues in Oral Poetry: Criticism, Teaching and Translation', in K. Barber and P. F. de Moraes Farias, ed., *Discourse and its Disguises: The Interpretation of African Oral Texts*, Birmingham: Birmingham University Press.

8 Theatre in Portuguese-speaking African countries

LUÍS R. MITRAS

There are five countries whose official language is Portuguese. These were all former Portuguese colonies. Angola and Mozambique, the largest two, are in southern Africa; Guinea-Bissau is on the west coast of Africa; and the remaining two (Cape Verde and São Tomé and Príncipe) are island archipelagos in the Atlantic. Portuguese colonialism left these countries with distinctive educational, legal, cultural and linguistic legacies, and to an extent this inheritance sets them apart from other African countries. The most potent of these legacies is of course language. Portuguese functions as a language of 'national unity' in those countries that have important regional languages, and it is also the language that binds the five Portuguese-speaking countries into some kind of associative unity.[1] But there is also a temptation, because these countries all speak Portuguese (or a Portuguese-based Creole, in the case of Cape Verde), to regard them as a sort of cultural bloc. If the regional differences in the larger countries are wide enough to provoke wars – the conflict in Angola is also a regional conflict – what of the differences between, say, Guinea-Bissau and Mozambique, countries at the opposite ends of Africa?

Then there is the question of the nature of the colonial experience. The three countries on the continent had ancient cultures before they were subjugated to colonial domination; these African traditions were never obliterated, and this has contributed to the way theatre is made today. The islands, on the other hand, were uninhabited before the Portuguese settled them with slaves and white immigrants. The proximity of the islands to the African continent and a mutual anti-colonial struggle means that we should not be too ready to separate the islands from Africa. (At one time, for example, Guinea-Bissau and Cape Verde were both ruled by the same political party, Amílcar Cabral's PAIGC.) But these islands have also much in common with the Creole islands in the Caribbean, and the kind of theatrical manifestations that we encounter on the islands do suggest that they operate on a different paradigm from that of the continent. For that reason we shall discuss them separately from the countries on the African mainland.

Continental Africa (Angola, Guinea-Bissau, Mozambique)

Theatrical forms in the pre-colonial era

Guinea-Bissau, Angola and Mozambique have officially been colonised since the sixteenth century. But in earlier centuries the European presence was limited to trading posts or slave ports along the sea coast – for these are all countries with extensive coastal areas. The hinterland only began to be colonised after the Conference of Berlin. (There were parts of Mozambique that were occupied only in 1917, at the time of the invasion of what was then German Tanganyika.) It was at the Conference of Berlin (1884–5) that European countries carved up Africa for themselves and drew up what are today's national frontiers. The importance of this is that many of the traditions that exist within modern African nation-states belong to ethno-linguistic groups that reside in more than one state; they need not be specific to Portuguese-speaking countries. For example, the Makonde people live in northern Mozambique and southern Tanzania. The Shona will be found in Zimbabwe and central Mozambique; the Shangaan in South Africa and southern Mozambique. The Kikongo people from the north of Angola are related to the Bakongo nation of the Lower Congo.

Theatrical forms, many of them of ancient origin, certainly did exist at the eve of colonialism. There was obviously no tradition of theatre with the support of a written text, since these were oral cultures.[2] It is perhaps the lack of a written text that makes some commentators suggest that the theatrical manifestations that existed in Africa were not real theatre, but represented theatre in some kind of 'embryonic' form. José Mena Abrantes, Angola's foremost playwright, for example, writes that the performance elements of traditional Angolan society – music, rhythm and body movement – reveal that there is no 'traditional Angolan theatre as such' (Abrantes, 1995: 33; my trans.), although he adds that the incorporation of these elements can contribute towards the creation of a more 'universal' Angolan theatre. Writing about Mozambique, Machado da Graça, a noted theatre director, states that mimetic dances and oral storytelling never developed to the point of actually becoming theatre as such. He writes that neither 'has given the qualitative leap that will permit us to affirm that it was already theatre' (Graça, 1995: 44; my trans.).

What these writers state is perfectly true in a sense: theatrical manifestations are not the same thing as theatre. But theatre need not be a play. In the 'embryonic theatre' of pre-colonial African society in the areas that constitute modern-day Angola, Guinea-Bissau and Mozambique, we can see two important forms of cultural expression where theatrical elements are identifiable, the ritual dance and oral storytelling.

Theatrical forms in traditional society
The first ritual dance I shall look at is the *Nyau* dance of the Maganja and Zimba peoples who live in the Tete province of Mozambique, an area bordering Zimbabwe and Zambia. This dance was first described by Edouard Fóa at the end of the nineteenth century and much of what we know about it is derived from his observations. The Nyau is a secret ritual performed before a society of initiates. That is to say, the dance has a 'liturgical' function – although it is important to point out that 'liturgical' in rural African culture might not be strictly limited to the holy. Some of the dancers are masked. Others hide inside animal figures made of straw. (For some reason, these straw figures are immediately destroyed after the dance is over.) What is interesting, for our purposes, is that the dance also functions as a story spectacle where people and situations are satirised. The danger of using the word *liturgical* to describe this dance is that it does not allow us to see that the dance spectacle is also the iconic ostension of a narrative, very much like ballet can be.

The second set of ritual dances that we shall speak of comes from the Makonde tribe who live in northern Mozambique and southern Tanzania. Most of the information comes from Jorge and Margot Dias's study of the Makonde tribe, and from Margot Dias's more specific work on Mozambican music (see references below). Two of these dances relate to circumcision ceremonies. The first is the dance of the *vanalombo* (circumcision masters). Their faces are painted with thick white lines that accentuate their features; their torsos are painted with speckled white dots in what looks like an obvious representation of a garment. The dance is full of acrobatic displays – it is usual for one of the *vanalombo* to catch a coin with his mouth. It is also usual for the dancer to take a break from the acrobatics and perform interludes of a more theatrical nature, where scenes from real life are enacted. The *nalombo* (apprentices) will often join in these.

The second circumcision dance is perhaps better known. It is the *mapiko*, the dance of the initiated. The dancer will be using an expressionistic wooden mask – not untypical of Maltonde sculpture – as well as a hat and a neck scarf He will often break away from the highly formalistic dance by letting go of the mask and, through mimetic gestures and acrobatics, act out dramatic or comic scenes from daily life. Margot Dias calls this 'the first cell of what can be called theatre' (1986: 219; my trans.).

In speaking of the Makonde, final mention should be made the dances with stilts, the *shilo*. These are performed by women. Like the initiated in the *mapiko*, they are also masked, and their hair is covered with a kerchief or headscarf. The dancer wears colourful clothes and is fully clothed, as if to conceal her real identity. Like the *mapiko* and the dance of the *vanalombo*, this is also an acrobatic dance.

The final dance I shall look at comes from the Bijagós islands of Guinea-Bissau, the *Dança do Boi* (The dance of the bull). This dance is especially famous, perhaps because it is the best example of the kind of folkloric spectacle nurtured by the colonial state, to the detriment of other forms of theatre. This is not to deny the intrinsic interest of the dance and its dramatic potential. Here two men play the role of two bulls. The dance tells a story. Initially the bulls are grazing and the dance is appropriately dignified, that is, until they catch sight of the cow and fight furiously about who should lay claim to her. Their costumes are rich in iconic significance. This is how Carlos Vaz describes them:

> They present themselves in the square dressed the part with their faces specked variously with white lead and red lead, the raffia skirts, the many necklaces around the neck, the animal hides tied at the waist, the chicken feathers in the ankles, and the bells at the knees. Sometimes they use skeletal wooden imitations of bulls' heads or else many-coloured helmets.   (Vaz, 1999: 46; my trans.)

In sum, a provisional claim can be made that these ritual dances, insofar as they act out story sequences and insofar as they employ a wide range of theatrical subcodes – the ones that are possible in a rural society – suggest a version of the theatre. Because these were not spoken texts, the dramatic possibilities were derived from the gestural, kinesic and mimetic aspects of the *dance*. Interestingly, the dramatic potential of narrative dances – so much akin to ballet – has begun to be exploited in the plays that have been produced in the last fifteen years, and many of the more innovative plays rely on danced-out sequences to achieve their full dramatic effect. It is perhaps worthwhile to point out that the Companhia Nacional de Canto e Dança (National song and dance company) in Mozambique has done much to promote the interaction of drama and dance.

Different from the dance is oral African storytelling, which ostensibly privileges the *word* and makes the word the vehicle of the performance. Oral storytelling is normally told by a single speaker, but that speaker often uses a wide range of para-linguistic resources to convey or *ostend* (show) the story: singing, intonation and facial mimicry – this is often allied to characterisation. Again, whilst this cannot be regarded as 'drama' in any sense, the theatrical potential is clearly there. It is significant that, as with the dance, traditional oral storytelling with its reliance on declamation or intonation has become an integral part of many recent theatre productions.

Dramatic forms in traditional society
Finally, I turn to what I have called 'scripted ritual performances'. These occur in a particular social situation, where certain roles are played in accordance with a prior socially endorsed script of responses and cues. The playing of these roles suggests a prior (though obviously unwritten) dramatic script. For example, among the Mundombe people from Benguela, in the south of Angola, it is possible, during mourning rites/ceremonies, to deduce a person's degree of kinship to the dead by the manner in which they cry or display their suffering. Abrantes talks about the existence 'of a prior formal score known and accepted by all, and according to which they express their true feelings' (1995: 33; my trans.). In other words, people act out according to some predetermined framework – their responses obey dramatic logic. But that is not to say that the existence of a socially accepted dramatic text really renders this theatre. One reason for this is that even though people really are performing roles, they are also expressing their very real mourning. This is an instance of something that might have a sense of the drama but not of the theatre.

Colonial period

Autos *and the role of the Church*
European-style theatre was first introduced into the territory that is today Lusophone Africa by Catholic missionaries. Missionary endeavours started as early as the sixteenth century. A bishopric was established in São Tomé

in 1534, which included the present-day area of Angola and the Congo. By 1596, with the erection of the diocese of São Salvador do Congo, the present-day area of Angola already had its own bishop. The diocese of Mozambique was established in 1612, detached from India. This, if anything, reveals that the cultural efforts associated with the church are long in date, at least in the coastal areas. And neither should the quality of these cultural efforts be underestimated. By the mid-1700s the missions in Guinea were already producing musicians and composers on a par with those of mainland Portugal. Many of these scores still exist and have been revived in concerts in recent years. The same cannot be said about the plays which were performed, most of which must have been destroyed or, because they were transmitted orally, were lost over the years.

The sort of theatre cultivated by Catholic priests and friars were *autos* ('acts', plays) representing biblical stories or incidents from the life of Christ. Judging from those autos that are still extant – and São Tomé, for all the particular reasons to do with its history and which render it a living museum, is the repository of many of those autos – the style and structure were not too different from that of the English miracle or morality play of the late Medieval period. What we see are the same didactic ends to which the stories are put. Very often the purpose of representing the autos was catechetical, that is, they served as a way of propagating the faith or of familiarising the faithful with Catholic doctrine and dogma. But this is not to deny the intrinsic subtlety of many autos: the rich theological and iconic subtext is often conveyed through what, to modern spectators, would be mundane verbal signs.

There is no evidence that the sort of autos produced through the auspices of the church changed much over the centuries, for versions of them continued to be produced well into the twentieth century. But it is probably true to say that the Christianised population in the more rural areas became familiar with them only after the mid-nineteenth century, when the great missionary endeavours began. This was also the period when Protestant missionaries established themselves in Angola and Mozambique. Some Protestant denominations played an important role in educating future African leaders, people like Graça and Samora Machel. The emphasis placed on African culture and its languages also had positive and beneficial aspects (see Marshall, 1990: 72–3). But we cannot be sure whether some of these churches and sects, many of them heirs to the worst excesses of the Puritans, ever nurtured theatre. Commentators often speak broadly of theatre in the 'Christian' missions, Protestant and Catholic, but no concrete details are ever provided.

Even though they served to deepen spectators' understanding of the Christian faith and, perhaps more importantly, to familiarise the indigenous population with western dramatic forms, church autos also had a more insidious underside. They functioned as a tool of colonial ideological domination. The Colonial Act of 1930 made it clear that the Catholic missions were instruments in civilising the 'natives'. The concordat signed in 1940 between Portugal and the Holy See granted the church many privileges, but it also transformed bishops into mere functionaries paid by the state. Adrian Hastings, the English church historian, writes that the church in Portuguese Africa willingly became a 'deliberate instrument in the colonization of millions of Africans' (1974: 14; my trans.). There were certainly exceptions, such as Sebastião Soares de Resende, the courageous bishop from Beira in the 1950s, or Manuel Vieira Pinto in Nampula in the 1970s, but we cannot be sure whether there were any practical spin-offs from their stands. The generalised ethos suggested that the white man and his religion were morally superior. We see this manifested in the casting of roles in nativity plays. It had become convention, and in Angola this continued as late as 1967, for blacks to play the roles of Judas and Satan and sometimes even Herod. The roles of baby Jesus, Joseph, Mary and the angels were reserved for whites. It is significant that it is these conventions that a more 'Africanist' theatre would want to overturn. For example, the first play written in a native language was also a Christmas morality play: Domingos Van-Dúnem's *Auto de Natal* (Christmas play), which was performed in Luanda in 1972, was written in Kimbundu, one of Angola's tribal languages.

Indigenous European-style theatre

The earliest reference to native European-style secular theatre comes from around 1898, when Carlos da Silva produced a tragicomic operetta, *Os Amores de Krilólu* (Krilólu's Loves) in Lourenço Marques (now Maputo).[3] António Rosado, in his reminiscences about the early days of Mozambique's capital city, tells us that Torre do Vale, a well-known settler, played the role of a black man, but also that João Albasini played the role of a prissy Goan very much proud of his second-hand Lusitanian heritage (Graça, 1995: 44). This small reference is interesting because João Albasini was a mulatto and a journalist who wrote for the early black nationalist newspapers *O Africano* (The African) and, later, *O Brado Africano* (The African outcry). João Albasini was a vocal opponent of the abuses of the colonial system, the contract worker system and discrimination against blacks (see Marshall, 1990: 48). His playing before a settler audience – and according to Rosado the entire 'town' (read whites) came to watch the play – is probably revealing of a certain fluidity in racial relations in the early years of the twentieth century. In those early days there were still significant mulatto oligarchies. Whites would only become the dominant class from the 1930s, when the fascist apparatus began to pass all types of bills, beginning with the already mentioned Colonial Act of 1930. The kind of theatre that got to be performed in that period onwards was written for and reflects the tastes of the dominant white settler class.[4]

Theatre of the variety or vaudeville kind was to become very popular among the white settler class. The genre spawned many plays of doubtful quality, but two from Mozambique are worth recalling: *O Império da Laurentinas* (The empire of the Lagers) from 1936 and *Palhota Maticada* (Walled-up hut) from 1939, both of them by Fernando Baldaque and Arnaldo Silva. The period also produced what got to be called *teatro colonial* (settler theatre), in other words, theatre about the lives of the settlers. A curious example of this sort of theatre is *O Mato* (The bushveld), performed around 1941. It was written by Caetano Montez, a lieutenant in the army. Rodrigues Júnior, a cultural critic writing in the 1950s, had this to say about the play:

> Everything in this play seems to be about the revenge of the 'bush' [bushveld] – the 'bush' seems to get off on ruining and destroying the white man. And his own revenge has something that is almost diabolical because, when he tortures the 'bush', he feels a joy that is like a spasm, a convulsion, the final letting go, exhausting, dominating.   (quoted in Graça, 1995: 45; my trans.)

These different theatrical manifestations reveal the extent to which Lourenço Marques was a lively and cosmopolitan centre. In Lourenço Marques, for example, there was even an amateur English theatrical society that managed to perform in South Africa. But this city was probably the exception rather than the rule. There are records of plays having been staged in Luanda and in Bissau, as well as in other provincial towns, but usually on a sporadic basis and without the support of any infrastructure, such as permanent theatre houses. Lourenço Marques's proximity to South Africa might have something to do, perhaps not so much with the quality of the work, but with the attempts at creating a wider range of cultural possibilities. An example will suffice. The Núcleo de Arte, which was to become a theatre house for quality shows, was started in order to provide a place for Jascha Heifetz to perform. This name probably does not mean much nowadays, but at the time Heifetz was also a world-famous violinist and virtuoso performer. He had been performing in Johannesburg. The good citizens of Lourenço Marques thought their city also worthy of a visit by a world-class performer, and so they created a theatre house.

Tours by Portuguese companies

Spectators, especially in more cosmopolitan centres like Luanda and Lourenço Marques, were further familiarised with European-style theatre through the tours of Portuguese-based theatre companies. There are records of tours from as early as 1910. These became more frequent from the 1930s onwards. The sort of shows they performed were the vaudeville or variety kind popular among white society. It was only in 1971, with a tour by the Teatro Experimental de Cascais, that Angolan theatre-goers at least became more familiar with the more innovative aspects of Portuguese theatre.

African nationalism and theatre

The factors that I have discussed – church autos, European-style plays and variety shows and tours by foreign companies – all contributed to helping spectators become more familiar with theatrical conventions and dramatic form. When the first native theatre got to be written, it betrayed the formal influences of the kind of theatre that had been around until then. By 'native theatre' I mean theatre produced, not by foreigners or settlers, but by people who had grown up in those countries and who wrote, in some way or another, about the social realities they themselves experienced. This sort of theatre was by its very nature political.

The period following World War Two saw the rise of a more vocal and articulate African nationalist consciousness and also of a more systematic programme of resistance. It was in this period that the three main liberation movements were established: PAIGC (African Party for the Independence of Guinea and Cape Verde), MPLA (People's Movement for the Liberation of Angola) and FRELIMO (Mozambican Liberation Front). Many of the future leaders of these movements were studying in Lisbon in the 1950s, and they were associated with the activities of the Casa dos Estudantes do Império, a university residence for African students. These activities were as much cultural as they were political. There was a considerable overlap between the two. (For example, Agostinho Neto, Angola's first president, was also a distinguished poet.) Anti-colonial struggle, nationalism and a new-found pride in Africa were powerful themes to be deployed in literature. A number of very bright and talented people started publishing in the 1950s and 1960s. There was something of a literary renaissance. The appearance of a native theatre was probably not unrelated to this since, in Angola at least, many poets and writers also wrote plays.

But the poetry that got to be written was bold, articulate and experimental. Very often it employed the full resources of indigenous traditions of oral recitation. It also appropriated the images and metaphors of African cultures. One thinks of the work of José Craveirinha. The same could be said of Luandino Vieira's highly poetic fiction from Angola. These are just two examples. The point is that in the context of such sheer creativity one would expect some sort of cross-over into the theatre. The sort of drama that was written or the sort of theatre that was performed did not break any ground; its formal qualities were those of the theatre that had been produced by and for whites.

Norberto de Castro and Domingos Van-Dúnem started the Clube de Teatro de Angola sometime after World War Two. The group did not survive for long, but it was the impetus behind the Companhia Teatral de Angola, another short-lived group, and also Ngongo, an amateur dramatic society that staged traditional tales and sketches, this from 1961 to the mid-1970s. Ngongo produced at least one play of merit, *Muhongo-a-Kasulo*, an adaptation of a short story from Óscar Ribas's *Ecos da Minha Terra*, this in 1962. All these endeavours were geared towards an urban or semi-urban audience, but there are records of plays performed for rural people in the early 1970s.

Similarly with Mozambique, plays whose subject matter dealt with the local reality only began to appear in the early 1970s. The two principal theatre groups – Teatro dos Estudantes Universitários de Moçambique and Teatro de Amadores de Lourenço Marques – were open to all races, but in the main they performed experimental plays from the European canon. The first play dealing specifically with the 'African' reality was Lindo Lhongo's *Os Noivos Ou Conferência Dramática sobre o Lobolo* (Bride and bridegroom, or a dramatic discourse on bride-money), performed in 1971. The work spoke positively in favour of the *lobolo* – or 'lobola', as it is known in South Africa. Lhongo also wrote *As Trinta Mulheres de Muzeleni* (The thirty women from Muzelini), which is about the clash of European and African cultures. According to some nationalist commentators at the time the play was too tied to the now outdated principles of *negritude* (Graça, 1995: 46). In an interview he gave at the time Lhongo said his play was about 'the anguish of this acculturated class, which is called "evolved", and which has one foot in Western culture and the other foot in the ancestral customs and traditions, in that culture that is really part of their own make-up' (quoted in Vaz, 1999: 61; my trans.). In 1973 João Fumane wrote *Feitiço e Religião* (Sorcery and religion), about a Christianised black man who is still tied to his ancestral beliefs.

There are probably three factors which would account for the kind of theatre that was being produced from the 1950s through the mid-1970s: the negative views of African folk traditions on the part of the African élite; a climate of terror and police surveillance; and the guerrilla war. I shall talk about each of these items separately.

The first factor relates to what I have previously said about theatre being formally indebted to the European models spectators were familiar with. African theatrical traditions (dance, music, mimicry) did not find their way into this kind of theatre – and, in fact, it is only in the late 1980s that they are added to the repertoire. This can be explained by two different motives. The dominant ethos among the liberation movements – by and large Marxist-Leninist in orientation – was that tribalism was something divisive and negative, which needed to be eradicated. Those theatrical manifestations of which I discussed a few were probably seen as being too closely related to specific tribal cultures, and maybe not fit for the 'new de-tribalized Africa'. As it was, it was precisely these 'folkloric' spectacles that the colonial state most often encouraged and nurtured. There is the example of the the Dance of the Bull, mentioned above, which was often performed for colonial dignitaries. Carlos Vaz makes the legitimate point that the same state that was vigorously opposed to the appearance of a revolutionary African theatre also cultivated these expressions of African folklore (1999: 47). We can understand the reluctance of playwrights and directors to be seen to be pandering to colonial tastes.

The second factor was the ever-constant vigilance on the part of the PIDE, the Portuguese security police. It was easier to hide a typewritten poem than to hide a public performance of a play. This probably discouraged writers from either tackling themes that were too bold or even attempting to have them performed.

The third reason was the colonial war, which started in Angola in 1961, in Portuguese Guinea in 1963, and in Mozambique in 1964. Many of the most talented writers left for exile or joined the guerrillas at this time

An indication that these writers might have turned to the theatre had things been different is the observation that the noted poet Costa de Andrade and the writer Pepetela were both involved in theatre work in the MPLA-controlled areas of Angola. The sort of work they produced was along the line of children's plays. These plays would be staged, often with improvisations, before adult audiences. They were used to explain why the MPLA was waging its war against colonialism. Theatre had become a very useful and practical tool to educate entire sectors of the population. This sort of lesson would be brought in when theatre was reconstituted in the period after independence.

Post-independence

Theatre in the service of the revolution
Angola, Mozambique and Guinea-Bissau became independent in 1975, a year after a *coup d'état* by the armed forces brought down the fascist régime of Marcello Caetano. The new governments that were established in these countries were Marxist-Leninist in orientation. Independence was regarded as the achievement of a people's revolution. This influenced the nature of the theatre in the early 'post-revolutionary' years. In Mozambique and to an extent in Angola theatre served, first and foremost, didactic or ideological ends.

Before independence, theatre, its playhouses and groups, had been dominated by whites and they constituted its biggest client group. The mass exodus of whites and Asians from Angola and Mozambique in the period around independence left these countries with something of a cultural vacuum. This was filled up with new groups fervently committed to the principles of the 'revolution'. In the early years of the 'revolution' the FRELIMO combatants theatre group Grupo Cénico das Forças Populares de Libertação produced an exciting series of plays. One of these was the 1975 production of *Chibalo*, written by Marcos Francisco Tembe, which was an attack on colonialism/imperialism, which, the play showed, ended up by corrupting those whom it oppressed. The play ends with a chorus uttering rather predictable slogans, which makes clear that the function of the staging was also to educate the populace:

Long live FRELIMO!
Long live the Unity of the Mozambican People!
Long live the Independence of our People!
Down with racism!
Down with tribalism!
Down with alcoholism!

(quoted in Vaz, 1999: 89; my trans.)

The same group also produced *Javali-Javalismo* (Wild hog and being a hog), another play about colonialism. This play has the dubious honour of having been banned by the new régime – not because it criticised the colonial heritage but because it also pointed to what was amiss in the new society. The group did not last long. With the demobilisation of army personnel, who returned to their homes in the rural districts of the country, it ceased to exist.

Other important plays from this period include two works by Orlando Mendes, a noted Mozambican poet and novelist, both of which were performed in 1975: *Um Minuto de Silêncio* (A minute's silence), which is about the social degradation, selfishness and self-destruction that ate into people who were impotent to resist colonialism; and *Na Machamba da Maria* (In Maria's small plot), the purpose of which was to 'conscientise' people to the fact that the revolutionary ideal was the only valid one. Also performed in 1975 was Orlando de Albuquerque's *O Filho de Nzambi* (Nzambi's child), a play about the new Angolan society.

But this sort of 'people's' theatre is not limited to the immediate post-revolutionary period. Much of the theatre that was produced until the late 1980s was didactic (or propagandist) in nature. Even Pepetela, Angola's premier novelist, turned his hand to plays that were probably somewhat skewed in their fulsome support of the dominant order: *A Corda* (The rope), published in 1978, and *A Revolta da Casa do Ídolos* (Revolt in the idol-worshipping house), published in 1979. This is also true of most of the other important plays that were published – that is to say, texts that were published, although not necessarily performed – during the fifteen-year period. Such is the case with João Maimona's *Diálogos com Peripécia* (Dialogue with incidents), published in 1987, a text about social injustice in a rural area in the Uíge province of Angola; Domingos Van-Dúnem's rather didactic or 'pamphleteering' *O Pamfleto* (The pamphlet) on the anti-colonial struggle, published in 1989; and Casimiro Alfredo's patriotic *Pátria* (Nation), published in 1992. All these are Angolan texts. There never was a tradition of publishing plays in Mozambique.

Guinea Bissau is the smallest of the countries under discussion and its theatre production has been the most meagre. In the period around independence Afrocid, an amateur dramatic society, staged at least one important play, *Chassô* (Truth), which dealt with torture at the hands of PIDE. Members of the same group produced *Se cussa Murri, Cassa cu Matal* (Nothing dies without a cause), which also concerns itself with the colonial legacy of tyranny. This play was directed by Carlos Vaz, Guinea-Bissau's foremost actor and a specialist on African theatre. Vaz left Guinea-Bissau for political reasons. The stagnation of theatrical production is probably not unrelated to his departure.

Theatre in recent years

Mozambique Throughout the 1980s Mozambique was involved in a bitter civil war against RENAMO (Mozambique National Resistance). Armed insurgency continued until October 1992, when a peace treaty in Rome ended the civil war. Multi-party elections were held in 1994. Although FRELIMO won the elections, Mozambique could no longer be regarded as a one-party Marxist state.

The 'opening up' process started much earlier, however, in the late 1980s, with the fall of the Berlin Wall, changes in South Africa and the dismemberment of the Soviet state and the changes it implied to geo-political reality. It was in the late 1980s that the nature of the theatre in Mozambique started changing. It is probably true to say that the most innovative and technically proficient work in Mozambique has been produced in the last fifteen years. But a broad look at the theatrical scenario shows that the quality of the work remains uneven. There is still no tradition of writing and publishing plays, and companies tend to rely on foreign (European, Portuguese, Brazilian, South African) texts. In addition, theatrical productions are mainly limited to the capital city of Maputo, a southern city very close to South Africa.

It is only relatively recently (1998) that Cena Lusófona, a Portuguese theatrical company, ran writers' workshops in Mozambique (see Mosse). Comic plays, sketches and vaudeville pieces remain quite popular – forms that are not always appropriate when dealing with complex subject matter. The sorts of themes Mozambican theatre has tackled include the question of *lobolo* (bride-money), ancestor worship and sexual mores. But it is also true to say that the more experimental companies are equally popular. Recent theatre relies greatly on oral traditions for its subject matter. There is much emphasis on singing and dancing, making the theatrical performance a much more integrated affair.

Theatre companies are various, and some of them are professional. The oldest is the Associação Cultural Casa Velha founded by João Manuel Machado Da Graça in 1982. This group has produced 'classical' works, including works by Molière, Strindberg, O'Neill, Chancerel, Soyinka, Diop and Pirandello.

The world-renowned and experimental Mutumbela Gogo was founded by Manuela Soeiro in 1986 and is based in Teatro Avenida in the centre of Maputo. It has produced plays based on literary texts, including *9 Horas* (Nine o'clock), adapted from a poem by Rui Nogar, *O Funeral de um Rato* (A mouse's funeral) by Mia Couto in 1990, a version of *As Mãos dos Pretos* (The hands of black men) by Luis Bernardo Honwana in 1991, and, more recently, *O Despertar do Guarda Nocturno* (The awakening of the night-watchman), a Henning Mankell version of Ludvig Holberg's *Jeppe Pa Berget*.

In 1992 Gilberto Mendes founded the Companhia de Teatro Gungo. Mendes was originally a member of Mutumbela Gogo. A talented writer and director, his productions include *Coração d'Lagoa* (Lagoon heart), *Oh Sô Ministro* (Oh, Hon. Minister), and, more recently (2001), *E Tudo a Água Levou* (Everything's gone with the water), which interweaves a modern story about corrupt officials with a traditional Chokwe tale from north-eastern Angola.

Other theatre groups of note include the Associação Cultural Tchova Xita Duma, which has performed Brecht and Fugard and Chico Buarque de Holanda, the Brazilian writer; Grupo Cénico dos Caminhos de Ferros de Moçambique, more dedicated to variety theatre; Grupo de Teatro M'beu, which has performed versions of traditional folk-tales (1989) and also, in 1995, *Joaquim Chofer* (Joaquim the chauffeur) by José Craveir-inha, Mozambique's most important poet; and Grupo Hopalangatana, which has dramatised a version of *Ualalapi*, a novel by Ungulani Ba Ka Khosa.

Angola It is probably not untrue to say that Angola has been at war almost continuously since 1961, the start of the colonial war. After the MPLA had declared independence in 1975 it found itself at war with both the FNLA (National Front for the Liberation of Angola) in the north and UNITA (National Front for the Total Liberation of Angola) in the south. With the help of Cuban troops, the MPLA defeated FNLA and managed to ward off a South African invasion. Throughout the 1980s large parts of Angola continued to be occupied by UNITA. There were also constant South African invasions.

A peace agreement between UNITA and MPLA was signed in May 1991 and multi-party elections were held in September 1992. The MPLA won the elections, but UNITA refused to recognise the results and went back to war. It took control of about 70 per cent of the territory. In 1997 many UNITA deputies took up their seats in the National Assembly and a government with UNITA members was sworn in. The constant war was an obvious hindrance to theatrical production and theatre is basically limited to the capital city of Luanda. This is not the only parallel with Mozambique. Recent Angolan theatre frequently adapts folk-tales for the theatre, but also local literary works. Plays often deal with aspects of social reality, although it has also become something of a tradition in Angola to write plays about important historical incidents. There are also many more local dramatists in Angola compared to Mozambique; these continue to be few in number, however. In addition, the country seems to have a more enduring tradition of institutional theatre in the period after independence.

A national theatre and dance school was established in 1976. A group that grew out of this was Grupo de Amadores de Teatro, which was run by Cuban instructors and which produced *O Círculo de Giz de Bombó* (The Bombo chalk-circle) by Henrique Guerra and Pepetela's *A Corda*, of which I have already made mention. The same Cuban instructors were behind a group that emerged from this first group, GIT or Grupo de Instrutores de Teatro (1978), which produced at least one important play, an adaptation of *A Vida Verdadeira de Domingos Xavier* (The true life of Domingos Xavier) by Luandino Vieira, the well-known Angolan novelist. A spin-off from this group was GET or Grupo Experimental de Teatro, founded in 1981 and tied to the Angolan Ministry of Culture. In 1983 this group performed *A Panela de Ko-Ka-Mbala* (Ko-Ka-Mbala's pot) by Guy Menga, the Cameroonian playwright, and in the following year *O Barqueiro* (The boatman), an adaptation of a traditional Chokwe (north-east Angola) folk-tale. Jorge Macedo's *Tutumbagem* was performed in 1985. In 1989 GET performed an adaptation of a Sãotomense legend, *O Eclipse do Sol* (The eclipse of the sun). Also in that year it staged one-act plays based on the short stories of Uanhenga Xitu: *O Alfaiate* (The tailor) and *Kahitu, Che Felito, Saldos* (Bargains).

Another important reference in Angolan theatre is José Mena Abrantes. Probably Angola's most important living dramatist and director, he returned from exile at the end of 1974 and helped to found the Tchinganje theatre group, which was to perform the first play after independence, *O Poder Popular* (People's power). In 1977 Abrantes co-founded the Xilenga-Teatro company, which was to perform a play based on a Chokwe folk-tale. In 1988 he founded Elinga Teatro. The first play it performed was Pepetela's *A Revolta da Casa dos Ídolos*, which I have already mentioned. Elinga Teatro has toured Spain, Italy and Portugal. It has also performed many of the important plays written by Abrantes, some of which I will mention.

Ana, Zé e os Escravos (Ana, Zé and the slaves), first performed in 1986, is a play about a woman slave trader (Dona Ana Joaquina) and her relations with a social outcast who becomes a settler (José do Telhado), this during the period that extended from the termination of the slave trade (1836) to the abolition of slavery itself (1878). The play was awarded the Sonangol Literary Award in 1986. *Nandyala ou a Tirania dos Monstros* (Nandyala or the tyranny of monsters), which dates from 1992, is inspired by a traditional tale from the south-west of Angola. *Sequeira, Luís Lopes ou o Mulato dos Prodígios* (Sequeria, Luís Lopes or the wondrous mulatto), performed in 1995, is about a Portuguese mulatto army officer who destroys three Angolan kingdoms which, in the seventeenth century, had opposed settler incursions into their territory. A two-volume edition of Abrantes's plays was published in Portugal in 1999.

Other important theatre groups worthy of mention include Nzinga Mbande, Makote, Oásis, and Serpente. I shall talk about each of these separately.

Colectivo de Artes Horizonte Nzinga Mbande was founded in 1986 by José de Sousa Sobrinho. The company was made up largely of former frontier guards. It is best known for its historical play on the seventeenth-century African warrior-queen, *Njinga, Rainha da União* (Njinga, Queen of Unity) and *Fabiana*, written by Jeli Costa in 1992.

Makote was established in the late 1980s by Correia Domingos 'Lobão'. *Kakila*, written by 'Lobão' himself, was the winning entry at the First National Theatre Contest in 1989. The play is about the feuds between two neighbouring kingdoms in the Kongo region during the pre-colonial era. A Romeo and Juliet scenario is the glue that holds the story in place. The integrated use of drama, dance, poetry and music has made this play especially original.

Oásis has performed a version of Boaventura Cardoso's *A Morte do Velho Kipacassa* (The death of old Kipacassa). Serpente, founded in Lisbon in 1991, has toured many countries performing Portuguese versions of the Fugard–Kani–Ntshona plays.

An interesting feature of post independence Angolan theatre is that plays are performed not just in Portuguese but also in Kimbundu. Grupo Teatral da Assatij, ETU-LENE and JULU all perform plays in these languages, as well as other local languages such as Lokue, Umbundu and Kikongo.

Guinea-Bissau In the 1980s an amateur Guinean group visited various communist countries. According to Leopoldo Amado, the author of a study on Guinean literature, to this day not a single European-style theatre house has been built in Guinea-Bissau (see 'Teatro' 2000). Amateur groups continue to exist, however.

The Islands (Cape Verde and São Tomé and Príncipe)

The Cape Verde archipelago, situated off the west coast of Africa, São Tomé and Príncipe, situated on the Gulf of Guinea, all have distinctive Creole cultures. The present-day population of Cape Verde, for one, is largely mixed-race. Its culture includes elements derived from both African and European sources. There is considerable debate about what is borrowed from what culture (see Ferreira, 1985: 95–112). The presence of many European-derived religious customs, alimentary methods and social rituals and institutions (see Filho, 1995) suggest a predominance of European influence at least at the level of the aforementioned. Cape Verde's relationship with Portugal was always ambiguous. Because of their level of education or cultural proximity to the Portuguese, Cape Verdeans often held subordinate positions in the Portuguese colonial administration in other African colonies; some, indeed, rose to occupy high positions. There is still a lot of debate in Cape Verde today about whether independence in 1975 was really in the islands' best interests.

In São Tomé there has also been considerable cultural hybridisation over the centuries. The population is predominantly of black origin, many the descendants of slaves brought over to work on the cocoa plantations. Contract labourers from the other Portuguese colonies continued to be brought to São Tomé well into the middle of the twentieth century. Most of the people were cut off from their tribal roots and integrated into pre-existing São tomense society, which had early on developed its own codes of behaviour and social rituals. But São Tomé is unusual because, unlike other colonies, it had its own black aristocracy. In the colonial period there were proportionally far more *assimilados* (indigenous people who basically had full citizenship rights) than in the other Portuguese territories in continental Africa. Along with other Portuguese-speaking countries, São Tomé and Príncipe became independent in 1975.

Romarias in honour of the saints and autos on the deeds of Charlemagne

I have already spoken about the role of church plays in the context of continental Africa. In a sense these missionary endeavours were no different from those on the continent. A diocese was established in Santiago (Cape Verde) as early as 1533 and, the following year, in São Tomé. But a consideration of the nature of religious experience in these areas in the last three hundred years hits upon the fact that the religiosity of these people and their popular manifestations of religion have much more to do with specifically Portuguese folk religious traditions (see Filho, 1995: 87–144). Many of these traditions verge on the unorthodox and they would not have been the sorts of things that missionaries in their post-Tridentine zeal would have wanted to inculcate to pagans and heathens. The nature of the religious experience is very similar to what we find in rural northern Portugal, and in those territories settled by immigrants from this region, namely Brazil and the uninhabited islands of Madeira and the Azores.

Central to the religious and social experience of all these people is the *romaria*. The word literally means 'pilgrimage', and it often revolves around a pilgrimage to a shrine dedicated to a particular saint, this on that saint's feast-day. Cape Verde, for example, has a number of pilgrimage shrines (see Filho, 1995: 87–95; Casimiro, 1939: 23). But a romaria is also a popular festival, one where the boundaries between the secular and the sacred blur. What is interesting is how many of the original features of the romarias are preserved in parts of rural Brazil and Cape Verde. (Various church attempts to purge the popular festivals from the nineteenth century onwards probably left them as more purely religious affairs in their places of origin.) Once the church activities – the procession to the shrine, the novenas said along the way, the masses – were over the faithful would be entertained with autos and dances. The most popular auto that was performed revolved around a story from the time of Charlemagne and the Moorish invasion of Spain. The Princess Floripes is abducted by the Moors and Christians lead an assault to recover their princess. The Moors are eventually defeated and submit to the Christian law by being baptised. The fight between the Moors and the Christians was often done on horseback. This was the *cavalhada*, and it was an important part of the spectacle.

Romarias with the staging of this Carolingian-inspired story continue to be staged in many parts of Brazil. Alba Zaluar, a Brazilian sociologist, argues that the staging of autos was a means by which social conflict and class tensions could be expressed (1983: 77–9). She mentions how easy the enacted fights turned into real fights. Also, the conflict between Christians and Moors replicated the conflict between rich and poor, one of which had to bow to the law of the other. Two points need to be made. The first relates to Cape Verde. Here the auto has, over the last hundred years, basically disappeared. On the other hand, the romaria remains an intrinsic part of Cape Verdean social life, as does the cavalhada, which continues to follow the pilgrimage. But the cavalhada is no longer part of any story; it has been removed from the nexus which gave it meaning. In São Tomé and Príncipe, on the other hand, the Carolingian-inspired autos remain popular and very much alive. The explanation for this is probably the sociological one Zaluar provides for Brazil. Traditionally, Sãotomense society was divided into two basic classes, plantation owners and slaves, and my use of the word *slaves* is not entirely metaphorical, since slavery in different forms continued well into recent times; modern-day slaves were called 'contract labourers'. Cape Verde, on the other hand, traditionally a poor country subject to periodic droughts, really only had dynastic families in the eighteenth and nineteenth centuries, but nothing on the scale of São Tomé, since Cape Verde had no agricultural riches to speak of. Baltasar Lopes, who wrote a study of Cape Verdean Creole and its social origins, speaks about the existence of 'a meagre superstructure' (1957: 42) on the islands. A certain sense of social egalitarianism, produced by historical and economic circumstances, might explain why the autos disappeared completely.

Morna and the theatre in twentieth-century Cape Verde

If it can be said that theatre occupies a central space in the cultural arena of Sãotomense society, the same is not true of Cape Verde. Here the emphasis is on music, and more specifically on the uniquely Cape Verdean *morna*. Morna has something of the Portuguese *fado* and the blues – although one commentator has described it as 'neither the *fado* nor the blues' (Rodrigues, 1993: 78). Like the fado and like the blues, the morna is an expression of sadness and longing. This is particularly relevant in a society where immigration is a fact of life and where poverty is so widespread that the remittances of Cape Verdeans outside the country constitute an important segment of the state revenue. The centrality of music might explain why, until recent times, theatre has not really thrived in Cape Verde. Interestingly, in recent times music has become a central ingredient in Cape Verdean theatre, not only the sad, wistful *morna*, but also the upbeat *coladeira*, another local music form. Other music forms, all of them derived from the mixed heritage of Cape Verde and all of which find their way into recent theatre, include the African-inspired *batuque* with its cowhide drums, the *finançon*, the *lundum*, and the *mazurka*, originally of Polish origin.

Theatre in the more European mode, not surprisingly, had a late start in Cape Verde. Jaime de Figueiredo wrote *Terra de Sôdade* (Land of longing) in the 1940s, a play on the quintessential Cape Verdean theme of emigration. There is no record that the play was ever staged. In the 1960s there was an amateur theatre group in Praia (on the island of Santiago). In the mid-1970s, around the time of independence, there was another amateur group in Mindelo. Generally speaking, theatre was basically left to student groups. The year 1979 saw the publication of the first play written in Cape Verdean Creole, *Descarado* (Shameless) by Donaldo Pereira de Macedo, this in the United States, where there is a considerable Cape Verdean immigrant community.

A more recent development centres around the city of Mindelo on the island of São Vicente, where MINDELACT, a cultural association, has since 1995 held an annual theatre festival. This has been the result of the work of João Branco, a theatre director who has done much to revitalise theatre on the islands. Plays of note that have been performed in recent years include *As Virgens Loucas* (The crazy virgins), an adaptation by Cândido Ferreira of a story by António Aurélio Gonçalves, a Cape Verdean writer, this in 1996; *Destino Cruel* (Cruel fate) by Jorge Martins, and *Rabecindade de Família* by José F. Martins, both in 1997; *Adão e as Sete Pretas de Fuligem* (Adam and the seven soot-black women) by Mário Lúcio Sousa, and *Agravios de um Artista* (An artist's troubles) by the novelist Germano de Almeida, both in 2001.

Renaissance drama in the Gulf of Guinea

Tchilôli

Autos were probably introduced on the island of São Tomé by immigrants from the Portuguese island of Madeira who settled there in the sixteenth century to work on the sugar cane plantations. They are at the origin of the *tchilôli*, which remains a popular and living theatrical form. Tchilôli is a 'hybrid' theatre. It retains the complete Portuguese Renaissance text, the original characters and the 'unities', but it adds many elements of African origin: the music, the choreography, the costumes, the musical instruments, the dances, the many mimed scenes and the pantomime (Vaz, 1999: 49).

The most important tchilôli is *Tragédia do Marquês de Mântua e o Imperador Carloto Mangano* (The tragedy of the Marquis of Mantua and the Emperor Charlemagne),[5] which was written by Baltazar Dias, a blind sixteenth-century Madeiran poet and playwright who wrote in the manner of Gil Vicente. (Vicente was a Portuguese Renaissance playwright; his handling of dramatic convention was late Medieval.) The play tells us how the Marquis of Mantua discovers that his nephew has been stabbed to death, and how Prince Charlemagne, who is guilty of this misdeed, is condemned. The *Tragédia* lasts for six hours, although there are shorter versions that last between one and three hours.

Interestingly, tchilôli observes two long-obsolete European conventions: female roles are played by males and actors take off their masks only after sunset. There have, however, been attempts to modernise these plays, at least insofar as props and costumes. We now encounter telephones, typewriters and modern army and navy uniforms. Although commentators are critical of these changes (see Vaz, 1999: 51), they are probably valid from a different perspective. Tchilôli seems to have survived precisely because it was also a ritualised critique of the dominant class; and it is through iconic signs (telephone, uniforms) that spectators can perceive these apparatuses, the privilege of the rich, as referring to that class. Françoise Gründ says that the sixteenth-century slaves memorised the words of the plays of their Portuguese masters, because in them they encountered the same pains of injustice expressed in a most eloquent manner – 'suprême élégance', she writes – and began to stage them in order to deride their masters and also 'pour revendiquer une justice magnifiée par d'autres' (1993: 123).

São Lourenço *or* Auto de Floripes *of Príncipe*

The *São Lourenço* (lit. 'Saint Lawrence') is the name by which the *Auto de Floripes* is known on the island of Príncipe and where it is performed annually on the feast-day of St Lawrence (10 August). The Auto de Floripes is the auto discussed above, which used to be performed after certain romarias or pilgrimages and which continues to be performed in parts of Brazil. Like the tchilôli, it also arrived via Madeira and is a hybrid form that draws on many African elements.

Danço Congo

Another theatrical manifestation from São Tomé is the *danço congo*, which is also known as the *Tragédia do Capitão Congo* (The tragedy of Captain

Congo). The dança congo is a huge dance sequence telling the story of the sufferings of a Congolese king who was deported to the islands as a slave. The story makes no use of oral texts and relies instead on mimicry, dance and song. Although the figures of this dance sequence are derived from classical European theatre (the Fool, the Devil, the Hangman), the manner in which the dance is performed is clearly of African origin.

Contemporary Sãotomenese theatre and the dança congo

Although theatrical production in São Tomé and Príncipe has, for centuries, tended to stay content with the glories of forms that have become national institutions, there has, in recent years, been an attempt at reappropriating the folk myths and old theatrical traditions in plays with a more modern subject matter. This is especially evident in the work of Fernando de Macedo, whose work, like that of Abrantes, has also been published in Portugal, this in 1999. His plays, Rei de Obó (King of Obó), Cloçon Son (Ground heart) from 1997, and most particularly Capitango, from 1998, exploit all the resources of the dança congo, including the choreography, music and dance. In a sense what these plays do is add the missing text to the danced-out story sequence that is the dança congo.

Notes

1. The CPLP (Community of Portuguese-Speaking Nations) is an example of an international organisation based on a shared linguistic identity rather than economic or political imperatives. It includes the five countries in Africa, as well as Brazil, East Timor and Portugal.
2. It needs to be pointed out that before the Portuguese arrived in Mozambique the coastal regions were under the influence of the Arabs. The most important legacy is the Islamic religion: today 40 per cent of Mozambicans are Muslims. I have not been able to find any documented evidence that makes the connection between the Muslim inheritance and theatrical manifestations among, especially, the Makua people.
3. The date is given by Carlos Vaz (1999: 57). He does not explain which play was performed that year. Most other authors state that Os Amores de Krilólu was Carlos da Silva's first performed play (cf. Graça, 1995: 49).
4. This should not be seen to imply that this was the end of Carlos da Silva's efforts. He was to write and produce two more plays, Crime de Anica (Anika's crime) and Madalena, a comic opera, As Aventuras de um Herói (A hero's adventures), a comedy, Sua Alteza – O Criador (His Highness – the Creator), and an operetta, Os Cavaleiros de Arcabuz e Era Eu (The knights of Arcabuz and It was me).

5. Other *tchilôli* which get to be produced regularly in São Tomé include: *Tragédia Formiguinha da Boa Morte* (The ant-sized tragedy of Boa Morte), *Tragédia Madeirense de Madre Deus* (Madeiran tragedy of the Mother of God), *Tragédia Benfica de Bom Bom*, *Tragédia de Caixão Grande* and *Tragédia Santo António de Madalena*.

References and further reading

Abrantes, José Mena. 1995. 'Breve Olhar sobre o Teatre Angolano'. *Setepalcos*.

Anjos, Frederico Gustavo dos. 1993. 'Les Autres Manifestations Théâtrales'. *Notre Librairie: Revue du Livre: Afrique, Caraïbes, Océan Indien*, 112.

Casimiro, Augusto. 1939. *Ilhas Crioulas*. Lisbon: Editorial Cosmos.

Dias, Margot. 1986. *Instrumentos Musicais de Moçambique*. Lisbon: Instituto de Investigação Científica e Tropical.

Elam, Keir. 1980. *The Semiotics of Theatre and Drama*. London: Methuen.

Ferreira, Manuel. 1985. *A Aventura Crioula*. 3rd edn. Lisbon: Plátano Editora.

Filho, João Lopes. 1995. *Cabo Verde: Retalhos do Quotidiano*. Lisbon: Editorial Caminho.

Graça, Machado da. 1995. 'O Teatro em Moçambique'. *Setepalcos*.

Gründ, Françoise. 1993. 'Le Tchiloli'. *Notre Librairie: Revue du Livre: Afrique, Caraïbes, Océan Indien*, 112.

Hastings, Adrian. 1974. *Wiriyamu*. Porto: Afrontamento.

Lopes, Baltazar. 1957. *O Dialecto Crioulo de Cabo Verde: Dialectos Portugueses do Ultramar*. Lisbon: Imprensa Nacional.

Marshall, Judith. 1990. *Literacy, State Formation and People's Power: Education in a Mozambican Factory*. Belville: CACE, University of the Western Cape.

Mosse, Marcelo. 1998. 'Termina Hoje em Maputo a Primeira Oficina de Escrita Teatral'. 21 June http://www.instituto-camoes.pt/arquivos/teatro/liberteatro.htm (17 November 2001)

Rodrigues, Moacyr. 1993. 'Ni Blues Ni Fado: La Morna'. *Notre Librairie: Revue du Livre: Afrique, Caraïbes, Océan Indien*, 112.

Serpieri, Alessandro. 1989. *On the Language of Drama*. Pretoria: University of South Africa Press.

'Teatro é Tema de Debate em BH'. 15 August 2000. http://www.estadao.com.br/divirtase/noticias/2000/ago/15/182.htm (17 November 2001)

Vaz, Carlos. 1999. *Para um Conhecimento do Teatro Africano*. 2nd edn. Lisbon: Ulmeiro.

Zaluar, Alba. 1983. *Os Homens de Deus: Um Estudo dos Santos e das Festas no Catolicismo Popular*. Rio de Janeiro: Jorge Zahar Editores.

Dramatic texts

Abrantes, José Mena. 1999. *Teatro*. 2 vols. Coimbra: Cena Lusófona.

Dias, Baltazar. 1859. *Tragedia do Marquez de Mantua, e do Imperador Carloto Magno*. Porto: Typografia da Revista.

Macedo, Fernando de. 1999. *Teatro do Imaginário Angolar*. Coimbra: Cena Lusófona.

9 Mauritius and Réunion

ROSHNI MOONEERAM

The islands of Mauritius and Réunion, not only the smallest African countries but also cut off by thousands of miles from mainland Africa, with no indigenous populations and with histories of settlement that go back a mere few hundred years, are islands which, as succinctly put by Vergès (1999: xii), suffer from the 'traumata of insignificance.'[1] Indeed known mainly as exotic tourist destinations – and albeit in the case of Mauritius, as an economic success and stable democratic model for the region – these islands remain on the outskirts of the post-colonial historical, political and cultural investigations that have over the past three decades, in particular, addressed the literary and cultural productions of (mostly) mainland Africa. Out of this context of cultural insignificance, this chapter aims to draw attention to these sister-islands' idiosyncratic theatrical forms informed by histories that at once converge and diverge.

Born out of common revolts, the theatre of Mauritius and Réunion are initially militant and reflect overlapping concerns with other African nations. Mauritian and Réunionnais theatre are, however, moving beyond militant politics to creating their own myths, which are essential in defining their post-colonial identities. In doing so, they rely on neither Négritude nor its progeny, the Créolité of the French Caribbean, with which there are historical parallels, but resources specific to their own historical, geographic and cultural make-up in the Indian Ocean. The selection of texts looked at in this chapter do not by any means represent the whole corpus of Réunionnais or Mauritian theatre, but rather allow a glimpse into the main developments in the Réunionnais and Mauritian play consciousness. Since Théâtre Vollard (TV)[2] in Réunion and Dev Virahsawmy in Mauritius have not only played pioneering roles but continue to be the most prolific and influential figures in defining and developing local theatre, this chapter will concentrate on their works, although reference will be made to the works of other playwrights and groups.

Political and demographic history

French settlement in Réunion started in 1638. Slavery was forbidden and marriage between whites and blacks – workers brought mostly from Madagascar – was common until 1690, when the introduction of the Code Noir turned all blacks into slaves. In a growing spirit of French imperialism, the neighbouring island (now Mauritius) was taken over in 1715 and a first colony of French and their slaves from Réunion despatched there for permanent settlement. For the purposes of agricultural development, a larger number of slaves were brought from Madagascar, east and west Africa as well as a small number of free workers and slaves from the south of India. During the Napoleonic Wars, the British, eager to prove their sovereignty in the Indian Ocean in relation to France, captured the island, renaming it Mauritius, while it was settled that Réunion would remain French. The abolition of slavery in Mauritius in 1835 and in 1848 in Réunion was marked by an immigration of workers from India and to a lesser extent from China. Since the Indian immigration to Mauritius was on a much larger scale – almost half a million – drastic changes occurred in the Mauritian demographic composition.

This brief historical overview contextualises the confluence of various cultural elements on the islands. Réunion and Mauritius shared two main determining historical periods, despite being under different colonial rulers from 1810 onwards – both islands knew a system of slavery and indentured labour, which led to potent exchanges among the cultures of four continents. The ethnic composition of each island is, however, slightly different, and race and class in Réunion interact differently than the way they do in Mauritius. While Franco-Mauritians[3] maintain their positions as 'sugar-barons' (Eriksen, 1998: 13) and other positions of economic power, in Réunion the traditional colonial scheme has been subverted by the proletarianisation of a large part of the white population. From the mid-eighteenth century onwards poor white farmers had their land taken over by richer landowners so that those – black or white – who did not belong to the world of the plantation and had, therefore, lost a place in the economic system sought refuge in 'Les Hauts', away from the residential areas of the white Réunionnais élite and French expatriates.

Creolisation

Creolisation can be identified in ethnic, linguistic and cultural terms. In terms of ethnic denomination, *Creole* in Réunion refers to mostly *petit blancs* and in Mauritius to individuals of African or Malagasy origin, and on both islands to individuals of mixed ancestry, the *métis*, whom it is often difficult to pigeonhole into specific ethnic categories.

Linguistic creolisation, born out of the necessity for communication not only between master and slave but also among all slaves, gave birth to the Creole language. According to Chaudenson (1995),[4] a French lexicologist, Creole first originated from slave–master and slave–slave interactions in Réunion. In Mauritius, Creole underwent further development, which would result into a distinct Creole from that of Réunion (formerly known as Bourbon). French and Creole have coexisted in Mauritius since the eighteenth century, and from this time onwards various factors have contributed to the autonomous development of Mauritian Creole (hereafter MC). In fact, MC has grown increasingly distant from French and now incorporates words of English, Indian and Chinese. Although Mauritius is one of the few to be officially part of both the Commonwealth and the Francophonie, it remains above all Creolophone. The mother tongue of more than 70 per cent of the population, MC remains officially unacknowledged by the state, but has since independence been transformed into a literary language. Although Réunion Creole (RC) remains much closer to French in terms of both grammar and lexicon, it shares many of the socio-linguistic conditions of MC.[5]

The cultural creolisation of Mauritius and Réunion can be said to refer to the process by which diverse cultural elements from various continents have been adapted to an insular environment and created new parameters, a new language, culture and social organisation. Too complex to do justice to in a brief description, aspects of Réunionnais and Mauritian cultural creolisation, or *métissage*, will be demonstrated through the histories of their theatres.

Contemporary sister-islands

Despite having originally shared a similar colonial history, these southwest Indian Ocean islands have pointed differences. Mauritius became independent from Britain in 1968 and a republic in 1992. On the other hand, Réunion changed status from French colony to *département* in 1946. Following *départementalisation*, the massive intrusion of French media, the growing presence of metropolitan French[6] and the reinforced links with France posed a further threat to Réunion culture. Moreover, the legislative texts of 1946 denied the presence of a plural Réunionnais identity, acknowledging and promoting exclusively French language and culture.

Geographically distanced from France but politically integrated with it, Réunion is neither strictly speaking a colony nor a post-colony. Réunion is referred to aptly by Vergès (1999: xiv) as a recolonised post-colony, having moved from economic and cultural underdevelopment to an ultimate consumer society where goods imported from France give the island the look of French suburbs in the tropics. The economic structures, however, are close to those of the Third World and include high rates of unemployment, increasing costs of living, a culture of dependence on France and an all-powerful and crippling French bureaucracy. The relations between Réunion and France oscillate between the desire for complete integration with France, and increasing autonomy and belonging instead to the Mascarene archipelago.[7]

In Mauritius, however, British colonialism did not try to transform subjects into British citizens or Anglicise the island and, since independence, major socio-economic and political changes have taken place that have, in turn, brought changes to the ethnic division of economic and political power.[8] From the 1980s, Mauritius made a significant leap from an agricultural economy to becoming a so-called Newly Industrialised Country. Once the backbone of the economy, the sugar industry has given way to more dynamic and lucrative sectors: industry, tourism and offshore financial services. Fast economic growth has led to a near eradication of unemployment and, moreover, encouraged women to join the labour market.[9] Social mobility has been witnessed among all communities. From the end of the nineteenth century, the Indian majority has progressed most in economic and social terms, and, since 1957, has largely dominated the political scene.

Breaking out of a colonial past in Réunion and Mauritius
In Réunion, the official theatre of the eighteenth and nineteenth centuries, which mostly replicated Parisian scenes onto an exotic background, was a conformist theatre in standard French and was reserved for an intellectual and bourgeois élite. The presence of any coloured actors was stigmatised if not generally prohibited, even for the purposes of an authentic representation of blacks on stage. Joubert (1991: 203) notes the derogatory comments of a journalist (1839) on the opera version of Bernardin de Saint-Pierre's *Paul et Virginie* (1803)[10] as to the presence of blacks and the *sega*[11] on stage. This absence of coloured actors persisted until the 1980s and was a powerful cultural manifestation of the colonial need for censorship in an environment where it was deemed dangerous to provide the inferior classes with too much importance. Next to this theatre imported from France, in the twentieth century

there was also a popular theatre in RC which in the style of the boulevard theatre represented situations from daily life – weddings, adultery, relations between rich and poor Creoles – and where RC functioned primarily as a laughter-provoking device.

In Réunion, prior to the regional reforms of 1981[12] and the proclamation of respect for the right to difference, any assertion of a Réunionnais culture was seen as a political attack on France. Certain writers, such as Jean Albany (1917–84), were, however, already encouraging thought and research into a Réunionnais identity independent of, and even antithetical to, French culture. In 1977 the writer Axel Gauvin published *Du créole opprimé au créole libéré*, highlighting the struggles for a national language and developing theories of a national Réunionnais literature. An emerging cultural voice soon manifested itself in several ways: the affirmation of RC as a language; the rejection of the *zoreille* lifestyle;[13] the desire for greater cultural, political and economic integration with the surrounding countries. Music groups and musicians such as Ziskakan and Danyel Waro were particularly active in the rediscovery and promotion of *Maloya* – a mixture of African and Indian rhythms. Known as the blues of Réunion and banned until the 1960s, Maloya has now come back with a vengeance as a major aspect of both traditional and contemporary Réunionnais culture. The theatrical genre was to combine all these cultural elements into one event, both in terms of form by using RC as the linguistic medium, incorporating Maloya music and including coloured actors, and in terms of content. The 1980s was a time of hope and cultural revolution, allowing for the first time all the cultures present to express themselves and encouraging an exploration of history.

The theatrical scene in Mauritius underwent a parallel revolution. Until independence the stage remained heavily dominated by English and French dramatic culture. The historian Decotter (1983: 7) highlights forty years of performances of *The School for Scandal*, *Sinbad the Sailor* and *Julius Caesar*. It was the historical and ideological developments brought by political independence and highlighted by Dev Virahsawmy,[14] described by Eriksen (1998: 21) as a 'cultural one-man movement', which led to the emergence of a theatre of protest. Virahsawmy claimed that MC, an autonomous language, could fulfil the role of national cohesion and bring further cultural and political liberation: 'We Mauritians have something in common. It is a very useful tool for the creation of a nation. It can release the feelings of loyalty, self-respect and complete participation. It is the creole which we speak'

(*L'Express*, 5 October 1967). Virahsawmy's insistence on referring to MC as 'Morisiê' sought to invalidate the association between the language and the Creole ethnic group and included everyone on the basis of nationality rather than ethnicity. To reinforce the point that Mauritius had a national language to fall back on in the challenging task of nation-building, he engaged in creative writing in MC, starting with *Li* (1972), the first modern play in MC, and has not stopped. Since the 1980s several other playwrights realised it was time to break away from a literature exclusively aimed at an educated élite.

Militant theatre

The early protest theatre written in Creole, the language of the majority, is associated in Réunion from the 1980s onwards with Théâtre Vollard; in Mauritius with Dev Virahsawmy, Azize Asgarally and Henri Favory. The place of language in the playwright's conscience is itself of a militant nature, functioning as a self-conscious defiance of the colonial language. Furthermore, since French (and English in the Mauritian case) remain important linguistic barriers, their linguistic choice achieved far greater accessibility to a wider public. Indeed, by recuperating a language that had traditionally contributed to the marginalisation of the majority of the population, the theatre of protest provided a space for a voice so far repressed and unheard and is, therefore, an essential dimension of the struggle for the construction of a coherent sense of identity for the two Creolophone societies. Moreover, this new theatre, political in intent, far from using MC and RC for self-parody, addressed serious historical and anthropological issues.

Recovering history: slavery, marronnage *and* métissage

Eager to address the problems of decolonisation and identity, the starting point of the Réunionnais theatre of protest was to explore history and drag out a past heavily marked by slavery. Revisiting the past becomes an important means of fighting against a memory loss organised officially and interiorised by part of the population which feels ashamed of its past. Indeed, Emmanuel Genvrin blames the Réunionnais youth's ignorance of local history on the persisting colonial education: 'On n'apprend pas la colonisation. On apprend "nos ancêtres les Gaulois"' (We do not learn about colonisation. We learn 'our ancestors the Gauls').[15] Before his first original play, *Marie-Dessembre* (1986), Genvrin produced *Tempête* (1969) in 1980, a rewriting of *The Tempest* by the Martinican, Aimé Césaire. Symbolic in terms of the abuse of power and slave–master relations, and highly real in terms of geographical location on an isolated island regularly visited by cyclones, the play had a powerful hold on the imagination of the public.[16] It must be noted that the authorities initially banned the play, throwing the scenery and the actors onto the streets, in fear of the revolutionary power of this political theatre. Genvrin has been cast as a revolutionary ever since.[17] His position as white zoreille – from France – makes his endeavours to create a post-colonial, political, national Réunionnais theatre in RC all the more subversive.

Marie-Dessembre, a key play in the history of Réunionnais theatre,[18] was written specifically to mark the first celebration of the abolition of slavery. *Marie-Dessembre* was to use Réunion itself and its early historical origins as a source of inspiration, reviving both the barbarity of slavery and the exhilaration of freedom. In particular, the play focusses on slave resistance and escape into the mountains – *marronnage* – which allowed the people to create another system in opposition to the dominant régime. It is, in fact, due to marronnage that elements of Malagasy culture have survived despite the assimilative efforts of colonisers in Réunion.[19] On a plantation, Marie-Mirandine, a young female slave, is pregnant from her lover, the master's son. Her pregnancy having caused a scandal, she elopes to join other runaway slaves in Les Hauts region. Although she dies in childbirth, her daughter, born on the very day when the abolition of slavery is officially announced in 1848 and named Marie-Dessembre, is the daughter of freedom.

Furthermore, in this and other plays, Genvrin insistently highlights the role of *métissage* as a biological and cultural reality which forms the very basis of Réunionnais society. Recuperating the image and the reality of the *métis* – here, through Marie-Dessembre the half-caste heroine – is a reaction to both colonial fiction in which, Vergès (1999: 99) points out, the métis was an object of pity and contempt, and to a contemporary society where Creoles often reject their non-white legacy (Chane-Kune, 1993: 41). Indeed, in Réunion, as in Mauritius, the term *batard* remains charged with the prejudice of a colonial world, where the term was used to humiliate those born out of relations seen as illicit.[20] The inclusion of coloured actors on stage, an event non-existent before the advent of the TV, further illustrated a post-colonial rewriting of history. *Marie-Dessembre* was highly successful and has been brought back to the stage half a dozen times since it was first produced. Moreover, for the past twenty-five years, the 20th of December, considered the main national Réunionnais celebration, is celebrated with more enthusiasm than Christmas in some families. In addition, the fact that a hospital in Réunion has recently been named after Marie-Dessembre suggests the impact of a theatre which, inspired by historic and social reality, builds up a legitimate Réunionnais mythology.

In Mauritian theatre cultural decolonisation also took place through historical figures such as Ratsitatane in Azize Asgarally's play (1984) and an exploration of a different form of slavery, indentured labour, in those of Henri Favory's *Anjalay* (1980)[21] and *Tras* (1983). It was previously triggered off by Virahsawmy's *Li*, a crucial landmark in the history of Mauritian theatre where he was to prove that a serious, thought-provoking political dramatic literature could be written in MC, especially in contrast to the existing tradition of burlesque sketches.[22] Issa Asgarally in *Littérature et révolte* (1985: 90) highlights the impact of *Li* in breaking away from canonical colonial influences and initiating a popular theatre close to social and political realities. The first post-colonial play was a reaction to the climate of political oppression at the time, as well as a reminder of the strike by the Union of Bus Industry Workers which had paralysed Mauritius on 12 August 1971 and had led to Virahsawmy's own imprisonment in 1971/2. *Li*, a one-act play, revolves around a political prisoner deemed dangerous by the state and held in a detention room at a police station. The unnamed prisoner is referred to as *li* – the third-person pronoun in MC – by the other characters. Whilst Li persists in a hunger strike, people outside the station, for whom he represents a saviour, demonstrate for his release. The level of official corruption becomes increasingly obvious as the sergeant, himself a victim of higher powers, assassinates the prisoner in the belief that this will lead to his own promotion. Outside the police cell, the crowds demand justice. Given the militant profile of Virahsawmy and the revolutionary message of the play, the play was banned by the National Censorship Board on the eve of its first performance, in 1977. The banning of the play brought it into the limelight and reinforced its position as a militant landmark. In addition, in 1979, the Réunionnais press dedicated a few articles to Virahsawmy and his play while Carpanin Marimoutou – Réunionnais poet, critic and academic – published a tri-lingual version of the play in MC, RC and French.[23] Virahsawmy submitted the play to the eleventh Concours de Radio-France International and won first prize in 1981. Four years later, *Li* was translated into English and published in a bi-lingual version as *Li – The Prisoner of Conscience* (1985).

Favory has written and staged numerous plays with great success. He writes in MC so as to reach the widest audience irrespective of class background.[24] *Tras* (1983) is one of his best known and the only one to have been published. Described as an act of 'rendre l'histoire à ses véritables propriétaires' (*Le Mauricien*, 31 January 1983), it is the manifestation of an emerging post-colonial identity attempting to reclaim its history. The play takes place in a courtroom where a sugar estate, a powerful institution which is still under the control of the Franco-Mauritians, referred to in MC as *tablisman*, is being sued by the labourers who have been dismissed without payment or compensation. The sugar estate, however, bribes its way into the support of the field supervisor, the police and even that of the court. In this conflict, the exploitation of the proletariat is closely and clearly linked to a neo-colonial form of exploitation, a continuation of plantation power relations by an economically powerful white hegemony, where generations of slaves have been succeeded by generations of indentured labourers and yet more exploited workers into the twentieth century.

An attempt to reclaim history directly, Azize Asgarally's *Ratsitatane* is until today regarded as 'la première pièce de théâtre à caractère historique', 'the first historical play' of Mauritius (*Weekend*, 29 January 1984). In line with Asgarally's militant agenda in writing *Ratsitatane* (1983),[25] his main aim was to allow a rediscovery of Ratsitatane, the nephew of Radama, king of Madagascar, exiled to Mauritius on suspicion of conspiracy against the British authorities. In Mauritius, while on the run, Ratsitatane was betrayed, tracked down and executed in public. In the recounting of these historical events, Asgarally challenges the persisting popular colonial image of Ratsitatane as the savage who abducted a French woman, raped her and drove her to suicide,[26] portraying, instead, a shrewd and committed politician determined to set his country free from British colonial power. In line with this post-colonial rewriting of history, the play is also deeply philosophical, challenging both the colonial perspective and its ideology.[27]

Réunionnais and Mauritian playwrights have seized on the idea that history only exists and can be understood through representations. Their re-enactment of history through performance is clearly an intellectual construction eager to provoke a reassessment of their respective identities. Virahsawmy, who started his dramatic career from an initially didactic perspective with *Li*, soon moved to satire. In fact, after a few initially serious militant plays, the theatre of both Réunion and Mauritius has successfully provided reflection on contemporary politics through laughter.

In *Zeneral Makbef* (1981), another major play by Virahsawmy, political satire and burlesque are used to address the internal corruption of Mauritius and the imperialism of the major world powers. The journalist and critic Seebaluck comments that 'here Dev Virahsawmy the writer should not be mistaken for Dev Virahsawmy the politician' (*Weekend*, 6 September 1981), highlighting a switch from didactic to creative dramatic writing. Makbef, who makes himself emperor of a republic, with a lust for power matched only by an unnaturally intense sexual appetite for both men and women, is a satirical reference to leaders such as Bokassa and Idi Amin Dada. Makbef is reduced to being the comic victim of the rivalry between two superpowers, the Yankidola and the Rusputik.[28] *Zeneral Makbef* warns against two types of oppression facing post-colonial countries, the risk of becoming a puppet in the hands of the superpowers and of becoming the victim of their own leaders. Although *Zeneral Makbef* is deeply political, the success of this three-act play relies on the satirical and humorous exploitation of relevant issues of protest for a local public.[29]

Similar in style and no less biting in the sharpness of its political comments, is Théâtre Vollard's *Votez Ubu colonial* (1994), one of the most successful plays in the history of Réunionnais theatre. Having played the original *Ubu Roi* by Jarry in 1979, Genvrin successfully adapted Jarry's antimilitarism and mockery of power games, ambition and administrations, to the specificities of Réunionnais politics and culture. The character, Bebel, an obese and stupid porter, wants to be elected king of the island, as Ubu. Mother Marcelle who runs an eatery with her husband, attracted by the financial gains, organises the elections. The Ubu is here played by a black actor to remind viewers that corruption and tyranny come from all sides, as seen in *Zeneral Makbef*. Ubu's political campaign revolves around the philosophy of *faire tatane*, 'to do nothing' and make the most of *l'argent gratuit*, 'free money', the term used for the unemployment and social benefits from *la grosse mère poule*, 'the mother-hen'. The latter term parodies the colonial image of France as 'a pure essence of love'.[30] Genvrin's political theatre is both insolent in its comments on the culture of dependence nurtured by France in Réunion and the corruption of bureaucrats, and festive as actors mingle among the spectators, distributing voting bulletins and even serving food. Virahsawmy's and Genvrin's plays seek inspiration from both local and foreign cultures, transcending – but not shunning – a Mauritian and

Réunionnais reality. By linking local to foreign cultures through Shakespearean and Jarry references, for example, many of their plays illustrate that while an intense and specific sense of time and place allows theatre to be oppositional and relevant to the audience, it need not reduce the appeal of the performance to a small number of spectators or limit it to an exclusively local source.

In *Votez Ubu colonial* the serving of local dishes during the interval by actors and actresses turned waiters and waitresses is a distinctive and polyfunctional trait of Genvrin's dramaturgy. The kitchen corner, the focus of the play, is not only the literal and metaphorical space where electoral as well as judicial matters are 'concocted', it is also one of the spaces where a miscegenated Réunionnais identity assumes itself.[31] Carpanin Marimoutou (1988) points out that Réunionnais food at once integrates and goes beyond ethno-cultural practices, which oppose one another in other areas. In the case of *Lepervenche chemin de fer* (1996),[32] performed in the village of La Grande Chaloupe, the inclusion of dinner in the ticket price benefitted the village locals, who were paid for the culinary responsibilities. Furthermore, Genvrin explains that through local food, he brings a Réunionnais festive dimension to the experience of theatre, as he does with the inclusion of the sega to which actors invite the spectators to dance on stage in several plays.[33] The celebration of the sega, local food and RC, cultural legacies of ancient slaves – important manifestations of a Réunionnais culture until recently believed to be non-existent – is the more relevant in a political and cultural context where some Réunionnais feel they are in exile in their own country, poised – as Françoise Lionnet (1993: 104) describes it – between a regional *Francité* and an international *Francophonie*. TV works towards counteracting this exile and defying a French hegemonic system within Réunion. The inclusion of local cuisine can, in fact, be seen as a reaction to the replacement of local dishes based on rice, grains and curries in schools by steak and French fries, which had already caused uproar.[34]

The Réunionnais' desire to regain and inhabit fully their own islands is also manifested through the use of space in theatre. Although both Théâtre Vollard and the Réunionnais Théâtre Talipot (TT) try to take theatre where it does not usually go, preferring to avoid classical theatre venues, TV's style in creating its own scenographic space in old garages and cinemas, in an open air theatre which avoids the play of light and sound effects, is distinctive. *Lepervenche chemin de fer*, a historical play situated in 1937–47, was an ambitious and successful project, performed appropriately in the train station of Grande Chaloupe that had been in disuse since 1964. Tracing the history of the trade union movement through the life of an aristocratic communist, Léon de Lepervenche, the play is a reminder that *départementalisation* had been the achievement of the left. Performed first in 1990, then in 1991, 1992 and 1996, the play reached 40,000 spectators. Performances involved the restoration of one of the old trains, which transported spectators in a literal travel across 6 km to the stage and a symbolic time-travel to an important page of Réunion history. This community theatre project initiative engaged and employed local people, a lot of whom were unemployed at the time. Moreover, spectators were forced to take the ration tickets which the Réunionnais would have had to collect during the Second World War and to move from one place to another within the old station for different scenes. The location of the play and the physical involvement of the public symbolised a reappropriation of the island's history and geography.

The solidarity reflex of Réunionnais society – itself highly heterogenous – under threat from the Francophone world informs both the content and the form of Réunionnais theatre and results in a distinct dramaturgy. In reflections on the issue of cultural miscegenation, playwrights from both islands have had to create further theatrical semiotics, of which two more aspects stand out – the play on languages and the construction of new inter-textual myths.

Language and cultural miscegenation

In Creole-speaking islands where there is already a close link between the lingua franca, which cuts across all ethnic groups, and a history of cultural miscegenation, the language of theatre becomes the locus of cultural contacts, the expression of a plural dialectic in a limited shared space. Indeed, the imaginary space of theatre informed by a multi-cultural consciousness, in both Réunion and Mauritius, proposes a language that sustains the transformed presence of all languages and cultures. TT, which has been established since 1986 and is directed by Philippe Pelen, is dedicated to the themes of travel, exile and the need to find one's identity within oneself rather than in a lost home. This theatre group often makes use of Indian, Comoran and Malagasy words to several effects, particularly in *Mâ* (1996), a musical play about a young couple's difficult journey to conceive a child, during which they come across the sorceress Kalla and the maternal figure of Mâ.

In the opening scene of *Mâ* there is no linguistic text, only performance in terms of body language, music and dance functioning as an invitation from the artists to the spectators. Equally, in scene 2 we witness the ceremonial entrance of musicians, followed by the spectators and finally the artists. In the third scene, the creation of the world is accompanied by an incantation of Sanskrit syllables:

A I OU E O
KA KHA GA GHA GNA
CHA CHAH JA JHA NGA
TA THA DA DHA NA
TA THA DA DHA NA
PA PHA BA BHA MA
YA RA LA VA SA SHA . . .

Sanskrit not only confers an ancient dimension to the scene, but indicates Pelen's idiosyncratic trait of using rhythmic pulses from different cultures rather than language to convey meaning. He forces the spectator to look beyond the text in terms of information, to the energy behind sounds, whether in terms of incantations in Sanskrit, Malagasy or Comoran. By representing words as music, that is, not only as a series of concepts but also as an aural emotion which acts on the body and the mind, the play transcends linguistic barriers. TT work on oral traditions, musical instruments from Africa, Europe and India as witnessed in the first two scenes particularly, to create a universal dramatic language, a miscegenated art form akin to jazz and flamenco.

Pelen's theatre veers automatically away from mainstream theatre, refusing to be pigeonholed in relation to a particular style or politics, and acknowledges parallels to Peter Brook's theatre.[35] However, TT's exploitation of cross-cultural forms of theatre through dance, music and languages – regional as well as international – rather than links with France, runs deeper than the parallel to Brook. Given a context where the di-glossic asymmetry between RC and French has been less seriously challenged in Réunion and other French DOM-TOMs (Départements d'Outre-Mer, Territoires d'Outre-Mer, which include Réunion, Guadeloupe and Martinique) than in Mauritius, Pelen's attempt to get away from an exclusive cultural and linguistic relation with French in the search for a Réunionnais theatrical semiotics has the more relevance. Since there is an underlying assumption that 'one people and one language are the prerequisites for living together as a nation' (Lionnet 1993: 101), that the French language makes Réunion French, Pelen's use of multi-lingual theatrical discourses captures the multi-cultural Creole world of Réunion, thereby legitimising an anthropological truth previously unacknowledged and even deliberately suppressed by French cultural imperialism.

In Mauritius, Virahsawmy also writes self-consciously within a multicultural context and plays on the range of languages spoken and written on the island in a creative fashion. In *Toufann* (1990), his rewriting of *The Tempest*, several words are borrowed from Indian and Chinese languages, such as the title itself, which is borrowed from Bhojpuri.[36] Moreover, Dammarro and Kaspalto (the equivalents of Stephano and Trinculo) occasionally code-switch to English. For example, when asked by Dammarro if he wants a drag of his spliff, Kaspalto replies: 'Never! Whiskey is all I take' (Act 1, scene 5), before resuming in MC. This code-switching to English reveals both subalterns' belief that the only way they can aspire to prestige is through the colonial language, a belief which is reinforced by the fact that politically powerful characters themselves speak in English cliché phrases. After the royal ship has been wrecked and trapped on Prospero's island, at a time of crisis when Lerwa Lir (in lieu of King Alonso) is expected to come up with a solution or, at least, a profound analysis of the situation, he declares melodramatically, 'Power corrupts . . . Absolute power corrupts absolutely' (Act 2, scene 3). Similarly, the only words of wisdom that the counsellor, Poloniouss, can think of when Lir is at his most desperate are, 'where there is a will, there is a way' (Act 2, scene 5). Far from casting on Lir and Poloniouss an aura of the knowledgeable and powerful, the repeated use of clichés – which function explicitly as cultural quotations where the form is more important than the content – reveals, instead, a mental lethargy, the inability to express thoughts and feelings in more creative and expressive ways, and, consequently, an inability to find solutions.

Whilst many writers in Mauritius use the mediums of English and French interspersed with MC idioms for a local flavour, and many translations retain indigenous words for an exotic flavour, Virahsawmy turns the situation around by rewriting the *Tempest* into *Toufann* in a confident MC with, instead, a Shakespearean flavour where bits of English carefully scattered become the exotic. Code-switching in *Toufann* is, therefore, of parodic nature, serving to undermine the assumption that in a di-glossic situation it is the dominant culture that imposes its conception of literariness. Thus, code-switching in *Toufann* is not merely a register choice which sheds light onto the characters, but is here manipulated as a complex and sophisticated literary device to deconstruct the very concept of (canonical/colonial) literariness.

Myths

Whilst early plays focussed on political and historical figures, in more recent plays juggling with myths of various cultural origins becomes a way of exploring cultural creolisation. In *Mâ*, Pelen brings together the various aspects of two female mythical figures, Mâ and Kalla, across continents. Mâ, of Sanskrit etymology and common to a lot of languages to refer to 'mother', is the universal divine mother, the guardian of all sources and traditions in Hinduism. Moreover, in the days of slavery in Réunion, it was also the term of respect used to address slaves who could not be addressed as 'Madam'. Next to Mâ there is also the legendary Réunionnais figure of Kalla or Gran Mère Kal, the sorceress who eats badly behaved children. This myth is based on the historic figure, Kal, a slave woman who was violently separated from her young child, killed and thrown away without any burial rites. According to Réunionnais folklore, her restless soul still roams in search of her child. Kal also exists in Madagascar as a potent female spirit, and in India she represents one of the forms taken by the Goddess Kali, the destroyer of evil, with red tongue and dishevelled hair. By simultaneously drawing from these diverse sources, Pelen's theatre brings together on stage what is separate elsewhere and contributes to the creation of myths both specific to the Réunionnais space and accessible to a diverse community.

In Mauritius, whereas previous feminist plays, such as Favory's *Anjalay*, were strongly rooted, and rightly so, within post-colonial outrage, in Virahsawmy's recent trilogy of the late 1990s and early 2000s, *Mamzel Zann* (1996), *Ti-Marie* (2000), *Romeo ek so Ziliet* (2001), it is a feminist agenda that comes to the fore. Virahsawmy's belief in *konpran feminin*,[37] 'feminine reasoning', informs his creation of new inter-textual feminist myths, particularly in *Ti-Marie*. In *Ti-Marie*, literally *Little-Mary*, myths from the Old and New Testaments and Hinduism are revisited. The prologue concludes with the single line: 'Sans ti'ena Ti-Marie', 'Thanks God, there was Ti-Marie', announcing a rewriting of the main events of the New Testament with Ti-Marie as prophet. The play opens with M-M Capricorn, a dressmaker who runs her own workshop and employs a few assistants. She is the mother of Ti-Marie, born on the 25th of December and whose father, Jeri Capricorn, is on a secret mission to avert the colonising ambitions of another planet, Jalsa Douniya.[38] The play ends with the revelation that M-M Capricorn's first name is Marie-Madeleine.[39]

The name Ti-Marie is highly significant. It allows a feminist rewriting of the myths surrounding the Virgin Mary and Mary Magdalene in the

New Testament. Jeri Capricorn's initials clearly indicate that he represents Jesus. Marie-Madeleine, Mary Magdalene, is Jeri's wife, by whom she has a child, Ti-Marie. Virahsawmy deconstructs the bi-polar myth of the saint and the sinner by presenting Marie-Madeleine in the roles of both Jeri's lover as well as Ti-Marie's mother. The passive motherhood associated with the Virgin Mary, who only functions as mother of the Saviour, is dismissed and replaced instead by Ti-Marie, who, neither saint, nor sinner, neither passive, nor mother, is a feminist rebellious adolescent. The limelight which Ti-Marie as title and name of the main protagonist benefits from is part of an attempt to subvert the dominant discourses of patriarchy and religion which place men at the centre of the universe, presenting women as marginal and only existing in terms of the roles they fulfil towards men, both in Mauritius and beyond. The playwright does the same in the rock-opera *Dropadi* (1982),[40] which he incorporates in the form of a mask within *Ti-Marie*. Dropadi is the name of an Indian princess in the millennia-old Sanskrit epic, *Mahabharata*.[41] Whereas the *Mahabharata* is known for its (male) warriors, kings and princes, Virahsawmy focusses on the female character of Dropadi. The inclusion of *Dropadi* in *Ti-Marie* both reinforces the feminist slant of the latter play and reflects new possibilities of redressing the balance of power between the representation of men and women on a universal basis, by drawing from various cultural sources. The chorus of *Dropadi* backs this up:

> Dropadi finn ne, Halelouya;
> Dropadi finn ne, Soubhaan Allah;
> Dropadi finn ne, Shanti, Shanti, Shanti.
>
> Dropadi is born, Halelouya
> Dropadi is born, Soubhann Allah
> Dropadi is born, Shanti, Shanti, Shanti.   (Scene 6)

Halelouya, Soubhaan Allah and *Shanti*, used to welcome the birth of Dropadi, represent the acclaim of Christianity, Islam and Hinduism. Rewriting past patriarchal myths into feminist myths becomes a means of reconceptualising the future.

The specificity of Virahsawmy's theatre lies in its self-conscious revelling in inter-textuality and the fact that his obsessive reference to canonical works is far from being paradoxical to his development of a Mauritian theatre. Indeed, whilst, on one hand, his plays maintain a literary link with master-narratives, including Shakespeare, the Bible and the *Mahabharata*, across various plays, on the other hand, he also maintains a linguistic and socio-cultural connivance with a Mauritian audience, bringing to the literary canon Mauritian and post colonial and cultural references that are alien to it. He seeks inspiration from the colonial cultures but refuses to be cornered within their confines, let alone assimilated. This is clearly demonstrated by his focus on code-switching to English and French as highly punishable by laughter and a strong form of resistance to Anglophilia or Francophilia. The ability to use MC without feeling the need to constantly code-switch to English and French is valued as a symbol of a Mauritian identity that has broken loose of a linguistic and cultural inferiority complex instilled by colonisation. Moreover, as Virahsawmy puts it himself, his particular focus on translations from Shakespeare reflects his intentions to 'Use Shakespeare to enhance my language' (Wilkinson, 2001: 113). In addition to original works and adaptations in MC, Virahsawmy has engaged in translations of plays from English, mostly, but also from French into MC.[42]

Like Pelen, Virahsawmy seeks to explore cultural creolisation, neither in the condescending terms of acceptance or tolerance of one another, nor in assimilation, but rather, through the discovery of the universal within individual cultures. Playing with the literary and cultural myths of diverse cultures allows playwrights to ease out different functions and statuses than those ascribed by the cultures which gave birth to them, 'in defiance of the classical canonical closures' (Said, 1992: 3). Theatre in both Réunion and Mauritius provides a reflection on the fact that individuals in these heterogenous societies often affirm a plural identity rooted in choice and preference rather than in pigeonholed cultural allegiances. In Virahsawmy's case, the dissociation of feminist from other colonial issues is indicative of a culture that is moving on from, or can at least distance itself from, the scars of a colonial past and an external colonial aggressor, to address contemporary political and cultural issues of its own making and find redemptive ways of life.

Conclusion

In Réunion and Mauritius, the move away from a theatre relevant exclusively to a minority English and/or French speaking élite, in terms of linguistic medium and issues addressed, combined with the valorisation of previously ignored local material, entailed what Baz Kershaw terms a significant 'democratisation of culture' (1992: 10). The act of recovering history and denouncing colonial and neo-colonial political scandals through theatre was an important part of affirming a national identity. The theatre of both Réunion and Mauritius in an attempt to define cultural specificity has, however, evolved beyond the master–slave polarisation to focus on the ethno-cultural originality of the islands, achieving a synthesis between the revalorisation of history and research and analysis of contemporary questions.

Latest developments in theatre examine the specific Réunionnais and Mauritian cultures without privileging exclusively the European input and literary culture, which is, nevertheless, an important part of the history of both islands. Theatre has been an important factor in creating a certain political awareness and self-awareness that are necessary to the construction of a collective Réunionnais identity and the concept of cultural miscegenation. Whilst in Mauritius there is less of a threat to the various ethnic groups, which retain their cultural specificities in terms of language, religion and other cultural practices, the more repressive political system of Réunion has led to interesting theatrical experimentation, which is now a distinct aspect of the Réunionnais dramaturgy. Since a revaluation of the cultural identity of a people is inevitably a powerful attack on the standardisation of culture and consciousness, Réunionnais theatre can be seen to be working to stop a French imperial rule as being universalised as common sense, and to highlight – within this peripheral Francophonie – a centre of cultural resistance and creolisation. Contemporary theatre in both islands is indicating that the future lies not only in the post-colonial assertion of a miscegenated and plural identity free of Francophilia, in the case of Réunion, and of both Francophilia and Anglophilia in the case of Mauritius, but equally in the empowerment of women. In Mauritius the theatre of Virahsawmy, in particular, aims at stopping patriarchy from being seen as a *sine qua non*.

All the plays discussed in this chapter have been successful not only within the region but also in mainland Africa, Australia and Europe, and many of them have been translated into various foreign languages. There is also a crucial link between theatre and the Creole language on both islands. Theatre, initially one of protest, has not only benefitted from the use of Creole but also, in turn, has valorised RC and MC. In Réunion, it is generally acknowledged that Théâtre Vollard has transformed the language into an important means of communication and a cultural vehicle. Mauritian theatre has also been highly influential in redefining the role of MC as the *de facto* national language and the symbol of a cross-ethnic national identity. Virahsawmy (Tranquille, 2000) even affirms that MC is now a fully-fledged language that has shed many of its Creole structures, which is why it should be referred to simply as Mauritian.

Kafka's observation that the memory of a small nation is no shorter than that of a large one and that the smaller nation reworks available material all the more thoroughly, certainly holds true for Mauritius and Réunion. His comment that theatre will be less the concern of literary history than that of the people is less so. It is precisely because theatre has positively affected and influenced the lives of those who live in Réunion and Mauritius and travelled beyond those confines that it informs, in powerful and complementary ways, the history of world theatre, starting with that of Africa. Having summarised some of the political and cultural achievements and revelations made by theatre in Réunion and Mauritius,[43] I must shed my starting point of insignificance.[44]

Notes

1. This phrase is actually from Patrick Bellegrade-Smith, quoted by Françoise Lionnet in her introduction to *Autobiographical Voices* (New York: Cornell University Press, 1989) and in turn quoted by Vergès.
2. The name comes from Ambroise Vollard, a Creole from Réunion, friend of Alfred Jarry (1873–1907), author of the *Ubu* plays. In twenty years thirty-five performances have been undertaken by Théâtre Vollard. They have worked with 280 artists, and have reached over 300,000 people, almost half of the population of Réunion. Emmanuel Genvrin, a Frenchman now settled in Réunion, is the writer and director. In Mauritius, Dev Virahsawmy is a linguist, ex-politician and creative writer. Seeing himself as an organic intellectual, his dedication to creative writing in Mauritian Creole is informed by his belief in the links between this language and socio-economic, political and cultural national development. He has more than forty literary *œuvres* published, including twenty-odd plays.
3. Mauritians of French origin.
4. There has been an on-going debate between Chaudenson and Baker (1982) as to the genesis of Mauritian Creole (hereafter MC). Baker rejects Chaudenson's hypothesis of Creole as an approximation of an approximation of dialect-influenced seventeenth-century spoken French, and focusses instead on the input of African languages on the structure of MC.
5. Vergès, 1999: 194 comments that every year in Réunion thousands of schoolchildren leave school barely literate, due to an education which has remained foreign to both the island's language and culture. The rate of illiteracy is also high in Mauritius. Although educational material has been adapted to the local reality, the medium of instruction is still a foreign language, namely English.

6. The French working in Réunion are entitled to twice the pay of local Réunionnais for the same job.

7. Given its schizophrenic political make-up, it is hardly surprising that Réunion also holds an ambiguous position within the Indian Ocean. Réunion is both commiserated for not having achieved independence and viewed with envy as a mercenary minority of France. Moreover, given its membership of the European Economic Community it is viewed in the African environment with suspicion, as France's watchdog and a base from which France potentially operates as a regional sphere of influence.

8. Despite over one hundred and fifty years of British colonisation – 1810 to 1968 – Chaudenson, 1995: 246 notes the 'theoretical' nature of the British presence on the island. Not only was Anglophone immigration almost non-existent, the few English families who did settle in Mauritius were soon integrated culturally and linguistically into the Franco-Mauritian community.

9. Despite this major socio-cultural change, however, Mauritius remains a strongly patriarchal society.

10. The context of the novel is slavery in Mauritius.

11. The music and dance forms of the slaves are an important legacy to both Réunionnais and Mauritian cultures.

12. Réunion became a *région d'outre mer*.

13. *Zoreille*, meaning literally 'ear', is a tongue-in-cheek term used by the Réunionnais for the metropolitan French, alluding to their hearing difficulty experienced in understanding the Creole-speaking locals. This term, therefore, subverts the colonial myth that RC is gibberish by shifting communicative difficulties on to 'inadequate' French ears.

14. After post-graduate studies in linguistics in the UK – 'Towards a Reevaluation of Mauritian Creole' (Applied Linguistics Diploma, Edinburgh, 1967) – on his return to Mauritius, Virahsawmy wrote a series of radical articles, inspired by his M.A. dissertation, in the Mauritian daily *L'Express* (April 1967–April 1968), creating the awareness that MC was the national language of Mauritius.

15. For Genvrin see www.regards.fr/archives/1998/. The subject matter of Théâtre Vollard's plays have often explicitly reflected the decisive stages in the history of the island's population:

- The French Revolution in *Etuves* (1989)
- The abolition of slavery (1848) in *Marie-Dessembre* (1986)
- The *départementalisation* in *Lepervenche Chemin de fer* (1996)
- Violence and corruption of local politics in *Votez Ubu colonial* (1994)
- 1991 riots, which caused eight deaths in Chaudron, in *Emeutes* (1997)

16. *The Tempest* continues to wield immense influence on post-colonial island literatures in particular. In Mauritius, Dev Virahsawmy's *Toufann* (1990), a

reworking of the Shakespearean play, was a success and the subject of an international conference, 'Toufann and Other Tempests: Shakespeare in Postcolonial Contexts', London, 1999.

17. Although dependent on French and local authorities for subsidies, TV is at war with the latter and, consequently, is made to pay for its anti-conformist views. An offical report, the Wurtz Report (1992, http://www.vollard.com/ ecrits/Wurtz.html), from a general inspector at the Ministry of Culture, acknowledges the pioneering role played by TV to Réunionnais theatre, but explains that they will not be given the direction of the CDR, the Centre Dramatique Régional established in 1998, due to the 'provocative character' of Genvrin. Following this, TV lost one-third of its sponsorships and the support of the Ministry of Culture.

18. Prior to *Marie-Dessembre* there had been a few playwrights working in isolation.

19. The issue of marronnage also dominates a large proportion of the works of French Caribbean writers, such as Maryse Condé and Edouard Glissant.

20. Virahsawmy also recuperates the métis in *Toufann*. Whereas Césaire, in *Tempête*, had focussed on a black Caliban to the obvious detriment of a conformist métis Aryel, in Virahsawmy's text, Caliban is an intelligent, resourceful and good-looking young métis who not only wins the heart of Prospero's daughter but also becomes King of Naples.

21. This play is named after an Indian-descent pregnant agricultural worker who was shot by the colonial police. In September 1943 in the village of Belle-Vue Harel, police opened fire on striking workers attending a religious ceremony. Four labourers were wounded and five killed, including Anjalay. Favory's play was performed on stage and also turned into a documentary film by Atelier de Théâtre Pierre Poivre.

22. Hookoomsing points out that until the emergence of the protest theatre in MC, the stage had been restricted to brief comical sketches revolving around the burlesque (1984: 397).

23. The tri-lingual version was published by Les Chemins de la Liberté – specialising in the publication and diffusion of literature in Creole – under the direction of Firmin Lacpatia. Several of Virahsawmy's works have been spread thus in Réunion and the group Ziskakan still use his early poems as song lyrics.

24. Favory referred to numerous occasions when he assessed the reactions of young adults to the language used in drama. His main observation was that a theatre in English would be shunned, one in French would be only partially accessible, while a theatre in MC was fully accessible and more enjoyable to a local audience, cutting across all classes and ethnic groups. Personal communication, September 1997.

25. In an interview for *L'Express* (18 February 2001), Azize Asgarally explains:

> J'écris . . . *Ratsitatane* en créole, c'était en 1982 ou 1983, parce qu'à l'époque je ressens le besoin profond d'exprimer une certaine révolte et un certain engagement dans ma langue maternelle.

> I wrote *Ratsitatane* in creole, it was in 1982 or 1983, because at that time I felt the deep need to express a certain rebellion and an engagement in my mother-tongue.

26. The colonial version is from Lucien Brey's account of the Malagasy prince in *Voleur Mauricien*, a literary journal which appeared in 1889.
27. For more details on *Tras* and *Ratsitatane*, see Mooneeram, 1999b.
28. Both *Yankidola* and *Rusputik* are examples of word-play. The first evokes the bargaining power of the American dollar (Yankey dollar) over a Third World country, the second evokes the Russians through the first and last syllables.
29. For Virahsawmy's other political plays, see Mooneeram, 2001.
30. Vergès, 1999: 152 observes: 'The dominant conservative fiction was that France loved her colonized children. France was idealized and transformed into a pure essence of love.'
31. See Baggioni and Marimoutou, 1988.
32. See below.
33. See Genvrin at www.regards.fr/archives/1998/. Since music is the most popular art form in both Réunion and Mauritius, and musical comedies are particularly popular, particular priority is given to music (particularly the *sega*) across most plays and theatre companies. In the plays of Théâtre Talipot (TT), several musical influences have aesthetic as well as semiotic functions. TV insists that all its actors should also be musicians. Local songs predominate in *Votez Ubu Colonial* and piercing Malagasy songs in *Marie-Dessembre*, for example.
34. See www.regards.fr/archives/1998/.
35. TT situate their works alongside the dramatic works of Peter Brook. Indeed, the semiotics of Mâ reflect Brook's (1987: 239) 'culture of links . . . between men and society, between one race and another, between the microcosm and the macrocosm, between humanity and machinery, between the visible and invisible, between categories, languages and genres.'
36. Bhojpuri, originally brought from north-east India, is the mother-tongue of around 15 per cent of the population. *Toufann* is the equivalent of 'tempest'. As opposed to *siklonn*, an established MC lexical item used by all speakers, both urban and rural, the word *toufann* is restricted to rural areas.
37. Also the title of a book co-written by Dev and Loga Virahsawmy (2001).
38. Bhojpuri for 'World of Fun'.

39. Virahsawmy often portrays Jesus and Mary Magdalene as lovers in line with his belief that chastity or sexual repression is a form of destruction.

40. *Dropadi* has not yet been performed. This on-going delay is due to the strong objection of extremist members of both the Creole and Hindu groups in Mauritius. On one hand, Virahsawmy and Sullivan were accused by the Creoles of 'Indianising', on the other, they were accused by the Hindus of 'westernising' their culture.

41. The *Mahabharata* recounts the injustice done to a righteous family by a rival one, and the former's final triumph via the help of the God Krishna after a bloody war.

42. Some examples are *Enn ta Senn dan Vid* (*Much Ado About Nothing*) (LPT, 1995); *Trazedji Makbess* (LPT, 1997); *Tartchif Froder* (*Tartuffe*) (Boukie Banane, 1999); *Zil Sezar* (*Julius Caesar*) (Boukie Banane, 1999); *Les Misérables* (unpublished but produced in 1999). Translations and rewritings of Shakespeare contribute towards redefining a di-glossic situation (typified by linguistic insecurity) into one of co-lingualism (which highlights a relationship of equality), encouraging the complementary position of MC next to French and English.

43. A further sign that theatre is healthy on both islands is the diversity of sub-genres and various theatre forms. In 1999, in Réunion, Hazaël-Massieux notes twenty-two registered theatre companies, including both small companies set up over the past fifteen years without much professional training and groups which operate on a fully professional basis. Komela Théâtre, which focusses on visual arts, objects, puppets and sees itself as popular street theatre, seeks to reach a more heterogeneous public by taking theatre to the people (rather than vice versa) and revalorising the function of the spectator and the receiver. There is also the CDR. In Mauritius, various theatre groups are thriving – Henri Favory, Atelier de Théâtre Pierre Poivre and a group of some of the best Mauritian actors brought together by the firm Immedia to export staged Mauritian humour to Paris and London in March 2002 (Fun under the Sun – 100 per cent Mauritian humour).

44. Borrowed from Vergès, 1999.

References and futher reading

Anderson, Benedict. 1991. *Imagined Communities: Reflections on the Origin and Spread of Nationalism*. London: Verso.

Armand, Alain and Chopinet, Gérard. 1983. *La Littérature réunionnaise d'expression créole 1828–1982*. Paris: l'Harmattan.

Asgarally, Azize. 1984. *Ratsitatane*. Rose-Hill: Loyster.

Asgarally, Issa. 1985. *Littérature et révolte*. Mauritius: Le Flamboyant.

Baggioni, Daniel and Jean-Claude Carpanin Marimoutou, eds. 1988. *Cuisines/Identités*. Saint-Denis: University of Réunion Press.

Baker, Philip, with Chris Come. 1982. *Isle de France Cresle: Affinities and Origin*. Ann Arbor: Karoma.

Beniamino, Michel. 1999. *La Francophonie Littéraire. Essai pour une théorie*. Paris: l'Harmattan.

Brook, Peter. 1987. *The Shifting Point*. New York: Harper and Row.

Chane-Kune, Sonia. 1993. *Aux origines de l'identité réunionnaise*. Paris: l'Harmattan.

Chaudenson, Robert. 1981, *Textes Créoles anciens (La Réunion et l'Ille Maurice). Comparaison et essai d'analyse*. Hamburg: Helmut Buske Verlag.

Chaudenson, Robert. 1995. *Les Créoles*. Paris: Presses Universitaires de France.

Cherel, Guillaume. 1998. *Fête de l'humanité*. www.regards.fr/archives/1998/

Decotter, André. 1983. *Le Plaze un demi-siècle devie théâtrale*. Rose-Hill: Précigraph.

Devonish, Hubert. 1986. *Language and Liberation: Creole Language Politics in the Caribbean*. London: Karia Press.

Eriksen, Thomas Hylland. 1998. *Common Denominators: Ethnicity, Nation-Building and Compromise in Mauritius*. Oxford: Berg.

Favory, Henri. 1983. *Tras*. Port-Louis: Piblikasyon Grup Enn.

Gauvin, Axel. 1977. *Du créole opprimé au créole libéré*. Paris: l'Harmattan.

Genvrin, Emmanuel. 1987. *Marie-Dessembre*. La Possession: Théâtre Vollard.

Genvrin, Emmanuel. 1994. *Votez Ubu Colonial*. Saint-Denis: Editions Grand Océan.

Genvrin, Emmanuel. 1996. *Lepervenche Chemin de fer*. Saint-Denis: Editions Grand Océan.

Hazaël-Massieux, Marie-Christine. *Le théâtre créolophone dans les DOM: Traduction, adaptations, contacts de langues*. www.superdoc.com/

Hookoomsing, Vinesh. 1984. 'Langue créole, littérature nationale et mauricianisme populaire', in *Anthologie de la nouvelle poésie créole*, ed. Lambert-Felix Prudent, Paris: l'Harmattan.

Joubert, Jean-Louis. 1991. *Littératures de l'océan indien*. Vanves: Editions Classiques d'Expression Française.

Kershaw, Baz. 1992. *The Politics of Performance: Radical Theatre as Cultural Intervention*. London and New York: Routledge.

Lionnet, Françoise. 1993. 'Créolité in the Indian Ocean: Two Models of Cultural Diversity', in *Postcolonial Conditions: Exiles, Migrations and Nomadisms*, ed. Françoise Lionnet and Ronnie Scharfman, New Haven: Yale University Press.

Mooneeram, Roshni. 1999a. 'Prospero's Island Revisited: Dev Virahsawmy's Toufann'. *Kunapipi*, 21.

Mooneeram, Roshni. 1999b. 'Theatre in Development in Mauritius: From a Theatre of Protest to a Theatre of Cultural Miscegenation', in *African Theatre in Development*, ed. Martin Banham, James Gibbs and Femi Osofisan, Oxford: James Currey.

Mooneeram, Roshni. 2001. 'Shakespeare in Africa', co-written with Martin Banham and Jane Plastow, in *The Cambridge Companion to Shakespeare on Stage*, ed. Sarah Stanton and Stanley Wells, Cambridge: Cambridge University Press.

Mooneeram, Roshni. 2002. 'Creative Writing in Mauritian Creole: The Emergence of a Literary Language and its Contribution to Standardization'. Unpublished Ph.D. thesis, University of Leeds.

Moura, Jean-Marc. 1999. *Littératures francophones et théorie postcoloniale*. Paris: Presses Universitaires de France.

Pavis, Patrice. 1992. *Theatre at the Crossroads of Culture*. London and New York: Routledge.

Pelen, Philippe. 1996. *Mâ*. Saint-Denis: Editions Grand Océan.

Ramharai, Vikram. 1990. *La Littérature mauricienne d'expression Créole: essai d'analyse socio-culturelle*. Port-Louis: Editions les Mascareignes.

Rose-May, Nicole. 1996. *Noirs, cafres et créoles*. Paris: l'Harmattan.

Said, Edward. 1992. 'Figures, Configurations, Transformations', in *From Commonwealth to Postcolonial*, ed. Anna Rutherford, Sydney: Dangaroo Press.

Tranquille, Danielle. 2000. *Interview with Dev Virahsawmy*. http://pages.intnet.mu/develog/

Vergès, Françoise. 1999. *Monsters and Revolutionaries: Colonial Family Romance and Métissage*. Durham: Duke University Press.

Virahsawmy, Dev. 1977. *Li*. Rose-Hill: MMMSP; MC, RC, French trilingual version, Saint-Louis: Chemins de la liberté, 1979; *Li/The Prisoner of Conscience*, Moka: Editions de l'Océan Indien, 1982.

Virahsawmy, Dev. 1981. *Zeneral Makbef*. Rose-Hill: Bukié Banané, 1981.

Virahsawmy, Dev. 2001. *Ti-Marie*. Rose-Hill: Boukie Banane, 2001.

Wilkinson, Jane. 2001. 'Interviews with Dev Virahsawmy and Michael Walling', in *African Theatre, Playwrights and Politics*, ed. Martin Banham, James Gibbs and Femi Osofisan, Oxford: James Currey.

10 Surviving the crossing: theatre in the African Diaspora

OSITA OKAGBUE

Africa and the Atlantic world

Between 1562 and 1807 the Atlantic slave trade saw millions of sons and daughters of Africa transported across the 'middle passage' to the plantations and homes of the New World. In the process, a cultural umbilical cord was established linking most Diaspora peoples of African descent to Africa; this bond, in spite of the intervention of time and distance, has remained. However, forcibly leaving home and enduring the horrors of the Atlantic was a traumatic experience that left indelible marks on the individual and collective psyches of the unfortunate slaves. As James Walvin points out, 'many never forgot the hell of those ships. Even among their descendants, the slave trade became a haunted refrain in collective folk memory, periodically revived and recollected by the chroniclers of slave culture' (1999: xiv). The conditions of the 'middle passage' initiated the systematic and prolonged deculturation process which the African slaves endured in the New World. However, this chapter is a celebration of the resilience of the African cultures which went across to the New World, as well as an acknowledgement of the tenacity of the slaves in retaining their humanity by clinging on to aspects of their respective African customs and traditions when they arrived at their respective destinations in the New World. Emmanuel Obiechina expresses this tenacity and courage very well when he says that Africa 'was a vibrant reality in the soul of her expatriate children during the era of the slave trade . . . [it] remained deeply etched in the consciousness, not always as something of pure pleasure and joy, but as part of themselves, as part of their emotional and spiritual existence without which their integrity as human beings would have simply disappeared' (1986: 101). Thus we see that Africa managed to survive in the souls of its enslaved and dispersed children to provide them, not only with mechanisms for survival, but also with tools for fashioning a new identity for a new environment.

This chapter will concentrate on two things: an examination of the contributions made by African cultures in the creation of Afro-Caribbean and

Afro-American cultures in the Caribbean and South America; and an assessment of the influences on and the manifestations of these cultures in the performances and theatres of the Caribbean and South America. The chapter will specifically look at theatres from Brazil, Haiti, Martinique, Guadeloupe, Cuba and the whole of what is often referred to as the 'Commonwealth Caribbean'. Emphasis will, however, be on key dramatists, such as Aimé Césaire, Errol Hill, Derek Walcott, Trevor Rhone, Eugenio Hernández Espinosa, Daniel Boukman, Oduvaldo Vianna Filho, Michael Gilkes, Dennis Scott and Felix Morisseau-Leroy. As this book is a history of theatre in Africa and its Diaspora, the approach in the chapter, whether in tracing the influences of African cultures and folk forms on the subsequent development of theatre in South America or the Caribbean, or in identifying dramatic trends in each country, will be more historical than analytical, placing trends, plays or playwrights within appropriate and defining historical contexts.

Surviving slavery: African cultures and New World theatres and performances

Atlantic slavery, without a doubt, had entailed a high degree of personal physical and psychic cruelty visited on African slaves. However, there is much evidence to suggest that slaves refused to resign themselves to being simply passive victims of their situation (see Reynolds, 1985; Davis, 1995; Thornton, 1998). They adopted various strategies of resistance to deal with their predicament; some, we learn, resisted by acts of suicide, others by escape, sabotage or through surreptitious disobedience to the law in matters of social conduct, religious association and worship.

But in whatever manner they resisted, a majority clung on to their African cultures, using these as a basis for negotiating their positions in the new social and cultural order in which they found themselves. The last mode of resistance was vital for the survival and subsequent contributions of African cultures in the Atlantic world. Davis argues that 'the strength of African culture, despite the oppressive impact of slavery, is demonstrated by the recreation of African societies in the areas of the New World that remained beyond the control of the Europeans' (1995: xiv). Maroon or *quilombo* (runaway slave) settlements definitely played a significant role in the preservation of African cultures, especially in Brazil, Cuba, Guyana, Jamaica, and of course in Haiti, where there was eventually a successful slave revolt. Notable among the maroon settlements was the Republic of Palmeras (1630–82), made up of about twenty thousand people of mainly Angolan origin who lived exclusively governed by west and central African customs and a few Portuguese cultural elements from their previous slave society (Davis, 1995: xiv). There was also a well-established maroon society on the hills on the outskirts of Jamaica, where west African, mainly Akan and Yoruba names were retained and the customs and lifestyle were almost exclusively African. Some of these societies of 'African nations' had their kings, queens, high priests and, sometimes, governors (Thornton, 1998: 202).

Even in the slave societies of the New World, Africans still managed, especially in places where their numbers were significantly higher than those of other population groups, to retain elements of their African cultures and identities. These provided them with sources of inner strength to cope with the terrors of up-rootment and displacement. In Brazil, for instance, the predominantly Yoruba slaves from the Dahomey and Oyo empires brought with them a worldview which provided the basis for *Shango* worship and other Afro-religious affiliations. Yoruba religion became *Cadomble* in Brazil, *Shango* in Trinidad, *Santeria* in Cuba, Puerto Rico and Panama, while in Haiti it was the basis for *Vodou*. A similar transformation of other African religions produced *Umbanda, Jare and Kongo* in Brazil and Haiti respectively. The syncretism between African cultures among themselves, and with other contesting cultures of the New World, mainly European and the native Indian, produced Afro-Caribbean, Afro-Cuban, Afro-Brazilian, Afro-Haitian, or what can be collectively termed the Creole cultures of the New World. These cultures provide founts for life and artistic expression.

Thus, African religious practices and philosophies had provided the strongest and most effective weapon and context for resistance, as is demonstrated by the strength and continuing role of Afro-religious practices in Brazil, Cuba, Haiti and across other Caribbean islands. These new religions not only provided avenues and mechanisms of knowing and negotiating with the other world, but also acted as the roots and depositories of African cultural identities for peoples of African descent in the New World. The performative potentials of African religions and their Afro-New World derivatives have had significant aesthetic implications for the theatres of peoples of African descent in the New World, as shown by calls in the 1950s and 1960s by scholars and theatre specialists such as Hill for a 'theatre of Exuberance' which appropriates the 'colour and celebrative nature of carnival and various indigenous masquerade traditions' as well as religious practices; and Louis Mars, who advocated the use of Vodou as a 'basis for an autochthonous

Haitian drama and theatre' (Balme, 1992: 183). A similar call was made in the 1970s by Marina Maxwell, co-founder of the Yard Theatre in Jamaica, who began to blend 'carnival and ritual' in her productions. For her, Vodou ceremony, with its throbbing African drums and spirit possession, was the most expressive metaphor of Afro-Caribbean identity and thus should provide 'the seedbed of West Indian theatre' (Balme, 1992: 183–4). Dramatists such as Walcott, Scott, Gilkes and Zenos Obi Constance successfully made creative use of Afro-Caribbean folk forms to create a unique 'theatre of ritual' in plays such as *Dream on Monkey Mountain*, *An Echo in the Bone*, *Couvade*, and *The Ritual* in the late 1960s and 1970s. Pepe Carril's *Shango de Ima* (1969) also belongs to this style of theatre, as does Edgar White's *The Nine Night* (1983).

Theatre has always had a complex and dialectical relationship with religion and ritual; all are performative and African religious practices are even more so, as they demand a high degree of interactive performance between the human officials, devotees and the characters of the other worlds. Thus, it is not surprising that many of the folk performances of the Caribbean and South America are religious in origin, just as they are in Africa. And for the slaves, adapting their African customs and religious practices to their new environment and circumstances enabled them to use their Afro-Creole religions and rituals as integral parts of their survival and resistance strategies against European domination. Afro-religious practices of the New World, such as Vodou, Pocomania, Santeria, Jare and Shango, Umbanda and so on, and especially those involving possession and spirit mediumship, have retained these highly performative qualities. Also, the tendency to anthropomorphise the deities and spirits and venerate them through play, characteristic of most African religions and which has given rise to a variety of theatre forms in Africa, such as the masquerade, the *Wasan Bori* of the Hausa and the *Masabe* of southern Zambia, has been retained in Afro-New World religions. And even where, as in Brazil, Cuba and Haiti, Catholic saints have been adopted or merged, as often was the case, with African deities, the same playful and sometimes irreverent relationship between African gods and their worshippers is maintained. However, although religious practices provided the strongest link and retention of African cultures in the New World, and also although the slaves' personal and private lives suffered greatly under the slave system, other Afro-secular cultural practices and activities were possible for the slaves. Traditions of storytelling, such as the *Anansesem* tradition of the Akan, the *griot* tradition of Mali and Senegambia, survived intact and some, such as storytelling, verbal contests, riddling and various dances, are still practised by folk performance artists such as Louise Bennett from Jamaica, the famed calypsonians and the Brazilian popular performance company, Solano Trinidade. Anansi, the central hero, was already part of the Jamaican pantomime by the 1940s. This folk narrative tradition is also the inspiration for Afro-Caribbean dramatists such as Walcott in *Ti Jean and his Brothers* (1957) and *The Odyssey*, his 1992 adaptation of Homer for the Royal Shakespeare Company in Stratford-upon-Avon, Rhone in *Old Story Time* (1979) and Kendal Hippolyte in *The Drum-Maker* (1985).

In the main, other African cultural and folk forms went through a syncretic process similar to that undergone by the religions, giving rise to exciting Afro-New World folk forms. In Brazil there evolved performance forms such as the acrobatic *capoeira, maculele* (a stick dance), samba dance and music, *afoxes*. In the Caribbean we have *calinda/laghia* (spectacular stick fights that are definitely of west African origin) which are celebrated in Hill's musical, *Man Better Man* (1960), warrior trials of strength, verbal contests such as Talk Tents, calypso, *Cannes Brulles* (*camboulay*), *jonkonnu* (John Canoe), plus a host of other secular ritual performances. There were also the unique African rhythms and dances which form the base for carnivals and other street performances. These forms, which evolved whole from African cultures or which were the result of syncretism with native Indian and/or European forms, represent the folk traditions of Afro-Caribbean and Afro-American peoples. They, as we shall see later, provide the fount from which many contemporary theatre artists attempt to fashion indigenous Afro-New World theatre traditions and styles.

Theatre and constructions of Afro-New World identities

Apart from folk performances, the first formal theatre activities in both Caribbean and Latin American colonial societies were European-style theatre productions, either by visiting European and American theatre companies or by local amateur theatre groups, often white, mulatto and middle class, who merely copied the theatre fashions and models of Europe or North America. According to Keith Noel, most of the plays produced were European, although a few locally written plays were staged. Even in the latter case, the plays differed little in content and style from their European models (Noel, 1985: 6). Thus, in the Caribbean there were no plays that dealt with local themes and characters until about the late 1920s and early 1930s. In a sense, the development of Caribbean theatre, like that of most other colonised societies such as those in Africa and Asia, followed the pattern of first presenting European theatre pieces by visiting European or American companies or local amateur groups of mainly expatriates for the exclusive entertainment of the élite. This phase was usually followed by local writers copying European models, sometimes in both content and form, but the style always remained European. Good examples of dramatists of this phase are C. L. R. James, Aimé Césaire, Una Marson and Wilton Rogers, who all wrote in the late 1930s and 1940s. This second phase happened at different times across the Caribbean and South American colonial societies. In Cuba, the first play to copy the Spanish style was Santiago Borroto's *The Gardener Prince*, which was written and produced around 1732, and in Haiti, the romantic style influenced dramatists such as Auguste Nau, Liautaud Ethéart and Alibee Fleury, who wrote and published many plays between 1851 and 1876. Brazilian theatre seemed happy to simply produce European and North American plays, a practice still going on today despite the emergence of native playwrights since the late 1950s. This phase and style of theatre was, however, for the élite minority, of either descendants of the European plantocracy or the western educated black upper and middle classes. But for the non-European community of former African slaves and indentured workers from Asia, non-literary theatre and performance traditions from their respective homelands and cultures provided the main form of theatrical activity. Thus, the literary European and the oral (mainly African, Asian and native Indian) traditions existed side by side and were later to become the building blocks for the development of contemporary native theatres of the Caribbean and Latin America. Of more relevance to this chapter, however, are the African inputs in this theatrical evolution.

According to Banham, Hill and Woodyard,

> Up to the abolition of slavery in 1834, and beyond, Caribbean theatre was merely a reflection of English and European. British, and occasionally French and American players, travelled to the then colonies with an established repertoire including Shakespeare, Molière and a quantity of farces and melodramas . . . From time to time plays romanticising Caribbean life, by foreign authors, would be produced, such as Richard Chamberlain's *The West Indian* (1771) set in London, Isaac Bickerstaffe's comic operetta *The Padlock* (1768), and the romantic *Inkle and Yarico* (1787) by Coleman Younger, set on a plantation in Barbados. (1994: 146)

The first genuine attempts to develop an indigenous Caribbean theatre can be traced to the pioneering efforts of the Jamaican politician and Pan-Africanist, Marcus Garvey, and C. L. R. James, between 1930 when Garvey wrote and produced his open air theatrical shows in Kingston, Jamaica, and 1936 when James's *Toussaint l'overture* (revised and produced as *The Black Jacobins* in 1967) was premièred in London. Garvey's plays of this period were *The Coronation of an African King*, *Roaming Jamaicans* and *Slavery: From Hut to Mansion* (all three written and produced in 1930) and *Wine, Women and War* (written and produced in 1932). All four plays were a marked departure from the type of plays mentioned above, as they dealt with issues about and relevant to Afro-Caribbean life, especially the black experience of slavery, as well as issues of nationhood. James's *Toussaint l'overture* deals with the successful slave revolution in Haiti and was also a very significant work, in terms of both the thematic and structural development of Afro-Caribbean theatre. Here for the first time was a play about African slaves written with some awareness of African theatre and performance structural devices – there are songs, drum music, dances and mimed sequences as part of the dramatic structure of the play – even though James's inspiration and models were essentially European.

Marson's *Pocomania* (1938), a play about the influence on a middle-class young woman of a Jamaican Afro-religious cult, *pocomania*, took up the interest in Afro-Caribbean themes as a way forward in the development of a truly Caribbean theatre. Other plays with distinctly Afro-Caribbean flavours were Tom Redham's *San Gloria*, Frank Hill's *Upheaval* and Roger Mais's *Hurricane*. The most successful dramatist of this period, however, was Archie Lindo, with two original plays, *Under the Skin* and *Forbidden Fruit*, and two adaptations, *The White Witch of Rose Hall* and *The Maroon*. Noel points out that before 1930 there was no

> 'Caribbean' drama to speak of. The black population brought with them from Africa . . . rituals and revelries which had then evolved into something unique, but this could hardly be labelled as 'Caribbean drama'. The ruling classes, too, had their forms of theatrical entertainment, but this could not be labelled as truly Caribbean. (1985: 5)

The drama was to evolve together with the emerging Caribbean society and nations. The 1940s to 1960s marked a significant period, in both the political and cultural evolution of Caribbean society, for although the 1930s had signalled the beginning of political nationalisms, it was not until the 1960s that real Caribbean nations were born, starting with the attainment of independence by Jamaica and Trinidad in 1962. The national consciousness engendered by the independence movements, and the scintillating politics of the period, transferred into the cultural and artistic spheres. The idea of a Caribbean federation (1958–62) was both a political as well as a cultural statement of identity by Caribbean peoples. However, the failure of this federation after just four years did not kill off the idea of a cultural union among the emerging nations of the Caribbean archipelago, as is evident in the continuing survival of institutions and events, such as the University of the West Indies (with campuses in Jamaica, Trinidad and Barbados) and Carifesta, a festival of Caribbean creative arts.

Interestingly, this drive to promote a unifying Caribbean culture and theatre encouraged theatre artists to tap into the folk culture of music, dances, storytelling and the various traditions of open and street processions which 'contained pronounced performative components' (Balme, 1992: 181). Another interesting outcome of this drive was that the local patois and dialect, the first languages of the Caribbean, hitherto deemed backward, were now seen as stage-worthy and began to be adopted by many dramatists to explore very serious issues. In fact, one of the closest links to Africa that Caribbean theatre has is the predominant use of the dialect or patois by both Anglophone and Francophone literary dramatists. These developments in the 1960s helped provide the impetus for the enormous influence that African cultures began to have on the new Caribbean theatre. These cultures provided the bulk of the folk forms from which the theatre could draw; indeed, they had also contributed significantly to the shaping of both the syntactical and lexical structures of the patois and dialects spoken across the islands of the Caribbean.

By the late 1950s folk forms were being thematically and structurally incorporated into the new theatre. Hill, who in 1972 argued for carnival as the base for a Caribbean national theatre, exploited the theatrical potential of the rituals of Shango, the physicality of the *batoniers* (stick fighters), the rhythms of calypso, and the colourful atmosphere of carnival in his musical comedy, *Man Better Man*. Prior to that, however, Walcott had used both African and Caribbean themes and structural techniques in *Drums and Colours* (a play commissioned to mark the birth of the federation), and *Henri Christophe* (1950), another play on the Haitian slave revolt. His latter plays, such as *Ti Jean and his Brothers, Dream on Monkey Mountain* (1967) and *The Odyssey*, show more evidence of Caribbean folk and African theatre sensibilities. In *Ti Jean*, he draws heavily on St Lucian folklore and rituals, but at the core is African storytelling (the Anansesem tradition of the Akan). *Dream on Monkey Mountain* is a play which 'incorporates ritual elements such as spirit possession, revivalist faith-healing, masking and Shango dancing' to weave the fabric of Makak's dream (Balme, 1992: 183). Other dramatists in the late 1960s and early 1970s continued this interest of creatively appropriating folk forms to serious levels in order to usher in a 'new development in Caribbean theatre'. These dramatists include Michael Gilkes, who wrote *Couvade* in 1972, and Scott, whose *An Echo in the Bone* (1974) explores the Nine Night ritual in which dance, drum music and possession provide the context for communication between the living and the dead and a journey into tragic knowledge. These two plays, together with *Dream* and others, represent the best examples of 'theatre of ritual' (see Stone, 1994).

Judy Stone identifies four other styles: 'theatre of realism', under which come playwrights such as Errol John in *Moon on a Rainbow Shawl* (1957), Trevor Rhone in *School is Out* (1975), *Old Story Time* (1979) and *Two Can Play* (1982) and Aldwyn Bully in *Streak* (1976) and *The Nite Box* (1977); 'theatre of the people', which includes Sistren (a Jamaican working-class women's theatre collective based in Kingston) and Pat Cumper in *The Rapist* (1977) and *Coming of Age* (1983); 'total theatre' brings together Roderick Walcott's *The Harrowing of Benjy* (1956) and Earl Lovelace's *Jestina's Calypso* (1978); Derek Walcott comes under 'classical theatre'. To Walcott, Scott, Gilkes and White should be added Rawle Gibbons in theatre of ritual. There was, of course, the 'theatre of exuberance' advocated earlier and exemplified by Hill in many of his other plays. There are a host of other highly successful Caribbean dramatists who do not fit into any of these categories, and of those who do, there are constant overlaps, such as Walcott's *Dream*, in which within the dream, Makak and the other black characters undertake a ritual return to Africa to discover the root of their Afro-Caribbean identity. There are also Diaspora dramatists such as Edgar Nkosi White and Caryl Phillips whose plays such as *Trinity: The Long and Cheerful Road to Slavery* (1982), *Redemption Song* (1984), *Orefo in a Night World* (1993) and *Strange Fruit* (1981), *Where there is Darkness* (1982) and *Shelter* (1984), written from the distorting distance of exile, do not fit neatly into any of the categories, yet are about issues and problems affecting Caribbean society and peoples. What all these dramatists have in common, however, is their acknowledgement of and use of Afro-Caribbean cultural and folk heritage as a basis for attempting to fashion a uniquely Caribbean dramaturgy and theatrical tradition, while articulating shared Afro-Caribbean cultural and national identities.

Cuba, Haiti and Martinique follow the same pattern as the Anglo-Caribbean in that folk forms significantly influence the development of contemporary theatre practices and dramaturgy. As pointed out earlier, in the same way that theatre scholars and theorists such as Hill and Maxwell had called for artists in the Anglophone Caribbean to mine the rich folk cultures, especially the religious rituals, carnival and other street processions, Louis Mars had made a similar call in Haiti in 1966, when he argued that Vodou rituals should provide the basis of an indigenous Haitian drama and theatre. However, the movement towards an authentic indigenous Haitian literature and theatre had been made more urgent by the occupation of Haiti by the United States between 1915 and 1934. Many Haitian writers at the time began to extol and include local customs, cultural practices and the local language in their works. Of these, the most successful was Dominique Hippolite, who wrote a series of political, historical and satirical plays in the early part of the twentieth century. Another major effort to create an indigenous Haitian theatre was Felix Morisseau-Leroy's *Antigone in Creole* (1953), in which the playwright tried to disprove the notion, then prevalent, that the Haitian Creole, which, like the dialect and patois, was the language of the ordinary people who are mainly of African descent, was not suitable for the stage. Syntactically and structurally, these languages were shaped by the African languages of the slaves. The play was highly successful, with performances in Haiti and further afield, and it marked a watershed in the development of an indigenous Haitian dramaturgy. Morisseau-Leroy's other play, also in Creole, was *King Creon*. Other plays which followed his examples were Franck Fouche's *Bouki in Paradise* (1960), *General Baron of the Cross or Masked Silence* (1971) and Franketienne's *Kaselezo* (Womb Waters Breaking, 1985). The last two plays, as well as being in Creole, appropriated the performance potentials of Vodou to explore the problems of Haitian people. *Masked Silence* uses the subversive atmosphere of carnival to both put forward Fouche's theories of theatre and to suggest a way out for Haiti from the clutches of the Duvalier dictatorship, while *Kaselezo* is about the problems of a Vodou priestess and her two daughters, and the appalling condition of women in Haitian society (see Banham, Hill and Woodyard, 1994; Rubin, 1996).

The greatest writer to have emerged from Martinique is, without doubt, Aimé Césaire. His African cultural heritage is a major part of his creative sensibility. But it is in his drama that he makes the strongest use of this heritage. His first play, *And the Dogs were Silent*, written and performed in 1946, is informed by an Afro-Martinican ritual. But the major plays to date remain *La Tragédie du Roi Christophe* (1963), about the Haitian revolt in which Césaire explores the issue of decolonisation in relation to black and African independence movements of the 1950s and 1960s, and *A Season in the Congo* (1967), about Patrice Lumumba's attempts to establish an independent socialist African state in the Congo, and similar to the earlier play in its views on European collusions in the politics of decolonisation which were going on in Africa in the late fifties and sixties. *Un Tempete* (1969) refocusses *The Tempest* so as to highlight the subtextual colonial theme of Shakespeare's play. Césaire's Prospero is a white settler while Caliban is a black slave and Shango devotee, both locked in a power struggle in which only Caliban will emerge victorious. Césaire's theatrical eyes were totally on Africa and the plays, it seems, were his contribution to the process of African decolonisation. A dramatist of significance from Martinique is Daniel Boukman, who, according to Carole-Anne Upton (1998), is descended from a line which begins from Césaire and which runs through Frantz Fanon. His plays, which usually explore notions of créolité, include *Songs to End the Days of Orpheus* (1970), *Full Bellies, Empty Bellies* (1971), *Negro Orpheus* (1973), *The Slavers, to the last beat of our Hearts* (1976) and *Delivrans!* (1995). Another is Edouard Glissant, whose major play is *Monsieur Toussaint*, one of the many plays on the Haitian slave revolt. What unites these latter two dramatists is that even though they each use their plays to challenge the Négritude of Césaire, they still espouse their Afro-Martinican identity in the way they make use of Afro-Martinican folk forms and the Creole language, as well as the Afro-centred trajectory of their themes. Of the younger generation, the most successful Martinican dramatist is Ina Césaire. Although based in France, she, like White and Phillips, is very much influenced by her Afro-Martinican cultural background. Her best plays are *Mémoires d' isles: Maman N et Maman F* (Island Memories, 1981) and *Child of Passage, or The Epic of Ti-Jean* (1987), which explores the famous Afro-Caribbean folk hero celebrated by Walcott thirty years earlier.

Unlike the other Caribbean islands, but like Haiti a century earlier, Cuba needed a revolution in order to look inwards to discover its true Caribbean identity. Cuban theatre prior to Fidel Castro's revolution in 1959 was simply a copying of Spanish models. But with the revolution and its encouragement of a national consciousness and cultural identity, theatre and the other arts were galvanised in a search for an authentic Cuban artistic and cultural expression. Because of the strong African cultural influence in Cuba, it was inevitable that African religions, rituals and folk performance styles played a significant role in the development of the theatre. The first appearance of a black character in Cuban theatre is credited to Francisco Covarrubias, who in the late eighteenth century created the *negrito* (black boy) and the *mulatto.* Although a black type-character, the negrito was always represented by a white actor in a painted black face and part of his sketch was to racially satirise supposed black manners. During the war of independence years, when the *bufos habaneros* were banned, this character was modified by Jose Marti (1853–95), whose Teatro Mambi transformed the negrito from the buffoon of the popular tradition into a 'strong dramatic hero' with a well-defined national and social identity (Rubin, 1996: 217). Marti's black hero was based on the griot, the storyteller, mimic, minstrel and clown brought over on the slave ships from Africa (see Versenyi, 1994: 70). The new negrito was to become a central feature of the many processions, ritual ceremonies, religious dances and the *diablitos* (devil myths) in which the African cultures brought to Cuba by slavery were celebrated.

The revolution also brought about the emergence of radical theatre groups who believed in using the theatre as an instrument of the political and cultural change the country was undergoing. Teatro Escambray, founded in 1968, is the best example of this style of theatre. Escambray's early work was very similar to the theatre-for-development philosophy in Africa, as well as to Boal's theatre of the oppressed in some countries of South America. Of the other groups outside of Havana, Cabildo Teatral Santiago is the most noteworthy, for its African and Cuban folk influences. Cabildo, according to Rubin, uses songs, dances and changeable spaces to create spectacles which, 'without being folkloric reproductions, establish very clear direct contacts with the Afro-Cuban working district audiences of Santiago de Cuba'. In their performances, short, everyday stories are used to 'offer a contemporary vision of reality' in a carnivalesque and popular musical style that transforms their performances into group parties that are often close in structure and flavour to the popular Afro-Cuban *conga* (Rubin, 1996: 226). Cabildo's most successful piece remains the 1974 performance of Raul Pomare's *De como Santiago Apostel puso los pias en la tierra* (About How the Apostle James Set Foot on Earth), in which they combine pantomime and dance with African and Cuban rhythms and movement. There are clear African theatre influences on Cabildo's repertory, not only in terms of the performance structure but also in terms both of staging and the dynamics of the spectator–performer interaction within his often mobile and fluid theatrical spaces.

Although, in keeping with the socialist ethos of Cuban society since the revolution, most of the theatre tends to be collectively created pieces, there have been successful individual playwrights. Carlos Felipe's *Requiem por Yarini* (Requiem for Yarini, 1960) is a play set against a Cuban-Yoruba background and very strongly reflects the pervasive African influence on contemporary Cuban culture and theatre. Pepe Carril exploits his Afro-Cuban cultural heritage in *Shango de Ima: A Yoruba Mystery Play*, written and produced in 1969. It is episodically structured as a series of stories, legends or histories strung together to show a flawed Shango, one of the Yoruba *orishas* to arrive with the slaves in Cuba. It is a typical mystery play in which Shango is tried and punished as a representative symbol of sinful humanity, and not just as a man who has emotionally and sexually abused three women, Oshun, Oya and Yemaya (three goddesses in the Afro-Cuban religious pantheon). The play not only explores an aspect of the Yoruba myth but also shows the dramatist's awareness and use of African theatre sensibilities, such as an *Alarinjo* opening glee, ritual invocations to Elegua (Eshu Elegba) with Yoruba music and songs, as well as dances, acrobatics and mime. However, of all the Cuban dramatists, Hernández Espinosa is the one most influenced by his Afro-Cuban cultural and theatrical heritage. His major plays are *Maria Antonia* (1976), *La Simona* (1977), *Oba y Shango* (The King and Shango, 1980) and *Odebi el cazador* (Odebi the Hunter, 1980). All four plays are deeply rooted in a mythical Afro-Cuban universe, which enables Espinosa to reflect with 'great authenticity the world of the blacks' in Cuba (Banham, 1994: 164). Three other Cuban dramatists with significant African influences in their works are Virgilio Piñera, Eduardo Manet and Jose Triana. The last is best known in Cuba and abroad for his *La noche de los asesinos* (Night of the Assassins, 1965), while Manet is known for *Ma dea*, a play that transfers the ancient Greek myth of Medea into a Caribbean context. This is performed in what Carlos Solorzano describes as 'a kind of black mass' (Rubin, 1996: 19), in which a group of wailing mourners and the hypnotic possession of an Afro-Cuban religious ritual provide the context for the symbolic killing of Jason's yet to be born children.

Brazilian theatre is a combination of 'assimilated post-war European cultural currents' and African ceremonies, 'which, similar to Haitian voodoo rituals, remind us that all theatre is an act that attempts to isolate spectators from immediate reality so as to help them enter a state of contemplation and leave behind rational awareness' (Rubin, 1996: 19). This functional character of performance in African contexts seems to have survived in many African Diaspora communities. But given the significant size of its descendant African population and the ubiquity of Afro-Brazilian cultural forms, one is rather surprised at the absence of a concomitant African influence in contemporary Brazilian dramaturgy. Perhaps this could be to do with the post-slavery and post-colonial social structure of Brazil, in which the majority of the descendants of the slaves languish on the margins of the socio-economic playing field. Thus it seems that this social structure has retained some of the racism of the slave period, with a perception of blacks and African cultures as being inferior to those of Europe. There is ample evidence that the colour issue is still very much alive in Brazil, with white at the top, black at the bottom, and other shades in between. The same superior–inferior status assignation seems to attach to the literary and popular street performances in Brazil, with the literary owing its origin to Europe, while street performances such as carnival and samba are infused with mainly African elements.

But the emergence of Afro-Brazilian theatre began when the Teatro Experimental do Negro (TEN) was co-founded in the 1940s by Afro-Brazilian activist Abdias do Nascimento and Ruth de Souza, the first black actress of the Brazilian theatre. In the forties and fifties, TEN was in the forefront of Negro consciousness awareness following in the wake of Marcus Garvey's 'Back to Africa' and the Négritude movement of Césaire and Sedar Senghor. In the 1940s through the 1960s the same movements seem to have provided the impetus for the nationalist politics in the Caribbean in which there was a good measure of Afro-Caribbean cultural revival and reclamation. Although TEN was a product of the Brazilian cultural matrix, it was essentially a call for the recognition and acceptance of an African cultural heritage by all Afro-Creoles of the Caribbean and South America. TEN began as a theatrical group whose aim was to promote Afro-Brazilian issues through the theatre and other arts. Its journal, *Quilombo*, was used as a forum for putting across and discussing black ideas and issues within Brazilian society. Their first play was Eugene O'Neill's *The Emperor Jones* at the Municipal Theatre. Souza, particularly, wanted to create an opportunity for herself and other black actors to do serious theatre work, which they could not do because of the racism of the society and the limited choices that Eurocentric plays offered to them. Other groups followed TEN's example, such as Brasilianse, a dance group, and Solano Trinidade, a popular theatre group interested mainly in researching and performing Afro-Brazilian folklore (see Davis, 1995: 257).

As already pointed out, the mainly white élite continued the colonial practice of producing European and North American plays or of copying European and North American dramatic models when they wrote, even when they dealt with Brazilian themes. But having said that, the pervasive influence of African cultures on Brazilian society and cultural life, especially in matters of religion and entertainment, was gradually becoming evident in the theatre as well. Thus, the most important writers and directors in Brazil, such as Ariano Suassana, Oduvaldo Vianna Filho (better known as Vianninho), Augusto Boal, Antunes Filho and Gerald Thomas, all reflect, unconsciously perhaps, this pervasive African influence, either through the carnival processions and samba rhythms, the folk-tales and their heroes, or the ritual and possession ceremonies of the many Afro-Brazilian syncretic religions often found in their works. Both Suassana and Oduvaldo Filho 'follow in the footsteps of Brecht in their references to social problems, but where Brecht recommended that music should explain the text and not idealize it, the works of the authors show a direct union between text and music, a direct influence of the black African ceremonies on the theatre' in Brazil (Rubin, 1996: 20). Filho worked with Boal and Gianfrancesco Guarnieri at the Arena Theatre in San Paulo. Arena's *Arena contra Zumbi* (the outcome of the Arena collaboration) is a series of plays that signalled Arena's search for a functional theatre for Brazil, away from the passive aristocratic Aristotle and beyond the also passive politics of Brecht. Boal was to later develop this into the 'theatre of the oppressed', which resembles African theatre in its functionality and its insistence on an active and creatively involved audience in a constantly changing and evolving play that only exists in the moment of encounter between all the participants. Like Teatro Escambray in Cuba, theatre of the oppressed is very similar to theatre for development in Africa, in which communities and artists make theatre as part of understanding themselves and dealing with issues that are of great importance to the communities involved.

It is not only Brazilian playwrights who are influenced by their multi-cultural context. Directors such as Antunes Filho and Thomas are also influenced in the styles and choices of plays that they produce, with the result that even though they produce foreign, mainly European and North American plays by Shakespeare, Kafka, Pirandello, Miller and so forth, they seek in different ways to impose a uniquely Brazilian language and performance sensibility on the texts. Thomas, whose post-modernist style has echoes of Robert Wilson, is the best example of this tendency, with productions such as Heiner Müller's *Quartet* (1986) and his unique Kafka trilogy *O Processo* (*The Trial*), *A Metamorfose* (*Metamorphosis*) and *Praga* (*Prague*), all done in 1988; *Carmen com Filtro* (Carmen with Filter, 1986) and *Carmen com Filtro 2* (Carmen with filter 2, 1990), *Electra com creta* (Electra with Crete, 1986), and his best-known work, *Flash and Crash Days* (1992). As David George says, Thomas 'borrows from a Brazilian cultural matrix closely bound up with ritual . . . (mainly of) Brazil's African cultures, a culture in which Thomas participates . . . One might say, then, that even Thomas's rehearsals have something of the character of Afro-Brazilian rituals' (2000: 20). Filho, for his part, is best known for his internationally successful *Macunaima* produced in 1978 and a very powerful *Macbeth* in 1992. In *Macunaima*, which is an adaptation of an earlier novel by Mario de Andrade, the rich colour, symbolism and rhythmic physicality of carnival are used to achieve a uniquely Brazilian theatre sensibility, and it, in many ways, helped set the tone for subsequent developments in Brazilian theatre of the 1980s and 1990s.

Conclusion

So, whether it is in Brazil, Cuba, Haiti, Martinique or in the Anglophone Caribbean, what emerges from a study of the history of the performances of peoples of African descent in the Diaspora is that some African theatrical sensibilities have, like the African cultures, been transferred and underpin most theatre practices. The most significant is the idea of function or relevance. Historically, the folk forms served as rallying contexts for reaffirming African identities for the slaves, who used the performances, whether religious or secular, to keep alive memories of an African home. The same sense of function is present in the plays of contemporary dramatists of African descent, from Walcott in *Dream on Monkey Mountain* to Ina Césaire in *Island Memories*, and from Carril in *Shango de Ima* to Scott in *An Echo in the Bone*. Theatre in the African Diaspora is strongly connected with issues of politics and cultural identity. Both the popular folk forms and the contemporary literary theatres are in most cases used as sites and instruments for articulating and expressing collective Afro-Caribbean or Afro-American identities. It is also a context for engaging with the current socio-political issues of the respective Diaspora societies.

But in doing this, dramatists recognise and work within the framework of a theatre that deploys many languages; from mime and dance to acrobatics, from the symbolism of ritual to the lyricism of words. And in accomplished dramatists such as Walcott, Hill, John, Scott, Rhone, Obi Constance, Espinosa, White, Gilkes and Morisseau-Leroy, a perfect balance is achieved between these mediums, so that at the height of the drama words become a dance of images and movement transforms into a dialogue of ideas and symbols through which personal and communal histories unfold. The plays, in different ways, achieve a flexibility of structure and form which allows the easy passages between different realities, different time schemes and different geographical spaces. This is the hallmark of African performance, and it is very much alive in the African Diaspora of the Caribbean and South America.

References and further reading

Balme, Christopher. 1992. 'The Caribbean Theatre of Ritual', in Anna Rutherford, ed., *From Commonwealth to Post-Colonial*, Sydney: Dangaroo Press.

Banham, Martin, Hill, Errol and Woodyard, George, eds. 1994. *The Cambridge Guide to African and Caribbean Theatre*. Cambridge: Cambridge University Press.

Browning, Barbara. 1998. *Infectious Rhythm: Metaphors of Contagion and the Spread of African Culture*. London and New York: Routledge.

Davis, Darien, ed. 1995. *Slavery and Beyond: The African Impact on Latin America and the Caribbean*. Wilmington: Scholarly Resources Inc.

George, David. 1992. *The Modern Brazilian Stage*. Austin: University of Texas Press.

George, David. 2000. *Flash and Crash Days: Brazilian Theatre in the Post-Dictatorship Period*. New York: Garland.

Grimshaw, Anna, ed. 1992. *The C. L. R. James Reader*. Oxford: Blackwell.

Hill, Errol, ed. 1985. *Plays for Today*. Port of Spain: Longman Caribbean Writers.

Hill, Errol. 1997. *The Trinidad Carnival: A Mandate for a National Theatre*. London: New Beacon Books.

Kanneh, Kadiatu. 1998. *African Identities: Race, Nation and Culture in Ethnography, Pan-Africanism and Black Literatures*. London and New York: Routledge.

King, Bruce. 1995. *Derek Walcott and West Indian Drama*. Oxford: Clarendon.

Noel, Keith, ed. 1985. *Caribbean Plays for Playing*. London: Heinemann.

Obiechina, Emmanuel. 1986. 'Africa in the Soul of Dispersed Children: West African Literature from the Era of the Slave Trade'. *Nsukka Studies in African Literature* 4.

Okagbue, Osita. 1996. 'Language and Identity in West African and West Indian Theatre', in Suzanne Stern-Gillet et al., ed., *Culture and Identity: Selected Aspects and Approaches*, Katowice: Wydawnictwo Uniwersytetu Slaskiego.

Okagbue, Osita. 2001. 'Exile and Home: Africa in Caribbean Theater', in Dubem Okafor, ed., *Meditations on African Literature*, Westport, CT: Greenwood Press.

Reynolds, Edward. 1985. *Stand the Storm: A History of the Atlantic Slave Trade.*
London: Allison and Busby.

Rubin, Don. 1996. *The World Encyclopedia of Contemporary Theatre,* vol. II, *The Americas.* London and New York: Routledge.

Rubin, Don, ed. 1997. *The World Encyclopedia of Contemporary Theatre,* vol. III, *Africa.* London and New York: Routledge.

Stone, Judy. 1994. *Studies in West Indian Literature: Theatre.* London: Macmillan.

Thornton, John. 1992. *Africa and Africans in the Making of the Atlantic World, 1400–1800.* Cambridge: Cambridge University Press.

Upton, Carol-Anne. 1998. 'French-Caribbean Theatre', in Richard Boon and Jane Plastow, ed., *Theatre Matters: Performance and Culture on the World Stage.* Cambridge: Cambridge University Press.

Versenyi, Adams. 1993. *Theatre in Latin America: Religion, Politics and Culture from Cortes to the 1980s.* Cambridge: Cambridge University Press.

Walcott, Derek. 1998. *What the Twilight Says: Essays.* London: Faber and Faber.

Walvin, James. 1999. *The Slave Trade.* London: Sutton.

Warner-Lewis, Maureen. 1996. *Trinidad Yoruba: From Mother Tongue to Memory.* Tuscaloosa: University of Alabama Press.

Index

448